"God Cannot Do Without America"

Matthew Simpson and the Apotheosis of Protestant Nationalism

By

Darius Salter

God cannot do without America: Matthew Simpson and the apotheosis of Protestant Nationalism
Darius Salter.

First Fruits Press, ©2017

ISBN: 9781621716280 (print), 9781621716297 (digital), 9781621716303 (kindle)

Digital version at http://place.asburyseminary.edu/academicbooks/15/

First Fruits Press is a digital imprint of the Asbury Theological Seminary, B.L. Fisher Library. Its publications are available for noncommercial and educational uses, such as research, teaching and private study. First Fruits Press has licensed the digital version of this work under the Creative Commons Attribution Noncommercial 3.0 United States License. To view a copy of this license, visit http://creativecommons.org/licenses/by-nc/3.0/us/.

For all other uses, contact:

First Fruits Press
B.L. Fisher Library
Asbury Theological Seminary
204 N. Lexington Ave.
Wilmore, KY 40390
http://place.asburyseminary.edu/firstfruits

Salter, Darius, 1947-
　　God cannot do without America : Matthew Simpson and the apotheosis of Protestant Nationalism / by Darius Salter. -- Wilmore, Kentucky : First Fruits Press, ©2017.
　　　　xxiii, 733 pages : illustrations, portraits ; 21 cm.
　　　　1. The outliner from Cadiz -- 2. The child of Providence -- 3. Cellars, garrets, and soot -- 4. A highly ordered life -- 5. Becoming an orator -- 6. A jubilee in Hell -- 7. A political and spiritual tightrope -- 8. An astute politician -- 9. In case of any accident -- 10. The high and the low -- 11. Headquarters at the White House -- 12. "God cannot do without America" -- 13. Hero, martyr, friend, farewell! -- 14. The broken arrow of patronage -- 15. All the kings horses and all the kings men -- 16. A withered olive branch -- 17. Anything for a Methodist -- 18. "He will draw you to your feet" -- 19. Feuding friends and competing paradigms -- 20. The ideal Christian gentleman -- 21. Epilogue and reflection.
　　　　Includes bibliographical references (pages 670-733).
　　　　ISBN - 13: 9781621716280 (pbk.)

　　　　1. Simpson, Matthew, 1811-1884. 2. Methodist Episcopal Church--Bishops--Biography. 3. Methodist Church--United States--History--19th century. 4. United States--Church history--19th century. 5. Nationalism--Religious aspects--Christianity--19th century. 6. I. Title.
BX8495.S55 S34 2017　　　　　　　　　　　　　　　　287/.092

Cover design by Jon Ramsay

Dedication

To the three Churches of my first pastorate:

Booneville, Warren's Chapel, and Clifty United Methodist Church of Owsley County, Kentucky,

And

Joe G. & Beulah Mainous Campbell and Edward, Jr. & Martha Rose Gabbard Campbell,

who gave me my greatest gift, Brenda Rose Campbell.

Darius Salter

Acknowledgements

The debt I have incurred in writing this project is overwhelming. The Library of Congress houses twenty-four containers of Simpson letters, diaries, reading notes, sermons, lectures, orations, articles, newspaper clippings, poems, and other memorabilia. Reading Room supervisor, Jeffery Flannery, and his able assistants Jennifer, Bruce, Patrick, and many others enabled me to wade through this material.

Dale Patterson, Mark Shenise, Chris Anderson, and Frances Bristol-Lyons offered constant assistance at the United Methodist Archives Building located on the campus of Drew University in Madison, New Jersey. There I was able to explore the Matthew Simpson, George Crooks, Clarence Wilson, Gilbert Haven, Clinton Fisk, and John P. Newman papers. Mark, who more than anyone may possess first-hand knowledge of nineteenth century Methodist documents, responded on countless occasions to my desperate requests for pieces to the Simpson puzzle. Chris Goodale and Susan McElrath assisted in tracing Simpson money that went to their respective schools, Simpson College and American University.

Donna Miller assisted me with the two boxes of approximately 1,000 Simpson letters at the Old St. George's United Methodist Church in Philadelphia. Wesley Wilson and his staff at DePauw University, Greencastle, Indiana, enabled me to explore Simpson's presidential years at what was then Indiana Asbury University. John Oyler and head librarian, Logan Wright, St. Paul's School of Theology in Kansas City before it was dismantled, traced long hidden American Methodist documents and loaded appropriate Methodist microfilm, especially the *Western Christian Advocate*. Linda Bailey of the Cincinnati History Library and Archives provided actual copies of the *Western Christian Advocate* and other materials shedding light onto Simpson's years as an editor.

Matt Strauss and Art Louderback at the Heinz Center in Pittsburgh helped to explore Simpson's years in Pittsburgh, as well as his connection to the city for the entirety of his life. The historians at Philadelphia City Hall made copies of Matthew Simpson's and Matthew Verner Simpson's wills, and maps of Mount Vernon and Arch Streets, where he resided. The libraries of Oakmont and Monongahela City, Pennsylvania, provided information on the Verners, and acquainted me with Williamsport (now Monongahela City). David Ninemire of the Free Library of Philadelphia pulled esoteric maps and dust-covered books and also sent me scanned materials. On numerous occasions, he graciously retrieved relevant information, responding to my desperate phone calls. William Waybright at Allegheny College, Meadville, Pennsylvania, volunteered his evening hours, enabling me to learn more about Simpson's brief teaching tenure at the School.

The Denver area libraries include Colorado History, University of Denver, Iliff School of Theology, the State Historical Society and the Central (downtown) Denver Public Library, where James Jeffrey helped me find information on the McCullough family. The John Evans papers are housed at History Colorado. Kerri Dvorak at Lincoln Nebraska Wesleyan University provided critical materials on John Chivington. Gary Leland Roberts is the world's foremost authority on the Sand Creek Massacre, and I was fortunate to benefit from his perceptions during the time he had been commissioned by the United Methodist Church to do a new study on that unfortunate event.

Before her retirement from Iliff School of Theology, Laura Harris forwarded me unpublished minutes of the Colorado Conference's early years. Micah Saxton at Iliff was especially helpful in enabling me to explore the Henry Warren papers.

Harvey Geerts of the Fulton Historical Society and Dawn Young from the Whiteside County Recorder's Office, both in Morrison, Illinois, provided deeds and abstracts for Simpson's many business transactions in that area of Illinois. The Monmouth County Hall of Records, Freehold, New Jersey, assisted me in finding the wills of the Simpson children, and able researchers at Pittsburgh City Hall traced the deeds and transactions on the Verner-Brown property at Liberty and Penn Avenues. Laura Poll, Librarian at the Historical Society of Monmouth County, Freehold, New Jersey, provided maps of Long Branch, enabling exploration of the location of Simpson's cottage and the surrounding area.

The archivists at the Kansas State Historical Society in Topeka provided materials on Cherokee County, Kansas, helping me to better comprehend Simpson's investments through James Harlan, Josiah Grinnell, and the American Emigrant Company. Barbara Davis at New Rochelle, New York Public Library and The Reverend Robert E. Gahler, Priest at Trinity St. Paul's Episcopal Church, provided both conversations and written materials on the Richard Lather family, in-laws of Matthew Verner Simpson. Kevin Crain of Pasadena Public Library helped in establishing birth and death dates of Eva Nelson Groff and her whereabouts while and after she was married to Matthew Verner Simpson.

It was my fortune to be introduced to Terri Neccai, architectural historian, who enabled me to visualize Simpson's house in Philadelphia, and the church which he pastored in Monongahela City. Chautauqua archivist Johnathan Schmitz from Jamestown New York sent information on Simpson's dedication of the pavilion at Chautauqua, as well as other preaching engagements at the summer resort. Historian Wayne Bell located Simpson's endorsement of Ocean Grove.

My discussions with Dr. Richard Stowe who has developed a keen interest in Simpson because of his primary research on Edward R. Ames have been invaluable. He transcribed hundreds of Simpson-Ames letters and guided me to several important documents.

Several local historians have stuck with me throughout this project. Without Dr. Scott Pendleton, President of the Harrison County Ohio Historical Society, Cadiz, Ohio, Simpson's native home, this project would have never been launched. Dr. Pendleton chauffeured me around Harrison County and beyond, pointing out houses, churches, cemeteries, and other Simpson localities, which are critical in understanding Simpson's developmental years. Cadiz, nestled in the Eastern hills of Ohio, still retains much of its nineteenth century charm not yet destroyed by modernity.

Arch Street United Methodist Church historian Dale Shillito gave tireless hours enabling me to navigate Philadelphia, in what seems like countless trips to that city. Dale accompanied me to City Hall, West Laurel Hills Cemetery, the Free Library of Philadelphia, Old St. George's United Methodist Church, Simpson House, and the Spring Garden neighborhood in which Simpson lived, and above all, Arch Street United Methodist Church, a beacon of light in inner-city Philadelphia. Dale often responded to my frantic phone calls and retraced our steps to uncover a lost or forgotten item.

Tom Gavigan, monument restorationist and stone mason gave me a personal lecture on Simpson's crypt as we stood in front of it and discussed its state of needed repair. Dave Adam, historian of Simpson House, Philadelphia, shared oral history with intriguing anecdotes.

Martha Boyd at Wesley College in Dover, Delaware, aided me in finding books that belonged to Bishop Matthew Simpson and his son-in-law, Charles Buoy. My friend, Reverend Ron Parker from Salisbury, Maryland, accompanied me to Dover, and has been my guide over the last twenty years to many historical sites in the "Garden of Methodism."

Teresa Gray at Vanderbilt University and Debra Madera, Special Collections Reference Assistant in the Manuscript Archives and Rare Book Room at Emory University, offered gracious southern hospitality. They both helped me to comprehend Simpson's uneven relationship to the Confederacy and Reconstruction. Debra provided access to the John McClintock papers. The archivists at the Howard Gotleib Archival Research Center at Boston University made available the William Warren papers. James W. Gerencser, archivist at Dickinson College, Carlisle, Pennsylvania, provided me with Board Minutes relevant to Simpson's relationship to that institution.

Obviously, several libraries and historical societies which I have been unable to visit, have furnished me information and materials. Among them are the Warren County Historical Society, Lebanon, Ohio, the Western Reserve Historical Society in Cleveland, Ohio, and Baldwin-Wallace College in Berea, Ohio.

It was my fortune to research the details of the Lincoln Funeral as the Abraham Lincoln Presidential Library and Museum prepared to re-enact the Lincoln Funeral in Springfield, Illinois, May of 2015. Within one half-hour of arriving at the Library, Curator James Cornelius had placed on my desk approximately fifteen items which enabled me to gain a clearer perception of what actually took place in Springfield during those mournful days. I also visited Northwestern University in Evanston, Illinois, during the time that the University had commissioned eight senior scholars to investigate John Evans' complicity in the Sand Creek Massacre. Northwestern Archivist Kevin Leonard quickly pointed me to pertinent materials and provided further information via email.

The Newberry Library in Chicago and Washington University in St. Louis are among the most comprehensive research institutions in the Midwest. Of course, I often invaded libraries around Kansas City who extended help to a complete stranger: the Nichols Library at the University of Missouri at Kansas City, the Watson Library at the University of Kansas, the Mid-Continent Library branches in Kansas City, the Missouri Valley Special Collections Library at the Central Public Library of Kansas City, and the Genealogical Library of Independence, Missouri. Jennifer McCullough and Sara DeCaro of Baker University, Baldwin City, Kansas, aided my efforts at that institution which now houses the most complete collection of Methodist materials in the Kansas City area.

No institution has been more helpful than Nazarene Theological Seminary where I was previously a professor. Library Director Deborah Bradshaw did her utmost to put my hands on needed resources or to find historical tidbits floating in cyberspace. Inter-library Loan Specialist Alexandra Duenow ordered countless books and items. She also did much word processing, utilizing her high-level cutting and pasting skills.

Nancy Beverage, one of the fastest typists I have ever known, worked on early manuscript copies. Josiah Ragan, "Production Service Expert" at Office Depot, ran off thousands of manuscript pictures and rescued me from several bewildering computer jams. Our neighbor Bart Nitz, resident technology guru, came to our aid on several occasions.

The following persons read all or parts of the manuscript, making valuable suggestions and typo corrections: Scott Pendleton, Stella Harris, Stephen Lowe, Wesley Wilson, Steve McCormick, William Dean, William Miller, Russell Richey, John Wigger, Gary Leland Roberts, Stephen Gunter, Richard Stowe, and Kenneth Kinghorn. Dr. Richey, my former history professor and American Methodism scholar par excellent, shared several perspectives which have made this book more accurate. To those who wrote endorsements and exaggerated my scholarship, I am truly grateful. I thank

Robert Danielson and his staff at First Fruits, Asbury Theological Seminary, Wilmore, Kentucky, for translating my efforts into a finished product.

Three special people have been of particular help. My spiritual director David Wilson has enabled me to maintain my sanity (I think) while attempting something for which my capabilities do not measure up. My closest life-long friend, Edwin (Bud) Salter (no blood relation until six generations back) just so happens to have a daughter living in the Baltimore-Washington area. I kept track of his travels to Maryland, and often leaned on him to retrieve information at the Library of Congress, which during my previous research visits I had overlooked. Bud also accompanied me to Sand Creek, Colorado, November 29, 2012, which was my first venture into the Simpson narrative. To our delightful surprise, we participated with the descendants of those native Indians who were killed on that tragic morning, in the first memorial service ever conducted on the site.

All the persons, whom I have mentioned, do not compare to my wife Brenda Rose Campbell Salter, who has stuck with me during this arduous task. Her typing skills, emails, research knowledge, and finding a parking spot while I ducked into an archive, have been essential. Brenda is the single most critical evidence in my life that there is a God. No one is a better example of fulfilling those vows we took four decades and four years ago at Danforth Chapel on the campus of Berea College, Berea, Kentucky. As a wife, help-meet, mother, and "Grammy" she is unsurpassed.

To God Be the Glory!

Darius Salter
September 2016

Table of Contents

Dedication	i
Acknowledgments	ii
Introduction	1
1. The Outlier from Cadiz	**11**
Ominous Beginnings	11
The Simpsons and Cadiz	14
The Remarkable Uncle Matthew	20
The Blessing of Escapism	26
A Pious Mother	29
Other Important Mentors: John McBean and Joseph Tingley	31
2. The Child of Providence	**37**
Courthouse Entertainment	37
The Methodist Invasion	38
Piety Avenue	41
Matthew and God	44
Spiritual Doubts	46
A Brief College Experience	49
Simpson as a Medical Doctor	53
The Call to Ministry	56
3. Cellars, Garrets, and Soot	**63**
The Circuit Rider	63
Young Men of Great Promise	65

Simpson Steps into a Hornet's Nest	67
Early Romantic Feelings	71
Simpson's Future In-Laws: The Prominent Verners	74
Marriage to Ellen	78
The Struggling Young Pastor	83
Faithfulness and Popularity	85
Pastoral Initiative and Revival	88

4. A Highly Ordered Life — 93

Finneyism and Other Isms	93
Spiritual Conflict and Depression	95
Lincoln and Simpson "Push Hard"	99
Total Commitment and Then Some	102
Utterly Confounded at Simpson's Appearance	107
A Faithful Last Charge	109

5. Becoming an Orator — 115

Allegheny College	115
Becoming an Educator	117
Conflict with Uncle Matthew over Abolition	119
Elected as President of Indiana Asbury	123
Pulpit Triumph	125
Oratorical Leadership	129
The Beginning of a Life-long Mantra	132
A Contagious Hypnosis	134
The Competition	138
Benevolent Paternalism	141
Storming Through Indiana	147
Indiana Becomes Insolvent	150
Beginning Tension with Edward Ames	153
Cousin Joseph Tingley	156

6. A Jubilee in Hell 159

The Tinderbox	159
A Delegate to the Critical 1844 General Conference	162
Simpson Begins a Life-long Friendship with the Harper Brothers	164
An Inescapable Agenda - Slavery	167
It Just So Happened	170
Schooled by Southerners	172
Non-negotiable Cultures	174
The Unprecedented Significance of the 1844 General Conference	178
Simpson Attends Southern Methodism's First Conference	179
Simpson Resigns from Asbury	181
The Loss of Four-Year-Old Jimmy	182
Simpson and the Northern Reversal	184
Simpson's Ecclesiastical Ascendency	186
Simpson Replaces Charles Elliott as Editor	188

7. A Political and Spiritual Tightrope 195

He Arrived Broke	195
America's Fastest Growing City	198
Conquering Distance	200
A Spirit of Kindness and Universal Charity	202
An Over-whelmed Novice	204
Unavoidable Conflict	205
The Specters of Calvinism and Catholicism	208
Titillating Sensationalism and Quotidian Mundaneness	210
The Fugitive Slave Law	214
The Elusive Middle Crowd	216
Anti–Slavery without Abolition	218
A Janus-like Response	222
A Myopic Triumphalism	224
A Conflicted Conscience	226

8. An Astute Politician — 231

Carefully Playing His Political Cards — 231
Why Simpson? — 233
One Great Sermon — 238
The Realities of the Job — 240
Hell with the Lid Off — 243
The Building Tension between Husband and Wife — 244
Long Distance Parenting — 246
Spiritual and Physical Hypochondria — 247
The Systemic Sins of Ecclesiastical Life — 249
Continuing Domestic Guilt — 251

9. In Case of Any Accident — 255

Mundane Obligations — 255
The Refuse of Creation — 257
The Night of That Terrible Storm — 259
Never "Sene" A Bishop — 263
Against the Current — 264
The Martyrdom of Anthony Bewley — 266
The Kansas-Nebraska Act and an Impotent Church — 268
A Bleeding Nation — 269
The Stevens-Simpson Conspiracy — 272

10. The High and the Low — 277

A Dream Come True — 277
Historic Trails — 279
The Holy Land — 281
At Death's Door — 284
John Evans Enters Simpson's Life — 286
Beginnings of Northwestern and Garrett Biblical Institute — 288
Simpson's Influence on Frances E. Willard — 292
Simpson and Benjamin Titus Roberts Collide — 293
The Ouster of Benjamin Titus Roberts — 295

A Huge Fault-line in the Methodist Episcopal Church	297
Not A Good Day to be a Bishop	299
Civil War Detonators	300

## 11. Headquarters at the White House	305

Simpson Ready to Step on the National Stage	305
Lincoln and Methodism	309
Simpson Begins His Washington Treks	310
Simpson Becomes the Protestant Patronage King	313
Besieged by Desperate Requests	317
Simpson and the Emancipation Proclamation	321
Religious Pressure on Lincoln	324
Simpson's Conversion to Emancipation	327
Ecclesiastical War within the Civil War	330
Simpson Becomes a Southern Persona non Grata	333
Lincoln Reverses Johnson	334

## Illustrations	340

A Young Photograph of Matthew Simpson	340
Uncle Matthew- polymath and Ohio State Legislator who raised Simpson	341
Two-story house where Uncle Matthew raised the future Bishop	342
Charles Elliott- Guided Matthew Simpson toward ministry	343
A Photograph of Ellen Vernor Simpson	344
An Early Painting of Matthew Simpson	345
Henry Bascom, who influenced Simpson's preaching style	346
Edward Ames- Fellow Methodist Bishop and envious adversary	347
James Harlan, United State Secretary of the Interior who "tipped" Simpson on railroad investments	348
John Evans, Simpson's closest friend implicated in the Sand Creek Massacre	349
Frances Willard, a great admirer of Simpson, who was converted under his ministry, but was later disappointed at his lack of support for her "causes."	350

John Chivington- Methodist Elder who led the Sand Creek Massacre and was never brought to justice by Simpson and the Methodist Episcopal Church   351

James Harper, founder of *Harper's Weekly* and mayor of New York   352

Metropolitan Memorial Methodist Episcopal Church in Washington, D.C.   353

Daniel Drew- benefactor of Drew Theological Seminary and Wall Street manipulator   354

An Older Matthew Simpson   355

A Group Photograph at the Milan Conference in 1875   356

Picture in *Leslie's Illustrated Magazine* of Simpson praying the Dedication Prayer for the 1876 Centennial Celebration in Philadelphia   357

Bishop Matthew Simpson Portrait   358

1334 Arch Street Mansion in Philadelphia   359

Simpson mausoleum in West Laurel Hills Cemetery   360

The Simpson House, Philadelphia   361

Statue of Bishop Matthew Simpson on front lawn of Simpson House in Fairmount Park, Philadelphia   362

12. "God Cannot Do without America"   365

The Preeminent Clerical Voice   365
The Cross and the Flag   366
Lincoln-"I Prefer Simpson to Speak for Me"   368
The War Speech   370
"God Cannot Do without America"   373
Simpson's Millennial Nationalism   375
A Theological Miscue   378
No Pen Can Adequately Describe the Speech   380
The Cosmic Affirmation   383

13. Hero, Martyr, Friend, FAREWELL !   **389**

A Deserved Rebuke	389
The Second Inauguration's Official Parade	391
The Good Friday Assassination and Christian Nationalism	393
Simpson Chosen as the Preacher for the Springfield Memorial	395
The Lincoln Funeral	396
The Eulogy	400
A Glaring Contradiction	401
Simpson's Civil War Legacy	403

14. The Broken Arrow of Patronage   **407**

The Indian Crisis in the West	407
Simpson and the Appointment of John Evans as Territorial Governor of Colorado	409
Evans Over His Head	413
Enter John Chivington	415
"The Fighting Parson"	416
A Soldier's Soldier	418
Simpson and Chivington	421
Escalating Tension and Explosion	422
Defenseless Women and Children	425
The Damaging Testimonies of Edward Wynkoop and Silas Soule	426
The Official U.S. Government Censure of John Evans and John Chivington	427
Evans Ultimately Indicts Himself	429
Simpson's Intervention for Evans	430
The Close Friendship of Evans and Simpson	434
Chivingon Maintains His Ministerial Credentials Inspite of His Sordid Past	436
Simpson's Financial Investments and Conflict of Interest	440
Methodism Attempts Amends	443
Simpson, Evans, and the Collusion of Silence	445

15. All the King's Horses and All the King's Men 449

The Primary Worry of the Simpson Family 449
Tension Between Simpson and McCullough 452
The Move to Philadelphia 453
Looking Older than His 55 Years 457
So Violent a Break and Continued Bitterness within Methodism 462
Simpson Recommends the Eccentric John Baldwin 466
"A Noble and Christian Cause" 470

16. A Withered Olive Branch 473

The Overture of Simpson and Janes 473
James Lynch: Simpson's Most Powerful Southern Voice 475
The Deaths of Charles and Mother Sarah 478
Edwin Stanton and Matthew Simpson Align Themselves Against Andrew Johnson 480
Stanton Begs Simpson for a Recommendation to a Seat on the U.S. Supreme Court 484
The Failure of Simpson and Methodists to Oust Johnson 485
Simpson Prays at the Republican National Convention 488
Simpson and the Methodists Support Grant 490
James Riley Weaver-The Son Simpson Never Had 492

17. Anything for a Methodist 497

An Architectural and Finanical Crisis 497
Simpson's Summer Resort 501
Simpson Endorses Ocean Grove 502
Simpson and the Founding of John Vincent's Chautauqua 503
Daniel Drew and the Founding of Drew Theological Seminary 506
Durbin and Simpson Disagree 508
The Consequences of Drew's Bankruptcy 510
Phoebe Palmer Attempts to Push Simpson into Holiness 513
Simpson and the National Camp Meeting Association for the Promotion of Holiness 518

The White Protestant Establishment as America's Foremost
Identity   522

18. "He Will Draw You to Your Feet"   527

The Golden Age of Oratory   527
The Deluge of Invitations   529
They Wept, Shouted and Danced for Joy   531
The Timelessness of Simpson's Preaching   533
Simpson's Biblical Hermeneutic   536
Simpson's Sermons Could Be Seen   538
Simpson's Christology   541
Simpson's Pneumatology   543
Justification of the Ways of God   546
A Utopian Ecclesiology   549
Simpson's Eschatology and Progressive Nationalism   550
Prosperity and the Anglo-Methodist Victory   553
Experiential Disconnects   557
A Crisis Impossible to Ignore   558
The Humanistic Inheritance   560
Preparation and Delivery   563
High Spirituality and Low Theology   564
"He Will Draw You to Your Feet"   566

19. Feuding Friends and Competing Paradigms   571

Suspected Crime at the Publishing House   571
One of the Botchers May Have Been Simpson   572
Lanahan Arrested   575
Simpson Exonerates Carlton   577
Simpson and Lay Representation Triumph   578
Merchant Princes of the Land   580
Women's Suffrage, but …   581
Simpson the Lecturer   583
Off to Europe and the Death of Uncle Matthew   587
The Evolution Explosion   591

Simpson Missed a Critical Opportunity   593
Broad and Catholic Views   595

20. The Ideal Christian Gentleman   599

America's Centennial Celebration in Philadelphia   599
Rutherford Hays and Simpson   604
The Favorite Preacher of American Presidents   607
The Colorado Iliffs   609
Cyclopaedia   612
The First World Methodist Ecumenical Conference   614
Methodism's Distinguished Doctrines Muted   617
Simpson's Tribute to an Assassinated President   619
Physical Collapse in San Francisco   621
Unofficial Chaplain to the U. S. Government   622
The Bishop's Last Sermon   623
The Simpson's Purchase a Mansion   626
Women in Ministry   627
Valedictory   628
Death and Funeral   629

Epilogue and Reflection   637

The Biography Squabble   637
Ellen's Influence   640
Matthew Verner Simpson   643
The Daughters and Final Distribution of the Estate   647
Blindsided by Modernity   652
Simpson's Nationalistic Agenda   654
The Theological and Sociological Critique   659
Historical Responses and Consequences   661
Final Legacy   665

Bibliography   670

Secondary Sources   670
Primary Sources   703
Archives   712

Newspapers	719
Journals	724
Unpublished Dissertations	729
Magazines	730
Websites	731

Index **734**

Introduction

The official Sunday service for Abraham Lincoln's second inauguration took place on March 5, 1865. On March 4, the date of the inauguration, the breaking of the clouds and appearing of the sun evidenced heaven's blessing on the most theologically profound speech ever given by a United States President. "Yet, if God wills that it continue until all the wealth piled by the bondsman's two hundred and fifty years of unrequited toil shall be sunk, and until every drop of blood drawn with the lash shall be paid by another drawn with the sword, as was said three thousand years ago, so shall it must be said, the judgments of the Lord are true and righteous altogether." Chosen to preach the "Congressional Sermon" the next morning in the House of Representatives chamber, Matthew Simpson's eloquence rose to the occasion. Simpson chose as his text, John 12:22, "If I be lifted up, I will draw all men unto me." Simpson did exalt Christ, but also proclaimed the righteousness of the Northern cause, the providence of God, the assurance of God's future blessing, and the centrality of America in God's plan for the redemption of the world. In response, Abraham Lincoln wept, stomped his feet, and tapped his agreement on the floor with a cane. Less than two months later, Simpson preached Lincoln's funeral in Springfield.

The argument of this book is that Matthew Simpson, the most prominent Bishop in America's largest denomination, was a decisive force in both the political and religious life of Civil War America. According to his contemporaries, Simpson was the most influential clergyman in the life of Abraham Lincoln. If that is so, why has he been given so little historical attention? His "War Speech," more than any other linguistic event, galvanized the North, yet few Lincoln–Civil War scholars recognize Simpson's contribution.[1] Civil War scholars, Richard Carwardine and George Rable,

---

1   For example, given his subject manner, Harry S. Stout should have at least

"God Cannot Do Without America"

are among the few exceptions who weave Simpson into their narratives. Carwardine writes, "Bishop Matthew Simpson, who crisscrossed as an evangelist of patriotism, was unsurpassed in his power to melt an audience to tears or rouse it to the heights of passion and enthusiasm for the war-torn flag."[2] Rable alludes to Simpson's "War Speech," but offers no extended analysis, even though his survey text thoroughly explores religion during the Civil War. Rable's conclusion concerning the voluminous historiography on the Civil War is accurate: "The grand and sweeping narratives of the sectional crisis and Civil War from James Ford Rhodes to Bruce Catton, to Shelby Foote and beyond, have seldom paid attention to religion, much less try to create a religious narrative of the conflict. Yet many devout people of the time would have considered this a curious omission."[3] Rable argues that almost all Americans held to a providential view of history, God's oversight in human affairs. The following pages will contend that Matthew Simpson, more than any other person, championed God's intervention in the Civil War, and the ultimate victory of the North.

Lack of tabloid fodder is a partial explanation for Simpson's obscurity. As Debby Applegate argues, Henry Ward Beecher, Simpson's contemporary, was "The Most Famous Man in America."[4] Simpson could not compare to either Beecher's platform flamboyancy or his licentious reputation. Preaching before "eleven mistresses," fathering at least one out-of-wedlock child, and enduring a year-long defamation trial is the stuff of intriguing biographies. Sin sells more print than does righteousness. It is my impression that for every ten times Beecher is referenced in American historiography, Simpson is mentioned once. This neglect would also prove true for homiletical texts published in the century following Simpson's death. For instance, the primary text for preaching during my undergraduate years, *The Preparation*

---

mentioned Simpson, but such was not the case. Harry S. Stout. *Upon the Altar of the Nation: A Moral History of the Civil War* (New York: Viking Adult, 2006). Doris Goodwin, Michael Burlingame, David Donald, James McPherson, and a host of other Lincoln and Civil War scholars, make no mention Simpson, other than he preached Lincoln's funeral.

2   Richard Carwardine. *Lincoln: A Life and Purpose and Power* (New York: Vintage Books, 2006) 279-280.

3   George C. Rable. *God's Almost Chosen Peoples: A Religious History of the Civil War* (Chapel Hill: The University of North Carolina, 2010) 5.

4   Debby Applegate. *The Most Famous Man in America: The Biography of Henry Ward Beecher* (New York: Doubleday, 2006).

and Delivery of Sermons by John Broadus and Jesse Weatherspoon, refers to Beecher six times and Simpson none.[5]

Others conjecture that Simpson's obscurity may include the Calvinistic bias of historians, or the lack of heresy accusations that were thrown at the likes of Theodore Parker, Ralph Waldo Emerson, and Horace Bushnell. Also, Simpson has been hidden by the bureaucracy of a denomination, rather than giving himself to the popularity of the "Lyceum Circuit." Neither did Simpson peculiarize himself by a radical stand on slavery or anything else. Normalcy and moderation do not make for riveting reading.

In no full length treatment of Simpson now existing would we find out exactly where he lived, who were his children, anything regarding his many economic investments, his tense relationship with his wife, Ellen, as well as the influence which she and the Verner family made upon his life. Though others have referred to his depression which constantly hounded him, no one has explored it. And maybe most importantly, though Simpson was primarily known as a preacher, no one has theologically and homiletically analyzed the content or methodology of his preaching.

George Crooks, a late contemporary of Simpson, wrote a biography immediately after the Bishop's death, *The Life of Bishop Matthew Simpson*.[6] Crooks' biography contains much original Simpson material such as letters and *Diary* entries, but offers little historical context or interpretation. It also suffered as the "authorized biography," and thus, Crooks could say nothing that would displease the Simpson family. The other two full-length treatments of Simpson were academically-driven, institutional projects limited in scope and interpretation. It may seem arrogant for me to claim that at the present time, no comprehensive biography of Simpson exists, at least according to my interpretation of what needs to be the salient features of a biography, reflections on both Simpson's private and public life.

---

5   John Broadus and Jesse Weatherspoon. *On The Preparation and Delivery of Sermons* (New York: Harper and Roe, 1944).

6   George Crooks. *The Life of Bishop Matthew Simpson* (New York: Harper and Brothers, 1890).

4 | "God Cannot Do Without America"

In 1956, Robert Clark published an abridged edition of his Ph.D. dissertation, *The Life of Matthew Simpson*.[7] Clark did extensive research and has left us the most factual and chronological account of Simpson. Clark excelled in capturing the essence of Simpson's moral and ecclesiastical influence, but failed to explicate the context and momentous events that swirled around him. Clark crammed his biography full of events, but gave little evaluation of Simpson's spiritual and psychological interaction with these events. We are left with a very busy Simpson who breathlessly, with little reflection, jumped from appointment to appointment. Clark does not allow us to know Simpson, or as one reviewer of Clark's work critiqued, "We miss the psychological and pathological, and especially the pathological. Did the good Bishop have no fixations, no frustrations, alas, no libido?"[8]

I assure you that Simpson had plenty of libido, as well as neurotic tendencies, was a man of romantic passion, and fulfilled a vocation which entrapped him in emotional turmoil and spiritual conflict, if not massive contradictions. Writing biography demands both exploring the uniqueness of the individual, and simultaneously identifying the frailties and foibles which assure us that our subject fully participated in that universal condition referred to as humanity. Like all "great people," Simpson transcended his contemporaries while at the same time remaining a "representative man." These two qualities were especially true of both Simpson and Abraham Lincoln, whose lives paralleled one another in numerous ways, which I will explore.

A more analytical and objective work than the publications by Crooks and Clark, is an unpublished Ph. D. dissertation by James Edmund Kirby, Jr., *The Ecclesiastical and Social Thought of Matthew Simpson*. Kirby argued that Simpson reflected an American, if not humanistic optimism, which was more representative of middle class morality than Wesleyan theology. Simpson espoused an active theology of doing good with a radical optimism

---

7   Robert D. Clark. *The Life of Matthew Simpson* (New York: McMillan and Company, 1956), based on his Ph.D. dissertation, *The Pulpit and Platform Career and The Rhetorical Theory of Bishop Matthew Simpson*, presented to the Faculty of the Graduate School, The University of Southern California in partial fulfillment of the requirement for the degree, Doctor of Philosophy, March 1946.

8   Alexander Mackey, "The Life of Matthew Simpson by Robert D. Clark," *Pennsylvania History* Vol. 23, No. 4 (October 23, 1956) 535-536.

for every soul finding a divine destiny. Although Simpson preached a manifest destiny that bordered on utopianism, he was realistically "attuned to his inner sense of influence and obligation to both his country and the Church; both which he dearly loved and served. No one was more representative of revivalistic Protestantism and American culture which occurred in the last half of the Nineteenth Century."[9] Kirby's astute analysis of Simpson's thought and ministry is helpful, but does not serve as a "biography."

Because Simpson believed the Church to be God's ordained instrument for moral reformation and never forgot his debt to Methodism, increasingly believing that his denomination was God's supreme institution for defeating Catholicism and every other "theological aberration" on the American continent, Kirby argues that Simpson knowingly rejected the prestige that could have been enjoyed through government patronage or public speaking for a fee. Kirby's point is well taken, but only partially correct. Though Simpson never accepted any official position within the United States Government, no clergyman without official portfolio had more effect on the course of the Union during and immediately after the Civil War. In spite of the deficiencies in all three of these works (My own work will demonstrate no less.) I stand on the shoulders of these authors. They have been invaluable for checking dates, the wording of a transcription, and tracing resources. Crooks did a monumental job in transcribing Simpson's illegible handwriting, and I have heavily relied on him. Another reason for utilizing Crooks is an "Autobiography" to which he had access, a document which he did not return to the Simpson family. Clark, Kirby, and I have not been able to access this narrative supposedly penned by Simpson.

Two hagiographies have been far less reliable: E. M. Woods' *The Peerless Orator*, and Clarence True Wilson's *Matthew Simpson: Patriot, Preacher, Prophet*, the latter riddled with errors, and most responsible for Simpson myths, which need to be reexamined and corrected.

Historian Timothy Smith placed Simpson in the vanguard of humanitarian reform, along with Edward Norris Kirk and Albert Barnes, who "never tired of glowing descriptions of the social and economic

---

9   James Edmund Kirby. *The Ecclesiastical and Social Thought of Matthew Simpson* (Unpublished Ph.D. dissertation, Drew University, 1963) 280.

millennium which they believed revival Christianity would bring into existence."[10] Smith demonstrated his Wesleyan bias by designating Simpson as one who "enjoyed the reputation of being America's greatest preacher." This book will reference many of Simpson's contemporaries who thought the same. Simpson proclaimed his millennial optimism at the Centennial Celebration of the Methodist Episcopal Church, "Another hundred years the earth shall stand in beauty and glory; a hundred years and the banner of the cross shall shine triumphant over every mountain top and every valley and the islands of the sea shall give their treasures to Emmanuel; a hundred years they will be singing in choirs and throughout the earth Halleluiah! The Lord God omnipotent reigneth."[11]

No historian whom I have read has charged Simpson with heresy, much less blasphemy for his claim that "God cannot do without America." Robert Handy (though he does not name Simpson) places Simpson's ethnocentric theology within the normative patriotic religion which prevailed during the Civil War and has never ceased to thrive in, at least, some segments of American society until this day.[12] When Simpson proclaimed to vast throngs, perhaps the largest addressed by any person of that era, his conviction that God seemingly needed America as much as America needed God, there was no clanging discord, no incongruity within the American ethos and scant hint that the ways of America may be at odds with the sovereign wisdom of God, as the fifty-fifth chapter of Isaiah suggests. Perry Miller wrote, "That is what is really astounding. Most of the ardent celebrators of national America sincerely continued to be professing Christians. Or really the amazing fact is that they so seldom hardly ever had any inclination that the basis of their patriotism and those of their creed stood in the slightest degree in contradiction."[13]

"God's favor" has been one of the predominant themes of American identity since the Separatists landed on Plymouth Rock and John Winthrop

---

10   Timothy L. Smith. *Revivalism and Social Reform in Mid-Nineteenth Century America* (New York: Abingdon Press, 1957) 151.

11   Ibid., 234.

12   Robert T. Handy. *A Christian America: Protestant Hopes and Historical Realities* (New York: Oxford University Press, 1971).

13   Perry Miller. *Errand in the Wilderness* (New York: Harper & Row, 1956) 219.

proclaimed, as he sat in the cabin of the *Arbella*, that America would be the "New England", the "city set upon a hill" for all the world to see.[14] America as the "new Jerusalem," God's ultimate communitarian experiment, reached full flower in nineteenth century utopianism, transcendentalism, Finney-Wesleyan revivalism, and above all, the triumphalism of the Methodist Episcopal Church, America's largest denomination, of which Simpson was the preeminent leader. From early colonial days to present time, in particular the nineteenth century, this energizing myth of a people favored and destined by God, left little doubt that Christian moral effort would bring the Kingdom of God to earth and America would be the primary actor in the transformation. Smith traced the streams of transcendentalism, Wesleyan Perfectionism, evangelical revivalism, and a millennial fervor that was distinctly American, into a confluence of romantic optimism that ruled antebellum America. Simpson, as much or more than any other person, would propagate this optimism in post-bellum America, until his death in 1884.

The title of this book is ambitious, if not brazenly hypothetical. Though others thought it, no one blatantly and forthrightly claimed that "God cannot do without America," not Ralph Waldo Emerson, Horace Bushnell, Theodore Parker nor Henry Ward Beecher. Without serious theological contemplation and sustained Biblical inquiry, the historical context of mid-nineteenth century America supported the ideals of a democratic society built on theocratic aspirations. Americans set about with due diligence definitively answering the question posed by Lincoln at Gettysburg,

---

14 Simpson escapes the notice of several authors, who would be expected to make him exhibit A of American Protestantism's penchant for confusing American manifest destiny and imperialism with the claims of the Bible. Simpson is absent from Martin Marty's *Righteous Empire*, Ernest Tuveson's *Redeemer Nation*, Mark Noll's *History of Christianity in the United States and Canada*, and Edwin S. Gaustad's *The Religious History of America*. A handful of historians have alluded to Simpson, if not giving him due credit. Sydney Ahlstrom's 1,000 page otherwise credible and comprehensive, *A Religious History of the American People* makes only one mention of Simpson. Ahlstrom observed that when California became a state, Simpson claimed that the American flag over Monterey "was a sure sign of God's special role for the United States," but made no mention of Simpson's role in the Civil War. Then Ahlstrom, from my perspective, made an egregious error, when he argued that Beecher and Brooks were in a class by themselves as "princes of the pulpit." Sydney E. Ahlstrom. *A Religious History of the American People* (Garden City: New York: Image Books, 1975) 79. The consistent slight of Simpson by hundreds of American church historians demands rectification.

"Whether any nation so conceived and so dedicated can long endure." Evangelicals believed the Civil War to be the ultimate crucible, God's test as to whether America would be true to the Biblical covenant which had been handed down to them by their Puritan forefathers. James Moorhead argues that the Civil War, a "holy war," brought about a "new conception of national unity. Most Protestants had held that the essence of U. S. nationalism was adherence to the democratic creed and that all people, whatever their origin, might become true Americans."[15] Out of all groups, religious or otherwise, the Protestant establishment of Presbyterians, Baptists, Congregationalists, and Methodists would understand itself as most representative of American nationalism. Methodism was by far the largest of these groups, and Matthew Simpson its most influential spokesman. The belief that America would redeem the world reached its apotheosis during and immediately after the Civil War. No one incarnated, proclaimed and popularized this conviction more than did Matthew Simpson.

Never did self-congratulatory chauvinism and ethnocentrism uncritically capture the American imagination more than in the waning days of the Civil War and the following two decades, which preceded the capital-labor embattlement. Reconstruction, urban blight, political corruption, and the "robber barons" would dim the glow of Simpson's enthusiasm, but in spite of much revisionist history, his nationalistic theology endures to this day. However, as uninformed as the American church may be concerning American nativism, imperialism, and colonialism, the most fervent fundamentalist of the 21st century probably would not forthrightly and blatantly say, "God cannot do without America." In other words, how did Simpson get away with it? We will explore why and how post-bellum America and Matthew Simpson reached the apex of Protestant nationalism, unmatched by any other period. Eminent Methodist historian, Russell Richey, answers his own question in the affirmative: "Had Methodists conflated the kingdom of God with the nation, construed denominational purposes in terms of those of a Christian America, and in making the church subservient to Christian nationalism intimately tied the former's health to the latter's?"[16] Simpson's

---

15   James H. Moorhead. *American Apocalypse: Yankee Protestants and the Civil War* (New Haven: Yale University Press, 1978) II.

16   Russell E. Richey. "History as a Bearer of Denominational Identity: Methodism as a Case Study," *Perspectives on American Methodism: Interpretative Essays*, eds. Russell E.

populous proclamation promoted an exact correlation between America's prominence in the world and Methodism's prominence in America. Right or wrong, no one did it better.

Richey, Kenneth E. Rowe, and Jean Miller Schmidt (Nashville: Abingdon Press, 1993) 480.

Chapter One:
The Outlier from Cadiz

Ominous Beginnings

Some events are best not remembered. The one-year-old boy held by his mother at his father's burial would never know his dad; much less remember the suffering which the father had endured for years. Infant Matthew, not long after his birth in June 1811, had been taken by his parents to Pittsburgh, so that his father could take advantage of better medical care. The move proved futile. James Simpson only got worse and died June 15 of 1812.[17] The sorrow was as smothering as the heat and humidity which shrouded the Allegheny Mountains. As Matthew would read years later in one of his medical books concerning tuberculosis: "It is melancholy to reflect how very little this disease is under the control of medicine and before I can enter upon the consideration of the principles which are to guide us in its treatment, I must record the failure of every plan for its effectual cure, which human ingenuity has yet devised."[18] The 31-year-old Sarah with her three children in tow moved back to Cadiz, Ohio, where support of family and friends awaited them. Under such calamitous circumstances the future seemed dark, if not hopeless, for her one-year-old son, five-year-old, Hetty, and three-year-old Elizabeth.

In 1787, the Northwest ordinance, an act of Congress, designated the land northwest of the Ohio River as the Northwest Territory. In 1803, the territory became the state of Ohio with a population of 60,000. The first

---

17 LOC, Simpson papers, "Notes on Family History," Matthew Simpson, Container twenty. The Allegheny County record of deaths and births does not extend back to 1812. There are no extant court records or newspaper articles regarding the death of James Simpson. His place of burial is unknown.

18 George Gregory. *Elements of the Theory and Practice of Physic* (Philadelphia: Towar and Hogan, 1829) 433.

12 | "God Cannot Do Without America"

steamboat paddled from Pittsburgh to Cincinnati in 1811; it was also in 1811 that the Erie Canal, Dewitt Clinton's "ditch" was begun, by 1825 linking Albany with Buffalo, New York. Most historically memorable, is that 1811 was the year of the New Madrid earthquake. The first series of quakes, approaching 8.0 on the present-day "Richter Scale," took place during December in southeast Missouri in the vicinity of New Madrid. "The Mississippi River was churned into a virtual maelstrom with miles of banks caving in, boats being swamped and sunken, and even an entire island disappearing, along with their human occupants."[19] New Madrid scholars David Stewart and Ray Knox claim that the 8.9 magnitude shock on January 23, 1812, could be felt throughout two-thirds of the United States, from the Rockies to the Atlantic seaboard. It was detected in three other countries, Mexico, Canada, and Cuba. "Chimneys fell in Cincinnati, sidewalks buckled in Baltimore, church bells rang in Boston."[20]

The earthquake reaped an evangelistic harvest. James Finley, who was the Methodist most influential in the area of Simpson's nativity, remarked, "This year will long be remembered as the one in which the whole region was shaken by a mighty earthquake. On the night of the twelfth of February, I was awakened by the rocking of the house in which I slept. It seemed as if my bedstead was on a rough sea, and the waves were rolling under, so sensible were the undulations. Slight shocks were felt about every day and night for some time. One day, while I was preaching a funeral the house began to rock, and the cupboard doors flew open. The people became alarmed and commenced shrieking and running. It was a time of great terror to sinners."[21] The Ohio Conference between 1810 and 1813 demonstrated a greater percentage growth during that three year period, than any ten-year epoch in the nineteenth century.[22]

---

19   David Stewart and Ray Knox. *The Earthquake That Never Went Away: The Shaking Stopped in 1812, But The Impact Goes On* (Marble Hill, Missouri: Gutenberg–Richter Publications, 1993) 17.

20   Ibid., 21.

21   James B. Finley. *Autobiography of James B. Finley* (Cincinnati: Methodist Book Concern, 1872) 238.

22   John Barker. *History of Ohio Methodism* (New York: Eaton and Mains, 1898) 123. Walter Posey calculates, "In the Methodist Church the Western Conference in 1811 was composed of the whole of Tennessee, Kentucky, and contiguous sections of Mississippi, Arkansas, Illinois, Indiana, Ohio, and West Virginia, nearly all of which lay in the seismical

In 1750 John Wesley, the founder of Methodism, preached a sermon, "The Cause and Cure of Earthquakes." Earthquakes were God's means to get the attention of sinners. Wesley's world view represented eighteenth century cosmological and theological understanding.[23] Eighteen hundred eleven was a dooms-dayer's delight. There were plenty of reasons for eschatological enthusiasts to ravage the *Book of the Revelation*. Historian Jay Feldman tracks the 1811-1812 climatic disturbances, bewildering and horrifying to a culture without the Weather Channel and not acquainted with El Nino. Massive flooding that summer took place in the Ohio and Mississippi River valleys. Intense heat and humidity smothered the Eastern seaboard cities. Tornadoes raked towns and cities from Maine to Georgia, including a storm, which killed more than a dozen in Charleston, South Carolina. Ominous portents emerged from land and sea, and stretched across the heavens. On September 17, an almost total eclipse of the sun darkened the skies on an otherwise clear and cloudless day, "so that its appearance was the most solemn and impressive that we could conceive." But all these cosmic signs paled in comparison to the Great Comet, fifteen million miles wide with a tail one hundred million miles long, that was visible from September through December. Those with a theological bent, which was almost everyone, waxed poetical:

> More than six months have past and gone,
> And still the earth keeps shaking;
> The Christians go with bow'd down heads,
> While sinners' hearts are breaking.

---

region of 1811 and 1812. In 1811, the Western Conference had a total membership of 30,741. This same territory (divided in 1812 into Tennessee and Ohio Conferences) at the next Conference reported 45,983, a net gain of 15,242, while in the years of 1811, 1812, and 1813, the whole of the country outside of the West increased its membership from 157,419 to 164,616, and to 168,324—additions of only 7,197 and 3,708 respectively." Walter Brownlow Posey. "The Earthquake of 1811 and Its Influence on Evangelistic Methods in the Churches of the Old South" in *Tennessee Historical Magazine* (January 1931) 111.

23 John Wesley. "The Cause and Cure of Earthquakes," *The Works of John Wesley* Vol. VII (Kansas City: Beacon Hill Press of Kansas City, 1978) 386-399. See Samuel W. Watkins. "The Causes and Cures of Earthquakes: Methodists and the New Madrid Earthquake 1811–1812," *Methodist History* (July 1992) 242-250.

The great event I cannot tell,
Nor what the Lord is doing;
But one thing I am well assur'd,
The scriptures are fulfilling.

The prophets did foretell of old,
That great events are coming;
The Lord Almighty's bringing on
The days of tribulation.[24]

The Simpsons and Cadiz

James Simpson, born in Tyrone County, Ireland, arrived in America in 1793. After a brief stop in Maryland he moved to Pittsburgh, where with his brother, Matthew, and John Wrenshall, opened a general merchandising store.[25] In 1804, James moved to Cadiz, Ohio, where he found treed hills, clear streams, rich soil and enough flat ground for a nascent village. Building foundations would be stabilized by solid limestone and rich veins of coal. Ohio topographical scholar J. A. Caldwell wrote of nineteenth century Harrison County: "The soil is generally pliable, calcareous loam in the valleys, rich in vegetation and everywhere well adapted to the growth of wheat." Caldwell also claimed that by 1875, Cadiz had "an intelligent thrifty

---

24   J. Feldman. *When the Mississippi Ran Backwards: Empire, Intrigue, Murder, and the New Madrid Earthquakes* (New York: Free Press, 2005) 12-13, 234.

25   Elmer T. Clark. *The Journal and Letters of Francis Asbury* Vol. II (Nashville: Abingdon, 1958) 405, 612. This Wrenshall was quite likely John Wrenshall who was rebuked for administering the sacraments without ordination. This infringement did not prevent Asbury from ordaining him at Hopewell Academy, Jefferson County, Ohio, September 9, 1803. He lived in Pittsburgh, and it was at his house that the Pittsburgh Society first met. John Wrenshall was the principal founder of the Methodist Church in Pittsburgh. "His name should always be highly revered by Pittsburgh Methodists. He was born in England, December 27, 1761, and came first to Philadelphia in 1794 and to Pittsburgh in 1796. He was for forty-one years, a local preacher in the church and was at all times, its strict supporter. He was a medium-sized man who talked and sang well, though with a clearly marked English accent. He was the first American ancestor of a large and well-known family, among them who was Mrs. Ulysses S. Grant, who was his granddaughter. Wrenshall died on December 25, 1821 at his home on Fourth Avenue, and was buried in a vault at the rear of the First Presbyterian Church on Ward Street." John Newton Boucher. *A Century and A Half of Pittsburgh and Her People* Vol.II (Pittsburgh, Lewis Publishing Co., 1908) 213.

population of about 1,600 and it's said to be the wealthiest town of its size in the Ohio state."[26] Ohio historian Henry Howe described the Cadiz area as, "very hilly, these hills usually beautifully curving and very cultivated. The soil is clayey in which coal and lime-stone abound." In 1847, Harrison County was one of the foremost wool producing counties in America, with 102,971 sheep.[27]

James Simpson came to Eastern Ohio with the thousands of other Scotch-Irish seeking their fortune in the early 19th century.[28] In Baltimore, 1803, a Scottish immigrant stated of his fellow immigrants, newly arrived highlanders, making their way through the port to settle in the back country, "They expected riches and liberty, but found nothing but a struggle to keep themselves alive."[29] Other than the Appalachian foothills reminding him of the Irish hillsides when he was a boy, in all likelihood James came to Cadiz because his brother John had moved to the upper reaches of Short Creek, Harrison County, around 1802. After James arrived, the brothers opened another general merchandising store in newly-founded Cadiz. The population was hardly sufficient to supply enough business to support two families. By going one hundred miles further west, they could have plowed the rich, fertile, black soil of the Muskingum River Valley.

But the Simpson family consisted of highlanders, not lowlanders. Streams ran through the hills, moss grew on the rocks, and the mist shrouded the early-morning sheep as they grazed in the valleys. Shallow wells yielded

---

26   J.A. Caldwell. *Caldwell's Atlas of Harrison County* (Condit, Ohio: self-published, 1875) 10-11.

27   Henry Howe. *Historical Collections of Ohio* Vol. I (Columbus: Henry Howe and Son, 1891) 173.

28   Bishop Matthew Simpson recorded, "Of my grandfather's people, I have little information. He died in middle life of a strain, from attempting to raise a huge pole on a building. He left five sons and one daughter. In 1793, the family immigrated to the U.S., sailing from Londonderry, and landing at Baltimore, after having encountered near America, a French vessel which took everything they had, France and England being at war. After landing, they settled in Huntington County, Pennsylvania. . . . later to western Pennsylvania, Washington Co., then Ohio, Jefferson County." Helen A. Simpson. *Early Records of Simpson Families* (Philadelphia: J. B. Lippincott & Company, 1927) 269. Also see Ellis Paxson Oberholtzer. *Philadelphia: A History of the City and Its People-A Record of 225 Years* (Philadelphia: The S.J. Clarke Publishing Company) 5.

29   Christopher Clark. *Social Change in America: From the Revolution to the Civil War* (Chicago: Ivan R. Dee, 2006) 97.

sweet water and tree-covered hills provided abundant timber for building houses. The hamlet of Cadiz was surrounded by a variety of topography, bottom land for the farmer and wooded hills for all who cared to hunt, trap, and fish. The foliage of the chestnuts, oaks, maples, and sycamores painted a picture of God at his seasonal and creational best. East central Ohio was not too hot and not too cold, not too flat and not too mountainous. It was sort of like Scotland and Ireland, or what the Scotch-Irish immigrants had heard about Scotland and Ireland. The hills of eastern Kentucky, eastern Ohio, western Virginia, and West Virginia are to this day still populated by Campbells, McDonalds, Simpsons, McCormicks, and, yes, Hatfields and McCoys. At the age of nineteen, Matthew recalled the bucolic surroundings of his nativity:

> The month of June with summer's ardent heat
> Has made another year for me complete
> Has brought around in annual course the day
> In which I commenced my earthly stay
> In which I first beheld the rays of light
> Which burst upon my tender orbs of sight
> Then first I saw fair nature's neat array
> With all her beauteous charms in full display
> When ripening crops and rising fields of corn
> The spreading landscape richly drest adorn
> When greenest foliage ornaments the groves
> Where tuneful birds are warbling of their loves
> When growing fruit on virent branches placed
> Though not unripe provokes the long taste
> Just such a time I first on nature gazed
> I looked, nor understood, but was amazed
> My birthplace Cadiz then an infant too
> Of houses scarce and small intended view
> Not yet a county seat had raised its name
> Or splendid mansions served to spread its fame.[30]

---

30   LOC. Simpson papers, "Reminiscent Lines of Matthew Simpson Jr. on His Nineteenth Birthday," Container fifteen.

On October 29, 1804, Zacchaeus A. Beatty laid out 141 lots in Cadiz, and James Simpson immediately purchased lot 100 for $30 and on it built a small frame house.³¹ In this house were born three children: Harriet (Hetty), April 3, 1807; Elizabeth, February 2, 1809; and Matthew Tingley Simpson, June 20, 1811.³² In his *Reminiscences*, Henry Boehm claimed that Francis Asbury baptized baby Matthew. There are several problems with this claim: Asbury recorded only one visit, August 1814, to Cadiz, making no reference to the Simpsons, and Boehm, who accompanied Asbury, mentioned nothing about Cadiz or the Simpsons at the time of the visit. Born in 1775, Boehm lived until 1875. Only after Simpson became famous, did Boehm recall that Asbury had baptized the infant. Boehm stated, "In 1811, when traveling with him (Asbury), near Xenia, Ohio, we were kindly entertained by a family named Simpson, and Bishop Asbury baptized a little infant and called him Matthew."³³ Was Boehm implying that Asbury christened the child? Xenia was two hundred miles from Cadiz, on the other side of the state. The elder Christian statesman was peering through years of cloudy nostalgia. The faulty memory of an almost one hundred-year-old man may have committed a historical inaccuracy, but certainly not a sin. The mother stated that she did not remember who baptized her son.

Mother Sarah recalled little Matthew was always falling down the stairs or stone steps. He once remarked she said, "To a friend, who afterwards twitted her about it, that it would be a mercy if I should die, as she did not believe, if spared, I would ever have any sense."³⁴ A Cadiz resident remembered that little Matthew was anything but precocious. The child did not exhibit any marked ability in learning: "When first placed in school, he was, if any difference may be allowed, a little slower than the ordinary child."³⁵ Walter Gaston Shotwell, a native of Cadiz, recalls the town of

---

31   H. J. Ackley and William T. Perry. *History of Carroll and Harrison Counties* (Chicago: Lewis Publishing Company, 1921). Also see Charles Hanna. *Historical Collection of Harrison County in the State of Ohio* (New York: privately printed, 1900).

32   Helen A. Simpson, 262.

33   J.B. Wakeley. *The Patriarch of One Hundred Years: Being Reminiscences, Historical and Biographical of Rev. Henry Boehm* (New York: Nelson and Phillips, 1875) 446.

34   Crooks, 10.

35   UMA, Drew University, Crooks papers, Letter from Mary McElroy to George Crooks, July 13, 1887.

Matthew's childhood as,

> a small frontier village. Its streets were unpaved and unpiked; and in the deep lime-stone soil of the locality, constantly cut up in winter by wagons hauling coal and wood, they became quagmires of mud, that were at times impassable. The houses were generally log or frame, with a few of the better class of homemade brick. The street crossings were of ashes. The stores were small. There was no railroad and being an inland town, there was no river communication. Two coach roads crossed at the public square and brought periodic mails; and these were almost the only means of communication with the outside world. The long winters of deep snow and mud, hemmed the residents in, for six months of the year, and the sole places of interest then were the Church and the Court House. The annual revivals of the former broke the monotony of the winter nights and the periodic terms of the latter attracted some outsiders and gave to the place an air of some little importance.[36]

At Simpson's birth, Cadiz was a crossroads for what are now Highways 22 and 250. Drovers bound for New York and Philadelphia markets turned northeast off the National Road at Cambridge, came through Cadiz, and headed for Steubenville, where they forded the river at Wellsburg, Virginia, approximately four miles below Steubenville.[37] Travel was a challenge; an early act of the Ohio legislature limited stumps left in the road to a foot high. In the swampiest places logs were laid side-by-side across the road to form what were known as corduroy roads. Because metal-spring suspension had

---

36   Walter Gaston Shotwell. *Driftwood: Being Papers on Old-Time American Towns and Some Old People* (Freeport, New York: Books for Libraries Press, INC., 1966) 176.

37   One of those cattle drovers (who would play a prominent part in Simpson's life) was a thirty-year-old named Daniel Drew, the first man to cross the Allegheny Mountains with two thousand head of cattle. Though he probably never ran them over salt flats so they would slake their thirst before market (hence, watered stock), he did buy the Bulls Head Inn in New York City, so that it would become the city's foremost watering hole for the cattle drovers. Drew's biographer Clifford Browder claims, "If this was not the first cattle drive over the mountains, it was surely the first successful one of its magnitude, and it established Drew as the foremost cattle dealer in the city." 30. This was Drew's first monetary speculation, a propensity for risk that would establish him as "Uncle Daniel" on Wall Street, a sobriquet that would be both a blessing and a curse to Methodism and Simpson. We do not know when Drew and Simpson first met, but both of them would be the most auspicious persons at the Centenary of American Methodism, symbolized and celebrated by the founding of Drew Theological Seminary in Madison, New Jersey, in 1867, the first time that Methodism would attach the word "seminary" to an institution. Clifford Browder. *The Money Game in Old New York: Daniel Drew and His Times* (Lexington: The University Press of Kentucky, 1986) 75.

not yet been invented, the only shock absorbers were large leather straps for a stage coach or wooden springs for wagons; both were fragile, often leading to breakdowns. The National Road reached Wheeling, Virginia, now West Virginia, by 1818 and Columbus, Ohio, in 1833. By 1838, Ohio owned about half the stock in the thirty-six turnpike companies which existed in America.[38]

Walter Beebe settled in Cadiz in 1813, and became Harrison County's first prosecuting attorney. He wrote to his parents, "I am in a land abounding in many of the good things in this life. I have seen good pot-turkeys weighing 20 pounds, sell for 15 cents; hens and chickens, 6 cents. Money is very plentiful in this state, probably more plentiful than usual, owing to its being near the N.W. Army."[39] On October 19, 1819, a Doctor Richard Lee Mason recorded of Sears (a tavern on the land of Ephraim Sears near Cadiz), "roads extremely rough .... Log cabins, ugly women, and tall timber." And of Freeport "nothing fit to drink, not even good water."[40] By 1816, the *Ohio Gazetteer* reported, "Cadiz, a post town and seat of justice for Harrison County, is a thriving town, situated in the township of the same name, containing a large brick courthouse, eight stores, seven taverns, 125 dwelling houses, and 531 inhabitants."[41]

The Scotch-Irish were fond of sheep and imported them for the rocky, hilly terrain, topography on which sheep could survive like few other animals. Sheering, farming, gathering, hunting, fishing, and home manufacturing such as spinning, sewing, and soap-making made up the subsistence, which knew little of hard currency. In 1817, a Joseph Steward was paid 68 1/2 cents per day, or nine dollars per month for general farm work. During the early 1820s tenant workers earned $.50-$.75 per day harvesting wheat.[42]

---

38   George Taylor. *The Transportation Revolution: 1815-1860* (New York: Rinehart and Company, 1951) 15.

39   *Ohio Sesquicentennial Celebration: 1813-1963* (Freeport, Ohio: The Sesquicentennial Historical Committee, Harrison County, Ohio, 1963) 8.

40   Ibid., 8.

41   Ibid., 8.

42   R. Douglas Hurt. *The Ohio Frontier, Crucible of the Old Northwest: 1720 to 1830* (Bloomington: Indiana Press, 1998) 350.

John, the first of the five Simpson brothers, was a tough physical specimen.[43] One of the pioneers of Harrison County, he cleared 160 acres of thick forest on rough, hilly terrain in what would later be called Stock Township. It was told that the mother of the boys "rode horseback on one occasion from Harrison County, Ohio to Washington County, Pennsylvania and thwarted three rivers carrying a child all the way on her lap."[44] Matthew Simpson recalled,

> My grandmother was of Scotch-Presbyterian descent and educated her family strictly in the faith and practice of the Irish-Presbyterian Church. But shortly after she was left a widow, she heard Mr. Wesley preach on one of his visits to Ireland. She joined the Methodist Society and her children became Methodists. She had a wonderful memory. Often did I listen to her reminiscences of Scotch and Irish life, of the persecution of the Protestants by the Catholics; and often have I listened to her stories of fairies and ghosts, the common tradition of the North of Ireland till my hair stood on end. She was happy at ninety, with spinning wheel and hymn book.[45]

The Remarkable Uncle Matthew

It sounds macabre, but the death of James Simpson was one of the most fortuitous events in his son's life. When the forlorn wife and children returned to the vacated house in Cadiz, James' older brother, Matthew, for whom the nephew was named, moved in with them.[46] The confirmed bachelor and celibate was an autodidactic of the rarest sort. He mastered Latin, French German, Greek, Hebrew, mathematics, as well as improvising a machine for manufacturing weaver's reeds. The uncle would provide for the family until

---

43   Waunita Farrier Groh. *Simpson Sons and Daughters: 1735–1986* (Punta Garda, FL: Waunita Farrier Groh, 1987). Thomas Simpson married Mary Elizabeth McFarland who migrated from Scotland to County Tyrone, Ireland, and gave birth to six children, all of whom migrated to America, five of them eventually settling in Ohio: Andrew, born sometime before 1770; John, 1770; William, 1774; Matthew, 1776; Mary, 1780; James, 1782. William, of whom the least is known, lived and died in Erie, PA.

44   *Commemorative Biographical Record, Harrison County, Ohio* (J. H. Beers and Company, 1891) 334.

45   Crooks, 28. Thus anti-Catholicism was early on ingrained in Simpson.

46   James had not yet paid for the house. Sarah gave two hundred dollars to a John Prichard and a John Malcolm, for the land to be placed in her name. LOC, Simpson papers, Deed-Harrison County, Ohio, July 4, 1816, Container twenty.

the daughters married and the nephew left home. Uncle Matthew would be the foremost reason for Matthew, the future celebrity Bishop, becoming an outlier.[47] Uncle Matthew was born in June 1776, unknown location, and came to America in 1793, arriving in Cadiz sometime around 1807.

Since their store did not supply sufficient income, the brothers John, James, Matthew, and the rest of the family reverted to weaver reed making. A weaver's reed was a necessary apparatus for a loom, the spinning instrument which almost every family owned in the age of homespun. Every loom required several reeds, because the reed determined the fineness or coarseness of the cloth. Harrison County excelled in homespun, because it excelled in wool.

The Simpson home, under the management of Uncle Matthew, distributed weaver's reeds throughout the surrounding counties in order for families to spin "linsey-woolsey," a fabric made of linen and wool of which there were many grades. (They obviously did not pay much attention to the biblical injunction in Leviticus 19:19: "Do not wear clothing woven of two kinds of material." NIV) The reed, approximately two feet long and six inches high, provided the frame for six to ninety tightly strung metal strips per inch, connecting the bottom and top of the frame. Uncle Matthew had discovered a faster and more efficient means to forge, cut and connect the metal to the frame. Much of the process necessitated pulling the strips of metal through steel rollers, until the desired shape and thickness were achieved. The more strips per inch on the reed, the finer the texture of the cloth. Thus, most houses owned several reeds and used them accordingly to produce both dress and work clothes, the latter being coarser in texture. Cotton, which few Ohio homes imported, hence fewer cotton clothes, demanded reeds with as many as ninety metal wires per inch.[48]

For the gentrified, linsey-woolsey was a metaphor for unrefined. When Arthur Saint Clair, governor of the Northwest Territory, named the

---

47   The term "outlier" is anachronistic, but no less accurate. Malcolm Gladwell has popularized the term, by arguing that individuals do not become "successful" in a vacuum, but are accomplished because of a particular set of circumstances, which include people and opportunities at the right time and place. Malcolm Gladwell. *Outliers: The Story of Success* (New York: Little, Brown, and Company, 2008).

48   https://en.wikipedia.org/wiki/Reed_(weaving)

Methodist preacher, Philip Gatch, as a magistrate of Clermont County without Gatch's knowledge, Gatch responded, "It was like wearing a linsey-woolsey garment."[49] It was no honor. The less refined, but no less educated, James Finley was more appreciative: "If a man was blessed with a linsey-woolsey hunting shirt, and ladies with linsey dresses, and the children with the same, it was counted of the first order, even if the linsey was made of the wool of the buffalo."[50]

Young Matthew spent days, weeks, and months on end, "splitting and shaping the half round wooden strips for the framework, splitting the canes and dressing them to the required thickness, and for tying them in place."[51] As a young teen, he was also given the task of keeping the business accounts. The work was tedious and boring, but there was a huge payoff. The nephew had won a tutorship with a polymath, a renaissance man who was able to converse intelligently about anything, especially religion and politics. Nineteenth century historian Henry Howe stated that Uncle Matthew was, "a state senator for many years, and by profession, a school teacher, and a man of peculiar acquirements, a walking encyclopedia, unprepossessing in appearance, small head and body."[52] Uncle Matthew believed in his nephew more than the nephew believed in himself. A Cadiz inhabitant said of the nephew, "The bishop was an awkward, barefooted boy, and when about seventeen, so shy that he was afraid of society, and so miserable in health, that it was supposed he would perish of consumption; tall for his age and round shouldered. He wrote an acrostic for the *Harrison Telegraph*, and was fond of visiting the printing office. The people here were astonished of his success in life."[53]

---

49   Elizabeth Connor. *Methodist Trailblazer Philip Gatch: 1751-1834* (Rutland: Academy Books, 1970) 203.

50   Finley, 70.

51   Crooks, 34.

52   Howe, 73.

53   Ibid., 891. An acrostic was a poem, each line beginning with a successive letter of the alphabet. There are no accessible copies of the *Harrison Telegraph* from this period.

In 1826, Uncle Matthew opened a private academy on Market Street, because Ohio had no public school system.[54] Naturally, the uncle leaned on his fifteen-year-old nephew. The two story house, which Uncle Matthew had built for the family in 1816 and stands today on Lower Lincoln Avenue, served as a reed factory, a school and a residence.[55] In 1829, the school moved to the "old academy building" on Gimlet Hill, where it lasted only three years, the building being sold in 1832. (This building still stands as a private home on a lane north of Charleston Street.) Uncle Matthew then relocated the academy in his house, where he taught until 1835.

Not having enough to do as a reed maker and a teacher, Uncle Matthew served in the Ohio Legislature. During the legislative sessions in Columbus, the nephew at age fifteen was the sole proprietor of the academy. The senior Matthew Simpson served as State Senator, 1816-1820, and 1822-1828. In 1825-1826, he served on the board of equalization, which ensured that the state was getting a fair exchange on its goods and money, and both persons and commodities were fairly taxed. Thus, the Senior Matthew Simpson was an expert in the language of compromise and appropriation, a wordsmith who adumbrated the parliamentary skills for which the nephew would become renowned.[56] As a member of the Ohio Senate, William Henry Harrison,

---

54   This is an understatement. There was no public normal school in the United States until 1839, when one was established in Lexington, Massachusetts, because Horace Mann was Secretary for the Board of Education in Massachusetts. See Lawrence A. Cremin. *The Republic and the School: Horace Mann on the Education of Free Men* (New York: Teacher's College, 1957). Bob Pepperman Taylor argues that there are two kinds of education: first, that which is partisan and portends, or creates an ideology. And second, that which produces critical thinking, autonomous individuals. Taylor states, "For the civic educator, the task is to produce a particular kind of citizen; for the educator released from political goals, the end of education is less to shape students than to develop their reason and knowledge to such a degree that they are able to take personal responsibility for shaping themselves as free and independent individuals-thinking through their own views, cultivating their own tastes, developing their own life plans, and becoming unique people." Bob Pepperman Taylor. *Horace Mann's Troubling Legacy: The Education of Democratic Citizens* (Lawrence: University Press of Kansas, 2010)x. My opinion is Uncle Matthew represented the best of both of these educational philosophies. Certainly, he wanted his nephew to be Christian, but at the same time open, tolerant, and liberal-minded. Bishop Matthew Simpson would personify all of these traits.

55   Uncle Matthew purchased the property from James and Nancy Barnes for the sum of four hundred ninety-seven dollars and twenty five cents. LOC, Simpson papers, Deed recorded May 17, 1816, Container twenty.

56   Elliott Gilkey. *The Ohio Hundred-Year Book* (Columbus: Fred J. Heer, 1901) 305.

"Old Tippecanoe," made an eloquent speech. Uncle Matthew said while shaking the General's hand, "I wish I had the eloquence that you have." The general responded, "I wish I had the logic that you have." John Bingham, who lived in Cadiz during his teen years, recalled of the older Simpson, "It was peculiar of Uncle Matthew's character, that he judged all men by their sincerity and each without respect to their outward circumstances."[57]

Matthew Simpson's legislative actions included voting for the establishment of poor houses; for appointing a committee to inquire into the agriculture and manufacturing interests of the country; for voting in a losing cause for the appointment of tax assessors for each county; for the establishment of medical societies to regulate the practice of "physic and surgery;" for various roads including a road from Steubenville to the National Road in Guernsey County; for borrowing not less than $3,600,000 and not exceeding 5% interest for navigable canals; against suspending excavations on the Ohio Canal south of Licking; for internal improvements on navigable canals; for exempting certain students from working on the roads. When he amended a bill for building a road from the town of Steubenville to the Ohio Canal with "respect to the present route," he was voted down.[58] He voted against renaming Western Reserve College, Western Reserve Theological Seminary.[59] The bottom line for Matthew Simpson, the State Senator from Harrison County, is that he was progressive politically and economically, lived beyond reproach ethically, and represented the interests of his constituents as well as benefiting himself.

After closing the academy in 1835, Uncle Matthew and his sister-in-law moved to just south of East Liverpool, Ohio, where they would live with Sarah's daughter, Hetty, and her husband, George McCullough. Uncle

---

57   UMA, Drew University, Crooks papers, Joseph Tingley, "Reminiscences," March 25, 1887.

58   Regarding, "respect to the present route," Scott Pendleton, President of the Harrison County, Ohio, Historical Association explains: "The Canal came within 35 miles of Cadiz at Dover (Ohio and Erie Canal segment opened in 1828) and it connected with the Ohio River at East Liverpool less than 25 miles from Steubenville (Sandy and Beaver Canal chartered in 1828 opened much later and was a disaster from the beginning). I suspect that since he was a shareholder in the Steubenville-Cadiz Pike, he was trying to make an amendment that gave some advantage to that route and his stock in it." Email from Scott Pendleton, May 8, 2013.

59   Journal, Senate, Ohio; http://booksgoogle.com/books

Matthew gave an exact location of the farm, seven miles above the mouth of Yellow Creek, between the towns of Wellsville and Faucettstown, "three miles from the former and one from the latter." At this point in his life, after having been quite public, Uncle Matthew went into seclusion: "We are all in our usual health and I spend my time in weaving foundations for stocks and in setting and keeping things to rights. The solitude is not disagreeable. I know nobody, and nobody, or but few, seem to know me."[60]

Especially during the early years of his ministry, the nephew received long letters of advice, encouragement, and theological interpretation from the man, who for all practical intents and purposes, had been and still was, his father. (In his early years, the nephew signed his name, Matthew Simpson, Jr.) Few people have made so profound an influence on another as did Uncle Matthew on his nephew. And few people have expressed more sentimental appreciation as did the nephew. When nineteen, he honored his uncle with verse.

> My dearest Uncle, how shall I recite
> How frequently you taught me with delight
> Commenced with small, then larger things explained
> That thus with ease, true knowledge might be gained
> Still as my mind began to gather strength
> And make excursions of greater length
> Your care increased, then double your delight
> To lead me still to new and greater light
> For minds like eyes increasing light can bear
> Though over-powered with too great a share
> While I my infancy you undertook
> To make me learn the value of a book
> Selected such as I could read with ease
> Acquire knowledge and my fancy please
> Whatever tastes for reading I acquired
> Thy constant care promoted and inspired
> To walks of science too you then inclined
> My youthful and unscientific mind.

---

60   LOC, Simpson papers, Letters, Uncle Matthew to Matthew, January 19, 1835 and April 18, 1865, Container three.

>Then from these works to him who these designed
>You early strove to turn my youthful mind
>And frequently you walked with me abroad
>And talked of nature and of nature's God
>Told me of animals both small and great
>Their different uses, structures, and their state
>Some dull, some cunning active and alert
>And others spiteful and inclined to hurt
>Told me of plants and when and where they grew
>Their various orders and their classes too
>Each principle in nature show in turn
>You so exhibited that I might learn
>Then with a view to show to what good end
>Such knowledge, wisdom, and such learning tend
>You told of man in all their diff'rent states
>In moral and in intellectual rates
>Then showed that men of wisdom always raise
>To higher ranks than those who spend their days
>Without improvements and without a case.[61]

The Blessing of Escapism

Matthew Simpson, Jr.'s introverted personality was compounded by not having a father, wearing ill-fitted clothes, lack of athletic prowess, and a high-pitched voice that sounded more unpleasant to him than others. He possessed a mortal fear of both one-on-one conversation with strangers, and standing up before a group of people, whether at church or school. To prevent panic attacks, he gave anxious contemplation to any excursion through the village, planning a route in which he was least likely to encounter another individual. Another contemporary observed, "Simpson was tall; he had extremely angular features, a reddish, freckled face, and very red hair . . . was of a retiring, diffident disposition; more fond of books than of society, and in going to and from his recitation, having to pass quite through the village, he invariably chose the path least traveled."[62] The self-effacing lad

---

61 "Reminiscent Lines of Matthew Simpson Jr. on His Nineteenth Birthday."
62 "The American Pulpit Magazine," *American Magazine Company* Vol. VI (1887)

had several places where he could hide: the local library, the courthouse, where his uncle William Tingley was the county court clerk, and at times, presiding judge, when the circuit judge was not present in Cadiz on court days. (Cadiz was the county seat for Harrison County, and still is today.) Joseph Tingley, editor of the *Harrison Telegraph*, especially welcomed his nephew, the son of his sister Sarah, and offered him a free apprenticeship in typesetting.

But most of the time, the boy escaped into books; the nephew was a sponge, reading and absorbing everything on which he could get his hands. One of his peers remembered Simpson being "extremely round-shouldered from his habit of stooping over in studying. His friends feared he might injure his lungs and die of early consumption. A primitive chair rest was constructed for him, but came too late to remedy the evil already accomplished, and he remained very much stooped the rest of his life."[63] In spite of claiming that he ran, jumped, wrestled, and engaged in other boyish activities, as well as working outdoor jobs in the summers, Matthew was not the all American boy.[64] He was an arch-typical nerd (before nerd was a word), and his physical development projected little masculinity. Referring to his early teens, "I had confined myself closely at an age when I was growing rapidly. The study of the Greek at that time was wholly through the Latin; my lexicon, an old Schrevelius, was printed in very small type and on very poor paper and the result was, I was troubled with inflammation of the eyes and a pain in the head for several years afterward."[65]

The trajectory of Simpson's life evidenced that, if he did not possess a photographic memory, he exhibited something close to it, though he never made the claim for himself. Social immaturities made him seem intellectually

---

629.

63   William McConnell, *Scrapbook*, Harrison County Historical Society.

64   Young Matthew may have worked on the "National Road," or other roads to pay off the Simpson family property taxes, but I could find no records verifying such employment.

65   Crooks, 18. Historian Henry May wrote that, "The common languages of the learned were obviously necessary for those who would make the slightest pretentions to gentility. They were indispensable for the ministry, the law, or medicine. They were required for entrances to colleges; the effort of mastering them sharpened the faculties; classic texts suitably selected, inculcated moral truth." Henry F. May. *The Enlightenment in America* (New York: Oxford University Press, 1976) 33.

slow. At an early age, Simpson was keenly aware of his intellectual acuity, no doubt affirmed by most of the adults with whom he associated. His immediate family smothered him with affection, and sheltered him from company and influences which they perceived detrimental. At age three, he could read, and when he was four or five years of age, was incredulous when visiting preachers asked him about that particular ability. "From my earliest childhood, I had an intense desire to read. In Cadiz, a public library had been opened, to which I had access, and between five and ten years of age I read a large number of its volumes on travel, history, and biography."[66] As the twelve-year-old isolated himself in his introversion, he was not alone. He fought alongside Alexander the Great, conquered the Alps with Napoleon, and fled the British with Washington across the Delaware River. These alter-egos enabled him to dream of greatness, but into what form his greatness would morph, he possessed not the faintest idea.

Simpson would transcend Cadiz with military generals, explorers, and riverboat captains. More than any other tangible objects in his life, books would catapult him into the future, a recurrent theme in his preaching and repeated exhortations to young people. While Matthew squirreled away in the Cadiz library, the Rev. Joel Hawes stood before the "young men" of Hartford, Connecticut, and stated America's primary means for self-improvement: "At pleasure, he can call around him the best of company--the wisest and greatest men of every age and country--and feast his mind with the rich stories of knowledge which they spread before him. A lover of good books can never be in want of good society, nor in much danger of seeking enjoyment in the low pleasure of sensuality of vice."[67]

Reading was one of the most significant activities for rising above and beyond native mediocrity. Karen Halttunen writes, "Popular biographies of self-made politicians, even artists and intellectuals—proclaimed the faith that in the boundless American social environment, any man might rise to any position in life."[68] Even though one could not separate fact from fiction in

---

66 Ibid., 11.
67 Joel Hawes, "Lectures Addressed to the Young Men of Hartford and New Haven." http://catalog,hathitrust.org/apl/volumes/oclc/1189231.html.
68 Karen Halttunen. *Confidence Men and Painted Women: A Study of Middleclass Culture in America: 1830-1870* (New Haven: Yale University Press, 1982) 28.

the lives of George Washington and Benjamin Franklin, mythology inspired, no matter how elusive and illusive the mythology may have been. Matthew further recalled as a boy, "While I disliked writing, I had a still stronger repugnance to declamation, which was one of the duties enjoined while studying grammar and made my schoolmates say that I could study, but I could not speak."[69] But when it came to academic performance, Matthew Jr. so outdistanced the competition, some of the parents became envious and accusatory. After one exam, on which Matthew did better than everyone else, they concluded, "Certainly the uncle must be favoring the nephew."[70]

A Pious Mother

Winning the genetic lottery for Matthew Simpson pertained to not just the paternal side of the family. Sarah Tingley, born near Amboy, New Jersey, May 23, 1781, arrived with her family in Pittsburgh, sometime before 1806. Her father, Jeremiah, had lost his money and any hope of financial solvency during the Revolutionary War. On June 10, 1806, Sarah married the young James who walked with a limp and already chronically coughed. The marriage took place at Short Creek in Jefferson County which is now part of Harrison County. No doubt, the Methodist Church brought them together. This woman exhibited uncommon wisdom, perseverance and love for God, all instilled into her son.[71] Mother Sarah's spirituality leavened the entire village of Cadiz. William Tingley's son, Joseph, wrote of his aunt,

> The Bishop's mother was my ideal saint. Always calm. Always peaceful and happy. Always kind and cheery. Always waiting for the final summons, yet was longing to cross over to the other shore. No one could be long in her presence without finding her secret of 'perfect peace' through perfect love. She constantly professed and enjoyed the blessing of entire sanctification, though not in the noisy, ostentatious way of some that make that claim.[72]

The first school in Cadiz was begun by Sarah Simpson's brother William Tingley.[73] He began holding school sessions in Cadiz about 1807. He was

---
69   Crooks, 12.
70   UMA, Drew University, Crooks papers, Joseph Tingley, "Random Recollections."
71   Groh, 458.
72   UMA, Drew University, Crooks papers, Joseph Tingley, "Random Recollections."
73   Charles A. Hanna. *Ohio Valley Genealogies: Relating Chiefly to Families in Harrison,*

no "rude border man being recognized by the Cadiz citizens as a scholar and a gentleman. It is unclear where he held classes. He probably utilized both his own house and that of his sister. He possessed to a marked degree the requirements of a teacher, knowledge and exactness."[74] It was this same William Tingley who served for some thirty years as a county court clerk and part-time judge; court reporter 1814-1829, and clerk, 1815-1838. Born in New Jersey in 1787, Tingley arrived in Cadiz in 1806 and married Rachel Paulson in 1814.[75]

Matthew's maternal grandfather Jeremiah Tingley married Esther Leddel on July 5, 1778, and to that union were born six daughters and two sons. One of the daughters, Sarah, born on May 23, 1781, grew up to be a pretty hazel-eyed, sweet girl. Even though she was of gentle spirit, recalled a relative, she was demonstrative at times in worship and "toward the close of life, her religious experience was so rich, she had such an abiding sense of the all-cleansing blood of Christ and was so constant in the enjoyment of the blessing of 'perfect love' as she called it, that hers was indeed the confidence of the just."[76] Mother Sarah nurtured the spirituality of her only son, a gift which he never forgot. No son ever revered a mother more than did Matthew Simpson.

Belmont and Jefferson Counties, Ohio, and Washington, Westmoreland, and Fayette Counties, Pennsylvania (Baltimore: Genealogical Publishing Company, 1968) 120.

74   Rupert B. Thumb. "History of Education in Cadiz from the Beginning of the Town," *Cadiz Republican* (March 30) 1911.

75   Hanna, 376. "Jeremiah Tingley was born August 28, 1755, in Plainfield, Union County, New Jersey. He was the son of Joseph Tingley and Christina Manning. He died in 1803 in Jefferson County (which still contained what is now Harrison County) at age 58." He "served in the New Jersey Militia as a private in Summerset County, New Jersey." After the Revolutionary War, he moved (1790) to Winchester, Virginia. In 1801 he moved to Short Creek, Ohio, where he lived the remainder of his life. He is buried in Hopewell Cemetery, Jefferson County, where a "Revolutionary Patriot Marker" was placed at his grave in 2004, by the Jefferson County Chapter of the Ohio County Genealogical Society. It reads, "Hopewell Cemetery, Graveside Services for Revolutionary Patriot, Jeremiah Tingley, 2011." On September 10, 1803, Asbury preached at Hopewell Chapel on 1 Peter 5:10. "We had love feast and sacrament. There was a cry raised very soon and it was with difficulty I could keep the thread of my discourse, whilst they were singing and shouting on top of the hill. At candle light the cry began again and continued until the break of day on *Monday morning*, (over two days later). It is judged, there were twenty souls converted to God." Clark. *Asbury Journal*, II:405. Also see Betty Pokas, "Hopewell Project to Create Noise," *The Times Leader*, Martins Ferry, Ohio (May 6, 2012) B1 and B3.

76   Tingley, "Random Recollections."

You kindly gave and watched me at my play
The thousand simple questions I would ask
You still would answer, though a tiresome task
None but a mother e'er the task could bear
And keep a temper still unmoved and fair
Soon as my mind was strong enough to know
You often strove the right and wrong to show
You told me God who reigns above the skies
Heard all my words and saw my thoughts arise
That if I loved him and would serve him well
To Heaven he'd take me with himself to dwell
But if I loved him not, and bad would be
I must forever from his presence flee
And oftentimes you warmly prayed that I
Might holy live and so be fit to die
Nor did your love e'er with my childhood cease
But with my years still kept on the increase
Unlike the brutes, whose love (if love it be)
Is one as soon as is their infancy
Thy love was great, thy government was mild
To me, thy only son thy youngest child.[77]

Other Important Mentors: John McBean and Joseph Tingley

When at his Uncle Tingley's school, the young Matthew came in contact with another influential person, John McBean. McBean took a circuitous route through life. Born in Scotland, orphaned as a child, he went to live with an uncle in the West Indies. Around 1820, he visited relatives in Harrison County, found employment at William Tingley's academy and stayed.[78] It was during this time, that McBean attended Jefferson College in Cannonsburg, Jefferson County, Pennsylvania, and graduated with a degree in classical languages. The school became Washington and Jefferson in 1869, when it was combined with Washington College in Washington, PA, where it is now located.[79]

77   "Reminiscent Lines of Matthew Simpson Jr. on His Nineteenth Birthday."
78   H. J. Eckley and William T. Perry, 862.
79   The biographical and historical catalogue contains the following history: "McBean,

McBean's mastery of Latin and Greek brought him into an intriguing conflict with his young student Matthew. The teacher paired students into couplets, with the intention that each would encourage and challenge his peer. Simpson quickly discovered that this arrangement was not mutual and that his study partner was, "fonder of amusement than of his studies."[80] Matthew pleaded with McBean to release him from this impediment, but the teacher refused. On Saturdays the students were required to submit an essay of choice, and Matthew wrote the following thinly veiled allegory:

> Two boys set out to climb the hill of knowledge. They had an able and experienced guide who held them both together. One of them was earnest to see all that could be seen on the hill and anxious to breathe the pure air upon the top. The other was easily tired and disposed to rest by the way thinking he had time enough by-and-by to look at its sites. The one who was anxious to gain the top plead often with the guide to let him go on. The guide refused advising him to hunt for choice pebbles and to gather some flowers by the way while his mate was resting.[81]

McBean got the point and released Simpson to fly solo. McBean was not a person who easily changed his mind. Being stubborn and frugal, he refused his diploma at Washington College because it cost too much. The result for Matthew was that in the remainder of that summer session, "I finished the *Graeca Minora*, read the first volume of the *Graeca Majora*, a part of the poetry of the second volume and a number of books of Homer, completing what then was marked out in the neighboring colleges as the entire Greek course."[82]

J.–son of John A. and Jane; born Dundee, Scotland; medical student Cadiz, Ohio; practiced medicine Freeport, O., 1825-29, Cadiz; Judge of Court; President Board Examining Physicians; Married Belinda Johnson; Died Cadiz, O., January 7, '80. Physician." *Biographical and Historical Catalogue of Washington and Jefferson College,* 20. http://archive.org/stream/biographicaland00eatogoog/biographicaland00eatogoog_djvu.txt

80   Crooks, 16. From the *Harrison Telegraph* we learn about the Cadiz Academy run by William Tingley. "This institution is incorporated by law and is under the superintendence of a president and trustees; two have taken great pains to procure the best of teachers and every necessary accommodation to make the student comfortable. Tuition is only $16 a year or $8 a session; and board in the best of families can be procured at the most reasonable rates. Its situation is one of the most healthy in the western country, and the society in the town is most pleasant and agreeable." Charles B. Wallace. *Excerpts from the Harrison Telegraph of Cadiz, Ohio 1821, 1823, 1828, 1832* (The Harrison County Historical and Genealogical Society, 1994) 17. *Harrison Telegraph* (October 8, 1823) 3.

81   Crooks, 17.

82   Ibid., 17.

Joseph Tingley, Sarah's brother, also served as a mentor for Matthew. Joseph, of whom we know little, other than he was the youngest brother in the family, founded the *Harrison Telegraph* in 1821, Cadiz's first newspaper, a four-page sheet weekly, composed of mostly local news and advertisements. The ten-year-old nephew helped set type, but mostly kept subscription accounts. At the end of the first year Joseph was quite discouraged: "We need not say that our support has been very limited, but considering the dullness of the times and the many instances which the people of this county have been trifled with by strangers and new beginners in our present line of business, we have to acknowledge that our undertakings have met with as much success as could be expected."[83]

Within three years, Joseph Tingley had to sell the paper, seemingly because of ill health. On May 29, 1824, Tingley announced, "The present volume of the *Harrison Telegraph* will expire on 3, July next, after which time the establishment will be transferred to Mr. David Christie of the county." He reserved his last issue for a scrant against slavery and the candidacy of Andrew Jackson, whom John Quincy Adams defeated in the 1822 presidential election.[84] Tingley wrote, "I do consider it inconsistent in a people renowned for their principles of liberty and freedom, justice and equality, in other respects to be promoting men to the highest offices within their gift, who hold their fellow beings in an abject state of slavery and ignorance as are the subjects of the most princely and radical monarchs of any part of the world."[85] In all likelihood, Uncle Joseph was the first person to introduce the nephew to slavery, an issue on which he would waffle until the Civil War thirty years later. After surrendering the newspaper, Joseph attempted to collect back payments from subscribers with little success. In December 1824, Tingley announced that because of the distance he was moving, he would be prevented from attempting any such business personally." He did not exaggerate the distance. He died within the week.

---

83   Wallace (October 8, 1823) 55.

84   This election always haunted Henry Clay, because most pro-Jacksonians believed that Clay had promised his support to John Quincy Adams, in return for being appointed as Secretary of State. See Robert Remini. "The Corrupt Bargain," in *Henry Clay: Statesman for the Union* (New York: W. W. Norton and Company, 1991) 251-272.

85   Wallace (July 3, 1824) 27.

"God Cannot Do Without America"

No Ohio boy born in 1811, could have been gifted with a more salubrious and stimulating family than was Matthew Simpson, Jr. In his days of popularity, he never allowed hubris to overshadow his humble, but fortunate childhood.

Chapter Two:
The Child of Providence

Courthouse Entertainment

Cadiz, as the county seat of Harrison County, was invaded by two very distinct and contrasting groups of people, preachers and attorneys. The boy Matthew went to court regularly, as anticipatory as today's teenager would attend an afternoon matinee at the cinema. The lad attended sessions of the court to watch the order of business and listen to the pleadings of the lawyers. "Such men as Tappan, Wright, Hammond, and Goodenough were in their prime and I have never in any part of the country seen a court, I think, whose attorneys, were equal orators."[86]

Simpson's facile assessment deserves another look. The "Goodenough" must have been John Milton Goodenow, who sued Benjamin Tappan for slander, a case which went all the way to the U.S. Supreme Court, where the plaintiff won. Tappan coughed up six hundred dollars for claiming that Goodenow, "fled his country (Is New Hampshire a country?) to escape from justice, and disguises himself under a borrowed name; he is unfit to be trusted . . .he is a d. . .d rascal, and an immoral and base man, and unless the law makes a lawyer, he is no lawyer." Goodenow was further angered when Tappan, as a judge for the United States District Court, ruled "English common law" could be applied in the United States. Goodenow responded by writing a lengthy book with a lengthy title: "*Historical Sketches of the Principles and Maxims of American Jurisprudence and Contrast with the Doctrine of English Law on the Subject of Crimes and Punishments.*"[87] Tappan, as a United States Senator, was censured by the United States Senate for leaking in 1844, a proposed treaty with Texas to the press.[88]

86   Crooks, 15.
87   SCO Home–SCO Former Justices. John Mills Goodenow, http://www.supremecourt.ohio.gov/SCO/formerjustices/bios/goodenow.asp
88   "Benjamin Tappan," *Biographical Directory of the United States Congress*. http://

John Crafts Wright, brother-in-law of Tappan, established a law practice in Steubenville in 1809, served in the U. S. House of Representatives, and also occupied a seat on the Ohio Supreme Court. He was honorary president of the "Peace Conference" which in 1861, attempted to pre-empt the Civil War.[89] He went down in history as the father of the "popular vote." In 1827, Wright demonstrated to the U.S. House of Representatives by using a statistical table, that Andrew Jackson had won the 1826 presidential election. He referred to his statistics as "popular votes."[90]

In 1823, Charles Hammond was appointed as reporter for the Supreme Court of Ohio. He spent his life as an out-spoken advocate for the "common school system." He is best remembered for serving as editor of the *Cincinnati Gazette* and lived by the personal maxim, "He should distinctively comprehend that those who differ from him might be as honest as himself, and as well informed, too; and he should know how to respect while he opposes them." Hammond was a poet of considerable talent, and not hesitant to impale his opponents with sarcastic verse. "Flogging taught him caution, but did not dull his satire–caution as to the manner in which he published his verses; but, in reference to personalities, exasperating, because felicitously descriptive, neither flogging in early, nor threats and bitter abuse in after-life, could teach him discretion."[91] Indeed, the boy Matthew was exposed to some influential, if not eccentric attorneys.

The Methodist Invasion

The persons who created the foremost collective unconscious for young Matthew were the Methodist itinerants, who descended on the Northwest with a soul-seeking intensity unrivaled by any other religious group. They left an indelible impression which Matthew would carry with him for the rest of his life. In terms of personal sacrifice and singularity of purpose, there was nothing like them in the entire world. In zeal, the Jesuits in the northeastern United States and eastern Canada were their closest rivals.

---

bioguide.congress.gov/scripts/biodisplay.pl?index=t000039
89   http;//www.ohiohistorycentral.org/w/Wright,_John_C.?rec=423
90   http:www.ourcampaigns.com/NewsDetail.html?NewsID+49165
91   William T. Coggeshall. *Poets and Poetry of the West with Biographical and Critical Notices* (Columbus: Follett, Foster and Company, 1860) 68.

As a missionary enterprise, the Methodist itinerancy which had been set in motion by Francis Asbury seemed to be almost ubiquitous, especially to the settlers who crossed the Appalachian Mountains. In this transient culture, Methodist preachers understood themselves to be trackers, rather than shepherds. On one occasion in 1812, the itinerant preacher Richmond Nolley was following fresh wagon tracks in order to encounter new settlers. He successfully located a newly-arrived family. The father, upon recognizing Nolley's clerical garb, exclaimed, "What, have you found me already? Another Methodist preacher! I left Virginia to get out of reach of them, went to a new settlement in Georgia and thought to have a long whet, but they got my wife and daughter into the church; then in this late purchase (Choctaw corner), I found a piece of good land, and was sure I would have some peace of the preachers, and here is one before my wagon is unloaded." Nolley replied, "My friend, if you go to heaven you will find Methodist preachers there, and if to hell, I am afraid you will find some there; and you see how it is in the world, so that you had better make terms with us and be at peace."[92]

General Richard Butler, who was sent to Warrenton, Ohio, to dislodge squatters, recorded in his journal October 2, 1785, "The people of this county appear to be much imposed upon by a religious sect called Methodists and are become great fanatics."[93] George Callahan preached the first Methodist sermon in Ohio in September 1787 at Carpenter's station near Warrenton, Jefferson County, which included Harrison County until 1813. Callahan, upon reaching Carpenter's Station, found a congregation already assembled with, "fifteen or twenty hardy-back woodsmen armed with rifles, tomahawks and scalping knives, totally outside of the assembly, as protection against alarm." After the sermon ended, a "pressing invitation was given the preacher to visit Carpenter's Fort again, and he cheerfully acceded to the request."[94]

Francis McCormick, a Revolutionary war veteran from Virginia, received a Methodist exhorter's license and moved in 1797 to Milford,

---

92 Quoted in Darius Salter. *America's Bishop: The Life of Francis Asbury* (Nappanee, Indiana: The Francis Asbury Press, 2003) 161-162.
93 John M. Versteeg. *Methodism: Ohio Area, 1812-1862, Ohio Area Sesquicentennial Committee* (Nashville: Parthenon, 1962) 40.
94 Barker, 82-83.

Clermont County. Here he formed the first Methodist society in the state of Ohio. McCormick's house became the New Testament Antioch for Ohio Methodism. Francis' father was a distiller, and the son grew up a "wild and wicked youth." He ran from Methodist preaching with a heart "filled with madness." He forbade his wife to attend Methodist services, but when she joined, "I was so angry that I went off home and left her." But upon hearing Lewis Chasteen preach on "The Axe is Laid unto the Root of the Tree," McCormick recorded that, "A trembling seized me as though all my flesh would drop from my bones." His father propositioned that if he would recant Methodism, he would be given the family farm. "He then flew into a great rage and told me to be gone or he would burn the house over my head." Upon being rejected by his father, Francis began to reflect on, "the trouble he had been in," but yet he did not "grieve" for his sins. "At last I discovered by faith that they were all forgiven. Then the Spirit bore witness with my spirit that I was a child of God; the peace and joy that followed no language could express."[95] This pattern of conversion was repeated ad infinitum in early nineteenth-century American Methodism.

In 1798, Asbury appointed John Kobler to begin an Ohio Circuit. Kobler recorded, "The houses here are very small often with only one room and fireplace around which the whole family and children, dogs and all crowd, and seemed to claim the same privileges and possess equal rights. Frequently I sit on one stool or bench and eat off another which serves as a table."[96] When Kobler crossed the Ohio River, "he fell upon his knees upon its shore and prayed for divine blessing for his great mission."[97] Kobler had a lot of territory in front of him, behind him and all around him. "The Western Conference was described back in those days, as being bounded

---

95   Abel Stevens. *History of the Methodist Episcopal Church in the United States of America* Vol. IV (New York: Eaton and Mains, 1864) 318-321.

96   Abel Stevens. *History of the Methodist Episcopal Church in the United States of America* Vol. III (New York: Eaton and Mains, 1864) 141. Henry Smith wrote of John Kobler, "He was always and everywhere the same humble, common, unassuming, sweet-spirited, heavenly-minded man. Oh how often we retired together from log cabin, to a lonely place for private prayer and embraced, and wept over each other's necks and sometimes shouted aloud for joy, that we were accounted worthy to suffer a little in the cause of Christ!" Henry Smith. *Recollections and Reflections of an Old Itinerant* (New York: Carlton and Phillips, 1854) 293.

97   Barker, 87-88.

on the East by the Alleghenies, on the South by the Gulf of Mexico, on the North by the Aurora Borellis, and on the West by the setting sun." In 1812, this entire domain was divided into two conferences, the Tennessee and the Ohio. Jacob Young pleaded at the 1816 General Conference, to allow, "The Alleghenies to be the dividing line between the Ohio and the Baltimore conferences contending, 'since they have given us sparsely populated ground, not well prepared to support members, we should have some of the rich territory also.'"[98] His request went unheeded.

Around 1809, James Finley arrived in the Cadiz area, and reported preaching to a Roman Catholic family. "I took out my Bible reading part of the third chapter of John. I spent an hour explaining to them the nature and necessity of the new birth. The family listened to what I had to say with the most profound attention and silence was only interrupted by their sighs and tears." On a return trip, "the old gentleman experienced religion," but not before he had gathered up a "large collection of people" to whom Finley preached. "The Lord attended his word with power to the hearts of the people; many were converted and a good work begun."[99] One family was so poor that Finley pulled off his "leggings" and told the mother to make a coat for her son. He then handed the widow with four children 37 and 1/2 cents, all the money he had.[100]

Piety Avenue

In 1809, Finley built a 12 x 14 foot cabin at Zanesville. "My finances were all exhausted. I sold the boots off my feet to purchase provision with, and after making all the preparation that I could render my family comfortable, started out again upon my circuit to be absent four weeks." Somewhere between Cambridge and Cadiz he again overnighted with a Roman Catholic family. "They occupied one side of the fireplace and a calf which was busy eating a mess of pumpkins occupied the other.[101] In May of 1812, Finley made his home in St. Clairsville, fifteen miles southeast

---

98   Versteeg, 38-39.
99   James Finley. *Autobiography of Reverend James B. Finley* (Cincinnati: Methodist Book Concern, 1872) 194-196.
100 Ibid., 199.
101 Ibid., 194.

of Cadiz, and in 1814, was appointed to the Cross Creek Circuit which included the towns of Steubenville, Cadiz, Mount Pleasant, Smithfield and several other villages, embracing all the county of Jefferson and parts of Harrison and Belmont County.[102] Finley recalled, "It took four full weeks to travel around it …. We had to preach thirty-two times every round and meet fifty classes." The Simpson home became a prophet's chamber for itinerant Methodists, and James Finley may have been the first preacher that Matthew remembered from his childhood. The street on which the Simpsons lived became known as "Piety Avenue," because of the numerous Methodists who resided there.

In all likelihood, Henry Smith, arch-typical Methodist itinerant, wandered into Cadiz sometime around the arrival of the Simpsons. Smith reported sleeping in a cabin where the inhabitants kept a bear, in a shanty where a horse had been lodged, on a bearskin where the fleas almost devoured him. He caught the itch, and bathed himself in a concoction of sulfur, rosin, black pepper, and hog's lard. It strongly "affected my nerves, and I had a restless night but it effectively cured me of the itch."[103] Smith testified, "If I was but poorly qualified for a missionary in every other respect, I was not in one thing; for I have long since conquered my foolish pretense about eating, drinking, and lodging. I could submit to any kind of inconvenience when I had an opportunity of doing good."[104] At Pee-Pee, Ohio (yes, that's right) it was boasted of a young Methodist itinerant, thought to be too tired to preach, "Try him; I'll be bound he'll preach, for a Methodist preacher can run up hill a quarter of a mile and give him time to draw five breaths and he is ready to preach."[105]

Of all the preachers who visited the Simpson home, none was more impressive than Valentine Cook. Cook, as a young preacher, bested a seasoned Calvinistic-Scotsman in a theological debate, before a large crowd in a Kentucky wood. Cook's voice "rolled on in thunder-tones over the crowd, and echoed far away in the depths of the forest while his countenance lighted up, kindled and glowed as if he were duly commissioned from on

---

102   Ibid., 268.
103   Smith, 72.
104   Ibid., 328.
105   Ibid., 321–322.

high to proclaim the salvation of God."[106] But Cook did not have to open his mouth to gain attention. "He possessed no symmetry in his figure; awkward appendages ... stoop-shouldered to such a degree that his longneck projected from between his shoulders almost at a right angle with the perpendicular of his chest. His head which was of particular formation, being much larger than usual from crown to the point of his chin, seemed rather suspended than supported by the neck."[107] What the young Simpson remembered most about Cook, was that in family prayer, as was his custom, he read out of the Greek New Testament, which he always carried with him, translating as he read.[108] The services at the Simpson home consisted of singing, prayer, Bible study and testimonies, with the circuit rider leading service and preaching once every six weeks.

In 1815, the small Methodist congregation in Cadiz elected a board which consisted of Uncle Matthew, William Tingley, Joseph Tingley, and Thomas Inskeep. By April 20, 1816, the church had purchased a lot for $60 at the southeast corner of Roan Avenue and N. Buffalo St., and in September, 1816, the congregation dedicated a 20 x 35 foot church. It had a boxed-in pulpit, straight-backed seats, and wooden candle holders on the walls, a women's side and a men's side divided by a main aisle, a large stove about halfway back in the room and a mourner's bench.[109] This particular building lasted until 1966. In 1803, Francis Asbury sent William Burke to form the first Ohio District, an area that included what would become Cadiz in 1806. He classically described the Methodist itinerancy:

> This was a field of labor that required about eleven weeks to accomplish, and many privations. The Methodists were, in those days, like angel's visits, few and far between, and we were half our time obliged to put up in taverns and places of entertainment, subject to the disorder and abuse of the unprincipled and half-civilized inmates, suffering with hunger and cold, and sleeping in open cabins on the floor, sometimes without bed or covering, and but little prospect of any

---

106   Abel Stevens. *The History of the Religious Movement of the Eighteenth Century Called Methodism* Vol. IV (New York: Carlton and Porter, 1858) 478.

107   Ibid., 401.

108   Crooks, 19.

109   Marcia Carter and Carol Spiker. *200 Years of Methodism in Cadiz and the Two Hundredth Birthday of Matthew Simpson* (Cadiz, Ohio: Scott Memorial United Methodist Church, 2011) 3.

support from the people among whom we labored, and none from any other source; for there was no provision in those days for missionaries. But, not-withstanding all the privations and sufferings that we endured, we had the consolation that our labor was not in vain in the Lord.[110]

Matthew and God

As to his personal relationship with God, Simpson recalled, "From the earliest period of my memory religious ideas were deeply impressed upon my mind. Instructions I received from my mother and from my uncle and the religious services at which I was present, so influenced my heart that I had a deep reverence for God, and often, if I was conscious of any area or act of impropriety, did I in early childhood passed seasons of severe mental suffering. Many times have I lain awake at night thinking of divine truths especially of the question which all hearts will turn over: What must I do to be saved and to come to Jesus?"[111] This spiritual confession was strange, given the Methodist preaching he had heard, preaching that always ended in a verdict and an invitation to salvation. As a teenager, there would have been numerous opportunities to make a profession of faith. Did Matthew's low self-esteem and sense of unworthiness prevent him from falling into the river of grace?

The boy's salvific anxiety was compounded by the intense preaching and worship of the Methodists, an overly scrupulous conscience, his delicate constitution, a deep-seated inferiority complex which, in all likelihood, was the cause for poor posture and not his constant reading, exclusion by his more masculine peers, the doting of a mother on her youngest child and only son, and in Freudian terms, the adolescent was overwhelmed by a strong super ego personified by Uncle Matthew. While the senior sincerely loved his nephew, he also was an overly protective, strict, and stern disciplinarian. Joseph Tingley, William Tingley's son, who later taught for President Matthew Simpson at Indiana Asbury, recalled that the uncle accompanied Matthew, "in his recreation and walks, and never allowed him to play out of his sight. In fact, he discouraged play almost altogether, but delighted in making the young happy in their duties and studies. Matthew was an apt

110   Barker, 112 – 113.
111   Crooks, 12.

pupil and naturally and wholly fell in with this mode of life."[112] When in the classroom, the nephew was never punished because the uncle "was too greatly feared and respected, and moreover, his mode of instruction forbade inattention by reason of its absorbing interest."[113]

A portrait of Uncle Matthew reveals a man with a glowering countenance, an exceedingly gaunt face over which was mounted a towering forehead. He "was a good disciplinarian, kind and gentle with his pupils, though at times seemingly severe with the unruly. His corporal punishment was a stroke or two upon the open palm with the flat side of a light pine 'ruler,' aptly named."[114] Was young Matthew naturally compliant and docile? Was there no spirit of adventure in him? Or was he already so politically astute, that as a child he chose a quid pro quo approach to life? Good behavior has its rewards, and there was no greater reward for the nephew than approval. The uncle recalled the nephew never disobeyed his mother, himself, or any other authority figure, for that matter.[115]

In Methodist terms, young Matthew was under conviction. In Dorothy Day's words over a century later, "I was always haunted by God." The question about his relationship with God was brought to a crisis during a camp meeting held at the Dickerson farm, about three miles outside of Cadiz.[116] "I felt deeply interested in the scene, and wondered why I, who had been so righteously educated, and whose life had been so guarded by Christian influences, should not experience the same religious emotions as they. I drew near the railing and was standing absorbed in thought when I saw a short distance from me standing near the railing a young man of a religious family with whom I had formed a pleasant acquaintance, but

---

112   Ibid., 56.

113   Ibid., 35.

114   Ibid., 35.

115   LOC, Simpson papers, Letter, Uncle Matthew to nephew, March 17, 1838, Container three.

116   The historical marker at Dickerson Church reads: "Matthew Simpson; Born in Cadiz, Ohio, June 21, 1811; Died Philadelphia June 18, 1884; Bishop of the Methodist Episcopal Church; Counselor of Lincoln; Peerless Orator; Ardent Patriot; Converted at the Camp Meeting held a short distance southeast of this church. From Bishop Simpson's oration at Lincoln's tomb; 'Hushed is thy voice, but its echoes of liberty are ringing throughout the world, and the sons of bondage listen with joy. We crown thee as our martyr and humanity enthrones thee as her triumphant son. Hero, Martyr, Friend, Farewell.'"

who like myself, was not a professed Christian."[117] The two of them went forward to pray at the altar, the friend leaving with a conviction that he had found salvation, an experience which eluded Simpson. Christian conversion of early nineteenth-century Methodists normally consisted of a convulsive paroxysm, a sudden crisis certified by the "witness of the Spirit" that one was a child of God.

Spiritual Doubts

The "witness of the Spirit," was a cornerstone doctrine for early nineteenth-century Methodism.[118] American Methodists believed that at the moment of regeneration, or the experience of entire sanctification, one would receive an undeniable certitude from God that the supernatural work was completed. After all, John Wesley had felt "his heart strangely warmed," on May 24, 1738. His Moravian friends, such as August Spangenburg and Peter Bohler, persuaded him that the new birth would be accompanied by an indelible impression, a knowledge that one was a child of God. From personal experience and empirical investigation, (Wesley's letters were often spiritual questionnaires.) Wesley seemed to have changed his mind on this issue. He concluded that a person could believe for salvation, receive life from God and not experience an unquestionable convincement of one's acceptance by God, if receiving convincement at all. Wesley parted with his Moravian friends over their claim that the knowledge of salvation was invincible, and their denigration of the "means of grace."

---

117 Crooks, 25-26.

118 Obviously, exact epistemological and psychological correlations for the doctrine of the "witness of the Spirit" are complex, if not impossible. For us, historical assessments will have to suffice. Randy Maddox states that Wesley, "Began to encourage publicly those whose despair over the absence of full assurance led them to doubt their justification, as earnestly as he had previously challenged those who had presumed that no such assurance was available …. In short, the mature Wesley rejected his immediate post–Aldersgate assumption of an absolute connection between being the recipient of God's pardoning grace and having a clear assurance of that pardon." Randy Maddox. *Responsible Grace: John Wesley's Practical Theology* (Nashville: Kingswood Books, 1994) 126–127. Apparently, Simpson did not get the memo. Indeed, the doctrine was confusing. I respectfully disagree with Randy Maddox when he states, "I do not believe that Wesley should be accused of duplicity here." Maybe not duplicity, but contradiction.

As important and historical as "Aldersgate," May 24, 1738, was in Wesley's life, he wrote the following October, "I have not that joy in the Holy Ghost; no settled, lasting joy. Nor have I such a peace as excludes the possibility either of fear or doubt .... I nevertheless trust that I have a measure of faith, and am 'accepted by the Beloved'. I trust .... that I am 'reconciled to God' through his son."[119] In January of 1739, he was even more doubtful of his salvation: "That I am not a Christian at this day I assuredly know as that Jesus is Christ. For a Christian is one, who has the fruits of the Spirit of Christ, which (to mention no more) are love, peace, joy, but these I have not."[120] Late in life, the reflective, seasoned founder of Methodism wrote a guilt-tinged letter to his friend Melville Horne: "When fifty years ago, my brother Charles and I in the simplicity of our hearts, told the people of England that unless they knew their sins were forgiven, they were under the wrath and curse of God, I marvel, Melville, they did not stone us!"[121]

The seventeen-year-old Matthew's atypical conversion resulted in a more profound commitment to the role of God in his life. He would overcome his doubts by stricter attention to religious duties. Four weeks later he initiated a young men's prayer meeting which only made absence of the assurance of faith more pronounced. "As I did not enjoy consciousness of my acceptance with God, it was a cross for me to engage in the exercises of a prayer-meeting, and yet I felt it to be a duty."[122] At no time in his life did Simpson give an account of a definitive conversion experience, i.e., exact time and place. In January of 1830 in poetical form, he expressed his doubts to his sister, Hetty, and requested prayer for his salvation:

Since last New Year's I have been brought to see
my urgent need a savior's love to feel
To know that he has surely died for me

---

119   John Wesley. *Works* Vol. XIV, ed. W. Reginald Ward (Nashville: Abingdon, 1990) 20.

120   Wesley, *Works* Vol. XIX, 29-31.

121   Robert Southey. *The Life of Wesley* Vol. I (New York: W.B. Gilley, 1950) 258. See Richard P. Heitzenrater's excellent essay, "Great Expectations: Aldersgate and the Evidences of Genuine Christianity," *Aldersgate Reconsidered*, ed. Randy L. Maddox (Nashville: Kingswood Books, 1990) 49-91.

122   Crooks, 26.

And that his blood the worst disease can heal
That I his love shed in my heart abroad
May feel and know my sins are all forgiven
That I can say my Father and my God
And view a place prepared for me in heaven
For this an interest in your prayers I crave
When you approach before a throne of grace
And when this life is over that God may save
And take me hence to view his glorious face
And I in turn will not forget to pray
That you in grace and love may more abound
Advancements made in knowledge day by day[123]

Pinpointing the time of one's conversion is often a problem for individuals who have never known themselves not to be Christian. Throughout life, Matthew Simpson would question his relationship with God. His certitude ebbed and flowed according to circumstances, emotional fluctuations and physical health. Observing his Uncle William Tingley's buoyant spirit during sickness, he recorded, "I was indeed wonderfully struck; it was such a contrast to the feelings and conversation of others whom I had lately seen afflicted .... Yet it made me feel sorrowful that I had not that clear sense of my standing, which I could wish."[124] At other times, he was more positive. After attending a camp meeting with many conversions, he recorded as a twenty-one-year-old, August 13, 1832, "At this meeting I obtained, I humbly trust some fresh spiritual strength. I was enabled in a greater degree to yield my heart to Jesus. I felt an application of these words: 'Come unto me all ye that are weary and heavy laden and I will give you rest,' and I felt in a good degree that I could come. Peace flowed into my heart but little joy."[125] Joy was not a commodity in which Simpson's melancholic temperament would often, if ever, luxuriate.

After initiating the young men's prayer meeting, the seventeen-year-old envisioned a Sabbath school for the village children. Upon approaching the trustees and requesting use of the church, he was rebuffed. Some members

---

123   LOC, Simpson papers, "Matthew Simpson's Address to Hetty McCullough," Container twenty.

124   Crooks, 39.

125   Ibid., 44.

of the church thought that day schools were sufficient and that teaching was not proper work for Sunday. The church would be soiled by the children and rendered unfit for service. "But we at last succeeded in getting the use of it and started our school."[126] Matthew obtained use of the church by promising to sweep and thoroughly clean it after use. Thus, there would be no evidence that children had ever been there. Cousin Joseph retained distinct memories of sitting in his older cousin's Sunday school class. "I remember well the impressive as well as popular style of his religious instructions. The class was very large, filling the entire piano corner of the church." Joseph also recalled Matthew's teaching at his Uncle Matthew's school. "He was called upon to 'talk to the school'. One of these occasions I remember well. He came into the room holding in his hand a bouquet of wilted wild flowers. He was in a tender mood, and that lesson of the fading flowers, melted many hearts and produced impressions never to be forgotten. It was a lesson of mortal and immortal life in a model object lesson on the subject."[127]

A Brief College Experience

In the summer of 1828, Charles Elliott of Madison College at Uniontown, in the vicinity of Pittsburgh, passed through Cadiz. His summer travel was for the expressed intent of promoting the college, a school sponsored by the Pittsburgh Conference of the Methodist Episcopal Church. Elliott lodged in the Simpson home and persuaded the teenager to attend Madison. In November, with little encouragement from his family, he left home to become a college student. "So, tying up what clothes I needed and a few books in a little bundle which I carried, I set out for college with eleven dollars and twenty-five cents in my pocket." He made the whole journey on foot, ninety miles, "traveling in the most economical way and arrived at Uniontown on the afternoon of the third day."[128] Thirty-five years later he recalled his only formal attempt at higher education:

> Uniontown to me has some pleasant reminiscences. Nearly twenty year ago, I entered it one afternoon as a poor student, having just walked from Cadiz, thus carrying my clothes and books in a

---

126 Ibid., 27.
127 Tingley, "Reminiscences."
128 Crooks, 19.

knapsack on my back. I left home with a few clothes, a few books and but eleven dollars in money to enter upon a college career among strangers. I could not afford a stage passage nor could I well afford to pay for regular meals, and however, I ate one meal a day, and lived on cakes for the other two until I reached the town. Then I called on Dr. Elliott; entered upon my studies, was needed as a teacher, and in a few weeks was elected tutor. Change after change has since occurred until this evening. I enter it again by the same road as I traveled then.[129]

Simpson's total college education lasted less than two months. His peers were not motivated as he thought they should be, and he had mastered just about everything the college had to offer. Thus Elliott, noting Matthew's boredom because he was not challenged, offered him a tutorship. He could teach and earn a college degree at the same time. But things were not going well at home. Elizabeth had contracted tuberculosis from which she would die five years later.[130] Hetty was engaged and soon to be wed. Uncle Matthew was sick. On November 30, the young student wrote his uncle asking his opinion as to the tutorship: "And now the question is whether I shall apply for the office or not; and upon this I desire you to send me a letter and let me know what your judgment upon that subject is. If you think it would be better for me to continue here, so send me word, and if you think not, let me know that, and also send Mr. Elliott a letter stating as a reason for my non-continuance, disappointment in circumstances at home so that he may not think hard of me."[131]

We have no record that Uncle Matthew responded to either the nephew or Elliott. The boy trekked back home for Christmas break, never to enroll in college again, never to earn a degree from an accredited educational institution during the entirety of his life. Matthew easily rationalized dropping out of college. Having never been more than ten miles outside of Cadiz that he could remember, he was homesick. The Cadiz inhabitants thought the teenager had been gone for six months which was understandable, for why should a college education take more than six months for someone as smart as the town bookworm? But Matthew did not return with a glow on his

---

129 UMA, Drew University, Simpson papers, Letter, Matthew to Ellen, June 9, 1852.
130 Elizabeth married Curtis Scoles, a physician who became a Methodist preacher. She died August 24, 1833.
131 Tingley, "Reminiscences."

countenance. Cousin Joseph remembered him sauntering back into Cadiz as, "tall, slim, hollow-breasted and round shouldered. And somewhat uncouth yet of a commanding appearance that inspired respect and admiration even then."[132] The brief stay at Uniontown was not in vain.

First, young Matthew stayed in the home of Charles Elliott, a person whom he would come to revere and with whom he would cross paths until Elliott died in 1869. Charles Elliott, then thirty-six years old, modeled the best in scholarship and piety. He was an excellent preacher and teacher. When later that summer Simpson listened to Elliott's sermon for the ordination service at Annual Conference, he recalled that he preached with remarkable power which "made a deep impression on my mind." Each morning Elliott gathered with his boarders for devotions, adopting a plan that each one would read from the Bible in a different language, the Vulgate in Latin, the Septuagint in Greek, as well as Hebrew, French, and German translations. "After prayer, the various readings of the several versions were a subject of more or less extended conversation."[133]

Second, Henry Bascom was president of Madison College in Uniontown. Simpson heard Bascom preach both at Madison College and the following summer at Annual Conference. Bascom may have been the most eloquent preacher of his day. Simpson sat spellbound listening to the seasoned preacher. Henry Clay, a friend of Bascom's, pronounced him the greatest natural orator of his age. (Clay was the person most responsible for Bascom becoming Chaplain of the House of Representatives.) Simpson would later echo Bascom's references to nature and his visual speech. Bascom's biographer, M. M. Hinkle, stated, "He loved to hold communion with the cloud crowned mountains, the wild cataract, the surging sea, the dark storm cloud, the harsh thunder and the tornado."[134] Hinkle further asserted that Bascom's discourses, "were full of deep thought, the gorgeous imagery of ardent fervency; and the understanding, the imagination, the passion were at once excited to the intensest degree." [135] As did Simpson

---

132   Tingley, "Reminiscences."
133   Crooks, 20.
134   M.M. Hinkle. *The Life of Henry Bidleman Bascom* (Louisville: Morton and Griswold, 1854) 347.
135   Ibid., 349.

later in life, Bascom painted word pictures: "If the tincture of his pencil was brilliant and pleasing, the force of his argument was irresistible. If his colors were glowing, the thunders of his eloquence were astounding and if the ear was delighted, the heart was softened and subdued."[136] The following from Bascom could have been placed in a later Simpson sermon without incongruence or discontinuity:

> Polished Greece, therefore and Imperial Rome owed their distinction to letters. For what is it knowledge cannot achieve? It has transformed the ocean into the highway of nations. Steam, fire, wind and wave all minister to the comforts and elegance of life. The cold and insensible marble speaks and breathes. The pencil of Raphael gives body and soul to color, light and shade. The magnet, the mysterious polarity of the lodestone, conducts man over the bosom of the deep to the islands of the sea; while the glass introduces him to the heavens and kindles his devotion amid the grander of a thousand worlds.[137]

Bascom would lay the cornerstone for the first building of Indiana Asbury University, where Simpson would eventually become President. Bascom served as President of Transylvania University in Lexington, Kentucky. The school's attempt to place itself under the auspices of the Methodist Episcopal Church was never achieved. Simpson later wrote of Bascom, "At one point he was perhaps the most popular pulpit orator in the United States. His sermons though long, did not weary the people. They were evidently prepared with great care. As is often the case in reading his sermons, we miss the brilliancy and vivacity of the living speaker. Bascom was a man of remarkable fine personal appearance and had a voice of great compass and power."[138] Bascom recorded after a fitful stay at the home of an impoverished family: "Had a breakfast that might've substituted as an emetic prepared by the good wife who might, had she floated down the Nile, been safe from molestation by alligators, if filth would frighten them."[139] Like all great preachers, Bascom had mastered hyperbole. For a couple of years Bascom was the chief spokesman for the American Colonization

---
136   Ibid., 180.

137   Ibid., 187.

138   Matthew Simpson, ed. *Cyclopaedia of Methodism: Embracing Sketches of Its Rise, Progress, and Present Condition with Biographical Notes and Numerous Illustrations* (Philadelphia: Lewis H. Everts, 1881) 92.

139   Hinkle, 207.

Society in which he firmly believed. Bascom may have exerted a greater influence on Simpson's homiletical subconscious than any other preacher. Unfortunately, Bascom died at the early age of fifty-two, exhausted by work, exposure to the elements as an itinerant, and crushed by the contention in the church for which he had given his life in sacrificial service.

Simpson as a Medical Doctor

At the age of nineteen young Matthew's life took a strange turn, which would be both to his betterment and to his detriment. What was he going to do vocationally? Ministry was ruled out because he possessed a mortal fear of standing in front of people. And the only way to be a successful attorney was arguing cases before a jury. His penchant for science, both biology and botany, made him believe he could become a medical doctor. By a three-year apprenticeship, reading a few medical books, and passing a non-standardized exam administered by his mentor, he would be qualified by the state of Ohio as a physician. Unfortunately, this occupational direction partially preempted the needed theological training for the vocation which he eventually chose. After John McBean taught Simpson in the Academy, the former classical languages professor had become a physician and was practicing in Cadiz.[140] Thus, Matthew could become a physician without ever having to leave home. That's what he thought until McBean moved his practice some twelve miles away to Freeport. But the young man may have chosen medicine in order to sublimate a neurotic fear of death.

---

140 John McBean had hung out his shingle on October 1, 1825. His first office was in the "northeast corner of Mr. Bingham's house." McBean died in January of 1875, after slipping on ice. He is buried along with his physician son in the Cadiz cemetery. His obituary stated, "Besides being a learned and skillful physician Dr. McBean was a thorough scholar, well-versed in the languages, and possessing a vast store of general information. In this respect, our community has probably never produced any man equal to him." *Cadiz Republican*, Cadiz, Ohio (January 17, 1878). Simpson never forgot the debt to his mentor, and on February 10th wrote the widow: "Dear Mrs. McBean: - I received the mournful tidings a short time since of the death of your estimable husband, and of my esteemed friend, Dr. McBean. It seemed to come very near my own heart, for he was for so many years my teacher, both in academic and medical studies. I had for his talent and honesty so high regard …. Years rolled rapidly away. As I look back, it seems to me but a little while since I was for a short time an inmate in your family when you resided in Freeport, Ohio, and yet, when I count the years, they are rapidly approaching the half century." UMA, Drew University, Simpson papers, Letter February 10, 1875.

"God Cannot Do Without America"

In a pre-antibiotic and pre-antiseptic age with little understanding of how diseases were transmitted, any family could expect to lose one or two children out of every five before they reached adulthood.[141] On January 21, 1831, Simpson recorded, "This day I am twenty. The one fifth of a century has elapsed since I was born. In that period, I have but been acquiring necessary information for a journey which I shall probably never take. Though I am young, I feel in myself the shafts of death."[142]

Among the texts which Simpson was required to purchase and study were Sir Ashley Cooper's *Surgery*, Christopher Williams Hufelord's *On Scrofula*, W. P. Davies' *A Compendious System of Midwifery*, William Gibson's *Institutes and Practice of Surgery*, Anthelme Richerand's *Physiology*, Sydney Thompson's *System of Medicine*, and George Gregory's *Elements of the Theory and Practice on Physic*.[143] These books were filled with both benign and dangerous information. The remedy was often worse than the disease. Simpson purchased George Gregory's thousand page tome in two volumes for six dollars.[144] Gregory recommended for kidney pain: "When pain is very acute, blood may be taken from the loins by cupping even from the arm, the patient should be placed in a warm bath and a full dose of opium given every second or third hour according to the urgency of the symptoms."[145] For rheumatism, "Sixteen ounces of blood may at first be taken from the arm and repeated two days afterwards if the pain continues urgent."[146] For hepatitis, "bleeding from the arm and locally by leeches …. But the employment

---

141 There are no U.S. mortality rates for the early nineteenth century. In 1850, the life expectancy for a white person was less than forty years, and only twenty-three years for a black person. A white woman had 7.04 children, and 216 children out of every 1,000 died in infancy, or over one out of five. In 1830, the mortality rate must have been just as high as 1850. Michael Haines. *Fertility and Mortality in the United States*, EH. Net Encyclopedia, Economic History Association. http://eh.net/encyclopedia/article/haines.demography

142 Crooks, 35.

143 Robert Clark. "The Medical Training of Matthew Simpson: 1830-1833," *Ohio State Archeological and Historical Quarterly* Vol. LXI, No. 4 (October 1952) 371-379. Simpson's notes on Richerand and Thompson are found in LOC, Simpson papers, Container nineteen.

144 George Gregory. *Elements of the Theory and Practice of Physic* (Philadelphia: Towar and Hogan, 1869). The volumes are in the possession of the Harrison County Historical Society.

145 Gregory, Vol. II, 384.

146 Ibid., Vol. I, 487.

of saline purgative is also a very essential benefit."[147] The observations in the medical books were often less than profound: "We presume that in dysentery the primal seat of the disease is in the inner membrane of the great intestine for morbid appearances chiefly present themselves in part of the alimentary canal."[148] One would not have to read a medical text to reach the following conclusion: "In some cases indeed there can be little doubt that after a certain time, inflammation of the mucous membrane of the stomach does come as in consequence of arsenic."[149]

Nineteenth-century America misunderstood and underappreciated medical doctors. They and attorneys were far too numerous. *The Western Journal of the Medical and Physical Sciences* asserted in the late 1820s that "wherever one went, he would find twice as many lawyers or doctors as was needed."[150] Fees were low, because before the Civil War, no state in the U.S. had established enforceable standards for the practice of medicine. Medical schools abounded, twenty-six founded between 1810 and 1840, but not anything close to a universally-accepted curriculum existed. One could matriculate through Yale "Medical School" in six months.

Simpson practiced little medicine. If he ever delivered a baby or performed surgery, he did not record the events. Medicine required probing and intrusion into private spheres, physical, emotional and spiritual preserves, making Simpson uncomfortable. His communication gifts, which would one day reach thousands in one setting, failed him in the intimate conversations of medical diagnosis. During his apprenticeship he plugged teeth for his brother-in-law, Curtis Scoles. (Dentistry was not a separate specialty.) He applied an electrical machine with a galvanic battery to his sister, but did not record the results. (She died within the year of tuberculosis).[151] August 19, 1825, he billed Isaac Layfort for 33 1/3 cents per day for attending him when sick. He billed him the same rate for attending his wife and daughter for 11 days. The total bill came to $6.66 and 3/4 cents. The bill brings us

---

147   Ibid., Vol. II, 478.
148   Ibid., Vol. II, 465.
149   Ibid., Vol. II, 451.
150   John Duffy. *The Healers: A History of American Medicine* (Chicago: University of Illinois Press, 1979) 179.
151   Clark, "Medical Training," 375.

to two conclusions: Simpson was exact, and he was not going to become rich practicing medicine.[152] On July 25, 1833, the apprentice received the following certificate: "Mr. Matthew Simpson, Jr. has studied the science of medicine under my direction for the period prescribed by state medical law; and I have no hesitancy in saying that I consider him an eminently-qualified member of the medical profession, and altogether deserving of the public patronage. John McBean."[153]

In the early morning hours November 13, 1833, a meteoric shower provided fireworks for much of the United States. As many during the New Madrid earthquake of 1811, observers thought the world was coming to an end. A thousand meteors a minute, emanating from the constellation Leo, brought the people of Cadiz out into the streets. As they watched the fiery torments, some were simply bewildered while others were so badly frightened that they fell on their knees and prayed. The blacks were especially terrified, uttering shrieks of terror and cries for mercy, while throwing themselves prostrate on the ground.

The young medical doctor, Matthew Simpson, understood the phenomena, and while marveling at the display of God's creativity, calmed the fears of at least a few that surrounded him. Others were not to be dissuaded that the rapture was taking place, and this would be a good time to confess their sins. A Mrs. Congreve exclaimed to her husband, "My dear husband, that dear boy, John, you think so much of is not your boy. He belongs to the shoemaker across the street." Her husband responded with, "That's enough, that's enough! Blow your horn Gabriel, blow, blow. I'm ready to go now."[154] (Sounds apocryphal, but it's a great story.)

The Call to Ministry

Simpson's meteoric benediction may have been one of his last official or unofficial acts, as resident physician within Cadiz. He was now ready to begin the vocation, that as in God's promise to the Apostle Paul, he would

---

152   Probate file of Isaac Layfort is in the Harrison County, Ohio Historical Society.

153   LOC, Simpson papers, Container twenty.

154   Charles B. Wallace. "Meteors and Consequences," *The Jimhinker* Vol XL, No. 1 (April 2010) 6. Harrison County Historical Society, Cadiz, Ohio.

carry Christ's words before "Gentiles and their king" (Acts 9:15.) Two people whom he trusted prompted or goaded him to test the waters. Sometime in his late teens, the exact year he did not recall, as one of the teenagers attending the Sunday evening youth service, he had the distinct impression that he should address his peers. "While I was discussing the matter with myself, Uncle Matthew came into the room and after a moment's hesitancy said to me 'Don't you think you could speak to the people tonight?' I was surprised and startled and asked him if he thought I ought to? He said 'yes, I think you ought. I think you might do good.' That night, by some strange coincidence, the house was crowded and I made my first religious address to a public congregation which was not written, was not very well premeditated. It was a simple and earnest out-gushing of a sincere heart."[155]

Amanda Wood of Springfield, Ohio, recalled, "I suppose there were some in that well filled little church who wondered at his self-possession as he arose to speak in the presence of the village wiseacres. But soon the power of his pulpit took hold and took the attention of his hearers."[156] Because the itinerant pastor showed up only once a month, young Matthew had many opportunities to preach in his home church. The boisterous worship of the Methodists and sing-song cadence of the young preacher earned the ridicule of the Presbyterians, even to the extent that a local amateur artist caricatured Matthew preaching with mourners at the altar.

> But this it seemed was not enough, and a young artist of the village employed his talents in caricaturing the mourner's bench. The picture was gotten up in good style and was privately circulated among the artist's (an engraver named Anderson) friends, causing a good deal of amusement. The principal figure was a very striking caricature of the young preacher (Mr. Simpson) whose lank, and stooping form and somewhat odd appearance made him a fine subject for the artist. He was represented in the act of administering comfort and advice to the absurdly agonized (in the artist's opinion) mourners. The artist and his "set" were always supercilious in word and action toward this plain and uncouth young man, who so far outstripped them in learning and true manliness. We was often publicly snubbed and jeered by them, and their petty jealousies gave him considerable annoyance although "none of these things moved him" or caused him to change his manner of tactics for a moment.

---

155 Matthew Simpson. *Lectures on Preaching* (New York: Nelson & Phillips, 1879) 50.
156 UMA, Drew University, Simpson papers. "Recollections of Amanda Wood," March 25, 1887.

> The leader in these youthful persecutions was the artist above named, whom I remember as a fine looking young gentleman, brilliant and popular among the reckless young men of the period, and a leading spirit in their social gatherings and "sprees." In later years he became a sot, and finally died by suicide.[157]

Second, providentially in the summer of 1833, Simpson was living with the McBean's in Freeport in order to study for his final medical exam. Charles Elliott rode up to the hotel across from the doctor's office and alighted for breakfast. Matthew was glad to scamper across the street and dine with him. "Our conversation turned especially upon the educational facilities we thought to be afforded to our youth and the doctor urged me to engage in some specific literary work. Before the conversation ended he asked me, if I did not think I was called to preach." Simpson admitted that he had had thoughts upon the subject, "but that I had in my own conscience, decided to obey the action of the Church. I intended to do what I could. I had devoted my life to the service of God, but I designed simply following the openness of his providence. If the church desired me to preach I believe the way would be open without any agency of mine."[158] Added to his fears of becoming a Methodist itinerant was the necessity of leaving his aging mother. Over a half century later, he recalled his mental anguish and spiritual doubts:

> After I had told her my mental struggles, and what I believed God required, I paused. I shall never forget how she turned to me with a smile on her countenance, and her eyes suffused with tears, and she said: "My son, I have been looking for this hour ever since you were born." She then told me how she and my dying father, who left me an infant, consecrated me to God, and prayed that if it were his will I might become a minister. And yet that mother had never dropped a word or intimation in my hearing that she ever desired me to be a preacher. She believed so fully in a divine call, that she thought it was wrong to bias the youthful mind with even a suggestion, so much as uttered in vocal prayer. That conversation settled my mind. What a blessing is a sainted mother! I can even now feel her hand upon my head, and I can hear the intonations of her voice in prayer.[159]

---

157   Tingley, "Random Recollections."

158   Crooks, 29. I agree with George Crooks that Charles Elliott deserves a fuller record than he has been given as one of the pioneers of Methodist education. Crooks is accurate when he claims that Elliott was indifferent to office and sensitive to the sense of right.

159   *Lectures*, 63-64.

Simpson indeed put God to the test, no less than did Moses in the wilderness. "I had been licensed a few weeks before as an exhorter and had spoken in the church at Cadiz on a few occasions."[160] Without applying, he received notification that he had been recommended for a license as a local preacher and he was summoned to attend the next quarterly conference which was to meet at New Athens. (Elliot had surreptitiously forwarded his name.) The Presiding Elder insisted that he preach before the Conference; in that preaching was the only way that the conference could assess his qualifications. Simpson refused. "I said to him that if he could show me any rule in the discipline authorizing persons to preach before they were licensed, I would yield, otherwise, he must excuse me as I had determined that I would take no step towards the ministry unless called out by the church."[161] In spite of his obstinacy, the credentialing committee examined him upon "doctrine and discipline." Some questioned his delicate health, while others advocated that Simpson was a "child of Providence." The detractors relented, and the conference recommended him for admission to the Pittsburgh Annual Conference. God had opened a wide door, and Matthew Simpson had no other option but to walk through it.

Simpson's first attempts at preaching were less than stellar. But a few early efforts brought success and no one was more surprised than the young twenty-two year old Matthew. In a camp meeting outside of Cadiz in the fall of 1833, Simpson chose Acts 2 as his text. One of Simpson's relatives wrote to George Crooks after the Bishop's death, claiming this was only Simpson's second attempt at preaching.

> A young lady in the audience, Peggy Simpson by name, A second cousin of the Bishop's and a niece of mine, was gloriously converted while on every hand arose shouts of praise to Almighty God, And truly it might be called a Pentecostal time. It seemed to be similar to the time when Moses beheld the burning bush, yea, truly it was holy ground whereas we stood because of the abundance of the Spirit poured out.[162]

---

160 The certificate reads, "This is to authorize, the bearer Matthew Simpson, Jr., to officiate, as an Exhorter in the Methodist E - P - Church, on St. Clairsville Circuit–Done by the consent of the Society At Cadiz, April 1st, A.D. 1833-Wm Tipton /P in charge." UMA, Drew University, Simpson papers.

161 Crooks, 29.

162 UMA, Drew University, Crooks papers. Letter, Mary McElroy to George Crooks, July 13, 1887.

God knew that the twenty-two year old Matthew's reticent, stammering tongue needed a huge dose of encouragement.

Chapter Three:
Cellers, Garrets, and Soot

The Circuit Rider

Even though Matthew Simpson had been given a local preacher's license by the "Quarterly Conference," he was yet to be granted an appointment by the Pittsburgh Annual Conference. The session, which met July 1833 in Meadville, Pennsylvania, consisted of several delegates who doubted Simpson's devotion to ministry and his fitness for it. Charles Elliott pleaded Simpson's case, and the Conference appointed him to a circuit surrounding his home town of Cadiz. Part of the rationale was his aging mother and his dying sister Elizabeth. Some persons thought that the gangly 22-year-old was not ready to survive without the support of family and home. Bishop Robert Roberts, who presided over the Annual Conference, may have been alerted by either Uncle William Tingley or Uncle Matthew Simpson, to retain the young pastor in the vicinity of Cadiz.[163]

The first crisis of Matthew Simpson's ministry was whether pastoring was going to be a part or full-time endeavor. The bi-vocational prospects were promising. He could continue to practice medicine, and/or he could accept a clerk's position with his Uncle Tingley in the county courthouse for a thousand dollars a year. Facing the possibility of a life defined by a bifurcated vocation of preaching part-time, the novice made a history-changing decision. "I felt that God had called me to a more active service, and that it was my duty to relinquish all secular business and to devote myself wholly to preaching. Accordingly, in March, 1834, I closed my office,

---

163   Roberts may have been well acquainted with both the Simpsons and the Tingleys. In 1808, Roberts served on the Shenango Circuit in the area of Wheeling, Virginia, now West Virginia. When Roberts left for Natchez, Mississippi, his wife Elizabeth stayed with an "Aunt Worley" in the vicinity of Cadiz. Worth Marion Tippey. *Frontier Bishop: The Life and Times of Robert Richford Roberts* (Nashville: Abingdon, 1958) 96,111.

64 | "God Cannot Do Without America"

and the circuit having earnestly requested my entire time to be spent upon it, I took my horse and saddle bags and began traveling."[164]

Simpson covered a six-week circuit with 28 churches and within four months his prodigious labors had added six others.[165] The stops included a schoolhouse, with a "single tallow candle" and "the small room of a private house." By the end of the first six weeks the delicate circuit rider was physically whipped, his feelings of inadequacy exacerbated by the warnings of his family and physicians with whom he consulted, that he would kill himself. Curiously, a Hicksite Quaker physician (a follower of Elias Hicks who did not believe in the validity of Scripture nor the deity of Christ), told him the wisest thing he could do, "was to travel a circuit that required me to ride from 8 to 10 miles and to preach once every day."[166] At the end of his first four months of service, Simpson had received $18.25, $6.75 short of the financial salary promised, but not guaranteed. "Friends and home and business had been given up and I had determined to choose reproach and privation and even suffering if I might be successful in winning souls."[167] Elizabeth died in the summer of 1833 and her husband, Curtis Scoles, quit his practice of medicine and served the rest of his vocational life as a preacher in the Pittsburgh Conference of the Methodist Episcopal Church.[168]

Simpson began his circuit in the summer. Riding up and down hills on a horse (and Simpson was not a horseman), battling the heat and humidity, was no easy task. Wet with sweat during the day, drying off in a stale, stuffy cabin at night, eating whatever was set before him, were the perfect ingredients for dysentery, colds and whatever contagious viruses infected the host family. Western cabins were incredibly crude and unsanitary, a contrast to the neat,

---

164   Crooks, 67.

165   Appointments for Simpson during his four years of pastoral ministry were 1833, Steubenville District to the St. Clairsville Circuit; 1834, Pittsburgh District to the Pittsburgh Circuit; 1836, Pittsburgh District to Liberty St. Church.; 1836, Pittsburgh District to Williamsport Church. Grafton T. Reynolds. *Manual of the Pittsburgh Conference of the Methodist Episcopal Church* (Pittsburgh: Pittsburgh Conference, 1928) 93, 94, 95, 97.

166   Crooks, 69.

167   Ibid.

168   Unfortunately, Scoles' pastoring days were short-lived. He lasted in the ministry only five years, dying in Brownsville, Pennsylvania, Feb. 8, 1847 at the age of 43. *Pastoral Records of the Western Pennsylvania Conference of the United Methodist Church: 1784-2013* (Pittsburgh: Commission on Archives and History, 2013) 1156.

clean domesticity that had been provided by his mother and uncle, a retreat that he was now able to enjoy only once every six weeks. In all likelihood, the physician-preacher maintained a small pharmacy in his saddle bag, so he could attend to his own body as well as the bodies and souls of his parishioners.

Young Men of Great Promise

At the 1835 Annual Conference held at Washington, Pennsylvania, Simpson requested of the Presiding Elder that he be sent to a "healthy district" (healthful area). He was stunned when the appointments were being read to learn that he was assigned to cholera-infected Pittsburgh. "My lungs being weak, my health poor, the city smoky and dirty and an epidemic spreading, my relatives were very unwilling that I should go and thought it almost equivalent to death to send me under such circumstances to such a place."[169] Pittsburgh was not yet the Bessemer–belching, fiery furnace that it would become in the 1870s, but there were enough ashes and cinders in the air from the iron ore smelting, that the putrefied air left one's palate coated with a sickening film of pollution.

Michael Chevalier, a Frenchman, recorded in the 1830s that, "Pittsburgh is a manufacturing town, which will one day become the Birmingham of America; one of its suburbs has already received the name. It is surrounded, like Birmingham and Manchester, with a dense, black smoke, which bursting forth in volumes from the foundries, forges, glass houses, and the chimneys of all the manufactories and houses, falls in flakes of soot upon the dwellings and persons of the inhabitants; it is, therefore, the dirtiest town in the United States."[170] He also prophetically observed, "American society, taking for its point of departure labour, based upon a condition of general ease on one side, and on a system of common elementary education on the other, and moving forward with the religious principle for its lode-star, seems destined to reach a degree of prosperity, power, and happiness, much superior to what we have attained with our semi-feudal organization and our fixed antipathy against all moral rule and authority."[171]

---

169   Crooks, 71.
170   Michael Chevalier. *Society: Manners, and Politics in the United States*, Letter XV (Boston: Weeks, Jordan, and Company, 1839) 169.
171   Ibid., 174–175.

"God Cannot Do Without America"

At Simpson's arrival, Pittsburgh boasted of more foundries than any city in the United States. Former Governor of Ohio, Arthur St. Clair, built the Hermitage Furnace in Pittsburgh, in 1803. He went broke, and spent his last days living in a small cabin on the outskirts of the city. But others discovered efficiency enough to make money by using three to four bushels of charcoal, cheaper than coal, to smelt one ton of ore. Three tons of the best ore yielded one ton of pig iron. The first blast furnace in Pittsburgh was built by George Anshutz in 1792. In 1811, *The Navigator* reported that, "the manufacture of ironmongery has increased in this place beyond all calculation. Cut and wrought nails of all sizes are made in vast quantities. We think about two hundred tons per year. Fire shovels, tongs, drawing–knives, hatchets, two feet squares, augurs, chisels, adzes, axes, claw hammers, door hinges, claws, hackles, locks, door handles, spinning-wheel irons, plow irons, flat irons, etc., tons of the these together with a number of other articles in the iron way, are exported annually."[172] The docks of Erie Pennsylvania, 150 miles above Pittsburgh, made Pittsburgh the center of the iron and steel industry of the New World.[173]

A continuous line of travel and transportation was opened between Pittsburgh and Philadelphia as early as 1834. The line consisted of a railroad from Philadelphia to Colombia, 82 miles; a canal reaching from Columbia to Hollidaysburg, 172 miles; the Portage Road from Hollidaysburg to Johnstown, 36 miles, and a canal from Johnstown to Pittsburgh, 104 miles. This made the distance 394 miles, a trip of 5-6 days, not much faster than a stage coach. But the transportation revolution made little difference to Simpson at this point in his life. The young minister made no trip east during these first four years of pastoring. In 1834, Simpson did not travel beyond his circuit, a four point charge. His colleague, Thomas Hudson, described the arrangement: "At that time Pittsburgh and Birmingham composed one station and employed three preachers. There were four places of worship connected with the charge. Smithfield Street, Liberty Street, a schoolhouse in the fifth ward, and a small house in Birmingham." At some time, a fifth appointment was added to the charge. Hudson was complimentary concerning his fellow pastors:

---

172   John Newton Boucher. *A Century and A Half of Pittsburgh and Her People* Vol. II (Pittsburgh: The Lewis Publishing Company, 1908) 16.
173   Ibid., 47.

Brothers Simpson and Hunter, my colleagues, made their home with my family, which was a very convenient arrangement for our work, and afforded me pleasure. They were young men of great promise, their talents and devotion to their work foreshadowing their future eminence in the ministry. They had been favored with good educational advantages, and their attainments in literature and theology were very respectable. Their habits of industry were remarkable; they were always usefully employed, and no duty neglected. If not engaged in the immediate work of the ministry, the time was faithfully improved in reading and study. They were laborious, acceptable, and useful. Their gentlemanly deportment and fine genial spirit rendered their sojourn in our family a season of delightful memories, which we shall ever cherish.[174]

The primary responsibility of pastoring on a multiple-point charge was preaching. The young preachers were required to schedule the entire conference year for the five preaching points. For the Conference Year 1834–1835, Simpson preached one hundred fifty-eight times. On most Sundays, he preached only twice, but on twelve Sundays, he preached three times. When Simpson preached only twice on Sunday, he would preach again at one of the churches that hosted a mid-week service.[175]

Simpson Steps into a Hornet's Nest

Dennis Dorsey resembled a scarecrow more than a human being. The Baltimore Annual Conference of 1837 lowered the boom on this tall, gaunt, sickly man with eyes sunk back in his head, for being away from his circuit during the year, "under the pretense of being afflicted, but had been traveling extensively circulating a work derogatory to the interests of the church."[176] It

---

174   Thomas M. Hudson. *Life and Times of Rev. Thomas M. Hudson* (Cincinnati: Hitchcock & Walden, 1871) 38, 142.

175   LOC, Simpson papers, "A Plan of Appointments for Pittsburgh and Allegheny town: 1834-1835," Container twenty. The five preaching points were Liberty Street, Smithfield Street, Allegheny town, Birmingham, and Bayardstown.

176   Edward J. Drinkhouse. *History of Methodist Reform* (Norwood, Massachusetts: Norwood Press, 1899) 105. In spite of Dorsey being schismatic, Simpson gave him a long, laudatory biographical sketch in his *Cyclopaedia*. Dorsey, a physician, exhibited "Composure under elaborate thought, clearness of intellectual vision, activity, justice of judgment, and metaphysical acumen associated with great simplicity of mind. His learning was considerable as a self-made man, particularly in theology had he fullness of knowledge.

was the Conference that was guilty of pretense and not Dorsey. Dorsey fully admitted that he had been distributing the periodical, *Mutual Rights*,[177] a monthly magazine founded in 1824, advocating laity rights, women's rights, Annual Conference rights, preachers' rights, and lambasting the power of the Bishops and the rigid hierarchy and autocracy of Methodism, especially the appointing of Presiding Elders by the Bishops. *Mutual Rights* entered into an editorial war with Methodism's leading periodical, *The Methodist Magazine*, edited by conservative heavy-weights Nathan Bangs and John Emory. As the presiding Bishop of the Baltimore Annual Conference stood above Francis Asbury's body, which was interred under the pulpit of the famed Eutaw Street Church, had the corpse possessed a smidgen of consciousness, it would have twitched at this repeat of the 1792 James O'Kelly schism, the most agonizing episode in Bishop Asbury's life. The conservative Baltimore Conference set out to make an example of the weakling Dorsey by stripping him of his credentials. Dorsey appealed his case to the General Conference which was to meet April 1828 at the Smithfield Street Church in Pittsburgh.

Smithfield Street was the mother Methodist Church of Pittsburgh. When Asbury preached while standing on the foundation of the church in its beginning days of construction in 1810 to whom he said were one thousand people (Asbury exaggerated crowds) he noted that they were "lively and increasing in numbers."[178] The leading Methodists of the area attended Smithfield, in particular Henry Sellers and James Verner, both of whom would make long-lasting contributions to very different aspects of Matthew Simpson's life.

Asa Shinn, a respected member of the Pittsburgh Conference and former pastor of Smithfield, 1824-1825 (the same circuit that Simpson pastored with two others in 1834) defended Dorsey and the other reformers who had been kicked out of the Baltimore Conference. Of course, the appraisals of

---

His writing was voluminous; and he left a great mass of manuscripts on a large range of subjects." *Cyclopaedia*, 307.

177   "The Mutual Rights of the Ministers of the Methodist Episcopal Church," in Laura A. Grotzinger's *Guide to the Archives of the Western Pennsylvania Conference of the United Methodist Church* (Pittsburgh: Western Pennsylvania Conference, 1988) 12.

178   Quoted in Norman Young. *Church Records: Western Pennsylvania Conference of the United Methodist Conference* (Pittsburgh: Western Pennsylvania Conference, 2013) 690.

Shinn's performance were biased,[179] but by any estimate, it went down as one of the most impassioned speeches in American Methodism's history. Even a New England delegate, who said he hated Shinn "like fire," declared that he had never heard "such an argument" in all his life. Bishop Robert Roberts stated that he did not remember, "To have heard a speech surpassing Mr. Shinn's for argumentative eloquence."[180]

Shinn's speech was in vain. Political maneuvering, and the vote being delayed until the next day, resulted in the General Conference upholding the expulsions which had taken place at the Baltimore Annual Conference. The decision probably did not make much historical nor practical difference. The "Methodist Church in the City of Pittsburgh," without the word "Episcopal," had already been incorporated by the legislature of Pennsylvania on March 8, 1828. The Methodist Protestant Church had its formal beginning six months after the Methodist Episcopal General Conference, when a "general convention of Methodist reformers," met in Baltimore on November 12, 1828. No amount of oratory could have prevented the schism. The forming of a new denomination did not quiet the Pittsburgh Annual Conference. Asa Shinn suffered a nervous breakdown, and Matthew Simpson stepped into a hornet's nest when he went to Allegheny County to pastor in 1834.[181]

---

179   Drinkhouse, 162. Asa Shinn married one of John Wrenshall's daughters, Mary Bennington. Another daughter, Ellen Bray, married Col. Frederick Dent, who became the parents of Julia Dent, the wife of Ulysses Grant. Biographical article on John Wrenshall at the end of *Wrenshall Journal*, microfilm: Manuscript Division-Heinz Center, Pittsburgh, PA.

180   This was not the only occasion at which Shinn's speaking was noted. A German lady stated of a Shinn sermon that, "it was as easy to tell the difference between a preacher vat preached over the spirit, from one vat preached over the letter as it was to tell the difference between pone-bread and pound-cake." George Brown. *The Recollections of Itinerant Life Including Early Reminiscences* (Cincinnati: R.W. Carroll and Company Publishers, 1866) 73.

181   Evidently Shinn had suffered two nervous breakdowns before the "separation." See Rev. C. Cooke. *Discourse on the Life and Death of the Rev. Asa Shinn* (Pittsburgh: Wm. S. Haven, 1853) 10. D.W. Clark glosses over the evolvement of Elijah Hedding in the events at Pittsburgh. "The complete vindication of Bishop Hedding was regarded by his friends as still more triumphant, because in the Pittsburgh delegation there were at least two individuals who had all along sympathized with the radical movement, and had at the outset, placed the same construction upon the bishop's address that "Timothy" did in his article; and, in fact, stimulated him to the course he pursued and eventuated in his withdrawal from the Methodist Episcopal Church. We refer to the Rev. Asa Shinn and Rev. H.B. Bascom." D.W. Clark. *The Rev. Elijah Hedding* (New York: Carlton and Phillips,

The Methodist Protestants attempted to retain possession of the newly-built Smithfield Street Church in Pittsburgh, by placing George Brown in the pulpit. Brown recalled that, "Previous to my arrival, N. Holmes (Nathaniel Holmes, another Methodist who would be highly influential in Simpson's life) and J. Verner, the two anti-reform trustees had served notice on the reform parties of the board (members of the Board of Trustees who wanted to join the Methodist Protestants,) threatening them with legal consequences if they dared to put me into the pulpit of the new meeting house."[182] Brown did manage to preach on June 7, upon being marched down the aisle by the chairman of the Board of Trustees, Thomas Robinson, and Secretary of the Board, Stephen Remington.[183] On June 25, James Verner, true to his threat, brought charges against all of the reform trustees for violating "the charter and for contempt of authority." In the summer of 1829 the case went to court.

Before the issue was resolved, the situation became ugly, culminating in a physical fight with members of the reform group throwing out the sexton and taking his keys. "The old side Sexton came at Stephen Remington with his cane aiming heavy blows at his head. He fended off bravely with his uplifted arms, still working around until he got his back towards the door . . . the Sexton following up with blow after blow until in the door he snatched the bunch of keys."[184] In September 1831, a three-day trial took place, resulting in the case going to the Supreme Court of Ohio where it was heard October, 1832. The court ruled in favor of the reformers, and against the Methodist Episcopal Church's "Deed of Settlement," which claimed that all property belonged to the parent denomination no matter

---

1855) 359. Bascom's biographer rightly argues that though during the 1828 General Conference, Bascom believed that "imparity in the ministry is created in contravention of the arrangements settled in the church by its Head." Bascom changed his mind. He stayed within the Methodist Episcopal Church (though he became a Bishop in the Methodist Episcopal Church South after 1844) and in 1850 wrote, "that ours is a legitimate Presbyterian episcopacy instituted and created as a separate distinct order by conventional consent." M. M. Hinkle. *Life of Henry Bidleman Bascom* (Nashville: E. Stevenson and F.A. Owen, 1856) 375.

182   Brown, 204.

183   John Boucher. *A Century and A Half of Pittsburgh and Her People* Vol. II (Pittsburgh: The Lewis Publishing Company, 1908) 204.

184   Ibid., 210.

what the disposition of the local members. The two parties contending for the Smithfield church reached a truce when the anti-reformers agreed to pay $2,000 and "surrender their claim to a cemetery which occupied the ground up over which the Union Station of the Pennsylvania Railroad now stands."[185] James Verner confiscated his church, but with it, a large dose of humility.

Early Romantic Feelings

Simpson's musings written in poetical verse, revealed a young man who lived in a fantasy, yet chaste world, concerning the opposite sex. His reflections were shrouded in mystery. Were they fiction, or in some way related to reality? On January 28, 1830, Matthew wrote a 64-line poem, "This Must Be Love," revealing his struggles in relating to women, part of which read,

> T'is then I feel a restless mind
> Yet t'is not sorrow, guilt, or woe.
> but some strange feeling then I find
> The name of which I do know.
> Sometimes when Gena comes in sight
> This feeling changes into joy.
> But when she disappears like light
> Then thoughts confused my mind employ
> Wherein I pass where Gena dwells
> My head will turn without my lead.
> To fancy in her whispers my lead.
> To fancy in her whispers tells
> Some glimpse of her I may receive.
> Wherein in company we meet
> My eyes in spite of me will roll.
> In quest of her command complete
> This something would have over my soul.
> Yet when it comes my lot to speak.
> Unwilling, diffident, and shy.
> A meaning timorous and weak

---

185   Ibid., 472.

From converse I would almost fly.
Yet go I can't my voice must out
Then trembling, quivering like a leaf.
My eyes go wandering about
And this you know must give no grief.
Now what is this I ask my mind
It says t'is friendship t'is esteem.
T'is tenderness, t'is feeling kind
T'is charity's inspiring beam.
I ask my heart there is no reply
But gentle feelings through it move.
I feel arise an anxious sigh
And this responds it must to be love.[186]

The second piece written in poetical form was titled "The Lover's Farewell," August 21, 1830.

And when a friend has ceased to live, In spite all that art would give
As in their ears the sad knell, So in this heart a sad farewell.
What! Must I say farewell to thee, And never in thy presence be
Never hear the music of thy voice, Nor thy sparkling eyes rejoice
Not one sweet moment with thee spend, And fondly dream I had a friend
Does not my sorrow move thy heart? Hast thou not felt such anguish smart,
Or never didst thy bosom feel, The pangs of woe like darts of steel?
Suffer thou those within my heart, As did the fatal poison dart
Since you command the way I go, And start to wade through seas of woe
Thus, I no pleasure here can find, Where grief and sorrow seize my mind
Away, away to bowers unknown, I'll wonder wretched and alone.
And think that thou not all the while, Thou shalt enjoy kind fortune's smile
That she will still remain thy friend, And still her choices favor sin
She yet may turn and make thee feel, Some words too fatal e'er to heal
You often see in starry nights The splendid meteors dazzling night.
And you have seen though bright their fire, Their race is short–they soon expire
And leave the stars to guild the night, If faint yet with certain light
Just as thy breast their tortures feel, To me too powerful to conceal
Then wouldest thou condescend, To common folks be a friend

---

186 Matthew Simpson, "This Must Be Love," LOC, Simpson papers, Container fifteen.

You remember how we walked, When until the time was quite forgot
And how I listened when you sung, And through my heart the music rung
And now let all things be forgot, And let them be as they were not
The moon will set the sun will shine, The stars under concert will combine
And evening zephyrs gently play, The funeral of each passing day
But I will not to you repair, And with you take the evening air
No more our thoughts together flow, No social pleasure with you know
This is the last I'll say to do, Henceforth I'll say to you
Henceforth farewell, Henceforth adieu.[187]

The following was either an attempt at fiction, a secretive letter to the idealized girl of Matthew's fantasy, or a letter never sent to an actual person in Cadiz, the name camouflaged.

January 14, 1832
To Susan Snowdrop:

>   Dear girl, you know Jim Thumper, don't you? If you do, why I'm the very fellow, and if you don't, why I live with Jacob Thumper at the crossroads. When I go to church I wear a blue coat that I got made at Schneider's sometime last summer, and my hat tapers like a tin bucket turned upside down. Besides that I'm the fellow that looks earnestly at you. Oh! How I love to see your sparkling, shining, star-like eyes look out from under your smooth, pretty brow. While your lips just look as though they were made to be enticing. Now, Susan, dear, lovely, beautiful, handsome, bewitching, enticing Susan I wish to believe that you could make a house happy and me too if I was in it, but that will leave for another time.[188]

Young Matthew's personality traits tell us that any attempts at pursuing and wooing a female companion must have been quite awkward. Matthew's first cousin, Joseph, son of William Tingley, and named after his uncle, remembered that his relative, "was especially timid in the presence of ladies, not acquaintances, but especially free, easy, and entertaining among his lady friends–who admired and revered him for his many excellences and attainments. Not the least were his consistent and cheerful, practical piety

---

187   Matthew Simpson, "The Lover's Farewell," LOC, Simpson papers, August 21, 1830, Container fifteen. The Harrison County Courthouse records for births and deaths do not extend this far back, and thus, it is impossible to identify this person, if indeed, the person existed.
188   Matthew Simpson, "To Susan Snowdrop" LOC, Simpson papers, January 14, 1832, Container fifteen.

which was not hidden under a bushel during social conversion. Neither was it ostentatiously displayed nor out of place at any time."[189]

As Simpson began his circuit riding days there must have been more than one eligible maiden. Who would have had more prospects than a young preacher-medical doctor visiting churches and scores of homes while traveling a 50 mile radius, as the following scenario represents:

> To stand at Perrine's and look around, their farm appears to be surrounded upon three sides with majestic hills, whose sides are skirted with woods, and upon whose summits improvements can be distinctly seen; upon the fourth side if you trace the creek wandering down mist smiling meadows. A handsome mill is on the place, running three pairs of stones, also a small stone house in which preaching is held. I was shown in and waited upon by Miss A. A. T. P____, a sprightly young damsel, who, her mother tells me, is just seventeen, neat in her person, handsome-faced, and amiable in her manners. I was very agreeably disappointed in finding some evidences of literary taste upon her writing-desk, which was very neatly furnished, lay some poetry in her handwriting, while upon her table were the files of the *Western Gem*. After meeting I heard her in another room teaching an orphan girl who lives with them how to spell.[190]

Simpson's Future In-laws - The Prominent Verners

Wow! Beauty, works of piety, gifts of poetry, a pristine romantic setting and the sincere introduction of a hoping mother could not offset the collection of a "worldly" periodical. Either the young preacher was not desperate enough, or he had visions of marital bliss that were somewhat unrealistic. But that would change when he stayed in the home of James Verner, (whom we have already met,) a lodging necessity when he first came to Pittsburgh. He was now vocationally away from home for the first time in his life. Loneliness crowded in on his melancholy spirit and the thought must have occurred to him that without a spouse he would be fighting the sirens of temptation for the rest of his life. The young pastor was smitten by the slender, spritely, seventeen-year-old daughter of James Verner, Ellen Holmes Verner, but recorded nothing about his initial attraction.

---

189   Tingley "Reminiscences."
190   LOC, Simpson papers, 1834 *Diary* April 5, 1834, Container one.

James Verner III was born a Methodist at Verner's Bridge in Northern Ireland in 1778. Both of his parents lived to be 95 years old. In spite of the adamant protests of both sets of parents, James married Elizabeth Doyle, a Catholic, and migrated to America in 1806. In 1816 the couple gave birth to a daughter whom they named Ellen Holmes. The name Holmes came from Nathaniel Holmes, a family friend who emigrated with them from Ireland. This was the same Nathaniel Holmes who defended the Smithfield Street Church against the Reformers, and would remain one of Matthew Simpson's friends for the rest of Holmes' life. As the father of modern banking in Pittsburgh, Holmes became wealthy. Pittsburgh historian George Fleming recorded that, "The firm of N. Holmes & Sons is the oldest private banking house west of the Allegheny Mountains; and with one exception the largest in continuous existence under the name of the founder in the United States. The house was founded by Nathaniel Holmes, who was born in the north of Ireland."[191] John Wrenshall recorded in his journal, "However, in the month of October 1807 we received another increase to our society in the arrival of Nathaniel Holmes and Edward Hazelton with their families from Ireland, men of steady habits and afterwards useful in the society."[192]

James Verner went into a partnership with another Scotch-Irishman, James Brown, in both a brewery and lumber business, a partnership which lasted approximately 40 years. Brown had every reason to continue to hold to the predestination of his Presbyterian upbringing. His life was indeed a series of miraculous events. John Knox's Presbyterianism almost completely displaced Scotland's Anglicanism, prompting Walter Scott to refer to the latter as a "shadow of a shade." As a 17-year-old, Brown had already saved 300 pounds by selling linen, and made his way to America. While on the voyage he became deathly ill and the ship's captain, fearing contagion, jettisoned his passenger on the nearest land which he spotted, the shores of Delaware. After lying around helpless for perhaps months, he recovered sufficient strength to make his way to Brooklyn, funds exhausted. In 1803,

---

191   George Fleming. *Pittsburgh and Environs* Vol. II (New York: The American Historical Society, 1922) 152. A life-size portrait of Nathaniel Holmes hangs in the Library Reading Room of the Heinz Center, Pittsburgh, Pennsylvania. Also see Catherine E. Reiser. *Pittsburgh's Commercial Developments: 1800–1850* (Harrisburg: Pennsylvania Historical and Museum Commission, 1951) 164 and 186.

192   *Wrenshall Journal*, Manuscript Division–Heinz Center, Pittsburgh, PA.

"God Cannot Do Without America"

he arrived in Pittsburgh and immediately went into the dry goods business. Brown was a visionary, buying up much Pittsburgh real estate and dying a wealthy man at the age of 95.[193] James Brown sat on the original city council when Pittsburgh was incorporated as a city in 1816. "Penn Ave. in those days of extension of the city boundaries became to be a favorite locality for houses and business ventures at a high price for lots and in this quest lots took on the foremost prices thus far obtained for municipal reality."[194] On this street Verner lived, and Brown and Verner established their brewery.[195]

Verner's and Brown's business ventures were not without crisis. Monday, December 13, 1835 a fire destroyed both the home of Verner and the brewery. The only death that occurred was that of a 12-year-old girl who was crushed to death by a falling wall of the brewery. "The wind was high and carried flakes of fire over a large portion of this city presenting a most appalling spectacle to the eye of every beholder and exciting the most awful anticipation of far greater distress and devastation that it has been our melancholy lot to witness." Out of the 30 houses and 18 businesses which were destroyed, the newspaper reported that "Messrs. Brown and Verner, Mr. Joseph Barclay and Mr. John Thompson have sustained the greatest amount of loss."[196] Verner and his family were not living in this house at the time of the fire.

In 1833, James Verner moved his family to 450 acres of land on the Allegheny River, which became known in the early days of the railroad as Verner's Station at the present-day site of Verona.[197] Verner with his son

---

193   Robert Cushing. *History of Allegheny County PA* Vol. VII (Chicago: A. Warner & Company, 1889) 272-73. See also Fleming, Vol. II, 58.

194   Fleming, Vol. II, 213.

195   Verner and Brown purchased this land September 26, 1828 for $1,747. Allegheny County, Pennsylvania, Department of Real Estate Deed Book Vol. 37, 133. In January of 1841, Brown and Verner divided their property. Deed Book Vol. 61, 276-278. I conclude that James Verner came under Methodist condemnation for being in the business of alcohol. Thus, Brown kept the brewery and Verner kept the land on which he would build a new house.

196   http://www.genealogybank.com/gbnk/newspaper/doc/v2%3A12A7E3496BF...h%2BBarclay%3B%2BSt.%2BClair-street%3B%2BCalamitous%5D/print.html

197   Fleming, Vol. II, 757. "Verona was incorporated as a borough May 10, 1871, it previously having formed a part of Plum and Penn Townships. The area was extended to include Iona, Verona, Oakmont, Hudson and Edgewater stations on the Allegheny

James cleared the timber from the acreage and built a house. A newspaper described the property as occupying, "A commanding situation on the left bank of the Allegheny River, the valley of which stream is unsurpassed, for the grandeur of its beauty, anywhere in western Pennsylvania. The lofty hills rise forest-clad before us, and here and there a deep and dark ravine, and a gray patch of rock lend diversity to the picture, and the whole is mirrored in clear waters of the upper branch of 'La Belle Reviere.'"[198] The son would profit from the land. James Verner, brother of Ellen, became wealthy and one of Pittsburgh's foremost civic leaders. He also entered the brewery business. In 1859, at the age of 41, he founded the Citizens Passenger Railroad Company, the first street railroad in operation west of the Allegheny Mountains. He then founded the Pittsburgh Forge and Iron Company and served as its president. James bred hunting dogs, loved to hunt and had a state-wide reputation for his accuracy in killing birds on the fly. He, like his father, was a leader in the Methodist Episcopal Church.[199] He was not a Christian before Matthew came into the family. On December 5, 1840, he wrote the following to his sister and brother-in-law:

> I really cannot say for myself that the Lord has pardoned my sins, but I trust that he will if I seek him with all of my heart. Now to tell

---

Valley railroad which was opened to Kittanning on January 30, 1856. At an early day James Verner (Ellen's brother) plotted the tract of land into village lots, and for a time it was known as Verner. At the time of the opening of the railroad the site of the borough on the south bank of the Allegheny River overlooked a valley unsurpassed for beauty; this gained an increase in population that soon made it a commercial and industrial center." Fortune struck Ellen's brother when the Allegheny Valley railroad ran through a portion of his property. James sold this parcel of land to Colonel William Phillips for 160 thousand dollars, at which time the two formed a corporation to "layout" the village and sell lots. James attended Allegheny College at the behest of his brother-in-law who taught there. "Mr. Verner was a man of considerable talent and industry. He attended a private school at Allegheny College at Meadville. He was married to Anna Murray, daughter of General James Murray of Murraysville," *Advance Leader* (June 6, 1946). Also see, Helen Barr, Alena Zaccaria, and Georgey Reed, *Verona Album 1871-1971: One Hundred Years of Memories* (Verona: Verona Centennial Book Committee, 1971). Also see, *Deed–DBV 249*, page 553, on file at Oakmont Carnegie Library, Oakmont, PA.

198   *Advance Leader* (June 6, 1946) as included in Kathy Ferguson, et.al. *Verona, Then and Now: A Commemorative Pictorial Book in Honor of Verona's 120 Year Anniversary* (Verona: July 11, 1991) unnumbered. https://www.riversofsteel.com/_uploads/files/alle-final-report.pdf

199   Cushing, 272-273. Also see *Charles Scaife Papers*, Manuscript Division-Heinz Center, Pittsburgh, PA.

you the truth of the affair, I am sometimes almost persuaded to become a Christian, but there is a selfish pride that keeps me back from going straight forward. This is the only reason I can give for not going to church.[200]

Marriage to Ellen

The young Simpson turned to poetry to express his feelings, presumptuously addressing his wife to be as Ellen Simpson. The 120-line poem proposed marriage, part of which read:

> We only can tell what might probably be
> By judging from things which around us we see
> Permit me to notice a subject or two
> Which may not be amiss to present to your view
> Perhaps ere this earth round the bright burning sun
> Shall complete the rotation it now has begun
> As a bird fully fledged flies away from its nest
> And seeks through the world for some pleasure of rest.
> So you may have left this your present abode
> And be seeking your fortune in some other mode.
> For thy heart may return an affectionate sigh
> To him who perchance for thy heart may apply
> And love's fed by sighs and blown into a flame
> By answers & looks here too tedious to name
> Till this question he puts from a love-smitten heart
> Though his tongue from his palate's unwilling to part
> "My dearest & fairest & loveliest & best
> Deign to listen in kindness to this my request
> Dost thou think in thine heart that thou e'er couldst consent
> That with me and for me thy days should be spent."
> Should you give your consent arrangements come then
> For adjusting the marriage & fixing the when
>
> Already I see you in future cast thought
> Arrayed in pure white and trimmed off with-what not.[201]

---

200   LOC, Simpson papers, Letter, James Verner to Matthew and Ellen Simpson, December 5, 1840, Container three.

201   Matthew Simpson, "Address to E. Simpson," LOC, Simpson papers, Container

It was the house on Penn Avenue in which Matthew Simpson married Ellen Holmes Verner.[202] The event merited little more than a parenthesis in his schedule. On November 3, 1835 he recorded,

> This day road about 12 miles into the country and married a young man of my acquaintance. Returned the same afternoon and at 6 o'clock was united in matrimony to Miss Ellen H. Verner daughter of James Verner in the city. Rev. Costen performed the ceremony. We had been engaged since the 19th of September and I trust that the union may be beneficial in a high degree to ourselves and to others. On Wednesday morning started to see my people in the beaver. Arrived about 4 o'clock. Remained with them until Friday.[203]

George McCullough, while working in the County Clerk office of William Tingley, had married Hetty Simpson in 1834. The McCullough's, living with Uncle Matthew and mother Sarah, had not completed their two-story house in Wellsville, and were still living in a one room log cabin. The newly engaged pastor immediately informed his family of his impending marriage. Uncle Matthew wrote on September 28, 1835, "Yesterday I received yours bringing the important information of your having come to your moorings and so our anxiety on that subject is over and we are very well pleased and hope all this is of God....We do not expect to have a room ready much short of six weeks, but if you should think proper to take a wedding trip you know what for a house we have we will be very glad to see you and Ellen and we will try to make her as comfortable as circumstances will admit but let us know the week before."[204] The race was on to provide a honeymoon retreat. On October 15 Uncle Matthew wrote, "All is usual here the house is in progress the frame is up and the front is nearly weather boarded and shingles made ready."[205] But the house was not ready to receive the honeymooners on the sixth of November. Where Matthew and Ellen stayed while visiting his uncle and mother is unknown.

---

fifteen.

202   Why the couple chose the Penn Avenue address, rather than the Verona location for their wedding is not clear, since the Verners were living at the Verona estate at the time of the wedding. Also note that this house burned down six weeks later.

203   LOC, Simpson papers, 1835 *Diary*, Container one. The Beaver was the name of the district on the Pittsburgh conference in which his family now lived in the area of Wellsville.

204   LOC, Simpson papers, Letter September 28, 1835, Container three.

205   LOC, Simpson papers, Letter October 15, 1835, Container three.

The events surrounding Matthew and Ellen's wedding were strange in that Simpson had not only performed another marriage that day, but had paid a $140.25 fine the week before, for performing an illegal marriage. One hundred and forty dollars was a huge sum for someone whose salary was $200 per year. Maybe James Verner bailed him out. There is little doubt that James Verner provided financial security for his daughter and son-in-law. After the wedding, Matthew moved in rather than Ellen moving out. On July 8, 1837, when at Allegheny College, Matthew wrote his wife in Pittsburgh, "And now Ellen, be sure to keep to yourself what I have written. If Father should ask you anything about things, give such answers as you think best, but do not tell the particulars of my circumstances, as I can work along without any help, though if he offers you anything, you need not refuse."[206] Of course, penury was Simpson's circumstance, and he was attempting to save face.

Twice Simpson mentioned his "scrape," the illegal marriage, in his *Diary* and once in a letter to his family. He wrote his family on September 4, 1835, "The marriage I had solemnized turned out badly. I have been prosecuted–if it is pushed, which is very doubtful, shall have to pay about $140. But my friends here will not let me suffer for money. There is no concern whatever against me in the minds of my friends as they all are satisfied that I acted honestly. So, let this give you no uneasiness."[207] On October 19 he recorded, "On my return I learned that the father of a young man whom I married not long since, had prosecuted me. This occasioned me great anxiety of mind. The matter is not yet settled."[208]

Simpson had no formal education for ministry. It was learn by trial and error. The tuition in this case proved to be expensive. While living in a boarding house, the green-horn preacher was approached by a young couple, requesting that he marry them. Presumably, Simpson knew nothing about the couple, and asked few to no questions. He also had done little work, if any, in acquainting himself with the marriage laws for the state of Pennsylvania. Simpson performed the marriage on the spot, and afterwards,

---

206   LOC, Simpson papers, Letter July 8, 1837, Container three.
207   LOC, Simpson papers, Letter September 24, 1835, Container three. There is no record of this incident in the archives of the Allegheny Court House, Pittsburgh, PA.
208   LOC, Simpson papers, 1835 *Diary*, Container one.

found himself victim of a lawsuit, filed by the groom's father. The man was enraged, in that the preacher had married his son to a young girl of a much lower socio-economic class, and more critically, the bride, somewhere in her background, had Negro heritage. The father failed to appreciate the beautiful Mulatto whom his son had betrothed, and took his wrath out on the twenty-four-year-old preacher.[209]

Simpson had definitely married above himself. Ellen, for the entirety of their marriage, provided the grace, charm, and etiquette, which her husband lacked. She was also the antitype to the normative Methodist preacher's wife. No anecdote better demonstrated her undermining the stereotype that most Americans had of a Methodist preacher's wife, especially before the Civil War, than the following story. Shortly after moving to Philadelphia, a Presbyterian banker's wife entertained the Simpsons. Thinking that the only way to not belittle the Simpsons was by identification with the lowly, the hostess tied her hair in a knot, removed her rings and put on a white apron. Ellen Simpson had been shown to her room by a servant girl. Upon being called for dinner, the Bishop's wife "swept down the stairs, a tall stately woman in black silk ruffled to the waist, with expensive laces and jewelry and her hair done in the latest style." While Ellen effervescently talked throughout the meal, her hostess sat in stunned silence.[210]

Ellen would have not been considered a beautiful woman. At least two portraits survive her: a full-head portrait, which hangs in the Simpson House in Philadelphia and a full-length in The Methodist Home for Children adjacent to the Simpson House. The full-length was damaged by fire, and the bottom, knees down, has been removed. Ellen was probably at least sixty years old when both of these portraits were painted. Her facial features were not dainty, but somewhat rugged, defined by an elongated nose. Her self-esteem was not bolstered when her brother jested that the looks of her first child James would be "passable enough if he did not have a nose like his mother."[211]

---

209   UMA, Drew University, Crooks papers, Letter from Caroline Hampton (Henry Sellers' daughter) to George Crooks, March 15, 1887.

210   Clark, *The Life of Matthew Simpson*, 276.

211   LOC, Simpson papers, Letter December 5, 1840, Container three.

According to Proverbs 18:22 Matthew had found a "good thing." Ellen set her husband on a refinement course for the rest of his life, and there was much room for improvement. On October 22, 1861, he duly reported that he was paying more attention to his hair as she had requested. He also asked her if he should purchase some new clothes.[212] The arrangement was somewhat mutual. He exhorted his wife to weigh herself often, and see how she gained.[213] Ellen was tenderly solicitous. Years later, Matthew recalled, "You recollect my state of health when you first knew me, and you will recollect also the constant care which I was obliged to take of it. The drying of socks–warming of feet, washing my skin in salt & water–rubbing with the flesh brush, use of pearl, ash, and charcoal–daily walking in the morning, etc., etc., foreknew the result under the blessing of providence."[214] Ironically, the "blessing of providence," i.e., his marriage, may have been the foremost reason as to why Simpson would later lose his primitive, Methodist moorings.

In 1841 James Verner and family moved back to the city and turned the farm over to his son. He located "in the district known as Lawrence, on the East Liberty Turnpike--later a part of Penn Avenue. A Mrs. McCargo as a young girl remembered that there was a long lane, with flowers leading to the house from the street. Murray A. Verner said the house stood until around 1915, on the SE corner of Penn Ave. at 38th St. and the grounds occupied an entire square--his younger brother Robert (1789-1860) lived diagonally across Penn in a less pretentious place."[215] James Verner died of cholera in July, 1849 and his wife died in July, 1851. When the bodies were exhumed in 1866, to be moved to another cemetery, the myth was spread that James Verner's hair had continued to grow until it ran almost completely over his shoulders.

Ellen brought a newly found spiritual stamina into her husband's life. He recorded shortly after their wedding, "I seldom have enjoyed more liberty in preaching than I had on the Sabbath before and after my marriage. For this I was truly thankful as it would prevent any idea of my being less useful and devoted than formerly. The whole arrangement appears to be peculiarly providential for although people are apt to be dissatisfied with

---

212 UMA, Drew University, Simpson papers, Letter October 22, 1861.
213 UMA, Drew University, Simpson papers, Letter June 23, 1860.
214 UMA, Drew University, Simpson papers, Letter Date unclear.
215 Heinz Center-Pittsburg, PA, Manuscript Division, Charles Scaife Papers.

their ministers getting married. Yet in my congregation up to this time (November 26) I have heard nothing but approbation."[216] Dr. Henry D. Sellers, aforementioned brother-in-law of Bishop Emory, commented that, "if marrying had that effect on preachers, he wished they all would get married."[217]

The Struggling Young Pastor

It was not long after marriage when self-doubt again consumed Simpson. "I see very little fruit of all my labors. My principal hindrances are first, indolence-I do not fill up my time as carefully as I ought; secondly, timidity--I suffer myself, for fear of offending people, to have my time run away with, I pray too little and visit too little and when I do visit do not converse as closely as I ought."[218] The spiritual leader found himself full of conflicting motives, broken promises and self-serving agendas. He was in conflict with both God and his parishioners. He chafed against the unreasonable demands that he preach three times on Sunday rather than twice. He was an "abomination" in the sight of God. His spiritual aspirations floundered, echoing Paul's sentiment in Romans seven. "When I would do good, evil is present with me." The introspective 25-year-old confessed, "I am indeed, a strange compound: now full of good wishes and desires; again, lost to all feelings of spiritual ambition. Now I resolve to abound in every good work and again yield to slothfulness; now I promise how much I will do this very day and this night finds me with nothing done."[219] Simpson suffered from spiritual angst, a psychological and spiritual malady, common to Wesleyans who tended towards works-righteousness. Wesleyans explained that works were a means of grace, but did not merit grace; for Wesleyans true faith produced outward righteousness, but did not increase one's standing with God. The delicate tension was difficult for timid souls to balance.[220]

---

216   LOC, Simpson papers, 1835 *Diary,* November 26, 1835, Container one.

217   Clark, *The Life of Matthew Simpson*, 49.

218   LOC, Simpson papers, 1835 *Diary,* November 30, 1835, Container one.

219   LOC, Simpson papers, 1836 *Diary,* February 2, 1836, Container one.

220   Finding moderation between the Apostle James and the Apostle Paul has been particularly challenging for Wesleyans. Randy Maddox provides this historical insight: "Surely the strongest form that Wesley ever put this point was in the infamous *Minutes* of the 1770 Conference. Here he argued--in direct rebuttal to antinomian uses of the

Age and maturity would mollify Simpson's guilt feelings, created by the gap between his spiritual aspirations and the realities of ecclesiastical work, but never entirely eliminate them. The superego, a composite of Wesley, Asbury, his Uncle Matthew and the authoritarian, Charles Elliott, was his taskmaster.[221] That combined with a frowning God, personified by Methodist itinerants, that blasted their way into human consciousness by way of metaphorical shock, as did the Old Testament prophets, brought the newly minted pastor to his knees lamenting, "I feel that I am far from God; almost dead in sin and a hardness of heart .... My prayers, my sermons, my all, are, I fear, abominations in the sight of God."[222] He was always coming up short and resolutions to greater devotion, watchfulness and punctuality were of little avail.

Simpson rarely perceived parishioners as a gift from God, but as fetters slowing him down, obstacles between him and accomplishing an agenda

---

idea of imputed righteousness--that both inner and outer good works are required in our Christian life 'as a condition' of final salvation. These *Minutes* created an immediate furor of accusation about a return to works-righteousness and led to a final split between the Calvinist and Wesleyan branches of the Methodist revival. They have caused consternation to Wesley scholars ever since. Yet, while the specific terms chosen might be questioned, the general point in the 1770 *Minutes* is surely consistent with Wesley's larger theological convictions. He was not asserting that we must "merit" final salvation, or that our works are a prerequisite to God's acceptance. He was simply insisting that God's *gracious* empowering acceptance enhances rather than replaces our responsive and *responsible* growth in holiness." Randy L. Maddox. *Responsible Grace: John Wesley's Practical Theology* (Nashville, TN: Kingswood Books, 1994) 171-172.

221   Allow me to disavow any attempt at a psycho-history of Simpson. Psychohistories began with a hypothesis and fit or bend the facts to fit that hypothesis. Erik Erikson's *Young Man Luther* argues that a stern, overbearing God was created in Luther's spiritual consciousness by an over demanding, critical and displeased father. Robert Moore, in *John Wesley and Authority: A Psychological Perspective*, attempts to identify Wesley's allegiance to the Church of England with the indebtedness to the maternal matrix as personified in his mother Susanna. There was no overwhelming debt or negative relationships in Matthew's growing up years that shaped his personality or destiny. I do not find the ultimate psycho-history theme in Simpson's life, that he translated his unique crisis into a universal patienthood. Erikson concluded that both Gandhi and Luther "were able to translate their personal conflicts into methods of spiritual and political renewal in the lives of a large contingent of their contemporaries." Erik H. Erikson. *The Life Cycle Completed* (New York: W.W. Norton and Company, 1985) 82. Eric H. Erikson. *Young Man Luther: A Study in Psychoanalysis and History* (New York: W.W. Norton & Company, 1958). R. Laurence Moore. *John Wesley and Authority: A Psychological Perspective* (Missoula, MT: Scholars Press, 1982).

222   LOC, Simpson papers, 1835 *Diary*, March 8,1835, Container one.

such as he expressed January 11, 1835: "I commenced studying Hebrew this morning, in order for a more critical reading of the Bible, than I ever have given it before. I now every day have a lesson in French and German and Latin and frequently consult Greek and mathematics." Four days later he recorded, "Company often tedious and unprofitable, runs away with time and prevents the accomplishment of what I might other words perform, but it is difficult to dispose of some company. It seems impolite to leave and it murders time to sit and hear the whining against time."[223] No one ever expected more of Matthew Simpson than he expected of himself. While pastoring, Simpson had not yet discovered that spending time with God and spending time with others may be one and the same. And one wonders how studying French and Hebrew enhanced the spiritual welfare of his Pittsburgh parishioners. Simpson's proclivities and aptitudes were at odds with the relational skills required for pastoring. But giving the benefit of the doubt to Simpson, the tension was healthful in that he was well aware that fragmentation of time can produce mediocrity.[224]

Faithfulness and Popularity

The rancor became so great between Smithfield and Liberty Street Church that the churches, being pastored by the same men on the same circuit, had to be separated. Charles Cooke was sent to Smithfield.[225] Simpson was

---

223   LOC, Simpson papers, 1835 *Diary,* January 15, 1835, Container one.

224   Though he may have never achieved it, Wesley was always aiming for moderation, balance between extremes. No statement better exemplified this than the following: "Preach our doctrine, inculcate experience, urge practice, and enforce discipline. If you preach doctrine alone, the people will be antinomians; if you preach experience only, they will be enthusiasts, if you preach practice only, they will become Pharisees; and if you preach all of these and do not enforce discipline, Methodists will be like a highly cultivated garden without a fence, exposed to the ravages of the wild boar of the forest." Quoted in Randy L. Maddox, "Wesley's Understanding of Christian Perfection: in What Sense Pentecostal? "Randy L. Maddox's Response to Laurence Wood," *Wesleyan Theological Journal* Vol. 34, No. 2 (Fall 1999) 108.

225   Charles Cooke, D.D., "was born in St. Mary's Co., Md., September 3, 1799, and died in Philadelphia, August 24, 1875. His parents were members of the Episcopal Church. In 1815 he entered the academy at Georgetown, D.C., and during the vacation of that year was converted at a camp-meeting, and united with the Foundry M.E. church, Washington, D.C. He was licensed to preach in 1819, and employed under the elder on Lancaster circuit, Virginia. In 1820 he was received into the Baltimore Conference, and appointed to Westmoreland. At the organization of the Pittsburgh Conference he fell into that Conference. He was elected as a delegate to the General Conference of 1836, and in

appointed to Liberty St. Church, built in 1831 at the corner of Liberty and Fourth Streets, in all likelihood, one of Pittsburgh's largest church structures. The one metropolitan area of Allegheny City and Pittsburgh in 1835 represented 22,000 people. Simpson's age and inexperience were greeted with scorn, criticism and above all envy by the church from which Liberty had split, Smithfield Street Church. "The charges being divided under a spirit of rivalry, it seemed to me almost impossible to maintain the pulpit of the church over which I was placed."[226] He also chafed over having to preach four new messages each week, three on Sunday and one on Wednesday.

As always in the early years of his labors, the young pastor turned to his Uncle Matthew for advice with the plea, "Still write to me as often and as much as you can for there is no person here that can in any degree supply your place."[227] The novice preacher need not have feared his Uncle's neglect, because the older the senior became, the more neurotically attached he was to his nephew. Uncle Matthew wrote, "You will excuse my solicitude I feel the anxiety of affliction and weakness incident to age and you are to me nearly all that is in the world." He then exhorted his nephew to transcend the opinion of others, be true to himself and above all, be faithful to his Lord. "Jesus is your Commander-in-Chief, he knows what you have left so follow him and he knows all that you are and all you have for he made you what you are and gave you what you have and O my son let this consideration keep your heart at ease nay let it make you joyful independent of other men's opinions be meek and patient under opposition avoid throwing out any hints which could be construed unfavorably to your present colleagues."[228] Adversity and criticism were proofs that he was doing God's will. "Could Luther or Wesley ever have been so great without opposition? Not at all. The most precious of metals by polishing will be lightened metals and even brass and iron may be polished by friction so as to become mirrors. So,

---

1840 was elected editor of *The Pittsburgh Christian Advocate*. After this he was transferred to the Philadelphia Conference, and served some of its most important appointments. At the session of 1870 he preached his semi-centennial sermon. His last appointment was St. George's, Philadelphia. He was gentle and amiable, and yet firm, an able preacher, and greatly beloved by his friends." Matthew Simpson. *Cyclopaedia of Methodism* (Philadelphia: Everts and Stewart, 1876) 254.

226   Crooks, 77.

227   LOC, Simpson papers, Letter November 10, 1834, Container three.

228   LOC, Simpson papers, Letter July 11, 1835, Container three.

opposition gives a luster to both the character and talents of a good man, which they never would have had without it."[229]

One of the few rebukes that the nephew ever received from his Uncle concerned his participation in a Masonic funeral. "If I am not mistaken in this, you would be considered in this to have given your countenance to the fraternity and their foolish funeral parade." Even though it was a funeral solemnity, the meeting of the Odd Fellows "may have been for the purpose of conviviality and for things secret and therefore are not known to the public or to the preacher."[230] The nephew did not inherit his Uncle's contempt for the "Masonic order," in that some of his future rich friends were "Masons," in particular, John Evans. And when Simpson laid the cornerstone for Metropolitan Church, Washington, DC, October 23, 1854, the public event was overrun with Masons.

The Presiding Elder attempted to oversee the division of members between Smithfield and the newer church. Simpson wrote on August 14, 1835, "About three hundred have joined each church and leaving about two hundred yet undecided; the probability is the division will be very near even."[231] But a week later he wrote, "In the division of members I received more than I anticipated."[232] On Sunday morning the twenty-four-year-old pastor looked at 400-500 people, one of the largest congregations of any denomination in the city. Of course, this only increased the antipathy between Liberty and Smithfield and the envy of his peers. He recorded in his *Diary* that considering his youth, want of experience and blessing of the Holy Spirit on his ministry during the last year he "expected the opposition of the Smithfield Church and also the jaundiced views, and expressions of my brethren in the ministry."[233]

Simpson was a faithful pastor. He frequently called upon the poor, "in cellars, in garrets as well as in the alleys and back streets who complained

---
229   LOC, Simpson papers, Letter August 17, 1835, Container three.
230   LOC, Simpson papers, Letter July 3, 1835, Container three.
231   LOC, Simpson papers, Letter August 14, 1835, Container three.
232   LOC, Simpson papers, Letter August 21, 1835, Container three.
233   LOC, Simpson papers, 1835 *Diary*, Container one. Thomas Hudson described Liberty Street Church which was built in 1831 as a "large and durable building but the style was antiquated, and more substantial than elegant." Hudson, 40.

that they had never been visited by a minister before."[234] He sponsored revivals, but did not simply leave the evangelistic work to the Holy Spirit and the guest speaker. "Visiting the people almost every day I found myself acquainted with the condition of nearly all who were seeking Christ and was able to give them such advice as I thought their condition required."[235] Out of concern for disciplining young men for the ministry he kept a supply of books on hand. He was joined by Charles Elliott in the endeavor which was the unofficial beginning of the Pittsburgh Book Depository. "I had also felt a deep interest in the young men, some of whom I thought would probably prepare for the ministry. I had organized our association among them; a few met once a week and I endeavored to direct them in their course of reading, and to inspire them with a thirst for knowledge. Of that little company several subsequently became ministers."[236] He appointed leaders to conduct prayer meetings in different areas of the town. He organized Sunday school for the children. "I obtained the names of the children of the church, formed them into classes, appointed leaders who met them every Saturday afternoon and I personally met with them as frequently as possible."[237]

Pastoral Initiatives and Revival

Simpson entered into two collaborative enterprises exceptional for a young Methodist pastor in those days. One of his first acquaintances in Pittsburgh, Henry Sellers, enjoyed a high reputation as a physician.[238] "When Asiatic cholera plagued Pittsburgh in 1832, Henry Sellers was appointed as a consulting physician to the sanitary board in order for the city to pass ordinances for a rigid enforcement of sanitary measures."[239] The young pastor had discovered a spiritual guide, "a gentleman of far more than ordinary character and intellect whose subsequent counsels and advice were of no little service to me."[240] Sellers had been brought up on the eastern shore of Maryland, and had married a sister of

---

234 Crooks, 73.
235 Ibid., 74.
236 Ibid., 79.
237 Ibid., 82.
238 Fleming, 115.
239 Ibid., 270.
240 Crooks, 72.

Bishop John Emory. Immediately before the 1828 General Conference Sellers had moved from Baltimore to Pittsburgh, involving himself in the ecclesiastical skirmishes in both places. Since he was sympathetic to the "reformers," he would have been at odds with Matthew's future father-in-law James Verner.[241]

Simpson met with Sellers each Monday morning for the latter to critique his sermons. This process required no little strength of character. The mentor strongly suggested that the pastor drop the "ahs" from the end of his sentences, a habit which he had adopted in Ohio. (This inflection is still today the *sine qua non* of preaching for some Appalachian pastors and evangelists.) Jacob Gruber parodied this style, as told by W.P. Strickland.

> A young preacher, desirous of improving his style as a pulpit orator, and having great confidence in Father Gruber, who, we believe, at the time was his Presiding Elder, wrote to him for advice. The young man had contracted the habit of prolonging his words, especially when under the influence of great excitement. Deeming this the most defect in his elocution, Gruber sent him the following laconic reply:
>
> "Dear Ah! Brother Ah!---When-ah you-ah go-ah to-ah preach-ah, take-ah care-ah you-ah don't-ah say-ah Ah-ah!" Yours-ah,
>
> Jacob-Ah Gruber-Ah[242]

Simpson also met weekly to discuss texts and prepare outlines with his pastoral colleagues in the Pittsburgh area. This practice cut across the conventional wisdom for sermon preparation. For most Methodists the

---

241 "Sellers, Henry D., M.D., was born in Hillsborough, Md., July 28, 1790, and early entered the church. While living on a farm, in the connection with some school facilities, he acquired a good education, and subsequently attended medical lectures, in 1820, at Baltimore, and entered upon the practice of medicine. In 1825 he removed to Pittsburgh, and at once became active in the church. He rose to eminence in the medical profession, and for forty years he stood among the highest. In general church interests he was a leader and molder of men, and from the organization of Liberty Street church until he assisted building Christ church, he led all of its aggressive steps. He occupied every position possible in the church, and as a class-leader he was pre-eminent, and his instructions were like ripened and rich fruit. For many years he held the office of a local preacher, exercising with great favor his functions chiefly at Liberty Street church, then the most important city charge. He was an active member of the Centenary Board, and aided in consummating its mission of securing the fund, which is now yielding a fruitful income, and for many years he was its president. He was a trustee of Western University of Pennsylvania. He was also deeply interested in the Pittsburgh Female College having been one of its earliest trustees and most devoted friend." Simpson. *Cyclopaedia*, 793.

242 W.P. Strickland. *The Life of Jacob Gruber* (New York: Carlton & Porter, 1860) 356.

selection of a text and its development were so personal and private that no clues as to what was to be the sermon were ever indicated beforehand. No pre-Civil War Methodist Church in America prepared a worship program which informed the congregation of the order of service and the pastor's text and sermon title. Simpson submitted himself to being mentored by others and the submission bore fruit. While the 23-year-old pastor served a circuit, which included the "whole of the northern part of Pittsburgh," a city wide revival, 1834, was sponsored. The meetings "continued for about three months during which time about three hundred members were added to them."[243] On February 2, 1836 he recorded, "Mr. Dighton assisted me in holding a protracted meeting the middle of last month, which resulted in much apparent good—fifty-two joined society and many professed conversion."[244] Erasmus Wilson in his *Standard History of Pittsburgh, Pennsylvania* stated:

> The most important era of moral quickening in the history of the city occurred during the early part of the decade of the thirties. The churches greatly increased in numbers and in interest. Sabbath schools were greatly improved, temperance societies were arranged, tract and Bible societies circulated many thousands of their publications; the crimes of dueling and slavery were realized, exposed and denounced and in many other ways this community gave evidences of great moral advancement.[245]

Matthew Simpson began his ministry with diligence, a fervent devotion to God, faithful pastoral visitation, and a mind quickened by avid reading and keen observation. Above all, he was a preacher, and he would have made any Presiding Elder both grateful and proud.

---

243   Crooks, 74.
244   Ibid., 117.
245   Erasmus Wilson. *Standard History of Pittsburg, Pennsylvania* (Chicago: H.R. Cornell and Company, 1898) 931.

Chapter Four:
A Highly Ordered Life

Finneyism and Other Ism's

Simpson's pastoral success was part of a much larger phenomenon, a religious conflagration that was consuming western New York and beyond. A little known converted attorney with almost no theological training had held a six-month revival in the small town of Rochester, New York, on the shores of Lake Erie. America had not seen the likes of him or it. Charles Grandison Finney would become the most famous religious person in America between the Revolutionary and Civil Wars. Pittsburgh was 300 miles from Rochester, a long distance in the 1830s, but not so far as to prevent snail mail and newspapers from informing Westerners of the sensational methodologies of evangelicalism's latest celebrity. Finney arrived in Rochester in September 1829 and began a "protracted" meeting at the Brick Presbyterian Church. This meant that the church would hold services night after night as long as the members thought the revival productive, and Finney did believe in production. Finney taught that if the right spiritual methodologies were used, the evangelistic yield would be as sure as correctly planning and cultivating a field of corn. "The door-to-door canvass, the intensification of family devotions, prayer meetings that lasted until dawn, the open humiliation of sinners on the anxious bench: all of these transformed prayer and conversion from private communion into spectacular public events."[246]

Paul E. Johnson, who did a meticulous sociological and demographic study of the Rochester Revival, claims that when Finney "gestured at the room people ducked as if he were throwing things. In describing the fall of sinners he pointed to the ceiling and as he let his finger drop people in the

---

[246] Paul E Johnson. *A Shopkeeper's Millennium: Society and Revivals in Rochester New York 1815–1837* (New York: Hill and Wang, 1978) 97–102.

rear seats stood to watch the final entry into hell. Finney spoke directly to the anxious bench in front of him. At the close of the lecture he demanded immediate repentance and prayer."[247] Gilbert Barnes, an astute historian of Finney and the resulting reform minded millennialism that ushered in the "benevolent empire" assessed that, "At the turn of the decade in the 1830s the revival burst all bounds and spread over the whole nation, the greatest of all modern revivals."[248]

No doubt the heat of the "burned over district" could be felt in western Pennsylvania, when Simpson began his Pittsburgh pastorate. The spreading revival was not without its aberrant edges: spiritual rappings, Shakerism, Mormonism, Swedenborgianism, sexual communism, Milleriteism, and many shades of perfectionism.[249] On February 24, 1835, Simpson recorded, "Thursday, had a long conversation with Mrs. B., a lady of considerable intelligence and energy, who is desperately perplexed with spirit rappings. She now promises to get freed from the delusion, but what will be the result, the good being alone knows. The spirit delusion is doing immense injury all through the Western Reserve, and is spreading infidelity in many hearts."[250]

Contemporaries Finney and Simpson would take highly divergent paths. Finney's new measures found receptive churches in Pittsburgh, but on Simpson's ministry trajectory, Finney's influence was negligible. Finney would later preach in the famed independent Broadway Tabernacle in New York, and become second president of radical Oberlin College populated by former students from Lane Theological Seminary in Cincinnati. Simpson would become an ecclesiastical bureaucrat, operating within a religious paradigm increasingly defined by America's market economy. Finney's preaching was in the style of an attorney: left-brained, logical, propositional, direct and accusatory, a discourse which arrived at a verdict. Simpson's preaching would increasingly become right-brained: romantic, idealistic,

---

247 Johnson, 102.

248 Quoted in H. Shelton Smith, Robert T. Handy, and Lefferts Loetscher. *American Christianity: A Historical Interpretation with Representative Documents* Vol. 2 (New York: Scribner's Sons, 1923) 12.

249 See Whitney Cross. *The Burned-over District: The Social and Intellectual History of Enthusiastic Religion in Western New York, 1800-1850* (Ithaca, New York: Cornell University Press, 1950).

250 LOC, Simpson papers, 1835 *Diary*, Container one.

picturesque, inspirational, and on the same frequency as the prevailing cultural ethos. Both would influence predominant strains within American evangelicalism.

Spiritual Conflict and Depression

Simpson was becoming a poet, not in the sense of the limericks and doggerels that he wrote as a 12-year-old for his Uncle's newspaper or even the romantic odysseys which recounted his youth, but in his ability to make language sing, to offer the hope and inspiration of what Walter Brueggemann would a century and a half later call a "prophetic-poetic construal of another world."[251] Admittedly, Simpson often confused the constructs of God's kingdom with the structures of the kingdoms of America. But no one ever listened to a Simpson sermon that did not feel she could be better and that the world in which she lived could and would be better. (Simpson exaggerated these possibilities, but so does Walter Brueggemann.) Simpson's preaching would enable persons to sing a new song, to envision a new world, to possess a new energy and above all a new reality within the inner person, the righteousness of Jesus Christ. Brueggemann writes, "The truth of God's ways with the guilty is no common routine reality. Our speech about it can be no common routine speech, but must be utterly uncommon. That is why the claim for God requires poetic speech that is costly and demanding."[252]

Simpson paid that price, a steep price to pay. Some have argued for a high correlation between artistic expression and melancholy, but not necessarily a cause and effect. Many artistic people are not depressed, and certainly most depressed people are not artistic. The Scottish poet Lord Byron wrote that, "We of the craft are all crazy. Some are affected by gaiety, others by melancholy, but all were more or less touched."[253] Kay Jamison claims, "Recent research strongly suggests that compared with the general population, writers and artists, show a vastly disproportionate rate of manic

---

251   Walter Brueggemann. *Finally Comes the Poet: Daring Speech for Proclamation* (Minneapolis: Fortress, 1989).

252   Ibid., 33.

253   Kay Jamison. *Manic Depressive Temperament and the Artistic Temperament* (New York: MacMillan, 1997) 2.

depressive or depressive illness."[254] Jamison goes on to write, "The depiction of a warring within of different minds, personalities, emotions and values reached its height in the 19th century; the artistry and shifting borders between the rational and irrational, the inhibited and uninhibited were captured particularly well by Robert Louis Stevenson in Dr. Jekyll and Mr. Hyde."[255]

Simpson was not the schizophrenic depicted by Stevenson, but keep in mind that he did exasperate on his 24th birthday, "What a strange compound I am." He confessed, "Of late, I have not visited enough from house to house, nor talked enough upon religious subjects. I would commence anew. I would appoint my time better. I would be more serious, more earnest, more persevering. But of myself, the good that I would do, that do I not. Lord, give me perfect victory the ensuing year, that with all my heart I may glorify thee, and that my life may be spotless."[256] Perfect victory? Part of the required reading for the Methodist "course of study" was John Wesley's *Plain Account of Christian Perfection*. Wesley quoted from his own tract, "The Character of a Methodist" that the entirely sanctified person,

> . . . is one who loves the Lord his God with all of his heart, with all his soul, with all his mind, and with all his strength. God is the joy of his heart, and the desire of his soul, which is continually crying, 'Whom have I in heaven but Thee? And there is none upon earth whom I desire besides Thee.' My God and my all! 'Thou art the strength of my heart, and my portion forever.' He is therefore happy in God; yea, always happy, as having in him a well of water springing up into everlasting life, an overflow in his soul with peace and joy. Perfect love having now cast out fear, he rejoices evermore.[257]

Always happy? Rejoices evermore? According to Wesley, not even the apostle Paul reached the state of grace referred to as "entire sanctification." The Father of Methodism offered disclaimers: "We believe that there is no such perfection in this life as implies an entire deliverance either from ignorance, or mistakes in things not essential to salvation, or from manifest

---

254   Ibid., 5.
255   Ibid., 121.
256   LOC, Simpson papers, 1835 *Diary*, June 21, Container one.
257   John Wesley. *A Plain Account of Christian Perfection* (Kansas City, MO: Beacon Hill Press of Kansas City, 1966) 18.

temptations, or from numberless infirmities, wherewith the corruptible body more or less presses down on the soul."[258] Though Wesley later disowned that he preached "sinless perfection," he wrote, "It remains, then, that Christians are saved in this world from all sin, from all unrighteousness; that they are now in such a sense perfect, as not to commit sin and to be freed from evil thoughts and evil tempers."[259] Or to state it more positively, "By perfection I mean the humble, gentle, patient love of God and man ruling all the tempers, words and actions, the whole heart and the whole life."[260] It was a difficult doctrine to understand and even more difficult to attain. Giving Wesley the benefit of the doubt, all theologies consist of at least some contradictions. Trying to solve the problem of evil for both the individual and society at large has been Christianity's greatest challenge.

John Peters cites the time in which Simpson entered ministry as the nadir of holiness preaching within American Methodism. The "Bishop's Address" at the 1832 General Conference asked "Why ... have we so few living witnesses that the blood of Jesus Christ cleanseth from all sin? .... Only let all who have been born in the Spirit seek, with the same ardor to be made perfect in love as they sought for the pardon of their sins."[261] Peters

---

258   Ibid., 36.

259   Ibid., 28.

260   Quoted in Kenneth J. Collins. *The Theology of John Wesley: Holy Love and the Shape of Grace* (Nashville: Abingdon, 2007) 302. David Stark studied the nomenclature used by 652 persons who experienced "entire sanctification" during the Wesleyan Revival in England, 1758-1763. Some, such as Alexander Mather in describing his experience of entire sanctification, almost exactly used Wesley's language. "What I had experienced in my soul was an instantaneous deliverance from all those wrong tempers and affections which I had long and sensibly groaned under; an entire disengagement from every creature, with an entire devotedness to God and from that moment, I found an unspeakable pleasure in doing the will of God in all things, I had also the power to do it, and the constant approbation both of my own conscience and of God. I had simplicity of heart, and a single eye to God, at all times and in all places; with such a fervent zeal for the glory of God and the good of souls, as swallowed up every other care and consideration." But for as many as found fulfillment in their spiritual pursuit, possibly even more found spiritual disillusionment. Stark states, "However aspiring the endless pursuit of Christian perfection may have been posed to be, there were many early Methodists (and sadly many more beyond) who suffered intense despair and disappointment because of their failure to experience the version of full salvation they were told and believed was happening in others." David Thomas Stark. *The Peculiar Doctrine Committed to our Trust: Ideal and Identity in the First Wesleyan Holiness Revival, 1758-1763.* (Unpublished Ph.D. dissertation, University of Manchester, 2011) 94, 103.

261   John L. Peters. *Christian Perfection and American Methodism* (New York: Abingdon,

claims that "little was said about the doctrine, for instance, in the principal denominational journals ... but by and large the 'old Methodist doctrine' was becoming a denominational curiosity."[262] Of course, this drought would be partially remedied by Phoebe Palmer's famed "Tuesday afternoon parlor meetings" in the late 1830s and the post-Civil War founding of the National Camp Meeting Association for the Promotion of Holiness in 1867.

Jamison's claim that the nineteenth century boasted more than its fair share of neurotics, may seem arbitrary. But Julius H. Rubin has written an essay, "What Hath God Wrought? Religious Melancholy in the Second Great Awakening."[263] Rubin argues that evangelical conversion morphed into a unilateral experience which was instantaneous, rapturous, highly emotional and often defined by erratic behavior. Individuals testified to conversions, especially in Methodist "love feasts" with exuberant expressions, such as claiming that they loved God with all of their heart and they possessed a constantly abiding peace. The experience of feeling was central to Methodism's experiential piety, a religious sensation that was empirical and emotionally validatable. As has been said by historians of American religion, "experience has often triumphed over dogma."

The hegemony of revival and camp meeting conversions was solidified by religious periodicals such as *The Christian Advocate*, *The New York Evangelist* and *The Methodist Magazine* (the last which Simpson was "required" to read). "Ministers or pseudo-anonymous converts submitted conversion narratives, stylized renditions of the act of conversion, conforming to an idealized prescriptive portrayal of evangelical religious experience."[264] In other words, in nineteenth century American revivalism, conversion became codified and systematized. The universal standard for entering the kingdom of God was accented both by Wesleyan-Arminian theology and the Taylor-Finney disavowal of original sin. Rubin writes, "Should a person experience doubt, or manifest a lack of faith or the absence of grace, these personal inadequacies in the face of manifold divine mercy represented a stubborn

---

1961) 98.

262 Ibid., 100.

263 Julius H. Rubin. *Religious Melancholy and Protestant Experience in America* (New York: Oxford University Press, 1995) 125-155.

264 Ibid., 129.

unwillingness to choose God. The abject sinner could only look inward to locate the source of guilt and unhappiness. In this manner Taylor's doctrine of moral agency posited an Omni causal self who created the condition of his or her own temporal and eternal misery."[265] Heavy doses of freedom of the will and self-determination produced their own peculiar side effects, symptoms that Simpson in his quest for righteousness would exhibit for the rest of his life.

Lincoln and Simpson "Push Hard"

Simpson's disconsolation resembled that of a man whom he had not yet met, but whose path he would cross when they both resided in Illinois. Both Abraham Lincoln and Matthew Simpson, the latter two years younger, were self-conscious about their gangly, irregular physiques which looked as if they had been thrown together by some laughable accident of nature. Both had constitutional tendencies to melancholy. Lincoln's mother was an illegitimate child, a fact that he kept hidden as much as possible.[266] No less was the grief at her death when Abraham was nine years old. Then there was the loss of his first love, Ann Rutledge, and the death of two sons.

Simpson's losses were neither as personal nor severe as were Lincoln's, but as a pastor, he was constantly surrounded by death. He recorded an inordinate fear of death due to his ill health, weak constitution and anxiety accented by his medical training. The loss of his father, though he could not remember him or the event, must have had some effect on him. His only extended reference to his father's death appears in the odyssey which he wrote on his nineteenth birthday.

> To earthly parents in this world
> Honour thy father and thy mother too
> Is a command in Holy writ we view
> And is a duty pleasing to the mind
> Which is enlightened virtuous or refined
> My Father Ah! No father now I claim

---

265   Ibid., 150.

266   Catherine Clinton. "Abraham Lincoln: The Family that Made Him, the Family He Made," in *Our Lincoln: New Perspectives on Lincoln and His World*, ed. Eric Foner (New York: W.W. Norton and Company, 2009) 49-266.

> Before in my infant life could I lip his name
> The King of Terrors summoned him away
> From dwelling in his tenement of clay
> And only moved him to a happier place
> For Death's sting was drawn by sov'reign grace
> And God who sees the fatherless from on high
> And hears the widow in affliction cry
> Leave me an uncle in my father's stead
> To guide my steps and teach me where to head
> Assist my mother to instruct my youth
> And fill my heart with knowledge love and truth
> My filial love to her is justly due
> For kindness past, and kindness recent, too.[267]

Remember that as a twenty-year-old, the young Matthew had confessed that he felt within himself the "shafts of death."[268] When he was twenty-four years old he wrote Uncle Matthew, "When I reflect upon the course which has been marked out for me by Providence these few years, I think that he either designs me for a short life or else one marked with peculiar incidents and an arduous responsible character."[269] The thoughts of death coupled with visions of greatness may sound ironic, but are not unusual. The only thing that would stand in the way of greatness would be death. The ambitious fear death because they have a lot more at stake in life, and both Lincoln and Simpson were ambitious.

Joshua Shenk claims that the word "individualism" first entered the American vocabulary in 1835 by way of Alexis de Tocqueville's *Democracy*. The Frenchman wrote, "Individualism is a novel expression to which a novel idea has been given birth." Every person could "sever him-self from the mass of his fellows" and be something or somebody, a vision which class conscious, aristocratic Europe did not afford.[270] After his first four years in Springfield, Lincoln told his law partner, William Herndon that he felt destined to be

---

267 Simpson, "Reminiscent Lines on His Nineteenth Birthday."
268 Crooks, 35.
269 Ibid., 106-107.
270 Joshua Shenk. *Lincoln's Melancholy: How Depression Challenged a President and Fueled his Greatness* (New York: Houghton-Mifflin Company, 2005) 72.

a great man and at the same time he said that he feared he would come to ruin. The ruin would be suicide, urges that consumed him during two nervous breakdowns when he was 26 and 32. Shenk argues that by Lincoln's early 30s, he faced a lifetime of depression. "Dramatic public avowals of his misery gave way to a private, but persistent effort to endure and transcend his suffering. Yet, the suffering did not go away. As we will see in his middle years, Lincoln demonstrated signs of chronic depression and even when he began to do the work for which he is remembered and took evident satisfaction in finding a great cause to which to apply his considerable talent he continued to suffer."[271]

To overcome melancholy Lincoln and Simpson took very similar paths: they would work harder than their colleagues and competitors, long hours and conscientious attention to detail. They would transcend depression and reward their efforts with success. What future success entailed, neither had little idea. Hard work was American and it was Methodist, but not necessarily "Christian." Psychologist Hagop Akiskal argues that chronic depressives "seem to derive personal gratification from over dedication to professions that require greater service and suffering on behalf of others."[272] *The Sangamon Journal*, the paper in Lincoln's hometown of Springfield, Illinois published "How to Succeed," which exhorted, "Push long. Push hard. Push earnestly .... The world is so made–society is so constructed that it's a law of necessity that you must push. That is if you would be something and somebody."[273]

Lincoln pushed. He pushed in two directions, away from his past and towards his future. It is no wonder that he became the American archetype of the self-made man in that he had done hard labor as a late teen. The rail splitter had split rails, but only for part of a winter, helping his cousin. He had used an ax plenty, helping his father clear land for a new farm whenever the family moved. The short-lived episode of rail splitting was sufficient to create a myth and a campaign slogan. The banners hanging from the rafters of the Chicago "Wigwam" would read in 1860: "Abraham Lincoln–The Rail Candidate for President."[274]

---

271   Ibid., 23.
272   Ibid., 103.
273   Ibid., 73.
274   Ibid., 3.

Simpson had no reason to push away his past, but he pushed ahead hard enough to make his mother and uncle worry about his health. On January 11, 1835, Uncle wrote, "God is not obligated to work a miracle to save neither the health nor life of a man who contrary to all that reason and experience can teach, rushes himself into a situation or country for which his constitution and health are altogether insufficient and shall I say presumptuously trusting that Providence will preserve him."[275] In other words, God would not take care of that which the young pastor willfully neglected.

Total Commitment and Then Some

Theoretically, Eldership in the Methodist Episcopal Church demanded total commitment. A Methodist preacher was to preach in the morning when he could get hearers. "We recommend morning preaching at 5 o'clock in the summer and six in the winter whenever it is practical." He was to be diligent. "Never be unemployed. Never be trifling employed. Tell everyone under your care what you think wrong in his conduct and temper." And then the well-known charge, "You have nothing to do but save souls. Therefore, spend and be spent in this work." At his Elder ordination, which took place in the Annual Conference of 1836 at Liberty Street Church in Pittsburgh, Simpson was asked,

> Are you going on to perfection? Do you expect to be made perfect in love in this life? Are you groaning after it? Are you devoted wholly to God's work? Do you know the rules of societies of the bands? Do you keep them? Do you deny yourself every useless pleasure of sense? Of imagination? Are you temperate in all things? Instance in food? Do you use only that kind in that degree which is best both for the body and the soul? Do you eat no more at each meal than is necessary? Are you not heavy or drowsy after dinner?

Some of these questions were carryovers from when Wesley preached to the miners at 5 o'clock in the morning. To be employed at all times was unrealistic, if not impossible, since Asbury himself took hot spring bath trips to western Virginia. The questions concerning the bands, three or four people who met together once a week for spiritual direction and absolution were equally unrealistic. "Do you desire to be told of your faults? Do you

---

275   LOC, Simpson papers, Letter January 11, 1835, Container three.

desire to be told of all your faults and that plain and home? Do you desire that every one of us should tell you from time to time whatsoever is in our heart concerning you? Consider! Do you desire we should tell you whatsoever we think, whatsoever we fear, whatsoever we hear concerning you? Do you desire in doing this we should come as close as possible, that we should cut to the quick and search your heart to the bottom?"[276] No wonder that within a half century of American Methodism's founding, bands and classes were almost completely a spiritual practice of the past. Individualism, privatization and a mind your own business mentality would not stand for such spiritual scrutiny. The threshold for membership entrance into an American Methodist church was exponentially dropping, even before Daniel Drew came along. Spiritual accountability was quickly dissipating, but not for Matthew Simpson. He piled on a few more rules of his own.

> What should I refrain from:
>
> 1. Never injure the feelings of any person with whom I converse or am associated, unless that injury be the result of the declaration of a truth which it becomes my duty to utter.
>
> 2. Speak evil of no one; never utter disrespectful words, or indulge in a conversation wherein anyone is unnecessarily spoken against.
>
> 3. Suffer myself not to give way to a jesting or jocose spirit, or talk upon unimportant subjects.
>
> 4. Spend no more time at any place than may appear indispensable.
>
> 5. Endeavor to refrain from lengthy conversations with my family and intimates, ever remembering 'Dum luquor, tempus fugit.'
>
> What I should do:
>
> 1. Rise at four every morning, and if I cannot retire at a corresponding hour sleep a sufficient time to make up the deficiency during the day.
>
> 2. Dress as expeditiously as possible, and then devote a considerable time to reading the English Scriptures and to private prayer.

---

276 *The Doctrines and Disciplines of the Methodist Episcopal Church* (New York: B. Waugh and T. Mason, 1832) 31-37, 80-85, 127-139.

3. If possible, devote some time to studying the Scriptures in their originals.

4. Fill up all my leisure hours with useful reading, always keeping some book in my hand.

5. Visit and pray from house to house, and talk pointedly and faithfully.

6. Reprove sin whenever I may find it, always in the spirit of love and meekness.

7. Always endeavor to give a religious direction to every conversation.

8. Ask no questions concerning myself, nor suffer the conversation to turn upon me.

9. If commended, pray for humility; if insulted, pray for love; if apparently successful, be thankful to God, and pray to feel my own unworthiness.

10. To preach, exhort, and pray as though in the immediate presence of Jehovah himself. Lord, help me to do all these things, and thy name shall have all the glory. Oh, keep me by thy power, or I shall assuredly fall.

M. Simpson
Williamsport, Jan. 11, 1836[277]

If anyone could have honestly and sincerely passed the rigors of the Methodist requirements for ordination, it was Matthew Simpson. His was a *highly-ordered life* defined by comprehensive note taking on everything he read, detailed reminders to himself as what needed to be done, effusive recordings of the events which surrounded him, whether they be denominational functions or foreign travels, and above all, reminders to himself as to how life could be more expeditious and efficient. Nothing was left to happenstance. He recorded,

Thoughts for Health and Comfort, Necessary for Health and Action.

I. Personal

1. Return always as early as ten.

---

[277] "What I Should Refrain From, "LOC, Simpson papers, Container nineteen.

2. Get sleep enough but try to rise regularly, at say 6.

3. If possible, get regular hours for meals. To facilitate this, get good check both for kitchen and sitting room. Also allow for bedroom at home.

4. As far as practical, avoid night traveling and unpleasant hours.

5. Use salt sponge bath every morning.

6. Full tepid bath once a week.

7. Change underclothes very frequently–home daily, travel two or three times per week

8. Keep from being chilled if possible-ask for conveniences when from home.

9. Be firm to talk less.

10. Refrain firmly all outside labor unless reasonably pleasant

11. Arrange papers for office to sign.

12. Get all clothing comfortable for season, no matter about cost-so to all changes.

II. Conveniences

1. Trunk arrange with hat box.

2. Case for parchments, etc.

3. Writing materials for Conf.

4. Traveling case, brushes, combs, razor, etc. Not to be used at home-always.

5. Round top desk at home.

6. Bureau for my clothes.

7. Closet or wardrobe for clothes.

8. Umbrella for traveling-lettered.

9. Umbrella for home-lettered.[278]

---

278 "Thoughts for Health and Comfort," LOC, Simpson papers, Container nineteen.

Of course, Simpson listed everything he needed to purchase whether for himself or for Ellen, when he was in a convenient shopping city such as New York or Philadelphia.

> Things to be got: 6 new shirts, 12 bosoms, 2 drawers, 2 flannel shirts, 12 handkchiefs, 1 cravat, 1 hat, 1 coat, 1 vest, 2 pantaloons, 1 overcoat, 1 slippers, 1 boots, 2 night shirts, 1 light coat, 1 double razor, 4 drawers, 6 chemises, 2 pr stockings, 2 pr shoes, 2 dresses, 6 handkhs, 2 pr gloves.[279]

When Matthew Simpson was ordained, the "course of study" varied from conference to conference. For instance in 1832, the Indiana Conference added to the General Conference requirements Richard Watson's *Theological Institutes*, Johann Mosheim's *Ecclesiastical History*, Thomas Reid's *Philosophy*, William Paley's *Natural Theology and Evidences of Christianity*, Isaac Watts's *Logic*, and the *Methodist Magazine*.[280] Despite a lack of uniformity, one could count on a heavy dose of Wesley, including the *Sermons, Notes on the New Testament* and *The Plain Account of Christian Perfection*, along with Fletcher's *Checks*, Baxter's *The Soul's Everlasting Rest*, Law's *Serious Call*, and Josephus' *Antiquities*. But William Cannon claims that since the course was not uniform throughout the church, ministerial education was irregular, often even spasmodic. "There was a wide gap between the law and its enforcement. Very seldom did a conference committee reject an applicant because he had failed to master the contents of the books assigned him."[281]

In 1834, Methodist Elder La Roy Sunderland accused the New England Conference of adopting a course of study, "but without any benefit, I believe, to any one, as it was never, to my knowledge, used to any extent in this conference, either by the candidates or the examining committee through the course of even one examination."[282] "Methodist itinerants before the Civil War joked that they had been trained in "brush

---

279 "Things to be Got," LOC, Simpson papers, Container eighteen.
280 Russell E. Richey. *Formation for Ministry in American Methodism* (Nashville: The General Board of Higher Education and Ministry, The United Methodist Church, 2014) 35.
281 William Cannon. "Education, Publication, Benevolent Work, and Mission," *The History of American Methodism* Vol. II, ed. Emory Bucke (Nashville: Abingdon Press, 1964) 566-567, and Frederick Norwood. *The Story of American Methodism* (Nashville: Abingdon 1974) 221.
282 Richey, *Formation*, 115.

college" or "swamp university." This was only a partial truth. Russell Richey has cogently argued that young candidates for the ministry trained within an intentionally designed program of apprenticeship, working under a Presiding Elder or alongside an older pastor. Richey writes, "The Methodist community or system as a whole—preaching, classes, disciplines, mutual oversight, testimony, the counsel of 'mothers-in-Israel,' quarterly meetings, and love feasts—shaped its leadership. And the system moved talent up the ministerial ladder as quickly and as far as character, grace, gifts, and fruit warranted."[283]

In 1831, Simpson did a thorough study of Calvin, taking over twenty pages of notes. He was struck by the argument that God does not simply permit the damnation of the lost, but wills it. Even Satan acts according to God's will, just as do the angels. The fall of man was by the will of God, and any attempt at understanding God's reasoning is useless. Absalom's incestuous adultery was the work of God. Simpson included none of his own thoughts or commentary on Calvin's argument. Of course he may have been discouraged from doing so, since Calvin states, "The devil hath no fitter instruments than those who fight against predestination." And further, "It cannot be but the enemies of God's predestination are stupid and ignorant, and that the desire hath plucked out their eyes"[284] Hard to imagine that James Arminius and John Calvin would have had good Christian fellowship.

Utterly Confounded at Simpson's Appearance

Of course, the Simpsons and McCulloughs, who now lived in Wellsville, were proud of the rising star of their immediate relative, who pastored the largest Methodist Church within a two-hundred mile radius. When the Methodist Church in Wellsville was built and dedicated, the Simpson family had just the person to preach the dedication sermon. At this occasion, Simpson began a pattern which would be true for years to come. The invitees would be utterly confounded at his appearance when he showed up, a disappointment that he would quickly dispel by his preaching. One attendee at the dedication recalled, "It was announced that he was to preach

---

283   Ibid., 20.
284   LOC, Simpson papers, "Extracts on Calvin," Container seventeen.

in the Methodist Church. This arrival was expected with some considerable interest, but 'the brethren' were much disappointed in his personal appearance and then expectations as to the sermon were disappointing." The "plain, humble, and unprepossessing" Simpson perceived the displeasure which spread over the congregation when he stepped to the pulpit. "But the sermon proved to be one of the most eloquent efforts and he was transformed into such a wonder of pulpit power that many of his disappointed auditors felt compelled to apologize to him for their first impressions." Years after the dedication, Mrs. George McCoy of Wellsville recalled,

> The Methodists had built a new brick church, and as we all felt proud of our boy preacher, it was resolved that he should dedicate the church. He consented, and I remember only the results of those two sermons; but you may readily conceive he was striving for more than dollars and cents. We had, as a farm hand, in our employ, a young Protestant Canadian; and as every member able to attend Church was expected to go, of course "Jimmy" went. Under that first sermon of Matthew Simpson he was convicted. After the night service he retired in bed, but not to sleep. His moans and prayers kept the entire household awake. At length my saintly mother (long since in heaven) called up-stairs: "Jimmy, my dear boy, cast your burden upon the Lord." He in reply said, "O, ma'am, do send for that young preacher to pray for me, for I am sure I shall be in hell before morning." A cousin of mine was sent, and he returned with the preacher. It was then 11 o'clock. How long they prayed with our "Jimmy" I don't recollect, but this I do know, that that night he was powerfully converted to God.[285]

A sample of Simpson's preaching, at this point in his life, may reveal why Jimmy was under "conviction." In the early days of his ministry, Simpson's pulpit performances were typical of Methodist preaching during the 1830s. The fiery young preacher was far more dichotomous, confrontational, and evangelistic, than in his later years. As Simpson matured, the combativeness of the following would lose its haranguing tone:

> Are we prepared? Remember time shall soon be no longer—This year is nearly gone and with it have fled many hope & joys. Should this year close your life how would it be with you? God may soon say to you Time shall be no longer. Thou fool this night shall thy soul be required of thee. The lady dying at her toilette—Sargent fell in the pulpit. Where will you be in another year, some here, some abroad, some

---

285   UMA, Drew University, Crooks papers, *Western Christian Advocate,* Letter to the Editor, n. d.

sick, some dying, some in heaven, some in hell—1 every second, then in 2 hours 24/60/1440. 2880 have died since we came here. Hundreds have fallen while [I]have been exhorting, listen to their voices, one cries Glory to God—another...Oh God I can't die—I won't die & dies with the words in his mouth. Oh! Sinner Time shall be no more ... now you may repent; now you may be saved. Oh! Be saved to night.[286]

A Faithful Last Charge

The last church which Simpson would ever serve as a pastor was Williamsport, now Monongahela City, about twenty miles south of Pittsburgh on the Monongahela River. The only thing for which Williamsport was known was the "whiskey rebellion" in 1794.[287] It almost seemed like a banishment when compared to the Liberty Street Church. Simpson had been assigned to Williamsport the year before, but the Liberty Street Church made such a ruckus that it secured his services.[288] Perhaps the Presiding Elder and Bishop colluded that they would not be intimidated by Liberty at the next Annual Conference. Also, a personal item favored the appointment. Ellen Holmes Verner was born in Williamsport and spent the first four years of her life there. Though her memories were faint, there was sufficient nostalgia to make the prospects pleasing, especially taking into account the clean air and beauty of a river town nestled under the umbrage of ash, oak and maple trees.

Matthew and Ellen moved into a small and dilapidated parsonage, "a little one-story frame house just below where Dr. and Mrs. Biddle lives, then owned by Judge White's father." A half century later a parishioner still had vivid memories of his young pastor, "He reduced the early and rather chaotic stage of affairs in a young church to a perfect system. Everything had to be done according to rule both in church, government proper and in its business affairs." His "persistent piety and devotion to his work" initiated "a prayer

---

286   Clark, *Pulpit and Platform*, 70. This sermon was titled, "Time Shall Be No More." I agree with Clark that the sermon was preached in the early part of Simpson's ministry.

287   "Parkinson's Ferry (in Williamsport) was a hotbed of rebellion during the whiskey insurrection, and there on August, 1794 was held the famous mass meeting which was attended by 200 delegates from the four western counties in the insurrection. The place where the meeting was held is on the high bluff just in the rear of the Bentley Theatre of Main Street and is still known as 'Whiskey Point.'" Earle R. Forest. *History of Washington County, Pennsylvania* Vol. I (Chicago: The S. J. Clark Publishing Company, 1926) 714.

288   LOC, Simpson papers, Letter July 21, 1835, Container three.

meeting of the official body and during his entire pastorate met with them, at my house, at daylight every Sabbath morning to pray for blessing on the day's work. That was in earnest of his devotion to his work. Earnestness pervaded his whole conduct and each branch of his duty and brought him finally to the head of our church."[289]

Again his self-perception varied widely with the memories of his parishioners. While at Williamsport March 1, 1836, he recorded, "This day I've seen my own faithfulness in a very reprehensible light. Indeed, I've not sought the weak. I've not prayed, nor preached, nor anything else as I ought to have done. What will become of such a wretch as I?"[290] Regarding his parishioners, he did not have confidence in their intellectual potential. When his Uncle Matthew suggested starting an academy in Williamsport, the nephew discouraged him by saying,

> As to a school here, I can say nothing. They are not a literary people, and there is no good school among them. James Mills resides here, and he would be very anxious for you to come and think there would be no doubt of success. I, however, am not so sanguine as he.
>
> I do not want you to calculate with certainty on teaching, but I want you to come, and when here you can judge of matters for yourself and be governed accordingly.[291]

Williamsport provided Simpson with a financial challenge, pecuniary responsibilities, which until this time had not been his. He had no training in budgetary oversight, but somehow managed to pay off the mortgage of a church which had overextended itself. The church had been founded in 1813, but had not built a house of worship until 1833, under the leadership of Charles Cooke. Simpson inherited a debt for the 50 x 80 foot church in the town of six hundred and attacked the deficit with a vengeance. It was great training for the future college president, whose primary task would be maintaining financial solvency. Over the years Simpson would become involved in countless financial schemes with ever increasing awareness of economic forecasts and trends on the national level. The 1837 Panic was just around the corner. He wrote his Uncle Matthew, "If you can sell your farm

---

289   *Daily Republican*, Monongahela City, PA: Vol. 4, No. 954 (June 23, 1884).
290   LOC, Simpson papers, 1835-1840 *Diary*, March 1, 1836, Container one.
291   LOC, Simpson papers, Letter September 26, 1836, Container five.

under the road, I would unhesitatingly say you want to do it. For times are becoming alarming to all intelligent men. In New Orleans, New York, in Philadelphia there have been failures in three weeks to the amount of near thirty million dollars and they are increasing every day."[292]

Most important to the introverted, self-effacing Simpson during those first four years of ministry, is that he was forced to deal with people. He may have avoided the unlikable, but he could not avoid everybody. He had chosen a vocation that was more people oriented than any other occupation. A great deal of emotional and spiritual energy had to be extended in order to build a bridge between his innate temperament and the requirements of shepherding the flock. Many American pastors have lived within the tension of the introversion congruent with reflective study and the extroversion required for political glad-handing. Alexis De Toqueville observed that in America where he expected to find a priest, he found a politician.

All the spiritual striving seems strange if not contradictory in light of Lincoln's "doctrine of necessity" and Simpson's constant use of the word "providence." Like most Americans, both may have believed in the sovereignty of God, but saw no disconnect between their theology and the practical philosophy of self-improvement. God's sovereignty was being replaced by a combination of enlightenment philosophy and Arminian theology, allies of human initiative. As Daniel Walker Howe states, "For their part the evangelical Christians beginning with Princeton Presbyterian Academies, but also including popular preachers like the Methodists, came to embrace the Enlightenment goal of self-improvement."[293]

In his sermon, the "Love of God Secures Good Fortune," Simpson stressed loving, knowing, and obeying God. To not do so would result in eternal damnation. It would better to come into the world a "driveling idiot," than to be forever lost. But the stress of the sermon was the possibility of turning evil into good by serving God. "There is something in the very fact that a man loves God to make all occurrences a blessing to him. Men are

---

292   LOC, Simpson papers, Letter April 4, 1837, Container three.
293   Daniel Walker Howe. *Making the American Self: Jonathan Edwards to Abraham Lincoln* (Cambridge, MA: Harvard University Press, 1997) 260.

affected by the facts that transpire around them, much according to their own characters respectively. Life is what we make it."²⁹⁴

"Making it" was to turn disadvantage into advantage by working harder and longer than the next person. Such compensation was Lincolnesque and Simpsonesque, both American and "religious." But industriousness played more into the hands of self-determination than it did God-determination. As we will see when we examine Simpson's theology, extracting original sin from the evangelical equation removed the shackles from human potential. America's and Methodism's God became increasingly civil, domesticated, politically correct and less concerned with rebuking and eradicating sin. No one more faithfully transitioned with Him than did Simpson. He led Methodism's charge into the land of self-improvement, not exactly the holiness territory that Wesley had in mind. Asbury's and Coke's *Methodist Discipline* not only became increasingly irrelevant, but it also represented the rudeness and intrusiveness of a by-gone era. Obviously, the *Discipline* would accommodate to culture, rather than the other way around.

---

294   UMA, Drew University, Simpson papers, "The Love of God Secures Good Fortune," underlining made by stenographer.

Chapter Five: Becoming an Orator

Allegheny College

Timothy Alden, a polymath graduate of Harvard, founded Allegheny College in Meadville, Pennsylvania in 1815, where he served as the first President and Professor of Oriental Languages and Ecclesiastical History. He jump-started the institution by a money begging tour of the Northeast, raising a total of $1,312.26, but only $461 in cash. Among his donors was former President John Adams, but it is not known how much the senior statesman gave. Alden was formally inaugurated president on July 28, 1817. The exercise consisted of an attorney, Patrick Farelly presenting an address in Latin, to which Alden responded in Latin. Later in the program, "pre-college probationers" rendered orations in Hebrew, Greek, Latin, and English.

The college took two giant leaps forward when in 1817, James Winthrop, a descendant of the Puritan founder, deeded his library, one of the largest private collections in America, to the infant institution. The Winthrop bequest included the French Encyclopedia of Diderot, and the holdings of Jonathan Mayhew, in total weighing three tons. Then in 1819, William Bentley deeded his library to Allegheny, and six months after notifying Allegheny of his gift of "classical and theological books, dictionaries, lexicons and Bibles," he died. Thomas Jefferson had offered Bentley the presidency of the University of Virginia, but he did not accept the position.[295] Jefferson wrote Timothy Alden February 18, 1824, "I had not expected there was such a private collection in the U.S. We are just commencing the University of Virginia, but cannot flatter ourselves with the hope of such donations as have been bestowed upon you."[296]

---

295   Ernest Ashton Smith. *Allegheny: A Century of Education 1815–1915* (Meadville, Pennsylvania: The Allegheny College History Company, 1916) 32-33.

296   Charles Homer Haskins and William Isaac Hull. *The History of Higher Education in Pennsylvania* (Washington: GPO, 1902) 10.

This collection proved a boon to a young professor who arrived on campus in 1837.

But the voluminous library did not ensure permanence. In 1828 the College Board came to the conclusion, "Although we may be out of debt, we are without funds, we are without teachers and professors except the Pres. Fac. Arts, or the means to employ them. We have at present no students and no prospect of attaining any until we have the necessary teachers and professors in the different branches necessary to carry on a regular course of collegiate studies."[297] Not surprising, since the requirements for entrance were "an ability to construe and parse Tulley's *Select Orations*, Virgil and the Greek Testament, to write Latin grammatically, to refer with promptness any example of common arithmetic, a sufficient testimonial of a blameless life and conversation and a bond for the payment of college dues."[298] The Presbyterians were not going to gamble on the quality of their students and went out of the education business, at least in Meadville.

In 1805, future Bishop Robert Roberts established Methodism in Meadville, by preaching in a tavern. It was so cold that Roberts kept on his overcoat. The deprivation of the whole situation caused Roberts to spin out, "If a man wants pleasure, he need not go to Satan for it, as he has been a stranger to it for more than 5,000 years. If he would want riches, were to sweep Hell, he could not find a sixpence." A man sitting in the corner of the tavern interrupted by exclaiming, "Well, Sir! Then money is as scarce there, as well as here."[299]

---

297   Ibid., 11.

298   Ibid., 8.

299   Charles Elliott. *The Life of Rev. Robert R. Roberts* (New York: G. Lane and C. B. Tippett, 1844) 137. Robert Roberts donated the first one hundred dollars for Indiana Asbury University, and he became the ecclesiastical cheerleader for the University. It was at Indiana Asbury University, by the prompting of Simpson and Ames, that Roberts' portrait was painted and now hangs in East College Hall. On July 21, 1842, he recorded, "I spent ten or twelve days at Greencastle, preached several times while there and had my likeness taken in full length and some persons think that it is a good one." When Roberts died, March 26, 1843, he was buried in a cornfield on his own farm. The spot was "in a remote corner of Lawrence County, Indiana, in a secluded neighborhood, to or near where no leading road conducts the traveler. Narrow horse paths or scarcely visible wagon tracks lead to the farm." The Indiana Annual Conference which met at Crawfordsville, October, 1843, moved that Roberts' remains be removed to Greencastle, Indiana, and "a suitable tombstone or monument be erected." Matthew Simpson was charged with the responsibilities of

In 1831, the Pittsburgh Conference of the Methodist Episcopal Church assumed the patronage of Allegheny, and closed Madison College in Uniontown, the only school of "higher education," which Matthew Simpson ever attended. In 1829, Timothy Alden resigned, and closed out his career as the pastor of Pine Creek Church in Sharpsburg, Pennsylvania, dying in 1839. Among noted graduates of Allegheny were Clarence Darrow and William McKinley. One legend claimed that McKinley in 1866 coaxed a cow up the stairs of Bentley Hall all the way to the bell tower, as a student prank. Allegheny claims to be the oldest college west of the Alleghenies with a continuous name. Martin Ruter, the first President under Methodist auspices (He had been President of Augusta College in Kentucky.) was an autodidact, proficient in French, Latin, and Greek. In 1822, Transylvania University granted Ruter a Doctor of Divinity degree, the first American Methodist so honored.

Becoming an Educator

When Simpson came into the Pittsburgh Conference, Ruter was pastor of Smithfield Street. Remembering the precociousness of the young pastor, Ruter pursued Simpson as professor of Chemistry and Natural Sciences, "to receive a partial salary" and depend for the remainder of his support "upon his lancet." This was the first invitation, October 1834, to which Simpson responded "no." Ruter again wrote Simpson on January 26, 1837, "The object of the letter is to say that it is intended to have a person appointed to a professorship in the college, embracing Chemistry and some other branches–perhaps in Mathematics and Natural Philosophy–and it has appeared to me that you might fill the chair as well as anyone else."[300]

---

carrying out the details of the transition. He contemplated writing a biography of Roberts, but his Uncle advised against the enterprise. The older Matthew understood the liabilities of hagiography. "It is, however, proper that a memoir should be written having the utmost regard to truth, which I fear is not often the case. Let Brother Elliott write. He is an older man, longer acquainted with the deceased. Beside all this, your time can be much more usefully employed, and you already have too much to do for your health." UMA, Drew University, Simpson papers, Letter May 2, 1843. Simpson interviewed Roberts during the 1842 portrait session, and began a biography for which he wrote 38 pages, approximately 15,000 words. The manuscript is in the LOC, Simpson papers, "Notes on Bishop Roberts," Container sixteen.

300   LOC, Simpson papers, Letter January 26, 1837, Container four.

The 25-year-old Simpson began his duties at Allegheny May 1, 1837, for $500 per year. It was not difficult to pull him away from the outpost at Williamsport. Because of no immediate family housing, Ellen, and the infant James, headed to her folks in Pittsburgh. When Ruter left for Texas in 1837, Homer Clark was named President and the 26-year-old Simpson Vice-President.[301]

Simpson was a popular teacher, but was somewhat disappointed in the quality of his students, as most of them were in preparatory classes. However, some were "bright young men who have since made their mark on their country's history." The professor's responsibilities included "six classes, embracing those in natural science, sometimes once or twice in mathematics, and occasionally one in languages." He was especially delighted with a library, "large for those days and among other books had a collection of the church fathers in Greek and Latin which I prize highly and carefully read." [302] While at Allegheny, the young professor formulated a principle that would inform his preaching for the rest of his life. The study of Greek and Roman Classics provided, "The advantages of elevated style, correct knowledge of construction of language and great command of words …."[303] Simpson excelled as a hands-on teacher, especially delighting in field trips.

> I went with several of my classes today, to a spring about a mile east of the college, to collect some specimens of a peculiar kind of worms in tubes of conglomerated sand. They're about one inch in length and tube is an oscillation of small gravel in the inside, it is perfectly smooth. The animal is enclosed within and is a slippery appearance and whit-ish color, except about one fourth of an inch of its exterior extremity, which it frequently elongates it's brown. It is furnished with three pairs of tentacles-all of which it used what elongated from the tube. Its head is small and hard.[304]

At Allegheny College Simpson was the quintessential scientist, an investigative pursuit that knew no limitations, other than those imposed by the school's isolation and lack of finances. Simpson kept eclectic notes on whatever grabbed his attention: elephants, lightning rods, electric magnetic

---

301   Smith, 110-113. At the 1834 Commencement on Sept. 25, Allegheny College conferred on Alfred Brunson and Matthew Simpson an honorary Master of Arts.
302   Crooks, 130.
303   LOC, Simpson papers, 1838 *Diary*, Container one.
304   Ibid.

engines, steam engines, buckwheat cakes, Yankee-pudding, black tea and various medical remedies. Joseph Tingley recalled, "I was shown the large electrical machine, which he had reconstructed and used in his teaching. Professor Simpson had found much of the laboratory equipment in bad condition, but he repaired and supplemented it so effectively as to gain the reputation of being a remarkable ingenious scientist."[305] Simpson also taught classes in surveying, which prepared the way for the hiring of a West Point graduate, T. P. Allen, to begin a curriculum in civil engineering. (Most West Point graduates were civil engineers, such as Robert E. Lee, which made the military academy the leading engineering school in America.) Simpson wrapped his scientific studies in theology, knowledge which would inform much of his future preaching.

The highlight of Simpson's week was the opportunity to preach in the surrounding churches. "Little of moment occurred in my college life. I have, however, a deep interest in the work of the ministry, visiting the charges from 16 to 20 miles of Meadville, and assisting also in quarterly and protracted meetings, and in the founding and dedication of churches."[306] It is doubtful that Simpson took a Sabbath day's rest, and his tireless labors along with the unmerciful Meadville winters wore on him. "As my health was poor and I was suffering from trouble with my chest and cough, I thought well of a change of climate .... A severe cough, pain in the side and chest and other symptoms of pulmonary disease led me and my friends to think that I needed a warmer climate."[307]

Conflict with Uncle Matthew Over Abolition

When the "Lane Rebels" emptied out Cincinnati's Lane Theological Seminary in 1833, and fled to the newly founded Oberlin College in Oberlin, Ohio, shockwaves vibrated throughout American colleges. The last thing a college President wanted on his hands was an abolitionist uprising. Thus, when Simpson came to Allegheny, Martin Ruter wanted to know exactly where this new faculty member stood on the issue of abolition. Many in the

---

305 Smith, 117.
306 Crooks, 131.
307 Ibid., 134.

Pittsburgh Conference were against abolition, especially Nathaniel Holmes. William Hunter had heard that Nathaniel Holmes talked of "blowing up Allegheny College ... he and Hudson are the most anti-abolitionists in the Conference."[308] And Simpson would not cross Holmes, because the banker served as the sugar daddy when Ellen was in Pittsburgh. Simpson preferred that his wife be dependent on Holmes, rather than throw themselves on the mercy of his in-laws.[309] When Simpson wrote Nathaniel Holmes requesting fifteen dollars, to be given at the call of his wife, he had to include the request on the same piece of paper he sent to Ellen. "Be sure and cut out this letter to Holmes so as not to leave all the black marks that I have made on this sheet—and especially cut off close at the bottom, so on those lines that I crossed out. I wrote them as an apology for not writing a separate letter, and I thought the apology only made it worse."[310]

As always, the nephew wrote his uncle for advice, in this instance resulting in an exchange of misunderstandings and apologies. The elder was steadily becoming an abolitionist, while the junior was adopting colonization. The young professor thought he was being condemned when the uncle wrote on March 2, 1838, "They (abolitionists) will not hold their peace. They will not cease to agitate till the whole Christian Church be purged from a participation in the guilt of slavery, the most abominable institution that ever disgraced humanity whether in Christian or heathen countries."[311] Uncle Matthew added that his nephew's ambivalence had caused him to weep. "In some weak moment, the enemy gained an advantage over your intellect. Oh, may he in whom are all the treasures of wisdom save you from such delusion."[312]

To his uncle's ultraist position the nephew responded, "I received yours this morning and hastened to reply. It is not pleasant for men to differ, to differ from my friends in sentiment much less to hold a controversy with

---

308   LOC, Simpson papers, Letter, William Hunter to Matthew Simpson, February 23, 1838, Container four.
309   LOC, Simpson papers, Letters March 12, 1838 and June 8, 1852, Container three.
310   LOC, Simpson papers, Letter March 12, 1838, Container three.
311   LOC, Simpson papers, Letter March 2, 1838, Container three.
312   Ibid.

him."[313] But differ he would! If the Uncle had said, "The slavery authorized by the Bible whatever it was, is not wrong in itself, I should have been saved a good deal of painful or at least tearful feeling." And as to abolitionists, they "Say many times what I cannot say on a point in our church they have taken several steps to which I disapproved- I speak my disapprobation and at once am set down as fawning slavery?" Was it necessary to use physical force against slave holders, in order not to be called a "friend of slavery?" Simpson then wrote down a credo concerning his thoughts on slavery, nine statements on which he would stand, anti-slavery without abolitionism until it became clear that war was a necessity.

> One-I believe slavery as it exists in our land is a sin against God– That it might possibly exist under some circumstances without being a sin. Two-I believe it should be abandoned, in fact immediately and in appearance as soon as the slaves can be prepared to enjoy full freedom. Three-That the North can exercise considerable influence over the South by reason and argument in the matter, and that influence ought to be exerted. Four-But the harsh and reproachful epithets should be abandoned as calculated to defeat the design and a kind spirit should be cultivated. Five-That freemen should continue to petition Congress until Congress shall abolish slavery in the District of Columbia, in the territories, and if it have power, put an end to traffic between the states. Six-As a Methodist, I believe that the rules of our Discipline should be enforced, if they are not, let the General Conference be petitioned to adopt measures to have the Discipline enforced. Seven-That all the other assemblies to discuss such questions on Conference rights ... Should be discontinued as were productive of more evil than this good. Eight-That questions respecting our economy and administration, in addition to the Discipline, should not be brought before the people in an agitating manner. They should be investigated as general principles-and not as a temporary connection with a party question. Nine–That ministers of the Gospel should not engage in agencies on this subject, to the neglecting the proper work of the church, but all should move in the sphere and order that the Church expects.[314]

The uncle was wounded in that according to him, he had been misunderstood. "When I wrote you last you seemed to have read a meaning which I did not intend you to understand. It never entered my mind that you should interpret my letter into any abatement of confidence much less

---

313 LOC, Simpson papers, Letter March 9, 1838, Container three.
314 Ibid.

a want of confidence."³¹⁵ It was a controversy that bore fruit. The nephew was forced to clarify exactly what he thought about the major issue facing American society. But ill health and a troubled conscience about slavery were not the only problems facing Matthew Simpson. A rebellion among the students took place over dissatisfaction with a professor; the details are not clear. The frigid temperature, 19° below zero, loneliness without Ellen and James, and his financial embarrassment all led him to confess "I don't know when I have so much wished to be away."³¹⁶

Financial panic had swept across America, which placed Simpson as well as the rest of the Allegheny staff in a pitiful paucity. "It is almost if not entirely impossible to get any money here. There is none in the treasury. You know–I had the promise of enough to do me on a loan and was resting easy. When the evening before last I was informed that I could not get it–I've since made every effort to borrow some but ineffectively."³¹⁷ On March 9, 1839, Simpson resigned. Allegheny historian Ernest Ashton Smith concluded, "Simpson's departure brought deep regret, for his influence was most prominent in the college and in the religious life of the community and the county. He was much attached to his associates in the Faculty and to the Students as well. He often said that only the climate sent him to another field."³¹⁸ Either Smith or Simpson was not being entirely truthful. The future bishop was moving on up. The students were kind enough to request of him a farewell address, and passed the following resolution, "Resolved, that in view of the distinguished ability, and the kindness and regard for us as a community, and as individuals, which have uniformly marked the course of Professor Simpson during our college connection–we cannot refrain from an expression of sincerest regret of the necessity which requires him to leave us."³¹⁹

---

315 LOC, Simpson papers, Letter March 17, 1838, Container three.
316 LOC, Simpson papers, Letter, Matthew to Ellen, March 15, 1838, Container three.
317 Ibid.
318 Smith, 122.
319 LOC, Simpson papers, Letter March 18, 1839, Container four.

Elected As President of Indiana Asbury

At the 1835 Indiana Annual Conference, John Cowgill, Mayor of Greencastle, Indiana outbid Rockville, Indiana with a subscription of $20,000 for the location of a new college, Indiana Asbury University. He further swayed the Conference delegates by adding that "people never die in Greencastle, although for convenience they have a cemetery there."[320] Dr. A.C. Stevenson served as the first Board President. As an early physician in Putnam County, the surgeon had amputated a man's leg with a fine tooth saw and a pocket knife.[321] The first faculty member, Cyrus Nutt, traveled for two weeks by stage, steamboat, wagon and foot in order to reach Greencastle. Joseph Tomlinson, a graduate of Transylvania, became professor of mathematics. Because he had served as President of Augusta College, Tomlinson was offered the presidency of Indiana Asbury, but refused the office. The 27-year-old Simpson was recommended by Charles Elliott and was offered the job, sight unseen. Board member Allen Wylie's invitation read, "Bro. Charles Elliott attended our last Conference a part of the time, and stayed at my residence which gave me an opportunity of presenting our wants and wishes to him, and he named, and recommended you to me, as a man, a Christian, a minister and a scholar, everyway fitted to answer our purpose in any department in which we might call you."[322]

One of Simpson's foremost ingratiating characteristics was his non-pretentious and unassuming personality. His ego divestment, which rarely communicated, "I should be treated better than this," took in stride whatever circumstances threw at him. At no time was this more evident than when the new College President arrived in Greencastle.

> I accordingly left Meadville the latter part of March. Sent my goods to Franklin and down the Allegheny River. My goods were shipped from Pittsburgh for Terre Haute according to directions given me, but unfortunately the Wabash River was low that spring, and they were detained at Vincennes until the next fall. The roads were extremely

---

320   William Warren Sweet. *Indiana Asbury-DePauw University, 1837-1937: A Hundred Years of Higher Education in the Middle West* (New York: Abingdon Press) 32.
321   Ibid., 35.
322   LOC, Simpson papers, Letter January 24, 1838, Container four.

bad; much of the way they were what was termed corduroy that is in marshy places made of sticks laid crosswise over which the stage jolted. Sometimes the sticks were misplaced or broken and then the wheels went down deep into the mud; once we were upset but without any serious harm. Reaching Putnam, we secured a private conveyance 6 miles across to Greencastle where we arrived on Saturday afternoon in the latter part of April 1839 …. I asked to be driven to the best hotel was taken to a two-story log building, weather boarded; but it was court week and the house was full. We were sent to the next best hotel, a small frame building on the public square. It boasted a small bell but as that was cracked its tones grated harshly on the ear and I felt despondent. That hotel was full also but some of the guests were to leave in the evening and they agreed we might stay. They were scrubbing the floors and we were shown to the back porch, where I was compelled for a time to sit with my wife and little boy. I ask in vain for a room, but finally learning that one of the best was occupied by an attorney from a neighboring county seat attending court, I took the responsibility of entering it, and getting a place where my wife could rest until his return from court.[323]

What Simpson found upon arrival in the muddy village was, "Less than one hundred students from all grades from preparatory to sophomore, two teachers, and only an old seminary as the home of the institution and the new building in process of erection, with a debt growing faster than an endowment fund"[324] For temporary housing the family settled in a two-story log house, until an eight room house with a central hallway could be readied. When finished, the structure was the nicest home in Putnam County, and would be the best house in which the Simpsons resided until moving to Philadelphia, other than staying for a few months with his sister Hetty and her family on Mount Auburn in Cincinnati.

Of course, Simpson showed up wearing his homespun "linsey-woolsey," which further accented his homeliness and lack of sophistication. Those who first observed the new College President recorded their less than favorable impression. One individual noted that, "Simpson looked as if much study had made him thin, and there was nothing prepossessing in his whole appearance. His forehead was low and un-prominent, his hair swinging in all directions as if it had been a stranger to a comb for a week;

---

323   Crooks, 145-146.
324   "The Arrival of Dr. Simpson at Greencastle," LOC, Simpson papers, Unidentifiable author, Container twenty.

his eye was dull and his countenance indicated a total disregard for all restraints of fashion and comeliness." Another description gave him "a face which was elongated, his shoulders round, his arms at first always seeming in the way and his lower extremities correspondingly loose and shuffling." Another observer claimed that Simpson's head "gave the lie to phrenology, a countenance that physiognomists would say, exhibits nothing remarkable, and a voice sometimes used in a singing tone like Quakers; with all these defects and drawbacks he astonishes the natives by his pulpit and platform performances." This was not the only time when someone stated that Simpson's head betrayed phrenology.[325]

Pulpit Triumph

Ellen bristled at the slights and condescending attitudes of the Greencastle villagers. She complained to her husband. He responded, "Never mind. Do not say a word, even if they should throw mud on us, we will only stay one year." After her husband was dead, Ellen insisted that her

---

325   See Reverend C.W. Pepper, "Bishop Simpson's Oratory", LOC. Simpson papers, Scrapbook C, Container twenty-three. Between 1838 and 1840, a Scotsman, George Combe, spent nearly two years in the United States studying phrenology. Phrenology taught that the brain was physiologically divided into faculties such as feelings and intellect. Under the first, would belong propensities and sentiments, and under the second, knowing and reflection. Most important for a person's intellectual and moral sensitivities was the shape and size of the head. A person with a small dome above the forehead, such as William Hare, was of deficient moral qualities. Because he had a small "coronal region," Hare killed sixteen people for the sake of selling their bodies for dissection. Combe went on to say: "We find that in all countries hitherto explored, a long head of which the circumference taken a little higher than the orbit does not exceed thirteen inches, which the distance from the top of the nose backwards over the top of the head to the occipital bone is less than nine inches, is in the existing races of mankind, invariably accompanied by idiocy." George Combe. *Notes on the United States of America during a Phrenological Visit in 1838–40* Vol. I: 92, Vol. II: 252–253 (Philadelphia: Carey and Hart, 1841). In fact, Simpson's forehead was so low, which may have been accented by his hairstyle swept across his brow, that it was important for a photographer to make him look as intelligent as possible. After he sat for a portrait in 1864, he received the following note from the photographer, "We have received from Mr. Whipple your photographe. It appears there was a misunderstanding as to your position in the group, for we wished it facing to the right instead of the left as taken. We think the picture also defective in other respects. The head is thrown back too much. This shows the forehead smaller than its due proportion, and shows the neck too open. Your former picture was taken with a black neck scarf or stock. We think that better than white. The engraving will cost us a thousand dollars, and we are, of course, anxious to get exactly the right thing." UMA, Drew University, Simpson papers, Letter June 4, 1864.

husband did not show up at Asbury "wearing linsey-woolsey, but he was wearing black, and that his pants were not too short."[326] She also objected to biographer Crooks using the word "uncouth" in describing her husband as the new college President.[327] Arriving on Saturday, he preached the next morning in the Methodist Church, and managed to subdue the prejudices of those who expected to be greeted by a man but "found only a stripling." Nephew Joseph Tingley probably did not exaggerate when he claimed that the "He won't do" was changed to "He will do."[328] Facile appraisals were immediately reversed because, "In the pulpit Simpson was on his throne and he lay on his hearers the spell of his eloquence. They were charmed, melted, conquered."[329] No doubt, whatever Simpson preached, he had preached before, and the sermon was well honed. His next public presentation was not as successful. Cyrus Nutt recalled that, "A large congregation was in attendance to hear the new President. The President preached a very plain, fair discourse, but not remarkable for brilliancy or power. He indeed felt it was a failure, and the great men of the Conference who had a disposition to treat us a little cool as important teachers were more distant on the next day than ever."[330]

If the disposition was cool, the weather was not. It was ninety degrees in a "house crowded with tired and sweltering men and women." Simpson was not informed that he was to preach in Indianapolis for the 1838 Indiana Annual Conference, until he arrived on Tuesday evening, after traveling all day on horseback. The Asbury Board met on Wednesday, both morning and afternoon, with a service planned that night. Simpson was so ill-prepared and worn out that, "He failed, utterly failed, and the verdict was that the young man had been vastly over-estimated as a preacher."[331] An observer claimed that Simpson "Resolved never to attempt to preach merely to

---

326   UMA, Drew University, Crooks papers, Letter, Sarah Elizabeth Simpson to George Crooks, December 28, 1888.

327   Ibid.

328   Tingley, "Reminiscences."

329   Crooks, 155.

330   George B. Manhart. *DePauw through the Years* Vol. I (Greencastle, IN: DePauw University, 1962) 88.

331   "The Arrival of Dr. Simpson"

gratify curiosity and when exhausted by overwork."[332] This proved to be a vain resolution.

Simpson displayed his mettle at the 1839 Indiana Annual Conference. Ezekiel 47, the vision of water flowing from the Temple, provided a text from which Simpson could take oratorical flight. An attender left a first-person account:

> It was the centennial year of Methodism, and Dr. Simpson was appointed to preach on the occasion in the little brick church the largest and best in the town. This "text" was the vision of waters flowing from the sanctuary into the desert. The opening hymn was "Saw ye not a cloud arise?" No pen or tongue can do justice to that occasion. On even ordinary occasions a congregation of less than 500 containing 150 Methodist preachers–such preachers as those were, from their large circuits and numerous revivals, and each more or less imbibing the theory men very prevalent concerning the near approach of the millennium, which culminated three years later in the Millerite Craze, would be an excitable body, but when the silver tongue of the young man before them began to recount the going out of the waters into the desert, and to portray the rich verdure and fruitage it brought, getting deeper and wider at every measurement, this tide of emotion rose to an uncontrollable pitch and at one time, he had to stop a few moments to allow it to subside. One very intelligent sister being, for the moment, entirely insensible to earthly surroundings. That sermon was never forgotten by those who heard it until one by one the fathers passed over; and those who were mere children thus have not forgotten it. That fixed the standing of the young president as a preacher, and gave him a rank which he retained, in Indiana until his death.[333]

Thomas Goodwin, a member of Asbury's first graduating class, represented an outstanding story of perseverance in order to attend the school. On a Wednesday afternoon he left his home expecting to arrive in Greencastle two days later. Sloshing through rain and mud, the open wagon broke down 6 miles outside of Indianapolis; Goodwin hopped on one of the wagon horses, and the driver with another passenger mounted the other horse. In Indianapolis Goodwin with the other passengers boarded a stage, which enabled an arrival in Putnamville where Goodwin spent the night at a Mr. Townsend's tavern, and listened to the proprietor condemn Indiana

---

332   Ibid.
333   Ibid.

Asbury University. Greencastle is "out of the way, away off the national road; no stage runs through it or to it. How could it ever amount to anything not being on the national road?" The next morning Townsend dropped Goodwin off at Lundy's Tavern on the Greencastle town square for a fare of two dollars. The tavern keeper told Goodwin, that he did not exactly know the school's location, and "you will not find it much of a University, I reckon."[334] Goodwin would graduate from Indiana University and would become President of two Indiana colleges and editor of the *Indiana American*.

In the meantime Simpson's brother-in-law, George McCullough, had vacated Wellsville sometime in 1840 and had moved his wife with mother Sarah and Uncle Matthew to Cincinnati. George had gone into business with a man named Miller at the corner of sixth and Main Street.[335] Here Ellen would spend several summers as she refused to travel with her husband on his fundraising endeavors. Depression and spiritual doubts continued to haunt Simpson. May 11, 1840 he recorded, "May the creator impress my mind with solemn views of eternity, the shortness of time and the strictness of judgment." And on June 8, 1840, "I labor too much to please myself and others and too little to please God."[336] Simpson's God kept his children on a strict schedule. On May 11, Simpson arose at 4 a.m., on May 14 at 4:05, but on May 22 at 4:45. "By some means I am prone to become irregular in my habits." He then exclaimed, "Oh, that I could gain the height of perfection, the depth of humble love."[337] Perhaps the rock candy from George McCullough's store in Cincinnati cheered him up.[338]

During the summers, Simpson was often accompanied by an agent appointed by the trustees for the purpose of fundraising, one of them being Rev. Samuel Cooper. Joseph Tarkington recalled, "The people often took Cooper to be the President of the University and Simpson the agent or circuit rider. Cooper was large and of imposing presence. Simpson, in

---

334 Crooks, 166-167.
335 LOC, Simpson papers, Letter, George McCullough to Matthew Simpson, January 27, 1840, Container three.
336 LOC, Simpson papers, 1840 *Diary*, Container one.
337 LOC, Simpson papers, 1840 *Diary*, Container one.
338 LOC, Simpson papers, Letter, George McCullough to Matthew Simpson, December 21, 1841, Container three.

those days angular, stooped somewhat of the shoulders and was utterly unpretentious. But when they spoke from the pulpit, who was who was manifest."[339] Simpson's eloquence was not sufficiently impressive to send him as a delegate to the 1840 General Conference. Goodwin recalled that, "In the first place he was not in the 'regular work' and then, he was only a recent transfer, and he never had any experience as a circuit rider. Besides, as self-sacrificing as the preachers of that period were in behalf of the young Asbury University, they took so little stock in education as a qualification for the ministry, that at that very General Conference (1840), by a large majority, voted against authorizing theological schools."[340]

Oratorical Leadership

It was a big day for Greencastle, an almost non-locatable village, forty-eight miles west of Indianapolis. Though Simpson had been in the presidential harness for a year, he had not been officially installed. Simpson's Inauguration coincided with Asbury's first commencement, the Indiana Annual Conference of the Methodist Episcopal Church, and the completion of the "Edifice," a three-story administration, classroom, library, and chapel building.[341] The Edifice with its cupola of five-foot clocks on each side could be seen for miles, and comprised the entire physical plant known as Indiana Asbury University. Indiana Governor, David Wallace, traveled from Indianapolis and after making a brief address, ceremonially presented Simpson with the keys to the University. Also on the program, was a 26 year-old preacher named Henry Ward Beecher, who lectured that evening to the "literary societies." His father, Lyman, was President of Lane Theological Seminary in Cincinnati, and would become known as the man who genetically produced the most brains in nineteenth-century America.[342]

---

339 Joseph Tarkington. *The Autobiography of Joseph Tarkington* (Cincinnati: Curtis and Jennings, 1899) 133.

340 Thomas Goodwin, "Introduction," *The Autobiography of Joseph Tarkington*, 19.

341 Clifton Phillips and John Baughman. *DePauw: A Pictorial History* (Greencastle, Indiana: DePauw University, 1987)10–11.

342 Lyman Beecher fathered thirteen children by three wives, most who distinguished themselves. The flamboyant Henry Ward Beecher pastored Plymouth Church in Brooklyn, New York. Edward Beecher pastored the famed Park Street Church in Boston, and was the first President of Illinois College in Jacksonville, Illinois, and distinguished himself as

Simpson's "Inaugural Speech," delivered September 16, 1840, at Indiana Asbury University was everything that Presidential oratory in the mid-nineteenth century should have been: pedantic, erudite, verbose, obtuse and long. It was the exact opposite of his preaching. The over 14,000 word speech took two hours to deliver, a testimony to the endurance of the auditors and their appreciation for monological entertainment. Simpson had given long hours to both composition and memorization. He referred to 63 historical figures, most from antiquity, and most of whom his listeners had never heard: Praxiteles, Apples, Nestor, Euripides, Sophocles and Aeschylus. Simpson's sweeping generalizations demonstrated his unbounded optimism for formal, institutional education. Education had eternalized Rome, brought light to the dark ages, freed the serfs, ushered in the Reformation, awakened Russia and above all triumphed in the formation of America. All of this was in contrast to South America which lacked intelligence and virtue and at this moment was "suffering from opposing and controlling factions."[343] Simpson boasted, "But our Union has arisen as a sun in its strength, her internal order scarcely disturbed, her external rights esteemed sacred. Her commerce is as wide as the earth, as she presents the sublime spectacle of a free nation, unembarrassed by debt, uncontrolled by religious monopolies, at peace with all the world, rising in intellectual and moral grandeur and throwing open her territories to receive the distressed immigrant as he flies from despotic power."[344]

Simpson's inflated statements arguing the value of education were naïve, simplistic, exaggerated and at times even preposterous. "There is scarcely a more pernicious influence operating against our learned professions than one who enters that profession without a college degree. Viciously disposed young men cannot generally be found engaged in college pursuits. If trustees have done their duty, the preceptors will always be men of irreproachable

---

an author and editor. Katherine Beecher founded Hartford Female Seminary in Hartford Connecticut, and gave her life to educational opportunities for women. *Webster's American Biographies* (Springfield, MA: G. & C. Merriam Company Publishers) 80-82.

343   Matthew Simpson. "Address Delivered upon the Author's Installation as President of the Indiana Asbury University." (Indianapolis, IN: University Board of Trustees, 1840) 15.

344   Ibid., 15.

habits and unblemished piety."³⁴⁵ Simpson translated a college degree into a panacea for almost all societal problems. The college-educated will have, "a spirit to brook difficulties–a dauntless energy to urge them perpetually forward, till they stand upon the pinnacle of the temple of fame, while their supported colleagues will be lingering around the basement waiting for fair hands to open each bolted door and sweet smiles to cheer them at each ascending step."³⁴⁶ Had he meditated in the Book of Proverbs, much less fast-forwarded to Freud's "pleasure principle" a century later, he would not have assumed, "The desire for happiness contains a thirst for knowledge."³⁴⁷

The address almost entirely preempted the existence of original sin, undermining Orthodox theology, postulating a much more positive view of human nature than did the Church Fathers and even our Forefathers, who instituted a government of checks and balances, because humankind cannot be trusted to act rightly. Simpson proclaimed, "Man in the creation was made in the image of God in distinction from animated nature, not that he was purer, for all was pure, but he was wiser. He had knowledge for government, power to control himself." Simpson did not clarify that it was the power of self-control that humankind had irrevocably lost, except by the affective transformation of the Holy Spirit. Ironically, Simpson denied or forgot the nurturing of his uncle, who was of far greater value and pedagogical effectiveness than the influence of an educational institution, when he postulated, "The father who neglects or refuses to send his son to school or to college, only chooses for him an education at home. He entrusts him not to men of intellectual attainments and high moral worth, but permits him to associate with the licentious and profane. He is taught no science but the science of wickedness."³⁴⁸ The uncle had cautioned his nephew about overstating the case for education:

> You say "education makes man all that he is." Not exactly. For his capacity for education is a part of what he is. And it is not the creature of education. Could a beast by education, be turned into a man, possess the instinctive powers of common animals. You will need to take care in comparing man with beast lest you draw points of comparison where there

---

345   Ibid., 24.
346   Ibid., 37.
347   Ibid., 6.
348   Ibid., 6.

is not one. For the one naturally possessing more perfect reasoning powers and the other such perfect instincts as to do what man by his reason and science could scarcely accomplish. Again you say, "The kind of education he receives determines his character." This is generally so, but there have been some individuals who attained to an improvement and elevation of character far above that which might have been expected from any example they had received; and others have exceeded in the downward course.[349]

Unintentionally, the uncle had made an argument against evolution, a conclusion which would elude the nephew, decades later. Uncle Matthew then reminded his nephew of what the college President and American Methodism increasingly forgot, that "Wesley's preachers were nearly all destitute of such an education and still they were useful and whoever preached with more success and usefulness."[350]

The Beginning of a Life-long Mantra

The "Inaugural" served as a launching pad for the themes that would later define the preaching career of Matthew Simpson: technology, progress, happiness, the contentment of those who sought to better themselves through hard work and procurement of knowledge, a millennial interpretation of history, and the dominance of the Anglo-Saxon race.[351] "Her (Britain) possessions are extensive in every quarter of the globe, and small as she is, she wields an almost omnipotent influence. What has produced this mighty change? Education is there. The schoolmaster is abroad. Her venerable universities have illuminated her sons, and widely diffused the spirit of

---

349   LOC, Simpson papers, Letter August 8, 1840, Container three.

350   Ibid.

351   The idea of progress and the discoveries of science coalesced in the 18th century. Alexander Pope's epitaph on Isaac Newton read "Nature and nature's laws lay hid in night. God said, let Newton be and all was light." A phrase crypted by Ernest Tuveson, "Nature's simple plot: The credo of progress," was exemplified by the following from Edward Law in 1745, "The following discourses were originally part of a larger design, tending to show that arts and sciences, natural and revealed religion, have on the whole been progressive from the creation of the world to the present time; as also that they have been suited to each other as well as to the circumstances of mankind, during each eminent period of this their progression." Tuveson writes, "At the time of Bacon, the question was one of the possibilities of progress; within a hundred years possibility had become certainty in man's faith." Ernest Lee Tuveson. *Millennium and Utopia: A Study in the Background of the Idea of Progress* (New York: Harper & Row Publishers, 1964) 147, 152.

enterprise. They have discovered and practically applied the maxim that 'knowledge is power.'"[352] Unfortunately, suggesting that enterprise, discovery and invention are the routes to happiness, which Simpson did throughout much of his life, was theologically vacuous. Of course, there was much in his preaching that contradicted notions of progress as axiomatic to happiness, but Simpson's theological and technological disconnect was often glaring.

Simpson spent approximately 1,600 words of his address touting the power of language, in particular, oratory. Simpson could not have completely disregarded himself when he proclaimed. "Our only security is in the intelligence and virtues of our citizens and every man who aspires to eminence should seek such an acquaintance with language as shall enable him to pour forth truth in all its strength and beauty; to clothe it in its own heavenly habitants of loveliness and to acquire the power of holding thousands entranced with the resistless magic both of thoughts that breathe and words that burn."[353] And did he really believe that, "Comparatively few can be writers, but all may be orators?"

On the positive side of the "Inaugural," Simpson was plausible and cogent as he explained how a school could be confessionally Christian and not be sectarian. "If by sectarianism be meant that any privilege shall be extended to youth of one denomination more than another, or that the faculty shall endeavor to proselyte those placed under their instruction or dwell upon the minor points controverted between the branches of the great Christian family, then there is not and we hope there never shall be sectarianism here."[354] And Simpson had a succinct retort for those who would label the school sectarian, because it chose Christianity as its guiding ethos. "The only persons who are properly free from sectarianism are those who either believe all things or who believe nothing."[355] Of course Simpson could not conclude his discourse without a financial appeal. To those who would support the fledgling institution were given a promise of reward in a crescendo of peroration that has probably never been equaled in the history of fund raising. What Simpson lost in eschatological clarity, he gained in pecuniary imagination.

---

352 "Simpson Inaugural," 14.
353 Ibid., 22.
354 Ibid., 38.
355 Ibid., 39.

> Nor can we conceive of but few more interesting scenes than the return of the disembodied spirits, after the lapse of ages, to revisit the place of their former benefactions. As hovering over those classic halls, they should witness the preparations for noble action-and should gaze intensely on those bright intellects, which even in their youth sparkle with celestial fire, and ardently burn to subdue the world to Christ, and to usher in the millennial glory-overwhelmed with the resistless rush of holy feeling, they would fly back to the palaces of bliss, to join in still more enrapturing anthems of praise unto Him who had enabled them, while on earth, to perform such illustrious deeds, and bear such a noble part in advancing the Redeemer's Kingdom.[356]

Simpson's speech was so sublime and eloquent that one wonders whether the content of the two-hour presentation was even heard, much less analyzed. Bishop Hamline unequivocally assessed that it was the greatest and best inaugural ever made by a Methodist preacher at the head of a college (which was not saying much). Charles Elliott, who possibly wrote more than any Methodist in the nineteenth century (Nathan Bangs and Abel Stevens would have been close competitors), appraised that the speech could have been improved, though he, himself, could not have done better. Again, perhaps the President should have listened more astutely to his uncle, to whom he had sent an early draft, who responded, "some generalizations ought to be qualified."[357]

A Contagious Hypnosis

The paramount result of the Indiana Asbury Inaugural was that Simpson, in the public mind, became an orator. Before that performance, he had only been a preacher. But if a hearer of Simpson's address would have been asked to draw a line between the person who was an orator and one who was not, the explanation would have fizzled into a tautology. The words were magical because they worked a certain magic, mysterious because of some indefinable aura, charismatic because the speaker demonstrated charisma, and eloquent because it sounded pleasing to the ear. Simpson had discovered in this event, if there was a particular point of discovery, that he could hold

---

356 Ibid., 40.
357 LOC, Simpson papers, Letters, Uncle Matthew to nephew, June 19 and August 8, 1840, Container three.

people spellbound because his speech was, well, spellbinding. True, he did have a lyrical quality in his voice, a naturalness of delivery, and a command of language that would propel him into a very small cadre of masters of the spoken word, in an age when the spoken word still mattered. Most of his auditors would have concluded as did Robert Clark, "Matthew Simpson had, in short, a quality of self-hypnosis which spread contagion-like to his audience."[358] A "contagious-hypnosis" is empty of rhetorical analysis, and tells us nothing about substance. Nonetheless, Simpson intentionally utilized substantive figures of speech.

Rhetorical devices abounded in the "Inaugural" in visual, sensual, concrete analogies: as the "spirit of the storm," as a "sun in a universe," as a "whale in the ocean," as a "star hitherto invisible," as "polished marble pillars." Imagination translated abstractions into concrete objects, causing much of the speech to be seen as well as heard: "tall trees," "tempestuous seas," "blood gushing forth," "white-topped mountains," "flashes of lightning," "history--the gray-headed chronicler of years," "volcanic violence," "summit of the temple," "plate of steel," and "cloud-capped mountains." Simpson utilized language that pulsated with transitive, active verbs, rather than intransitive, passive verbs: "the fowls of the air constructed their nests," "the beaver built his dam" and "our ancestors waded through seas of blood." Simpson lifted the vagaries of America's founding documents from their lifeless pages: "These elements of character are the same which shone so conspicuously in our brave sires, whose gigantic intellects planned the colossal fabric of our Constitution--whose hands toiled in its erection--whose blood cemented its parts, and calls upon us to preserve uninjured its massive pillars and its encircling dome."[359]

For most of the "Inaugural," Simpson's images carried their intended meaning. At other times, the symbolism was so overwhelming, that clarity was almost completely lost, spraying the attenders with obfuscation. "But although heated air will invariably rise, yet blot out the sun from existence, or direct its rays from the earth, and thick-ribbed ice would hold universal dominion, blot out colleges, and a Cimmerian darkness would overspread

---

358   Robert Clark. "The Oratorical Career of Bishop Matthew Simpson," *Research Annual: Speech Monographs* Vol. XVI, No. 119 (November 1, 1949) 49.
359   "Simpson Inaugural," 36.

the land, and the huge icebergs of the frigid zone, would but faintly represent the more intense indurations of all the feelings and powers of the mind."[360] Metaphors and tropes can be so vivid and abundant that the concept is lost.

The above should not leave us believing that Simpson's speech was opaque and incoherent. He could send an auditor home with not only a memorable sentence, but with an aphorism or epigram which would be remembered for years. "America's happy because she is enlightened and virtuous." "The harmlessness of the dove must ever be united with the wisdom of the serpent." "Education without morals is pernicious, and to have morals without religious instruction is impossible." "Great men are generally the birth of great times."

Simpson excelled in the passion of congruence. His listeners believed what he said, because *he* believed what he said. No one doubted Simpson when he began his "Inaugural:" "Your speaker cannot be insensible to the interest of this moment. The surrounding circumstances, the eloquent, impressive charge, the high trust committed to his care, and the immeasurable responsibility connected with it, stand vividly before him."[361] He believed himself to be about an ultimate cause, which both temporally and eternally mattered. "The great cause in which we are engaged, which have convened this assembly is of utmost importance."[362] For Simpson, this importance held life/death implications, and he accented his speech with decisive and consequential language: "Gray hairs with sorrow to the grave," "the battlements of Heaven," "the glories of a heavenly inheritance stand forth in bold relief," "blood rushing warm from its hidden fount," "triumphant enthrallment from the yoke of bondage," and "strangle liberty in her cradle."

Passionate ideas are filled with passionate language and passionate illustrations. Who could forget Simpson's allusion to Archimedes who, "Going into a public bath while intent on solving the problem of Hiero's crown, suddenly discovering the method sprang from the bath, and rushed naked into the streets crying, 'I have found it, I have found it.'"[363] Even if

---

360	Ibid., 25.
361	"Simpson Inaugural," 3.
362	Ibid., 4.
363	Ibid., 19.

the dubious illustration was obscure, as distant as the name of Archimedes would be to the average person, the imagery was not lost. The eureka of the "Inauguration," the arrival at the speaker's podium was not so eagerly anticipated, that Simpson forgot to dress as did Archimedes. Though his sartorial splendor may not have been as radiant as some of his more refined supporters desired, one thing was for sure: Simpson believed what must be the conviction of all effective speakers, "If it does not matter to me, it will not matter to them." Simpson believed what he said and hardly anyone, other than the most prejudiced cynic, ever doubted the man's sincerity.

Henry Ward Beecher immediately exclaimed that the presentation should be published and distributed throughout Indiana. Such warmhearted sentiments between Simpson and Beecher would soon be cooled. Edward Ames had just moved to Greencastle as Presiding Elder of the new district, and the speech prompted the first of hundreds of letters between the two men over the next half-century.[364] He informed Simpson of the College Board's request to have 1,000 copies of the speech printed. "John Hammond was highly delighted with your address and intends to send his son to college!!! And young Harrison 'you're a hoss over drawn since you made that speech.' I think perhaps I had better stop now lest you be spoiled by over much praise"[365] But Uncle Matthew was not going to spoil his nephew. He cut the new college president down to size with some profound wisdom:

> But while I am exceedingly joyful at the success of your performance, I would admonish you to remember whence cometh thy help and in deep humility adore that fountain of light from whence a ray has enlightened thee. And remember too that popularity of any kind is very uncertain it is a variable breeze on which you may now float to the clouds and then sink to the bottom of the ocean and mere trifles may be the occasion of both the rise and the fall.[366]

---

364   Dr. Richard Stowe transcribed some four hundred pages of letters from the Library of Congress. Many of the letters were between Bishop Ames and Matthew Simpson, throwing much light on the relationship between the two men. My discussions with him about Edward Ames have been invaluable.

365   LOC, Simpson papers, Letter September 18, 1840, Container four.

366   LOC, Simpson papers, Letter December 27, 1840, Container three. Uncle Matthew may have been a bit contradictory at this point. He wrote his nephew on June 19, 1840, "Don't forget the Inaugural Address for next fall, your duty and reputation both require attention to that." LOC, Simpson papers, Letter June 19, 1840, Container three.

The Competition

One disavowal which Simpson made in his "Inaugural" was patently false. He claimed that, "Yet, she (Indiana Asbury University) assumes no attitude of rivalry .... The spirit of the times is a spirit of peace. The bitter jealousies and rancorous enmities that have subsisted between communities are changed into treaties of friendship and alliance...."[367] The impetus for founding a Methodist college in Indiana was a contemptuous remark by the Presbyterian lawyer Samuel Bigger, who asserted that the ignorant Methodists were not capable of managing a literary institution. The abrasive attorney further claimed that when Ohio University desired to obtain a Methodist professor they had to fetch one from Europe. Even though the Methodists outnumbered the Presbyterians in Indiana by 24,000 to 4,000, the latter dominated the board of the state college in Bloomington. William Sweet argued that the Methodists considered the "Presbyterians as extremely arrogant; assuming themselves to be the only competent educators of the people and under the existing system no Methodist could be placed on the board of the University of Indiana at Bloomington."[368] (Ironically, Cyrus Nutt would serve as President of the Bloomington School for fifteen years between 1861 and 1875.) Yes, Indiana Asbury University was an, "I'll show you we are not blockheads," initiative on the part of the Indiana Methodists.

Another slight occurred when the 1840 Indiana census, taken by a Presbyterian, did not recognize nor record the existence of a college in Putnam County. Simpson was further snubbed in 1842 when Presbyterian pastor Henry Ward Beecher and trustee Samuel Merrill of Presbyterian Wabash College sponsored a state educational convention, but did not invite Simpson. (The organizers later invited him, but only as an afterthought.) They instead named Gov. Samuel Bigger to preside over the convention. When Bigger envisioned himself being voted out of office in the next election by seething Methodists, he called a meeting with Simpson, Ames

---

He wanted the young college President to do well without being proud of doing well. Uncle Matthew may have been prouder than he was willing to admit.

367 "Simpson Inaugural," 33.

368 William Warren Sweet. *Circuit Rider Days in Indiana* (Indianapolis: W.K. Stewart, 1916) 61.

and Samuel Cooper to explain a way his contentious remarks about the Methodists.[369] But there was no retreat and the *Indiana Sentinel* fanned the flames between the Bigger Whigs and the Methodist Democrats.

Robert Clark claimed that Simpson on a speaking tour found himself, "embroiled in a political battle." Henry Ward Beecher and others denounced Simpson's electioneering tour. Beecher shot himself in the political foot when he publicly castigated Simpson at the Wabash College commencement. One overly enthusiastic Presbyterian further derailed the Bigger candidacy for a second term as governor when he said that if the Methodists voted in mass, "The Whig party will blow their college to hell." The Methodists shrugged off the threat of eternal damnation and sent Democrat James Whitcomb to the governorship in the election of 1842. The Bloomington Post condemned Indiana Asbury University for allowing its "holy head" to travel making political speeches in behalf of "so base a hypocrite as James Whitcomb."[370]

The practical result of the foregoing events was that Whitcomb granted a permit for Methodist John Evans to build a hospital for the insane in Indianapolis. And in 1851, Indiana named William C. Larrabee, then interim President of Indiana Asbury, as the first Superintendent of Public

---

369   We do not know what was said at this meeting, but we do know what Bigger said to Simpson in a letter dated March 14, 1843: "I got into a bungling sentence as I sometimes do and put my words together in such a manner as to furnish the inference which was drawn. That fact of the case was that the professor was a foreigner and I suppose I stated it so, as to be understood to say that they had to get a foreigner or go to Europe for him or words clearly conveying that idea although my intention was to merely state the fact as it occurred to me, ... And I am fully aware of President Simpson's position. Not only the Methodist Church, but the community from his public situation of a strong and deep interest in everything connected with him." UMA, Drew University, Simpson papers, Letter, Samuel Bigger to Matthew Simpson, March 12, 1843.

370   Robert D. Clark, "Matthew Simpson, the Methodists and the Defeat of Samuel Bigger," *Indiana Magazine of History*, Vol. 50, No. 1 (March, 1994) 23-33. Crooks down-played Simpson's role in dismantling the Bigger administration, "There is nothing in that Bigger affair that can well be utilized in the biography. The offense was committed in 1835-36, long before Simpson's time. It consisted in his refusing, as chairman of the Committee on Education, to report on a petition from the Indiana Conference, asking the legislature to so amend the law, as that the Legislature might fill vacancies in the Board of Trustees for the University (Bloomington), instead of allowing the Board itself to fill vacancies, by which it was left in the hands of the Presbyterians, to the exclusion of Methodists. True, in 1843, when he was a candidate for re-election, Bp Ames, then a most intense Democrat, used it against him. Simpson took little hand in that, but acquiesced because Whitcomb was a Methodist." UMA, Drew University, Crooks papers, Crooks to John Wheeler, Letter March 11, 1887.

Schools.[371] Most important to Simpson was the smile that curled on his lips when he reflected on the Methodists besting the Presbyterians. But Simpson probably did not know James Whitcomb as well as he should have. Whitcomb was famous for saying, "Give the people plenty of whiskey and stir them up well with a long pole and their votes are certain." Indiana historian Paul Fatout described Whitcomb, "As much more the politician than the statesman, he was hampered by caution and timidity that prevented him from exercising the courage of statesmanship. Opponents called him a trimmer, adept at face saving turnabouts, and heartless as well."[372] At least Whitcomb had a heart big enough to leave DePauw 4,500 of his books.[373]

One of Simpson's fundraising techniques was a "we against them" mentality, or, in other words, setting up straw men. In an *ad hominem* circular letter sent to the ministers, members, and friends of the Methodist Episcopal Church in the Indiana Conference, he pleaded on behalf of raising funds for a new library,

> You know that as a community, we have patiently borne more than ordinary reproach. In our commencement, its pulpit, press, and mob were all against us, but arguments held in check the denunciation of the one and Christian meekness calmed the violence of the other. But when more direct attacks ceased, then the indirect commenced. The united voice of the literary were against us. We had no colleges, and though we increased in numbers, we were allowed no representation in the management of those institutions in which, as a part of the people, we had equal interest. If our sons were sent to college, the religion of their fathers was made a subject of derision, and many were drawn into the bosom of other churches, or ruined with the licentiousness of infidelity, and were branded as ignorant--as fanatics--as enthusiasts. What should we do? Just what you have done. Quietly leave others in possession of the public funds, patiently bear to remain unrepresented in the faculty of state institutions–and in answer to the charge of ignorance, incapacity, etc., get up institutions that should shun comparison with some around them. This,

---

371 One project on which Simpson and Beecher did see eye to eye was in their support of a school for the deaf, which was founded in Indianapolis in 1844. Both Simpson and Beecher served on its board. Logan Esarey. *A History of Indiana: From its Exploration to 1850* (Indianapolis: D.K. Stewart Company, 1915) 436. Also see Edward Moore. *A Century of Indiana History* (New York: American Book Company, 1910) 268.

372 Paul Fatou. *Indiana Canals* (West Lafayette, Indiana: Purdue University Studies, 1972) 111.

373 Manhart, 58.

brethren, has been your course. And as a church prospering greatly, but we must not stop until we possess every advantage essential to prosperity.[374]

What would fix all of the Beecher and Presbyterian slights and disrespect was "Doctor" attached to Simpson's name. On August 4, 1841, Wesleyan University in Middletown, Connecticut, bestowed on him the L.T.D. If receiving a M.A. along with Alfred Brunson did little for his ego, the honorary doctorate probably did even less, in that Jacob Gruber, Secretary of the Board, informed him of the honor, after the fact. Uncle Matthew wrote that "A.D.D. is as empty as an acorn shell and often conferred on those that know little about theology."[375] Though Uncle Matthew may have been confused about the exact degree, he was not misled about the sterility of the intended honor.

Benevolent Paternalism

Almost all colleagues and students had high regard for President Simpson. The warm conversationalist constantly had them in his home where Ellen was a gracious hostess. Simpson carried on a steady correspondence with the parents and was expected to be a surrogate father. Administering a nineteenth century college demanded nothing less than micromanagement as the following request from Edward Ames demonstrated: "I have this day forwarded to you by the hand of brother William Speak, $20 for to be used for the expense of my son as you may judge most expedient, and I wish it distinctly understood that I am to pay no debts of his contracting."[376] In all likelihood the President personally responded to the following that requested him to be both a spiritual director and personal physician:

Lawrence County March 28, 1846

Dear Sir: inasmuch as I have pute my son Jarvis under your Care and Protection I take the liberty to wright to inform you that ai intertain fears he is ingering himself by his stdeing. Laste fall he complained of his breste and eys J Rosewell later wrote by him the 10 March whare in he

---

374 LOC, Simpson papers, "Matthew Simpson to the Ministers, Members, and Friends of the Methodist E. Church in the Indiana Conference," Container thirteen.
375 Clark, *The Life*, 96.
376 LOC, Simpson papers, Letter March 9, 1846, Container four.

states he has something like the dead palsy in his righte arm hi leter was way badly rote he lefte oute letters in a grate ma(n)y of his words I know not whether you are apprised of his condition or not tharfore Sir I will be much oblige to you if you will see him and let me no if it would be proper to leve him thare the nexte secion wrighte to me as soon as this come to hand and oblige your friende

Wishing your health & happiness I remain your friend

Jesse Johnson[377]

The following requested Simpson to be a personal physician, private investigator, and assess the risk of financially investing in academia.

Cambridge Jay 24th 1847

Dr Simpson   Dr Sir

Henry left here two weeks since on tomorrow I heard that he was still at Indianapolis last week a thing that was very strange to us as he professed to be in great haste to regain his class. If this is so he is deceiving me & idling his time and I shall have no hopes of his progress. My losses in this flood is at least $8000. And I cannot bear the expense if his time shall be idle. I shall think the harder of him as he appeared to be in so great a hurry to set off after I got home. I hope Dr you will write me in the spirit of that candor which I would expect from you the whole truth in regard to him his habits his industry & his progress as I feel very uneasy since I know he delayed so long at Indianapolis under the circumstances.

friend--

James Rariden[378]

The President must have not given Henry sufficient attention, or he had little to no academic potential.

---

377   UMA, DePauw University, Simpson papers, Letter March 28, 1846.
378   UMA, DePauw University. Simpson papers, Letter January 24, 1847.

Cambridge July 10th 1847

Dr Doct

I recd ? a few days since enclosing Henry's Bills he has acted the part of promising Boy out there the money I remitted to him including what I handed you would have paid his room all the time and allowed him $2.25 per week for extra comforts enough I suppose he has ? ? of at least $5.00 per week more making his expenses while there about $9.00 per week exclusive of tuition. I had understood that it was against the ? of the institution to credit students without the leave of the faculty or weeks – those gentlemen who loaned him money & hired him Horses and Buggies do ? him & me & ? extremely ill favour. It is no credit to any gentlemans generosity to encourage in such a way, and for ? too the Idle & Extravagant propensities of such a Boy & I feel under no obligation to them & if I pay these Bills it will be when my sch-? ? off. I had no thought that he owed any thing of any amount. I had ? him money to pay Mr. Wheelers Bill which I suppose went for Buggy hire & here let me say he must have sold or gave away the Books he bought the first session & appropriated the proceeds the same way as he has none of them. I find him charged with Websters Dictionary $3.75– Taylors History $3 & a grammar? He says he left in the library of his society–in that much I doubt. It is settled with me that Henry goes back no more. It certainly took up his whole time expending ? $9.00 per week and would be too much to ask such a spirit to do that & study some into the bargain. It would ruin his constitution. I ? you $25.00 take your own advance out of it to pay his Boarding house bill & the student Morgan the loaned money–when I get more I'll remit and direct its appropriation–had I known Henry's habits there I would have arrested it at once I hope you have few who acquit themselves in this way.

Very respectfully   Your sincere friend

James Rariden[379]

As an administrator Simpson was paternalistic, and as a teacher of mathematics or anything else, peerless. One of Indiana Asbury's first students recalled, "He was a great teacher for he encouraged pupils to think. No book was authority. Whatever statement would not stand the test of argument was to be condemned. He encouraged students to challenge every

---

379   UMA, DePauw University. Simpson papers, Letter July 10, 1847.

statement which their judgment did not approve, and when challenged, the soundness of the statement was challenged in the classroom."[380] Another recalled that in conversation, "He was brilliant, magnetic. It mattered not what the theme was---abstract science, mathematics, logic, rhetoric, languages, history, politics---he was equally versed in all, and his classes were always delighted when he would lead them outside the routine of the hour."[381] Ex-Governor A.G. Parker of Indiana recollected: "I remember as if it were but yesterday the occasion when I first saw him. I was a bashful boy of 16 who would come to enter the preparatory department of the college and I called at his house. He looked to me like a plain, warm-hearted and hospitable farmer and in afterlife, he always looked to me so. He greeted me with overflowing kindness …. He called to his wife and introduced me to her; and they both invited me to visit them often, and assured me I should always be gladly received."[382] The word got out and the applications came in, of which the following is choice:

February the 4th 1845

Dear Sirs. Mr. Mathew Simpson

With pleasure I'll take my pen in
Hand to inform you that I want
To come to School two you
Providing we Can Agree on the
Terms of It
I want you to write to me and let
Me know What is the best terms
That you will let me Come
In the first place I will inform
You that there are two others
That wants to Come If they
Can Agree on your terms.
We want to know what you have
A Session or what you have a
Year We want to know what

---

380   Manhart, 29.
381   Crooks, 163.
382   Ibid., 165.

> For Chance there will be for
> Renting a room and upon what
> Terms we Can get one
> Well we want to Study Arithmetic
> English grammar & Latin and geography
> And writing
> Tuition or not
> And if there is I think probable
> That We Can Come
> We have some little money
> We want to (k)now Whither the
> Money has to be payed in advance
> Again Want to (k)now when the Spring
> Session will Commence
> Write as soon as you receive our letter
> And direct it to Georgetown Post Office
> Brown County. Indiana
> Yours untell death   Alfred H. Young
>   Isaac H. Walker
>   Robert Shanion[383]

No matter however low he had bowed to the shrine of education in his "Inaugural," Simpson provided spiritual leadership for his school. He believed that Christian nurture was as important, if not more important, than knowledge inventory. Col. John Ray recalled that, "Eminent as Dr. Simpson was in his position of President, teacher, friend; all his greatness was magnified, when he sought to teach the religion of the Lord Jesus Christ. He was more zealous to make Christians out of the students than to impart secular instruction."[384] In 1847, a revival broke out in the college and academics were mostly shut down for two weeks. "During this meeting none were so active and as constantly employed as Dr. Simpson. He seemed like a father, weeping with the penitent, and utilizing the matchless power of his eloquence to win souls for Christ; and with such success that the entire town was for days more like a camp meeting than anything else."[385]

---

383 UMA, DePauw University, Simpson papers, Letter February 4, 1845.
384 Crooks, 164.
385 Ibid., 164.

Naturally, some students for whatever reason identified with Simpson more than others, and he favored them, often becoming lifelong friends. James Harlan must have reminded the President of himself, when he trekked to Madison College a decade earlier. Harlan arrived at Asbury, dressed in "homemade shoes without stockings and in homespun cotton trousers and carrying all his belongings in a red bandanna handkerchief."[386] Years later Harlan wrote Simpson, "It will afford me the highest gratification to accept your kind invitation to call on you and Mrs. Simpson, whenever an opportunity may be presented. This cannot be otherwise, for as bad as human nature is, there are but few I think, who could forget or fail to appreciate the personal kindness with which you have favored me in bygone years."[387] Humorously, one of Simpson's first challenges consisted of defending student John Wheeler. The College Board as well as other conservatives within the community desired the President to censure Wheeler for "fiddling" on Sunday. Wheeler was a musical genius, capable of playing the guitar, bass violin, violin and accordion---maybe not all at the same time. Evidently, Simpson allowed such profaning of the Sabbath to take place at his home. The President took no action on the matter. No one regretted Simpson leaving Asbury more than did Wheeler, who was by then an Asbury professor.[388]

Though ethically conservative, Simpson transcended legalism and contentious nitpicking all of his ministerial life. And he had sufficient ego strength to allow himself to be the object of a practical joke, especially if he was allowed the last word. While walking after dark in Greencastle, he heard the words of a student who had not identified the College President. "Backup here, old fellow and carry me across the street." Simpson completed the task, startling his incarnational baggage with "John, I guess that is enough for one time."[389]

---

386   Irving Frederick Brown. "Indiana Asbury University: A History," *Bulletin of DePauw University*, Vol. X, No. 4 (November, 1913) 13.

387   LOC. Simpson papers, Letter January 5, 1856, Container six.

388   "The Arrival of Dr. Simpson."

389   Bishop David Moore. "Bishop Simpson–A Centennial Appreciation," *Pittsburgh Christian Advocate* (June 29, 1911).

But to be sure, Simpson did not make everyone happy. Evidently, Simpson was displeased with the teaching of John Weakly,[390] and planned either to fire him or so antagonize him that he would resign. He also desired to make room for William Larrabee on the faculty, a placement that the university could not afford without Weakly's removal.[391] Simpson and Ames colluded against Weakly, promising Nutt the chair of mathematics, if he would support them in the removal of Weakly. Weakly was asked to resign and left with considerable bitterness, later becoming President of Springfield High School and Female College, just outside of Cincinnati. Nutt did not receive the chair of mathematics as promised, but instead was assigned to teach Greek and Greek *littérateur*. The jaundiced Nutt left Indiana Asbury in 1843, but returned in 1847.

In his journal, Nutt charged Simpson with one of the most condemning indictments that we have on record. "He kept himself thoroughly posted in regard to the character of those about him and their movements. All the gossip of the town and the private affairs of the families and individuals of neighborhoods, he managed to have reported to him immediately and he was strongly suspected of employing a system of espionage not only over the students but over the citizens of Greencastle and the preachers of the Conference." Nutt further accused Simpson of being vindictive. "He was never known to conciliate an enemy, but it was a war of extermination. He was remarkably successful in throwing things in the way of those he did not like; and this was done secretly, the hand that gave the blow was always concealed."[392] Nutt was not alone in his assertion. Some of the students suspected that the President had a system of espionage, and possessed an "almost omnipresence in discovering their faults."[393]

---

390   Weakly's name is variably spelled, "Weakly, Weekly, Weakley, and Weekley."

391   Manhart claims that Simpson met Larrabee at the 1840 General Conference, but Simpson was not at the 1840 General Conference. In all likelihood, it was Ames who broached the invitation for Larrabee to come to Asbury. Manhart argues that Larrabee was more capable than either Simpson or Nutt. He had the reputation of working an eighteen-hour day. One visitor to Larrabee's home observed that he "wrote until midnight, then had evening devotions with a long chapter from the Bible and a long prayer, and then awakened his guest for morning devotions at 4 a.m." Manhart, 33.

392   UMA, DePauw University, "Cyrus Nutt Journal."

393   Clark, *The Life*, 91.

Storming Through Indiana

The main fight that Simpson had was not with students or faculty, but with finances. It was a day-to-day struggle to keep the institution afloat. The primary responsibility for the President of a small private institution was begging for money. Thus, Simpson spent his weekends and summers traveling to churches, camp meetings, Annual Conferences and whatever events took place in the sparsely populated Indiana, to incarnate the identity of the institution in the mind of the public. If public speaking was the best means for raising money and attracting students, the embryonic college could have not had a better representative. Thomas Goodwin described Matthew Simpson's appearance and his preaching at the Indiana Annual Conference in the fall of 1839. "His personal appearance was a perpetual disappointment. He was too youthful to meet expectations, being less than thirty years old, and his dress was of jeans neat and well-fitting; but not what most expected of so distinguished a man. His praise as a preacher was in all the land, and everyone desired to hear him."[394]

Simpson did not sit around waiting for a monetary gusher. He hit the trail. A contemporary recalled that Simpson preached, "In almost every town and hamlet in the state."[395] In June 1843 he wrote Ellen, "My health has been better than I expected considering my labors. I think that I am over the severest work. And though my voice is much broken I was able to speak twice yesterday with considerable ease. Since I left you I have delivered thirty sermons, and twenty-three lectures, and have traveled upwards of four hundred miles in twenty-three days .... Before I see you I've yet to travel two hundred twenty miles, to preach twelve or thirteen times and deliver some ten lectures."[396] Despite the duress of riding a horse, Simpson enjoyed the country side taking note of flowers and plants such as Sundial, Sweet William, Sweet Lydia, Golden Button, and French Pink Ladies Slipper. Even more remarkable were the few industrial endeavors

---

394   Goodwin. "Introduction," *The Autobiography of Joseph Tarkington*, 18-19.
395   UMA, Drew University, Crooks papers, John Smith's "Address at DePauw," June 12, 1887.
396   Crooks, 174-175.

taking place throughout Indiana: forge furnaces, flower mills, and Robert Owens' various manufacturing enterprises at New Harmony, which was the "nucleus of infidelity."[397]

Ironically, a man without a college education stormed throughout Indiana and beyond to sell illiterates on the value of a college education. But this irony worked to Simpson's and Indiana Asbury's favor. These illiterates knew good preaching, and Simpson could preach. And he could preach to the common person in spite of or because of having possessed none of the advantages of a genteel heritage. Maybe the children of homesteaders could become like Simpson, which resulted in aspiring parents not so much sending their children to Asbury, but rather sending them to Simpson. Thomas Goodwin, years later, recalled the essence of Simpson's effectiveness: "It is not extravagant to say that of the first thousand who attended this institution seven hundred would never have attended any school higher than the very poor country schools of the period but for the influence of the college agents, seconded by the faithful preachers of that day. To this must be added the wonderful magnetism of our first president. Wherever he went to preach he awakened an interest in our University."[398]

In no situation, was Simpson more effective than at a camp meeting. Asbury had referred to the methodology of camp meetings as Methodism's "battle axe."[399] No denomination used the instrument more effectively than Methodism, and the instrument fit Simpson's hands perfectly. At one such meeting in the summer of 1842 in the vicinity of Greencastle, Simpson

---

397   Clark, *Pulpit and Platform*, 170.

398   Thomas Goodwin. "Reminiscences of the Early Days of Indiana Asbury University," *Semi-Centennial Reminiscences and Historical Addresses: 1831-1887* (Greencastle, Indiana: DePauw University, 1887) 9.

399   The following from Russell Richey places camp meetings in American Methodism's historical and theological context. "They created, for a few days, a cathedral-in-a-grove, a community ordered as clearly around its central tabernacle as in any European city. They permitted garden-like, confessional times during which individuals and families could wrestle with the spiritual challenges that the grove preaching induced. And always they dealt with wilderness—the natural wilderness tamed by clearing the underbrush, the human wilderness of mischief makers and liquor sellers and ruffians constrained by the guards or watch, the spiritual wilderness faced by those unconverted, who came, perhaps under the pressure from mother or spouse, and the wilderness they created by bringing black and white together (and later Native Americans as well)." Russell E. Richey. *Methodism in the American Forest* (New York: Oxford University Press, 2015) 79.

spoke on the "Multitude in the Valley of Decision," and described the "soul of a glorified saint looking into the face of the Redeemer." An attender remembered that, "the young and the old, the black and the white, the polished student and the ignorant day-laborer, the earnest Christian and the Apostate, all shouting; laughing, crying, as their emotions moved them …. for more than an hour, the excitement was so intense, that all efforts to control it, even by singing, were unavailing."[400] In the vicinity of Indianapolis, Simpson preached from Revelation 20:12, "And I saw the dead, small and great stand before God," Reverend James Hill remembered, "The effect of the sermon was electric, awful, and utterly indescribable."[401]

Indiana Becomes Insolvent

There was not only the need to raise money, but to make available funds go as far as possible. From 1839 to 1843, the teachers were paid in college "warrants."[402] One professor reported that, "Frequently a whole year passed without so much as five dollars coming into the hands of any one professor. I did not receive money enough to pay my postage." The faculty took care of the shrubbery on the campus and for their pay were allowed to cut and keep the hay which grew on the grounds. The faculty was also charged with making sure that cows did not graze on the campus, and the President with preventing the students from "playing ball against the college building."[403] In the early 40s the college began to sell "subscriptions and contributors were given credit for delivering wood and food for the faculty and staff." In the middle 40s the President and trustees sold perpetual scholarships. By 1844, the school was $1,164.00 in arrears of Simpson's $1,000.00 per year salary.[404] If it was not already difficult enough to raise money among poor Methodists for a nascent college, Indiana found itself in a depression which had only worsened since the 1837 Panic.

---

400   Manhart, 28.

401   UMA, Drew University, Crooks papers, Letter, James Hill to George Crooks, n. d.

402   Phillips and Baughman. 24.

403   Irving Frederic Brown. "Indiana Asbury University: A History," *DePauw Bulletin* (November 1913) 13.

404   Phillips and Baughman, 24.

The completion and profitability of the 362 mile "Clinton Ditch" between Albany and Buffalo, New York, led several states to believe they could duplicate the transportation marvel. Indiana, in particular, "paid dearly for the delusion."[405] When on January 9, 1832, the Indiana legislature authorized the building of the Wabash-Erie Canal, cannon fired, and people whooped through the streets of Indianapolis, fireworks lit the skies, bonfires were built, and such a large boisterous crowd rushed into the home of Governor Noble, that the floor gave way. The construction superintendents contracted mostly Irish labor, who always had a, "wad of something tied up in a black greasy old pocket handkerchief and crowd you, and grease you, and stench you to death."[406] A "jiggerboss" walked the work line all day keeping the laborers supplied with whiskey.

An optimistic and myopic budget had the canal begun in 1832, finished in 1835, and paid for in 1836. Paul Fatout adroitly reminds us that, "As a careful job of close figuring, the exercise would have been perfect if human affairs and the forces of nature affecting canal building were as free from vagaries as sums in addition."[407] Further appropriations by the Indiana Legislature, January 27, 1836, authorized the borrowing of $10 million for twenty-five years at five per cent. Again, Fatout summarizes, "The mammoth Hoosier system of internal improvements was conceived in madness and nourished by illusion."[408] The $500,000 interest a year on the loan was more than the total revenue of Indiana taxation. Governor David Wallace, who spoke at Simpson's "Inaugural," was called, "One of the craziest, most ultra and whole hog advocates of the system."[409] It was also Wallace who ordered soldiers to drive the Pottawatomies out of Indiana into Kansas. "The two month journey harried by stifling weather, shortage of water, lack of food, and any humane treatment caused many deaths, variously reported as up to one-fifth of the tribe."[410]

In July 1841, Indiana defaulted on its mortgage payment, and was eventually left with an $18,000,000.00 debt. The canal was not only laden

---

405 Fatout, 12.
406 Ibid., 47.
407 Ibid., 45.
408 Ibid., 76.
409 Ibid., 87.
410 Ibid., 91.

with debt, but with depravity. A Western Seaman's Society missionary sent to the Canal Zone in the late 1840s despaired that, "There is more out breaking wickedness here than on any other thoroughfare of equal magnitude in the Union .... Not one boat in ten had either a Bible or Testament on board."[411] In the short-sightedness of political exuberance, Governor James Ray had hypothesized in 1828, "If the cost of building the Wabash Canal should exceed a million, the state had the means promised by the land; if additional sums were necessary, borrowing would not damage state credit if canal profits were sufficient to pay interest on the loans and extinguish the principal."[412] The canal builders should have listened to the Miami Indian, Chapine, who when his cabin was dismantled to make room for the canal said, "Can't do it; won't rain enough to fill it; white man a fool; the Great Spirit made the rivers."[413]

Andrew Jackson had already shut down the National Bank, which initiated the founding of scores of local banks. These banks were mostly west of the Alleghenies, and there was no federal agency to regulate currency and to prevent over-speculation. The inflation of money, the deflation of land, and excessive borrowing shut down banks almost as fast as they opened. No state was more excessive than Indiana. When in 1837 Jackson ordered that, "land offices would receive nothing but gold and silver in payment for public land making an exception for actual settlers," local banks were left with loans on depreciated farms and internal improvements. "By 1839, the state had got into such a financial condition that it could not meet its bills as they fell due .... The people of Indiana had speculated and piled mortgage upon mortgage on their properties, on the faith that the state would complete its internal improvements .... The state could get no money. To remedy the situation, Indiana printed money on red paper which became known as 'red dog currency.'"[414] This resulted in merchants, millers, plank

---

411   Ibid., 131.

412   Ibid., 40.

413   Ibid., 40.

414   William Henry Smith. *The History of the State of Indiana from the Earliest Explorations by the French to the Present Time: Containing an Account of the Principal Civil, Political and Military Events from 1763 to 1903*, Volume 2 (Indianapolis, IN: B. L. Blair Company, 1897) 610.

road companies, issuing their own money on blue paper called "blue pup."[415] Obviously, it became difficult to assign consistent value to either the blue or red paper, and inflation was rampant, not to mention unscrupulous currency investing and trading.

What the board of internal improvements did not expect to happen was a dramatic decline in the value of land. Assessed value per acre of land was $8.23 in the 1837 tax year. In 1842, value per acre had fallen to $3.73.[416] Simpson found himself President of a college appraised at one half the value than when he had landed on its campus. No wonder Simpson became fighting mad when the state legislature suspended interest on its $8,000 loan to competitor, Presbyterian Wabash College at Crawfordsville in 1842, in all likelihood by the influence of the Henry Ward Beecher cabal. At the end of his first year Simpson had to report to the trustees a deficit of $449, an indebtedness which by 1842 had increased to $4,610.[417]

Beginning Tension with Edward Ames

As if he did not have enough to do, the Indiana Annual Conference elected Simpson as its Recording Secretary.[418] Ames was secretary before Simpson, but his new job as Secretary of the Missionary Society called for extensive travel. Over the next four years Ames traveled some twenty-four thousand miles back and forth between Minnesota and Texas. He camped out much of the time, and on one occasion, had nothing but maple sugar to eat.[419] Simpson not only took copious notes during the sessions, but prepared them for publication. That responsibility, along with his college presidency almost assured him of being elected as a delegate to the General Conference of 1844. Quite likely, his preaching travels made him the most

---

415   Ibid., 610-611.

416   "Sovereign Default and Repudiation: The Emerging Market Debt Crisis in the United States: 1839-1843," cconweb.umd.edu/Wallace/paper/sovereign default and repudiation. 24.

417   Sweet, *Indiana-Asbury DePauw*, 56.

418   Simpson served as Secretary in 1843, 1845, 1846, and 1847. UMA, Drew University, The Methodist Episcopal Church, Indiana Conference Minutes, 1844-1851, see 188. These Minutes have been typed from the original manuscript copies by the Northern Indiana Conference Historical Society.

419   Charles Manning Walker. *History of Athens County, Ohio* (Cincinnati: Robert T. Clark and Company, 1869) 420–425.

recognizable person in the state of Indiana. Indiana pastor, Thomas Eddy, described Simpson as secretary of the Conference.

> He who sits at the secretary's table is Matthew Simpson. There is nothing in his appearance to suggest to the casual observer the vigor of his mind and the brilliancy of his genius. He is stooped in gait, and there is a hint of carelessness in his dress. When conducting public worship he reads his hymns and lessons in so plain and straightforward a manner that as yet there is no indication of his wonderful ability. Still his talents and piety have won him a reputation second to none in our church.[420]

Despite his disheveled appearance, Simpson was a master of order in his own life and that of his institution. The suspicions of his spying on both faculty and students were a result of his micro-management. Simpson meant for Asbury to be a well-ordered academy of higher learning, but he did not run it like a military academy. The following from Edward Edwards in 1846 tells us that although there was structure, it was not strictly enforced.

> We study in our rooms and recite in the college. The bell rings to awaken us at four in the morning, but we do not mind it much, but get up about 6 a.m., have breakfast, study a while, and at 9 a.m. go to the college for morning prayer … the recitations commence and continue till noon, when we return to our rooms and after dinner, are supposed to spend the afternoon in study till 4 or 5 p.m. Then we are free for recreation until after supper, we are expected to go to our rooms and study till the 9 p.m. bell, which means bedtime and lights out, but this is a question of honor among the students as there are no monitors or spies sent as to watch over us.[421]

No doubt, Simpson was the pride of Indiana Methodism, increasingly to the annoyance of Edward R. Ames. Ames was formally educated at Ohio University in Athens, Ohio. Five years older than Simpson he was robust in physique, handsome in appearance, fastidious in dress and second only to Simpson in oratorical ability. His second fiddle status would grate on him all of his life and at times, cause him to double-cross his "friend." Lucien Berry, an agent for the college and later President, could not understand Ames' about face, when Simpson had been encouraged by his board of trustees to attend an "Evangelical Christian Conference" in England, and had accepted

---

420   Charles Sims. *The Life of Rev. Thomas M. Eddy* (New York: Phillips and Hunt, 1880) 147-150.
421   John J. Baughman. *Our Past, Their Present: Historical Essays on Putnam County Indiana* (Greencastle, Indiana: DePauw University, 2008) 58.

the invitation.[422] "Brother Ames bearing on the whole subject in relation to your leaving the University was singular and mysterious …. Then again; there was something of superciliousness in his bearing which was wholly inexplicable."[423] Before Berry wrote his letter, Ames had attempted to diffuse some of the rumors about his duplicity on the trip. He wrote Simpson:

> A number of circumstances have conspired for some time past very much to perplex & mystify me until I had finally come to the conclusion that for some reason or other you had not only ceased to be my friend but had become my enemy. It is not necessary perhaps to dwell on these matters now any further than to say that I thought your letter in answer to the one which I wrote you from Salem did not breathe the same spirit which had previously marked our correspondence …. I wrote you a damning letter the other day, from the crustiness of which you will very rationally conjecture that I was in an ill humor.[424]

Ames had stirred up enough protest that Simpson decided against the trip. The relationship was patched up, but these cross currents would continue for the rest of their lives. Ames died five years before Simpson; thus, both of them lived to be just short of their 73rd birthday. Simpson recorded in his *Cyclopaedia* concerning Ames: "He was a man of broad views, an eloquent preacher, an able and skillful presiding officer, and a strong advocate of all church interests."[425] One of Ames' most lasting legacies was as the founding principal of Lebanon Seminary in 1828, Lebanon, Illinois under Methodist auspices. Peter Cartwright chaired the board and suggested a permanent name, McKendree College, which was adopted in 1830.[426] Simpson preached Ames' funeral which was held at Baltimore, April 1879, and stated, "Few

---

422   This action was taken by the Indiana Asbury Board of Trustees, March 19, 1846. "That should it meet the views of President Simpson, and should the way providentially open, it will be a source of high gratification, to the members of this Board and the community represented by them, to have him attend the world's convention, to be held in the city of London, in June next, for the purpose of further considering and promoting an evangelical alliance among the orthodox Protestant denomination of Christendom." UMA, DePauw University, Indiana Asbury University Board minutes, March 19, 1846.

423   UMA, DePauw University, Simpson papers, Letter, Lucien Berry to Matthew Simpson, April 15, 1846.

424   UMA, DePauw University, Simpson papers, Letter March 24, 1846.

425   *Cyclopaedia*, 34.

426   Patrick H. Folk. "McKendree College: The First 100 Years" in *McKendree College History 1928-1978* (Paducah, KY: Turner Publishing Company, 1996) 8.

men knew Bishop Ames as well as I did. I met him forty years ago, when he was in the prime of life in Indiana, and since then I have been almost constantly associated with him in the work of the church. We were delegates to the same conference, were elected on the same ballot, and our hearts have been ceaselessly knit together. He was then a man of vigorous frame and commanding presence with great powers of endurance."[427]

Cousin Joseph Tingley

The single greatest gift which Matthew Simpson gave Indiana Asbury University was Matthew's Tingley's son, Joseph Tingley, who taught in Greencastle for 30 years (1849-1879). Simpson persuaded his eleven-years-younger cousin to enter Asbury as a student in 1843. Tingley, when he arrived, observed that the town "presented a rude and uninviting appearance," leading the 21-year-old to conclude that the 900 inhabitants must have "expended their whole stock of enterprise and public spirit upon the one object of founding the University, and had nothing left for further improvement." Tingley taught astronomy, botany, chemistry, geology, meteorology, natural history, physics and physiology as well as playing the violin, the cello, the piccolo, clarinet, and flute. He also excelled at painting, having attended the Cincinnati School of Art before coming to Allegheny College. According to one student's calculation, "There is probably no institution in the world where the experimental sciences are taught more successfully, or a greater variety of scientific demonstrations are employed." Tingley also "acted as a civil engineer for Greencastle for several years, platting the streets and alleys and laying off lots for the newly-created Forest Hill Cemetery." He was in constant demand on the lecture circuit, entertaining his audiences with scientific experiments, explaining the positive relationships between science and religion, and adamantly denouncing Darwin.

The University Board thought Tingley not to be giving sufficient time to his academic duties. In 1879, the entire faculty was asked to resign behind a theological smokescreen. Tingley refused to offer his resignation and was fired in spite of the loud protest of his Bishop Cousin.[428] Simpson wrote

427   LOC, Simpson papers, Scrapbook D, Container twenty-three.
428   Manhart, 116.

Chairman of the Board, Judge Eglehart, with the plea that, "The chair of natural science in many institutions has been the source of skeptical speculation and it is important to have it filled with devout Christians." And if they were going to fire Tingley, could not they wait another year, so that his cousin could make "arrangements?"[429] But neither piety nor convenience was sufficient consideration. Tingley died at the age of 70, while teaching art at Campbell Normal University in Houghton, Kansas. One of his former students wrote, "Joseph Tingley was a man of rare and versatile genius, accomplished in many arts. He was an accomplished artist, a fine musician, a skillful mechanician, a thorough scientist, a popular lecturer on scientific subjects, a painstaking teacher and a tireless worker."[430]

It ran in the family.

---

429   UMA, DePauw University, Simpson papers, Letter July 14, 1879.
430   "Joseph Tingley: Professor of Natural Science," UMA, DePauw University, Tingley papers, March 29, 1993.

Chapter Six:
A Jubilee in Hell

The Tinderbox

Presbyterian Charles Finney declared that, "No doubt, there is a jubilee in Hell every year about the time of the meeting of the General Assembly."[431] If he had been a Methodist he would have said the same of the 1844 General Conference of the Methodist Episcopal Church. The ultraism of the 1830s which included temperance, sabbatarianism, Millerism, and all other issues of millennialism, was now almost completely focused in one issue, abolitionism. Simpson's neck was so tightly fastened to the yoke of attempting to pull a college through crisis after crisis that he hardly had time or energy to look up and detect the brewing storm. Plus, Simpson's temperament of moderation was incompatible with the alarmists who set dates for the appearance of Christ and the overthrow of slavery. There were rumors of schism, but the preaching, fundraising President was not yet putting his ear to the ground to catch the rumblings of ecclesiastical politics.

Gilbert Barnes argued that by 1842, congressional Washington had reached a turning point in its anti-slavery stance. The abolitionist, Joshua Leavitt, editor of *The New York Evangelist*, traveled to Washington in 1841, and buttonholed as many congressmen as would listen to him. The flame-throwing Theodore Weld, "logic on fire," as John Greenleaf Whittier referred to him, set up shop in the alcove of the Library of Congress located in the Capitol building. (The Library was located in the new Jefferson building in 1897.) Weld became a cheerleader and advisor for a coalition of congressmen, who led the abolitionist cause within the House of Representatives. Leading

---
431   Whitney R. Cross. *The Burned-Over District: The Social and Intellectual History of Enthusiastic Religion in Western New York, 1800-1850* (Ithaca, New York: Cornell University Press, 1981) 258.

the way in the formulation of anti-slavery petitions were Congressmen Joshua Giddings, Seth Gates, William Slade, and John Quincy Adams, the former President. After visiting Adams' house for dinner, Weld recorded that "The old patriarch talked with as much energy and zeal as a Methodist at a camp meeting. Remarkable man!"[432] Adams had spoken to the House for most of an afternoon, and Weld reported that he was as "fresh and chased as a boy."[433]

In the meantime, the Methodist Church was a tinderbox with more and more inflammatory resolutions from the Annual Conferences shoved into it. Eventually it would not shut. Orange Scott cried out in the 1836 General Conference, "When you can put your foot on one of the burning mountains and smother its fires—when you can roll back the current of the thundering falls of Niagara or stop the sun in its course, you may then begin to think about crushing abolitionism! Sir, the die is cast—the days of the captivity of our country are numbered! Its redemption is written in Heaven!"[434] William Lloyd Garrison called the Methodist Conference a "cage of unclean birds and a synagogue of Satan."[435] Mississippi slaveholders declared that anyone who circulated abolition papers was "justly worthy in the sight of God and man of immediate death."[436] Prior to the 1844 Conference, Northern Methodists responded by making the peace at all costs, Elijah Hedding "the butt of their ridicule and in some of their lectures, a mock slave auction was enacted with Bishop Hedding and his wife in burlesque, sold as slaves."[437]

The various periodicals within Methodism slung accusatory barbs. One editor referred to Luther Lee, one of the leaders of the 1843 Wesleyan Methodist schism, as "a metaphysical tadpole always wriggling to stir up the

---

432   Gilbert Barnes. *The Anti-Slavery Impulse: 1830-1844* (New York: Hardcover Art Brace, 1933) 180.

433   Ibid., 184. In fact, in June and July of 1838, the seventy-one year old John Quincy Adams held the floor of the House of Representatives for three weeks straight as he spoke against territorial expansion and slavery. See Fred Kaplan. *John Quincy Adams: American Visionary* (New York: Harper, 2014) 508.

434   Charles Bower Swaney. *Episcopal Methodism and Slavery with Sidelights on Ecclesiastical Politics* (New York: Negro University Press, 1926) 61.

435   Ibid., 65.

436   Ibid., 88.

437   Ibid., 89.

muddy waters of strife."[438] Another editor responded that some abolitionists "were morally and mentally deficient, and hence, totally incapable in conducting a process of thought." The Wesleyan abolitionist contingent assessed Thomas Bond, editor of the New York Christian Advocate, as so much below the common standard of Christian courtesy, that he resembled the "blackguardism of the grog shop."[439] That Thomas Bond did not drink alcohol was not of much importance in an irrational war of words. Probably not anymore rooted in fact was the accusation of abolitionists, who met in Holland, Maine, that within Methodism, "Two hundred traveling ministers held 1,600 slaves, 1,000 local preachers owned 10,000, and in all, Methodists held 207,900 slaves."[440] Where the abolitionists got their numbers was not as important as the anti-Southern attitude among Northern Methodists.

Little correlation has been made between the developing two-party system in the 1830s and the split of Methodism in 1844.[441] It is difficult to trace the voting patterns and party allegiances of the delegates to the 1844 General Conference. Whigs, though mostly located in the North, were not unilateral in their opinion on slavery. They were united in their bitter hatred of "King Andrew Jackson," no less than their revolutionary forefathers were united against King George III. Michael Holt, in his definitive treatment of the Whig party, writes, "From the Whigs' perspective, everything that Jackson had done demonstrated his intention to amass power in his own hands; to upset the constitutionally mandated balance among the branches of the federal government; to subvert or destroy the independence of other political leaders and voters through patronage, the influence of his pet banks,

---

438   Ibid., 109.

439   Ibid.

440   Ibid., 110.

441   Richard Carwardine argues that Methodists, "formed no political monolith, but cast their ballots full-range of political parties, losing electoral leverage as a result." But he afterward generalizes that, "We can confidently conclude that during the first party system, Methodists were very largely drawn into the ranks of Jeffersonian democracy. Under the succeeding party system, organized around the conflict between Jackson's democracy and its evolving opposition, the majority of Methodists probably maintained a democratic outlook, but a substantial body of the church rallied to Whiggery, including quite probably a majority of its ministers." In other words, according to Carwardine, about the time of the 1844 dividing Conference, Methodists were being converted from Democrats to Whigs. Richard Carwardine. "Methodist, Politics and the Coming of the American Civil War," *Church History* Vol. 69 (September 2000) 585, 590.

or intimidation; and thereby to crush popular liberty."[442] And even though in its early days Whiggery provided a coalition for "National Republican, anti-Mason and states' rights Southerners," by the 1844 Clay-Polk Presidential campaign, there had developed within the popular mind, "Polk, slavery, and Texas" versus "Clay, Union, and liberty." This popular perception brought more anti-slavery men into the Whig fold. One Southerner howled that, "The very continuance of an anti-slavery man will do the Whig Party more prejudice at the South than all other matters combined; there is more involved than even our great interest---they become questions of feeling---passionate---and reason is powerless to subdue or even alay them."[443]

Surely some of the above currents whirled around the 1844 General Conference. Holt claims that by 1840, "Abolitionists appealed to and showed the same moralistic fervor for reform that characterized the evangelical Protestant groups who normally supported the Whigs. The Liberty Party consequently cut into the ranks of Whiggery. It grew most rapidly in rural strongholds of Whiggery and revivalist sentiment like northern New England; upstate New York, western Massachusetts, the Western Reserve in northeastern Ohio, and Michigan."[444] Even if the two-party-system did not perfectly align with the northern-southern polarization of the 1844 Conference, it did nothing to broker a compromise.

A Delegate to the Critical 1844 General Conference

None of the above forebodings did anything to dampen the ardor of the thirty-three-year-old Simpson, who had never been east of the Allegheny Mountains, and was now about to make a 1,000 mile journey to America's largest city. The toughest part of the journey was the 100 miles by wagon from Greencastle to Columbus, Indiana. The trip was plagued with muddy roads, snow, holes which almost swallowed the wagon, and forded rivers, causing the ladies to gasp and groan. The corduroy road, bone jolting and posterior pounding, was the most violent invention ever devised for transportation. As the wagon fell into a trench, Ames' carpet bag fell off and the waggoneer

---

442   Michael Holt. *The Rise and Fall of the American Whig Party: Jacksonian Politics and the Onset of the Civil War* (New York: Oxford, 1999) 29.
443   Ibid., 313.
444   Ibid., 156.

was sent back to find it. On at least this one occasion, the farm-raised Ames out did Simpson. Simpson gave him due credit: "He mounted the saddle-horse, which, by the way had no saddle on him, and whose back was as sharp as a nor' wester, his feet were rested on the trace chains, for want of stirrups, and a large beech stick held erect over his shoulders served for a whip–and then the wagon, a red bed with a white muslin cover in hand–in road wagon style, well filled with livestock and lumber–altogether not a bad subject for a Cruikshank." The waggoneer, who found Ames' bag, and eventually caught up with the team, beat the saddle horse, "blind in one eye and very thin," with a fence rail, but even though the treatment evoked sympathy from Simpson, he admitted that the "beast of burden was completely cured for the rest of the journey."[445]

The rest of the trip would be by train and boat, but the peril was not yet over. Mother Sarah and Uncle Matthew boarded a paddle-wheeler at Cincinnati to accompany the Conference party as far as Wheeling, Virginia (now West Virginia). When helping his mother down the gangplank, Simpson stumbled and tore a hunk of flesh out of his leg. Upon arriving in Pittsburgh, the wound called for a week of convalescence at his in-laws, which was not all that bad. He needed the rest, and was visited by a constant flow of friends, who begged him to return to the Pittsburgh Conference. Simpson's travelogue gives us an accurate perception of what travel from the Midwest to the East Coast entailed in mid-nineteenth century America:

> It was the first time I had crossed the Allegheny Mountains and seen the Atlantic coast, traveling at that day was attended with difficulties unknown at present. I left Green Castle, Ind. where my home then was and traveled by private conveyance to South Columbus, Ind. Then the end of the only railroad in the state which extended from Madison, there we took the steamer to Cincinnati, and then a steamer from Cincinnati to Pittsburgh where I left Mrs. Simpson & two children. Passage from Pittsburgh was then by the canal which was navigable to Jonestown. The mountains were crossed by several inclined plains and the canal was taken again at Hollidaysburg, thence to Harrisburg, the journey from Pittsburgh to Harrisburg occupied from 3 to 4 days, at Harrisburg I took the stage to York and road through a beautiful section of country and at York, took the rail for Baltimore, the only portion of now is the Northern Central Road.[446]

---

445   LOC, Simpson papers, 1844 *Diary*, Container one.
446   LOC, Simpson papers, *Autobiography*, Container fifteen. The document covers

Simpson Begins a Life-Long Friendship with the Harper Brothers

While in New York City, Simpson boarded with Methodist James Harper, the mayor of the city, and founder of *Harper's Weekly*, which would become the most popular nineteenth century secular magazine in America.[447] The brothers, James and John, had started the business in 1817 under the business names "J. and J. Harper." When the brothers, Joseph and Fletcher, joined the firm in the 1820s, the corporate name became "Harper and Brothers." The earliest historian of Harper Brothers recalled the Methodist home in which the brothers were raised: "System and order ruled the household, and the Bible was read through in course at family prayers, genealogies, and all. To avoid a chapter, would've seemed to them like putting up a slight upon the word of God. The Sabbath was a solemn day, and the family was always regular at church."[448] Simpson may have observed that the Harper brothers were not the normative legalistic Methodists. John Harper was censured by Methodist conservatives when he allowed "his young children to participate in round dances at his home."[449]

---

the years 1844 to 1852, and was dictated to Simpson's stenographer, in all likelihood, Samuel Martin Stiles. Crooks wrote on the top of the first page, "Autobiographical: 1844–1852 contains account of his election to Episcopate. Very valuable." The 53 pages of this document are not numbered, and thus, I will refer to this resource as *Autobiography*.

447   Somehow a letter sent by Simpson in 1842 landed wrongly in the Harpers' hands and on returning it they invited him to "stay with them whenever in the City." LOC, Simpson papers, Letter, James Harper to Matthew Simpson, March 28, 1842, Container four. The postscript between the Harpers and Simpson did not take place until George Crooks published the Simpson biography with Harper Brothers. The Methodist Publishing House accused Crooks of betrayal. Simpson's hometown friends in Philadelphia stated, "We confess to a revulsion of feeling at the very thought of having the life of our great and good Bishop hawked around by book agents and used as a means of money making." LOC, Simpson papers, Scrapbook E, May 17, 1890, Container twenty- three.

448   J. Henry Harper. *The House of Harper: A Century of Publishing in Franklin Square* (New York: Harper, 1912) 22. Tyler Anbinder writes, "The defection of Democratic American Republicans to their former party, Harper's inability to reform municipal government, Whig determination to offer a credible opposition to the American Republicans and the fallout over the Philadelphia riots, all contributed to Harper's defeat in April, 1845." Tyler Anbinder. *Nativism and Slavery: The Northern Know-Nothings and the Politics of the 1850s* (New York: Oxford University Press, 1992) 12.

449   Harper, 59.

James Harper ran in 1843 on the newly-formed Nativist American Republican Party ticket, standing on a platform proclaiming that he would reform New York City. The *New York Enquirer* touted the "Great personal popularity of Mr. Harper ... and above all, the intense desire among all parties for a city government that should consult the welfare and promote the interests of the City."[450] Harper removed peddlers from the sidewalks, swine from the streets, beggars from the public markets, and racing carriages from New York avenues. But when he tried to enforce Sunday "Blue Laws," he found himself crossways with the First Ward, which granted itself 127 liquor licenses within a two-day period. When Harper added 200 police for a "day and night" watch, he had overplayed his New York reformation, and was voted out of office in April of 1845.

When James was asked, "Which of you is the Harper and which are the brothers?" he responded, "Each one is the Harper and the rest are brothers." *Harper's Magazine* founded in 1850 had a circulation of 50,000 within six months, and by 1853 a circulation of 150,000.[451] "They were among the first to employ steam as a motor power in the press room, and theirs was the first house in America that introduced the then almost unknown art of electric typesetting"[452]

In 1852, the entire publishing house burned to the ground, "the largest commercial loss by fire until that time in America."[453] James Harper's home may have been the most ostentatious house in which Simpson had ever stayed: "Five stories high, each story embellished with rows of four large windows. The house was previously owned by Lewis Tappan, the wealthy abolitionist merchant."[454] James firmly believed that the following three rules would ensure happiness: "Trust in God, pay your bills, and keep your bowels open."[455]

---

450   Ira M. Leonard. "Rise and Fall of the American Republican Party in New York City: 1843-1845," *New York Historical Society Quarterly* Vol. L (April 1966) 171.

451   Harper, 86.

452   Ibid., 9.

453   Ibid., 96.

454   Eugene Exman. *The Brothers Harper* (New York: Harper and Row Publishers, 1965) 189.

455   Harper, 248-249.

Harper's Weekly was the first periodical to give front-page coverage to a war, and in 1861 the Harpers were accused by Secretary of War Stanton of giving "aid and comfort" to the enemy, an offense punishable by death. Fletcher Harper scurried to Washington to placate Stanton's wrath. *Harper's Weekly* popularized the political cartoon by way of the skilled art of Thomas Nast. In 1867, Harper began publishing *Harper's Bazaar and Magazine*, aimed at upper middle-class America. No publication better typified Methodism's march into societal acceptance. "We perfected special arrangements with the leading European fashion journals, especially with the celebrated bazaar of Berlin, which at that time supplied fashion to the newspapers of Paris …. *Harper's Bazaar* was a pioneer fashion Journal of the country and in any true sense of the word, a paper for the family."[456] The day before James Harper was thrown from his carriage and killed, he was sufficiently prescient to sign a $10,000 insurance contract on his life, and the morning of his accident he had his photographic portrait taken.[457]

As Simpson sat in the Green Street Methodist Church for six weeks of debate, the moldy odor, stifling heat and tediousness of speech after speech transformed the honor of being a delegate into troubling disillusionment. His mind wandered as he looked around the sanctuary with its massive ten-foot wide pulpit and wrap-around balcony supported by white columns. It was possibly the most architecturally splendid Methodist Church in which he had ever sat.[458] At least he could write Ellen, and dispel his gloom with a bit of humor. "My acquaintance is small with the ladies of the city whom you mentioned in your last. Some of them are handsome, some ugly; many are very amiable and accomplished, but all in all, I wad'na gie my ain wife for any wife I see."[459]

---

456   Harper, 248-249.

457   In his *Cyclopaedia*, Simpson gave more attention to the Harper brothers than any other 19th century family. Large pictures and full biographical sketches of the four men were included. *Cyclopaedia*, 430.

458   Stanley J. Menking. *200 Years of United Methodism: An Illustrated History* (Madison, New Jersey: Drew University, 1984) 35.

459   LOC, Simpson papers, Letter May 25, 1844, Container three. This line comes from a poem, "I wad na gie my ain wife." Author unknown. LOC, Simpson papers, Scrapbook C, Container twenty-one.

Simpson was not quite as observant nor descriptive as Charles Dickens who stood on Broadway two years earlier, "Heaven save the ladies…how they dress. We have seen more colors in ten minutes than we should have seen elsewhere in as many days. What various parasols. Rainbow silks and satin! What pinking of thin stockings and pinching of thin shoes; and fluttering of ribbons and silk tassels and display of rich cloaks with gaudy hood and linings."[460] Guidebooks advertised New York as a place of "serious excitement." A young 1843 Union Theological Seminary student described Broadway as a street with "Faces and coats of all patterns, bright eyes, whiskers, spectacles, hats, bonnets, caps, all hurrying along in the most apparently inextricable confusion." The department stores, the newspaper headquarters, the monster hotels, made New York worthy of her pretensions as the metropolis of the Western Hemisphere[461] Simpson broke the conference monotony by shopping for Ellen. He bought a watch and key $60, shawl $6.25, print $1.76, gingham $2.94, skirt $1.20, alpaca $2.98, glove 0.56, handkerchief $2.04, which he carefully calculated to the grand sum of $77.73.[462]

An Inescapable Agenda - Slavery

Slavery walked through the door of the Green Street Church in the persons of Francis Harding and James Osgood Andrew and demanded full attention. The Annual Conferences had been deluged with anti-slavery petitions, and the New England Conference resolved to withdraw if slavery was not eradicated from the Church.[463] The Indiana Conference sent its

---

460   Charles Dickens. *American Notes* (Hazelton, Pennsylvania: The Electronic Classic Series, 2007) 83.

461   Edwin G. Burrows and Mike Wallace. *Gotham* (New York: Oxford University Press, 1999) 692, 688.

462   LOC, Simpson papers, 1844 *Diary*, Container one.

463   "The rumor and the threatened consequence created intense excitement. The Rev. James Porter (New England Conference) informed a 'prominent actor' in the subsequent proceedings that New England wanted, among other things, 'that Bishop Andrew should be required to purge himself of slavery or vacate the Episcopal office.' He was promised by this gentleman that the Baltimore Conference would go with New England in carrying its measures." Edward H. Myers. *The Disruption of the Methodist Episcopal Church, 1844-1846: Comprising a Thirty Years' History of the Relations of the Two Methodisms* (Nashville, TN: A.H. Redford, Agent, 1875) 42.

delegates with the support of fasting and prayer.[464] But either God was not paying attention or He willed that the Methodists provide the ecclesiastical arena for the showdown on American slavery. They showcased a shameful spectacle. In Donald Mathew's words, "All of the church had not been connected to abolitionist ideals, most certainly had been rudely shocked into viewing more honestly what the radical antislavery men had said was the character of Southern Methodism. Alienation and disruption clarified positions and made opposition simple; the South was now the enemy because it had decided to repudiate the Methodist heritage."[465] Caucuses were gathering even before the Conference began, positioning themselves and strategizing for the longest General Conference in the history of American Methodism, fifty days, May 1st- June 19th.

Simpson first spoke on the floor May 2, bringing a resolution from the Indiana Conference on "division," to divide the Indiana Conference into two parts, which was referred to the committee on Boundaries.[466] On May 4, he made his second foray into church politics with the innocuous motion, "Resolved that permission having been attained of the city authorities to have the street in front of the church covered with tan to prevent the disturbance of the Conference by the noise of vehicles & the Book Agents have the street so covered as soon as practicable."[467] Wednesday, May 15, was set aside for fasting and prayer. Simpson led morning devotions and the prayers were to be focused on the "six", who were to confer with the Bishops,

---

464 The resolution read, "We will recommend our people within the bounds of the Conference to observe Friday, the 26th day of April next as a day of fasting and prayer, with special reference to the meeting of our ensuing General Conference, fervently praying the Head of the Church as to direct that body in all their deliberations, that their minds may be to such conclusions as shall most tend to promote the glory of God and advance the Redeemer's Kingdom upon earth." Sweet, *Circuit Rider Days*, 326.

465 Donald Mathews. *Slavery and Methodism: A Chapter in American Morality, 1780–1845* (Princeton: Princeton University Press, 1965) 271.

466 In 1844, the Conference split into the North-Indiana and the Indiana Conferences along the National Road, approximately Interstate 70 today. Curiously, even though Greencastle was in the North Indiana Conference, Simpson stayed with the Indiana Conference as a member of the Indianapolis District. Indiana. Conference leaders wanted to keep their secretary and Simpson wanted to be visible in Indiana's capitol and seat of power. *Minutes of Annual Conferences of the Methodist Episcopal Church for the Years 1839-1845* Vol. III (New York: T. Mason and Lane, 1840) 527.

467 *Journal of the General Conferences of the Methodist Episcopal Church* Volume II, 1840, 1844 (New York: Carlton and Porter, 1856) 17.

and bring to the Conference a "permanent pacification plan." Ironically, James Osgood Andrew was chairing the session and called on his Southern colleagues to conduct the prayer meeting. Again Simpson played it safe on May 18 by moving that historical papers be collected and submitted to the next General Conference, in particular, "Correspondence touching the lives of any of our deceased Bishops or other ministers."[468] The Conference created an ad hoc committee of five to carry out the task.

Simpson addressed the Conference May 18 by bringing a resolution from the Education Committee, "Resolved that the committee on Sabbath schools be instructed to inquire as to the expediency of the Conference of electing a Board of Directors to superintend the general interest of Sabbath schools in our Church and the committee further consider the propriety of withdrawing from all connection with voluntary associations on the subject."[469] When P.P. Sanford opposed the resolution, in that there was already a Sunday School Union, Simpson responded that the "very object he had in view, was to withdraw from the Sunday School Union."[470] (The resolution was referred to the Committee on "Sabbath Schools and Voluntary Associations.") Simpson had given his fellow delegates their choice of committees:

> Ames selected for himself the Book Committee & Wiley a place on the Episcopacy, & I being on the Committee of Education and owing, however, to the excitement which subsequently followed, during General Conference, the Committee on Education met but a few times, and did but little business. Dr. Bascom, subsequently Bishop, was its chairman, & was also an active leader of the Southern party, and the author of the Protest, he was so occupied with those matters, the Committee on Education did nothing in the few meetings held, however, I formed a very pleasant acquaintance with Drs. Payne & Pierce, both of them subsequently Bishops in the Church South.[471]

After denying the appeal of Francis Harding, the Northerners began their verbal assault on James Andrew on May 22, and on that date he was requested to resign his office. On May 23, James Finley offered the motion

---

468	Ibid., 56.
469	Ibid., 68.
470	Ibid.
471	*Autobiography.*

that eventually passed: "That whereas Bishop Andrew has become connected to slavery by marriage and otherwise .... Resolved, that it is the sense of this General Conference that he desist from the exercise of this office so long as this impediment remains."[472] Over the next week a verbal barrage that was greater in quantity, if not intensity, than the artillery exchange that would take place at Gettysburg, threatened to shatter the chandeliers and crack the plaster on the walls of the Green Street Church. The Bishops believed that they could get around the impasse by moving to table the motion until the next General Conference. But the delegates would not accept postponement. The constant crossfire, laced with emotional and pathetic stories from the good old days, so agitated Simpson that he informed Ellen that another month would "ruin his health."[473]

It Just So Happened

On Monday, June 3, a Southern delegate reported that the treatment of James Andrew had produced "a state of things in the South which renders the continuance of the jurisdiction of this General Conference over these Conferences inconsistent with the success of the ministry of the slaveholding states."[474] Simpson's parliamentary prowess prevented a melee from breaking out on the Conference floor. He moved that "the Conference appoint brothers Olin, Durbin and Hamline as a committee to prepare a statement on the facts connected with the proceedings in the case of Bishop Andrew, and that they have liberty to examine the protest just presented by the Southern Brethren."[475] It was time to summarize what had transpired until now: The Baltimore Conference had immediately previous to the General Conference, March 13, ousted one of their ministerial members for owning slaves. One of the General Conference's first acts was to turn down Francis Harding's appeal for reinstatement, 117 to 56.[476] Thus, a precedent for the Andrew case had been set. Or maybe one should say that the kindling had been lit for the conflagration that was about to take place. Andrew had

---

472 *Journals*, 65-66.
473 LOC, Simpson papers, Letter May 25, 1844, Container three.
474 Journals, 109.
475 Ibid., 113.
476 Ibid., 33.

inherited slaves on three different occasions. Shortly, after his election to the Episcopacy, he inherited a young female mulatto who, when she was nineteen, refused to go to Liberia. Then at his mother-in-law's death, his wife had inherited a Negro boy. When his wife died, the boy became his. Through all of this, the Methodist Episcopal Church had paid no attention to the fact that Bishop Andrew owned slaves.

But it just so happened Andrew's wife died, and in early 1844 he remarried a woman who owned slaves. Even though he signed a deed of trust that secured the slaves to her, this particular inheritance was a detonator lit at exactly the right time for an explosion to take place in the 1844 Conference. Was the Conference going to allow a double standard for a Bishop owning slaves when an elder had been stripped of his credentials? Of course the Southerners could argue (which they did) that neither Maryland nor Georgia allowed emancipation. Plus, the Baltimore Conference was overriding a resolution of the 1840 General Conference:

> Resolved by the delegates of the several Annual Conferences in General Conference assembled, that under the provisional exception of the general rule of this Church on the subject of slavery, the simple holding of slaves or mere ownership of slaves in States or Territories where the laws do not admit of emancipation and permit the liberated slave to enjoy freedom constitute no legal barrier to the election or ordination of ministers to the various grades of office known in the ministry of the Methodist Episcopal Church and cannot therefore be considered as operating any forfeiture or right in view of such election or ordination.[477]

When Andrew inherited two slaves in his second marriage, he claimed to have kept them for "conscience sake." When asked why he did not simply have his wife turn the slaves over to her children he responded, "I would set them free, I'd wash my hands of them, and if they went to the devil I'd be clear of them. Sir, into such views of religion or philanthropy my soul cannot enter. I believe the providence of God has thrown these creatures into my hands and holds me responsible for their proper treatment."[478] After Andrew said, "I think a week is long enough for a man to be shot at and it

---

477   John Early. *The Methodist Church Property Case* (Richmond: John Early, 1851) 42.
478   Albert Redford. *The Methodist Episcopal Church South* (Nashville: A. H. Redford, 1871) 270.

is time the discussion should terminate," he offered to resign. The Southern delegation would not allow him.

Schooled by the Southerners

In the history-changing Conference of 1844, perhaps the most politically foreboding religious assembly held in the history of American Christianity, Simpson was dwarfed by seasoned ecclesiastics, who were only a little less articulate than the Webster-Clay-Calhoun triumvirate. Twice, he found himself verbally outmaneuvered. Simpson moved that, "While they could not admit the statements put forth in the protest, yet as a matter of courtesy they would allow it to be placed in the Journal; and that a committee consisting of Messrs. Durbin, Olin and Hamline be appointed to make a true statement on the case to be entered on the Journal," William Winans objected to the word "courtesy." He pontificated, "The minority asked no courtesy in the hands of the majority. They demanded it as a right."[479] When Simpson on May 27 asked the Chair to curtail a speech by Silas Comfort, Presiding Elder of the New York Oneida District, because it was, "Not in order to discuss the principles of a division under that resolution," Bishop Soule replied that the speaker was, "not more out of order than others had been, and he should allow him to proceed; the debate had taken a wide range." When Comfort continued his meandering incoherence, Simpson renewed his call to order and even wrote it out, presenting it to the Chair. But the College president was no match for Silas Comfort. Neither Simpson nor the Chair could stop him.[480] Simpson wrote a resolution which he never presented, a call for an 1846 General Conference, which would give its attention completely to slavery.[481]

---

479   *Report of the Debates in the General Conference of the Methodist Episcopal Church Held in the City of New York*, 1844. Robert West, Official Recorder (New York: G. Lane and C. B. Tippett, 1844) 212.

480   Luther Lee. *Debates of the Methodist Episcopal Church General Conference:* 1840-1844 (New York: O. Scott, 1844) 180.

481   "Whereas our brethren of the Southern Conferences have represented that such is the condition in which they are placed, that they are unable to remain under the jurisdiction of the General conference of the M. E. Church, and whereas this General Conference desires, if separation is unavoidable, that shall take place amicably and whereas the members of this Conference have not received full information as to the desire of our ministers and members throughout the connexion, on this subject-and whereas the Conference does not

Bishop James Osgood Andrew became a cause célèbre for the South and a symbolic target, a scapegoat for the North. James Kirby claims that in the case of Bishop Andrew, the question was whether slaveholding constituted a sufficient impediment to the exercise of Episcopal functions. He concludes, "It was certainly disingenuous, if not hypocritical to claim as some of his opponents would, that Andrew would be unable to serve the whole church. Bishops had not itinerated throughout the connection for twenty years." Kirby is essentially, but not technically correct.[482] Andrew had ordained Simpson as a deacon in the Pittsburgh Conference of 1835, and Joshua Soule had presided at the 1834 Pittsburgh Annual Conference. Stephen Olin attempted geographical compartmentalization of the problem. He responded with 5,000 words which could have been distilled into, "What's the big issue? Keep Andrew operative only in the South where he already is, and there will be peace." Or more formally stated, "Resolved, the General Conference recommend the Episcopacy to assign each superintendent his sphere of labor for the next four years."[483] The Conference perceived Olin's recommendation as only postponing the problem. Simpson apprised the leadership of the South as excelling the delegates from the North:

> During the controversy, the attention of the nation was considerably turned toward the proceedings, but more so in the South than in the North, as at that time Methodism had more influential friends among the leaders of the south than among those of the north. Dr. Capers was in correspondence with John Calhoun and other southern leaders who were watching over the phase of the slavery question, and the threatened disunion. The leaders of the south in the general conference were more shrewd and diplomatic than those of the north. The latter felt themselves strong both in the rightfulness

---

offer to possess full constitutional powers to act in the premises–Therefore, resolved, That we do call a General Conference to meet in two years to decide finally upon this subject, and that we also recommend this plan proposed by the committee appointed on this declaration if our Southern brethren, to this calm and prayerful consideration of the several Annual Conferences, and that they send their delegates prepared to act in the premises provided further that if the previous superintendents should be satisfied that there is no necessity for such a called Conference, they shall now have power to suspend the call." LOC, Simpson papers, 1844 *Diary*, Container one.

482   James E. Kirby. *The Episcopacy in American Methodism* (Nashville: Kingswood Books, 2000) 138.

483   Kirby, 106.

of their cause and the strength of their numbers. The others knew they were in the minority, and hence resorted to greater tact.[484]

The Southern delegates argued that the General Conference was promoting a double standard for an Elder and a Bishop. The former would be allowed to continue in ministry in the South as a slave holder, but the latter would not. Plus, to remove an Elder would require a trial, but the General Conference was going to defrock Andrew by fiat. The General Conference would not strip Andrew of his ministerial credentials; rather, it decided that Andrew would "desist" from exercising the office of Bishop. The reprimand was so light that the Conference concluded Andrew's office of Bishop would be left in the *Minutes, Discipline and Hymnal*, and a separate Annual Conference presiding schedule would include him, in case he decided to reverse his stance and release his slaves. (The alternate schedule was never created.) Curiously, the moral integrity and purity of Andrew's character was constantly affirmed throughout the Conference, even by Northerners. Most of the debate was not about the unrighteousness of slavery, but about the constitutional authority of the General Conference to remove a Bishop. Even the author and prime mover of the "desist" resolution, James Finley, was careful to defend Andrew's integrity.

> The resolution does not impeach the character of Bishop Andrew in any way; and as no brother here would deny the fact that he had become connected with slavery, the resolution is predicated on the principle, that the act had brought after it circumstances which would impede and prevent his circulation as an itinerant general superintendent. What do we request of Andrew in that resolution? We don't dispose him as a Bishop; we only say, it is the sense of the General Conference that he ought to cease to exercise the office till this embarrassment ceases. I do not wish the Bishop to resign.[485]

Non-negotiable Cultures

To refer to the Andrew situation as a temporary "embarrassment," was highly naïve, if not totally ignorant of the Southern ethos which ensconced the issue. Slavery was a way of life, the fabric of the South's economy and social order, a subjugation of a race, and a class strata that in the view of

---

484   *Autobiography*.
485   *Debates*, Lane and Tippett, 100.

Southern leadership was fully supported and practiced in Scripture. In the North, abolitionism had permeated society through a populist press. No wonder the first martyr to the cause was a printer named Elijah Lovejoy in Alton, Illinois. The North would no longer compromise its conscience, and the South would no longer be belittled by "holier than thou" abolitionists. Bishop Hamline got to the constitutional heart of the matter, "In church and in state there must always be an ultimate or supreme authority and the exercise of it must be independent, so far as systematic responsibility is concerned. But is the Episcopacy in regard to the question supreme? Certainly not! The General Conference adjunct in certain exigencies, with the Annual Conference is the ultimate depository of power in our church."[486] To be sure, this was an exigency!

The Conference rejected Olin's geographical compartmentalization of the problem. Neither could the eccentric Peter Cartwright douse the conflagration with colloquial irreverence: "Well, I want brethren not to go hanging their lips, and get afraid of a muckworm …. Why the Methodist Episcopal Church would not miss me anymore than an ox would miss a fly off his horn."[487] Was he the fly and Andrew, the muckworm? He was also amused at the Latin phrases he had heard. It reminded him of a constable who had been elected somewhere in Georgia, and had to serve a writ on someone who had escaped into the swamp. After the officer pursued the man far longer than he cared to, he returned with the explanation, "In swampum, et non, comoutum." He further said, "I want to pay my respects to the little learned brother that would not disturb the hair on the head of a bald-headed man."[488]

After being verbally roasted for a week, Andrew rose on Tuesday, May 28, and addressed his fellow delegates:

> The Conference can take its course; but I protest against the proposed action, as a violation of the laws of the discipline and an invasion of the rights secured to me by that book. Yet, let the Conference take the steps they contemplate; I enter no plea for mercy. I make no appeal for sympathy; indeed I love those who sympathize with me, but I do not

---

486   Ibid., 129.
487   Ibid., 157-158.
488   Ibid., 158.

want it now. I wish you to act coolly and deliberately and in that fear of God–but I would rather that the Conference would change the issue and make the resolution; depose the Bishop and take the question at once, for I am tired of it. The country is becoming agitated upon the subject, but I hope the Conference will act fourth in the resolution.[489]

"Agitated" was an understatement. To say that the Methodist General Conference was a microcosm of American society is inaccurate. It was actually a macrocosm, representative of the full American gamut of emotions and attitudes on the subject of slavery. "One hundred and eighty preachers elected as delegates from 33 Annual Conferences and representing 1,171,356 members of Methodist Churches came from all parts of the nation and from the Republic of Texas."[490] The 1844 quadrennial gathering of Methodists augered a holy war, conflicting righteous causes of sacred natures, sacred ideals, sacred characters, and sacred meanings.[491] No speech expressed the impending crisis and its threatening implications more than the impassioned plea of Joshua Soule:

> You may immolate me, but you cannot immolate me on a Southern altar; you cannot immolate me on a Northern altar; I can only be immolated on the altar of the Union .... Not for those men on my right hand and on my left hand, but for your sakes and for the Church of God of which we are members and ministers let me ask you, let me entreat you, not to rush upon the resolution which is now before you. Posterity sir,--review your actions, history record them, and whatever we may do here, will be spread out before the face of the world, the eyes of men will be fixed upon it.[492]

Joshua Soule, a direct descendant of a Mayflower Pilgrim, had been raised in the state of Maine by a sea captain turned farmer. Without a formal day of education, he had written the Constitution of Methodism at the 1808 General Conference. The Constitution had clearly stated the "six restrictive rules," but did not forthrightly clarify who had authority over whom, the General Conference or the Episcopacy. But no one could misinterpret where Soule stood. When the 1820 Conference elected him

---

489   Ibid., 150.
490   Norman W. Spellman. "The Church Divides," *History of American Methodism* Vol. II, ed. Emory Bucke (Nashville: Abingdon, 1964) 47.
491   Language borrowed from Harry Stout. *Upon the Altar of the Nation: A Moral History of the American Civil War* (New York: Penguin Group, 2006), xviii.
492   *Debates*, Lane and Tippett, 170.

Bishop, he refused ordination because the Conference had voted to place the appointment of Presiding Elders under a nominative and elective system. The Conference tabled the proposal until the 1824 gathering, and it failed passage by two votes. Soule was ordained Bishop; he had single-handedly maintained the right of Bishops to appoint Presiding Elders.

Until the 1844 General Conference, Soule lived in Lebanon, Ohio, but had mostly presided in the South and West. Firmly believing that the Episcopacy had been rendered impotent by the Andrew crisis, he moved to Tennessee, and became a Bishop in the Methodist Episcopal Church, South. But either Soule's memory failed him, or he was not being consistent. No doubt, he had read Bishop McKendree's encyclical just before the 1824 General Conference: "From the preachers collectively, both the General Conference and General Superintendents derive their power."[493] The preachers of the 1844 Conference did have the power to dispose of Andrew, but due process was not spelled out in the *Discipline* of the Methodist Episcopal Church. After Finley's resolution passed, that Andrew would "desist" from his Episcopal duties, almost completely along sectional lines (Simpson voted with the majority as he did on every resolution), the offended Southerners responded, "To request Bishop Andrew to resign, therefore in view of all the facts and revelations of the case, was in the judgment of the minority to punish and to degrade him; and they maintained the whole movement was without authority of law, is hence of necessity, null and void, and therefore, not binding upon Bishop Andrew or the minority protesting against it."[494]

The die had been cast. Southerner A.B. Longstreet pronounced that the "verbal suspension of Andrew from his office must produce a state of things in the South which renders the continuance of the jurisdiction of the General Conference over these Conferences (Southern) inconsistent with the success of the ministry of the slaveholding states."[495] On June 5, the Southerners J.B. McFerrin and T. Spicer, "Resolved, that the committee appoint to take into consideration the communication of the delegates

---

493   H. M. Dubose. *Life of Joshua Soule* (Nashville: Smith and Lamar, 1911) 167.
494   *Journals*, 196.
495   Jesse T. Peck. "The 1844 Conference," *Methodist Quarterly Review* Vol. 7 (April 1870) 165–188.

from the Southern Conferences be instructed, provided they cannot in their judgment devise a plan for an amicable adjustment of the difficulties now existing in the church on the subject of slavery to devise, if possible, a constitutional plan for a mutual and friendly division of the church."[496] The Conference responded by appointing a committee of nine, three each from the North, South and border states to compose resolutions for an agreeable separation. The committee composed twelve resolutions, among them that the capital of the Book Concern would be divided between the North and South proportionate to the number of preachers in each, and all people in the South "shall be forever free from any claim set on the part of the Methodist Episcopal Church." These fifth and ninth resolutions would cause various contentions and a long protracted lawsuit in the coming years.

The Unprecedented Significance of the 1844 General Conference

The 1844 General Conference set a historical precedent in that the legislative and judicial power of the denomination was to be found in the assembly of delegates and not the Board of Bishops. Without historical and legal argument and without citing historical precedents, the Conference assumed that it held ultimate authority over the Episcopal office. The General Conference made the Bishops and not vice versa. Asbury had established the precedent, although it is not recorded that anyone cited the event, when he requested that the Christmas Conference vote on his Episcopal office rather than simply accept the appointment by John Wesley. More than any other religious or ecclesiastical incident in American history, the 1844 Methodist General Conference portended and predicted the Civil War. If America's largest denomination could not morally and theologically process slavery without sectional schism, neither would the nation.

In essence, James Osgood Andrew served as a pawn for the South no less than did John Scopes for the ACLU when Clarence Darrow and William Jennings Bryan squared off at Dayton, Tennessee, in 1925. Andrew incarnated the agenda that the South forwarded and the North welcomed. The fight produced no winners, but a resulting conflict that would be the

---

496   *Journals*, 196.

most costly in the American experience. On June 1 by a tally of 110 to 68, the Conference voted that Andrew must forfeit his Episcopal functions as long as he remained a slave owner.[497] This cataclysmic fissure would have to be ratified by the Annual Conferences, and there was little possibility of that occurring. The final tally was 2,135 affirmative and 1,070 negative, short of the three-fourths majority needed for ratification.[498] The point of contention was the sixth restrictive rule that guaranteed the profits of the publishing house going to the worn-out preachers and their widows of the Methodist Episcopal Church, not some other schismatic denomination. Simpson accused John Early, a future Bishop in the Southern Church and brother to the famed Civil War Calvary commander, Jubal Early, of attempting to buy his vote.

> Dr. Early, subsequently a bishop of the south, frequently visited at Mayor Harper's, and would talk very freely upon the serious questions at issue. Near the time of the vote being taken, he came to consult as to terms for educating some of his near relatives, and spoke of the friendship of the south for the north, and how necessary it was to maintain full intercourse. As he had not spoken to me before as to my thoughts of sending his friends to Indiana, I feared at once that it was an effort to conciliate. I answered his questions briefly by turn; I said to him I did not expect him to send his friends to the University. He colored and asked me, why not. I simply replied it was far from home, other institutions were nearer and easier of access. The conversation at once ceased. I heard no more of the students.[499]

Simpson Attends Southern Methodism's First Conference

Before leaving New York, a Southern caucus planned a delegated Conference for Louisville, Kentucky in May of 1845. All Methodist Bishops were invited to attend. Why Matthew Simpson thought it imperative to travel to the Louisville Conference is not clear. Whatever, he would preach and make important contacts for the University along the way. He would also spend a week in Cincinnati with his mother and Uncle Matthew. The trip took three weeks with arrival in Louisville by paddle wheeler on May 8. Simpson sat in the balcony observing (spying on) the proceedings. More than he was willing to confess, ecclesiastical warfare was more alluring than

---

497   *Journals*, 84.
498   Robert W. Sledge. "Till Charity Wept–1844 Revisited," *Methodist History* 48.2 (January, 2010) 92.
499   *Autobiography*.

the confines of Greencastle, and the hack seed churches scattered throughout Indiana. (Hoosiers, of uncertain origin, possibly comes from *hoojers*, meaning ill-mannered rustics.) Simpson was on his way to becoming a persona non-gratis in the Methodist Episcopal Church South. The Convention resolved that "Bishop Soule and Andrew be, and they are hereby respectively and cordially requested by this convention to unite with, and become regular and constitutional Bishops of the Methodist Episcopal Church South, upon the basis of the plan of separation adopted by the late General Conference."[500] Simpson recorded in his journal:

> Pierce tried to show reconciliation hopeless and impossible; because the North would not concede. Charged ignorance of the Bible in Northern abolitionists and declared that they did not appeal to the Bible for the justness of their cause but to the writings of Jefferson. And that after all the movement of the Northern church was not so much against Slavery as against Episcopacy. That the Northern were radical in that they had ceased to use bread and water in love feast and their speeches were somewhat like those of the 4th of July toast and that in 10 years there would not be a vestige of the peculiarities of Methodism among them.[501]

What Pierce actually said was, "The North has taken their ground we have taken ours and cannot, will not, abandon it. Reunion has been impossible; we have no overtures to make. It is due to the church, to ourselves, to the country that we stand upon our rights, and until the North comes back to the Scripture ground, he, for one, would say, separation and independence, now and forever."[502]

Simpson Resigns from Asbury

The next two years were relatively quiet for Simpson other than a constant schedule of preaching and begging for money. In 1847, Simpson was debilitated by typhoid fever, and decided he needed a change of venue. Crooks, Clark, and Kirby all claim that Simpson had resigned Asbury before

---

500   Horace M. DuBose. *Joshua Soule* (Nashville: Smith and Lamar, 1916) 243.

501   LOC, Simpson papers, May 1845 *Diary*, Container one.

502   George G. Smith. *The Life and Times of George Foster Pierce* (Sparta, GA: Hancock Publishing Company, 1888) 153. William Cannon historically observed that George Pierce "was considered the most handsome preacher in Methodism, and one of the most charming and prepossessing young men in the entire nation. His speaking ability was extraordinary. Not only in appearance was he 'like a god, and aspect so divine' but his voice was as the voice of many waters–deep, rich, resonant, clear, and distinct." William Cannon. "The Pierces: Father and Son," *Methodist History* Vol. XVII, No. 1 (October 1978) 9.

leaving for the 1848 General Conference, but I can find no record of this assertion. He would have had to inform the Indiana Annual Conference in October, 1847, that he was resigning, but this would have been too long to serve as a lame-duck President. Evidently, Simpson made the decision while attending the 1848 General Conference. By 1848, Simpson had become a household name in every Methodist home in Indiana, and he was ready to be elected at the 1848 General Conference as the editor of the *Western Christian Advocate*. Edward Ames was offered the presidency of Indiana Asbury but deferred, in all likelihood harboring aspirations for the Episcopacy to which he was elected in 1852, along with Simpson. William Larrabee rendered interim leadership until Lucien Berry was elected President. Simpson, who was present at the inaugural commencement exercises in July 1850, reported that Berry's address on human progress was "full of strong thought forcibly expressed." When Simpson left in 1848, the financial stress, though not eliminated, had been alleviated. More importantly, during Simpson's presidency, the student body had grown from 22 to 268, making it the largest school of higher learning in Indiana.[503]

In 1846, tiny Woodward Female College in Cincinnati invited Simpson to be its new president. Simpson informed the Indiana Annual Conference of his intention to accept the invitation behind the smokescreen that Cincinnati would be more advantageous for his wife's health. Actually, he desired to live in the same city as his mother, uncle, and sister. The Conference leadership

---

503   Sweet, *Indiana Asbury-DePauw*, 59. In a letter John Wheeler wrote Simpson, while Simpson was at General Conference, May 25, 1848, he made no allusion to Simpson's intention of resigning:
    Pres. Simpson,   Greencastle, Ind. May 25, 1848
        Dear Friend,
I don't know how many times I have been asked if I have heard any news from the president; and as yet I cannot learn that anyone in this place has received a letter from you. I do not know but some of your friends are disposed to put this omission on your part on the ground that you don't care much about us here. I put it on the grounds and suppose that being unwell when you left here, as first you would feel a disinclination to do anything that was not absolutely necessary – and then soon coming into the society of friends and shortly afterward to General conference and then being engaged on committees etc. – having so much to say and do you have had no leisure. Under this charitable view of the subject and flattering myself that you might be interested in a line from the "ends of the earth", I have concluded to drop a line and hope you will pardon my breach of etiquette in "speaking before I am spoken to". LOC, Simpson papers, Letter May 25, 1848, Container five.

adamantly refused Simpson's resignation.[504] When Simpson returned from the 1848 General Conference (Pittsburgh), he brought news that no one in Indiana Methodism and especially Indiana Asbury University wanted to hear.

> The summer before the general conference I had a severe attack of Typhoid fever, which had been preceded with chills and fever, and the opinion of my physician's nurse that I must either change my sedentary habits of life or change my residence, I consulted physicians in whom I had great confidence & who knew me in Pittsburgh, and such being their judgment I felt it my duty to say to the delegates from Ind. that they must look for a new president for their university as my health would compel me to decline, my purpose was to return to the Pittsburgh conference, of which I had formerly been a member, but when it was rumored I was to retire from the presidency, I was nominated by a number of friends as Eastern editor for the "Christian Advocate," the delegates from the West learning this proffered me the position of editor of the "Western Advocate" and claimed I should remain in the West. Attending a preparatory meeting to nominate officers for the West, when named for the Advocate, I protested against accepting the position, urging that Dr. Elliott, who was my friend, and who had been Editor, should remain in the position & if desired, I would accept the position of assistant editor. The general conference, however, refused to appoint more than one editor & without my consent, elected me to fill the position.[505]

The Loss of Four-Year-Old Jimmy

The most critical event for the Simpsons, which took place during the Asbury years, was the loss of four-year-old Jimmy in January of 1842. As always when facing a crisis, Ellen, with the infant Charles in arms, fled to her parents in Pittsburgh. The college President was left to wallow in the self-pity of grief and loneliness. With good intentions, sympathizers offered their condolences, but like most explanations that attempt to make life's sorrows more palatable, they landed on dead end streets and fell on deaf ears. Uncle Matthew wrote, "He has taken his James to his heavenly paradise. He has reserved him from the entanglements and temptations of a world of sin and sorrow and death …. He has placed him beyond the reach of sin of pain and of death among the spirits of just men made perfect and angels who never sin."[506] Asbury Board

---

504 UMA, Drew University, *Methodist Episcopal Church, Indiana Conference Minutes 1844–1851*, 45–46.
505 *Autobiography*.
506 LOC, Simpson papers, Letter January 21, 1842, Container three.

Member, Allen Wiley, wrote, "My dear brother, I do not say grieve not but remember your sorrows could have been multiplied had your little boy lived to man's estate, been educated, and commenced a course of honor and usefulness and then fallen, your anguish would have been greater."[507]

This standard theodicy seemed to be saying that "If death prevents us from becoming bank robbers or axe murderers, it would be well if God would knock all of us off, before the age of accountability. We would then enjoy the eternal bliss of Disney World, rather than a life sentence in a penitentiary." Simpson was so overwhelmed with the loss of his firstborn, that he recorded nothing in his *Diary*, and as far as we know, did not verbally express his thoughts until he wrote a letter to Ellen, still in Pittsburgh, on May 1, 1842. To attempt to paraphrase or summarize Simpson's emotional and spiritual tempest would not do it justice:

> I could say a great a deal to you, which perhaps it is not prudent to write, of many things, and different plans which I have entertained since I parted with you. Whether the indolence arising from disease has given me more time to think or whether my spirits have received a deeper tinge than usual, from past and recent events I know not, but a stronger motley of feelings frequently crowd upon my mind. Sometimes as in a moment I seem to forget weakness, inability and lay large plans for future action and seem to enjoy the idea of mingling with the world and molding to some extent the public mind, and even dream of success in all my enterprises. But a change comes over me, and I feel my weakness, an inability to do anything, as if I were a mere drone in the great human hive that swarms around me, and that it was almost wrong for me to enjoy the smallest of the sweets that nature has prepared–that it was wrong for me possessed of such a nature as I have, so full of everything defective and impure, to pretend upon the resources of the Church, and talk to others of things that I know so little about and pretend to instruct when most of all I need to be taught. And then a sense of loneliness comes over me, and I feel as if there was not a heart in the whole universe that beats in unison with my own, as though I stood alone, like some solitary tree on a little island with the wild waves dashing around me, and washing away the soil from about my roots, while my head was already bending as though to fall in the giddy current–or like a tree struck in midsummer by the scathing lightning which has torn the bark and burned to yellow paleness the leaves that but yesterday were beautifully green.[508]

---

507   LOC, Simpson papers, Letter January 19, 1842, Container four.
508   LOC, Simpson papers, Letter May 1, 1842, Container three.

184 | "God Cannot Do Without America"

Simpson harbored the loss for the rest of his life, and periodically referred to James. On September 25, 1867, he wrote Ellen, "I have visited Greencastle---stopped today with Professor Tingley and visited the cemetery. How many tearful reminiscences gathered around my heart as I stood by the little grave, and thought of the dear little boy---his full round face---his prattling talk---the hoarse cough---the rainy weather---the absence---the little room---the pale still form in the coffin and the weary way to the graveyard."[509] As late as 1871, Simpson mused, "How strange is memory---above the memories of affection. They do not die---loved ones across the sea---loved ones across the sea of invisible---seem to come near. Back yonder there in Greencastle---in that small house---I can see little James climbing on my knee---, how plainly I see him now, as I write with the tears falling from my eyes---his little primer---his round, rosy cheeks---his soft voice---and then---and then---that forehead so smooth and cold that we kissed before we laid him away."[510]

The adulation of thousands could not replace the loss of a child.

Simpson and the Northern Reversal

In the 1848 General Conference, Simpson was one of the prime players in voiding the 1844 "plan of separation." Because the event was held at Liberty Street Church, his former pastorate and fifty miles from Cadiz, he may have been tempted to flex his leadership muscles. Many family and friends must have been present. On Friday afternoon, May 26, he made the following motion, which passed with only five dissenting votes: "The report of the Select Committee of Nine, on the declaration of the delegates in the slaveholding states, adopted by the General Conference of 1844, of which the memorialists complain, and the operation which deprived them of their privileges as members of the Methodist Episcopal Church, was intended to meet a necessity, which it was alleged might arise and was given as a peace

---

509 UMA, Drew University, Simpson papers, Letter September 25, 1867.
510 UMA, Drew University, Simpson papers, Letter April 9, 1871. Close scrutiny of the Greencastle newspapers during this time revealed no obituary reference to James' death. In fact, if one read the Greencastle newspapers for the period of Simpson's presidency, an individual would not know that Indiana Asbury University existed.

offering to secure harmony on our southern border."[511] In other words, the 1844 "plan of separation" was a moratorium with no legal, not even ethical obligations. Thus, the Conference concluded that "in view of these facts, as well as for the principles contained in the preceding declaration, there exists no obligation on the part of this conference to observe the provision of the said plan."[512] There were seven other sections in Simpson's motion, which included the necessity for a "three-fourths (votes) of the members of the several annual conferences for validation of the separation;" and establishment of boundaries separating the Northern and Southern Church, which was impossible, because both localities, especially the border states, contained churches loyal to the other side.[513]

The Methodist Episcopal Church had retracted its peace offering, a prelude to not sharing proceeds from the Book Concerns, and later confiscating Southern church property. In Simpson's mind, as well as most of the other Conference delegates, the Methodist Episcopal Church South was not a new denomination, enjoying the blessing of the mother church and its Wesleyan heritage, but a renegade faction, which because of carnal contention had stepped beyond the bounds of constitutional authority. There would be no justification for financial reparation to the Methodist Episcopal Church South, because the General Conference had no authority to act independently of the Annual Conferences. The final report from the "state of the church," a committee which Simpson had initiated, concluded that because the "said plan" was "incompatible with certain great constitutional principles elsewhere asserted, we have found and declared *the whole and every part of said plan to be null and void.*"[514] By sharing the funds of the two publishing houses, the Northern Church would be condoning the rebellion of the Southern churches, a rebellion motivated by slavery.

Of course, the Northern church justified their actions by claiming the Southern church had not been true to the plan of separation as conceived by the 1844 Conference. The Bishops began the 1848 Conference with a statement

---

511   *Journals of the General Conference of the Methodist Episcopal Church*, 1848-1856 Volume III (New York: Carlton & Porter, 1856) 80-81.
512   Ibid., 85.
513   Ibid., 81.
514   Ibid., 164.

of condemnation: "The Methodist Episcopal Church South has officially and authoritatively taught the infraction of the Plan by her Convention, her General Conference, her Bishops, her Annual Conferences, her Editors, and her leading Ministers." They then listed numerous infractions committed by the Southern church such as the,

> Kanawha District in the northwest part of Virginia is a part of the Ohio Conference. In 1845, that work was supplied from the Ohio Conference, as usual. Their preachers were received with one exception, as far as we know, namely, Parkersburg Station. A part of the members there refused to receive any preacher from the Ohio Conference. They rejected the preachers sent to them. Not for any objection to him personally, but because he came from Ohio; and by threats of violence, in preparation to execute those threats on a given day, compelled him to leave the place. And took possession of the chapel. He, however, returned after some weeks, and in connection with the preacher of the adjoining circuit, to which they were transferred, served the remaining members of the scattered flock in another house. These outcast members have since erected a chapel for themselves, in which they worshipped undisturbed; while the old chapel is supplied from the Kentucky Conference of the M.E. church, South.[515]

Simpson's Ecclesiastical Ascendency

Simpson was no longer a novice in church affairs. He had spoken freely and often. In the 1848 Conference, he had recommended the cessation of "fraternal relations" between the two ecclesiastical bodies. Even though Simpson's resolutions were only a reflection of consensus sentiment, it was his name more than any other that was attached to the reversal. Simpson's articulation of the Northern non-recognition of the Methodist Episcopal Church South only served to drive a larger wedge between Northern and Southern Methodism, and coupled with the future "McKendree Church" affair during the war, translated the name of Matthew Simpson into anathema in the South for the next twenty years. Having never traveled in the South, the soon-to-be editor had little understanding of Southern culture. He had been the major player in a game in which he had limited understanding of the rules, and minimal comprehension of what was at stake. It was one of the few times that Simpson overplayed his hand. He had no personal acquaintance with the growing number of Southern "fire eaters,"

---

515   1848 *Journal*, 168.

in particular, John Calhoun who for years had advocated "nullification." (Nullification championed state's rights, rights that could invalidate the federal government's demands on a particular state. Secession would be the ultimate act of nullification.)

The genesis of retraction did not originate with Simpson. The Conference had already rejected a plea from the Southern Church to divide the value of the Book Concerns in that it could not act "advisedly upon the communication in question, until they receive the official reports of all the Annual Conferences in relation to the change of the sixth restrictive rule as recommended by the last General Conferences."[516] The "sixth restrictive rule" designated profits from Methodist publications to be for the "benefit of the traveling, supernumerary and worn-out preachers, their wives, widows, and children, and to such other purposes as may be determined upon by the vote of two-thirds of the members of the General Conference."[517] The "other purposes" had been often appropriated. How to respond to the Southern churches' honest and well-validated appeal was foremost in the minds of the delegates to the 1848 General Conference. On May 25, one day before Simpson's adopted resolutions, George Peck, Chair of the Committee on the "State of the Church," brought the issue to a head. "The report of the Committee of Nine commonly called the Plan of Separation adopted by the General Conference in its session of 1844, having in its results practically contravened the above named principles, and having been dependent upon conditions which have not been fulfilled is hereby declared that said plan is and has been null and void."[518] The "State of the Church Committee" and the Bishops had provided the ammunition, but Simpson had crafted and calibrated the gun. William Daily was prescient when he wrote Simpson, May 24, 1848, predicting that his leadership in the 1848 General Conference would "immortalize his name."[519]

---

516   1848 *Journal*, 48.
517   Nolan Harmon. "The Organization of the Methodist Episcopal Church, South" in *The History of American Methodism* Vol. II, ed. Emory Bucke (Nashville: Abingdon, 1964), 128.
518   1848 *Journal*, 78.
519   Clark, *Pulpit and Platform*, 231.

Simpson departed the 1848 General Conference as a recognized leader in the affairs of the Methodist Episcopal Church. To summarize Simpson's Conference contributions, he had offered substitute motions for three long resolutions demonstrating his cogent facility for the English language, acute knowledge of parliamentary procedure, and his analytical insights into administrative complications. One of the key ingredients of leadership is to express the sentiments of those of similar concerns, and in so doing, provide a solution for an actual or perceived crisis. The substitute motion by Simpson, which followed a brief motion by J. Clark, requiring each church to appoint trustees by class, demonstrated Simpson's impressive circumlocution. The following was articulated extemporaneously, an impromptu creativity for which the future Bishop would become well known:

> *Resolved*, that the several annual conferences be requested to take proper measures to ascertain what changes, if any, are requisite in our deed of settlement and mode of appointment of trustees, so as to conform to the laws of the several states, and add to the security of the property of the Church. And when said annual conferences shall have agreed upon such changes, not affecting, however, any of the trusts contained in our present deed, and when such changes shall have been inspected and approved by the bishops, so as to secure uniformity as far as possible, then the Book Agents shall be authorized to publish copies of said deeds, to be furnished without charge to the presiding elders of the several states, who shall be charged with the duty of seeing that our Church property is *properly* secured, according to the form of said deed.[520]

Simpson Replaces Charles Elliott as Editor

On Tuesday, May 30, the Conference elected Matthew Simpson as editor of the *Western Christian Advocate*. Hopefully, he would be a more sedating voice than Charles Elliott, who was increasingly incurring the wrath of Southerners and anti-abolitionist Northerners. Historian Richard Carwardine states that, "Southerners particularly blamed the breakdown of understanding and trust on free-state editors, especially Thomas Bond of the *Christian Advocate and Journal* and Charles Elliot of the *Western Christian Advocate*. Their papers, regarded as threats to social peace, were regularly seized and even burned by magistrates at the post offices, their

---

520   1848 *Journal*, 65.

actions sustained by a combination of statute, grand jury endorsements and demands of vigilance committees."[521]

Methodist historian J. N. Norwood assessed, "When removed from the mellowing influence of that trying session (the 1844 General Conference) the North took a more cold-blooded vision of the issue; Northern Methodists concluded that their delegates had gone too far. Repudiation was born and grew lustily. If the Southerners wished to leave, let them leave as seceders. This feeling marked a violent reaction from the noble expression and action of the General Conference of 1844."[522] Norwood also placed much of the blame on Charles Elliott and Thomas Bond, who reneged on and invalidated the plan. He accused Elliott of executing "the most spectacular intellectual somersault during the entire debate."[523] Robert Clark is accurate in that Simpson, in spite of his divisive actions, was "conciliatory at heart, and for that reason, was chosen the editor of the *Western Christian Advocate*, some thought the most powerful voice in Methodism."[524]

Simpson had been appointed to a position in which he replaced his friend and mentor, Charles Elliott. Elliott's parting shot was apologetic: "And as offenses must come, we are aware we have offended some, this is inevitable in our circumstances. It would have been on our part an offense against God, did we not offend some, and we were bound to obey God rather than man." Elliott was charitable to his former student and incoming editor: "We take pleasure to present to our readers and correspondents our successor, the Rev. Matthew Simpson D. D., who we are persuaded will more than fill our place." In closing, Elliott in his valedictory (more accurately a maledictory) let his readers know what he thought of the job he was handing his successor:

> The duties of a circuit district or station, strange as it may appear to some, are more favorable to writing and solid study than the miscellaneous duties of editing. We can scarcely suppose a more unfavorable position

---

521 Richard Carwardine. "Trauma in Methodism: Property, Church Schism and Sectional Polarization in Antebellum America"; in *God and Mammon: Protestants, Money and the Market*, ed. Mark Noll (New York: Oxford University Press, 2001) 199.

522 John Nelson Norwood. *Schism in the Methodist Church: 1844* (Alfred University: Alfred, New York, 1923) 125.

523 Ibid., 108.

524 Clark, *Pulpit and Platform*, 239.

for systematic study or severe preparation for the press than the miscellaneous gatherings and vagrant researches of the weekly editor. Indeed most of what we have published, since our editorial course began, had been principally prepared while busied with the duties of large circuits or districts with a full share of ministerial labors of all kinds. Editing the weekly sheet is as Dr. Capers said, after a three-year trial of it, "the dog's drudgery." And we are sure that no man who can write anything better than the weekly editorial will ever engage in it, unless other reasons than literary tastes, will urge him to this course. The composition of weekly editorials, as a whole, we never liked. We do not like them now, and we are sure we never will. And we now are glad we are rid of this sort of labor. To which for fifteen long years we always sat down with reluctance, we performed it without delight, and reflected on it with little satisfaction.[525]

Elliott's farewell was partially sour grapes, but he was not without a job. The 1848 General Conference commissioned him to write a history of the last four years of the church, which resulted in two books: *Sinfulness of American Slavery: Proofs from Its Evil Sources; Its Injustice; Its Wrongs; Its Contrariety to Many Scriptural Commands, Prohibitions and Principals and to the Christian Spirit: And from its Evil Effects; Together with Observations on Emancipation and the Duties of American Citizens in Regard to Slavery* (1850), and *History of the Great Succession from the Methodist Episcopal Church in the Year 1845* (1855). The man never did anything halfway. Little did he realize that four years later he would again inherit the "dog's drudgery." James Dixon, the British delegate to the 1848 General Conference, observed that,

> Elliott was possessed of the vivacity, acumen, logical power and with all hatred of popery, which unite to distinguish the natives of the North of Ireland. In his editorial labors, as well as in his Delineation, he has done good service in the support of Protestantism. He is besides a perfect abolitionist. Slavery can have no favor in the sight of Dr. Elliott. It is an abhorred and detested evil: an unmitigated injury to the slaves themselves; a crime in the slaveholder to exact this oppressive wrong; and, moreover, an outrage against Christianity, and a sin against Almighty God, in the estimation of Dr. Elliott.[526]

Dixon also noted of Simpson:

> Dr. Simpson is a man of mark. I had the privilege of much friendly intercourse with the gentleman and witnessed with great admiration

---

525 "Valedictory," *WCA* Vol. XV, No. 16 (July 26, 1848) 62.
526 James Dixon. *Methodism in America: With the Personal Narrative of the Author*

the discharge of his public duties at the Conference. He is a very able man in every way, and being young is likely, it is hoped, long to bless the Church, and the world with the benefits of his valuable labours.[527]

What churned on the inside of Simpson having displaced the man who had most mentored him, other than his uncle Matthew, we do not know. Clark accurately chronicles Elliott's lifetime influence on Simpson, especially in the latter's developmental years: "He it was who had induced Simpson to go to college, who had persuaded him to enter the ministry, had been chief agent in securing a position at Allegheny College, and had almost entirely responsible for his election to the presidency of Indiana Asbury University."[528] It was with apologetic guilt that Simpson accepted the new office, a perplexity that he would recall decades later. No doubt, Simpson's claim that he had been appointed "without his consent," was an attempt to salve his conscience. After Elliott's death, Simpson credited Elliott as the primary person who encouraged and enabled him to enter the ministry. He then gave Elliott a somewhat underhanded compliment. "As a writer and a speaker, Dr. Elliott was strong and vigorous. Careless, possibly too careless, of all the graces of style or of manner, grasping the thought clearly and strongly, without care for either illustrations or ornament. In his palmy days, he often moved an audience as the wind bows the ripe grain in the harvest field."[529]

Simpson was politically gracious in leaving Asbury. He wrote the following to the Board of Trustees, July 18, 1848:

> In closing my official relations with the University, I should do violence to my feelings, did I not express my grateful acknowledgements to the Trustees, but to the different members of the faculty. For years we have labored together. In our official relations,---in our official decisions, there has never been, an uninterrupted unity of spirit and action---and much of that moral influence which has always so powerfully swayed the students of the University has been owing to the perfect unity of purpose prevailing of the Board. Permit me, Gentlemen, to render to you and through you to my colleagues of the Faculty, both officially and personally assurances of my kind regards and my ardent prayers that the Almighty may have you personally--

---

during a Tour through a part of the United States and Canada (London: John Mason, 1849) 382.

527 Ibid., 368–369.
528 Clark, *Pulpit and Platform*, 199.
529 LOC, Simpson papers, "Rev. Dr. Elliott" by Bishop Simpson, Container twenty.

and the Institution for which you labor, in his holy keeping, may his smiles rest upon you and may he crown all your efforts with abundant success.[530]

They in return responded on the same day:

> We reflect with pleasure on that harmony and mutual confidence that has ever existed between President Simpson and the board of trustees & we rejoice that our mutual labours have been blessed with abundant Success–And we must regret that other duties have devolved on Dr. Simpson by which we have been deprived of his able and efficient Services–And we wish in accepting the resignation of the President to express to him our acknowledgement for his efficient services.

Therefore:

> Resolved; the Board tenders to Dr. Simpson a vote of thanks for his efficient and able services as President of the University.[531]

No job within Methodism provided a better stepping stone to national leadership within the Methodist Episcopal Church than editor of the Western Christian Advocate. Simpson, more than any other person, would have the ear of the Methodists west of the Allegheny Mountains. As Americans flooded the Ohio River Valley, the denomination most ready to harvest them, in methodology and theology was the Methodist Episcopal Church. The new Methodists needed a weekly newspaper uniquely devoted to their ideals and interests. Who better could have met their needs than a young editor from the hills of eastern Ohio?

---

530   UMA, DePauw University, Simpson papers, Letter to the Trustees of Indiana Asbury University, July 18, 1848.

531   UMA, DePauw University, Simpson papers, "Minutes of the July 18, 1848, Board of Trustees Meeting, Indiana Asbury University."

Chapter Seven:
A Political and Spiritual Tightrope

He Arrived Broke

Nineteenth-century print historian Candy Gunther Brown claims that Cincinnati "emerged as a Western publishing Center for periodicals, as it was for all the other print forms. The Methodist *Western Christian Advocate*, published from 1834 to 1939 in Cincinnati, outstripped every religious and secular paper in the region by garnering fourteen thousand subscribers by 1840 and twice that number by 1880."[532] During Simpson's tenure, his weekly was perhaps the most influential periodical west of the Alleghenies. The *Cincinnati Examiner* in 1850 had a circulation of 15,000, serving a population of 115,000, while only 30,000 people lived in Chicago. Simpson was not unaware of the influence he exerted. In 1850, he wrote: "Thirty years ago there was scarcely a religious newspaper in existence .... Now, how changed is the scene! Each church has its organ through which religious intelligence is communicated and its enterprises advocated, and its triumphs made known."[533]

William Warren Sweet calculates that the official publications of the Methodist Episcopal Church (North) in 1860 totaled more than four hundred thousand subscribers.[534] Across the total denominational spectrum, the number of religious periodicals dramatically increased during the 1850s.

---

532   Candy Gunther Brown. *The Word in the World: Evangelical Writing, Publishing, and Reading in America: 1789-1840* (Chapel Hill: University of North Carolina Press, 2004) 147. Brown's numbers are slightly exaggerated, but her observation is essentially correct.

533   Matthew Simpson. "The Religious Newspaper," *WCA* Vol. XVII, No. 5 (Jan. 29, 1851) 18.

534   W. W. Sweet. *The Methodist Episcopal Church and the Civil War* (Cincinnati: The Methodist Book Concern, 1912) 111.

"In 1850, there were one hundred and ninety religious newspapers and periodicals: in 1860, the number had increased to two hundred and seventy seven, an increase of fifty-seven per-cent."[535] Donald Jones concludes that religious publications became the "chief dispenser of information and values to the American people."[536] It is almost impossible to exaggerate the influence of the press, and in particular the religious press, in a pre-radio, pre-television, and pre-internet world. Cyberspace consisted of the newspaper. According to Carl Russell Fish, "Before 1830, organized religion, with its regular sermons, its facilities for the publication of books, and its innumerable periodicals representing each form of activity of each denomination, was the most potent intellectual influence in the country. The next twenty years merely developed this activity."[537]

Simpson arrived in Cincinnati broke; thus, he moved in with his brother-in-law, George McCullough and sister Hetty in the Mount Auburn neighborhood, advertised as the "brightest jewel in Cincinnati's crown."[538] Mount Auburn Street angled northeast, five hundred feet above the "crumbling riverbanks, the burning kettles of the immigrants housed in flat boats which sent up long columns of smoke, where steamers now (in 1852) darken the air with thick clouds of steam and soot."[539] In his daily commute, much of the time in a hired hack, the 500 foot climb too steep to walk, Simpson passed wide grounds with palatial homes, a neighborhood which boasted of Alphonso Taft and his son William Howard Taft. Also living on the hill was William McGuffey, pedagogical pied piper for America. In 1852, the Methodists built a church on Mount Auburn. The city paid for part of the cast of the church bell, on the condition that it could be used for fire alarms and other civic purposes.[540] Matthew and Ellen had three

---

535   Donald G. Jones. *The Sectional Crisis in Northern Methodism: A Study in Piety, Political Ethics and Civil Religion* (Metuchen, New Jersey: The Scarecrow Press Inc. 1979) 21.

536   Ibid.,2.

537   Carl Fish. "The Rise of the Common Man," in *A History of American Life*, ed. Mark C. Carnes (New York: Simon and Schuster, 1996) 585.

538   G. J. Giglierano and Deborah Overmeyer. *The Bicentennial Guide to Greater Cincinnati: A Portrait of Two Hundred Years* (Cincinnati: The Cincinnati Historical Society, 1988).

539   Silberstein, 17.

540   Giglierano and Overmeyer, 190. Also see Clyde W. Park. *Mount Auburn Methodist Church: The First Hundred Years, 1852-1952* (Columbus: Historical and Philosophical

children, Charles age 7, Ella age 5, and Anna age 2. With the five of the editor's family, and the three of Hetty's family, along with Uncle Matthew and mother, Sarah, the living conditions were cramped. Matthew and Ellen, their three children with Uncle and Mother in tow, moved into a "boarding house" on Sixth Street some time in 1850.

Housing was a problem for Simpson throughout his tenure in Cincinnati. Upon his editorial election he wrote from Jeffersonville, Indiana, "I prefer housekeeping, but if I cannot get a house that will suit, I see no alternative but boarding." He soon after wrote Ellen, "Boarding for our family besides lights and fuel will cost $14.00 per week. House rent on Mount Auburn from 3–400. None at present to be had."[541] What Simpson could afford, he would not have, and what he would have, he could not afford. On October 2, 1850, he wrote, "D. Miller is very anxious to sell his house. Very low indeed, and on easy terms, but it is too far away."[542] He continued to seriously look, finding a house for which he drew a detailed floor plan. "It fronts Harrison Street, and has a beautiful yard, which runs back to the old burying ground in the rear of Wesley Chapel. I think it is now used as playgrounds for children." Ellen may have not been too keen about the burying ground–play ground concept. They did not buy the property.

When Simpson moved Ellen and the children down to the boarding house on Sixth Street, he had to be mindful that he was putting his family at cholera risk. The former physician, as well as others, did not know what caused cholera, but he learned while living in Pittsburgh that it was far more prevalent at lower elevations, as all water seeks the lowest level which it can penetrate. The "destroyer" of Cincinnati in the summer of 1849 swept whole families away and "large buildings are left desolate." Simpson wrote, "Directly between our office and residence, the disease assumed a most malignant aspect. The locality elevated from one to three hundred feet above the level of the river, and for a few weeks but little indication of sickness was manifest; but it came suddenly like the falling of an avalanche, and the whole hillside became a scene of suffering and death." Simpson recalled his pastoral confrontation with cholera which afflicted a family in Pittsburgh

---

Society of Ohio, 1952).
541   UMA, Drew University, Simpson papers, Letter June 8, 1848.
542   UMA, Drew University, Simpson papers, Letter October 2, 1850.

in 1834. "On Sunday their son, a lad of some 14 years, was severely attacked, and on Monday morning a daughter passed rapidly into collapse. We visited them on Monday, and the rest of the family appeared to be in good health. We expected to have called again, but that afternoon we were ourselves upon a bed of sickness. By the following Thursday the father, mother and three daughters were swept away, the son was slowly recovering."[543]

Whatever office Simpson held for the rest of his life, he never lost his pastoral heart. Willie Campbell, son of a widow, died during the 1850 cholera epidemic, and his mother was not able to find a pastor at Wesley Chapel, where she and her son attended. She sent her son's friend to find a preacher of any stripe. The lad wandered around the city for several hours until he stumbled into the Book Concern of the Methodist Episcopal Church. There he found Matthew Simpson "bent over his desk, very busy writing." The boy stated his need, and the editor responded, "My young brother, if you will go with me and show me the way, I will go." On a hot humid afternoon, Simpson followed the boy to a tenement house and preached a funeral message for the widow, to a small gathering of friends and relatives.[544]

America's Fastest Growing City

Cincinnati was a river town, growing faster on the eve of the Civil War than any other American city. The city's population increased by more than 2 1/2 times from 1820 to 1830, and quadrupled between 1830 and 1850. In 1850, Cincinnati was the sixth-largest city in the country, the third in manufacturing.[545] Daniel Drake, one of Cincinnati's first historians and founder of the Medical College of Ohio, described the city's inhabitants as: "Drinking to intoxication, public balls, theatrical amusements, horse racing, billiards, and various games of chance prevailed to a degree, exceeding unfavorable to habits of study, cards the most dangerous of all family amusements were part of the means of wasting time, by the majority of houses of the village and the whiskey bottle was a symbol of hospitality in the whole."[546]

543   Matthew Simpson, "The Destroyer," *WCA* Vol. XVI, No. 29 (July 18, 1849) 113.
544   "Bishop Simpson and the Widow's Son." UMA, Drew University, Simpson papers.
545   Silberstein, 31.
546   Ibid., 16.

In spite of its depravity, Cincinnati for both Matthew and his young son, Charles, was an exciting place. Steamboat whistles blew both day and night. Hundreds of people daily passed through Cincinnati bearing news from the East, or their hopes and dreams for becoming rich in the California gold fields. By walking only a few blocks from his office, the thirty-eight year old editor observed the busiest river port other than New Orleans, in all of America. Tons of cargo were being imported or exported by the hour. On a spring or autumn day, the river market was the perfect place to grab a sandwich or sausage, washed down with apple cider from one of the dozens of vendors. While eating, the editor conversed with a passenger or steamboat captain passing through the Queen City. On summer evenings, the docks took on a carnival atmosphere, each steamboat with intriguing and eccentric travelers, bearing tall tales from far-away places. The curious enjoyed the entertainment and hustlers earned small change by transporting luggage.

Cincinnati had justly earned its moniker, "Porkopolis." Charles Cist, Cincinnati's foremost statistician, stated, "Pork is our great staple and hogs to the number of 498,160 have been cut up in the market in a single year. Yearly average number of hogs put up during the last four years will not however exceed 375,000. That of 1850 was 324,539." Cincinnati boasted the largest slaughterhouse in America, if not the world, measuring 364 feet wide and 160 feet deep.[547] In the 1840s, a visitor from England described Cincinnati as a "city of pigs.... A monster piggery.... alive and dead, whole and divided into portions, their outsides and their insides, their grunts and their squeals meet you in every moment."[548] While most endured the stench, others smelled money. In the late 1830s, William Proctor and James Gamble moved to town to convert hog fat. By the early 1850s, P & G had its first factory producing soaps and candles. When Horace Greeley visited Cincinnati in 1851, his clairvoyance was limited, but nonetheless optimistic, "It requires no keenness of observation to perceive that Cincinnati is destined to become the focus and mart for the grandest circle of manufacturing thrift on this continent. Her delightful climate is unequaled in ever-increasing facilities for cheap and rapid commercial intercourse with all parts of the country and the world; her

---

547 Charles Cist. *Sketches and Statistics of Cincinnati in 1851* (Cincinnati: W.H. Moore & Co, 1851) 228-229.

548 Hessler Silberstein. *Cincinnati: Then and Now* (Cincinnati: The Value Service Education Fund, 1982) 35.

enterprising and energetic population; her own elastic and exulting growth are all elements which predict and ensure her electric progress to grand greatness."[549]

Conquering Distance

At the age of 38, Simpson had witnessed technological innovations, as revolutionary as any breakthroughs within the history of humankind. Steamboats had become the first internally-powered vessels for the transferring of goods and passengers, a transportation revolution no longer reliant on winds, tides and the downward flow of rivers. A steamboat traveled the thousand miles from New Orleans, turned East at Cairo, Illinois, and headed toward the burgeoning cities of Louisville, Cincinnati, and Pittsburgh. The Ohio River because of steam power had become the most prominent East-West thoroughfare on the North American continent.

On March 24, 1844, Samuel Morse sent a message from the Supreme Court chamber in the basement of Washington's capital to the Mount Clark railroad station in Baltimore. Though he had not invented the telegraph, Morse had introduced to America a practical device which could communicate over hundreds of miles within a few minutes. What this meant for Simpson is that he could obtain same-day news from a place such as Washington D.C., even though his readers would not receive his paper until approximately ten days later. For example, day by day news from the General Conference was edited and posted.[550] John O'Sullivan, coiner of one of America's most defining motifs, "manifest destiny", exuberated in 1846, "The magnetic telegraph will enable the editors of the 'San Francisco Union', the 'Astoria Evening Post', or the 'Nookton Morning News', to set up in type the first half of the President's Inaugural, before the echoes of the latter-half shall have died away beneath the lofty porch of the Capitol, or spoken from his lips."[551]

---

549   Henry Ford and Mrs. Kate B. Ford. *History of Cincinnati: With Illustration and Biographical Sketches* (Cleveland: L. A. Williams and Company, 1881) 331.
550   Gerald J. Baldasty. *The Commercialization of News in the Nineteenth Century* (Madison: The University of Wisconsin Press, 1992) 43.
551   Quoted in Frederick Merk. *Manifest Destiny and Mission in American History: A Reinterpretation* (New York: Alfred A. Knopf, 1963) 51.

But the telegraph in no way diminished the popularity of newspapers. In the 1840s the bulk of the mail consisted of newspapers, and as early as the 1820s the U.S. Post Office employed more people than all other United States government offices, and the United States had more newspaper readers than any other country. United States post-office scholar, Richard John states that "By 1828, the American postal system had almost twice as many offices as the postal system in Great Britain and over five times as the postal system in France. This translated into 74 post offices for every 100,000 inhabitants, in comparison with 17 for Great Britain and 4 for France."[552] When Simpson moved to Cincinnati, he came at a propitious moment that had witnessed triumph over what William Walker Howe refers to as the "tyranny of distance." This triumph only intensified America's most serious battle, the war of public opinion: "The political parties debated serious issues, economic and constitutional. Political divisions were sharp and fierce .... The evangelical movement prompted national soul-searching and argument over the country's goals and the best means to achieve them .... The communication revolution gave a new urgency to social criticism and the slavery controversy in particular."[553]

It was only a matter of time before steam would be connected to the printing press, what Bernard Weisberger christened as the "twin deities in the pantheon of progress."[554] Simpson inherited a cylinder press which had been invented by Frederick Koenig in 1813, and perfected by Robert Hoe in 1831. "It was a patent known as the Single Large Cylinder, the whole circumference of the cylinder being equivalent to the entire travel of the bed, forwards and backwards; the cylinder making one revolution for each impression in printing without stopping."[555] The "lightning press" was a huge step forward from the flatbed press for which Simpson had set the type as a 10-year-old for his uncle Joseph Tingley. Before the invention of

---

552   Richard R. John. *Spreading the News: The American Postal System from Franklin to Morse* (Cambridge, MA.: Harvard University Press, 1995) 5.

553   Daniel Walker Howe. *What Hath God Wrought: The Transformation of America, 1815–1848* (New York: Oxford University Press, 2007) 586.

554   Bernard Weisberger. *The American Newspaperman* (Chicago: The University of Chicago Press, 1961) 91.

555   Robert Hoe. *A Short History of the Printing Press And of the Improvements in Printing Machinery from the Time of Gutenberg up to the Present Day* (New York: Robert Hoe, 1902) 18.

the cylinder press, a printer put a publication together one letter at a time, lifting the smaller letters from a flatbed, and the capitol letters from an area above it; hence, lower and uppercase letters. If one ran out of a letter, he would have to substitute another word because he was "out of sorts."[556]

Simpson's particular press was marketed by A.B. Taylor, and hence referred to as the "Taylor Cylinder Press." The $25,000 apparatus could turn out 1,000 sheets per hour; the four- page *Advocate* which consisted of one sheet folded once, could be printed in two days. Each page of the four-page broad sheet consisted of seven columns across, each column two and five-eighths inches wide, the total page nineteen and one half inches wide and twenty-six inches tall. Only black ink was used for the paper, and sheets had to be fed into the machine separately. It was not until 1865 by the ingenuity of William Bullock, that a press could utilize a continuous role of paper.

A Spirit of Kindness and Universal Charity

The Western Christian Advocate was established in 1834 with Thomas Morris as the first editor. In 1820 the Methodists planted a publishing house in the promising city of Cincinnati at the corner of 5th and Elm. In 1840, the Methodists purchased the four-story mansion of Gen. Arthur St. Claire, who had served as governor of the Northwest Territory. (Remember, he had gone bankrupt and lived in a cabin.) To this building Simpson daily reported when he was in town. In addition to the mansion the Western Book Concern built another four-story building on the property for sales rooms, offices, and binding.[557] Also in 1840, the Cincinnati location was named the Western Book Concern, to differentiate it from the Methodist Publishing House in New York. In surveying Cincinnati's businesses, Charles Cist reported that "not the least in importance is our publishing establishments, although among the last referred to, is the Methodist Book Concern, Southwest corner of Main and Eighth streets. There are issued from their presses of the Western Christian Advocate, twenty-one thousand copies; Ladies Repository, sixteen-thousand five-hundred; Sunday School Advocate, twenty three thousand; Christian

---

556   William E. Huntzicker. *The Popular Press: 1833-1865* (Westport, CT: Greenwood Press, 1994) 165.

557   Walter Sutton. *The Western Book Trade: Cincinnati as a Nineteenth Century Publishing and Book-Trade Center* (Columbus: Ohio State University Press, 1961) 156.

Apologist, three thousand. They keep five steam presses in constant occupation; employ twenty five hands in the printing and forty six in the binding. Beside these periodicals, they issue various religious publications. Value of books and periodicals published last year, $125,000."[558] The paper was advertised in the city directory: "The Western Christian Advocate, published weekly at the Methodist Book Concern, corner of Main and Eighth streets, at $1.50 per annum, payable in advance, is edited by the Rev. Matthew Simpson DD."[559]

Simpson moved into his new job with alacrity, publishing one of the highest volume papers of any kind in America. During his four-year tenure as editor, Simpson almost doubled the circulation from 12,000 to over 21,000. By the end of each year Simpson had gathered, copied, collated, proofed and printed between 2,000 and 2,500 articles: national news, international news, poems, medical advice, missionary letters, camp meeting news, and revival reports. And there were a variety of issues beyond Methodism: temperance, anti-Romanism, tobacco, libraries, internal improvements, and reverence for the Sabbath. He had borrowed without permission (copyright was a non-issue),[560] but always giving due credit, from every conceivable source: *The Knickerbocker, Missionary Advocate, Ladies Repository, Sunday School Advocate, The Scientific American, Christian Parlor Magazine, The American Almanac, The Encyclopedia Britannica, Christian Chronicle,* and the numerous city newspapers throughout the country. Clark observes that Simpson jotted in his "memo book," subjects ranging from "parks in Cincinnati to Miama College, discovery of iodine, World's Industrial Fair, Sunday school singing, the poor in winter, church architecture, religious politics, and asylums for the insane."[561]

---

558   Cist, 234. Robert C. Williams claims that Horace Greely was the first to use the "Lightning press" which could produce 20,000 sheets per hour. When and if the *Western Christian Advocate* attained this level of production is unknown. Robert C. Williams. *Horace Greely: Champion of American Freedom* (New York: New York University Press, 2006) 61.

559   *Western Cincinnati Directory and Business Advertiser for 1850-1851*, second annual issue (Cincinnati: C. S. Williams College Hall, 1850) 207.

560   The federal copyright law of 1790 did not include newspapers, but only maps, charts and books. Music was added in 1831. See Lyman R. Patterson. *Copyright in Historical Perspective* (Nashville: Vanderbilt University Press, 1968) 197-201. Coincidentally, just after Simpson assumed his Cincinnati job, the Associated Press was founded in New York, May, 1849, with six member newspapers. Obviously, Simpson was not part of this elite group, whose members, for a fee, purchased news sent to a central telegraph office in Boston. Weisberger, 114-115.

561   Clark, *Pulpit and Platform*, 238.

Simpson's salutary remarks reminded readers that though the paper would "state clearly and forcibly Christian doctrine," the approach would be in "a spirit of kindness and universal charity." Simpson meant to cast no aspersion on his predecessor, but he would be far more placating than Elliott. Simpson never had a huge appetite for controversy. As ever the churchman, he viewed the weekly organ as an enabler of the body of Christ, Methodism and beyond: "To assist the pulpit in the diffusion of religious truth, to state clearly and forcibly Christian doctrine, to bring the truth to operate practically upon the conscience and life of the individual, so as to result in a change of heart and in the production of good works, to lead by instruction and exhortation the young convert to become a perfect man in Christ Jesus and to present the vast field of usefulness that opens before the eye of the Christian."[562] For the most part, Simpson would live within that purpose, a charge which he humbly accepted: "In conclusion we must ask the indulgence of our readers. We come to our present position without experience. We cannot expect to fill the place of the distinguished editors who have preceded us. We promise nothing, but to put forth efforts to do good. But in humble reliance for strength and wisdom upon the Almighty, we shall endeavor to go forward."[563]

An Overwhelmed Novice

Simpson's name first appeared on the paper's masthead August 2, 1848, and his first editorial was entitled, "Reading Sermons." Simpson stated, "This practice meets with no encouragement in the word of God. The great teacher did not read his sermons, and not one of the apostles indulged in the practice; it was unknown in the purest age of the Church, before innovations were introduced."[564] In other words, Simpson was against it. He could have just saved his ink. A "read sermon" was a contradiction in terms, an oxymoron for almost every ante-bellum Methodist.

Simpson was immediately overwhelmed with the job of turning out 12,000 copies per week with inviting and edifying material, a stretch compared with the 100 copies of the *Harrison Telegraph* with which he

---

562 "Salutary." *WCA* Vol. XV, No. 18 (August 2, 1848) 66.
563 Ibid., 66.
564 "Reading Sermons," *WCA* Vol. XV, No. 17 (August 2, 1848) 65.

assisted his uncle as a ten-year-old. He wrote his friend, Daniel Curry, a prolific writer throughout his life, for some efficiency tips.[565] Curry was not optimistic: "You are indeed kept in pretty close quarters by your agents, closer than was intended by the General Conference. And I think I may add closer than is compatible with the success of your paper .... No man living can properly conduct a large weekly without assistance, and if attempted by you I apprehend a twofold failure, your health and your paper."[566] Curry was correct. Within a year, Simpson's friends had begun to notice his haggard face, lost weight, and more slumped that usual posture. He wrote his wife, "I know I have cares and anxieties and difficulties, both from my public duties and my private embarrassments, but I did not know that the marks had presented themselves quite so strongly in my features. But let it pass."[567] Financial "embarrassments" would haunt him until the salary and fringe benefits of the Episcopacy.

Unavoidable Conflict

Thomas Morris, former *WCA* editor and now Bishop, offered his unsolicited ideas. He advised the new editor to write sparingly and cautiously: "By writing little, he (the editor) will have the advantage of doing it well, having it always read and redeeming time for other interests of the paper." In light of the intensifying sectional crisis, above all, Simpson was to be an agent of reconciliation: "The church needs rest from this painful conflict. She expects it and under present circumstances, I think she has good ground for such expectations both east and west."[568] Morris's plea was well-founded; the years between 1844 and 1860 were shredded by the "paper wars." Arthur Jones, Jr. assesses: "In the minutes of conferences and meetings; in speeches, sermons, and addresses; articles, pamphlets, and books; but above all, in the pages of the official Advocates and Journals, the charges and counter-charges, and the protests and replies poured from the presses. These were,

---

565   In 1854, Curry was chosen as president of Indiana Asbury University and in 1864 was elected as editor of the *New York Christian Advocate. Cyclopaedia*, 272.

566   LOC, Simpson papers, Letter January 20, 1849, Container five.

567   UMA, Drew University, Simpson papers, Letter September 12, 1849.

568   LOC, Simpson papers, Letter August 16, 1848, Container five.

indeed, the years of a paper warfare."[569] No doubt, those who had nominated and elected Simpson for the editorship of the *Western Christian Advocate* were hoping that he would be a balm in American Methodism.

Simpson must have been dumbfounded when he received a second letter from Morris, some three weeks later, complaining about an article written by Joseph Tabor, "Church Matters in St. Louis, Mo." A letter, falsely attributed to Morris, placed him in an unfavorable light. Tabor, in attempting to defend the senior Bishop, only further embarrassed him: "It is not my province, in a case grave and serious as this, which includes the veracity of old gray-headed Christians near the grave."[570] Morris wrote, "I trust that brother Simpson will not infer from anything in this private letter that I am offended by him personally; it is not so, though I am grieved by the course the thing has been suffered to take and therefore state my grievance to you, privately, not intending to say anything about it to others."[571] Staying clear of personalities was not as easy as Simpson thought. It pained him that he found himself at odds with the abolitionist editor of the *New York Christian Advocate*, George Peck:

> I deeply regret that our presses seem to be thrown into a controversial attitude towards each other. I cannot enter upon a discussion with my brethren (of the) Advocate, unless, absolutely forced into it. I love peace, and especially with my brethren, I may differ as to policy and with my brethren, but I never expect to condemn them. They have difficulties enough, without having them from members of our own family.
>
> On controversial topics I have "said my say," nor have I desired to say more. Yours of the 26th, I have just read. I do not except very materially to the rest of your views. Yes, I regret that a few of the expressions will probably be applied when you did not intend them and will be used by our common enemies to procure discord in our ranks. On <u>resistance</u> as an evil, but in "disregarding" a law under certain circumstances, I am not sure whether I clearly understood you.[572]

---

569   Arthur E. Jones, Jr. "The Years of Disagreement: 1844–61," in *History of American Methodism*, 145.

570   Church Matters in St. Louis, Mo," *WCA* Vol. XV, No. 20 (August 23, 1848) 77.

571   LOC, Simpson papers, Letter September 7, 1848, Container five.

572   UMA, Drew University, Simpson papers, Letter, Simpson to George Peck, December 27, 1850.

The above was not the only crossfire in which the new editor found himself. Edward Ames had turned down the presidency of Dickinson College in Carlisle, Pennsylvania. Simpson had said no to the same offer. In Jesse Peck's opinion (brother of George Peck), Ames had used the offer for "self-glorification" and in doing so, had spoken negatively of Simpson on the floor of the General Conference. Peck accused Ames of being consumed by his own popularity. "After this exhibition he furnished on the conference floor- after that almost malignant attack upon you, you can no longer be in doubt upon that subject."[573]

The trustees at Indiana Asbury were hoping that the "impossibility" of the new job would dawn in on their former president, and send him scurrying back across the state line. John Wheeler, who was now Chair of "Latin Languages and Literature," wrote Simpson on November 6, 1848, "Some of your friends fear that your health is failing–they think you cannot long bear the labor of your present position. They wish you to accept the presidency next July and move back to Greencastle."[574] According to Simpson, failing health was the reason he left Greencastle. But as already suggested, sickness was a thin rationale for moving to the city where his mother, sister, and uncle resided. The "Queen City" was a river town on hills, susceptible to infectious diseases, far more than Greencastle.

For long intervals, Simpson began the weekly edition with an editorial, mostly benign, but informational: the Jews, Easter, Josephine (the wife of Napoleon), Africa, Cuba, the Jewish Temple, etc. He espoused anything that he thought to be a good cause: literature, public schools, female education, temperance, condemnation of tobacco, and colonization. There were also ecclesiastical concerns such as pew rentals (on which he was neutral), the worth of camp meetings, the evil of church lotteries, the ventilation of churches, and lay representation at the General Conferences. He remained a non-combatant on the Church property suit, but made sure his readers knew which side exemplified righteous cause. He quoted Jesus as not retaliating in kind, and referred to the Southern litigates as "misguided and designing men," while congratulating the Northern Church on "the high moral

---

573   LOC, Simpson papers, Letter October 24, 1848, Container five.
574   LOC, Simpson papers, Letter November 6, 1848, Container five.

position which it occupies before the public."[575] Each edition concluded with "The Editor's Table," book reviews that would lead the Christian to profitable reading. Simpson was an omnivorous reader, more so in his early years than later in life.

The Specters of Calvinism and Catholicism

Simpson rarely waded into theological issues. The delicate nuances of theological controversy were not his forte; thus, he pulled out from an ongoing doctrinal debate, which Charles Elliot had conducted with Presbyterians, William Latta and Nathan Rice.[576] Simpson safely critiqued Pelagius, the representative man for heterodoxy in the last fifteen hundred years of the Church's history. "Our readers will at once perceive that if Adam's posterity is not corrupted by his sin-thus, such as those dying in infancy, have no need of a Savior, and can never enter the host of the redeemed. If the individual has arrived at years of accountability according to this theory, he may need atonement for sins committed, but he needs no help to enable him to keep God's commandments."[577] Downtrodden Pelagius has been one of the most utilized theological targets in the history of Christendom. In that Simpson targeted Pelagius is interesting, because the same charge, a minimal need for grace, would be leveled against him, and a stream of other nineteenth-century theologians such as Nathaniel Taylor, Charles Finney, and Horace Bushnell.

Although Simpson usually steered clear of doctrinal debate, he did bristle at a theological slight. When Albert Barnes promoted Calvinism at

---

575   Matthew Simpson, "The Property Question," *WCA* Vol. XV, No. 24 (September 20, 1848) 94.

576   It would have been impossible to continue the debate with William Latta, who died in 1847. Simpson would have been no match for these theological heavyweights. Latta was one of the founders of Princeton Theological Seminary, and served as its Dean. Nathan Rice had debated Alexander Campbell with the attorney, Henry Clay, acting as a judge. He was editor of the *St. Louis Presbyterian*, and served as moderator for the Presbyterian General Assembly when it met in Nashville. Rice actually lived and pastored in Cincinnati when Simpson was editor. That the two ever met is unknown. When Rice died in 1877, he was "Professor of Didactic and Polemic Theology," at Danville Theological Seminary. Alfred E. Nevin, ed., *Encyclopaedia of the Presbyterian Church* (Philadelphia: Presbyterian Encyclopaedia Publishing Co., 1884) 418, 760.

577   Matthew Simpson, "Pelagius and Pelagianism," *WCA* Vol. XVI, No. 39 (Sept. 26, 1849) 154.

the expense of condemning Methodists, comparing them with Buddhist priests and other forms of superstition, Simpson did not withhold his pen. "We cannot reconcile the language which he (Barnes) employed in this sermon, with that dignity and courtesy of character, for which we thought he was distinguished."[578] Simpson inferred that Barnes was comparing the ignorance of Methodist preachers with the refinement of Presbyterians and Congregationalists. Education, Barnes implied, would make one a Calvinist.

Simpson's tenure as editor corresponded with the height of nativism and in particular, anti-Catholicism in America. In 1847, Presbyterian Nicholas Murray poured out his vituperation on Bishop John Hughes, which resulted in unprecedented Catholic–Protestant exchanges, and unleashed Protestant fury on American Catholicism in the late 40's and early 50's. Murray wrote Hughes, "You are hoodwinked and manacled by a system of the grossest fraud and delusion; you are denied the common birthright of a citizen of the world–seeing with your own eyes and hearing with your own ears .... Oh! Suffer the entreaties of one who suffered as you now do under the galling chains of papal tyranny."[579] Upon Elliott climbing back into the editor's chair after Simpson was elected to the Episcopacy, he exhorted Methodists to, "Go and beard the lion in his den; and if they escape with life the first time, let them go again .... And renew the assault till it shall become clear to all men that the Pope is the greatest tyrant in Europe, and that American popery is the most perfect specimen of Hypocrisy and Turpitude the earth has ever seen."[580]

Simpson was not nearly as vitriolic as his mentor, but did cast aspersions on Catholicism. The progress of the Church of Rome, from an earlier period down to the present age, had been marked with blood. "The dreadful carnage among the Waldenses and the Albigenses, the torturers and dungeons of the Inquisition, the massacre of Saint Bartholomew, the bloody wars in the Netherlands, and the fires of Smithfield in the days of Mary, were but

---

578 Matthew Simpson, "Rev. Albert Barnes - Calvinism," *WCA* Vol. XVI, No. 22 (May 30, 1849) 86.
579 Ray Allen Billington. *The Protestant Crusade 1800–1860: The Study of the Origins of American Nativism* (New York: Rinehart and Company, 1952) 253–255.
580 Ibid., 275.

the exponents of her spirit in each succeeding age."[581] He was convinced Protestantism would triumph over Catholicism in America. This particular convincement shaped not only his interpretation of history, but also current events.

> The application of steam to ships and cars, the electric telegraph, the vast expansion of the arts and sciences, and the discovery of the vast mines of California, mark another era; and it is followed by the *wounding* of the Papal power .... California, while held by Papal power, hides its gold in her bosom, nor tells her hoarded wealth. She passes into the hands of a Protestant nation, and immediately she reveals her countless stores.[582]

Titillating Sensationalism and Quotidian Mundaneness

It was easy to pontificate from the chair of an editor and easy for us to blame Simpson, perhaps unfairly, for abstract and premature ideas, perspectives which would be contradicted by future interpretations and activities characterizing his personal and professional life. He would betray his call for simplicity in church architecture by his advice to Christ Church in Pittsburgh, which was recognized as one of the most gothic of American churches. Even the general Church began to waffle on the simplicity issue by adding a "practicality" criterion in 1852. "Let all our churches be built plain and simple and with free seats wherever practical."[583] And his condemnation of political patronage is curious, if not humorous, in a column entitled "Political Exultation." He condemned the practice "to the victor go the spoils," noting, "The patronage of our government is vastly increasing. With the extension of our territorial limits, offices are multiplied; and by the increase of population, the revenue of those offices is increased. We much doubt whether the framers of our government, could have seen its vast extension, would have placed such a tremendous power of appointments in the hands of the Executive. And we further doubt, where even the former purity and calmness of our Presidential contests will return until there is

---

581   Matthew Simpson, "The Intolerance of Rome," *WCA* Vol. XVII No. 5 (January 29, 1851).

582   Matthew Simpson, "The Great Western Thoroughfare," *WCA* Vol. XVI No. 9 (February 28, 1849).

583   *Journals of the General Conferences of the Methodist Episcopal Church 1848-1856* Vol. III (Carlton & Porter, 1856) 108.

a diminution of executive patronage."[584] During the Lincoln, Grant, and Hayes administrations, no clergyman in all of American Protestantism would be linked more to patronage than Matthew Simpson.

For weeks, which stretched into months, Simpson wrote no editorials, filling his editorial column with correspondence from various locations: Europe, Baltimore, New York, Pakistan, Iowa, New England, etc. At other times, he delegated the editorial responsibility to others with articles entitled, "The Poor," "Thoughts on the First Chapter of Genesis," and "Dancing," as well as contemporary pieces such as the U.S. President's "Address to Congress" (what became known as the "State of the Union") and the quadrennial "Bishops' Address," at the General Conference, their assessment of critical issues facing American Methodism. Simpson's editorial dereliction brought criticism. His preaching itinerary took him away from Cincinnati for weeks at a time. When Simpson requested additional funds to pay contributors and decorate the paper with woodcuts, the "Book Committee" protested. Charles Elliott had not needed such funds, but Simpson prevailed. "He hired correspondents in Washington, Philadelphia, New York (his friend, Curry) and Paris. He began to use cuts representing public buildings, colleges, churches, ordinarily with a woman in the foreground, her full skirts sweeping the street and her parasol delicately raised, or a carriage drawn by a spirited horse, his neck arched, his forefoot in midair at the beginning of the downward stroke."[585] It was difficult to draw the line between aesthetic appeal as entertainment and Methodism's middle class aspirations for societal acceptance. In all likelihood, Simpson did not contemplate the money and time for one of his fashionable woodcut ladies to boast of an eighteen-inch waist. Unwittingly, Simpson had advocated anatomical impossibilities, at least for most women. Halttunen notes, "The vertical lines, the simple sleeves, and necklines and the low, tight bodices" on gowns in pictures of "sentimental women," in 1848.[586]

---

584   Matthew Simpson, "Political Exultation," *WCA* Vol. XV No. 33 (November 22, 1848) 130.

585   Clark, *The Life*, 151. Simpson was no slacker in expending editorial ink. James Kirby lists 175 editorials and articles written by him during the less than four year stint as editor. Kirby, *Ecclesiastical and Social*, 335-343.

586   Halttunen, 77.

The Western Christian Advocate reflected both civil and ecclesiastical culture in America, mostly one and the same. Nothing was more unique in the periodical than a regular column, "Revival Intelligence," a term foreign to contemporary Methodism and any other mainline American denomination of the twenty-first century. A single issue of the *Advocate* included 36 reports of "revivals" and their conversionary and numerical efficiency. "We have just closed a protracted meeting in this charge of nine weeks continuance. The great head of the church was with us from the beginning to the end and has very gloriously refreshed our Zion. There were more than 100 clear conversions, 130 received on trial in the church and several professed the blessing of perfect love."[587] A church in the Cincinnati German district, reported: "One hundred sixty-three were added to the Church since Conference, and about the same number were converted, thirty-six from the Church of Rome."[588] Dubuque, Iowa, reported a revival which had begun nine weeks ago, still not stopped. "Many have experienced and professed the blessing of perfect love; ninety-five have been added to the church, the most of whom have been converted to God; making about one hundred fifty since Conference."[589]

Another cultural indicator was the paper's preoccupation with death, most of it represented by melodramatic poetry: "The Miser's Deathbed," "The Voyage Home," "Vision of the Poor," "Dies Idle," "The Death of Infants," "The Death of a Daughter", "Little Boy that Died." The poem "Not as a Child" read:

> Lay up nearer brother nearer for my limbs are growing cold
> And thy presence seemeth dearest when thy arms around me fold
> I am dying brother, dying, soon you'll miss me in your berth
> For my form will soon be lying Neath the oceans briny surf.[590]

Even more bizarre was "The Idiot's Grave":

---

587   *WCA* Vol. XVIII, No. 15 (April 9, 1851) 58.
588   *WCA* Vol. XVIII, No. 12 (March 19, 1851) 46.
589   *WCA* Vol. XVII, No. 12 (March 19, 1851) 46.
590   "Not As a Child," *WCA* Vol. XVIII, No. 23 (June 4, 1851) 92.

Now on the cold and pallid face a smile of heaven was seen
There was no longer any trace of the torn wretch she'd been
Doubtless her mind had seen the light as her worn spirit fled
And on her lone and darksome night her God his Ray had shed.[591]

Simpson recognized that in order to maintain his readership, he needed a steady stream of societal news. He attempted a balance between solemnity and sell-ability, titillating sensationalism and quotidian mundaneness. The steamboat George Washington exploded killing 18 people and badly scalding the captain. On the same day, the steamboat Martha Washington caught on fire, killing six people. "Both of these boats left Cincinnati at nearly the same time. Both were bound for New Orleans and both were burned up about the same hour of the night."[592] Shocks of earthquake were distinctly felt in New Bedford, Massachusetts and Providence and Warwick, Rhode Island. An epidemic of scarlet fever invaded Philadelphia.

Perhaps the most graphic and sensational news of Simpson's editorial tenure concerned the famine in Ireland. In the last eighteen months 1,000,000 people had died of starvation. In the trial of a man for stealing sheep, "One of his children had died of starvation and the wife of the man had fed upon the flesh of the child before he violated the law to procure food. Mr. Dobbins (the judge) has caused the body to be disinterred and the limbs were found to be picked to the bone."[593]

Simpson also added personal anecdotes, if he assessed them sufficiently interesting. During an early summer trip on the steamer *Wisconsin*, Simpson and family bested a storm. The boat when attempting to turn in the middle of the river was "struck by a hurricane, which almost capsized her, and which rendered her wholly unmanageable. For a few minutes the guards (rails) of the boat were 3 to 4 feet under water and in the opinion of the officers, the danger of capsizing was so imminent that we were only saved by the falling

---

591   "The Idiot's Grave," *WCA* Vol. XVIII, No. 19 (March 7, 1851) 76. Lincoln scholar, Michael Burlingame, cites Lincoln's fascination with the poetry of death. "Lincoln's own poetry and his literary taste indicate that his predisposition to depression was rooted in the death of loved ones in his early years." Michael Burlingame. *Abraham Lincoln: A Life* Vol. I (Baltimore: The Johns Hopkins University Press, 2008) 246.
592   *WCA* Vol. XIX, No. 4 (January 28, 1852) 15.
593   *WCA* Vol. XV, No 19 (August 16, 1848) 76.

of the chimneys of the boat which were torn off by the storm." The boat managed to make it safely to shore, and Simpson testified that he had never witnessed "such anxiety and alarm."[594]

The Fugitive Slave Law

When the Missouri Compromise was adopted by Congress in 1820, proposed by Henry Clay, "the great compromiser," no one dreamed that within a quarter of a century, the United States would increase its territory by a third, extending its boundaries all the way to the Pacific. The 36 degree-50 minute parallel ran almost straight through the middle of California. Would the state be half slave and half free? When the freshman congressman, Abraham Lincoln, had opposed Polk's Mexican war, which would acquire California, he appraised the President as an "insane man" further adding that "his mind, taxed beyond its power, is running hither and thither like an ant on a hot stove."[595]

Some six months before Simpson assumed the editorship of his newspaper, the United States signed the Treaty of Guadalupe Hidalgo, which ceded to the United States land from Mexico for $18,250,000 which included California, Nevada, Utah, most of New Mexico and Arizona, parts of Wyoming and Colorado.[596] After settling the boundary with Great Britain for the Oregon territory at the 49th parallel, the continental United States (except for non-contiguous Alaska and Hawaii) became the geographical location in which Americans live today. The settlements with Mexico and Great Britain increased America's land size from 1,787,159 square miles to 2,981,166 square miles, an addition of well over 1,000,000 square miles.[597] The only further change would be the 30,000 square mile purchase from Mexico in 1854, the "Gadsden Purchase," in order to provide a railroad

---

[594] *WCA* Vol. XVII, No. 31 (July 31, 1851) 122. Simpson did not know that hurricanes are coastal events which never occur in the Mideast or the Midwest. No doubt the wind was high, but not technically a hurricane.

[595] Robert W. Merry. *A Country of Vast Designs: James K Polk, the Mexican War and the Conquest of the American Continent* (New York: Simon and Schuster, 2009) 11.

[596] Arthur Schlesinger, Jr. *The Almanac of American History* (New York: Barnes & Noble, 1993) 254.

[597] Carl Russell Fish. "The Rise of the Common Man" in *A History of American Life*, ed. Mark C. Carnes (New York: Simon & Schuster, 1996) 609.

through southern Arizona to California. The slave status of these new land acquisitions, would consume American politics over the next dozen years.

Polk believed the compromise of 1820 sufficient to settle the slavery question, but the majority of Americans were dead set against slavery spreading to all of New Mexico, Arizona, one third of California and all of Texas. Though the Wilmot Proviso had never been adopted by Congress, it still dominated the thinking of the Northern states. On April 8, 1846 Congressman David Wilmot introduced a bill that would have banned slavery from all lands acquired from Mexico. The House of Representatives passed the bill, the Senate rejected it. Nonetheless, Wilmot had drawn a line, an issue that would not go away. Most Southerners were adamantly opposed to the Wilmot Proviso because it did not allow for a "permanent equilibrium of power in the Union."[598] The expansion of "free soil" into all the acquired territory from Mexico, other than Texas, created disequilibrium from which the South would never recover. During the 1850s, this alarming reality threatened to undo a culture built on what Southerners believed to be inalienable rights afforded them by the Constitution.

Henry Clay knew full well that, in Robert Remini's words, "If Christian churches could not maintain their unity, in the face of this momentous question, could the union itself long endure? It was a frightening apprehension that no doubt speeded Clay's determination to seek an amiable resolution to the immediate problem."[599] On January 29, 1850, Clay presented his "omnibus bill," eight resolutions, three of which would become law, but only after being separately presented six months later: the admission of California as a free state, a stricter fugitive slave law and the abolishment of the slave trade in the District of Columbia. On a cold February 5, Clay, consumed by tuberculosis, climbed up the Capitol steps with a friend holding his arm. Over the next two days Clay spoke for five hours plus, explaining and defending his proposals. When Southerners accused him of giving the North "all the trump cards in the pack," he responded, "I know

---

598   Major Wilson. "Ideological Roots and Manifest Destiny: The Geo-politics of Slavery Expansion in the Crisis of 1850," *Journal of the Illinois State Historical Society* Vol. LXIII, No 2 (Summer 1790) 143.

599   Robert V. Remini. *Henry Clay: Statesman for the Union* (New York: W. W. Norton and Company, 1991) 730.

no South, no North, no East, and no West, to which I owe my allegiance …. My allegiance is to this Union, and my own State; but if gentlemen suppose they can exact from me an acknowledgment of allegiance to any ideal or future contemplated confederacy of the South, I here declare that I owe no allegiance to it; nor will I, for one, come under any such allegiance, if I can avoid it."[600]

On April 8, Clay made the statement for which he is best remembered: "I go for honorable compromise when it can be made. Life itself is but a compromise between death and life, the struggle continuing throughout our whole existence, until the great Destroyer finally triumphs."[601] The "great destroyer" would win less than a year and a half later. Clay died, having left his beloved country with the fugitive slave law, a law which was impossible to enforce, and a compromise which would only intensify the Southern-Northern tension and eventuate into the war he had desperately tried to avoid.

The Elusive Middle Ground

Simpson first referred to slavery June 13, 1849, by reviewing Nathan Bangs' pamphlet, "Emancipation: Its Necessity and Means of Accomplishment." Bangs proposed that,

> Congress make a proposition to the several slave states, that so much per head shall be allowed for every slave, that shall be emancipated, leaving it to the state legislatures respectively to adopt their own measures for effecting the object for doing the time, age at and the circumstances under which emancipation shall take place. In respect to the aged and infirmed, it would be unjust, if not indeed inhuman to set them free without provision being made for their support and comfort, and the young and helpless infant ought to be provided for by some adequate means.[602]

Simpson agreed with financial reimbursement for freed slaves, and Lincoln himself held to a similar idea well into the second year of his Presidency. Simpson returned to emancipation again on August 1, when the state legislatures in Kentucky and Missouri were debating the issue. As always, Simpson could suggest no workable solution to America's foremost

---

600   Ibid., 740.
601   Ibid., 745. Or was it "I'd rather be right than President?"
602   *WCA* Vol. XVI, No. 24 (June 13, 1849) 96.

problem. He only knew that he was against slavery, a comfortable position north of the Ohio River.

> We deeply regret that any Christian, and especially any Christian minister, should arrange themselves upon the side of perpetual slavery. Whatever apology may be supposed to exist in behalf of Christian citizens of slave holding states, who are connected with slavery, such apology must cease whenever the opportunity to alter these laws occurs and are found opposing such alterations. They then become slaveholders, not from necessity of circumstances, but of choice. Such must ever rank among the friends and upholders of slavery.[603]

On October 9, 1850, Simpson condemned the fugitive slave law in that it denied trial by jury, did away with the writ of *habeas corpus*, bribed the judge, and demanded of all citizens to catch escaping slaves. (A judge was paid five dollars for freeing a slave and ten dollars when he returned the fugitive to his owner.) He then quoted *Zion's Herald*, "Is there a God-fearing man in the North who would hesitate to abjure such a law before heaven and earth at any penalty?"[604] Unwittingly, Simpson had suggested civil disobedience. From this assertion, the editor backed off two weeks later. He apologized in "Upon a given measure, viewed in its moral aspects, the Advocate has given free utterance, and will continue to do so, but it desires not to call into question the general patriotism and excellence of our leading men of both parties."[605]

Three weeks later, Simpson clearly disowned any suggestion of civil disobedience in that Christians are to suffer the law and not resist. He believed that Scripture did not teach or support civil disobedience. Simpson was unclear in his own mind and communicated equivocation to his readers. "Christianity does not require her votaries to obey laws that conflict with God's law. She does not even allow her disciples to conform to the mandates of any earthly power. At the peril of death in its most frightful forms, if those mandates are directly opposed to God's word, but she never teaches

---

603 Matthew Simpson, "Emancipation," *WCA* Vol. XVI, No. 31 (August 1, 1849) 122.

604 Matthew Simpson, "The Fugitive Slave Bill," *WCA* Vol. XVII, No. 41 (October 9, 1850) 160. Giving Simpson the benefit of the doubt, Scripture is also unclear on this matter, in that Peter and Paul resisted the law, but yet Paul wrote in Romans 13:1, "Everyone must submit himself to the governing authorities, for there is no authority except that which God has established. The authorities that exist have been established by God" (NIV).

605 Matthew Simpson, "Political Explanation," *WCA* Vol. XII, No. 43 (October 23, 1850) 73.

resistance." Simpson further argued resistance is not only unchristian; but in a democratic country, it is unwise. "If the majority is dissatisfied with the law, they have the power to repeal it. If the majority is satisfied, it is in vain for the minority to resist."[606] Simpson demonstrated no evidence of having read David Thoreau's pamphlet on "Civil Disobedience" written in 1849.

Daniel Webster on March 7, 1851, expressed his disappointment in Simpson and all other Methodists who mixed religion and party politics. "I was in hopes that the differences of opinion might be adjusted, because I looked on that religious denomination as one of the great props of religion and morals throughout the whole country from Maine to Georgia and westward to our utmost Western boundary."[607] Stephen Douglas was even more condemning of the intensifying, anti-slavery stance of Northern Methodism, a movement "which came forward with an atrocious falsehood and an atrocious calumny against the Senate, desecrated the pulpit and the sacred desk to the miserable and corrupting influence of party politics." Douglas accused Methodists of "profound ignorance on the questions upon which they attempt to enlighten the Senate as the same body of preachers."[608]

Anti-Slavery without Abolition

The "bill of compromises" for the sake of admitting California as a free state "came to Congress as several other states have come, and it seeks admission in the usual way." Simpson prophesied, "If these threats mean anything they indicate a settled purpose to seize hold of the first plausible pretext to form a separate organization. Surely we do not believe this to be the wish of the people of the South." Simpson then apologized for stepping beyond the parameters which he had originally proscribed when he accepted the editorial assignment. "But it is not our purpose to write a political homily." But that is exactly what he had done. He then justified the transgression. "We believe indeed that these moral questions come strictly within the province of the religious press, but we know that it is difficult to treat them,

---

606   Matthew Simpson, "Fugitive Slave Law–Resistance," *WCA* Vol. XVII, No. 46 (Nov. 13, 1850) 182.
607   William Warren Sweet. *The Methodist Episcopal Church and The Civil War* (Cincinnati: The Methodist Book Concern, 1912) 44.
608   Ibid., 45.

so as to avoid the appearance of party predilection."[609] Circumventing the most critical issue in America was an impossibility. During the 1850s, one well-traveled observer wrote, "Political life to an American citizen had all the fanaticism of religion and all the fascination of gambling."[610]

After Simpson had stepped outside his editorial camouflage, there was no retreat. One month later, April 3, he wrote, "But when moral principles are the ground of controversy, and when the whole discussion turns upon the great question of human rights, then no tongue should be dumb, no press should be silent." Then with astute prescience, Simpson stated what he did not want to happen, but would be the ultimate outcome. "California will certainly be admitted just as she is, unless by intrigue a number of bills should be blended into one so that territories must be admitted and fugitive slave bills passed by the same vote which admits the Golden State." After placing much of the blame upon Daniel Webster's apparent defection to the South, Simpson accurately predicted the results of a rigid fugitive slave law, the price of admitting California as a free state: "The fugitive slave bill will open the door to such a system of kidnapping the free colored population as will excite the whole community. Whatever the oath of an abandoned villain, who can be hired for a few dollars to deal in human flesh, shall be sufficient to throw in chains and hurry into slavery without the right of *habeas corpus* or a trial by jury, any colored man what must be the inevitable result."[611]

Simpson's stand against the above fugitive slave law did not translate into abolitionism. Other than "colonization" which placed him in the mainstream of Northern attitudes, Simpson, at no time previous to the Civil War, gave any practical solution to America's foremost problem.[612]

---

609   Matthew Simpson, "Doings of Congress," *WCA* Vol. XVII, No. 10 (March 6, 1850) 37.

610   William E. Gienapp. "Politics Seem to Enter into Everything: Political Culture in the North: 1840-1860," *Essays on American Antebellum Politics:* 1840-1860, eds. William E. Gienapp, et. al. (College Station: Texas A. & M. University, 1982) 16.

611   Matthew Simpson, "The Religious Press and Politics," *WCA* Vol. XVII, No. 14 (April 3, 1850) 53.

612   The African Colonization Society, as a practical solution to the slavery problem, never gained wide-spread popularity. Eric Burin argues, that, "Natural right ideology, evangelical egalitarianism, economic uncertainty, and African resistance, all slowed its proliferation. The Society was motivated more by whites who feared miscegenation, than

That Liberia was American Methodism's first foreign field of service was no accident. Simpson argued for continued attention to Liberia. Other places offered history, aesthetic enticements: Germany, France, Palestine, and Greece. But Liberia presented no such inducements. "No works of art, no ruins of the past, no valuable libraries, no association with the noble and the wise" would entice missionaries. Its inhabitants were "manumitted slaves, its houses frail, its lands uncultivated, and sickness and death, in almost every breeze!"[613] Simpson had to be aware of the sneering disdain of those who interpreted colonization as a compartmentalized denial of the real problem, what historian, Dwight L. Dumond, referred to as "a rationalization for the lazy intellect, a sedative for the guilty conscience, a refuge for the politician and the professional man."[614] Matthew Simpson held on to colonization for the rest of his life. On March 23, 1882, he wrote Edward W. Syle, Corresponding Secretary of the Pennsylvania Colonization Society,

---

it was blacks gaining liberty by exportation. Thomas Jefferson was not alone in his anxiety that emancipating millions of slaves in America would culminate in ethnic blood-letting or blood-mixing. (Recent history, aided by the science of DNA has shed light on Jefferson's ironic hypocrisy)." The "American Society for Colonizing the Free People of Color" was founded in 1816, by the likes of Henry Clay, Daniel Webster, and John Randolph. Malaria and harsh conditions killed twenty-nine percent of the first 1,670 immigrants who headed to Liberia between 1820 and 1830. Utopian dreams were quickly extinguished when an emigrant observed that Liberian graveyards, "always looked fresh." Blacks continued to immigrate under the aegis of the ACS until 1904. By then, approximately 10,000 former slaves had left America during the Negro diaspora, a nano-fraction of those who chose to stay in America, their rightful home. Eric Burin. *Slavery and the Peculiar Solution: A History of the American Colonization Society* (University Press of Florida, 2005) 17, 148, 169.

613   Matthew Simpson, "Liberia Mission," *WCA* Vol. XVII, No. 5 (January 30, 1850) 17. Methodism stubbornly held on to the Liberia idea for the next thirty years. In 1882, the General Missionary Committee, chaired by Simpson, came to the conclusion that the mission had been futile. Daniel Curry remarked, "that he hoped to see the African mission given up absolutely. It must be patent to all that Liberia was one of the greatest failures, both as a missionary station and as a colony, and he was willing to give it up wholly to the British as soon as opportunity offered. Dr. Fowler believed this to be true, but thought that while the mission there was not a success, it was altogether the best thing they had in Africa. They had failed to develop among their brethren of the Liberia Conference the energy to carry on the work in the interior." "Methodist Foreign Missions: The Appropriation for the Next Year to be $750,000 -Liberia and South America," *New York Times* (November 7, 1882).

614   Quoted in Sydney E. Ahlstrom. *A Religious History of the American People* Vol. II (New Haven: Yale University Press, 1975) 94.

> I most heartily wish you great success in advocating the cause of the American Colonization Society. The regeneration of Africa requires not only Christian Missionaries, but also Christian Colonists, who shall show the natives the superiority of Christian arts and civilization. Her sons, in our land, are gradually becoming so enlightened and so experienced in business, that they will feel it to be their duty to give a helping hand to their brethren who are in darkness. To your Society must they chiefly look for that assistance which they will need for settlement in Africa.[615]

The real problem for most Northerners was that moral indignation did not translate into respect for Blacks as equal human beings made in the image of God, much less love for brothers and sisters in Christ. American church historian Sydney Ahlstrom wrote, "Nowhere in Christendom was Negro slavery more heavily institutionalized, nowhere was the disparity between ideals and actuality so stark, nowhere were the Churches more deeply implicated."[616] For the rest of his life, Simpson tenaciously held onto the Liberian Mission at least until Methodism abandoned the miserable failure. Before Gilbert Haven went to Liberia in 1876, Simpson wrote him. "I have no doubt, that there are other parts of Africa that would be healthier, and better from which to reach the interior if we were not bound by strong ties to Liberia. We cannot, however, relinquish that colony whose religious care has seen so largely to devolve upon us."[617] Simpson's admonitions for Haven to beware of exhaustion and impure air, because of his age, were in vain. On this trip he contacted malaria from which he never fully recovered, dying three years later on January 3, 1880.

As Simpson stiff-armed abolitionism, he was keenly aware that he was walking a political and spiritual tightrope, while attempting to maintain "a conscience void of offense" without unnecessary alienation. Donald Jones argues that, "In resisting the succession of parts of the church and beguiling clergymen and members to stay with the northern Church, Simpson and others no doubt played the chief role in saving Maryland for the Union and succeeded in retaining many congregations in other border states for the Union cause."[618]

---

615   LOC, Simpson papers, Letter, March 23, 1882, Container thirteen.

616   Ibid., 92.

617   UMA, Drew University, Gilbert Haven papers, Letter, Matthew Simpson to Gilbert Haven, October 30, 1876.

618   Donald Jones, 36.

Simpson was playing the same role as many of his high ranking predecessors in Methodism. As Donald Mathews claims, "In 1835, every major Methodist publication except *Zion's Herald* of Boston, was enlisting in the colonization ranks." He further assesses, "In spite of their self-conscious Arminian devotion to the freedom of the will, Methodist colonizationists did not presume to pit themselves against society. If history were to be adjudicated on behalf of the black man, let it be done in Africa! As members of the master class, they could extend charity but not dispense justice."[619]

A Janus-like Response

Attempting fairness, Simpson printed a rebuttal to his own arguments against the fugitive slave law by Congressman William J. Brown, editor of the *Indiana State Sentinel*: "The editorial is full of errors, unintentional errors of course, but just such errors as editors will fall into, when they attempt to write upon subjects they do not understand. We have always admired Dr. Simpson for his eloquence in the pulpit and the simplicity and beauty of his style as a theological writer. But divinity, not law has been his study." Simpson had abandoned "the lipid streams of divinity to sail his bark on the turbid and boisterous ocean of politics. He must look out or he will have frequent collision with more experienced navigators." Simpson replied that the critical issue was the slave being denied a trial by jury. A slave was not allowed due justice of the law. "The fugitive from justice is kept in the hands of the law until indicted by a grand jury and tried by a petit jury, but the alleged fugitive from slavery is delivered into the hands of the irresponsible claimant who may put him in handcuffs and hurry him to the nearest slave market for sale."[620]

From his perspective, Simpson was not meddling in party politics, but carrying out the duties of humanity. He admitted to not being a lawyer, but he had read some law books and quoted from Blackstone. "If any human laws allow us or require us to commit crime we are bound to transgress that

---

619 Donald G. Mathews. *Slavery and Methodism: A Chapter in American Morality, 1780-1845* (Princeton: Princeton University Press, 1965) 104-105.
620 *WCA* Vol. XVII, No. 47 (November 20, 1850) 186. Also see William J. Brown, "Dr. Simpson and the Fugitive Slave Law," *Indiana State Sentinel*, Indianapolis (January 7, 1851).

human law." After quoting several other jurists, Simpson exploded off the page as if he were a Garrisonian disciple: "As long as our lips will have an utterance or our fingers make a pen, we shall fearlessly speak and write what our judgment and our conscience approve." But then in a Janus-like move, Simpson exonerated himself and the Methodist Church from any propensity "to resist" the law. "Neither the Conference nor ourselves as editor, interfere in any way with fugitives, but we do disapprove of a law which makes the whole North a hunting ground for kidnappers, exposes free men to the claims of slavery, offers a premium to corrupt officers, and takes and attempts to turn the whole population into slave catchers or kidnappers." For the time being, Simpson and Methodism would combat slavery in word only, not in deed.

Years later, Simpson refuted (or forgot) the ambiguity and equivocation, which had characterized his response to the fugitive slave law. "On public measures, the paper was outspoken for a very decided editorial on the fugitive slave law. It received the commendation of the Ind. Conference by a rising vote, & it defended against political assailants."[621] Simpson remembered that he had received supporting letters from Thomas Benton and Salmon Chase. In April of 1850, Chase had written him: "Never were truer words uttered than yours: The hours of trial are upon us, and though in the end humanity will triumph, yet humane duty demands free and full utterance now for every lover of liberty. Hardly any subject can now more worthily engage the action & the prayers of all true Christians."[622] Methodist scholar Ralph Keller correctly modifies Simpson's interpretation of his editorial stance on the fugitive slave law.

> When fellow editors Stevens, Hosmer, and Peck shortly became involved in bitter debate, Simpson refused to be drawn in. His position was that of a moderate, frightened by signs that discontent over the law might take a violent turn. Even the popular temptation to blacken forever the name of Daniel Webster for his part in passage of the law drew a mild rebuke. His disclaimers to the contrary, Simpson had also been constrained by the common view that political matters were not the proper domain of the minister. He had apologized so often for speaking on the law that readers may well have questioned whether his own mind was clearly made upon the propriety of his course.[623]

621   *Autobiography*.
622   LOC, Simpson papers, Letter April 26, 1850, Container five.
623   Ralph A. Keller. "Methodist Newspapers and the Fugitive Slave Law: A New

In summary, consequences for the Methodist Episcopal Church were more important than consequences for the American Negro.

A Myopic Triumphalism

Simpson and his newspaper entered 1851 with glowing optimism. All was well in America. "Why should we not be happy? Our government is a glorious one …. Unseen, the majesty of the law is constantly around us. Property is protected and life is secure. Our coasts are unguarded, yet, no hostile fleets descend upon them. Our cities are un-walled, yet, no ruthless host coming with torch and sword causes the inhabitants to tremble or to flee. Our vast territories are thrown open and the suffering and the oppressed from Europe's crowded cities seek among us shelter and asylum."[624] Again Simpson had to remind his readers of their monetary obligations or they would be "stricken from the list." Self-depreciatingly, Simpson promised, "Apart from our own contribution, the *Advocate* will be a rich source of instruction to every family circle."[625]

The above triumphalism indicates that in all likelihood, Simpson had never stepped into a Cincinnati slaughterhouse, and watched a "gutter" rip the internals from three hogs within one minute. The meaning of being splattered with blood and hog entrails all day for minimum wages would be left for Sinclair Lewis and the other "muckrakers." His paper hinted at no awareness that the "suffering and oppressed in Europe" were equally suffering and oppressed when they arrived in New York or even Cincinnati. Simpson did not report on the Irish Riot, that had stormed the Astor Place Opera House in 1849, resulting in twenty-two persons killed.[626] In fact, the above optimism adumbrated Simpson's ever increasing progressive nationalism and ethnocentricity, which somehow ignored the intensifying problems of labor, urbanization and class division. Simpson's insular isolationism, in keeping with his individualistic theology, never came to grips with the

---

Perspective for the Slavery Crisis in the North," *Church History*, Vol. 43 No. 3 (Sep. 1974) Cambridge England: Cambridge University Press on behalf of the American Society of Church History, 319-339.

624   Matthew Simpson, "The New Year," *WCA* Vol. XIII, No. 1 (January 1, 1851) 2.
625   *WCA* Vol. XIII, No. 3 (January 15, 1851) 10.
626   Schlesinger, 256, 259.

frightening complexities and deprivations which tortured those who lived on the margins of society.

In terms of his vocation, Simpson could feel good about the last four years. He had not only increased the circulation of the *Advocate*, but had also faithfully represented the sentiments of most Northern Methodists. He had tackled, but not placed a chokehold on issues such as the fugitive slave law, mixed seating for the sexes, free pews, lay representation in the General Conference, the societal advancement of women and the North-South Publishing House dispute. He recalled his resolution that "no controversy should begin by me, nor would I touch upon one already begun. I consequently excluded from the paper all communication of this kind announced in my salutary determination to avoid personalities and to make the paper strictly a church paper for the defense of the doctrine and polity of Methodism."[627]

Simpson's editorship of the *Advocate* was for him personally, the beginning of a journey toward what Will Herberg called "the fusion of Protestantism with the American way of life."[628] Whatever fangs with which Charles Elliott had endowed the *Advocate*, Simpson had extracted, with the forceps of denounce and then retract, declaim and then apologize. Unfortunately the *Advocate* had moved towards a "culture religion," which James Kirby insightfully interprets "as lacking sufficient normative content to bring any cogent criticism to bear upon society because of its identification with it."[629] The above political moderation and sagacity makes one an ideal candidate for the highest jurisdictional office within an ecclesiastical body. Charles Elliott was the lone exception to the first eight editors of the *Western Christian Advocate*, all of whom stepped into the office which Francis Asbury had instituted, Bishop of the Methodist Episcopal Church.

---

627   Crooks, 257.

628   Will Herberg. *Protestant, Catholic, Jew: An Essay in American Religious Sociology* (Garden City, New York: Anchor Books, 1960) 110.

629   Kirby, *Ecclesiastical and Social*, 307.

A Conflicted Conscience

No doubt, Simpson was aware that Cincinnati was the primary depot in the United States for the Underground Railroad. He would have also known of Levi Coffin, if he did not know him personally, as a prominent Cincinnati merchant and the chief Cincinnati conductor for the Underground Railroad. In 1850, Coffin claimed that he had assisted an average of 100 slaves per year over the last quarter of a century to escape to freedom. "We knew not what night or what hour of the night we would be raised from slumber by a gentle rap at the door. That was the signal announcing the arrival of a train of the Underground Railroad, for the locomotive did not whistle, or make any unnecessary noise." When a friend told him it was wrong to harbor fugitive slaves because they might have killed their master or committed some other crime, Coffin asked, "If the Good Samaritan stopped to inquire whether the man who fell among thieves was guilty of any crime before he attempted to help him?"[630] We do not know if the contemporary Cincinnatians ever met.

The editorship of the *Western Christian Advocate* smoked Matthew Simpson out of his comfort zone. Editing a newspaper available for public consumption by a readership rapidly populating the continent, was far different than administrating the affairs of a small educational institution whose influence hardly extended outside of Indiana. Though he was aware of the intensifying slavery conflict, he would have never imagined the editorial role in which he would be forced, a challenge to retain a modicum of integrity. Even as he penned his anti-fugitive slave law convictions, he wrestled with a conflicted conscience. It was not as simple as obeying God rather than man, because it was difficult to discern the mind of either. Simpson's perspective was a safe moderation, a stance which one New Englander described as loving, "the honor of a seat in so dignified a body–rich breakfasts, sumptuous dinners, exhilarating teas, good smokes in summer-houses, or shady bowers, downy beds,[and] seeing the lions and elephants."[631] Though this assessment

---

630 "The Underground Railroad," Levi Coffin, *http://www.nationalcenter.org/UndergroundRailroad.html*
631 Smith. *Revivalism and Social Reform*, 191.

would have not been completely true of Simpson, the editor made sure that the "lions and elephants" stayed on the other side of the fence.

If Simpson was enigmatic, it was partially due to his fumbling transition from an evangelical gospel of personal and individual salvation to having to grapple with systemic evil, the "peculiar institution", which betrayed America's most foundational beliefs. Also his waffling, unlike Levi Coffin, was due to the fact that American Methodism had never taken an unequivocal stand on slavery. Francis Asbury actualized his ambivalence when he removed the condemnation of slavery from the copies of the *Discipline*, which were shipped to South Carolina in 1808. "Asbury had voted for a growing, though incoherent church. It was better to have the largest in America, even if it was divided and afflicted by a malignant tumor. Asbury preferred to compartmentalize-two churches, two races, two disciplines, and in a sense, two Gospels."[632]

Only screwball fanatics who carried either a literal or verbal saber were completely convinced they possessed the mind of God. And nobody ever called Simpson a fanatic. In reality, Simpson, like most Americans, floated down a historic river, which channeled him more than he directed it. In ante-bellum historian Timothy Smith's words, "The conservative temper which preferred to let well enough alone rather than cope with thorny problems, became as strong in ecclesiastical assemblies as in the halls of Congress. Everywhere men of good will-whether saints or skeptics-rejected all thought of armed conflict, even while adopting measures, which in the name of human brotherhood, drove the country toward a brother's war."[633]

Editing the *Western Christian Advocate* served as a watershed in Matthew Simpson's life. At least part of the time, he lived in a comfortable house in an elite neighborhood. He no longer had to scramble for his own salary and stress as to whether the institution for which he was employed was going to financially crumble. He would never again live in rural America, in which Methodism had faced dire deprivation, and yet became the most numerically successful of American sects. In 1852, as Simpson stepped into

---

632   Darius Salter. *America's Bishop: The Life of Francis Asbury* (Nappanee, IN: Evangel Publishing House, 2003) 317.
633   Smith, 202-203.

his denomination's highest office, he had begun a cultural accommodation which would parallel that of the church which he served. No one personified over the next quarter of a century American Methodism's increasing prestige and institutionalization more than Matthew Simpson.

Though Simpson was already acquainted with Thomas Carlton, James Harlan, John Evans, and the Harper Brothers, as well as other influential Methodists, he would now participate in their world. The salary for a Bishop was not exorbitant ($2,000–3,000 per year), but more importantly, Simpson would become a member of Methodism's elite, with accompanying financial benefits. A small coterie of Methodists were becoming strategic players in America's economic and political life. As he and Ellen headed to Boston, his fears of an early death were being translated into the possibilities of becoming a man of destiny. Maybe God was going to spare him after all. John L. Smith, six years earlier, had told Simpson that he would be elected Bishop at the 1852 General Conference.[634] The forty-year-old editor had not forgotten.

---

634 Clark, *Pulpit and Platform*, 268.

Chapter Eight:
An Astute Politician

Carefully Playing His Political Cards

Simpson attended the 1852 General Conference with the intention of leaving the office of editor of the *Western Christian Advocate*. He had packed his belongings, before leaving Cincinnati, a city that had proved more unfavorable to his health than Greencastle. "The Cholera was very severe for several days …. & unusual gloom hung over the city. I visited some who had suffered, and I myself was prostrated by an attack which, thanks to a kindly providence, yielded to my will a vigorous treatment by Dr. Comegys. He was then my family physician. The following 2 years I had attacks of typhoid fever and I became satisfied my health would not permit me to remain an editor in Cincinnati."[635] While in Cincinnati, he had turned down the presidencies of Dickinson College, the planned North Western University in Evanston, and Wesleyan University in Middletown, Connecticut.

What Simpson expected in the Episcopal election is difficult to discern. If we believe what he said about his political possibilities were what he thought, he was convinced that his potential for becoming a Bishop was almost nil. Some thought him liberal on church architecture; others were concerned that he had not spent enough time in the itinerate ministry; Easterners believed that Simpson wanted to eliminate pew rents and surely two persons would not be elected from the same Conference. The election of Ames would eliminate Simpson and allow the many Edward Thomson supporters to install their man. Most of all was the fear that Simpson was too anti-slavery. "Delegates from the Border States sent a committee to question

---
635   *Autobiography*.

as to my position. I simply referred them to my course as editor and to the views I had publically expressed, and declined to make in further expression of opinion, whatever. I had resolutely and conscientiously refrained from any arrangement with any person looking towards securing a vote & declined to make any expression which might be interpreted as wishing to gain any favor whatever."[636]

Like all astute nineteenth century politicians, Simpson camouflaged his political ambitions and hedged on any issues where a clear declaration would jeopardize his possibilities. There was no guarantee against a further schism. The denomination still smoldered from the 1844 fissure, and slavery was not going to fade away. The era of combustion necessitated moderation as the paramount quality of one who would chair conferences in both border states and New England. Simpson exuded calmness in a church defined by a razor-sharp emotional edge. An article in the 1867 *Christian Advocate and Journal*, "Bishops as Partisans," stated,

> In accepting their positions, our bishops (and all others) accept their restraint and responsibilities, as well their authorities and dignities. The rights of one's individuality are sacred as long as the individual maintains his private and personal position, when he accepts a public position he voluntarily foregoes his individual rights, so far as they may be incompatible with his public position. Things are so obvious that we need only state them, and anyone is free to use them and make any legitimate inferences from them in practical affairs.[637]

In other words, an aspirant for ecclesiastical office must play his political cards close to his chest.

As a forty-year-old, Simpson was elected at the 1852 General Conference in Boston as a Bishop of the Methodist Episcopal Church in America. Bishop Elijah Heading had died, and Bishop Leonidas Hamline had resigned. With the increase of Conferences (now thirty-two), the delegates chose four new bishops, amazingly on the first ballot: Levi Scott 113 votes, Matthew Simpson 110 votes, Osman Baker 90 votes, and Edward Ames 89 votes, Tuesday, May

---

636 *Autobiography*.
637 "Bishops as Partisans," *New York Christian Advocate & Journal*, Thursday (November 4, 1867).

25th.[638] Equally surprising, was that two bishops had been elected from the same Conference, Indiana, certainly not the "hub" for American Methodism. Although a member of the Indiana Conference, Simpson did not reside in Indiana, but Cincinnati, where he was the editor of the flourishing *Western Christian Advocate*, an office from which twelve bishops would eventually be elected.[639]

Why Simpson?

But Bishop Simpson's election, as well as that of the others, still begs the question, "Why not Nathan Bangs or Abel Stevens," both also editors and writers of multiple volumes of Methodist history? Bangs increased the effectiveness of his sonorous voice by living in Canada for six years. He was elected a delegate to every General Conference from 1808 until 1856, with the exception of 1848. No one was of more regal appearance on the Conference floor than Nathan Bangs. His capable and tireless efforts enabled him to simultaneously edit two Methodist periodicals, the *Methodist Magazine* and the *Christian Advocate*. He founded the Methodist Missionary Society and for sixteen years, gratuitously served as its secretary, vice-president, and treasurer, but a failure marred his life.[640] In 1841, he was elected president of Wesleyan University in Middletown, Connecticut, where he lasted only a year. He also confessed that preaching was a real trial. "I was always constitutionally timid, and when I commenced preaching it was with much fear and trembling."[641]

---

638   *Zion's Daily Herald: Boston* (May 25, 1852). *Zion's Daily Herald* was published during the 1852 sessions of the General Conference of the Methodist Episcopal Church by the Boston Wesleyan Association–F. Rand, Rev. A. Stevens and Rev. E. Otheman, Editors.

639   "Twelve Bishops: Have Left the Western Book Concern for the Episcopate," *Cincinnati Enquirer*, 23 May, 1900 (Cincinnati, Ohio: 1872-1922) 7.

640   Carl Price wrote: "In managing the discipline of the undergraduates, President Bangs was not happy, as might have been expected of one so inexperienced in that delicate task, and as he himself had somewhat anticipated when he was considering his election to the presidency. A portion of the undergraduate body had become estranged from their president, and some of the boys began openly to question the value on their prospective diplomas of the signature of a president, who himself was not a college graduate. The complaints came to his notice and deeply wounded him. Hearing that Dr. Olin had at last recovered health, and realizing that the financial efforts, which he had not been able to bring to fruition, could in all probability be consummated more fully by Doctor Olin, Bangs resigned." Carl F. Price. *Wesleyan's First Century: With an Account of the Centennial Celebration* (Middletown, CT: Wesleyan University 1932) 68-69.

641   Abel Stevens. *Life and Times of Nathan Bangs* (New York: Carlton and Porter,

According to Bangs, he was asked to let his name stand for Bishop at the 1824 General Conference. Citing domestic responsibilities, he declined. But often, the reasons one gives for not accepting nomination for a political office, serve as a defense mechanism. Did Bangs fear he would be elected, or did he fear he would not be elected? Bangs claimed that had he allowed his name on the ballot, he would have been elected with little opposition. If his claim was true, why was he never again caucused as a nominee? Giving Bangs the benefit of the doubt, he may have feared emasculation. In Abel Stevens' appraisal, Bangs "believed that the position he occupied, in connection with the great enterprises of the Church–its missions, Sunday-schools, literature, and publishing house–an equally honorable, and a much more useful sphere of labor. Besides these considerations, there was throughout his noble nature–a nature robust for all useful labors, and courageous for all necessary contests–a vein of diffident modesty, which made him shrink from any promotion which, with whatever advantages of power and usefulness, imposed the conventional restrains of official dignity."[642] Though Bangs was appreciated, he was not a representative man. Nathan Hatch argues that Bangs personified upward mobility in Methodism.

> Bangs envisioned Methodism, as a popular establishment, faithful to the movements of original fire, but tempered with virtues of middle-class propriety and urbane congeniality. If Asbury's career represented Methodism's triumph as a popular movement, with control at the cultural periphery, then Bangs' career illustrates the centripetal tug of respectable culture. Dissenting paths have often, in America, doubled-back toward learning, decorum, professionalship, and social standing.[643]

Abel Stevens over his lifetime edited four different Methodist periodicals. But the *National Magazine* may have been his undoing in regard to the Episcopacy. This short-lived periodical was given to the "arts and literature,"

1863) 344-345.

642 Ibid., 280.

643 Nathan Hatch. *The Democratization of Christianity* (New Haven: Yale University Press, 1989) 202. Russell Richey makes this same point referring to Nathan Bangs as the "luminous star" of mid-19th century Methodism. He states: "Bangs labored effectively not only to speak on Methodism's behalf to 'its culture critics' and the religious establishment, but also to remake Methodism so that it might claim its place in the American religious establishment." See Russell E. Richey. *The Methodist Conference in America: A History*, 83, also see Richey, "History as a Bearer of Denominational Identity: Methodism as a Case Study," 486.

an out-of-bounds venture for old-time Methodism. Abel Stevens had also come across as an intemperate abolitionist at the 1844 Conference. At the bottom of the Episcopal politicking was a decided bias against Eastern urbanity. From the Western perspective, the city folk in the metropolitan areas back East simply thought they were better than other people. True or not, the "self-made man" came from the old Northwest rather than the East coast.[644] But who can predict or accurately analyze the whims of ecclesiastical politics? It may have been sour grapes that prompted Stevens to declare that the capabilities of both Simpson and Ames were wasted on a limited office. "If there is any oppression in the Methodist Church, it is on the bishops. No officer of any other enlightened body on earth, civil or religious, is so severely restrained; and it is indeed questionable that any man should expose himself to the liabilities which may result from such peculiar restrictions."[645]

Perhaps Bangs, Stevens, and others were too suave, too smooth and too elegant to be elected to their denomination's highest jurisdiction. Such ordered and outward perfection, which at times suggests ostentation, often promotes envy or disdain rather than emulation. Simpson's diffident personality and non-pretentious attitudes, approachability and unassuming presence were favorable for nineteenth century politics. Eccentricities, idiosyncrasies, and imperfections are often more attractive than sculptured artificiality, no matter how perfect the sculpture and gleaming the marble. Almost everyone who ever knew Simpson was taken by his charisma, a person who never pretended he was the most important person in the room. Simpson's personality traits offered their peculiar attraction. A contemporary recalled that Simpson's "social powers were good. He would sometimes indulge in a little irreverent playfulness which gave a zest to companionship, but never disparaged the preacher."[646] Stevens described the persona which communicated, "There must be something more to this person than I immediately perceive." Stevens wrote, "There are a great many

---

644   Frederick Turner in supporting his "frontier thesis" pointed out that beginning with 1860, six of the next seven presidents came from the old Northwest, and the one exception was from western New York. Frederick Jackson Turner. *The Frontier in American History* (New York: Dover Publications, 1996) 222.

645   *National Magazine: Devoted to Literature, Art, and Religion*, Abel Stevens, editor, vol. VII. July–December, 1855 (New York: Carlton and Phillips) 388.

646   UMA, Drew University, Crooks papers, Letter, R. Hopkins to Crooks, n. d.

fond temptations playing about our editorial heart to 'puff' him, but we must 'give in' respecting his face and head, he must consent, unconditionally, to take his seat among the respectable class of 'homely' men .... his voice is not good, and it usually assumes a shrill monotone, the result, incompatible with true eloquence, yet he is eloquent in defiance of the critics."[647]

On one of the evenings of the Conference, the nine editors dined together. They swapped war stories, sympathized with one another and genuinely enjoyed the conviviality. Abel Stevens could not resist comparing, or rather contrasting George Peck and Matthew Simpson:

> At the head of the editorial list, as conductor of the leading church organ, is Dr. Peck. His position is usually on the extreme left, near the altar. He is tall and well formed, with an incipient tendency to Episcopal development. His head, partially bald, presents a very good phrenological manifestation, the forehead is ample, and the "perceptive bumps" have prominent importance. His features are regular, and are set off by considerable nasal capacity. His general contour is decidedly prepossessing; there is a serene, reverence, and scholarly aspect about it and it is a genuine expression . . . .
>
> Dr. Simpson, editor of the *Western Christian Advocate*, sits a few pews in the rear of his *confrere* of New York. The Doctor, like our humble self, may very appropriately thank Dr. Watts for that sublime stanza, "The mind's the standard of the man." He is rather slight in form, but evidently lithe and strenuous; his mien is not commanding; he stoops a little; his facial contour is a sharp, small triangle; his forehead is a capital refutation, of phrenology. In fine, he is unquestionably a man of decided intellectual strength. He has delivered sermons and speeches in Boston which have excited no little interest .... He is one of "the noble army" of candidates for the Episcopacy which seems to have marched hither in overwhelming force and taken entire possession of the Conference.[648]

---

647   *The National Magazine* Vol. VII (July-December 1855) 291.

648   *Zion's Daily Herald* (May 24, 1852) 70. Note the reference to phrenology. Stevens referred to John McClintock, "His head is his capital attraction, figuratively as well as etymologically, so it projects out and rounds off prodigiously." In 1835, the young McClintock wrote the following about his head to a friend: "Perseverance must be your matter in this as everything else. By the way, writing the word, "perseverance" made phrenology to rise up before in all its length, and breadth, and majesty. I have been studying the sublime science somewhat, and have by way of experiment, (by way of experiments ala Bacon) had my own cranium examined. Well, phrenology must be true, for the man gave me a fine head, causality, comparison, ideality, etc., in abundance. Are you not convinced? I must say in justice to the man of phrenology that he pointed out not a few of my foibles and

Simpson's unvarnished peculiarities accented his authenticity. Part of that authenticity, the kind of authenticity that gets one elected to ecclesiastical office, calls for moderation. Simpson was conservative but not ideological, spiritual but not fanatical, western but not uncouth, anti-slavery but not abolitionist, gregarious but not superficial, progressive but patient. Those who are elected to the highest office of a denomination inexorably becoming middle-class must be fail-safe. He cannot operate on a wave length or track which goes against the direction of the popular vote which elects him. Nathan Hatch claims that, "By 1852, eleven Congressmen from Indiana were Methodists; as well as the Governor and one Senator. By 1870, twenty-four of thirty-seven states including ten of the original thirteen colonies had been governed by a Methodist."[649]

Election to secular office and election to sacred office were of the same kith and kin. Political appeal which requires a wide popularity may not admit of the radical monotheism which defined Wesleyan holiness or of its peculiarities. William Nast interviewed his German acquaintance Phillip Schaff in 1857 to gain the latter's understanding of Methodism. Schaff saw Methodists as "stamping and bouncing, jumping and falling, crying and bawling, groaning and sighing; all praying in confusion—a rude singing of the most vulgar street songs, so it must be loathing to an educated man and fill the sense with painful emotions."[650] Simpson was steadily moving away from Schaff's stereotype, as were Indiana's governors. The new style church bureaucrat would exercise political craftsmanship that earned him a "wily" reputation.[651] Sacred leverage for secular purposes would become his forte.

---

weaknesses in investigating the detrimental part of my character or rather my caput, and I am by no means prepared to say that phrenology is a humbug, and its professors, fools, or imposters." George Crooks. *The Life and Letters of the Rev. John McClintock. L.L.D.* (New York: Nelson and Philips, 1876) 59.

649   Nathan O. Hatch. "The Puzzle of American Methodism," *Methodism and the Shaping of American Culture*, eds. Nathan O. Hatch and John Wigger (Nashville: Abingdon, 2001) 30.

650   William Nast. "Dr. Schaff and Methodism," *Methodist Quarterly Review* 31 (1857) 431.

651   The term "wily," was applied to Simpson by the *Presbyterian Banner*, New York (March 6, 1880).

238 | "God Cannot Do Without America"

The "Report of the Western Book Concern to the General Conference" read, "We have since the last General Conference added three large Adams book presses, so that we now run five power presses–four for printing books and one for our *Western Christian Advocate, Sunday School Advocate.*" As to Simpson's work, the report stated, "We are however able to say that our *Western Christian Advocate* has been steadily on the increase. We are now issuing 21,000, making an increase since the last General Conference of 10,000."[652] Simpson's track record was notable, but even more impressive was the work of William Nast, who over the last four years had written, proofed or edited 3,976 pages including a Sunday school hymnbook and a grammar of the German language, as well as publishing the *German Christian Advocate*.[653]

One Great Sermon

If election to the Episcopacy necessitated being heard on the Conference floor, Simpson's silence would have negated his candidacy. He opened his mouth only seven times, none of them for an extended length, and he entered into none of the debates of the 1852 General Conference. He wanted clarification on building a book depository in Chicago; he brought a motion from the Indiana Conference for division of the Conference; a resolution for the formation of a German Conference; a statistical report from Georgetown Seminary; a report from the committee on lay delegation and a request from the Indiana and Erie Conferences for a ministerial course of study. His only impromptu remarks regarded denominational support for building a church in Washington, D.C. It was his opinion that Methodism had suffered in the nation's capital for want of better church accommodations. Methodists should be concerned that a Methodist had looked for a Methodist Church, and not being able to find one, fell into a "Baptist prayer meeting." (It must have been fore-ordained, though Simpson admitted that the Wesleyan seeker should be grateful that "he fell into so good a place".)

Simpson proceeded to state that, "he did not want a grand church. He did not ask for so fine a church as this; but still if such a one was built, he

---

652 Zion's *Daily Herald*, 133.
653 Ibid., 133.

would have no objection, 'save these bonds' (playfully pointing to the pew doors)." When asked if the church should have pews (rented pews), Simpson responded that he "hoped the pew question would not be introduced in this connection. At that locality, that under their circumstances, it was thought better to build a free church and rely upon some help from abroad."[654] (As we will see in Chapter 18, Metropolitan's overwhelming debt required the renting of pews.)

Out of this discussion came a resolution to build a Methodist Church "of convenient and prominent location, combining commodiousness in its size and attractiveness, in its interior and exterior style of architecture."[655] Simpson "laid" the cornerstone October, 1854, and preached the dedication sermon, February, 1869, before two thousand congregants which included President Grant, Vice-President Shuyler Colfax, and Chief Justice Salmon P. Chase. *Harper's Magazine* described the church as "pure Gothic. It is built of brown stone, roughhewed …. At the northeast corner of the structure is to be constructed a tower and a spire; the utmost point of which will be two hundred forty feet from the pavement." The magazine described the church as, "By far one of the handsomest and the most elaborate churches in Washington," and another newspaper designated it as, "The Westminster Abbey of American Methodism."[656]

Even though Simpson said little on the floor, the Conference granted him a preaching platform, and the *Advocate* editor did not waste the opportunity. Simpson was well aware that in past General Conferences it took only one great sermon to elect a Bishop. On Wednesday evening, May 12, he spoke at the Broomfield Church for the Sunday School Convention. He "gilded the lily" with graphic speech, picturesque language, analogies to nature and sentimental stories. A reporter recorded:

> Dr. S. next spoke of the influence of Sabbath Schools in their results, and mentioned the case of a lady teacher in England, who one day fell in with a bright-eyed but ragged little boy, whom she induced to attend the Sunday School, who there was converted, and eventually became a

---

654   Zion's *Daily Herald* (May 3, 1852) 31.
655   Ibid. (May 11, 1852) 31.
656   Kenneth Rowe. "Building Monumental Methodist Cathedrals in America's Capitol City: 1850-1950" *Methodist History* 50:3 (2012) 171.

prominent missionary to the heathen. Who can tell the influence of the Sabbath School as he considers the history of such a child, poor and forsaken, yet in time becoming given to God, then affecting the interests of hundreds, and they in turn thousands of human beings! Who could tell the influence of such small instrumentalities? They were like the polypi, of the hidden coral reefs, in the eastern oceans which work silently and unobserved beneath the waves, but in their security and continents broad and strong, that in time should block up harbors and impede the commerce of the world. He had been interested, some months since, in the experiments that were making in the towering monument; so raised that vast pile of rock that the suspended wire used in the experiment was moved from its position, and was restored again to its place only by the coolness of the day. Thus was that mighty mass of stone swollen and raised up by this simple and quiet influence of the noon day sun. So with the power of the Sabbath School he would bring the rays of gospel light to shine upon the hearts of the whole community, swelling them out and lifting them up, saying to all the people, be elevated, higher and higher, till the noon of millennial glory should burst upon the world.

We are not to despise the day of small things, and we cannot do better than spread light upon the youthful mind. It is told in early English history of Alfred who has the fame of founding the first universities of that realm. That when in his youth, his step-mother was passing through France; she received a present of a little book, which she promised to the child that she had first learned to read. The little Alfred strove for that prize, and was the one to win it. And so far as we are permitted by providence to scan human events, it was this little incident that resulted in raising Alfred to his high, proud position and gave his name the eminence it now has. Who, then, can estimate the influence of the thousands of similar little books that are now daily pouring forth from your power presses?[657]

The Realities of the Job

If the Episcopal election inflated Simpson's ego, there was also sufficient cause for letting the air out of his self-esteem. He was well aware of who were his enemies. "I had the active and uncompromising opposition of nearly all the Ohio delegation … most of the north Ohio to which was joined Cartwright of Illinois and Phelps of Rock River and also Haney

---

657 Only of Simpson's sermon at the 1852 General Conference did the reporter add, "The reporter is as keenly aware as is the reader of the disadvantage at which the eloquent Dr. is placed by having his remarks abstracted when not a syllable of his fervid and appropriate address should be admitted. But newspaper space is not always *ad infinitum*." *Zion's Daily Herald*, Boston (Friday, May 14, 1852) 41.

and Pilcher of Michigan."[658] Upon leaving the Conference he recorded, "On yesterday afternoon, I left Morgantown at one-half past three having waited for the stage from nine in the morning until that hour. When it came it was a miserable hack." From Uniontown he progressed only twenty-five miles in twelve hours. Ellen, who had joined him at the Conference, stopped in Pittsburgh and lived in a boarding house until July 26, at which time she found a residence to rent at 262 Penn Street for $362.50 per year.[659]

Eighteen fifty-two was a presidential election year, and on September 20, Simpson found himself on a train with Winfield Scott, "Old Fuss and Feathers." Simpson sized him up: "He is evidently not a man of the people, as was General Taylor. He is rather cold, and the effort to be friendly and familiar sits rather awkwardly upon him. At Cleveland he was received with firing of cannon and stopped for the night."[660] Political celebration carried risks. "One poor fellow loading too quickly was blown almost to pieces. His eyes were put out, his limbs broken and the flesh torn from part of his chest. Even the semblance of war has its horrors."[661] Certainly enough excitement for one day. When he arrived in Indianapolis, Simpson was in such pain, that he had to be given morphine.[662]

The 1852 General Conference of the Methodist Episcopal Church charged the Conference in which the Bishop lived with the responsibilities for his upkeep. A General Superintendent within Methodism did not preside over a diocese, was not a "resident bishop," and traveled, according to an Annual Conference plan, assigned by the General Conference. Simpson immediately assessed that the present mode of operation was inefficient and counterproductive. Because of lack of planning and communication, as many as three bishops would show up at events that merited far less attention. Simpson's pleadings were in vain, at least for now. "For several years I found

---

658 LOC, Simpson papers, 1852-1853 *Diary*, Container one.

659 Ibid. Penn Street still hosted the wealthy of Pittsburgh, but Michael Holt observes that by the 1850s "Because of the much improved means of transportation offered by the plank roads and passenger railroads the men of means moved to country homes to escape the crowded city." Michael Holt. *Forging a Majority: The Formation of the Republican Party in Pittsburgh 1848-1860* (New Haven: Yale University Press, 1969) 139.

660 LOC, Simpson papers, 1852-53 *Diary*, Container one.

661 Ibid.

662 Ibid.

a difficulty in the same way, and pressed upon my colleagues some regulation of our work to give more efficiency and supervision, but the judgment of the authority still remained decided that it was not best to attempt any plan other than what the General Conference had prescribed."[663]

Nineteenth century travel offered few conveniences. Conveyances included railroads, wagons, stages, horseback, steamers, barges, ferries, and foot. George Templeton Strong cursed the Long Island Railroad: "Long detention, rain, smoke, dust, cinders, headache again, all sorts of botheration--home at half-past nine and went straight to bed doubting whether I should ever enjoy the blessing of a clear face again."[664] And railroads continued to be dangerous. As late as 1888, "*Harpers* editorialized in a number of cartoons, the most graphic of which, entitled 'The Modern Altar of Sacrifice,' pictured a glowing car stove standing in the midst of a flaming wreck. Draped on top of the stove was a prostrate female figure. The wooden railway car and its demon heater were likened to the Prophet Elijah's fiery chariot."[665]

Itinerate Bishops could not accurately gauge how many days or even weeks a trip would necessitate. Discomfort was constant. Matthew wrote Ellen, "After we were fairly underway, you may imagine me in a sleeping car with high backs. My carpet bag under my head–my hat hung up–a handkerchief around my head, and thus with diver sensations of my feet going to sleep–changing my position–getting so far awake as to joyfully find that some predicament was not a reality." But there was the reality of a "rosy-cheeked" girl of about three-years-old, puking all over him. "We had quite a wiping scrape and I have a dirty handkerchief as my share of the profits."[666] Arriving hours, or even just minutes before a Conference began, was to have arrived without having bathed or shaved for days, clothes dusty and crumpled, hair even more unruly than usual. Twenty-four seven discomfort was the call and conviction of a denomination determined to not modify an itinerate episcopacy for the sake of convenience.

---

663 *Autobiography.*

664 Quoted in John Gordon. *The Scarlet Woman of Wall Street* (New York: Weidenfield and Nicholson, 1988) 39.

665 John White, Jr. *The American Railroad Passenger Car* (Baltimore: The John Hopkins University Press, 1978) 390.

666 UMA, Drew University, Simpson papers, Letter January 17, 1856.

Hell with the Lid Off

Simpson could live anywhere, within reason, he chose. Even though the Methodist Episcopal Church did not consist of a diocesan system, there was some consideration given to where a Bishop lived when the Episcopal Board divided the Annual Conferences. Thus, during his first year, Simpson presided at Morgantown, West Virginia; Washington, Pennsylvania; Jamestown, New York; and Delaware, Ohio. In his first full year, 1853, he chaired the Annual Conferences of Kingston, New York; New York City; Watertown, New York; and Madison, New York. The latter schedule meant that Simpson did not return home for four months.[667]

Health wise, Pittsburgh was the last place Simpson needed to live. It was not the Pittsburgh in which the Simpsons lived in the 1830s; it was a whole lot worse. Already designated by Charles Dickens as the Birmingham of America, Francis Trollope declared Pittsburgh the "darkest place I have ever seen." And someone else profanely called it, "Hell with the lid off." Andrew Mellon's biographer, David Cannadine, calculates that by the time of the Civil War, "The city fabricated locomotives, freight cars, steamboats, artillery, small arms, ammunition, armor plate, and clothing in unprecedented quantities, and 5.5 million tons of coal were mined in the vicinity to power the factories, foundries, and furnaces."[668] All of this manufacturing meant that Pittsburgh had to be accessible which was the only advantage Simpson's residence afforded. Besides the confluence of three rivers (Monongahela, Allegheny, and Ohio), "The Pennsylvania Railroad linked Pittsburgh to Philadelphia in 1852, thereby shortening the journey from two weeks to thirteen hours, and thereafter lines were built to New York, Baltimore, Washington, Chicago, and beyond."[669]

---

667   *Annual Conferences of the Methodist Episcopal Church 1852–1855* Vol. V (New York: Carlton and Porter, 1855).
668   David Cannadine. *An American Life: Mellon* (New York: Alfred A. Knopf, 2007) 33.
669   Ibid., 20.

The Building Tension between Husband and Wife

Listening to the hundreds of Conference reports, sitting for days behind a makeshift desk, periodically implementing parliamentary procedure and almost always staying in a strange home–all of this combined to produce a lonely and depressed man. Ellen did not identify with his loneliness, and through the entirety of their marriage, in her husband's estimation, she never wrote enough. Matthew's irritation regarding Ellen's long stays at her mother's began while the Simpsons still lived in Cincinnati. (Ellen's father, James Verner, had died in 1847.) On March 9, 1851, the husband wrote his wife, "You will see that you are needed at home in as early as you can with any propriety arrange to come."[670] On March 20, Matthew wanted Ellen to comprehend the urgency and faithfulness with which he wrote: "Yours of the seventeenth is just received. I have written every day immediately upon the receipt of your letter and have myself, carried the letter to the office."[671] All subtlety is removed from the following written March 5, 1851: "It is very unpleasant to be expecting you and then that you will stay longer. Fix the time deliberately, but when fixed let nothing let you alter it as a matter of life and death."[672]

From the husband's perspective, the communication irregularity did not improve during his Episcopal travels. On October 8, 1852, Matthew wrote Ellen, "You say in your second letter, forwarded to me yesterday from Cincinnati, that you wish me to write every day, as it comforts you in affliction. If I can add, by any act mine, to your comfort, I will gladly do it, and hence, while sitting in Conference, I steal a few moments to write. But let me say that I should enjoy a letter occasionally as well as yourself."[673] In spite of his aggravation, Simpson's letters never lost their solicitous affection. "Be careful of your health. Be cheerful. Look aloft. The stars display their beauty to us only when we look at them; and if we look down at the earth our hearts are never charmed. Be resolved to be happy today–to be joyful now and out of

---

670 LOC, Simpson papers, Letter March 9, 1851, Container three.
671 LOC, Simpson papers, Letter March 20, 1851, Container three.
672 LOC, Simpson papers, Letter March 5, 1851, Container three.
673 LOC, Simpson papers, Letter October 8, 1852, Container three.

every fleeting moment draw all possible pure and lasting pleasure."[674] Simpson took responsibility for his wife's and children's spiritual nurture; the father was the spiritual director for the family. He wrote Ellen, September 20, 1859,

> I hope you are better in health and in spirits. Look upward and I pray that God may give you the rich consolation of his grace. Life at best is short-its scenes will soon pass away-eternity will be our home-our only home-our permanent home. All we need be anxious about is to do our duty to ourselves, each other, and to those instructed to our care. Let us act as if God saw us, and heard us constantly-and does he not-? Is not his presence and his power always about us?[675]

Simpson did not want to move from Cincinnati to Pittsburgh, no matter how sick he had been. His mother, uncle, sister and brother-in-law still lived in Cincinnati, but Ellen won the argument in that the Simpsons owned no property in Cincinnati. After all, it was the Verners, even though Ellen's father and mother were dead, who had provided financial support. Ellen had the three daughters and Charles (two more children to come in 1853 and 1855), her brother and his family, as well as many friends living in the area. In his travels, Matthew had hardly anyone but strangers, and his first Episcopal trip proved to be frustrating. He forthrightly expressed to Ellen on October 11, 1852, "I have gone regularly to the office (post office), but have returned even as I came. In retaliation I have inflicted upon you the reading of an extra number (of letters?). Have I revenged myself sufficiently? What say you? I have showed at least that I think of you frequently whatever you have done of me."[676] All of this complaining by a husband did not mean that husband and wife did not love and even adore one another. Absence makes the heart grow fonder, and no one ever wrote more romantic letters to his wife than did Matthew Simpson. "Yes, my very dearest. There are those I highly regard and esteem-I love my kindred and I dearly love my children, but for you, it is more. You have become part and parcel of my life. And no day passes, and but few hours, that you are not before me-But enough of this. You will think I grow soft, as I grow older."[677]

---

674 LOC, Simpson papers, Letter October 8, 1852, Container three.
675 UMA, E. PA Conference of the UMC, Old St. George's UMC, Philadelphia, Simpson papers, Letter September 20, 1859.
676 LOC, Simpson papers, Letter October 11, 1852, Container three.
677 UMA, Drew University, Simpson papers, Letter March 15, 1861.

Long Distance Parenting

And of course having lost one son, Simpson constantly worried about his only son. Every letter to Charles was an essay on safety, decorum, and piety. On the same day, Hetty (Simpson's sister) and George McCullough, lost their daughter, Julia, August 7, 1854, the father wrote his son, "Be a good boy. Be careful of your health. Do not eat green fruits, and be careful where you go in the water. Read your Bible daily and be pleasant to all around you."[678] A month later he wrote, "Be careful of your health, avoid tobacco, don't use any in any way. Keep your skin clean, but do not go in deep or stagnant water. Don't race on horseback, you might get thrown or be killed or have your legs broken. Read your Bible. Attend your church and Sabbath School and be kind to all around you."[679] On September 21, 1854, "Be a good boy, read your Bible carefully."[680] It sounded as if the father wanted a pious and benign Little Lord Fauntleroy for a son. Not really. The worried dad was simply contradictory. He wanted Charles to grow up and be a man without taking any risks, without injuring himself or anyone else while he grew into a robust and mature individual.

Simpson's guilt for absence as a father ratcheted up the moralistic pleas. On September 13, 1853, "You must be very kind to her (mother), and you must do all you can to make everything pleasant about the house. Be kind to your sisters and keep everything quiet."[681] As he headed to California, the desperate father put the pressure on thirteen-year-old Charles, "I hope, Charles, that you will be loving and obedient to your mother. Endeavor to aid her all you can in my absence--be studious--be prayerful--read your Bible--be kind to your sisters--be regular at church and may God bless you, a wise holy and happy man."[682] Deep down the troubled father knew that no amount of letter writing could make up for his absence. If the father could not be at home, the son would represent him. "Remember that all

---

678 LOC, Simpson papers, Letter August 7, 1854, Container three.
679 LOC, Simpson papers, Letter September 9, 1854, Container three.
680 LOC, Simpson papers, Letter September 21, 1854, Container three.
681 LOC, Simpson papers, Letter September 13, 1853, Container three.
682 LOC, Simpson papers, Letter December 27, 1853, Container three.

eyes will be on you as my son and they will expect a manly, noble, consistent, and religious course of conduct from you. O I wish you were active. I wish you were active in religion. Are you teaching in the Sunday school? Are you trying to pray and to do good? Life is short; let it not run to waste."[683] As life headed into the 60s Charles became increasingly profligate and brought pain to his parents.

Spiritual and Physical Hypochondria

The newly elected Bishop continued to struggle spiritually. After all, if one fulfills the foremost jurisdictional distinction in his ecclesiastical body, he ought to possess the highest spiritual experience to which that denomination aspires. He had not experienced "entire sanctification," the primary reason for which Wesley believed God had raised up the Methodists. At the end of his first Episcopal year on December 28, he recorded, "For various reasons I am much depressed. My heart greatly needs a deeper work of grace …. It requires something not yet possessed to make me victorious over all my infirmities and temptations, and give me triumph in the Lord Jesus Christ." [684]A day later he recorded, "I feel less fatigued but I greatly need a purified heart, one washed and quickened by redeeming blood." Strange that a man who had arrived at the pinnacle of America's largest denomination would record on the last day of the year, "My time has gone to waste, my sands of life are ebbing out …. may *he* at the close of this year, even now while I write, wash away all my past offenses, forgive all my iniquities, and make me a *new creature.*"[685]

Again, it was difficult to parse out the moodiness of Simpson's temperament, his spiritual deficiencies, and the dejection inherent to the disjuncture and tensions between his office and personality. There were also unrealistic expectations and misapprehensions as to the content of true spirituality. On January 1, 1853, he reflected, "I think I felt truly grateful that I had been spared to witness the beginning of another year, and that the angel of Death had not been commissioned to cut me down as a cumbrance

---

683   UMA, Drew University, Simpson papers, Letter August 29, 1858.
684   LOC, Simpson papers, 1852 *Diary*, Container one.
685   Ibid.

of the ground…. I should redeem time, conversing less with others. I should deny myself every physical and intellectual pleasure that my judgment does not approve, as being in accordance with the highest growth in grace."[686]

Spiritual hypochondria and physical hypochondria were corollaries within Simpson's introspective temperament, anxieties intensified by Wesleyan experiential piety.[687] How one felt at a given time, the sensations of joy, peace, etc., were identified with the "witness of the Spirit," the certitude that one belonged to God, and was in good standing with God. As these emotions fluctuated so did spiritual anxiety. Preoccupation with spiritual consciousness was the downside of Arminian, if not Pelagian tendencies for an individual to serve as master of both his temporal and eternal destinies. Experiential piety demanded severe self-examination:

> Morning-Am I thankful for the mercies of the night-or the coming of the morning—is it my first thought to praise the name of God-do I feel the spirit of prayer ? am I looking to be sanctified? Am I really desiring this blessing? Can I think of any plan which will enable me to live more holy? What have I to do today? What private business? What official? Am I depending on God for help? Am I using all the means of improvement? Is my heart given to God? Am I placing my affections upon anything on the Earth? Do I feel humbled under a view of my unworthiness and unfaithfulness? Am I trusting altogether upon the merits of Christ for salvation?[688]

Ironically, the Wesleyan doctrine of "assurance" resulted in spiritual despair if one failed to perceive whatever elements which were supposed to formulate salvific certitude. Wesley scholar Stephen Gunter argues that Wesley, "through his crisis religious experience interiorized the meaning of justification by faith alone, but in his exuberance to communicate the newly found certainty of salvation, his sermons seemed to have induced

---

686   LOC, Simpson papers, 1853 *Diary*, Container one.
687   In an otherwise positive article, "John Wesley's Doctrine of Assurance," Mark Noll writes, "Thus the cognition that saving grace had worked in a life was seen as the final means to ascertain if saving grace had indeed been present. The implications of this teaching, taken by itself, seem to lead to a condition in which superficial self-analysis ("yes, I've got the witness") results in spirituality while the kind of doubt which assailed such people as Luther and even at times John Wesley himself results in a loss of the hope of salvation." Mark Noll. "John Wesley's Doctrine of Assurance," *Bibliotheca Sacra* (April 1975) 171.
688   LOC, Simpson papers, "Hints of Self-Examination," Container nineteen.

more consternation than consolation."[689] Gunter then quotes the late Bishop William Cannon, who interpreted Wesley's Anglican doctrine of faith as not a free gift of God, but rather an individualistic initiative which grew "through the watering of human achievement."[690] Even if Gunter and Cannon do not exactly represent the mind of Wesley, there is little doubt that the father of Methodism placed much spiritual pressure on his theological children. Was there an inherent contradiction between the adulation which Simpson constantly received as a preacher and the humility essential to the heart of cruciform theology? Adoration quickly dissipates into depression when the crowd has dispersed and one is left to the silence of a lonely night in a strange place. Fleeting popularity could never substitute for hearth and home filled with those who love one in disregard to performance and office.

The Systemic Sins of Ecclesiastical Life

The office of Bishop confronted the problems that are systemic to the proclivities of church life: the higher the office, the greater the problems, the more fires to extinguish, and the more contentions to subdue. John McClintock, who would become the editor of the *Methodist Quarterly Review*, first president of Drew Theological Seminary, and who accompanied Simpson on his first trip to Europe, wrote on January 17, 1839, "I know too that the Methodist Church affords few inducements to worldly ambitious spirits, but with all this, I have found the same petty jealousies, the same pursuit of individual aims, the same lust of power, the same envy of superior talents among Methodist preachers that I should have expected to find among the potsherds of the earth."[691] Simpson was amazed at one of his preachers, who desired to be Presiding Elder because, "His wife had rich and influential relatives in the East, who were expected to visit them the next summer, and he wanted them to find him in an influential position in the church. I had never met a case just like it."[692] But Simpson was not naïve about the reality of sinners posing as saints or the hypocrisy of preachers. In 1850,

---

689   W. Stephen Gunter. *The Limits of Love Divine: John Wesley's Response to Antinomianism and Enthusiasm* (Nashville: Abingdon, 1989) 72.

690   Ibid., 72.

691   Crooks, *John McClintock*, 83.

692   *Autobiography*.

Matthew wrote Ellen: "But Alas! One of our numbers is strangely fallen; Bro. Bayless it is reported has behaved himself scandalously and lustfully towards young men. He declined investigation, and has gone to Kentucky or Tennessee to the Church South. I think he must surely be deranged."[693]

Also, as American Methodism tumbled towards the Civil War, Methodism was in no way a solution to the impending crisis, but was part of it. Attempting to be holy within a denomination most representative of American society for which Simpson was a chief executive officer, presented a challenge. Personal holiness was at odds with the glaring imperfections of corporate and systemic evil. Richard Carwardine has perceptively written, "There is a sad irony in the fact that Methodism, a major instrument in the process of American national integration in the early republic, became a principal channel of spiritual alienation during the middle years of the nineteenth century."[694]

Methodism's "sins" were not benign abstractions, but malignancies which took their toll on both corporate and individual life. The mounting pressure over the slavery issue caused Elijah Hedding, who died just prior to the 1852 Conference, April 9, to confess, "I was oppressed with the business of the Conference. That business has affected my nerves for the past years so that sometimes I have been unable to speak or stand without trembling."[695] During the New England anti-slavery controversies, Hedding changed his residence to Lansingburg, New York, because in his estimation he had been, "unjustly and publicly held up to public view."[696] Hedding's spiritual journey may have not had the most salubrious beginning. When he was a small boy, Hedding had been asked by Benjamin Abbott, "Well, my boy, do you know you are a sinner?" He replied, "Yes, Sir." Then Abbott vociferated, so that everyone present could hear. "There is many a boy in hell not so old as you are." Later, Hedding writhed on the floor crying out, "I am going to hell! I am going to hell!" and then found relief in the realization that Christ had

---

693   LOC, Simpson papers, Letter October 8, 1850, Container five.
694   Richard Carwardine. "Methodist Politics and the Coming of the Civil War," *Church History* Vol. 69 (September 2000) 598.
695   James Kirby. *The Episcopacy in American Methodism* (Nashville: Abingdon, 2000) 121.
696   Ibid., 121.

died to save him from hell.[697] Methodism would steadily move toward more civil evangelism and more gentle conversions.

Continuing Domestic Guilt

On April 29, 1853, Simpson recorded, "This morning had made my arrangements to leave for New York Conference via Philadelphia, but Mrs. S. had been so sick through the night that she was unwilling for me to leave, so I remained until evening. At nine o'clock took cars. I was rather depressed leaving Mrs. S. so ill and to be absent from home so many weeks." [698]The sickness to which Simpson referred was the pregnancy of his wife with their sixth child, Matthew Verner. The Simpsons, having already lost James at four and one-half years old, moved to Pittsburgh after Simpson's election with four children: Charles thirteen, Ella twelve, Anna four, and Sarah two. The last child, Ida, was born to the Simpsons in 1854. This meant that Ellen would go full-term with seven pregnancies. She had her hands full with domestic responsibilities. Simpson, like most men, did not fully empathize with a wife while he was being feted by those who idolized him. Actually, the husband had more discretionary time than did his wife. He could write a letter while sitting on a train or during days while he was waiting for a Conference to begin, or even scribble a few lines while chairing an Annual Conference during a boring report. From all accounts, Ellen was an efficient household manager, having inherited the business acumen of her father, James Verner. There was not much opportunity to write sunset-over-the-ocean soliloquies while she was changing diapers.

Pangs of guilt followed his oft acrimonious communication, and with the probability of heated exchanges at home, Simpson was awash in a sea of doubt, the tension between domestic and ecclesiastical responsibilities which had tormented all Methodist itinerants who attempted wedded bliss. On July 27, 1853, the plagued husband wrote his wife in an attempt to placate his own guilt and provide a rationale for the tension in his marriage.

697　D. W. Clark. *Life and Times of Rev. Elijah Hedding* (New York: Carlton and Phillips, 1855) 48, 68-69.
698　LOC, Simpson papers, 1853 *Diary*, Container one.

> I have felt too that my example in conversation has not been governed with that care and devotion which would have been beneficial to you. I have tried to ask God for forgiveness wherein so ever I have erred, and I pray you also to forgive my errors, and negligence in this matter, and let us henceforth try to "perfect holiness" in the fear of God.
>
> My duties are pressing–God has laid them upon me and I dare not shrink from them, as I should sink beneath his curse. Yet these duties call me from home and you feel the burden imposed upon you, now you will not wish me to suffer by doing wrong, but unless you are blessed with a deeper work of grace, you will [not] feel joyful in your loneliness.[699]

For the husband, there would be no "deeper work of grace," at least deep enough to eliminate his irritation at his wife's non-communication. The following demonstrates the Bishop's non-empathy and non-understanding of his wife's plight. The sarcasm glared.

> Be a good girl--say your prayers--always keep in a good humor--keep every wrinkle off your brow, for time will make them too soon, anyhow--look at the bright side of the picture. Get into the fresh air, keeping good care of your feet--move about a little ever day--if nothing else, move the bed round as it used to be, and then, when you have looked at it, move it back again. Change the chairs and the divans and pull the piano over a little--just a *little*--farther over; and when you have nothing else to do, think of me, but *don't write too often*.[700]

The intense devotion of Matthew and Ellen to one another would more than endure the next thirty-two years. The deprivation of sexual intimacy and domestic comfort for months on end was a huge price to pay for a man in his early forties. Ironically, as for thousands of other American clergymen who have provided spiritual formation for the masses, they have not been able to provide the same for their families. The elation of ecclesiastical victory often slumps into the despair of victim. Matthew Simpson, the Bishop, had sufficient ego strength to be at his best self when the self on the inside felt otherwise. All vocations demand a persona, perhaps none more than church leadership. Nonetheless, throughout their married life, the husband was an incurable romantic:

---

699   UMA, Drew University, Simpson papers, Letter July 27, 1853.
700   LOC, Simpson papers, Letter September 27, 1853, Container three.

And now, Ellen, I bid you good night.
  Sweet be the dreams that cross your mind
  As some bright angel, fair and kind
  Shall whisper thoughts of truth and love
  Of peace on earth--of joy above.
    Tranquil and calm may be your rest
    As John upon his Masters breast
    If in your waking hours you sit
    With Mary at your Saviors feet.

FN #, UMA, Drew University, Simpson papers, Letter, October, 10, 1047.

Chapter Nine:
In Case of Any Accident

Mundane Obligations

In the mundane tediousness of bureaucratic maintenance, preaching was Simpson's only salvation. At the Genesee Conference held at Batavia, New York, in 1853, all of the surrounding churches cancelled their services to hear Simpson preach. "Near Main Street toward the Eastern part of the village .... The sermon was one of wondrous power of thought and emotion and to be remembered for a life time. The fame of the Bishop as a pulpit orator had preceded him to the Conference, but the high anticipations of all, were more than realized. Everyone was completely overwhelmed and carried away and melted down before the Lord."[701] In St. Louis, October 9, 1854, Bishop Janes and Simpson converged at the same Annual Conference. Janes reported to his wife the effectiveness of Simpson's ministry. His assessment was more subdued than that which emanated from the normal fawning adulation, but was probably more accurate: "The topics were the immortality of our soul and the resurrection of our bodies. Grand topics! It is one of my old texts and subjects. Of course we do not preach alike from the same texts. Two minds so unalike each other could not make two sermons alike. This was a very excellent one, and made a good and deep impression on the audience."[702]

Much of Simpson's time was spent in letter writing, as evidenced by his report to Ellen that he had written twenty letters in one day. William Daily had been accused of using intoxicating drink. In a letter dated July 2, 1852, Daily implied that the rumor originated with Edward Ames. Daily explained, "While in Boston I had diarrhea nearly all the time–I did get a

---

701   F.W. Conable. *History of the Genessee Conference of the Methodist Episcopal Church* (New York: Phillips & Hunt, 1885) 617.

702   Henry Ridgeway. *Life of Edmund S. Janes* (New York: Phillips and Hunt, 1882) 189.

phial of spirits at a drugstore. I used a little of it with peppermint. Also, used a good deal of laudanum for the same disease. Bishop Ames did the same. This much I am prepared to admit, but that I used spirits as beverage or so as to be under its influence I must deny." Daily further stated, "This matter has fully satisfied me that I have a most deadly enemy in Bishop Ames, and that in accordance with his general character. I may expect him in some way or other to pursue me as would a Jesuit–or as did the Jesuit in the 'wandering Jew.'"[703] Daily's persecution complex continued into the fall. On October 16, 1852, he wrote, "I have been most shamefully ostracized. I am a proscribed man .... Bishop Ames has done it by his own hand in his own cunning and crafty way."[704]

Lucien Berry was hanging by his fingernails to the presidency of Indiana Asbury University. Ames told Berry in a letter to Simpson, "Had the University been older when you (Simpson) expelled Mack, Good, Smith and others, they would have called you to account." Ames then assured Berry that he entirely approved of his administration. Shortly thereafter, Berry heard that Ames opined, "If Brother B. doesn't get more popular with the students and with the citizens, it may be necessary to have a new president." Simpson's friends expected him to be their ex-officio advocate. Berry inquired, "Would it be too much to ask you to write to Rev. J. L. Smith, Laporte; Rev. J. H. Hull, Indianapolis; and C. D. Davidson, Evansville?"[705]

Simpson intended to intervene on Berry's behalf, and on June 27, 1854, wrote John L. Smith asking if he could discover the "enemies of the University before the commencement of the Indiana Annual Conference."[706] Simpson further stated, "I have feared for some rumors that have reached me that prejudice has been excited against President Berry for strict management of the institution. He may have erred for all I know, but I know that in Greencastle, there are some determined enemies of Methodism who are trying to strike the Church through him. They did what they could to abuse me and only the detecting their plan early saved me from trouble with

---

703   UMA, DePauw University, Simpson papers, Letter July 22, 1852.
704   UMA, DePauw University, Simpson papers, Letter October 16, 1852.
705   UMA, DePauw University, Simpson papers, Letter June 9, 1854.
706   UMA, DePauw University, Simpson papers, Letter January 27, 1854.

them."[707] No doubt, Simpson remained anxious for the school which he had nurtured from infancy to maturity.

The Refuse of Creation

In California and Oregon, the Methodist Episcopal Church founded two new Conferences which necessitated an annual visit from a Bishop. Ames took the first trip in December of 1852.[708] The routes consisted of either six weeks crossing the Isthmus of Panama or six months around the Horn of South America. Panama was the only realistic option, but it was no nature hike. It was a three-day endurance across, "lofty and rugged mountain ranges and deep and pestiferous morasses." Panama historian F. N. Otis remembered, "The first thirteen miles beginning at Nang Bay was through a deep morass, covered with the densest jungle, reeking with malaria, and abounding with almost every species of wild beasts, noxious reptiles, and venomous insects known in the tropics."[709]

On December 17, 1853, Simpson left Pittsburgh, sailed from New York, stopped in Jamaica, and embarked for Aspinwall, Panama. Four ladies who desired to make the trip chose Simpson as a guide and chaperone, which made his labors only more burdensome. A train transported them from Aspinwall to the Chagres River where the party of twenty boarded a covered barge, and took the river trip to Chagres, which was not the hospitable and civilized town which Simpson expected. The anticipation of overnighting at Hotel Saint Charles turned to disillusionment, as there was no record of reservations. Simpson scurried back to the American Hotel where the ladies were given a decent room, but the men only cots. "These cots had no covering and no pillows. And from their appearance they had remained unwashed so long as it seemed to us that the memory of man runneth not to the contrary." After surveying a village filled with gambling houses and liquor stores, Simpson and his fellow travelers returned to the hotel for a night's rest.

---

707 Ibid.

708 Simpson had moved for the founding of the Annual Conferences of Oregon and California in the 1848 General Conference.

709 F. N. Otis. *History of the Panama Railroad and the Pacific Mail Steamship Company* (New York: Harper & Brothers, 1867) 21.

> But there was little sleep for us. It seemed that though the refuse of creation had been gathered into one room. There were from one hundred to one hundred fifty cots and bunks. And many of them were occupied with men highly excited with drink. Now and then when sleep was about to visit our eyelids, some rude remark was made and responded to, followed by a volley of oaths and obscene utterances of the most disgusting character. To add to the darkness of the picture, some lewd women occupied an adjacent room, separated by only a thin partition. Their jests and laughter and vile language were heard and responded to by men of the baser sort. In the bar-room beneath us men who could get no cots to lie on were drinking, swearing, and carousing, and making night more hideous by their revelry. In the native huts, long after "the noon of night" had passed, there were alternate singing and hallooing. One shrill voice near us kept up a song in loud vociferation the greater part of the night, as if someone were acting the part of an improvisator for the amusement of company. Add to this the noise of mules and donkeys collected for our journey and the confusion may, in part, be imagined. We felt as if we were in the very suburbs of Pandemonium.[710]

The mule trip, which began the next morning at 8 a.m., was something less than romantic. "The ladies never having been on mules before and to say the least our mules were mulish. Some took it in their head to go back to the starting place while others paused as if conceding the difficulties of the trip."[711] The mules only responded by being beaten with umbrellas and sticks and being gouged by spurs. The steep ravines and narrow gorges were more adventurous than for which the missionaries bargained. "Occasionally these passes are obstructed by a mule, falling beneath his load. It is said that in such cases, they are killed by the natives and cut in pieces in order to remove them out of the road."[712] The accommodations in Panama City were no better than those in Chagres. By the time Simpson went to bed, he was running a fever, and attempted to position his cot so that the current of air flowing through the door would not directly blow on him. "I laid me down to sleep but about eleven my cot gave way, and I came down head foremost. As it was useless to complain and impossible to get another bed, I laid upon

---

710   Matthew Simpson, "Notes on Trip to California," LOC, Simpson papers, Container fifteen.

711   Ibid.

712   Ibid.

the floor and rested as well as I could."[713] Simpson should not have been surprised at his fever. H. M. Brands claims, "So malicious was the Chagres fever, in fact, that the life insurance policies purchased by many immigrants carried a Chagres-exclusion clause if they slept ashore at Chagres, they voided their policies."[714]

Had Simpson read from J. M. Letts, who published *California Illustrated*, including a description of the Panama and the Nicaragua routes, he would have been better prepared to greet the natives. Letts wrote, "We crossed the river to Chagres, a village consisting of about thirty five huts constructed of reeds and thatched with palm leaves, the inhabitants, the most squalid set of beings imaginable. They are all good Catholics, but do not go to the Bible for their fashions. There are fig leaves in abundance yet they are considered by the inhabitants as superfluous, they preferring the garments that nature gave them, sometimes, however, adding a Panama hat." Upon reaching Panama City, Letts noted, "The people here have a great passion for 'fighting cocks.' There is not a house that is not furnished from one to a dozen."[715] Less than astute observation enabled Letts to conclude that Panamanians preferred pleasure over work.

The Night of that Terrible Storm

The *Golden Gate* sailed from Panama City on January 1, 1854 but the main shaft to the propeller broke, and for two weeks the ship was adrift with only back-up sails, which with no wind, provided little progress.[716] But the mishap allowed for observation and descriptive prose at which Simpson excelled, a forte which was the main ingredient of his preaching.

---

713   Ibid.

714   H. M. Brands. *The Age of Gold: The California Gold Rush and the New American Dream* (New York: Doubleday, 2002) 77.

715   J. M. Letts. *California Illustrated: Including a Description of the Panama and Nicaragua Routes* (New York: R. T. Young, 1853) 14.

716   The *Golden Gate* weighed 3,000 tons, accommodated 800 passengers and was 269' long. The San Francisco Press hailed the *Golden Gate* as, "The finest specimen of Naval architecture on the Pacific," and the "largest and swiftest steamer in our waters." James P. Delgado. *To California by Sea: A Maritime History of the California Gold Rush* (Columbia: University of South Carolina Press, 1996) 63.

> In the evening we had one of those glorious sunsets for which the Pacific is so famous. The sea was almost as smooth as a plain, save for the ceaseless undulation which ever moves its surface. Not a cloud was in the sky. The sun went down slowly, while a deep ruddy color spread around, and its last line of light suddenly disappeared. The sea from the reflection of light seemed like a mosaic pavement. Its color upon the summit of each swell was a purple shaded with blue; the sides of the swells inclining towards the west were covered with rings of yellow and green, while on the side of each swell eastward the colors shaded into black. I stood gazing at the scene until, under the dimming light, the colors faded away. On the other side the full moon cast her rays from the east, and the undulations were tinged with silver as they sparkled under her beams. It lacked only some fleecy clouds to display the various colors which I had seen a few evenings before to make it indescribably grand.[717]

The adventure was not over. The *Golden Gate* ran ashore in San Diego Harbor and had to ride out a storm. "Near twelve, the guards on the larboard side were split part of the way up; those immediately outside my room which was wholly above the guards, splitting up so that I could not get to it without great risk. A heavy sea striking after burst up the guards in the passage way, so as to throw the surges directly into the cabins, and wetting several of the rooms."[718] In order to dock the passengers, they were transferred to the *Goliad*, and then the weather worsened. The Captain rejected Simpson's suggestion of a prayer meeting, responding that collective speaking would only further alarm the passengers. But the opportunity to serve as a spiritual solace in time of storm was not lost. "Some of the wildest men came to me to converse on religious subjects, and I had an opportunity of pointing several to the mercy of God in Christ, who at other times were utterly careless."[719] There was reason for alarm: "Several, who had been in storms around the Cape of Good Hope and in the Atlantic and Mediterranean, said they had never witnessed a night so terrible."[720]

The storm subsided, port was made, and the passengers disembarked at one of the most inviting spots on the North American continent. Sunny San

---

717 "Notes on Trip to California."
718 Ibid.
719 Ibid.
720 Ibid.

Diego with its balmy breezes offered a much needed respite. Simpson made his normative keen observations: "Climbing a high hill overlooking a town in the bay, I walked over around the remains of Fort Stockton. It is situated on the point of the hill which rises into a low conical peak and consists simply of a ditch some 6', and a breastwork of the day which had been excavated. From the quality of hoop iron which remains in the ruins, I presume many barrels must have been used in its construction." As always he was observant of the local Catholicism, the priest saying mass, "a portly looking old padre, who evidently exceedingly enjoyed good living was dressed in his long white gown whose lace in the edging, with his embroidered surplice contrasted strangely with a heavy pair of thick boots–a young man also a priest, pale & sallow was busy reciting his prayers ...." For Simpson the food was as bland as the religion. "As I could get no breakfast immediately, I stepped into an eating house where some of the company were eating oyster soup–ordering a plate, I had one well filled with weak soup and bread and good crackers and butter, and plenty of good pure water–the soup was evidently oyster soup because in the plate were two or three oysters so stewed that no flavor remained in them .... But an excellent appetite served for flavor."[721] After the brief sojourn in San Diego, the *Goliad* uneventfully transported the Simpson entourage to San Francisco.

On January 30, the steamer *Antelope* transported Simpson up the Sacramento River to Sacramento. In spite of the friendliness of the California Methodists, Simpson was depressed. "A shade sometimes comes over my spirit when I think of the condition of my eyes, the spots of which have increased since I left home; but perhaps I may not need them longer than they shall serve me." He made sure his wife shared in his melancholy: "The night of that terrible storm I little expected to see you or the children or to preach again in the name of Jesus; but God who is rich in mercy, has allowed me to speak again, and possibly he may permit me to meet my loved ones. In the meantime, meet me at the cross, the blessed cross."[722] His melancholy turned to irritation when no letter from his wife greeted him at the port of call. He wrote from Sacramento, after having been in the foothills at Stockton, "Again I traveled my round, and this afternoon, after forty-five miles staging through frost and snow and mud,

---

721   James E. Kirby."Matthew Simpson's Diary," *The Journal of San Diego History*, Vol. 29 No. 3 (Summer 1983).
722   Crooks, 314.

I arrived at this place, where Conference will begin Thursday morning, and where Thursday evening I will meet the elders, but no letter meets me. Two months, save three days, have passed since I left home and no letter yet."

> My friends, do they now and then send
> A letter or thoughts o'er the sea;
> To tell me I yet have a friend,
> Who loves to write letters to me?[723]

Visiting Sutter's Mill in Corona, and standing near the spot where James Marshall discovered gold (we do not know the exact spot) and at Placerville, where he watched gold being panned, Simpson almost caught the gold fever.[724] He was amazed that a medical doctor could make $1,000 per month. He wrote Ellen, "What would you think of a home in California? I have been warmly urged to fix my residence here, and I confess, were you and the children with me, I think I could spend a few years very pleasantly in trying to lay the foundation of the Church on the Pacific coast."[725]

Upon returning to San Francisco, Simpson met and observed William Taylor who claimed to have preached 600 sermons on the streets. His preaching went something like the following, as he stood on a whiskey keg: "You have tried a great many sources, money-making and money-spending, rum drinking and gambling, with occasional bear and dog fights. Bills were posted all through your streets last week promising a rich feast for immortal souls on the Fourth of July. The intellectual feast was to commence a fight between a bull and grizzly bear. The second with as much whiskey as could be desired. The third course of dancing among the men because ladies were very scarce."[726] Much of his preaching was against alcohol: "He has long since sent his victim's shattered bloated carcass to a drunkard's grave, and his soul to a drunkard's hell. His family is in the poor house daily shedding fountains of tears more bitter than death."[727]

---

723   Ibid., 315.

724   Having personally visited Corona, I did not leave with the conviction that a specific spot for the discovery of gold could be located.

725   Crooks, 317.

726   William Taylor. *Seven Years of Street Preaching in San Francisco, California* (New York: Nelson and Hunt, 1875) 54.

727   Ibid., 100.

Never "Sene" a Bishop

On March 10, Simpson took the screw-propelled *Paytona*, one hundred seventy-feet long, up the coast to Astoria, Oregon. The ocean has always been able to convert the most hardened sinner and in this case, sanctify more fully the most sainted Bishop.

> We sat down to dinner but a sudden pitch of the vessel left me dizzy. I tried to take some soup but found I had occasion for nothing more, and leaving the table I deposited my soup *et dia biliosa* in the bucket of one of my companions and satisfied with my exploit laid down to rest. At supper time a half a cup of tea and a cracker shared the same fate and so dinnerless and supperless, I retired to roll another night. Serious feelings rested upon my mind, and reviewing my various errors, and imploring mercy for all my sins and iniquities I endeavored to commend myself to God. I had read a large portion of the Psalms, and I found the tranquilizing influence of God's word and of prayer. Solemnly did I vow a new and holier life, less of self and more of God in all my ways.[728]

Already late, Simpson boarded a boat going east to Portland up the Columbia River and then at Oregon City took a steamer down the Willamette River to Corvallis. The boat caught a sandbar, getting him only as far as Salem. He then hired a wagon for the trip to Corvallis. The wagoneer got lost, but eventually arrived at the home of a Mr. Collins, who agreed to take Simpson to Corvallis, leaving at 10 p.m. "Taking advantage of some sheaf oats put at the hinder part of the wagon, I laid down on them and, thus, rode a part of the way which was down through sloughs and mud, reaching Corvallis at 2:00 at night."[729] Renting a horse, he rode the fifteen miles to Belknap Settlement, where he found a log schoolhouse, the site of the Conference. Unbathed, unshaved, hair going a thousand different ways, spattered with mud and speckled with oats, and looking like he had not slept for days, and had not changed his clothes for weeks, the novice Bishop of the Methodist Episcopal Church arrived for the Oregon Annual Conference. "Alighting and divesting myself of my outer wraps, I stepped into the church just as the congregants engaged in prayer at the close of the Conference, as

---

728 James Kirby, "A Missionary Journey to Oregon," *Oregon Historical Quarterly* Vol. 102, No. 4 (Winter 2001) 458.

729 Crooks, 320.

I was informed of an excellent sermon by Brother Pearne, who had acted as President of the Conference."[730] Simpson preached that afternoon and ordained three deacons. The Bishop's presence was an unforgettable event for the Oregon pioneers cut off from civilization. Ketturah Belknap journaled,

> Many of us had never Sene a Bishop .... Just as Brother Pearne was closing the Morning sermond the Bishop stept in, someone near the Door gave him a seat .... Pearne thought by his look and the look of his grip that he looked like A Preacher. Pearne ceaces to Preach, Amid breathless silence utters these words .... if the stranger who had traveled all night over Corduroy Roads and stump Roots, and mud of varying depths, who had changed from Wagon to Saddle and badly be spattered with mud ... Advanced to the front amid shouts and Hallelujahs from all sides, I was there and surely the sene was beyond description.[731]

Belknap further noted of Simpson's preaching,

> And when the Bishop came to Portray Heaven and all its Beauties he Just Scared
>
> A way up and took the Congregation with him
>
> Then His Prayer (I feast on it yet) H K Hines said, Dews of Heaven could not Distill more sweetly, as he poured out his Prayr for them Preachers. And that community, then he seemed to Just take up Oregon in his Hand And Just Hold it up to the Lord so he could see how it needed his care and help....[732]

Against the Current

After reversing his route to Portland, Simpson conducted some church business and then went up the Columbia to check on an Indian mission. The Columbia River, which originates in the Cascades, is possibly the strongest river current in the United States, having cut the Columbia Gorge through the Cascade foothills thousands of years ago, as it rushes toward the Pacific. Thus, the wind can easily and frequently gust up to 50 mph as the cold air seeks lower elevations through the gorge. As H. M. Brands

---

730 Ibid., 321.

731 Elizabeth M. Smith, "William Roberts: Circuit Rider of the Far West," *Methodist History* Vol. 22, No. 2 (January 1982) 71.

732 Robert Moulton Gatke, "Ketturah Belknap's Chronicle of the Bellfountain Settlement," *Oregon Historical Quarterly* Vol. 38, No. 3 (Sept 1937) 294-295. http://www.jstor.org/stable/20611058.

observes: "Between the strait of Georgia in what would become British Columbia and the Gulf of California and Mexico, the Columbia is the only river to pierce the mountain range of the Sierra Cascade chain–which was a principal reason the early western immigrants went to Oregon .... The river's victory is carried in the walls of the present day Columbia Gorge."[733] To put it another way, rowing east against the Columbia current was almost impossible. At The Dalles Simpson recorded:

> There the steamer above the Cascades was broken, and, after having waited for a sail-boat until Monday, I was obliged to hire an Indian canoe, and with Brother Pearne, who accompanied me, to row up the river. About ten o'clock at night we reached the Indian camp, where, as it rained, we were compelled to lodge in a miserable Indian hut, among the filthy natives, until the morning light appeared. The next day we reached The Dalles. There spent Wednesday, Thursday tried to get down the river in a schooner, but, the wind being adverse, after struggling for twenty hours, and being nearly capsized, and escaping by a hand's-breadth from being dashed upon the rocks, we left the schooner and took a small boat or skiff. We rowed all night, except three hours, when the crew gave out. Making a fire upon the shore, miles from any house, we threw ourselves upon the ground, and I had a good, sweet sleep. Friday reached the Cascades, and Saturday, by steamer, returned here.[734]

Pearne remembered that the canoe was forty feet long, and contained "fish nets, dogs, three squaws, two Indians, two half-drunken white men, myself and the bishop, to say nothing of innumerable fleas."[735] Amazingly, one of the drunks had been a student at Indiana Asbury. When Simpson asked him, "Do you think your mother knows what kind of life you are living?" the man began to weep. When in 1864, Pearne and this same person encountered one another on a river steamer, the latter testified that the Bishop's question had converted him and he was now a "happy man with a beautiful family, on his way to heaven."[736]

---

733 Brands, 162.

734 Crooks, 323.

735 Thomas Hall Pearne. *Sixty-One Years of Itinerant Life in Church and State* (New York: Eaton and Mains, 1899) 163.

736 Ibid., 165.

The Martyrdom of Anthony Bewley

Simpson returned to Pittsburgh, sometime in May. He did not chair an Annual Conference until August 23, which was in Tiffin, Ohio. He finished out the year by chairing Conferences in LaPorte, Indiana, September 6-11; Peru, Indiana, September 20-23 where his former faculty member Cyrus Nutt served as secretary; Greensburgh, Indiana, September 28. Ames presided over the Missouri Conference held at Hannibal, Missouri, with J. M. Chivington (whom we will meet in Chapter 14,) serving as secretary. Eighteen fifty-four was a travel year that Simpson did not care to repeat. His Episcopal itinerary in 1855 consisted of the following:

> New England Conference–Chelsea, Massachusetts, April 11-18, 1855;
>
> Troy Conference-Troy, New York, May 9-17, 1855;
>
> New York Conference-Danbury, Connecticut, May 16-23;
>
> Indiana Conference-September 12-17, Vincennes, Indiana;
>
> Iowa Conference–Keokuk, Iowa, September 30-October 3;
>
> Missouri Conference-St. Louis, October 11-13;
>
> Arkansas Conference-Timber Creek near Bonham, Texas, November 1-3.[737]

The trip to Timber Creek may have been the most anxious of Simpson's itinerancy. For the first and only time that Matthew ever shared with his wife his fear regarding an Episcopal sojourn: "When I stop for Sunday, I have no chance of stage for three days, but I may get a private conveyance. This is uncertain. *It is right, however, that you should know my route in case of any accident.*" (Italics mine)[738]

At the 1855 Arkansas Conference, Simpson appointed Anthony Bewley as pastor to the Texas District, a district in which there were only 200-300 Methodists. On October 18, 1855, Matthew wrote Ellen from Springfield, Missouri, "I arrived at Brother Bewley's, four miles from this

---

737   *Minutes of the 1855 Annual Conferences* (New York: Mason & Lane, 1855).
738   Crooks, 329.

place, a little after noon to-day. I had to walk and carry my saddle-bags, coat, and blanket some two miles and a half to reach his house. He was just starting for Conference. I got in his buggy, drawn by two young and small mules."[739] Simpson's anxiety was grounded in reality. The hatred between the free soilers and pro-slavery parties had reached a hot tempest. Bewley publically declared his allegiance to "The Methodist Episcopal Church of the United States" in the 1845 Missouri Annual Conference. Charles Elliott wrote, "From that very hour the demons of persecution went howling upon his trail, nor ever ceased till it was glutted with his life blood."[740] In 1855 the Southern *Nashville Christian Advocate* ran the following article:

> The office of the Luminary, Parksville, which paper was suspected of free soilers, was attacked on Saturday by two hundred citizens of Platte County. They destroyed the fixtures, threw the press in the Missouri River and the editor's absence saved him from a coat of tar and feathers. Resolutions declaring the paper a nuisance, denouncing the editor, and threatening their lives as other free soilers were passed. No Methodist preacher is to be allowed to preach in the county under a penalty of tar and feathers for the first offense and hanging for the second.[741]

In the 1860 Arkansas Conference Edward Ames and Anthony Bewley held a frank discussion as to whether the latter should return to Texas. Bewley decided to go, even though he thought "he would do little good." He stated, "Let them hang or burn me if they choose, hundreds will rise up out of my ashes."[742] Upon returning to his responsibilities the threat and duress upon Bewley's family became so great that he fled to Barry County, Missouri. A letter was forged in the name of a William H. Baily suggesting Bewley was planning a slave insurrection. Southern Methodist camp meeting in Missouri placed wanted posters on the grounds, "offering a $1,000 reward for Bewley and his return to Fort Worth."[743] A posse caught up with Bewley

---

739   Crooks, 328.

740   Charles Elliott. *South-Western Methodism: A History of the ME Church in the Southwest from 1844-1864* (Cincinnati: Poe and Hitchcock, 1868) 28.

741   Ibid., 60.

742   Elliott stated: "In 1855, Bewley was put in charge of the Texas Mission District." Ibid., 45. Simpson said 1858, but his memory failed him. Simpson himself placed Bewley in charge of the Texas Mission District in the Arkansas Conference of 1855. Simpson was not present at the 1858 Arkansas Conference. *Cyclopaedia*, 105.

743   Elliott, 160.

and hauled him back to Fort Worth where he was hanged September 13, 1860 at the age of fifty six. His bones were placed on the roof of Ephraim Dagget's store, where the children of Fort Worth played with them for years.[744] Before his death Bewley wrote his wife, "You will have to spend the remaining part of your life as a bereaved widow, with your orphaned children, *with one blind daughter*. Now my feelings I cannot describe, but I know there is a God that doeth right."[745]

The Kansas Nebraska Act and an Impotent Church

The 1852 General Conference hardly mentioned slavery. The Bishop's Address pretended that it did not exist. The Conference spent four days resolving that Methodism could remain respectable by allowing mixed seating among the sexes. And they could be more inclusive by less specificity on dress. "Give no tickets to any who wear high head, enormous bonnets, ruffles or rings," was changed to "Give tickets to no one who disregard the apostolic caution (I Timothy 2:9) by adorning themselves with gold, or pearls, or costly array."[746] Obviously, Pauline vagueness would be much more difficult to enforce, or maybe it would not be enforced. Perhaps the superficial legalism would sublimate the avoidance of outlawing slavery.

Much changed in America between 1852 and 1856, and much of the change was due to the Kansas-Nebraska Act. James McPherson, America's preeminent Civil War historian, assesses that, "Coming at the time as the Anthony Burns' case, this law may have been the most important single event, pushing the nation toward civil war. Kansas–Nebraska finished off the Whig Party, and gave birth to a new entirely northern Republican Party."[747] Stephen Douglas' attempt at pacification by way of popular sovereignty provided a battleground for the North and the South, ironically, in a state that was not defined by the Mason–Dixon line. Because the ballot did not achieve democracy in Kansas, the slavery question would have to be decided by artillery.

---

744   Donald E. Reynolds, "Reluctant Martyr: Anthony Bewley and the Texas Slave Insurrection Panic of 1860," *Southwestern Historical Quarterly* 96:3 (January 1993).

745   Elliott, 164.

746   *Journals 1848-1856* Vol. III, 76.

747   James McPherson. *Battle Cry of Freedom* (New York: Oxford, 1988) 121.

In 1820, the Missouri Compromise, which solved the slavery question in the newly acquired lands of the Louisiana Purchase, seemed sufficient to settle the issue for time and eternity. McPherson writes, "Clay simply took the southern boundary of Missouri, drew it straight through the Purchase, and decried that hereafter only land south of that line could be organized as slave territories, and admitted to the Union as slave territories, and with the neat partition everyone could, presumably, be happy."[748] But no one dreamed that a quarter century later, America would extend its boundaries to the Pacific Ocean. The slave states perceived themselves as becoming marginalized, since out of all the land acquired from Mexico, only Texas preferred slave status.

As we have already seen, getting to California was a torturous affair, and the only means for providing sufficient travel across no man's land was a railroad, the supreme capitalistic hope of the future. The new territories needed to become states, i.e. parts of the Union, with fully functioning governments, so that railroad right-of-way negotiations could take place. All of this was going to become a non-navigable morass of politics, with railroad progress stymied, because the South perceived the new non-slavery territory as a threat to their "peculiar institution." A huge chunk of land in the heart of America, Nebraska, henceforth would become two territories, Nebraska and Kansas. Nebraska, according to the Douglas scheme would become a free soil state, and the inhabitants of Kansas would vote as to whether they would live with or without slavery. Walter McDougall states that Douglas never did get his railroad, but thanks to him, "a new game called popular sovereignty would be played out on the frontier. Too bad, that nobody thought to draft rules."[749]

A Bleeding Nation

Popular sovereignty translated into an unpopular war in "bleeding Kansas," with two hundred people killed and two rival governments, the free soil in Topeka and the pro-slavery in Lecompton. While the 1856 General

---

748 Ibid., 99.

749 Walter A. McDougall. *Throes of Democracy: The American Civil War Era 1829-1877* (New York: Harper-Collins Publishers, 2008) 333.

Conference of the Methodist Episcopal Church met in Indianapolis, "border ruffians," also known as "bushwhackers" from Missouri and pro-slavery men from Kansas, sacked Lawrence, a community comprised of "free soilers," looting and burning much of the town. The Lecompton Guards, Doniphan Tigers, Platte County Rifles, and others who composed the five to eight hundred guerillas were not all that efficient. They "planted three cannons near the hotel, fired some thirty shots in a vain effort to batter it to pieces and tried to blow it up with a keg of gunpowder. Finally, after ransacking the rooms and seizing the stock of liquor, they burned it down."[750]

On May 21, an abolitionist fanatic named John Brown, along with his sons, retaliated by slaying with broad swords five men from a pro-slavery family that lived at Potawatomie Creek, in Franklin County, about five miles below Osawatomie County. Because of newspaper bias and out-right lying, the people back East did not know the exact circumstances of the Brown atrocity. "The New York Tribune's correspondent, with real dexterity, used the savage features of Brown's crime to exonerate Brown by arguing that the mutilation of Henry Sherman's body showed that he had been killed by the Comanche Indians, and that the pro-slavery men had tried to pin this atrocity upon the free-starters."[751]

It was not only bleeding in Kansas, but literally bleeding in the halls of Congress. The "Crime against Kansas" was supposed to be the speech of Charles Sumner's life, but it almost cost him his life. Stephen Puleo describes the scene: "All that was missing when Charles Sumner entered the Senate chamber on May 19, 1856, was a fanfare of trumpets. The throngs awaiting his words, the intense heat, the grand stage, the sectional tension, the magnitude of the moment, the nation's eyes upon him—all of this lent a drama that suited Sumner's thirst for attention and his irresistible desire to preach and moralize to the masses, all in the name of their enlightenment."[752] Sumner's moralizing became rather personal, leaving nothing to abstraction or imagination. Sumner charged Andrew Butler, Senator from South

---

750 Allan Nevins. *Ordeal of the Union Vol. II* (New York: Charles Scribner's Sons, 1947) 436.

751 David Potter. *The Imspending Crisis: 1848–1861* (New York: Harper and Row, 1976) 222.

752 Stephen Puleo. *The Caning: The Assault that Drove America to Civil War* (Yardley, PA: Westholme Publishing, 2013) 57.

Carolina, with choosing a mistress "to whom he has made vows, and who, though ugly to others, is always lovely to him; though polluted in the sight of the world is chaste in his sight, I mean the harlot slavery."[753] Sumner's choice of words such as harlot, virgin, and rape, was particularly galling to Southerners who had been often accused of sexual license with their slaves.

On May 22, Congressman Preston Brooks, stepped into the Senate chamber, to avenge the insult to his cousin Butler, who had been sick and not even present for Sumner's speech. "Mr. Sumner, I have read your speech over very carefully. It is a libel on South Carolina and Mr. Butler, who is a relative of mine." Brooks then reigned down approximately thirty blows with a "gutta purcha" cane on Sumner's head and body and when finished, turned around and walked out. Edwin Morgan, who caught Sumner as he slumped to the floor, stated that the Senator was as "senseless as a corpse for several minutes, his head bleeding copiously from the frightful wounds and the blood saturating his clothes."[754] Sumner battled for his life, and did not return to the Senate for three years. Allan Nevins historicized concerning Sumner's absence from the Senate, "That empty seat had spoken with rare eloquence."[755] Stephen Puleo summarizes: "Almost overnight, the caning crushed any hope of conciliation between North and South, and galvanized both sides. It transformed slavery from a legal, political, and economic issue, to a titanic moral struggle, replete with religious overtones—and it established Sumner and Brooks as anti-Christ figures to their opposing sides."[756] George Rable notes that Methodist, Gilbert Haven, "even compared the caning of Sumner to the flailing of Jesus, and blood guilt became a powerful theme in his preaching."[757]

Obviously, May of 1856 was not a pleasant time for religious or political convocations. The delegates arrived at the 1856 General Conference armed with sixty-three resolutions, most of them aimed at extirpating slavery from the Methodist Episcopal Church. The Board of Bishops attempted to preempt a discussion on slavery, by warning that any radical action or changes

---

753   Ibid., 64.
754   Ibid., 113.
755   Nevins, 446.
756   Puleo, 116.
757   Rable, 29.

in the Discipline, would alienate the "border states" and/or Conferences in Northern states where Methodists still owned slaves and in Southern churches who still belonged to the Methodist Episcopal Church.[758] But the attempted appeasement and pacification of the Bishops proved to be a frail barrier to the tsunami of emotions on the slavery issue, which was about to wash over the Conference. Though no physical blows were struck, there was a fight among the delegates to gain the floor, and pontificate about slavery. The cries of "Mr. President" from all over the legislative chamber of the Indiana State House, caused Ames, then presiding, to shout, "I will not recognize anyone until the Conference has come to order. Sit down, sit down, I will not preside in a mob."[759] In the very beginning of the Conference, when there was a prolonged discussion over a minor issue of procedure in choosing a secretary, Peter Cartwright exclaimed, "The brother is mistaken ... we always load a thirty-six pounder to the very muzzle to shoot at a mouse."[760]

A resolution was brought to the floor by the "committee on slavery" to outlaw slavery from the church as any other sin. "We believe that all men by nature have an equal right to freedom, and that no man has a moral right to hold a fellow being as property. Therefore, no slave holder shall be eligible to membership in our church hereafter, where emancipation can be effected without injury to the slave unless ownership was for the purpose of freeing the slave and ownership would be dealt with as any other case of immorality."[761] Dozens of speeches were given for and against the resolution, mostly repetitive with little new input or insight on the issue.

The Stevens-Simpson Conspiracy

Simpson and Abel Stevens, late into the night or several nights, drafted an argument against abolitionism. McClintock presented Stevens' argument

---

758 *General Conference Journal of the Methodist Episcopal Church held in Indianapolis, Indiana–1856* (New York: Carlton and Porter, 1856) 199.

759 *Proceedings of the M.E. General Conference held in Indianapolis, Indiana* (Syracuse: L. C. Matlack, 1856) 77.

760 Ibid., 2.

761 Ibid., 122.

on the Conference floor, with no hint that Simpson was involved.[762] After a detailed, historical journey through American Methodism's stand on slavery, Stevens concluded, "Let it come out, Sir, for the sake of frankness, for the sake of repentance, for the sake of amendment, let it be acknowledged historically, constitutionally, admittedly we have been a slave-holding, though an anti-slavery Church." If a blanket prohibition of slavery was adopted, "Our denominational history would close, Sir, with another such disaster."[763] Stevens, speaking through McClintock, closed with a warning that if said resolution passed, Methodism would lose the Border States. That exact fear had prompted Simpson to become Stevens' ghost writer.

After several others had spoken, McClintock publicly asked Stevens if he meant the abolition of the black laws was to be affected by the Conference. "By no means; I mean at the ballot box, in their capacity as citizen–Conferences have nothing to do with slave laws, and I have only named the matter in order to show our aggressive brethren that they have work enough at home, if they will do it, without troubling us with evil, which we have no power to correct."[764] Stevens further added that the Conference had, "No more chance to form a sound, practical judgment about the wise management (of slavery), than Mr. Asbury would have had to learn experimental chemistry in the field of a cotton farm or a rice plantation."[765] Stevens argued the non-feasibility of making a radical change in a church that was numerically growing and doing well. To surgically remove Methodism's malignancy would end like the man who had engraved as his epigraph, "I was well--would be better--took physic--here I lie."[766]

The tension rose when Abel Stevens and James Floy got into a shouting match. Floy retorted, "I did not interrupt you in your speech or during

---

762   According to historian Lucius Matlack, because Simpson could not argue on the Conference floor due to his Episcopal office, he helped Stevens draft his argument. This was the claim made by Bishop Edward Thomson in a letter written to Matlack, November 22, 1879. Lucius C. Matlack. *The Anti-Slavery Struggle and Triumph in the Methodist Episcopal Church*, 275.

763   *Proceedings of the M.E. General Conference held in Indianapolis, Indiana* (Syracuse: L. C. Matlack, 1856) 122.

764   Ibid., 309.

765   Ibid., 310.

766   Ibid.

the reading of Dr. McClintock, of your cogent and forcible recantation, if I may call it that."[767] McClintock found Floy personally offensive and obnoxious.[768] Stevens indignantly exclaimed, "Abel Stevens is not a coward; don't represent me as a traitor."[769]

The delegates to the 1856 General Conference of the Methodist Episcopal Church came as they left, with no new resolution or change regarding slavery in their *Discipline*. One could continue to be a respectable Methodist in good standing, though not a minister and still own slaves. Since a change in the *Discipline* would require a three-fourths favorable vote in all the Annual Conferences, the majority of delegates and especially the Bishops believed that any decision by the General Conference in the direction of eradicating slavery would be useless. No Conference in Methodism ever produced so much smoke with so little illuminating fire as did the 1856 General Conference.

Other than Simpson's clandestine collusion with Stevens, he as well as the other Bishops had been rendered impotent during the impassioned speeches. They were only observers, other than calling time on those who exceeded their thirty minute allotment. They had attempted to muzzle or at least circumscribe debate by stating that, "[We] think it to be our duty to express our strong doubts whether in view of the restricted powers of a delegated General Conference, any measure equivalent to a change in the general rules can be constitutionally adopted without the concurrence of the Annual Conferences."[770] Their caution was as effective as a parasol in a monsoon. Frederick Jobson, a fraternal delegate from British Methodism, concluded that such verbal fireworks were normal for ecclesiastical debate. No doubt he had at some time visited the House of Commons. He may have assumed that the Bishops were supposed to remain aloof from such uncivil wrangling in that he filed the following favorable report:

> The general appearance of the Conference is very impressive. The Bishops are grave, dignified men, who bear in their very looks and demeanor, the care of the Churches. There is no haste or impetuosity in

---

767 Ibid., 350.
768 Ibid., 351.
769 Ibid.
770 Ibid., Appendix 22.

anything they say or do, that at all times they show great self-possession and wisdom. When appealed to on points of law and order, they showed themselves fully prepared to answer. And yet their response to a question is given in such a manner that it by no means tends to check free and full discussion by the Conference, or to place the party complained of for being out of order in a painful or humiliating position And if anyone appeals against their decision to the General Conference, they manifest no dogmatic authority, or tenacity of opinion; but calmly submit the case to the assembly of their brethren for final determination. The Bishops are very evidently humble and devout men who speak and act with reverence toward God, and with respect and affection towards their brethren. This ennobles them in the estimation of all throughout and candid observers and gives to them an aspect of apostolic dignity when seated before the general assembly of their brethren in ministry.[771]

Jobson's description brings to mind how different American Methodist Conferences were from British Methodism over which Wesley had presided. After listening to Conference discussion, Wesley reserved all decisions for himself under the controlling dictum, "We are no republicans." Fortunately for Simpson, the American delegates were "republicans," for they had voted him as a fraternal delegate to the ensuing British Conference at Liverpool.

---

771 Frederick Jobson. *America and American Methodism* (London: James S. Virtue, 1857) 202-203.

Chapter Ten: The High and the Low

A Dream Come True

Simpson was as giddy as a first grader on a field trip to the state fair, as he stood with seventeen-year-old Charles on the steamship *Africa*, waving at Ellen standing on the dock. They waved until they noticed no one else was waving, and Ellen faded from view as the leviathan churned through the New York Narrows and out into the Atlantic Ocean. On the first Sunday, a storm greeted the ship, but the turbulent sea worked to Simpson's advantage. The ownership company mandated a Sabbath service conducted by the "Established Church" of England. The rules also stipulated that the crew must be present, and because the sailors were attending their ship in peril, the Captain requested Simpson to conduct the service, permitting the Bishop to lead the service "wholly" in his own way. "Prayer books and Bibles were distributed, and I conducted the service in our usual method, and preached to a very attentive and sober company, closing with the doxology and benediction."[772]

The Bishop would now visit many of those places he had read about as he curled up in the small village library of Cadiz, what now seemed long ago. Upon arriving, he had to pinch himself to see if being in England was only a dream. In his amazement he penned Ellen, "Am I really here? I am ready to ask myself, for everything is so much like I have seen elsewhere, and so many marks of common civilization and a common Christianity are about me, and the same language which I have always heard I hear still."[773]

---

772   LOC, Simpson papers, "Notes of Travel and Reading," 1856-62, Container one.
773   LOC, Simpson papers, Letter May 25, 1857, Container three.

Yes, the British Isles were not "Merry Old England," and Simpson's fellow British Methodists did not dress as if they were Knights of the Round Table, doing the bidding of King Arthur's Court.

The quartet of Simpson, John McClintock, and the blind preacher, William Milburn,[774] with Charles tagging along, made their way to Ireland, with stops at Dublin and Belfast. It was then to Scotland, where he rhapsodized to Ellen, "In my vision of the day as I wonder over hill and dale, as I gaze at silver streams, clear lakes, wild mountains, beautiful edifices, or old ruins, how often I feel that my delight would be almost perfect could I have you to enjoy these scenes with me. And when I sit, as I do now, by a window overlooking the city and hear the noise of which in the street and the busy tread of feet in adjoining rooms I almost involuntary look around to catch a smile from you."[775]

The speaking appointments at both the British Conference in Liverpool and at the World's Evangelical Alliance in Berlin were somewhat uneventful with Simpson not at his best. Standing before the British, Simpson lost his composure for about fifteen minutes, befuddled in front of his auditors' cold stares and deafening silence. Milburn recorded, "Just as we were giving up all for lost, the speaker seemed to forget himself for a moment or two, as a happy illustration fell from his lips; his face lighted up, his eyes flashed, and every eye in the multitude answered him, and there was a murmur of 'hear, hear!' from all over the house. The Bishop's legs were no longer unsteady. He seemed to erect himself above himself, his voice lost its wavering inflection and uncertainty of tone; his sentences flowed freely in clear and higher

---

774   William Milburn was one of the most extraordinary individuals within the history of American Methodism. He became blind at age five and later testified, "I never saw the face of anyone with whom I spoke, although I have preached and lectured for over half a century." In 1837, he preached in Springfield, IL, with Lincoln in his congregation. The future President declared, "It was the most impressive sermon I ever heard. I believe it and wonder that God should have given such power to a man. The most wonderful thing to me was that sometimes I felt myself strongly involved in it." At twenty-two years old, Milburn was elected Chaplain of the U.S. House of Representatives. He made numerous trips to Europe, and in 1883, at the age of 70, claimed to have traveled 1,500,000 miles. He died in 1893, just short of his 80th birthday. Clarence P. McClellan. "William Henry Milburn: Blind Man Eloquent," *Journal of the Illinois State Historical Society* XLVIII, No. 2 (Summer 1955) 138, 140.

775   Crooks, 338.

form. The speech became earnest, effective, poetic, impassioned, thrilling."[776] McClintock recorded, "Bishop Simpson spoke first and grandly. My audience was raised to a high pitch of enthusiasm, and I succeeded in keeping it up during my speech, which was of the most successful I ever made in my life."[777] The English gave Simpson passing marks:

> There is something overwhelming in his abundant and vehement eloquence. His mind is keenly sensitive of the profound and various truths which the subject of his ministry brings before him, and his illustrations have a rude grandeur which reminds us of the scenery of his native land; that the characteristics of his preaching is intense moral power. He reaches upon the soul with all the weight of his important message.[778]

In Berlin, Simpson's preaching at the Garrison Church was the first time an American or Englishman had ever spoken in the established Church of Prussia. He preached one of his golden oldies, "Unity." An Englishman responded, "Aw, Sir that was preaching; what a backbone of hard, stout thinking was behind all that tenderness and unction."[779]

Historic Trails

At Herrnhut, the Bishop recalled the Moravian influence on Methodism: "The graves are marked by small slates lying flat upon the ground and the simple expression 'fallen asleep' with the name and date and age. All are alike except the graves of the family of Count Zinzendorf on which the slabs are placed on raised walls about three feet high. A little higher on the summit of Hutberg is a small summer house for which one may overlook the old estate of the Count and a little village where the Bishop now resides a mile distant." Simpson credited Peter Bohler with bringing John Wesley into a "closer knowledge of the fundamental doctrine of the gospel." He recalled that in 1738 when visiting Zinzendorf's colony at Herrnhut, Wesley had traveled much of Germany by foot, stopping in Cologne, Frankfort, Halle, Leipzig

---

776   Ibid., 335.
777   Manuscript Archives and Rare Book Library, Emory University, John McClintock papers, 1828–1910, Letter to Ellen, July 31, 1857, Container three.
778   LOC, Simpson papers, "Portraits of Our English Delegates," Scrapbook A, Container twenty-one.
779   Crooks, 344.

and Dresden. At Herrnhut, Wesley explored the Moravian understanding of religious experience and worship practices. "Though subsequently he (Wesley) was separated from the Moravian brethren, he unquestioningly received from them many valuable suggestions which he incorporated into the regulation of his infant societies." Simpson believed Methodism to be a synthesis, combining the "form and regularity of the Church of England with the simplicity and religious energy of the Moravian brethren." A visit to Prague brought to memory John Huss, the Protestant martyr, who was President of the University of Prague, "the great center in which the religious tenets of an early Protestantism were taught and under its influence the Bohemian people were alienated from the Romish Church."[780]

Simpson during his European tour was adept at digging up dirt on Roman Catholicism. "Thus by deluging the land with blood, Romanism triumphed in Bohemia." But he admitted that the followers of John Huss were not completely innocent. When Huss was burned at the stake, "a terrible persecution ensued. Bohemia was the scene of bloody conflicts. The Hussites rose in the terrible tumult and cast twelve senators from the windows of the Senate House upon the points of the lances of the people below. The Pope called upon the potentates of Germany for assistance and promised universal remission of sins even to the most wicked who should kill but one heretic." As Simpson placed his head upon his hotel pillow in Prague, the history lessons had been overwhelming:

> Resting at night I could scarcely rest--thoughts of the martyrs of Old Bohemia, the preaching of Huss and Jerome, the bloody contests, the thousands slain, the exile of the Bohemian brethren, their wandering into Moravia, their settlement at Herrnhut, the spread of the Moravian mission, the visit of Wesley, the growth of Methodism.--All became mingled thoughts in that old city of Prague while the songs that ring out so sweetly in the midnight air seemed to me to indicate that the spirit of the old martyrs were hovering around and the Prague, a battlefield for centuries, should again become a center which yet should spread throughout the Austrian dominions.[781]

---

780   LOC, Simpson papers, "Notes on Trip to Europe," Container fifteen.
781   Ibid. Both Jerome and Huss were burned at the stake within one year of each other, Huss on July, 1415, and Jerome on May 30, 1416. *The New Encyclopedia Britannica* Vol. 6 (New York: Encyclopedia Britannica, 2002) 168, 536.

Yet, Simpson did not catch the juxtaposition nor did he state the disconnect between a persecuted church and the societal adaptation of his own denomination which was shedding any peculiarities sufficient to incite sneering disdain, except from the most hardened skeptic. Over the last decade his thinking had not changed, but only reified. Christianity was synonymous with the defeat of Catholicism and the spread of American ideals and symbols. Simpson had written for the 1854 Annual Report of the Methodist Episcopal Church Missionary Society, "Providence has clearly designed this country as a land of Protestants; and God has prepared us to receive the nations of the world by the vigour and purity of our civil and religious institutions and by the successive and vast extensions of our territory."[782] When in Austria, he recorded, "A flame shall ascend from the ashes of these early martyrs which shall spread until … papal idolatry will perish from the land." He was convinced that "A large portion of the priests in Bohemia are anxious for deliverance from papal domination."[783] Incredulously, at least to us, he further noted, "American interests are not represented in foreign lands as the magnitude and honor of our country demands. Comparatively small, would be the outlay to secure in each Capitol, a permanent position from which the American flag should float and to which all eyes should be directed, as the center and safeguard of American institutions."[784] (He did not say, the cost would be "comparatively small," if a good-sized army could be cheaply deployed.)

The Holy Land

And now, the Bishop would fulfill a dream. Leaving Charles in Germany, McClintock returning to America, and Milburn continuing on a European speaking tour, Simpson began his journey to the Holy Land. He was accompanied by twenty-four year old William Warren, who would become the first president of Boston University, Joseph Wright's son,[785] and

---

782   Quoted in David Hempton's *Empire of the Spirit* (New Haven, Connecticut: University Press, 2005) 151.

783   Quoted by Scott Kisker in "Methodism Abroad: Matthew Simpson and the Emergence of American Methodism as a World Church," *Methodist History* Vol. LII, No. 1 (October 2014) 17.

784   Ibid., 28.

785   Joseph Wright would have at that time been foreign minister to Prussia and living

a Lutheran minister from Pennsylvania. As when he was in New York in 1844, he sized up the women, "The Greek and Armenian women look like our own. The Turkish are veiled in a kind of way, but with two or three exceptions, all I have seen are pale, feeble, and cadaverous."[786]

Warren detailed in his journal the constant fight with mosquitos, fleas, and spine-jolting donkeys and horses as well as "other wild beasts." He attempted to keep a sense of humor: "Once more in Jerusalem, slept but little last night, mosquitos having tormented and stung my face almost to desperation. It was evident that the monastic insects had not renounced the 'lust of the flesh,' however great had been their self-abnegation."[787] In spite of Simpson being constantly sick, the Bishop bored him "to death by his kindness." Warren was amused when on January 9, 1858, Simpson read from Isaiah 9 in a Greek Orthodox Church, where maidens kissed the Bishop's hand, the "second one a little beauty."[788]

For the first and only time in his life, Simpson grew a beard. "It is as white as a patriarch's, seventy years upon my chin, brown my cheeks and whiskers and strangly threatened to be sandy on my upper lip." On November 3, 1857, his wedding anniversary, he was in Beirut, Lebanon. "Twenty years ago this evening, yes, this very evening. Do you remember the little group which met in that parlor in Penn's Street, and do you remember the neat young woman, with the blush of health upon her cheeks who stood beside a tall awkward young man, and there and then before God's minister those solemn vows

---

in Berlin. As a staunch Methodist and former Governor of Indiana, he was a friend of Simpson. On October 23, 1854, Wright wrote Simpson informing him that at least two-thirds of Indiana Methodist ministers are "connected" with the Know Nothings. See Tyler Anbinder. *Nativism and Slavery: The Northern Know Nothings and the Politics of the 1850s* (New York: Oxford, 1992) 49.

786   LOC, Simpson papers, Letter from Matthew to Ellen, October 15, 1857.

787   The Howard Gotlib Archival Research Center, Boston University, William Warren papers, *Diary* 1857-1858.

788   Ibid. As well as covering most of Israel, which included Jerusalem, Joppa, Haifa, and Nablus, Warren and Simpson also visited Alexandria, Cairo, Corfu, Corinth, and Athens. Warren was elected President of Boston University in 1873, retiring from the Presidency in 1903, after which he became Dean of the Boston University School of Theology, a position which he held for eight years. During both his deanship and presidency, he served for thirty-eight years as Professor of Systematic Theology. He died on December 6, 1929 at the age of 97. Daniel L. Marsh. *William Fairfield Warren* (Boston: Boston University Press, 1930).

were irrevocably said?"[789] Evidently, Ellen did not wax as romantic about the occasion as did her husband. Sometime between then and the first of the year she expressed her aggravation at her husband's absence, "He lived to himself without any real thought for the happiness of his wife and family."[790]

But Ellen was more worried than perturbed. Somewhere on the Danube in Germany, her husband had picked up malaria or some non-definable virus. In Beirut, a physician administered "twenty leeches, mustard plasters, blisters and poultices." There were moments when the Bishop thought he was going to die, but that did not stop him from traipsing all over Palestine in the steps of his Savior on days when it would have been difficult for a man in full health to keep going. On the way to Sidon, Warren recorded, "Hunger came upon us, but we had nothing to eat; heat tormented us but we had nothing to drink. We dared wait for them to come up, less something had happened to prevent them from coming and then night would overtake us, far from our shelter."[791] Ultimately, the small party found shelter in a mosque, where they were warmly and hospitably lodged in a large "upper room." Listening to the waves lapping up on the shores of the Mediterranean, Simpson may have regretted all the Mohammedan bashing he had inflicted both as an editor and a preacher.

Continuing to be sick, Simpson still managed to climb the highest pyramid outside of Cairo. A letter from the Board of Bishops found him in Naples. His first Annual Conference was to be in Arkansas in March. Was Ames at it again? Was he jealous of his friend traveling on the other side of the world in places of antiquity where he would never go? Matthew complained to Ellen. Ellen wrote Colonel Alexander Cummings, who lived in Philadelphia, asking him to intervene, stating that her husband was "surprised and astonished" to find when and where the Conferences were to commence in the spring. "He left Greece forthwith by the first steamer, intending to come immediately to New York."[792] Even though the Bishops

789 LOC, Simpson papers, Letter November 3, 1857. Was the husband confused? Did he mean to write twenty-two years?

790 Clark, *The Life*, 205.

791 Crooks, 354.

792 UMA, DePauw University, Simpson papers, Letter, Matthew to Ellen, February 4, 1858. Clark seems to overstate the case here. "Ellen accosted Ames with a good deal of spirit," but there does not seem to be any evidence of Ellen's rancor poured out on the

assured Simpson that he need not be physically present in Arkansas, he denied himself a much coveted trip to Rome and headed home, with his son.

At Death's Door

But the Bishop would hold no Conferences throughout 1858. He was an invalid, home in bed, consumed by the prospects of death. His friends and family were not convinced that he was going to pull through. On May 5, 1858, Simpson wrote Ames that he was recovering his strength, but doubted he would ever be strong again. "I shall be glad to see you if you can pass through our 'smoky city'"[793] When Ames visited his "friend" in the fall, he was "shocked by the pale, gaunt figure stretched out on the bed." He wrote Janes, "I fear Bp. Simpson will never mingle again with us in labor."[794]

The future Bishop to Africa, William Taylor (the same Taylor, Simpson had heard preach in San Francisco) was a guest of the Indiana Conference at Mount Vernon, Indiana, September 30-October 5, 1858. He led the Conference in a fervent prayer for Simpson's healing, and certitude swept over the gathering that the Bishop's life would be spared. More than one person would later claim Simpson reporting "miraculously" beginning to recover on the day of Taylor's prayer.[795]

By November 5, Simpson felt well enough to write John McClintock in order to settle his financial accounts regarding the trip to Europe and the Holy Land: "I have no regular account of expenses which I can readily separate so as to know precisely what I spent in the service to the Church, as my zig zag course of travel was affected by my desire to visit Methodist and other localities in Ireland, Scotland . . . . I know precisely what my whole expenses were from leaving home until I left Berlin for the East, but I am troubled to separate my private sightseeing from the whole and to

---

Bishop. Clark, *The Life*, 206.
793   UMA, Drew University, Simpson papers, Letter May 5, 1858.
794   Ibid., 207.
795   Clarence True Wilson. *The Dedication of the Simpson Memorial Chapel, The Metropolitan Building, Washington, DC* (Washington, DC: Board of Temperance, Prohibition, and Public Morals, 1929). Also see "Bishop Simpson's Life Saved By Prayer," *Indianapolis Sentinel*, LOC, Simpson. papers, no date.

know exactly how to divide between the Book Concern and the Missionary Society."[796] Simpson requested McClintock to send him his accounting, but it sounded like a hopelessly muddled mess. Since Simpson sent accounts of his travels to Methodist publications, he could have rationalized the entire expenses charged to the Methodist Episcopal Church. As we will later see, McClintock was not a genius in financial matters. Though Simpson would later be blind-sided by systemic evil (Sand Creek), he was a person of unquestionable integrity in the miniscule details of everyday affairs.

Simpson defied the what-ever imported microbes and began to mend, in spite of not being able to breathe clean air. Pittsburgh was only getting worse. Even in the more fashionable neighborhoods "the smoke permeated and penetrated everything. If you placed your hand on the balustrade of the stair it came away black; if you washed face and hands they were dirty as ever in an hour. The soot gathered in the hair and irritated the skin …life was more or less miserable."[797] To escape the misery, Simpson moved his family to Evanston, Illinois, one of the most baffling and peculiar decisions of his life. But before moving, he had a party to attend.

Reception/Invitation to St. Paul's MEC, NY April 12, 1859.

Dear Sir: The restoration of BISHOP SIMPSON'S health is cause of gratitude to the church and country. In order to afford an opportunity to all who may wish to offer him their congratulations and respects, a Social Meeting will be held in the Chapel of St. John's M.E. Church, corner 4th Avenue and 22nd Street, on Thursday evening, 14th inst., from 8 until 10 o'clock. You and your family are cordially invited to be present.

JOHN Mc CLINTOCK,	GEO. R. CROOKS,
A.C. FOSS,	JOHN POISAL,
D. L. ROSS,	J. A. ROCHE,
JAMES BISHOP,	DANIEL DREW,
JOHN ELLIOTT,	JOHN FALCONER[798]

---

796 Manuscript Archives and Rare Book Library, Emory University, McClintock papers, Letter November 5, 1858, Container three.
797 David Nassau. *Andrew Carnegie* (New York: The Penguin Press, 2006) 66.
798 LOC, Simpson papers, Invitation April 12, 1859, Container seven.

John Evans Enters Simpson's Life

Sometime in 1841, John Evans heard Matthew Simpson speak in Attica, Indiana, and confessed that the Indiana Asbury President was "the first man who ever made my head swim in talking."[799] Soon thereafter he and his wife Hannah joined the Methodist Episcopal Church, in which he would be inextricably and abundantly involved for the rest of his life. Simpson and Evans would become best friends.

John Evans was intelligent and innovative in his own estimation, and fortunately for him, in the estimation of others. He lacked neither confidence nor initiative. On May 31, 1850, Evans called together eight other Methodists, which included three attorneys, three clergymen, and two businessmen, one of whom was Orrington Lunt. At this first meeting, "The men knelt in prayer to ask for guidance and blessing; and then resolved that the interest of sanctified learning required an immediate university in the Northwest under the patronage of the Methodist Episcopal Church."[800] During the 1850s, Evans was one of the movers and shakers in a small, but rapidly growing city named Chicago, on the southern shore of Lake Michigan. In an interview, which he granted Ashley Bancroft for the purposes of her uncle writing his history, Evans recalled moving to Chicago in 1848, and lecturing each winter at Rush Medical Institute for eleven years.[801] Serving on the Board of the Chicago–Fort Wayne Railroad, he was instrumental in establishing railroad service in and out of Chicago over the next decade. An early history of Chicago states that Evans was "actively engaged in railroad enterprises, and was largely instrumental in securing the right-of-way for the entrance of the Pennsylvania Railroad into Chicago, and also in the building of the Chicago & Ft. Wayne Railroad. He retired from medical practice in 1855, and devoted himself to extended real estate and business enterprises."[802]

---

799   Harry Kelsey, Jr. *Frontier Capitalist: Life of John Evans* (Denver: State Historical Society of Colorado & the Pruett Publishing Company, 1965) 32.

800   Harold F. Williamson and Payson S. Wild. *Northwestern University: A History 1850-1975* (Evanston, Illinois: Northwestern University, 1976) 2–3.

801   Hubert Howe Bancroft published a thirty-nine volume set of historical books on the "West" in which he included "Colorado." Obviously, he needed material from Evans. It is for him, the Bancroft Library at the University of California–Berkley, is named.

802   "Dr. John Evans." *Historical Review of Chicago and Cook County and Selected*

Evans bought sixteen lots in Chicago for $8,000.00, which he deeded to North Western,[803] with the requirement that the University trustees would not sell, but only lease them. At the time of the interview four decades later, they were worth $1,000,000. Serving on the Chicago city council, Evans was appointed chairman of the Committee on Public Schools, and was partially responsible for establishing the first high school in Chicago. Serving as a member on the Committee of "Streets and Alleys," Evans established standard grades for the roads and sidewalks in Chicago. He raised his own building six feet with fifteen hundred screws, and leased part of it to the *Chicago Tribune*. He and two other partners started a banking house, and in his spare time, he edited the *Northwestern Medical Journal*. Whether or not he accurately remembered, and honestly reported his relationship to Lincoln, his recollection needs to be quoted in full.

> I was acquainted with Lincoln but not very intimately, before he was elected president. He spent a night at my house in Chicago, once when he was there attending a lawsuit. And I met him there during the preliminary work of the campaign which elected him as President, that is to say when they were organizing all over the country, campaign clubs for Cameron and Logan. During that time he visited General Julius White, who was at Harper's Ferry, being in command part of the time.
>
> We became quite well acquainted at that time and on other occasions. I was one of the delegates from Chicago that first proposed Abraham Lincoln's name for President at the state convention of Illinois that nominated Dick Yates for Governor, and Abraham Lincoln for President. He was around and we sent for him to make us a speech. We had commenced the rail splitter Hurrah, and we had one of the rails that he split when a boy, leaning up there. We appointed delegates to the national convention at Chicago to present his name, killing the Cameron & Lincoln clubs at one fell sweep, because he went right away ahead of Cameron. Lincoln's speech there struck me most forcibly, by the honest candor of the man more than anything that he said. Now says he, I don't know whether I split that

---

Biography Vol. 2, ed. A. N. Waterman (Chicago: The Lewis Publishing Company, 1908) 280–281.

803   "The split word appeared in the institution's records until February, 1863, when North and Western were combined into a single word in the school catalogue. Beyond the school, however, the earlier spelling continued to appear in newspapers and magazines for a number of years." Email from Kevin B. Leonard, Northwestern University Archivist, August 22, 2015. http://www.library.northwestern.edu/archives.

rail or not, but one thing I do know, that down where that was made, John Hanks and I did in such a winter split a great many oak rails.[804]

Evans was not intimate enough with Lincoln to persuade him to visit Evanston during his presidential campaign in 1860. Lincoln declared that he had no desire to socialize with a, "lot of college professors and others, all strangers to me."[805]

Beginnings of Northwestern University and Garrett Biblical Institute

Sometime in the spring of 1853, Orrington Lunt wandered around the shores of Lake Michigan some dozen miles above Chicago. There he entered into conversation with Dr. John Foster who had determined to build a female academy on 370 acres of prime shore line property. Lunt shared with Foster the even bigger plans conceived by the Methodists, and Foster conceded that he might consider selling his land for such a proposal. Evans followed up the Lunt-Foster conversation with a call on Walter S. Gurnee, President of the Chicago and Milwaukee Railroad. Evans promised Gurnee a depot, on land purchased from Foster, in return for running a rail line north up the Lake Michigan shore. Evans then returned to Foster, who had to be persuaded to sell his prized piece of property. "Only when Evans described their educational idea in great and sometimes passionate detail did Foster relent–though he set a high price on the undeveloped land, $25,000." Foster offered terms of $1,000 down, and ten years to pay the rest, "We took it said Evans, who made the down payment on October, 1853, and provided his personal guarantee for the note."[806]

Almost a century later, John Evans, a grandson named after his grandfather recalled, "Dr. Evans wanted the village named in some way for Bishop Simpson, whom he admired very much, but the divine was modest and didn't want it done. Some of the trustees thought the town should be

---

804   "Bancroft Interview" on file, Northwestern Archives, Northwestern University: Evanston, Illinois.
805   J. Pridmore. *Northwestern: A History* (Evanston, Illinois: Northwestern University Press) 32.
806   Ibid., 19–20.

called 'Luntville,' for the man who had found the site, but Orrington Lunt was modest, too. Among them they settled upon Evanston, because of John Evans' generous gift which made possible the purchase."[807] Whether an invitation to become president of Garrett Biblical Institute was attached to Evans' first beckoning for Simpson to move to Evanston, we do not know. We do know that the idea of the move was broached sometime before March 15, 1858. On that date Evans wrote Simpson:

My Dear Bishop,

Accept my sincere congratulations upon your safe return and an expression of my devout thankfulness to our Heavenly Father for his protection and preservation. I desire thus early to notify you of our anxious solicitude for your early removal to our place. I have already apprised Mrs. S. of the fatal effects of the financial embarrassments of the country upon our Bishops parsonage. We however had almost enough subscribed to secure the object when the crisis came & thought it best to delay.[808]

Augustus Garrett served two different terms as Mayor of Chicago, while he invested in real estate and died at the early age of forty-seven. His well-off widow, Eliza, stipulated that a large portion of her wealth would go to a Bible institute, and the founders of North Western accommodated her with a piece of ground in the middle of their proposed campus. In faith or in hope of Eliza Garrett's early exit from this life, the newly-elected Board of Trustees for Garrett Biblical Institute, erected a building and opened its doors to students, January 1, 1855. Less than one year later, November 15, 1855, Eliza, seemingly in good health, died. A third of her estate went to Garrett in the amount of $300,000.00.[809]

By the date of the March 15 letter, because of the 1857 financial panic, Garrett was in economic trouble. The institution's insolvency made President John Dempster's desire to leave Evanston all that more pronounced. By August 1858, "Dempster was talking about traveling to California, the

---

807 "John Evans: Builder of Evanston and Northwestern University." *Evanston Review* on file, Northwestern Archives, Evanston, IL.

808 UMA, DePauw University, Simpson papers, Letter March 15, 1858.

809 Mrs. John A. Logan. *The Part Taken by Women in American History* (Wilmington, DE: Perry Nalle Publishing Company, 1912). Frederick A. Norwood. *From Dawn to Midday at Garrett* (Evanston: Garrett Evangelical Theological Seminary, 1978) 5.

land of promise. He did not get into the gold rush; but he felt the urge to make still another beginning in theological education. This man was never content, unless he was on the front edge."[810] By May of 1859, the invitation for Simpson to move to Evanston and the invitation to become president of Garrett Biblical Institute were one and the same. C. P. Bragdon, pastor of the First Methodist Church in Evanston,[811] enticed Simpson with a description of paradise:

> As to the healthfulness of this place, you nor your family need entertain any fears--Our doctor says: "It is disturbingly healthy"--affording him almost limited business. It is not biliary or pulmonic--but a golden mean--you know something of my past history--how my health was for years before coming west. I am naturally biliary and have also a pulmonary trouble; yet here I enjoy the best health I had after 20 years past. It is as near perfect as my organic constitution will permit me to enjoy.[812]

It is not surprising that John Evans would want to live near his friend, Matthew Simpson. They revered one another. In the 1889 interview, Evans recalled his relationship with Simpson and the beginnings of Northwestern. "In talking the matter over, he agreed with me that it should be a good idea to start a Methodist School at Chicago, and that we should put the matter before the leading members, and I commenced working on it before I left there."[813] This means that part of Evans' motivation for moving from Indianapolis to Chicago was to begin a school of higher learning under Methodist aegis. What was ironic about Simpson moving from Pittsburgh to Evanston, Illinois was quite apparent. First, he would be out on the Episcopal and camp meeting trail in the spring, summer, and fall, but shut in on the shores of Lake Michigan in the winter. When the fifty-year-old asthmatic stepped out of his house in January, the wind chill (a term not used then) blowing off of Lake Michigan would be fifty degrees below zero, a damp, chilling-to-the-bone wind. Second, Edward R. Ames resided in Indianapolis, or about 150 miles from Chicago. Two of the six bishops, one

---

810   Norwood, 26-27.

811   C.P. Bragdon became pastor of Evanston First Methodist Church in 1858. In all likelihood he served on the Northwestern board of trustees. He died on January 29, 1869. *History of Northwestern University and Evanston*, eds. Robert Dickenson Sheppard and Harvey Bostwick Hurd (Chicago: Munsell Publishing Co., 1906) 342.

812   UMA, DePauw University, Simpson papers, Letter May 29, 1859.

813   "Bancroft Interview," on file at Northwestern Archives.

third of the Episcopal board, would be living at the northwest corner of the Northwest Territory, an arrangement for which there was no financial or logistical rationale. How would this arrangement work in servicing the new churches in Kansas and Nebraska as well as the state of Texas, not to mention the majority of Methodists who lived on the East coast? But the trustees of North Western University, of which Evans was the chair, and the newly formed Garrett Biblical Institute prevailed.[814]

Whatever the sequence of the above events, the trustees and faculty voted Simpson President of Garrett Biblical Institute on January 2, 1861.[815] Simpson did not immediately latch on to the offer. Almost six months later on June 17, 1861, Simpson wrote Lunt, "After full reflection, I have concluded to accept this position to which you have invited me, understanding as I do that it is not in any way to interfere with my episcopal duties."[816]

---

814   The Rock River Conference extended the following invitation to Edwards Ames in 1853: "From the rapidly developing and extending character of the work in the North West, it is highly important that it should have the personal acquaintance and residence of someone of our Superintendents, therefore, resolve, that Bishop Ames is respectfully requested and warmly invited to reside within the bounds of the Rock River Conference." *Minutes of the Rock River Conference of the Methodist Episcopal Church* (Chicago: Northwest Advocate Office, 1853) 14. Ames did not accept the invitation. Simpson presided over the 1861 Rock River Conference. Garrett reported to the Conference: "The Institute congratulates itself on the acceptance of Bishop Simpson of its Presidency, to which he was long ago unanimously elected. His counsel and cooperation will be invaluable to the faculty. Nor will his advice to candidates for the itinerancy in the large compass of his Episcopal duties be less important." *Minutes of the Twenty-Second Session of the Rock River Conference of the Methodist Episcopal Church* (Rockford: Register Steam Printing Establishment, 1861) 12–13.

815   The official minute of Simpson's election was recorded May 2, 1861. "The President made communication to the Board in relation to the election of the President of the Board of Instruction whereupon Mr. Judson moved that we jointly with the faculty proceed to the election of the president of the Board of Instruction, Bishop Matthew Simpson, having received the votes of all present was declared unanimously elected. On motion it was resolved that Bishop Simpson be affectionately and earnestly requested to accept the presidency of the faculty of the Garrett Bib. Institute and that he signify his acceptance at the earliest day practicable." Orrington Lunt, Sec. Board Trustees. UMA, Drew University, Simpson Papers.

816   Garrett Evangelical Theological Seminary Archives, Letter June 17, 1861, "Autographs and Portraits."

Simpson's Influence on Frances E. Willard

In March of 1858, eighteen-year-old Frances E. Willard, whose family lived in Milwaukee, traveled to Evanston, Illinois, for the purpose of entering North Western Female Seminary. Over the next four years, she formed a relationship with the Simpson family, especially Ella, who was two years her junior. Between 1841 and 1846, the Willard family lived in Oberlin, Ohio, and "Frank" retained vivid memories of hearing Charles Finney preach. He was, "a combination of thunder and lightning; lightning in his looks, thunder in his voice .... who was very much given to rehearsing in our hearing the pains and penalties of the condemned."[817]

It was not the thunder of Finney but the "personal holiness" of Matthew Simpson which won Frances Willard to Christ. In December of 1859, Simpson held a revival at the First Methodist Episcopal Church of Evanston. On December 14, Simpson entreated "my dear friends, you have thought it a little thing to sin publicly, and it is just and right that you *publicly* declare by your action if not by your words, that you intend to stop sinning, that you intend with Christ's help, to live reconciled to God." Two nights later, Willard went forward and made a public confession of faith. Her conversion was not the normal Methodistic, emotional upheaval. Just as Simpson had invited his listeners to an act of the will, Willard's conversion was primarily volitional.

> I have commenced! O Lord! I am trying to redeem the solemn promise I have made to Thee, I have publicly declared my determination to forsake my sins—to seek forgiveness for the past and help for the future; to endeavor with Christ's help,--always with Christ's help,--to live a good, true, valuable life—a life that shall glorify God and be a blessing to my fellow toilers and sufferers on the earth.
>
> I have not yet the change of heart that Christ has promised to those who ask Him rightly, but I expect it.[818]

---

817   Frances E. Willard. *Glimpses of Fifty Years: The Autobiography of an American Woman* (Chicago: H. J. Smith and Company, 1889) 5.

818   Frances E Willard. *Writing Out of My Heart: Selections from the Journal of Frances E. Willard, 1855-96* (Chicago: University of Illinois Press, 1995) 54.

She later wrote:

> The Bishop, though at home only during brief intervals was the central figure and beloved hero of the town, where during his three or four years' residence he preached and lectured not less than thirty times. His eldest daughter, Ella, more like himself than any of his other children, was a school friend and companion in many a pleasant, confidential ramble through the woods and down by the lake shore.[819]

Simpson and Benjamin Titus Roberts Collide

In 1857, Benjamin Titus Roberts wrote three imprudent articles for the *Northern Christian Advocate*, and in his last essay "Causes of Religious Declension" stated, "This great declension in numbers is prima facie evidence that our spiritual condition is not good. We are a Conference low in spirituality. There is great want of the power and even of the form of godliness. In many and perhaps most of our charges, probably not one half of our members are enjoying justifying grace, according to the scriptural and the Methodist standard."[820] Roberts had called half of the Genesee Conference unregenerate, and needless to say, reaped antagonism. But many "old line" Methodist preachers in the Genesee Conference agreed with Roberts. Thus, a collective movement became known as "Nazaritism," though Roberts and his sympathizers never formally met together on a specific date to adopt the moniker. Those who opposed them were known as the "Regency", though they, too, never designated themselves as such. Representative of the "Regency" was Thomas Carlton, head of the New York Publishing House and financial advisor for Simpson. Ironically and coincidently, Thomas Carlton had displaced George Lane, by the vote of the 1852 General Conference, the latter with whose family Ellen Roberts had lived during her teenage years.

What Simpson had to say about Roberts and Carlton indicated on which side of the fence the Bishop stood. Simpson claimed that Carlton, as New York Book Agent and head of the missionary society, maintained a "high standard and displayed unusual talent as a financier."[821] Simpson allowed

---

819   Willard, *Glimpses*, 175.
820   Howard A. Snyder. *Populist Saints: B.T. and Ellen Roberts and the First Free Methodists* (Grand Rapids: William B. Errdmans Publishing Company, 2006) 245.
821   *Cyclopaedia*, 167. Carlton was one of the main advisors to the Niagara congregation

no specific article on Roberts in his *Cyclopaedia*, but under his essay, "Free Methodists," the Bishop identified the denomination with "Nazaritism" and pejoratively wrote, "In its early history, some of its leaders encouraged a spirit of wild fanaticism, claiming the power of healing by the laying on of hands. In many cases, the excitement connected with the meetings, passed into extravagance which was sanctioned by their leading men, as being evidence of the Holy Spirit."[822] Had Simpson forgotten about Freeborn Garrettson, Billy Hibbert, Benjamin Abbott, and all the other Methodist "shock troops" that had willed, sacrificed, and peculiarized Methodism into existence? Had he forgotten that uncontrollable holy commotion had, at times, broken out under his own preaching?

In 1843 when Simpson started his biography on Robert Roberts (a work he never finished because of the advice of his uncle) he interviewed the Bishop, while the latter was having his portrait painted at Indiana-Asbury University. Roberts (no relation to Benjamin Titus) recalled during his early days of preaching, when his listeners "Began shouting, jumping up and down and falling to the floor," he simply stopped. He further stated, "At one of our quarterly meetings, probably the second in Carlisle, the meeting-house small, the congregation large, we held meeting in the grove. Our presiding elder commenced preaching (a very neat man, wore a silk gown) and before he closed his sermon such was the effect on the congregation that they were falling in every direction like men in battle."[823] Simpson dutifully recorded Roberts' description of his early days in Methodism. Certainly the man, who was now a Bishop himself, was aware that a tranquilizing sedation was leveling out his denomination.

At the 1857 Genesee Annual Conference, at which Simpson was not present because of his European trip, Roberts was placed on trial, and accused of condemning Methodism's dead constituency, and among other things indicting the so called Regency, with "sneering at Christianity in a manner

---

which, after Roberts left, refurbished their church, went into debt, and subsequent bankruptcy, and shortly thereafter, closed its doors for good. When money could not be accounted for in the New York Book Concern, Simpson defended Carlton. See Matthew Simpson, *A Hundred Years of Methodism* (Hunt and Eaton, 1876) 248-249.

822   *Cyclopaedia*, 379-380.

823   Tippy, 79-80. Tippy quotes from Simpson's manuscript on Roberts, which is in the LOC, Simpson papers, "Notes on Bishop Roberts," Container sixteen.

not worthy of Thomas Paine, and that falls below that of Voltaire."[824] The Conference pronounced Roberts "guilty," but only slapped him on the wrist with a reprimand, hoping that the reformer would reform his contumacious ways. But there was not an ounce of conformity in Roberts, especially regarding theological and spiritual conviction. The 1858 Genesee Annual Conference again placed Roberts on trial, but this time "for un-Christian and immoral conduct," which biographer Howard Snyder correctly calls a "farce." Roberts was a person of ramrod integrity and profound spiritual intensity. But as a sailor on a ship, attempting to correct direction, Roberts could not provide a large enough rudder and create sufficient wind for the sails.

The Ouster of Benjamin Titus Roberts

When on trial at the 1858 Annual Conference, Roberts, who had trained as an attorney, defended himself with dignity and logic, and reminded the preachers who sat before him that "Galileo compelled by a council that claimed as much wisdom and infallibility as this body of ministers, to retract his statement that the earth moved instead of the sun. But after his recantation, he was heard to say in an undertone, 'but the earth does move after all.'"[825] The Conference voted Roberts guilty, and stripped him of his ministerial credentials. Edmond Janes was graciously charitable, if not prescient, to cordially shake the departing Roberts' hand and say, "Do not be discouraged Brother Roberts, there is a bright future before you yet."[826]

After being absent because of both travel and illness, Simpson chaired the Genesee Conference at Brockport, New York in 1859, where the "Nazarites" set up a rival tent a couple of miles away with as many as 5,000 in attendance. Simpson and the "Regents" interpreted the affront as a serious breach of ecclesiastical ethics. He wrote his wife: "Women had come by troops—one crowd by a canal-boat, others from Utica, and some; it is said, from St. Louis. They are in attendance in the galleries, and some have their knitting busily employed. They are all Nazarites, and use in their

---

824 Snyder, 401.
825 Ibid., 441.
826 Ibid., 448.

conversation, many epithets denunciatory of the Conference."[827] He then stood up before the Genesee Conference and stated:

> Brethren, I have been a Methodist from my youth up. I have lived to witness several secessions, but I never heard such doctrines professed by Methodist preachers as have been openly declared on this floor this morning. I have heard brethren declare their right to admit to their pulpits, and associate in labor with them, men who stand expelled from the Methodist Episcopal Church; and I have heard brethren appeal to their right of private judgment in justification of the same, and also of their right to preach when and where they will, and to enter within other men's fields of labor, and work without the consent of the pastor. In all my knowledge of Methodism, I have never heard such doctrines avowed till this morning.[828]

But Simpson's memory was weak, or he was dishonest, or he did not know his Church history. Wesley, Whitefield, Gilbert Tennent, and Finney, as well as hundreds of other flaming zealots, were condemned by the "Church establishment" for ignoring parish boundaries. Wesley had defended the right of Methodist preachers to invade the parishes of Anglican priests. "I look upon all the world as my parish: thus far, I mean that, in whatever part of it I am, I judge it meet, right, and my bounden duty to declare unto all that are willing to hear, the glad tidings of salvation."[829] But this was not a war between right and wrong; it was a contest between prophet and priest, reform versus maintenance, insiders versus outsiders, immediatism versus gradualism, authority versus submission, and endless interpretations of who and what the Church ought to be. Roberts was a bender; fossilized, calcified, and brittle churches most of the time refuse to bend which results in endless cycles of sectarianism, what Luther referred to as the Church "reformed and being reformed."

Simpson and Roberts were going in opposite directions, not that Simpson never changed course. But at the heart of Simpson's character and the peculiarity of his office, he was neither a reformer nor a prophet. As a protector of Methodism's rules, Simpson painted himself into a corner when he stated, "After such vow and covenant to surrender your private will to the

---

827   Ibid., 494.

828   Ibid., 495.

829   Nehemiah Curnock. *The Journal of the Rev. John Wesley* Vol. II (London: The Epworth Press, 1938) 218.

judgment of your seniors in the Gospel, a promise made without mental reservation, and freely. I am astonished to hear brethren assert a right of judgment in regard to the order and manner of their ministerial services against the judgment and decision of the Conference."[830] Simpson was asking his subordinates to do what Scripture does not require, to surrender right of conscience and privacy of opinion.

A Huge Fault-line in the Methodist Episcopal Church

By late 1859, Roberts was pastoring a group of people whom he organized as a Methodist church in November, emphasizing it was "free" which equated to no rented pews. At the 1860 General Conference, inundated by slavery petitions, the Roberts appeal got kicked around to several committees.[831] Finally it landed in the Committee on "Itinerancy," which had too much business for another agenda, and hence, "handed off" Roberts to the Committee on "Appeals." One could ask, why did not the case go there in the first place? This committee decided that because Roberts had continued to preach and had rebelled against the authority of the Church, and connected himself to another organization, that his appeal could not be considered. Snyder argues for the founding date of July 2, 1860, at Wayne, Illinois, as the official beginning of the Free Methodist Church. To no one's surprise, B. T. Roberts was elected as General Superintendent.

Holiness Movement historians Timothy L. Smith and Melvin Dieter both argue that the Wesleyan doctrine of "entire sanctification" was at the center of the schism. Smith states, "The rupture could scarcely have occurred had the conflict over holiness not been involved from the beginning with

---

830 F. W. Conable. *History of the Genesee Annual Conference of the Methodist Episcopal Church: 1810–1872* (New York: Nelson and Phillips, 1876) 652.

831 There was a real irony here. One of the axioms on which Free Methodism stood was its clear abolitionism: "free men." James Arnold Reinhard is perceptive in noting that Simpson in his article on Free Methodism did not mention abolitionism. He is also correct in accusing Simpson of misrepresenting the Methodist Episcopal Church's stand on slavery after 1844. Simpson wrote, "While not entering the political arena or taking part as a church in the excited elections, no other agency (the Methodist Church) was so patient in affecting the public mind and in preparing for the triumph of anti-slavery principles." James Arnold Reinhard. *Personal and Sociological Factors in the Formation of the Free Methodist Church 1852–1860* (unpublished Ph. D. dissertation: The University of Iowa, 1971) 125.

a struggle for place and power in which platforms of moral reform in the church and state played a major part. The doctrine of entire sanctification and the crusade to restore 'old-fashioned Methodism' were emotional symbols as well as issues vital to the fray."[832] Dieter, who reminds us that the "Free Methodist Church was the first organized church in history to specifically identify itself with the doctrine of Christian Perfection at its founding," summarizes that the newly-formed sect found its impetus by tying together the themes of the Wesleyan doctrine of perfectionism, the abolition of slavery, and the enforcement of a more stringent discipline.[833]

Free Methodism, though a small denomination both then and now represented a huge fault line in American Methodism. Free Methodism augured for both Simpson and the Methodist Episcopal Church an ongoing adaptation to middle-class values, and an erasing of social aberrations that had defined earlier worship practices and ethical strictures. Past splinter groups, the Republican Methodists, the Methodists Protestants, the African Methodist Episcopal, the Wesleyan Methodists, and the Methodist Episcopal Church South had originated because of constitutional controversy or the inability of American Methodism's governing process to deal with specific social issues. The genesis of Free Methodism was different, a first. B. T. Roberts and his followers claimed that they conformed to early American Methodism more than did its current leaders. The Free Methodists believed themselves to be more Methodist than either Simpson or Carlton. Free Methodism was paradigmatic of cyclical sectarianism within American religion, a restorationism which believes itself to possess a clearer perception of truth. Most schismatics view themselves as more representative of primitive Christianity, a biblical authority no longer freighted by the mother ship which has jettisoned its original identity and ideology.

Not a Good Day to be a Bishop

Roberts wrote Matthew Simpson September 15, 1878, regarding his *Cyclopaedia* article on the Free Methodist Church, "There are some fifteen

---

832 Smith, *Revivalism and Social Reform*, 133.
833 Melvin Dieter. *The Holiness Revival of the Nineteenth Century* (Metuchen, New Jersey: The Scarecrow Press, 1980) 52,125.

statements or re-statements which are utterly untrue, and some five or six statements which, though in a sense true, yet, are from the manner in which they are made, misleading."[834] The Bishop replied, October 23, 1878, "I am not aware of any incorrect statements in the article, but if you will furnish me with corrections and the accompanying proofs, I will gladly make any alterations in a future edition, should such editions be called for."[835] What Roberts called for, he elaborated in over three hundred pages, *Why Another Sect*, which we presume he sent to Simpson. As to the charge of fanaticism, Free Methodist historian Leslie Marston returned to Simpson's early days, when preaching on Ezekiel's image on water flowing from the Temple, that a "respectable" woman walked to the center aisle and cried out, "Sun, stand thou still and let the Moon pass by."[836] The crying and shouting almost drowned out Simpson's voice. But the Bishop had not blotted out these aberrations from his memory, when he condemned Roberts and Free Methodism. He was painfully cognizant that Roberts incarnated an essential aspect of Methodism that was in danger of being lost. Thus, at the end of the 1859 Brockport Conference, he rebuked, "coldness and formality" in worship, and assured his preachers that "hardy prayers and response", and "praising God aloud" were the true spirit of Methodism, but such equivocation offered no redemption. The proscription of Simpson's office called for protection rather than provocation. The confines of the Episcopacy entrapped him in one of his worst bureaucratic dilemmas, and there was no way out. Caretakers are seldom converted into reformers. It was not a good day to be a Bishop.

But the Genesee Conference would not let Simpson go unrewarded. When he chaired the Annual Conference in October of 1863, D.S. Seagar presented the Bishop a cane made of Palmetto wood, "the head ivory, with gold and silver mountings, beautifully carved after a design patented by Mr. (J.C.) Nobles." Inscribed on the cane was the picture of an eagle, strangling a serpent, symbolizing a rebuke to Copperheads and Southern traitors. Genesee Conference Historian C. S. Conable stated that the, "presentations were fine, and the responses most happy." Conable also noted that the Conference was, "short and pleasant, very little, of anything of the Nazarite

---

834   B. T. Roberts. *Why Another Sect* (New York: Garland Publishing Inc., 1984) 17.
835   Ibid., 17.
836   Leslie Marston. *A Living Witness* (Winona Lake, Indiana: Light and Life Press, 1960) 315.

element remaining in the Conference."[837] Maybe during the Civil War, it was good to attend something that was short and pleasant.

The antagonism between Roberts and Simpson included a quaint and curious sidebar. In 1876, the Federal Government decided that Roberts' home town of North Chili, New York, was unworthy of a post office. After its removal, Roberts wrote Simpson, asking him to intercede on behalf of North Chili. "Will you please give me such a letter of introduction to the President or will secure from him a hearing of the case upon its merits?"[838] If Roberts did not believe that Simpson was in favor with God, he had high confidence in the Bishop's influence on men.

Civil War Detonators

On March 6, 1857, the frail Roger Taney, seventy-nine-year old Chief Justice of the Supreme Court, held in his shaking hands a fifty-four page document, which he read in its entirety.[839] The speech delivered to all who could crowd into the small chamber on the ground floor of the Capitol was effective, i.e., if one wanted to start a war. Well, a large canister of gun powder to blow up the Capitol would have been much quicker than the two hours of legal minutia, which could have been distilled into one sentence: "Dred Scott is not a citizen of the United States and, therefore, cannot sue for his freedom." America's highest judicial authority, had decided Scott was not a person; he was a thing to be bartered, bought, sold, and owned, the same as a horse or cow. Taney, in cahoots with Democratic President, James Buchanan, had just handed the Republicans the White House in 1860. Republican John F. Potter called the decision, "Sheer blasphemy ... an infamous liable on our government ... a lasting disgrace to the court from which it issued and deeply humiliating to every citizen."[840] The *New*

---

837 Conable, 673-674.

838 LOC, Simpson papers, Letter May 8, 1876, Container ten.

839 Simpson was not an admirer of Roger Taney, in spite of him being a graduate of the Methodist Dickinson College in Carlisle, PA. He believed had Taney not been Chief Justice of the Supreme Court the Court would not have ruled against the Methodist Episcopal Church in apportioning proceeds from the publishing houses to the Methodist Episcopal Church South. *Autobiography*.

840 Kenneth M. Stamp. *America in 1857: A Nation on the Brink* (New York: Oxford

York Independent declared, "The decision of the Supreme Court is the moral assassination of a race and cannot be obeyed."[841] Because Taney and Buchanan had been seen whispering in one another's ear at the presidential inauguration, William Seward called the decision a "conspiracy."[842] Charles Sumner was not far from wrong when he prophesied that, "The name of Taney is to be hooted down the pages of history ... an emancipated country will fasten upon him the stigma which he deserves."[843]

We conclude the decade before the Civil War with an event which impacted Simpson and every other American. John Brown got the world's attention when he stormed the federal arsenal at Harper's Ferry, Virginia, and then was hung for his deed. Was the man insane? Yes, if insanity equates to being obsessed with an idea. Yes, if that obsession drives one to attempt a feat for which he has little to no practical means for accomplishment. But did Brown really believe that the feeble effort to capture Harper's Ferry would start a slave rebellion, amounting to a revolution, which would lead to emancipation, and he, more than any other person, would be the emancipator? Neither a psychiatrist nor a historian can give a definitive answer. However, if Brown intended to raise his life to the level of symbol, even as did a Spartacus or a William Wallace, no psyche has ever been more clearly grounded in reality than Brown's.

Brown's biographer, Evan Carton, reminds us that, "Those who answer Brown's or Thoreau's call with immoderate passion and abandon will always be controversial, always be extreme." They separate themselves from the rest of us, who stand exempt from examination and debate.[844] A few days after his arrest, Brown stated to Governor Wise, "There is an eternity behind, an eternity before, and the little speck in the center, however long, is but comparatively a minute. The difference between your time and mine is

---

University Press, 1990) 104.
841   David N. Potter. *The Impending Crisis: 1848-1861* (New York: Harper and Row, 1976) 284.
842   Ibid., 288.
843   Ibid., 289-290.
844   Evan Carton. *Patriotic Treason: John Brown and the Soul of America* (New York: Free Press, 2006) 346.

trifling."[845] These are not the words of a psychotic. No man ever died more gallantly or with such clear-minded purpose. Whatever Brown's deeds, there can be no doubt that he accomplished more in death than in life.

Brown became the final preeminently heard voice preceding the Civil War. As he exited the Charleston jail to walk to the scaffold, he handed a note to a guard: "I, John Brown, am now quite certain that the crimes of this greedy land will never be purged away, but with blood. I had as I now think vainly flattered myself that without very much bloodshed it might be done." Simpson's moderation brokered no sentiment for Brown's grandstanding. On the eve of the "bloodshed," no two personalities could have been more antithetical. Strange, that Simpson from his lofty perch could not see as far or as clearly, as a man who had groveled through life, and failed in just about everything he ever attempted.

---

845   Ibid., 318.

Chapter Eleven:
Headquarters at the White House

Simpson Ready to Step on the National Stage

The eve of the Civil War found Matthew Simpson at the height of his mental, physical, and elocutionary powers. The Nation's most formidable and defining event would bring the Methodist preacher into national prominence. Until now, Simpson's popularity was confined mostly to Methodism, but the Civil War would place him in the national spotlight, a visibility among America's clergymen rivaled only by Henry Ward Beecher. Beecher was already a household name because of his bombastic preaching, strategic location of his Plymouth Church in Brooklyn, his melodramatic displays such as "mock slave auctions," and outspoken abolitionism, known more for showmanship than for theological and biblical integrity. The time was right for Simpson, the most powerful preacher within America's largest denomination to become a major political player, beyond the confines of the ecclesiasticism which had nurtured and shaped him. His 1860 American "passport" listed him as six feet with blue eyes and mixed-colored hair, with no peculiarities.[846]

Ironically, as America careened towards an apocalypse, beyond anyone's darkest forebodings, a brutality and suffering that had not been seen on the face of the earth since the Napoleonic Wars some one-half century earlier, Methodism's national gathering in May of 1860 was even more benign and quotidian than usual. The Bishops began the Conference by confessing their impotence to eradicate slavery from the denomination. In fact, they had

---

846   LOC, Simpson papers, "Description of Person," Container twenty.

nothing new or insightful to say on the issue: "We find so little change in the relation of the church to the subject during the last four years that we refer you to the views which we communicated to the last General Conference in our Episcopal Address."[847] The 1860 Conference, because of the scores of petitions against slavery, resolved that

> We believe that the buying, selling, or holding of human beings to be used as chattels is contrary to the laws of God and nature, and inconsistent with the Golden Rule and with that rule in our Discipline which requires all who desire to continue among us to "do no harm, and avoid evil of every kind," we, therefore, affectionately admonish all our preachers and people to keep themselves pure from the great evil and to seek its extirpation by all lawful and Christian means.[848]

"Affectionately admonish" provided the resolution with the backbone of a banana. One could continue to be a Methodist in good standing and own slaves. The pundit who said, "Trying to abolish slavery through the church was like trying to pry up a stump with a bamboo crowbar,"[849] may have been referring to Methodism.

Simpson received a couple of kudos during the Conference, results of his visits to Ireland and England, in 1857-58. A report from the Irish Conference declared, "We recognize in Bishop Simpson, a Bishop of the primitive time and of the apostolic stamp, being in journeyings often, in labors more abundant, apt to teach, and mighty in the age-old doctrines."[850] Likewise from the British Conference: "In Bishop Simpson we have learned to more highly honor the Episcopacy of your church, and fervently do we pray that the chief shepherd may ever rise up men of like spirit and power to take the chief places in your ministry."[851]

But the glow of laudation was dimmed when the Conference indirectly indicted Simpson for his heavy-handed treatment of B.T. Roberts. "The Committee (on the Episcopacy) find that the ruling of Bishop Simpson in

---

847   *Journal of the General Conference of the Methodist Episcopal Church: 1860*, held in Buffalo, New York, edited by William Harris (New York: Carlton and Porter, 1860) 319.

848   Ibid., 255.

849   D. Reid Ross. *Lincoln's Veteran Volunteers Win the War* (Albany, New York: Albany State University of New York, 2008) 15.

850   1860 *Journal*, 323.

851   Ibid., 326.

this case is in accordance with usage and with previous Episcopal decisions, but to prevent misunderstanding upon the subject and to settle the principle involved ... while the counsels upon our Superintendents are to be highly respected and to be considered of great value in the administration of Discipline, their decisions are not to be regarded as having the force of law outside of the annual conferences."[852] Simpson's proscription of Roberts did not carry the authority of Methodism's Constitution which was ultimately enforced by the Annual Conferences, and not the General Conference.

By reading Simpson's *Diaries* and letters during the early 1860s, one would hardly know that America was engaged in a horrific contest for its very survival.[853] No mention of Fort Sumter and no lament of the embarrassing Union defeat at Manassas Junction in July of 1861. Methodically, Simpson continued to go about his ecclesiastical duties. In 1860, he chaired ten conferences: Baltimore, Kentucky, New Hampshire, New York East, Black River, Cincinnati, Ohio, Michigan, North Western, and Southern Illinois.[854] But in 1861, Simpson chaired only seven Conferences. Between the Wyoming Conference of April at Oswego, New York, and the Indiana Conference in September, Simpson visited no Annual Conferences. His whereabouts were largely unknown except by his family and close friends. The interruption in Simpson's schedule was caused by his designated turn

---

852 Ibid., 428. Interestingly, the final decision on B. T. Roberts' ouster from the Methodist Episcopal Church was made in Buffalo, New York, the site of the 1860 General Conference, the epicenter for the Roberts versus Methodism conflict. On May 31, the appeal of B. T. Roberts was rejected for the following reasons: "1) That B. T. Roberts, subsequently to his trial and condemnation, joined the Methodist Episcopal Church as a probationer, and thus, at least, tacitly confessed to the justice and action of the Conference of his case 2) That B. T. Roberts, since he was deprived by his expulsion of his ministerial authority and standing, has continued to preach and has rebelled against the authority of the Conference and the Church 3) That B. T. Roberts, since he declared his intention of appealing to the General Conference, has connected himself with another organization contemplating church ends independent and hostile to the Church whose General Conference he now appeals. Resolved–That the appeal of B. T. Roberts be not admitted." Ibid., 253.

853 Crooks stated concerning Simpson and the Civil War, "It is not the purpose of this volume to trace the vicissitudes of the War from 1861–1865 ..." Crooks should have said, "It is not our ability." Simpson's *Diary* entries were almost always sporadic, but they were especially irregular and sparse during the Civil War. Crooks correctly assessed, "Most unfortunately again the Bishop's letters and private memoranda failed to shed as much light as we might wish upon this important period of his life." Crooks, 371, 379.

854 *Minutes of the Annual Conferences of the Methodist Episcopal Church of 1860* (New York: Carlton and Porter).

to visit California and Oregon during the summer of 1861. The Episcopal assignment of Annual Conferences, which had been prepared upon the adjournment of the 1860 General Conference, did not allow for a Civil War.

The cross-continent journey still called for a voyage through Southern waters to the east coast of Panama. No one could predict the results of privateering, closure of ports, and mutiny by Southern sailors as well as other vicissitudes, on a boat built and owned by Northern shipbuilders. What kind of disruption would take place on the federally-funded delivery of both mail and passengers across the Gulf of Mexico and the Strait of Panama? The hypotheses concerning these liabilities ignited a heated contention within the Board of Bishops, and again brought Edward Ames and Simpson into direct, if not belligerent, contention. Ames' bellicose pomposity, in so many words, called Simpson a yellow-bellied coward. His acrimonious letter to Simpson pontificated, "For as I understand it: in accepting our office--I believe no instance has yet occurred in the history of our church in which one of her Bishops has refused to perform his official work through fear of personal dangers--for this thing of courage or cowardice is owing to physical organization." And "weak nerves" was a temperament with which Ames could not identify.[855]

In spite of all the other Bishops agreeing that California was a risky idea, Ames triple, double-dared Simpson, and the dare was too much for Simpson's sensitive soul to process. Thus, he took a train to New York for the purpose of booking passage to Panama. Upon arriving in New York, he met with J.P. Durbin, "Missionary Secretary" of the Church, who provided Simpson with an out. The Bishop could use his time more profitably if he would travel through the summer and by preaching and writing; replenish the depleted missionary fund of the church. John Durbin had served as Editor of the New York *Christian Advocate* and as President of Dickinson College. Simpson later wrote of him, "Few men ever equaled him in 'solid and wide spread popularity;' few have been his equal in ability, fidelity, and industry. He ranked among the first in the church as a pulpit orator, a Christian pastor, an educator, a writer, and an administrator."[856]

---

855 LOC, Simpson papers, Letter, Ames to Simpson, May 27, 1861, Container seven.
856 *Cyclopaedia*, 319.

Simpson postponed his West Coast trip, and for the summer of 1861, became a fundraiser beseeching Methodist Churches to become a global missionary enterprise. Simpson penned an urgent appeal that was to be distributed to every preacher. "Let no circumstances of church building, or repairing--no erection or furnishing of parsonages–no depression of business –or deficiency of ministerial support, prevent a personal appeal to every member or friend of the Church, in behalf of this great cause."[857]

Lincoln and Methodism

No doubt, Simpson knew Abraham Lincoln before the latter became President, and it is highly possible, because of their geographical proximity and John Evans' acquaintance with Lincoln, the religious leader and political leader met sometime in 1860. By Simpson's own testimony he was present at Lincoln's house on the morning of the "affectionate farewell" speech at the Springfield Depot on February 11, 1861, when Lincoln left for Washington.[858] In the late 1850s, Evans, because of his several municipal positions and real estate holdings in Chicago, was a major player in Republican Party activities. Simpson followed in the political steps of the man who had lured him to northern Illinois, and would become his chief financial advisor. Robert Clark claims that Simpson had met Lincoln, "earlier in the year (January 1861) at the Illinois Capital where he and John Evans had gone on behalf of a bill

---

857 UMA, Drew University, Simpson papers, Letter July 4, 1861.
858 "The New York Conference: Monday, April 24, New York," *The Methodist*, Vol. VI No. 18 (May 6, 186) 138. In all likelihood, Simpson was present for the Lincoln departure, but was fuzzy on the details. Lincoln had not stayed in his house for the previous two nights because the lessees had already occupied it. The Lincolns had stayed at the Chenery House, Springfield's finest hotel. It would have been very difficult for Simpson to have met with Lincoln that morning, as he claims, since the President and family left the hotel at 7:30 a.m. Stephen Thomas Jones described the morning and the thousand people who gathered at the Great Western Train Depot. "It was a dark, gloomy, misty morning, tending rain. The people assembled early to say their last good-bye to the man they loved so much. The railroad office was used as a reception room. Lincoln took up a position where his friends and neighbors could file by him in a line. As they came up, each took his hand in silence. The tearful eye, the tremulous lips, and inaudible words was a scene never to be forgotten. When the crowd had passed, I stepped forward to say good-bye. He gave me both his hands–no words after that." Scott D. Trostel. *The Lincoln Inaugural Train* (Fletcher, Ohio: Cam-Tech Publishing, 2011) 15.

to re-charter North Western University."[859] From this date, if not before, Lincoln was aware of the Bishop's identity, with a dawning recognition of Methodism's importance to his political future.

In his twenties, Lincoln was formally introduced to Methodism. In 1832, Peter Cartwright had beaten Lincoln for a seat in the State Legislature. In the 1846 United States Congressional Campaign, Lincoln had again run against Cartwright and won. In order to win, Lincoln had to defend himself against the Presiding Elder, who charged the future President with skepticism, if not atheism.[860]

In 1857, William Duff Armstrong was accused of killing James Metzger at a Methodist Camp Meeting at Walker Grove Mission, Mason County, Illinois. Lincoln defended Armstrong, son of a family who had once befriended him. Hannah Armstrong, William's mother, had sewn leather on Lincoln's pants to extend their usefulness, and Lincoln at times had lodged in the Armstrong house. Lincoln won the case by demonstrating from an Almanac, that the moon would have been too low in the sky for the witness to have made a clear identification of the murderer. This famous case had involved disorderly drunks at a Methodist event. Hopefully, Lincoln's total impression of Methodists did not consist of Peter Cartwright and camp meetings.[861]

Simpson Begins His Washington Treks

As we have seen, the summer of 1861 offered Simpson some discretionary time, and part of that time was spent in Washington, D.C. According to some, the Bishop was so often in Washington after 1861, that the White House seemed to be his headquarters.[862] In spite of the President's residence and the United States Government being located in this Mid-Atlantic city, the Nation's Capital remained non-hospitable, a disease-infested swamp

---

859   Clark, *The Life*, 218. Sounds plausible, but Clark offers no documentation for the information.

860   Burlingame, Vol. I, 238-40.

861   Daniel W. Stowell. "Murder at a Methodist Camp Meeting: The Origins of Abraham Lincoln's Most Famous Trial," *Journal of the Illinois State Historical Society* Vol. X, No. 3-4 (Fall-Winter 2008) 219-234.

862   David Rankin Barbee. "President Lincoln and Dr. Gurley," *The Abraham Lincoln Quarterly* Vol. V, No. 1 (March 1948) 4.

which enabled visitors to depart with cholera, malaria, and unforgettable memories of sub-standard lodging and food. Jerrold M. Packard writes that, "By 1860, the Tiber Creek and Canal were essentially sewers–filthy, dark, disease-carrying waterways, haven to an inexhaustible supply of mosquitos, the final resting place of members of dead and bloated animals, the receiving culvert for a large part of the city's ordure and chief creator of the foulest odors to be experienced anywhere on the Eastern Seaboard."[863]

According to Clinton Fisk, sometime after Fort Sumter in April, Simpson visited the White House. He found Lincoln and several Cabinet members in a quandary as how to enlist troops and how many to enlist. Would the "Civil War" be an overnight skirmish or a fight-to-the-death, obliterating the nation, eliminating the democratic experience and leaving the door open to Great Britain or anyone else to pick up the pieces? Simpson was both optimistic and realistic. He did not perceive either side laying down their arms at the first sight of blood. Lincoln thought 75,000 to be sufficient troops.[864] "The Bishop expressed the opinion that 75,000 were but a beginning of the number needed; that the struggle would be long and severe."[865] What makes Fisk's claim suspect is the Monday of April 15, on which Lincoln called for a militia; Simpson chaired an Annual Conference in Oswego, New York. He then went home to Evanston, Illinois, and spoke at the Wigwam, Chicago, on April 28.

Lincoln did not immediately declare war, but called for 75,000 one-hundred day volunteers to suppress the "combination" of the Southern

---

863 Jerrold M. Packard. *The Lincolns in the White House: Four Years That Shattered a Family* (New York: St. Marten's Press, 2005) 7.

864 On February 28, 1795, Congress empowered the President to "call forth a militia" whenever the law of the United States would, "Be opposed or the operation thereof obstructed in any state, by combinations too powerful to be suppressed by the ordinary course of judicial proceedings or by the powers visited in the marshals by the act." Simpson was certainly correct in his perception for additional troops. Fred Shannon depicted Lincoln's predicament, "75,000 raw, green militiamen, who could not be trained for the field by the time their three months term of service had expired, for the suppression of a rebellion thoroughly organized in seven of the strongest states of the Union and more than incipient in eight more." Fred Albert Shannon. *The Organization and Administration of the Union Army: 1861–1865* Vol. I (Cleveland:The Arthur H. Clark Company, 1928) 29–31.

865 Crooks, 373. Sounds plausible, but for this anecdote, Crooks relied on, "The Reminiscences of Clinton Bowen Fisk." For the present-day historian, these "Reminiscences" do not exist.

states which had seceded. The proclamation was a defensive rather than an offensive measure. Among the cabinet members, some advised 50,000 and others 100,000. Lincoln split the difference. One week after the "militia" proclamation, Lincoln insisted to the Mayor of Baltimore that "his proclamation had not been properly understood, that he had no intention of bringing a war, but that its purpose was to defend the Capitol, which was in danger of being bombarded from the heights across the Potomac."[866] Concerning the estimation of needed troops, all kinds of numbers were thrown at Lincoln; Stephen Douglas suggested 200,000, and Horace Greeley called for 500,000.[867]

But even if we cast doubt on Simpson's recommendation as to troops needed, Lincoln unquestionably respected Simpson's perception on a wide range of issues. Because of the itinerant Episcopacy, no denominational legate in America could offer a more accurate perspective on people and places. Elizabeth Todd Grimsley, a relative of Mary Lincoln, who spent six months at the White House, recalled that the "beloved-sainted Bishop Simpson" and New York Archbishop John Hughes were exceptions to the "importunities, meddlesomeness, impertinent censure and arrogance of preachers, politicians, newspaper writers, and cranks."[868] Thomas Bowman, Methodist Senate Chaplain, claimed that Lincoln "occasionally" sent for Simpson to feel the pulse of the nation. He quoted Lincoln, "Bishop Simpson is a wise and thoughtful man. He travels extensively over the country and sees things as they are. He has no axe to grind, and, therefore, I can depend on him for such information as I need."[869] Newspaper correspondent Noah Brooks, who between December of 1862 and the end of the Civil War had almost unlimited access to the President, referred to Simpson as an, "intimate friend of Lincoln."[870] After Lincoln's death, Simpson recalled, "Whenever I

---

866   Burlingame Vol. II, 136.   http://opinionatorblogs.nytimes.com/2011/04/14/lincoln-declares-war/

867   Ibid., 237.

868   Elizabeth Todd Grimsley. "Six Months in the White House," *Journal of The Illinois State Historical Society* (October-January, 1926-1927) 60.

869   Crooks, 372.

870   Noah Brooks. *Washington DC in Lincoln's Time* (Chicago: Quadrangle Books, 1971) 234.

have been preaching in Washington during the last two years, with but one exception, he (Lincoln) has been present at the service."[871]

One of the more believable stories of Simpson's influence on Lincoln was told by Charles Cardwell McCabe, the Financial Agent for the Church Extension Society, which Simpson chaired. McCabe was known as the "Grand Field Marshall of Methodism, and referred to himself as the Great American Champion Beggar." McCabe was elected Bishop in 1896. Simpson related to McCabe that, "Abraham Lincoln was a man of prayer, and that once in the darkest time of the war after a long conversation in the White House, Mr. Lincoln rose and turned the key in the door and said, 'Bishop Simpson, I feel the need of prayer; won't you pray for me'? Bishop Simpson told me they fell on their knees, and while he led in prayer, the President responded fervently all through it."[872]

Simpson Becomes the Protestant Patronage King

Though patronage has always been and always will define politics, no matter how "democratic" and "equitable," a political system claims to be, "whom one knows" is and always will be a critical factor for actualizing personal ambitions. For whatever reasons, cultural factors and historical circumstances, the Fathers of the two present-day political parties of America, Andrew Jackson and Abraham Lincoln were the kings of patronage. No doubt, rewarding offices to their respective constituencies, assured party loyalty more than did free whiskey.

At Andrew Jackson's inaugural reception, office seekers overran the White House, soiling, if not destroying just about everything except the chandeliers. They had every reason to be optimistic. During his first year in office, Andrew Jackson displaced 919 federal officials including 423 postmasters, more than all of his predecessors in the last forty years.[873] Thus, until Civil Service Reform under Chester Arthur (though Rutherford Hays

---

871 "The Annual Conferences: New York Conference," Fifth Day, Monday April 24 in *The Methodist*, Vol. VI No. 18 (May 6, 1865) 138.
872 Frank Milton Bristol. *The Life of Chaplain McCabe: Bishop of the Methodist Episcopal Church* (New York: Eaton and Mains, 1908) 215.
873 Howe, *What Hath*, 333.

headed in that direction), being a member of the winning political party often equated to employment. Politics was war and "to the victor, belong the spoils." At no time in American history were patronage and politics more conjoined than the Civil War, the rewarding of offices as formulaic as winning a battle. In patronage, Lincoln outdid Jackson. Phillip Paludan writes: "Lincoln rewarded Republican supporters very well. He removed Democrats from practically every office they held, replacing 1,195 out of the 1,520 president appointees he personally controlled."[874]

The difference between Lincoln and his predecessors was that he was going to interview all of the job applicants, at least as many as his daily calendar would allow. Doris Kearns Goodwin claims that on the first day in office the President was assaulted by a "crush of office seekers. Hundreds, perhaps thousands pressed in as soon as the doors were open ignoring the barriers set up to keep them in line."[875] When Lincoln was warned that he would wear himself out, he responded, "They don't want much, they get but little and I must see them."[876] According to Secretary John Hay, even though Lincoln tore down the makeshift barriers between him and the people, he, complained bitterly and frequently about the time he was compelled to waste on job hunters who lined the corridor outside his office and sometimes queued all the way down the staircase to the front door of the White House. He told Robert Wilson that, "he was so badgered with applications for appointments that he thought that sometimes the only way that he (could) escape from them would be to take a rope and hang himself on one of the trees in the lawn south of the President's house." If he would move his office to a "smallpox hospital" maybe they would stay away, but on second thought the office seekers would first get "vaccinated."[877]

Simpson lost no time in gaining an audience with Lincoln after the Inauguration. He indicated to Ellen that on March 8, he had met with

---

874 Phillip Shaw Paludan. *The Presidency of Abraham Lincoln* (Lawrence, Kansas: University of Kansas Press, 1994) 35-36.

875 Doris Kearns Goodwin. *Team of Rivals: The Political Genius of Abraham Lincoln* (New York: Simon and Schuster, 2005) 334.

876 Ibid.

877 Allen Guelzo. *Abraham Lincoln: Redeemer President* (Grand Rapids: William B. Eerdmans Publishing Company, 1999) 276–278.

Lincoln and interceded for John Evans.[878] Simpson quickly lost patience with Lincoln, in that Methodists were being slighted in the federal job handout. Three weeks after Lincoln's inauguration, Matthew again wrote Ellen, "As far as I can learn, no Methodist has been appointed to any office by the administration."[879] John Lanahan, Methodist pastor in Alexandria, stoked the patronage fire by writing Simpson:

> When I last wrote you I had supposed Gov. Chase was a real exception to the other members of the present Administration in regard to Methodists. It is so to a very small extent. I hold that the treatment of our people by this Administration is an open, standing insult to the church. Episcopalians and Presbyterians have the government & in the Border States the great body of their people are doing all they can to destroy the government. With us it is just the opposite in every respect. More of our people–good and true men–have been removed than appointed-Episcopalians & Presbyterians are seldom removed and always promoted.[880]

Eventually Simpson visited the White House with the complaint that Methodists were not getting their fair share of the political pie.[881] Clark claims that Simpson "took the opportunity to rebuke the President for rejecting Joseph Wright from Berlin without finding a comparable post for any other Methodist."[882] The word "rebuke" sounds out of character for Simpson. Nevertheless, the plea was sufficiently threatening or pathetic for the President to offer a Methodist, whom Simpson would name, an Ambassadorship to Honduras, a carrot stick not in the same class as the Berlin Consulate. A few days later, Simpson attempted to retract his impertinence, with a letter to Secretary of War, Simon Cameron.

---

878   UMA, Drew University, Simpson papers, Letter to Ellen, March 8, 1861.

879   UMA, Drew University, Simpson papers, Letter March 24, 1861.

880   LOC, Simpson papers, Letter November 1861, Container seven.

881   Clark, *The Life*, 225. This visit was arranged by Simon Cameron.

882   Ibid. Wright was the first person dismissed by Lincoln, and Norman Judd, the "first appointment to a diplomatic post sent by Lincoln to the Senate for confirmation. It was sent on March 6, two days after the inauguration." Harry J. Carman and Reinhard H. Luthen. *Lincoln and the Patronage* (Gloucester, Massachusetts: Peter Smith, 1864) 79.

Dear Sir.

I received your note last evening informing me that the President had kindly requested me to name a minister for Honduras.

Will you do me the favor as I am compelled to leave the city to tender to the President my thanks for the proffer so unexpectedly made and which I receive as a token both of his good will to me personally, and his intention to consider more fully the statements which I took the liberty to present to him?

At the same time please to assure him for me, that I have no wish to make appointments to office. I did not come to this city to present the claims of any person for any position; nor did I anticipate an interview with the President on any such subject. For as you stated, I speak on your invitation as reference to a matter of your own suggestion. I think too the President does not fully perceive my position. I am not seeking anything for my friends. I object alone to the patronage of the government being so dispensed as to attach a religious monopoly and to create unjust distinction between churches. This I believe has been done. Though I do not charge it as so intended by either the President or his Cabinet. Yet the injury to us is no less on that account.

I may say however that were the proffered appointment of the same grade, as that from which Gov. Wright was so summarily ejected--restoring us in this respect to the position which we held under the last administration--I would have ventured to suggest to the President the name of Col. Cummings, who I think has been overlooked by this administration.

Allow me also to add that I look with deep interest as to the issue of your application to the President in reference to the Chaplaincy of West Point. As I understood both you and the President yesterday, this appointment belongs to you. You had resolved to give it to Dr. McClintock because of his peculiar fitness, and you will so confer it, unless the President refuses you authority. This appears to me a _test_ point.

Arch Bishop Hughes was sent to England <u>because he is a Catholic</u>, and Bishop McElwain was sent <u>because he is a Protestant Episcopalian</u>. Yet though several leading citizens requested the appointment of Dr. McClintock he was rejected <u>for he is a Methodist</u>.

Now after you have avowed your purpose if permitted to appoint Dr. McClintock to this chaplaincy, if the President refuses you permission, we shall have a case of direct proscription, and a plain interposition of the President to prohibit a Methodist from receiving office. This I hope will not be the case. On the contrary I trust the appointment will be made, and if so, I shall feel that some of my apprehensions are groundless, and I shall have hope that our church may be regarded by the President or his cabinet, on equal footing with other churches.

However this may be, accept my thanks for the interest you have shown in this matter.

Yours truly,

M. Simpson[883]

Beseiged by Desperate Requests

In spite of Simpson's disclaimer written to Cameron and conveyed to Lincoln, a disavowal to become an office monger, the solicitation for the Bishop's intervention became relentless. Simpson's *modus operandi* for furthering the vocational and political aspirations of his Methodist children was usually not to write letters to Lincoln, but to write to a Cabinet member or simply make his request known in private conversation. Simpson's effectiveness for placing persons in office is difficult to gauge, but his friends as well as those he had never met, thought him to be omnipotent. Office seeker C. H. Comegys wrote, "I had a letter to Mr. Chase, to Judge McLean, Porter of Indiana, and our Representative, Gurley, and Bishop Ames wrote to Mr. Lane, but as I said to my nephew, who stays with me, 'I put my trust next to Providence in Bishop Simpson'."[884] The pleas for field and hospital chaplaincies, judgeships, tax commissioners, clerkships, consulates, territorial secretaryships, postal workers, custom-house collectors, and countless promotions within the military, were innumerable. Francis Gillette wanted his son to become assistant paymaster in the Navy.[885] Simpson's

---
883   LOC, Simpson papers, Letter November 27, 1861, Container seven.
884   LOC, Simpson papers, Letter April 15, 1861, Container seven.
885   UMA, E. Pennsylvania Conference, St. George's United Methodist Church,

nephew, Joseph Tingley, desired an appointment to the Smithsonian.[886] D. E. Crawford wanted the chaplaincy at West Point.[887] Henry Slicer wanted F.S. Carlson to become collector of the Port of Baltimore.[888] Alexander Cummings requested a Brigadier Generalship, which he got.[889] James Harlan did not have any qualms about asking Simpson to "date back" a letter to whomever on behalf of an ambassadorship to Bogota for Jesse Bowen. He closed his letter June 20, 1861 by asking, "How has our church fared in the appointments this year?"[890]

A flood of patronage letters deluged the Bishop. William Nast on February 23, 1861, requested the Bishop to procure an appointment for his son's a consulship in "my native city of Wattenberg. It is a small consulate worth about $1,000 that is."[891] Nast, after graduating from Tubingen University, came to America in 1821, and became the first President of what is now Baldwin Wallace College in Berea, Ohio. As publisher of the *German Christian Apologist*, William Nast had been Simpson's co-worker at the Cincinnati Book Concern. Another wrote, "Please give me a recommendation to President Lincoln for a chaplaincy in the Army or Navy of the U.S. As a denomination, we are poorly represented in appointment of our government. I understand that you are acquainted with Mr. Lincoln and I'm quite confident that your influence will secure for me such an appointment."[892] Others were bolder and more specific. Richard Boyle pleaded with Simpson to intercede on behalf of his brother. If his younger sibling could be mustered out of the Army and given employment "which he could readily do-at a salary of $1,200 per year," the two of them would be "very comfortable"[893] O.M. Spencer wrote "I have been desirous for some time past for obtaining a foreign appointment in Europe which would

---

Philadelphia, Pennsylvania. Simpson papers, Letter, December 5, 1864.
886   LOC, Simpson papers, Letter February 17, 1862, Container seven.
887   LOC, Simpson papers, Letter October 23, 1861, Container eight.
888   LOC, Simpson papers, Letter no date, Container eight.
889   LOC, Simpson papers, Letter November 3, 1861, Container eight.
890   LOC, Simpson papers, Letter June 20, 1861, Container seven.
891   LOC, Simpson papers, Letter February 23, 1861, Container seven.
892   LOC, Simpson papers, Letter May 17, 1861, Container seven.
893   LOC, Simpson papers, Letter January 1865, Container seven.

afford me a comfortable support and some literary leisure."[894] When Daniel Kidder requested an appointment for his son, Simpson responded, "I went to Washington and saw Presd. Lincoln. He informed me that the appts. had all been made in June and that there was no vacancy but added that some might soon occur and probably would."[895]

Clinton B. Fisk sent no less than ten letters to Simpson requesting intervention for procuring a Brigadier Generalship. He wrote, "The President I'm persuaded has a good opinion of me." Fisk not only wanted the Bishop to know that he was in favor with Lincoln, but God as well. "I believe in God and his Son Jesus Christ, my savior. I believe in the Holy Ghost, the resurrection of the dead and life everlasting. I believe in the United States and the blessed banner of liberty to all men. That's my creed. I'm willing to live and die by it."[896] Some sinecures bore fruit, and other appeals fell into a black hole. When Simpson requested a clerkship in the Treasury Department, Salmon Chase's office responded by saying that Simpson had no idea how many requests for clerkships they received. The fervency of the patronage battle was almost as heated as anything happening in the battlefield.

The patronage war was especially explosive when Simpson went head to head with Postmaster General Montgomery Blair. "Marty" was the son of Francis Blair, a trusted advisor to Andrew Jackson. The aristocratic, plantation and slave-owning Kentuckian, moved to Washington in the 1850s, built the "Blair House" (which presently serves as the guesthouse of the President) and an additional estate in Silver Spring, a favorite retreat for Abraham Lincoln. Marty was "tall, thin, and scholarly," and in spite of being the lead attorney in representing Dred Scott, never shed his privileged aristocratic cloak.[897] John Hay recalled that "the Blair's have to a universal degree the spirit of a clan. Their family is a close corporation--they have a going with a rush for anything they undertake."[898] When War Secretary Simon Cameron advocated the use of black soldiers, Blair accused him of, "nigger

---

894   LOC, Simpson papers, Letter January 13, 1865, Container seven.
895   Garrett Evangelical School of Theology, Bishops' Autographs and Portraits 1789-1897, Letter September 19, 1864.
896   UMA, Drew University, Simpson papers, Letter December 18, 1863.
897   Goodwin, 24.
898   Ibid., 314.

lobbying for political leverage."[899] Lanahan and Simpson called on Lincoln to complain about the lack of respect for Methodists by the Postmaster General.[900] Lanahan was no fan of the Blairs. When Roger Taney died, the Methodists feared that "Monty" would be appointed as Chief Justice of the Supreme Court. Lanahan described for John McClintock, his and Bishop Ames' visit to Lincoln:

> Judge Blair was named. Mr. Lincoln said nothing. I remarked that if that was likely to take place, the loyal people of the country, would at once go to their knees and pray, that it might not be done. Mr. L. made no reply.
>
> I then remarked Mr. B. had dishonored himself as a gentleman by telling falsehoods with the view of slandering, and prejudicing his colleagues in the cabinet, and that a man who could be guilty of such conduct was unworthy of any such high honor and responsible position, to say nothing of other matters …. Old man Blair is as cunning as he is ugly, and can maneuver beyond most other men.[901]

Simpson visited Blair, and requested a list of Methodist employees. Methodists, for the Postal Department, Blair assured Simpson, had been sufficiently considered and appointed. Simpson asked for proof and Blair refused, claiming that Simpson was making religion as a basis for office. He then added that he had nothing against Methodists since he employed them as, "kitchen workers and carriage drivers." The incensed Simpson responded with a blistering letter accusing Blair of prejudicial slander. Blair attempted to backtrack with a seven page letter, part of which read:

> My language even as reported to yourself, cannot be streamed into a disparagement of the Methodist Church. The fact of the lowly and humble being taken into the bosom of the church is not a reproach to it. Nor is my speaking of such a being made welcome to the bosom of my family a reproach to me. Nor can its simple expression even as given in your letter, be tortured to mean a derogation from the dignity of the church or an insult to its members. The gospel teaches that the lowly and humble are exalted by religion. They do not degrade it. Ought one then who invites their fellowship in however humble an employment and who refers to it as evidence of his sympathy with their religious creeds, be accused of

---

899   Ibid., 404.

900   Clark, *The Life*, 228.

901   Manuscript Archives and Rare Book Library, Emory University, McClintock papers, Letter October 27, 1864, Container four.

sneering at the humbleness of its votaries? And when you know moreover, that the best friend I or my family ever had are of that persuasion; that my father's sisters both belonged to that church, one who still lives, venerable for a long life of piety and worth ennobled by all the Christian character and I had not then or since, discriminated against the Methodists either in my own appointments having appointed many of them myself, or in my recommendation and support for office it is impossible that you should believe that I intended any disrespect to that church in what I then said.[902]

In conclusion, Blair requested a retraction of the accusation made by Simpson. "It will be sufficient for you to say that I had not at any time insulted you personally or said anything in your presence derogatory or inciting hostility to the Methodist Church. I should prefer that the correction should appear as an authorized statement in your church newspaper if that would be agreeable to you." Such a retraction was not forthcoming. Simpson immediately replied to Blair "It seems we differ totally as to the cause of my visiting your office. You pronounced my statement 'incredible' and impute to me unworthy motives and then say you are authorized to 'claim' that I publish that you never said anything derogatory to the Methodist Episcopal Church in my presence. This I cannot do and you must excuse me if I cannot recognize your authority or claim."[903]

---

902   LOC, Simpson papers, Letter, Blair to Simpson, May 30, 1867, Container eight.

903   LOC, Simpson papers, Letter June 5, 1867, Container eight. William Ernest Smith stated that, "Montgomery was much disturbed by a five-year-old controversy with Bishop Matthew Simpson. The Bishop was the Chrysostom of American Methodism during the Civil War. Bishop Simpson threw himself into the cause of the North, and brought thousands of people to the support of the Union. He was a zealous, proud Bishop, proud of the Methodist Church and resentful of any word against it." Smith accused John Lanahan of perpetuating and enhancing the story of Blair's depreciation of Methodists and concludes that Blair in 1867, "reopened the case with the Bishop, but found the stern old preacher, now a confirmed Radical, absolutely unmovable. The Bishop acknowledged that he had made the remark about the kitchen, but beyond that he could not be moved." William Ernest Smith. *The Preston Blair Family in Politics*, Vol. II (New York: Macmillan Company, 1933) 384–386. John Lanahan interpreted Blair quite differently than did William Smith. "I did not say that B. said our people would do for culinary purposes–but I did say his language admitted of that inference. Blair's letters to you only mark him with deeper infamy in my estimation." LOC, Simpson papers, Letter, Lanahan to Simpson, August 7, 1867, Container eight.

Simpson and the Emancipation Proclamation Myth

Within Simpson mythology, no claim looms larger than the assertion that Simpson motivated Lincoln to issue the Emancipation Proclamation.[904] The historical marker displayed on the grounds of the Harrison County Courthouse in Cadiz, Ohio, proudly proclaims in its brief biographical sketch of Matthew Simpson, "In later years, Simpson became a close friend of Abraham Lincoln. It was Simpson who urged the President to prepare and issue the Emancipation Proclamation." The story originated with Clinton Fisk, a person who constantly exhibited the tendency to think more highly of himself than he ought to think. George Crooks, quoting from "Fisk's Reminiscences," wrote, "In the summer of the same year, 1862–after the seven days fighting and McClellan's repulse, the Bishop had another interview with Mr. Lincoln confined to the point of the President's duty to issue a proclamation setting the slaves free in the rebellious states. Subsequently Mr. Lincoln showed him the proclamation; the Bishop was

---

[904] One of the primary perpetrators and perpetuators of the Simpson Emancipation Proclamation myth was Clarence True Wilson, "General Secretary of the Board of Temperance, Prohibition, and Public Morals," 1910-1936. He expended much time and energy attempting to prove that John Wilkes Booth was still alive. Wilson's brief biography of Matthew Simpson was riddled with errors, among them that Simpson "graduated" from Madison College; that, in the 1844 General Conference, Simpson distinguished himself, "By taking part in debate on the slavery question," and that the 1860 Conference, "fixed several cities as a residence of Bishops," implying this to be the reason Simpson moved to Philadelphia. In his article, "Bishop Matthew Simpson, The Man Who Inspired the Emancipation Proclamation," Wilson states, "Abundant evidence exists to show that Simpson was the man who convinced President Lincoln that he could issue the Emancipation Proclamation without violating the Constitution or the pledges he had given in his first Inaugural." Wilson claimed that he had discovered manuscripts, correspondence, and papers that had been lost in a number of trunks for almost forty-five years. Wilson recalled that Simpson and John Lanahan went to the White House on "April 8, 1861, when after the cabinet meeting of that week, he (Simpson) boldly told the President that he would have to get rid of slavery before God would ever let him end the war." What makes the claim suspect is that Simpson chaired the Providence, Rhode Island Conference, April 3–8, and the Wyoming Conference, Oswego, New York, April 11-16. Between the 8th and the 11th, Simpson would have made a torturous three-hundred-mile trip by stagecoach, the Hudson River, and the Erie Canal. He certainly would not have gone by way of Washington, D.C., a logistical impossibility. Clarence True Wilson, "Bishop Matthew Simpson: The Man Who Inspired the Emancipation Proclamation," in *Current History*, October, 1929, 99-106.

delighted with it. When it was read in the Cabinet meeting, Mr. Chase suggested its last sentence. 'Why, replied Lincoln: that is just what Bishop Simpson said. 'In their interview prior to the meeting of the Cabinet, the Bishop had suggested there ought to be a recognition of God in that important paper.'"[905] Crooks claimed that he received the narrative (orally) from Clinton B. Fisk. There is no paper trail between Fisk and Crooks, and more critically, no paper trail between us and Simpson. Simpson made no mention of any conversation between himself and Lincoln regarding any aspect of the Emancipation Proclamation in his *Diary* or letters. Nonetheless, the supposed conversation snowballed into a narrative that, not only had Simpson suggested an emendation to the "Proclamation," but Simpson had conceived and planted it in the President's consciousness.[906]

Lincoln had so many advice-givers concerning freeing the slaves that it was impossible to sort through the cacophony of voices. From the firing on Fort Sumter until the public issue of the Emancipation Proclamation, Lincoln was constantly assaulted by letters, telegrams, newspapers, Congressmen, delegations to the White House, radical Republicans, and clergy, informing the President that they were delivering to the President a divine revelation from God. Those who had put him in office claimed the right to tell him what to do. James Oakes writes,

> Lincoln could hardly have missed all the prophesying about slavery's doom among his follow Republicans. His own cabinet members were predicting that secession would lead to slave rebellion and emancipation. And Lincoln's mailbox was rapidly filling up with letters from politicians and pundits across the Republican spectrum, all of them telling the new president the same thing. In late April the radical William Channing wrote to Lincoln "advising (the) abolition of Slavery by martial law as the surest way to conquer rebellious States and preserve the border ones."[907]

---

905   Crooks, 374.

906   Fisk implied that he was present, when Simpson suggested the Emancipation Proclamation to Lincoln, which is questionable since Fisk wrote Simpson, November 19, 1862, "I'm not personally known to the President, that is, not well known." UMA, Drew University, Clinton Fisk papers, Letter November 19, 1862.

907   James Oakes. *Freedom National: The Destruction of Slavery in the United States, 1861–1865* (New York: WW. Norton & Company, 2013) 79–80.

Only Simpson admirers, writing from a Methodist perspective, have propagated the Bishop's influence on the proclamation.[908] Simpson's son-in-law, Charles Buoy, claimed that the Bishop prompted Lincoln to issue the proclamation.[909] But no respectable Lincoln biographer related Simpson to the Emancipation Proclamation. Yet, the lack of solid evidence did not prevent obsequious historians and eulogists from perpetuating Simpson's role in one of the most important acts in American history, even though Simpson never made any mention of it. The relationship between Lincoln, Edwin Stanton, and Bishop Simpson was exaggerated by Fisk. "After Mr. Stanton came into the Cabinet the Bishop's relations with the President became more intimate. The Bishop was of the same mind as the President (on a more lenient treatment of border state Confederate sympathizers), and it was sent to Stanton to bring him over to the President's way of thinking."[910] On November 24, 1862 by the intervention of Simpson, Fisk was promoted to Brigadier General. After Simpson's death, Fisk would play a critical posthumous role in the Bishop's life, as we will later see.

Religious Pressure on Lincoln

The first time Lincoln broached the possibility of emancipating slaves took place in a carriage ride on July 13 with Gideon Wells and William Seward.

---

[908] Randolph Foster said at Simpson's funeral, "He was a close and trusted friend of Mr. Lincoln and of the Great War Secretary, Mr. Stanton, more than once, when the cloud was darkest; he supported them with his prayer counsel. The Proclamation of Emancipation, if not his inspiration, was not made without his sanction--he had from early manhood pleaded the cause of the slave and worked in all honorable ways to secure his freedom, and when at last the cruel achievement of war had broken his chains. He has lived to secure for him all the benefits of emancipation and continued to work untiringly to that end for a score of years; but those who have stood closest to his head well knew that during all that time he cherished no bitter feeling toward his fellow countrymen who were on the opposite side of the great struggle." *Christian Advocate*, New York: Thursday (July 3, 1884). William Warren Sweet, American Methodism's most prolific author during the first half of the twentieth century, in his study on the relationship of Methodism and the Civil War, bought into the "seventy-five thousand" anecdote, but made no mention of Simpson's relationship to the Emancipation Proclamation. William Warren Sweet. *The Methodist Episcopal Church and the Civil War* (Cincinnati: Methodist Book Concern Press, 1912).

[909] Charles Buoy. *Representative Women of Methodism* (New York: Hunt & Eaton, 1892) 456.

[910] Carl Sandberg. *Abraham Lincoln: The War Years*, Vol. III (New York: Harcourt, Brace, and Company, 1939) 589.

Wells recorded that Lincoln, "dwelt earnestly on the gravity, importance, and delicacy of the movement, said he had given it much thought, and had about come to the conclusion that it was a military necessity, absolutely essential for the salvation of the Union, that we must free the slaves or be ourselves subdued, etc., etc." Wells went on to say, "It was a new departure for the President, for until this time, in all our previous interviews, whenever the question of emancipation or the mitigation of slavery had been in any way alluded to, he had been prompt and emphatic in denouncing any interference by the General Government with the subject."[911] On July 22, Lincoln submitted a "rough draft" of the Emancipation Proclamation to his cabinet but solicited no response.[912]

In September of 1862, when Lincoln submitted his Proclamation of Emancipation for the consideration of the Cabinet, he had not conferred with anyone about the phraseology of the instrument. He read the document through without a single interpretation or comment. They all concurred in that it was an admirable paper. On New Year's Eve, 1862, Lincoln again read the document to his cabinet, and Salmon Chase responded, "Mr. President, you have invoked the considerate judgment of mankind, but you have not invoked the blessing of almighty God on your action in this matter. I believe he has something to do with this question." Lincoln requested Chase to write a fitting conclusion. Chase wrote seven words, "And the gracious favor of almighty God." Lincoln added them to the end of the last paragraph which made it read as follows: "And upon this act, sincerely believed to be an act of justice; warranted by the Constitution upon military necessity I invoke the considerate judgment of mankind and the gracious favor of almighty God."[913]

---

911 Burlingame, Vol. II, 361.

912 John Talliaferro. *All the Great Prizes: The Life of John Hay from Lincoln to Roosevelt* (New York: Simon & Schuster Paperbacks, 2013) 58.

913 William K. Klingaman. *Abraham Lincoln and the Road to Emancipation*, 1861–1865 (New York: Penguin Putnam Incorporated, 2001) 224. Other recent books written specifically on the Emancipation Proclamation make no mention of Simpson. They include: Allen C. Guelzo. *Lincoln's Emancipation Proclamation: The End of Slavery in America* (New York: Simon & Schuster, 2004), Louis P. Masur. *Lincoln's Hundred Days: The Emancipation Proclamation and the War for the Union* (Cambridge, Massachusetts: The Belknap Press of Harvard University, 2012) and Todd Brewster. *Lincoln's Gamble: The Tumultuous Six Months That Gave America the Emancipation Proclamation and Changed the Course of the Civil War* (New York: Scribner, 2014).

In tracking Lincoln's march toward the Emancipation Proclamation, William Klingaman gives no indication that the President and the Bishop ever made contact. The absence of any mention of Simpson raises serious doubt as to any influence the Methodist Bishop had in the wording of the Proclamation, much less being a primary motivator. At the beginning of the War, both Lincoln and Simpson shied away from Emancipation not knowing how, once freed, the slave would be assimilated into society. They both lived in the dilemma, aptly described by Thomas Jefferson shortly before his death, "We have the wolf by the ears, and we can neither hold him nor safely let him go. Justice is in one scale and self-preservation in the other."[914]

Lincoln reluctantly entertained religious intruders who perceived themselves as having the mind of God. At times, he would respond with a deflecting anecdote which caused one Methodist clergyman to respond, "Tale-telling and jesting illy suit the hour and become the man in whose hands the destiny of a great nation is trembling."[915] To another clergyman, Lincoln believed the emancipation of the slave to be akin to the removal of a brain tumor: "My advice is to prepare the patient for the operation before venturing on it."[916] When a Quaker delegation beseeched him, the President responded, "Perhaps he might be an instrument in God's hands of accomplishing a great work and he certainly was not unwilling."[917] According to Ward Hill Lamon, who acted as Lincoln's bodyguard, "Clergymen were always welcomed by Mr. Lincoln at the White House with the respectful courtesy due to their sacred calling. During the progress of the war and especially in its earlier stages, he was visited almost daily by reverend gentlemen, sometimes as single visitors but more frequently in delegations. He was a patient listener to the words of congratulations, counsel, admonition, exhortation, and sometimes reproof, which fell from the lips of his pious callers and generally these interviews were entertaining and agreeable on both sides." And sometimes they were not, such as the time a delegation attempted to institute Sunday observance for the War or insist on, "a speedy proclamation of emancipation."[918]

---

914   Klingaman, 21.
915   Ibid., 175.
916   Ibid., 151.
917   Ibid., 133.
918   Ward Hill Lamon. *Recollections of Abraham Lincoln: 1847–1865*, ed. Dorothy Lamon (Chicago: A.C. McClurg and Company, 1895) 137.

Several persons, especially clergy, having visited the President, took credit for the Emancipation Proclamation. More likely to have hounded the President concerning emancipating the slaves was Byron Sunderland, pastor of the First Presbyterian Church in Washington, D C., whom Washington historian George Townsend referred to as, "a small, indignant gentleman with a fierce patriotism."[919] Sometime in December, 1862, Sunderland said to Lincoln, "We are full of faith and prayer, that you will make a clean sweep for the right." Lincoln responded, "Doctor, it's very hard sometimes to know what is right! You pray often and honestly, but so does those people across the lines, they pray, and all their preachers pray devoutly. You and I do not think them justified in praying, for their objects, but they pray earnestly, no doubt! If you and I had our own way, Doctor, we would settle this war without bloodshed, but Providence permits blood to be shed. It's hard to tell what Providence wants of us. Sometimes we, ourselves are more humane than the divine mercy seems to us to be."[920] Lincoln was theologically and intellectually superior to many of his clergy visitors.

In essence, Lincoln's Emancipation Proclamation was a pragmatic decision, with little moral, religious or theological force behind it. The Union was losing the War and daily hundreds of Union soldiers were abdicating their posts. Many, if not most, did not know for what they were fighting. Thus, Lincoln made a bargain with God, what evangelicals would call "putting out a fleece." If God would enable the Union Army to drive the Confederates out of Maryland, he would issue a proclamation freeing the slaves in states rebelling against the United States. The answer for Lincoln was not nearly as clear as it had been for Gideon, the Israelite deliverer, but nonetheless, there was a divine intervention or human error. A Union soldier found Lee's battle plans wrapped around three cigars lying on the ground. The foreknowledge was not of enormous benefit. Twelve thousand Union troops were killed or wounded as against 11,000 Confederate casualties, the bloodiest day of any American war. Antietam was not a clear victory, but Lee and Jackson *had* retreated out of Maryland.

---

919   George Townsend. *Washington: Outside and Inside* (Hartford, Connecticut: James Betts and Company, 1874) 714.

920   Burlingame, Vol. II, 68.

After Fredericksburg in December of 1862, perhaps the most lopsided victory by the Confederates, 13,000 Union casualties as opposed to 5,000 for the Southern victors, soldiers including officers and in particular chaplains left the Army by the droves. One Minnesota soldier confessed, "I lost a chunk of patriotism as large as my foot. I would do almost anything to get shut of the most unjust and ungodly, uncalled for war."[921] Lincoln's detractors came down so hard on him that the President was inclined to quit.[922] Pennsylvania governor Andrew G. Curtin found him "walking the floor, wringing his hands, and uttering exclamations of grief." The President was known to have despaired, "I wonder if the damned in hell suffer less than I do," and "if there is a worse place than hell, I am in it."[923] He was desperate to find something that would boost the morale and provide motivation for a demoralized Union Army. Lincoln signed the Emancipation Proclamation on January 1, 1863, in the presence of William Seward and his son, Frederick.

Simpson's Conversion to Emancipation

The only glimmer of possibility that Simpson had any input into the Emancipation Proclamation was provided by Salmon Chase, who stated that Simpson visited him on November 13, 1862: "Mr. Cummings and Bishop Simpson came in. The Bishop just from California, Oregon, Wash,

---

921   Marvel, 300.

922   T. Harry Williams argued that, "The Army of the Potomac was a seething mass of discontent and demoralization. The massacre at Fredericksburg, the culmination of a long line of failures and disasters, undermined their confidence in the generals and the government, and dulled their faith in the sanctity of the cause for which they fought. 'I am sick and tired of disaster, and the fools that bring disaster upon us,' a disillusioned captain wrote to his family. The correspondent of an abolitionist newspaper reported: 'The men are to an alarming extent discouraged, and anxious to go home. They are stupefied by continual reverses.' Many asked for leave and others simply drifted away from camp without permission. Eighty thousand were missing from the muster rolls, one half of them 'improperly absent.' One of the division officers later told the Committee: 'Desertions were very numerous; the general tone of conversation in the camps was that of dissatisfaction and complaint.' An agent sent down to Falmouth by the Connecticut legislature to look after the dead and wounded in the state's regiments reported in his home town newspaper: 'You have no idea of the depression there is in the army as the result of the third attempt to go to Richmond.'" T. Harry Williams. *Lincoln and the Radicals* (Madison: The University of Wisconsin Press, 1941) 237.

923   Burlingame, Vol. II, 246.

through homewards Utah and Nevada gave much information."[924] It seems unlikely that Simpson would have visited Chase without making a call at the White House. If Simpson did visit Lincoln, he did not record the event. The Methodist who had the most contact with Simpson when the Bishop visited Washington, was Alexandria pastor John Lanahan. When Crooks asked Lanahan for recollections of Simpson's life, Lanahan recalled, "Bishop Simpson's arrival in Washington was always occasion of interest and courtesies from the chief men of the government and Congress .... I know not that Lincoln consulted the Bishop upon the emancipation of the slaves .... I don't think Simpson ever urged upon Lincoln such a proclamation, though he desired it."[925] John McClintock rather than Matthew Simpson recalled discussing with the President the Emancipation Proclamation. Lincoln said to McClintock, "When I issued that Proclamation, I was in great doubt about it myself. I did not think that the people had been quite educated up to it, and I feared its effects upon other border states. Yet, I think it was right. I knew it would help our cause in Europe, and I trusted in God and did it."[926]

Simpson left no such testimony, but he was experiencing a conversion. He wrote Ellen from California, "Alas, how many shall fall before our government will and can strike an effectual blow I cannot tell. Hundreds have now fallen through Lincoln's unwillingness to strike a blow at slavery."[927] There is no clear evidence that Simpson had any direct input into the

---

924 John Niven. *The Salmon P. Chase Papers, Journals: 1829-1872* Vol. I (Kent, Ohio: The Kent State University Press, 1993) 424.
925 Crooks, 375-376. A copy of a confusing letter exists in the papers of Clarence True Wilson in the UMA at Drew University. The letter is dated War Department, Washington City, D. C., August 25, 1862. The location would have been impossible since Simpson was in California at that time. The letter reads, "My Dearest Ellen: I am waiting in an antechamber while the President is closeted with Secretary Stanton. I have been at Secretary Chase's office, but he is not yet visible. I do not know how I shall fare in reference to Henry Bannister, but I shall do what I can. Yours affectionately, M. Simpson."
926 John McClintock. "Discourse on the Day of the Funeral of President Lincoln," Wednesday, April 19, 1865, recorded by J. T. Butts (New York: Press of J. M. Broadstreet and Sons, 1865) 18.
927 UMA, E. PA Conference of the UMC, St. George's UMC: Philadelphia, PA, Letter August 29, 1862.

Emancipation Proclamation, though as did Lincoln, he gradually saw it as a necessity.[928]

One of the more fascinating stories was told by Cornelia Gray Lunt, daughter of Orrington Lunt, whom we have already met as a founder of Northwestern University. Late in life, she recalled that as a girl she had visited the Simpsons in Philadelphia. She recorded that one evening at supper, she heard the Bishop discussing the Emancipation Proclamation. She quoted Simpson's discussion of Lincoln, "I have urged on him that Proclamation, as have so many others of our best thinkers, and I am puzzled and disappointed over his dilatory attitude." She claimed that Simpson left for Washington at once, returned to Philadelphia, and reported that he had said to Lincoln, "Mr. President I shall no longer remain silent on a subject I deem so vitally important. I have come to tell you my firm belief that unless you issue that proclamation at once, the Proclamation and Country will both suffer, and you will be responsible for its unpardonable postponement. I have spoken to you first, and I let you see what I think and feel and now I go to tell the people."[929] The two problems with this story are first: the Simpsons did not move to Philadelphia until after the Emancipation Proclamation. Second, delivering a threatening ultimatum to a President would not have been consistent with Simpson's temperament.

---

928   Robert Clark persuasively argues that Simpson had nothing to do with the Emancipation Proclamation. Simpson was on the West Coast during the fermentive and formative period of the Proclamation's gestation. Simpson was not an emancipationist, and a private urging of emancipation would have been in contradiction of his public moderation stance. Simpson's social-political motivation unfortunately outweighed theological and ethical convictions. Clark writes, "The issue of slavery in the Border States facing Simpson and the other Bishops at the outbreak of the war was therefore very similar to that confronting Lincoln. Unable to achieve the social and economic detachment of the New England abolitionists and so to act from moral impulse, Simpson and his colleagues were forced to seek an accommodation between the expedient and the moral. In choosing compromise they undoubtedly prevented a much larger exodus from the church along the border states. The action which rallied support to the leadership of men like Battelle and Governor Thomas Hicks of Maryland, both of whom were Methodists, may have had political consequences in reinforcing Lincoln's efforts to hold the states in the Union." Robert D. Clark. "Bishop Matthew Simpson and the Emancipation Proclamation," *Mississippi Valley Historical Review* Vol. XXXV (September 19, 1948) 268.

929   Cornelia Gray Lunt. *Sketches of Childhood and Girlhood* (Evanston, Illinois: self-published) 217.

More plausible than bullying by Simpson or anyone else, is William and Jane Moore's narrative tracing the relationship between Owen Lovejoy and Lincoln. According to the Moores, both Lincoln and Lovejoy utilized the "language, symbols, and insights of the prevailing moral and religious ethos of the period-Protestant evangelicalism."[930] Lovejoy was patient with Lincoln, not goading him, but on Sundays taking his Bible to the White House for theological conversation.[931] Lovejoy stated, "I am for pouring all the steam that the machinery will bear; but it is better to get into port a few hours later than to risk the explosion of the machinery. If the President does not believe all I do, I believe all that he does. If he does not drive as fast as I would, he is on the same road, and it is a question of time."[932] After Lovejoy died on March 24 1864, Lincoln wrote "Throughout my heavy and perplexing responsibilities–here to the day of his death, it was scarcely wrong of any other to say, he was my most generous friend." The Moores argued that both Lincoln and Lovejoy believed that though they could not have the best of all imagined worlds, they could have the best of all possible worlds. (No evidence that either Lincoln or Lovejoy had read Gottfried Leibnitz.) It would take time, and any wise politician knows that timing is everything. Simpson fully understood that Lincoln was not going to be rushed into a rash immediatism. Perhaps the strongest argument for Simpson not having cajoled Lincoln into enacting emancipation is that no clergyman in America had more political sagacity than did the Methodist Bishop.

Ecclesiastical War within the Civil War

At no time in America's history was the interpretation of the First Amendment, the relationship between church and state, more confused than during the Civil War. When the North occupied such places as New Orleans, Louisiana and Natchez, Mississippi, the churches were expected to declare their allegiance and support for Abraham Lincoln, and this support was to be evidenced in worship services. When Episcopalian ministers Leacock, Goodrich, and Fulton complied with Jefferson Davis' proclamation for a day

---

930   William F. Moore and Jane A. Moore. *Collaborators for Emancipation: Abraham Lincoln and Owen Lovejoy* (Chicago: University of IL Press 2014) 55.
931   Ibid., 157.
932   Ibid., 137.

of fasting and prayer, Northern General Benjamin Butler shipped them off to New York, and when they tried to return, Butler denied them embarkment without pledging allegiance to the Union. Colonel B. G. Farrar ordered that, "any minister failing to comply with these orders (proper spirit towards the Chief Magistrate of the United States) will be immediately prohibited from exercising the functions of his office in this city and rendering himself liable to be sent behind the lines of the United States forces at the discretion of the Colonel commanding."[933]

Methodists were not alone in their endeavor to confiscate unused or misused church properties. Northern Presbyterians, Episcopalians, Baptists, and Catholics, who did not appreciate anything in the Southern culture worth salvaging, all invaded the South under the guise of missionary outreach and benevolence to both slaves and impoverished whites. The idea of reclaiming Methodist church properties did not originate with Edward R. Ames and Matthew Simpson. Of course, some conferences did not know whether they belonged to the North or South, such as the Holston Conference in western North Carolina and western Virginia, which resolved to transfer church properties "to the Methodist Episcopal Church in the United States."[934] The Conference further justified their actions by declaring, "That we accept Civil War in the course of Divine Providence as a result of national crimes, while the horrors of bloodshed and savage cruelty have deepened our purpose to labor and pray for that period when the nations of the earth shall learn war no more."[935]

On November 23, 1864, Tennessee Methodist layman L.P. Reed wrote Simpson that "most all the churches in Nashville and through middle Tennessee were left by their pastors on the arrival of our army and they

---

933   Edward McPherson. *The Political History of the United States of America during the Great Rebellion–1865* (Washington, D. C.: Philp & Solomons, 1865) 546, 538.

934   Russell Richey makes this same point. "Existing conference boundaries and the line drawn thereby between the MEC and MECS did not circumscribe sentiments and loyalties. The boundaries crossed state lines; the northern conferences encompassed slave-holding areas; some anti-slavery sentiment existed in southern conferences, notably in Kentucky; itinerants and presiding elders enjoyed close relations with circuits and congregations cut off by the new lines." Richey, *The Methodist Conference*, 111-112.

935   Ibid., 346.

are now standing empty or are occupied by the government."⁹³⁶ In January of 1864, Ames and Simpson put their heads together, the result being that Ames secured permission from Edwin Stanton for the Methodist Episcopal Church to occupy all churches "belonging to the Methodist Episcopal Church South, in which a loyal preacher appointed by a loyal bishop does not now officiate."⁹³⁷ Simpson traveled to Nashville and discovered that the McKendree Church was being occupied as a field hospital by General George Thomas. Samuel Baldwin from the Methodist Episcopal Church South had already staked claim to the church once it was abandoned by the Northern Army. It was not until February that Lincoln learned of Stanton's permission, and the President wrote his Secretary of War a letter of disagreement, but also equivocation:

> I have never interfered nor thought of interfering as to who shall or shall not preach at any church; nor have I knowingly or believingly tolerated anyone else to so interfere by my authority …. after having made these declarations in good faith, and in writing, you can conceive of my embarrassment at now having brought to me what purports to be a formed order of the War Department bearing date November 30, 1863 giving Bishop Ames control and possession of all the Methodist Churches in certain departments whose pastors have not been appointed by a loyal Bishop or Bishops and orders the military to aid him against any resistance which be made to him taking such possessions and control.⁹³⁸

In spite of reservations, Lincoln later endorsed church confiscation but limited the action to "states in rebellion" and in churches where there was no "organized worship."⁹³⁹ On February 13, 1864, Lincoln wrote to John Hogan, "I fear it is liable to some abuses but it is not quite easy to withdraw it entirely and at once."⁹⁴⁰

Lincoln was heavily indebted to the Methodists who had furnished more soldiers and chaplains than any other denomination. Compliance to the pressure of Northern clergymen was a simple quid pro quo. On May 18,

---

936   James Kirby. "The McKendree Chapel Affair," *Tennessee Historical Quarterly* Vol. 25 (Winter 1966) 361.

937   Ibid., 361

938   Roy P. Basler, ed. *The Collected Works of Abraham Lincoln* Vol. VII, (New Brunswick, New Jersey: Rutgers University Press, 1959) 179.

939   Ibid., 180.

940   Ibid., 183.

1864, the General Conference meeting at Philadelphia hand-delivered by committee a pledge of support to Lincoln, the delegation headed by Ames. The Methodist visitors standing in the White House, swelled with self-congratulatory pride, as Lincoln responded, "Though he would not utter anything invidious against any of the churches, the Methodist Episcopal Church, because of its numerical superiority was most important of all. It is no fault in others that the Methodist Church sends more soldiers to the field, more nurses to the hospital, and more prayers to Heaven. God bless the Methodist Church–bless our God–bless all the churches and bless the God who in our great trial giveth us the churches."[941]

Simpson Becomes a Southern Persona Non-gratis

In Nashville, Simpson was something less than a celebrity. He wrote Ellen, "I had an interview with Governor Johnson this morning. He is true Union but all these Southern people have a deep prejudice against the North. Tomorrow morning I've agreed to preach in the Hall of the House of Representatives. But my congregation I have no doubt will be chiefly soldiers. The citizens care nothing about us except to dislike us." Again he ribbed Ellen for not writing: "No letter yet--isn't it 'funny?'"[942] He informed Ellen that he had met Grant for the first time. "We had an interview with General Grant. He is not very communicative but I have no doubt he's both an able General and a talented man." Methodist John Cramer agreed to refit the church, but was not optimistic; it was in bad condition in that "all the pews were ripped out of it and it was surrounded by houses of prostitution."[943] A week later, Cramer informed Simpson that Grant had given permission for the Methodist Episcopal Church to occupy McKendree, and the Army was going to refurbish the structure since it was

---

941   UMA, Drew University, Simpson papers, Letter May 18, 1864. In a project headed by Daniel Stowell, with help from personnel both at the Library of Congress and Drew University by using the latest technological techniques to distinguish original manuscripts from lithograph reproductions, it has been determined that the original Lincoln speech to his Methodist delegation, is located in Series 4 of the Abraham Lincoln papers at the Library of Congress. See in Daniel W. Stowell. "God Bless the Methodist Church–A. Lincoln: Finding the Lost Speech," *Methodist History*, 50: 3 (April 2012) 179-184.

942   UMA, Drew University, Simpson papers, Letter January 16, 1864.

943   LOC, Simpson papers, Letter March 11, 1864, Container seven.

responsible for its deterioration.⁹⁴⁴ It did not hurt the Northern Methodist cause that Cramer was a brother-in-law of Ulysses Grant.

Simpson was warned by one of his informants, Northern Chaplain J.W. Hoover, that animosity against his intrusion was swelling into indignant belligerence at Simpson's arrogance and would result in the interest of the Union cause being seriously "embarrassed by your operation in this quarter when you are to be appealed to as a Patriot to abandon your enterprise in this place for the good of the country." Hoover further accused Simpson of forcing "a religion upon a people to which they were hostile." Hoover supported this last assertion by quoting Samuel Baldwin who had declared that, "sooner than submit to any attempt to thrust upon him any religion by the sword or bayonet he would shed his last drop of blood."⁹⁴⁵ Nonetheless, McKendree Church opened for services on June 12, 1864, with John Cramer, the appointee of Simpson, officiating. The large crowd was disappointed that Simpson himself was not present, but returned the next Sunday to pack out the place both morning and evening. (Evidently, Nashville had many Northern sympathizers.) Cramer was encouraged: "I have no doubt that we shall soon be able to gain a permanent foothold here." But Cramer also had a personal problem: he was broke and forthright with Simpson about his indigence. "I have written to you three or four times concerning the Church affairs here and concerning my finances but I've not yet received an answer. I feel very anxious to hear from you."⁹⁴⁶ Attempting to mollify Cramer's anger, Simpson immediately responded by sending him $200 out of his own pocket.

As the ecclesiastical air in Nashville became more toxic, new Bishop Charles Kingsley, to whom had been passed the McKendree baton, stated the obvious: "For some reason there's much odium attached to our occupancy of the church property in Nashville and it will require the very best management to get along without doing more hurt than good, as many Union men think we are not justified in the cause we have pursued."⁹⁴⁷

---

944   LOC, Simpson papers, Letter March 18, 1864, Container seven.
945   LOC, Simpson papers, Letter April 22, 1864, Container seven.
946   LOC, Simpson papers, Letter July 20, 1864, Container seven.
947   Kirby, "The McKendree Chapel," 365.

Bishop Levi Scott took the moral high ground, indirectly condemning Simpson. "We might by aid of military take the churches but I can have no part in that policy."[948]

Lincoln Reverses Johnson

On January 23, 1865, the Northern coup was ended (or some thought) by the decision of the Military Governor soon to be sworn in as Vice President of the United States. Andrew Johnson issued the following order, returning the Church to the Southern claimants:

> The Methodist Episcopal Church, denominated the "McKendree Church" in the city of Nashville, was taken possession of under an order of the Secretary of War, issued November 30th, 1863, and is now held by Bishop Simpson in pursuance thereof.
>
> Application has been made to the President of the United States, for the restoration of said Church, Parsonage, and other property pertaining to said church, therewith.
>
> The President thereupon referred the question of restoration to me for consideration and decision. It appears from a statement of facts, which have been filed in this office, in reference to the loyalty of the parties, who make the application for the restoration, that Bishop Soule, is, and has been, loyal to the Government of the United States, and that the Officiating Ministers and Trustees have long since taken the Amnesty Oath, and that there is no charge of any violation by them of the same, on the contrary there is proof, that it has been observed in good faith, and that they have complied with the Constitution and Laws of the United States.
>
> My decision is, that the Church, Parsonage, and other property pertaining to Said Church, be restored to the above parties as above indicated.
>
> Signed, Andrew Johnson
> Mil. Gov. & B. G. [949]

---

948   LOC, Simpson papers, Letter, Scott to Simpson, March 10, 1864, Container seven.
949   UMA, Drew University, Simpson papers, Letter, signed "Andrew Johnson Order," issued January 23, 1865.

On February 6, 1865, Lincoln tersely dismissed Johnson's order by replying, "Let the matter of the McKendree Church remain as it is without further action until you see me."[949]

After becoming President, Johnson needed the good will of America's largest denomination and sent for Simpson in order to smooth over his backtracking on the North's confiscation of Southern churches. The matter was further complicated by the fact that Northern Methodist A.A. Gee, who was now the pastor of McKendree Church, refused to vacate the church since, "The church and property in question were placed in the hands of Bishop Simpson and he is, therefore, responsible for the same. I have no authority to comply with your demand but would most respectfully refer you to him."[950] Kirby assesses that the early August meeting between the President and the Bishop "accomplished little but to antagonize one another." Even though Simpson immediately released the Church, irrevocable damage had been done, a searing memory which would last for decades. After the return of McKendree Chapel into Southern Church jurisdiction, the Bishops of the Methodist Episcopal Church South replied:

> The conduct of certain Northern Methodist bishops and preachers in taking advantage of the confusion incident to a state of war to intrude themselves into several of our houses of worship, and their continuing to hold these places against the wishes and protests of the congregations and rightful owner, causes us sorrow and pain, not only as working an injury to us, but as presenting to the world a spectacle ill calculated to make an impression favorable to Christianity. They are not only using, to our deprivation and exclusion, churches and parsonages which we have built, but have proceeded to set up a claim to them, as their property. By what shadow of right, legal or moral, we are at a loss to conceive. We advise our brethren who suffer these evils to bear them patiently, to cleave closely together, and not indulge in any vindictive measures or tempers …[951]

Simpson was well-intended in wanting to make full use of properties that had once belonged to the Methodist Episcopal Church. But at the same time, he was woefully ignorant of Southern culture and mores, and equally unsympathetic to Southern rights perspectives. But then again, 950

---

949 Basler, Vol. VIII, 264.
950 Kirby, "The McKendree Chapel," 367.
951 Ibid., 368.

neither Simpson nor anyone else in America had ever been involved in a "civil" war. "Civil" was extremely difficult to define.

During the war, Simpson did little that put him in harm's way. But, he was not totally uninvolved with the Northern troops. He did not have to travel far; three miles north of the White House he spoke to the Eighth Illinois Calvary camped on the banks of the Potomac. A reporter wrote that "although the bishop had a great press of business on his hands, he most cheerfully complied, and yesterday gave us one of those powerful, heart-searching sermons of his. There was scarcely a dry eye in that whole company of twelve hundred men, and come what may to them–temptation, sickness, and death–nothing will ever quite obliterate the impressions then and there made."[952]

No less than the nation, Matthew Simpson was an embattled man. Preaching provided a psychic and spiritual relief for his own soul and that of the nation for which he would become the primary spokesman.

---

952   "8th Illinois - Calvary," *Northwestern Christian Advocate* (November 23, 1861).

Illustrations

A Young Photograph of Matthew Simpson
(Courtesy of DePauw University Archives, used with permission)

UNCLE MATTHEW SIMPSON.

Uncle Matthew- polymath and Ohio State Legislator who raised Simpson (From plate in Crooks, *Life of Bishop Simpson* (1890), between pages 104-105)

(Image in the public domain)

Two-story house where Uncle Matthew raised the future Bishop. Still stands in Cadiz, OH (From drawing in Crooks, *Life of Bishop Simpson* (1890), page 4)

(Image in the public domain)

Dr. Charles Elliott.

Charles Elliott- Guided Matthew Simpson toward ministry
(from plate in Wood's *The Peerless Orator: Matthew Simpson, D.D., LL.D. Bishop of the Methodist Episcopal Church* (1908) between pages 90-91)

(Image in the Public Domain)

A Photograph of Ellen Vernor Simpson
(Courtesy of DePauw University Archives, used with permission)

An Early Painting of Matthew Simpson
(Courtesy of DePauw University Archives, used with permission)

Henry Bascom, who influenced Simpson's preaching style

(Photo in the Public Domain)

BISHOP EDWARD R. AMES.

Edward Ames- Fellow Methodist Bishop and envious adversary
(From plate in Crooks, *Life of Bishop Simpson* (1890), between pages 184-185)

(Image in the public domain)

James Harlan, United State Secretary of the Interior who "tipped" Simpson on railroad investments

(Photo in the Public Domain)

John Evans, Simpson's closest friend implicated in the Sand Creek Massacre
(Image in the Public Domain)

Frances Willard, a great admirer of Simpson, who was converted under his ministry, but was later disappointed at his lack of support for her "causes."

(Photo in the Public Domain)

John Chivington- Methodist Elder who led the Sand Creek Massacre and was never brought to justice by Simpson and the Methodist Episcopal Church

(Photo in the Public Domain)

James Harper, founder of *Harper's Weekly* and mayor of New York

(Image in the Public Domain)

Metropolitan Memorial Methodist Episcopal Church in Washington, D.C.-
Founded by Simpson and an architectural disaster (from image in Simpson's
Cyclopaedia of Methodism: *Embracing Sketches of its Rise, Progress and Present Condition,
with Biographical Notices and Numerous Illustrations* (1880) page 900)

(Image in the Public Domain)

Daniel Drew- benefactor of Drew Theological Seminary and Wall Street manipulator

(Image in the Public Domain)

An Older Matthew Simpson
(Courtesy of DePauw University Archives, used with permission)

356 | "God Cannot Do Without America"

A Group Photograph at the Milan Conference in 1875 (Matthew Simpson seated in front right)

(Courtesy of Drew University Methodist Collection, Madison, NJ- Matthew Simpson Papers, used with permission)

Picture in *Leslie's Illustrated Magazine* of Simpson praying the Dedication Prayer for the 1876 Centennial Celebration in Philadelphia from page 78 of the *Historical Register of the Centennial Exposition*, Frank Leslie, 1876)

(Image in the Public Domain)

Bishop Matthew Simpson Portrait

(Courtesy of Drew University Art Collection, Madison, NJ, used with permission)
(Painted by Cora Richardson in 1873)

Simpson's Home in Philadelphia,
Where he died.

1334 Arch Street Mansion in Philadelphia- Where Matthew Simpson lived the last two years of his life (from plate in Wood's *The Peerless Orator: Matthew Simpson, D.D., LL.D. Bishop of the Methodist Episcopal Church* (1908) between pages 198-199)

(Image in the Public Domain)

Simpson mausoleum in West Laurel Hills Cemetery

(Photograph courtesy of Donald Reese, used with permission)

The Simpson House, Philadelphia

(Photo by Ronnie Fluellen, used with permission)

Statue of Bishop Matthew Simpson on front lawn of Simpson House in Fairmount Park, Philadelphia

(Photograph in the Public Domain)

Chapter Twelve:
God Cannot Do Without America

The Preeminent Clerical Voice

One is tempted to assume that the M.E.C. Bishops would have immediately expressed unanimity in their response to Southern secession. Such was not the case. Bishop Janes was decidedly against pastors resigning their churches for Union chaplaincies, much less taking up arms. It is ironic that Matthew Simpson expressed no doubt nor evidenced any qualms to advocating a full military response. The man had never fired a gun in his life. If he ever hunted for squirrels or rabbits, he never mentioned the activity. His sensitive soul reverenced life; it was to be observed, not killed. Also, the state where he lived, Illinois; the state where he had lived, Indiana; and in particular the state where he was from, Ohio, was run over by "peace democrats" and Copperheads. To the contrary in the fall of 1861, Simpson and the Northwest Indiana Conference formally adopted the position that "The enemies of Constitutional liberty had resorted to arms. They boldly assumed the initiative, and nothing but a counter resort to the weapons of war upon the part of the loyal citizens of the Republic could save it from disaster and death." Conference historian, J. C. Reed, wrote of Simpson: "He had no criticism of the young itinerant who chose to lay aside his sacerdotal robes for the panoply of a soldier. The call of the country in this hour was supreme; her voice was the voice of God." Matthew Simpson became the preeminent clerical "voice" for the Union over the next four years.[953]

---

953   J.C. Reed. "The War of the Rebellion," UMA, DePauw University, Detzler papers. I thank Richard Stowe for alerting me to this source.

"God Cannot Do Without America"

Six rhetorical performances during the Civil War lifted Simpson beyond the parochialism of Methodism and transfigured him into a national celebrity, and ultimately into the most influential advocate for the Northern cause.[954] All six occasions were prompted or provided by his allegiance to the Republican Party and a progressive obligation to Lincoln. After the secession of the Southern states and the initial fireworks at Fort Sumter, the Illinois Republican Party decided that someone should place the present crisis in perspective, its perspective, and who better than Matthew Simpson who lived in Evanston, Illinois, and was a personal friend of John Evans. Thus, Simpson's first public pronouncement on the righteousness of the North and the sinfulness of the South took place before 6,000 people at the Wigwam in Chicago on April 28, 1861. The preacher theologically justified a military response to the treason of the Southern states. "The man who goes to war goes in the order of God, goes to hold the government ordained of God, goes for the right."[955]

The Cross and the Flag

The Wigwam occasion was transformative for Simpson, the Methodist Episcopal Church and, ultimately, the Union. Simpson's preaching thereafter became an exaltation of both the cross of Christ and the flag of the United States. At times, as Simpson stood before either a secular or sacred audience, it was difficult to distinguish which symbol was more important. Of course, Simpson clarified that the flag was below the cross, but it was "just below the cross." The object lesson of waving the flag as the peroration of his declamation may have betrayed his primary allegiance or what should

---

954   The six rhetorical performances were at the Wigwam, Chicago, April 28, 1861; The Sanitary Fair in Philadelphia, June 7, 1864; The Concert Hall in Pittsburgh, PA, October 20, 1864; The Music Academy, New York City, November 3, 1864; The U. S. House of Representatives, March 5, 1865; and the Lincoln Funeral in Springfield, Illinois, May 4, 1865.

955   *Northwestern Christian Advocate* Vol. IX, No. XVIII (May 1, 1861), *Chicago Evening Journal* (April 29, 1861), *Chicago Tribune* (April 29, 1861) *The Methodist* (October 12, 1861, March 8, 1862). Karen Armstrong would argue that at this point Simpson's nationalism became a religion. "If we can define the sacred as something for which one is prepared to die, the nation had certainly become an embodiment of the divine, a supreme value …. The Civil War armies have been described as the most religiously motivated in American history." Karen Armstrong. *Fields of Blood: Religion and the History of Violence* (New York: Alfred A. Knopf, 2014) 294-295.

have been his primary allegiance as a Christian minister of the Gospel. In summary, democratic government was ordained of God and America, now the Union, was the primary exemplar of that government, a loyalty which called for the ultimate sacrifice.

> The love of country is an exalted passion inspiring generous thought and heroic deeds; but it must pale before an intelligent appreciation and love of popular government, the best earthly hope of humanity. And now that both country and popular government are imperfect, we can conceive of no sacrifice that the nation ought not to make for their preservation. Let us be united firm, generous in supporting the measures adopted by government and above all let us look to the blessing of heaven in the enterprise which so nearly concerns the will of our nation and race.[956]

Simpson's text was Psalm 47: 1-2. He broached the God–country relationship, but the arrangement was more temporary and tentative than in the later Music Academy speech at New York in November of 1864. Simpson left no doubt that America, at least for this time and occasion, was God's primary instrument. "How can God blot out this nation from the map of the face of the earth? Reverently, I would say it; God cannot afford to lose this government. He will use it till the end of its creation has been worked out, when another may arise to stand in its stead; but till then, He may chide us as a father, he may scourge as his son but not destroy."[957] For the first time he used the "flag nailed just below the cross" phrase. The critical proximity between the flag of America and the cross of Christianity became Simpson's most graphic imagery over the next four years. What he did not say, nor have to say, but was plainly clear to his listeners, is that there was no other nation between America's flag and the cross of Christ.

America and its affairs were God's top priority. To his credit, Simpson was clear that a nation's power and triumph rested not on military prowess, but within God's sovereign plan. God could divert and stymie the greatest military power, and mighty armies and navies could become inept and impotent by God simply flicking nature's switch. "The invincible Spanish Armada sweeping down upon the defenseless coast of England was smitten and scattered. God spoke to the winds and Protestant England was saved." Simpson then turned to one of his favorite historical individuals: "When

---

956 *Northwestern Christian Advocate* (May 1, 1861).
957 *Chicago Daily Tribune* Vol. XIV, No. 258 (April 29, 1861).

Napoleon invaded Russia, a careful computation of the setting of the seasons for twenty years had been made by his order and all his calculations for the campaign had been based on nature's laws but when the time had come for God to say to the invincible conqueror, 'Thus far shall thou come and no further,' the stars and their course fought against him."[958] Simpson then offered a theodicy for the war:

> A cause for this war may be in the fact that it is necessary to give this nation a still higher position. If we are to be a missionary nation we must be pure. There are dark spots upon our national escutcheon that need to be removed, for they hinder our sending abroad the truth through the nations of the world. If Jefferson, in his day, could tremble when he thought of our national sin and deprecate God's justice, how can we wonder when it has reached its present magnitude and altitude? If, when this war shall come to an end, we shall be seen standing in power, having shown our strength, standing in purity, having cast away our sin, then can we proclaim the gospel of this salvation with pure hands, and speak more eloquently than in the former days.[959]

Simpson did manage to disavow slavery, but his solution was myopic and naïve, in fact, decidedly wrong. He believed until it was plain to see otherwise, that the slaves would be shipped back to their native land. The exodus of the slaves back to Africa would be similar to the Israelites marching out of Egypt. The only difference would be violent and protracted bloodshed. But the return shipment would pay huge dividends, the conversion of Africa. "It may be that thus Africa, oppressed Africa, shall secure her elevation through the instrumentality of her own children."[960] Unwittingly, Simpson had provided justification for American slavery. He simply forgot to ask the slaves, should they be freed, what would be their residential preference.

Lincoln: "I Prefer Simpson to Speak for Me"

Simpson's greatest honor, other than the Lincoln funeral, may have been provided by Lincoln's request for Simpson to speak on the opening day of the Sanitary Fair in Philadelphia, June 7, 1864.[961] Lincoln wrote

---

958   Ibid.
959   Ibid.
960   *NW Christian Advocate*, 129.
961   Richard Carwardine writes, "Bishop Matthew Simpson, who crisscrossed as

George Childs, "I want you to find Bishop Matthew Simpson, wherever he may be, and tell him that I would prefer to have him speak for me than anybody in the world."[962] Between June 7 and June 28, 1864, Philadelphia held its great central fair which raised over a million dollars to renew the Sanitary Commission's dwindling funds.[963] By the end of the War, roughly thirty sanitary fairs had been held, earning over fourteen million dollars. In 1864, Philadelphia boasted around thirty hospitals, possibly more than any other city in the world. Most of the hospitals had been built for Civil War purposes and, thus, Philadelphia provided the ideal location for the United States Sanitary Commission to hold its fair. A 200,000 square-foot pavilion was built to showcase and sell the largest mass of goods ever assembled on one location. It was the forerunner of the modern mall. "Union Avenue was the walkway that went through the center of the fair compound. The pavilion was 540 feet long and 64 feet wide, and the highest point of the central arch reached 51 feet above the ground. The building was an imposing sight in Logan Square."[964] The fair, which had been organized by eighty-four committees, served 9,000 meals per day, and raised over one million

---

an evangelist of patriotism, was unsurpassed in his power to melt an audience to tears or rouse it to the heights of passionate enthusiasm for the war-torn flag. There was nothing coincidental about the President engaging Simpson to substitute for him at the Philadelphia Sanitary Fair." Richard Carwardine. *Lincoln: A Life of Purpose and Power* (New York: Vintage Books, 2006) 279-280.

962   LOC, Simpson papers, A.C. Jeffries, "A Bishop Speaks for Lincoln."

963   The Sanitary Commission was aptly named. Its main business was the sanitation of the North's military encampments. "Eighty per cent of the privies were in good condition, properly arranged, kept in good order, and free from offensive odor. The remaining 20 per cent were a threat to good health. In 68 per cent of the camps men obeyed commands confining them to exclusive use of privies; in 32 per cent officers did not enforce the orders. That the men preferred to go off into the bushes was understandable. The sink was usually a pit surmounted by a rail; cleanliness meant throwing earth over the sink once a day and keeping its edges free of excrement. In 35 per cent officers allowed the men to urinate within camp limits at night. The British service provided one night bucket for each tent, but the Union armies apparently made no such provision. Soldiers disposed offal systematically in 77 per cent of the camps; they were very negligent in the remaining 23 per cent. Not infrequently stables were found within camp limits, a direct violation of Army Regulations. In general, camp police had improved since the summer of 1861." William Quentin Maxwell. *Lincoln's Fifth Wheel: The Political History of the United States Sanitary Commission* (New York: Longman, Green & Company, 1956) 38–39.

964   Alvin R Kantor and Marjorie S. Kantor. *Sanitary Fairs: A Philatelic and Historical Study of Civil War Benevolences* (Glencoe, Illinois: S.F. Publishing, 1992) 117.

dollars.⁹⁶⁵ By the time the fair closed, 253,924 ticket holders had made an estimated 442,658 visits an average of 29,510 each day.⁹⁶⁶

With solemnity and dignity, Simpson, along with the Mayor and the Chairman of the Executive Committee, marched down Delaware Avenue to a band playing "Hail Columbia." But then disaster struck: "The temporary platform upon which the ladies and gentlemen were to sing an anthem and The Star Spangled Banner, as a portion of the ceremonies, were seated gave way, and threw the singers and musicians to the ground on top of the wreck. Several persons were seriously injured by this unfortunate accident, and after a short delay, the committee decided to proceed with the regular program."⁹⁶⁷ The speech was not one of Simpson's better oratorical performances, but nonetheless, he played the occasion to the hilt, resonating with his auditors.

> Sherman is just now showing, from his onward career, that he is a Northern man with Southern proclivities (Cheers and laughter.) We have a *Thomas* who never doubts.(Cheers.) We have a Hooker who pushes his forces amid the clouds. (Cheers.) New England has given us her Howard, who, one-armed, is still within himself a host. (Cheers.) Pennsylvania has in her Hancock a tower of strength (cheers), and near her heart she bears her Meade of honor. (Cheer upon cheer.)While the giant West, from the shores of her broad Mississippi, sends us a Grant of unconditional victory! (Tremendous outbursts of applause, culminating in a "three times three," given with full emphasis) Nor are the seamen less brave. A gallant Foote has ended his labors, and peace be to his memory. But Porter, Dupont, and Farragut still marshal our fleet. (Cheers.) Our monitors have changed naval warfare, and have taught the world the value of hearts of oak in breasts of iron.⁹⁶⁸

The War Speech

The prelude for Simpson's New York speech was provided by his wife's hometown, Pittsburgh, Pennsylvania, in October of 1864. At the Concert Hall, an Episcopal clergyman presented Simpson by stating that the Bishop had promised that he would be on his good behavior and say nothing

---

965   www.youtube.com/watch?v
966   Ibid., 151.
967   Charles Stille. *Memorial of the Great Central Fair for the U.S. Sanitary Commission* (Philadelphia: United States Sanitary Commission, 1864) 26.
968   "The Great Central Fair," *The Philadelphia Inquirer* (June 8, 1864).

about politics. Simpson came off his chair like he was shot out of a cannon and declared when he reached the podium, "I desire it to be distinctly understood that I have given no one any assurance as to what I shall say and shall not say at this time: nor have I given anyone else authority to speak for me. I am here to utter my mind as a free American citizen, and I shall do so without restraint. If politics gets in the way, it will get its share with everything else."[969] Three thousand people cheered and shouted for several minutes before they let Simpson continue. The *Christian Advocate* reported, "The great idea of the lecture was to point out the finger of God in our national history, and to show that divine indications abound as an augury of continued unity and future greatness."[970]

Simpson spent two hours and twenty minutes working through the four options for the future of America, as people applauded, wept, shouted, and waved their handkerchiefs. An enthralled reporter exclaimed, "It was impossible to catch and retain just images of those vast thoughts that splashed and sparkled before an entranced audience. Here and there in the experiences of life we had had the pleasure of hearing eloquent men; the foremost of living orators; the most distinguished of those not long dead; but we have never heard anything like that Tuesday lecture; and we have but little hope that we shall here its like again."[971] At this event, Simpson articulated what would become the essence of the speech called by various titles: "The Future of Our Country," "The National Conflict," "The War Speech," which he presented scores of times. Clarence True Wilson claimed sixty times, but that number cannot be documented. It may have been at the Pittsburgh location that for the first time, Simpson spontaneously grabbed an American flag and waved it. Henceforth, the emotionally-laden object lesson became a highly calculated exclamation mark.

Methodist and Republican operatives Oliver and Mark Hoyt arranged for Matthew Simpson to speak at the Academy of Music Hall, New York City, November 3, 1864, five days before the national election. The covert purpose of Simpson delivering his "War Speech" was to erase any doubt

---

969   Charles W. Smith. "Bishop Simpson's Greatest Oratorical Triumph," *Pittsburgh Christian Advocate* (June 22, 1911).
970   *Pittsburgh Christian Advocate* (October 22, 1864).
971   Ibid.

that Lincoln would carry New York City and hence the State electorate.[972] Mark Hoyt wrote: "Speaking here at that time with the full report promised of the speech in the Tribune Times Herald and Evening Post is equivalent to speaking to the nation and will give ample time for it (the speech) to produce its result on the election."[973] The Hoyt brothers had prospered in the leather business, gaining the reputation of being among the most prominent merchants in New York City. The *New York Times* stated upon Oliver Hoyt's death in a carriage accident on May 4, 1887 at the age of 64 that, "In 1844 at the age of 20, he came to this city and, with his brother William, founded the leather house of W& O. Hoyt which later became the widely known firm of the Hoyt Brothers. Strict integrity and methodical habits of business resulted in a large measure of prosperity, and Mr. Hoyt became very wealthy."[974] Simpson wrote of Hoyt:

> He has made several large gifts to the purposes of the Church among which may be named his contributions to the building of the church of Stanford, Connecticut, a gift of $25,000 to Wesleyan University, and one of $2,000 to the Wesley Memorial Church of Savannah, Georgia. He has been for more than twenty years an active member of the Board of Managers of the General Missionary Society of the Methodist Episcopal Church and has also served as Treasurer of the Church Board of Education. He was one of the founders of the Methodist newspaper and takes an active part in all church work. He has also been a member of the State Senate of Connecticut.[975]

---

972 According to Michael Burlingame, Lincoln had reason to be worried about New York State. Lincoln expressed to gubernatorial candidate Reuben Fenton, "I am anxious for New York, and we must put our heads together and see if the matter can be fixed." Burlingame, Vol. II, 704-705. It is theoretically possible, but not likely, that Simpson influenced the New York State vote since it was won by only four thousand votes. Most of the attendees at the Simpson event would have already been committed to Lincoln.

973 LOC, Simpson papers, Mark Hoyt to Simpson, Letter November 4, 1864, Container seven.

974 *The New York Times* (May 6, 1887).

975 *Cyclopaedia*, 457. The propensity of Simpson to tout business personalities has, according to some, provided exhibit A as evidence for his enamored-ness with the "bourgeoisement" of Methodism. Morris Davis argues that, "This emphasis on material success and elite cultural social and professional status reinforces our understanding that Simpson was indeed one of a growing number of Christian leaders of the United States in the nineteenth century who considered these things of God's providence. This understanding of individual success carried over directly to their understanding of what it meant to be a successful nation and in what way God shined his providence on a nation. For Simpson, God chose those who would lead, and this was signified in both individual lives as well as

"God Cannot Do without America"

The event was billed as "The National Conflict," and the *New York Times* reported that the hall was jammed, and the doors were shut fifteen minutes before the commencement of the program, "to prevent any more from entering." The "War Speech" proceeded along its normative lines of argument, until Simpson came to the line which informs the title of this book. He had broached the concept of God's dependency on America in the 1861 Wigwam Speech and recent Pittsburgh presentation. But this time, Simpson was less tentative, more direct, more explicit, and his assertion was readily available for public consumption. "We were the great immigrant depot of the world. Did the people of other nations go elsewhere? No they came here till we had Irishmen enough to make us almost all Irish, German enough to hear the language of the Fatherland in every street. They were coming from Italy and Hungary, and on the Pacific coast they were coming from China and Japan. What nation could take their place? None. No, none. And he said with reverence, 'God cannot afford to do without America.'"[976]

At best, Simpson had proclaimed a theology of benign jingoism. At worst, he had proclaimed the idolatry of theological blasphemy, that God needed America was as important and critical to God's will as America needing God. The Methodist Bishop mouthed what most Americans

---

the life of the nation, in material wealth, and political power, and in elite social standing." Morris L. Davis, Jr. "From the Gospel Circuit to the War Circuit: Bishop Matthew Simpson and Upwardly Mobile Methodism."*Methodist History* 38.2 (April 2000) 207–208. Donald Marti has calculated that out of 347 laypersons given biographical descriptions in Simpson's *Cyclopaedia*, "The vast majority listed was because of their achievements in medicine, law, politics, education or some kind of business." Marti notes that Simpson listed 92 of the lay delegates to the 1872 General Conference in his *Cyclopaedia*, "including five governors, a dozen congressmen, at least fourteen college trustees, and one professor .... Almost all of the delegates enjoyed business or professional success." Concerning Simpson's rich philanthropists, Marti concludes that, "Thanks to the embellishments they provided, they no longer had to feel themselves inferior to Episcopalians or, at least, Presbyterians. Whatever Asbury or Wesley would have thought of the fact, they had become respectable." Donald B. Marti, "Rich Methodists: The Rise and Consequence of Lay Philanthropy in the Mid-Nineteenth Century" in *Rethinking Methodism*, eds. Russell E. Richey and Kenneth E. Rowe (Nashville: Kingswood Books, 1985) 165.

976   *New York Daily Tribune,* Monday, November 7, 1864. *The New York Times*, November 4, 1864, recorded "God could not do without America."

thought. It had just never been said by so public a figure in so public a setting in such a straightforward and blunt manner. Simpson was not alone in believing that the Union was critical, if not necessary, for God conducting his business. In a book published in 1864, Horace Bushnell had written,

> We associate God and religion with all that we are fighting for .... Our cause, we love to think, is especially God's and so we are connecting all most sacred impressions with our government itself, weaving in a woof of holy feeling among all the fibers of our constitutional polity and government .... The whole shaping of the fabric is providential, God, God is in it, everywhere .... every drum-beat is a hymn, the cannon thunder God, the electric silence, darting victory along the wires, is the inaudible greeting of God's favoring work and purpose.[977]

The primary proposition supporting American folk theology was that America was the new Zion, the New Jerusalem. In 1813 John Adams wrote Thomas Jefferson, "Many hundreds of years must roll away before we shall be corrupted. Our pure, virtuous, public, spirited, federative republic will last forever, govern the globe and introduce the perfection of man."[978] God had always needed a people to carry out his purposes, and He had simply traded instruments, Israel for America. This theme has been pulverized by a long list of American religion historiographers.[979]

---

977   Sidney E. Mead. *The Lively Experiment: The Shaping of Christianity in America* (New York: Harper and Row Publishers, 1963) 142–143.

978   Jurgen Moltmann. *The Coming of God: Christian Eschatology* (Minneapolis: Fortress Press, 1996) 171.

979   Charles Sanford in his *The Quest for Paradise* examined American Puritanism and its descendants, who were convinced that America was the "new Eden." Ernest Tuveson wrote: "Providence or history has put a special responsibility on the American people to spread the blessings of liberty on the earth and to defeat, if necessary, by force the sinister powers of darkness." According to Edmund Wilson's interpretation, "The Puritanism of New England was a kind of new Judaism, a Judaism transposed into Anglo-Saxon terms. When the Puritans came to America, they identified George III with Pharaoh and themselves with the Israelites in search of the Promised Land. They called their new called their new country Canaan, and talked continually of the Covenant they had made with God. Winthrop and Bradford were Moses and Joshua; and Hutchinson was pilloried as Jezebel." One of the most astute Protestant prophets of the twentieth century referred to such Messianic pretentions as idolatry. Reinhold Niebuhr wrote, "It would seem that the individual man is fooled by the greater majesty and the seeming mortality of collective man's achievements. Therefore he worships his nation as god. But there is always an element of perversity as well as of ignorance in this worship. For other nations and cultures are perversely debased and become merely the instruments or tools, the victims or allies of the nation of one's worship. There are no strictly pluralistic conceptions of history after the

Simpson's Millennial Nationalism

If the reader will grant this historian liberty of theological reflection, it can be argued from a Biblical perspective, that God uses people to carry out his purposes, and since God acts in historical context, which is a central truth of the Incarnation, such people by divine plan must be a specific people at a specific time and place. Since God is true to his character, and in that character is love of the other, and love always delights in the delight of the other, and inherent to that delight is the fulfillment of purpose, then God desires for all his children to clearly hear and realize, "But you are a chosen people, a royal priesthood, a holy nation, a people belonging to God, that you may declare the praises of him who called you out of darkness into his merciful light. Once you were not a people but now you are the people of God; once you had not received mercy, but now you have received mercy" (I Peter 2:9-10 NIV).

It was too easy within Simpson's nationalistic paradigm to trade the word mercy for the word merit. America was working its way into God's favor by ingenuity, initiative, technological prowess, and building more church structures per capita than any other nation. But what Simpson forgot and perhaps all of us forget, it is even more difficult to impress God spiritually than technologically. All human endeavors come across as quite pathetic at the foot of the cross. Simpson's triumphalism resonated with his audience because all self-righteous patriots routinely legitimatize their own sentiments as pious and those of the enemy as diabolical. Ronald Reagan a century later would do the same. The divine-evil dualism consisted of what Harry Stout calls, "a millennial nationalism as the primal religious

---

primitive period of culture, when every tribe remembers its own story without reference to any other story or tribal destiny. Since the beginning of ancient civilizations history is interpreted, not pluralistically, but in terms of false conceptions of universal history. The culture which elaborates the scheme of meaning makes its own destiny into the false center of the total human destiny." Charles Sanford. T*he Quest for Paradise: Europe and the American Moral Imagination* (Urbana, IL: University of Chicago, Press, 1961). Ernest Tuveson. *Redeemer Nation* (Chicago: University of Chicago Press, 1968) viii. Quoted in E. Digby Baltzell. *The Protestant Establishment: Aristocracy and Cast in America* (New Haven: Yale University Press, 1964) 88. Reinhold Niebuhr. *Faith and History: A Comparison of Christian and Modern Views of History* (New York: Charles Scribner's Sons, 1949) 114-115.

faith."[980] The Civil War was a religious war. Charles Dana once received the following battle report from a *Tribune* reporter in the early days of the war: "To God Almighty be the glory! Mine eyes have seen the work of the Lord and the cause of the righteous hath triumphed." Wrote Dana in reply: "Hereafter, in sending your reports, please specify the number of the hymn and save telegraph expenses."[981]

Ironically, among the few who did not adopt an ethnocentric theology was the politician, Abraham Lincoln. Somehow Lincoln's "doctrine of necessity" did not dissipate to the point of nationalistic idolatry as did Simpson's reliance on "providence." The Calvinism of Lincoln's childhood never lost its grip, not allowing him to be naive and sentimental regarding the motives that activate the affairs of humanity. Civil War victories, and there were never enough to the bitter end, did not allow the President to bask in halcyon sanguinity, that God was gloating over the triumph of the North. Lincoln fully held that divine favor played little part in triumph when industrial complexes were pitted against cotton plantations. On almost every occasion that Lincoln spoke and in every conversation of which we have record, the President was careful to not equate God's wisdom with the desires of American nationalism. To a preacher who had declared the Lord is on our side, Lincoln responded, "The Lord is always on the side of right, but it is my constant anxiety and prayer that I and this nation should be on the Lord's side."[982]

Simpson's God allowed humanity to control its own affairs more than did Lincoln's God. For Simpson, man needs only to cooperate with Providence and all things will work out in humanity's favor as individuals interpret favor from their vantage point. In Simpson's synergism, God's plans were as conditioned by the actions and attitudes of humanity as much as human plans are conditioned by God's sovereign will. Lincoln in his use of the words "almost" and "probably," was more tentative than Simpson in

---

980 Harry Stout, *Upon the Altar*, 405.

981 Robert C. Williams. *Horace Greeley: Champion of American Freedom* (New York: New York University Press, 2006) 224.

982 George C. Rable. *God's Almost Chosen People: A Religious History of the American Civil War* (Chapel Hill: The University of North Carolina Press, 2010) 187. The word "almost" which Lincoln used in the State House in Trenton, New Jersey, separated Lincoln from most American Protestants. Never did the word almost represent such a wide gap.

assessing the power of human volition to determine a particular outcome. Lincoln lived within the tension between nineteenth century romantic evangelicalism and the fatalism of Lord Byron, Shakespeare, and other poets, persons with whom Simpson had little acquaintance. Simpson was closer to the humanism and rationalism of the Enlightenment than was Lincoln. Stewart Winger concludes, "Despite his bouts of skepticism and his consequent Romantic reformulation, he (Lincoln) cast his lot in some degree with Reformed Doctrine and in particular with the Old School emphasis on predestination. The decision put Lincoln in conflict with Methodism and with the emergent 'New School' that made Arminian concessions to the Enlightenment belief that mankind was indeed free to shape its destiny if only it resolved to do so."[983] Or to put it another way, Lincoln was willing to dwell in the no man's land of paradox, a domain in which Jesus often trod, but American evangelicals have rarely frequented. Elton Trueblood wrote,

> Always, in Lincoln's matured theology, there is mature paradox. There is sternness, yet there is also tenderness; there is melancholy, yet there is also humor; there is moral law, yet there is also compassion. History is the scene of the working out of God's justice, which we can never escape, but it is also the scene of the revelation of the everlasting mercy. Lincoln knew that, if we stress only the mercy, we become sentimentalists, while, if we stress only the justice, we are driven to despair. The secret of rationality is the maintenance of the tension. The greatest possible mistake is the fatuous supposition that we have resolved it.[984]

How could Lincoln's theology have been so transcendent and Simpson's so ethnocentric? Did Lincoln's lack of church attendance enable him to listen to God more than to preachers?[985] The weekend retreats to the "old

---

983   Stewart Winger. *Lincoln, Religion, and Romantic Cultural Politics* (DeKalb, Illinois: Northern Illinois University Press, 2003) 181–182.

984   Elton Trueblood. *Abraham Lincoln: Theologian of American Anguish* (New York: Harper & Row Publishers, 1953) 124. Noah Brooks observed Lincoln at the New York Avenue Presbyterian Church, "His eyes were almost deathly in their gloomy depths, and on his visage was an air of profound sadness. His face was colorless and drawn and newly-grown whiskers added to the agedness of his appearance." Brooks, 9.

985   It is difficult to assess just how much Lincoln attended church. If he spent most weekends at the "Old Soldier's Home" and the Blair estate at Silver Spring, his church attendance was quite sporadic. When Lincoln did attend church, he went to the New York Avenue Presbyterian Church pastored by Phineas P. Gurley, as a result of asking if there was a church, "whose clergyman holds himself aloof from politics?" Burlingame, 256. When Lincoln was asked what he thought of Gurley, he responded, "I like Gurley. The

soldiers' home" may have born him through the war more than anything else. To those who were constantly attempting to inform him of the mind of God, he responded, "I hope it will not be irreverent for me to say that if it is probable that God reveals his will to others, on a point so connected with my duty, it might be supposed he would reveal it directly to me, for unless I'm more deceived in myself than I often am, it is my earnest desire to know the will of providence in this matter and if I can learn what it is I will do it. These are not however the days of miracles, and I suppose it will be granted that I am not to expect a direct revelation."[986] Lincoln's suspicion of the human liability to self-deception, the propensity for all of us to bend life to our own perceptions and desires was unnatural for any political leader, both then and now.

A Theological Miscue

From a theological perspective, the waving of the American flag became more problematic than salvific. No doubt, many of Simpson's auditors placed the flag over the cross rather than "just under it." Placing the flag within proximity of the cross may have been Simpson's single worst theological miscue. The flag represented military power, imperialism, and 'Captain America,'[987] a cult figure at odds with the lowly Jesus entering Jerusalem on the foal of a donkey. To plant the kingdom of God in both America and the

---

Doctor is a good man. He reminds me of a bank bill in a case I tried in Illinois, where a man had passed a counterfeit. His defense was that it looked to be sound. The Judge asked him if he had showed it to anybody to test it. 'Yes,' he said. 'I showed it to our merchant Jones.' What did Jones say? He said it was a pretty fair, tolerable sort of bill." Barbee, 24.

986   Rable, 194.

987   As Robert Jewett and John Lawrence have shown, Captain America resided in both the South and the North. "With mutually exclusive forms of zealous nationalism pitted against each other, and the expectations of world redemption with the destruction of the other side, the stage was set for a way whose ferocity and duration challenged the illusions of both sides. The biblical expectation that the enemy would be cowardly was belied by those dreadful and 'indecisive contests where overwhelming victory was impossible because neither side would run as they ought when beaten,' in the words of Oliver Wendell Holmes, Jr. It was a tragic cycle of destruction, with every prospect of increasing in brutality and injustice no matter which crusading army won the battle. Nothing short of the enemy's bloody annihilation could promise to appease the voracious appetite of such zeal." Robert Jewett and John S. Lawrence. *Captain America and the Crusade against Evil: The Dilemma of Zealous Nationalism* (Grand Rapids: William B. Eerdmans Publishing Company, 2003) 64.

hindermost parts of the world was thoroughly Wesleyan. Simpson was clear as to the objective, but muddled about the means.

The War Speech lasted more than two hours, but the stenographers were only able to record less than half.[988] Much of the meat on the skeleton has decomposed, but we do have the preserved bones. Simpson's outlined four possible outcomes of the Civil War. A) America would become so emaciated that it would be taken over by another nation. B) The War would forever split the union leaving two nations. C) The North and South would reunite but with "Southern institutions and Southern ideas established." He was correct in concluding that there were ideas and institutions other than slavery at stake. But there was a conflict between his cultural arrogance and cultural empathy and, thus, Simpson declined as far as we know to name the other institutions.[989] Simpson's fourth outcome prophesied the triumph of the North. D) "The Fourth and last possible issue is that our nation having passed through the fiery ordeal, may come out of it purer, stronger, and more glorious than ever before."[990] Of course, Simpson was betting his money on the fourth option.

The second constant of the speech beyond the four point outline, was an emotionally-charged conclusion, accented by the waving of an American flag. As Crooks described, "Its peroration was usually an apostrophe to the old flag, which, with consummate art he grasped in his hand and held to

---

[988] The two longest versions that we possess are the *New York Tribune's* version at 3,400 words, and the Clarence True Wilson version, around 3,800 words. An audible reading of the Wilson version takes approximately forty-five minutes.

[989] Edward Pollard, a confirmed Southerner from Virginia, distinguished what he thought were the clear differences between Northern and Southern institutions, "But the intolerance of the Puritans, the painful thrift of the Northern colonists, their external forms of piety, their jaundiced legislation, their convenient morals, their lack of the sentimentalism, which makes up the half of modern civilization, and their unrelenting hunt after selfish aggrandizement, are traits of character which are yet visible in their descendants. On the other hand, the colonists of Virginia and the Carolinas were from the first distinguished for their polite manners, their fine sentiments, their attachment to a sort of feudal life, their landed gentry, their love of field sports, and dangerous adventure, and improvident aristocracy that dispensed its stores and constant rounds of hospitality and gaiety." Edward Pollard. *The Lost Cause: A New Southern History of the War of the Confederates* (New York: E. B. Treat and Company, 1867) 50.

[990] Crooks, 380.

380 | "God Cannot Do Without America"

view."[991] Pulitzer prize-winning historian T. J. Stiles captures the significance of the flag to a Civil War military unit:

> For both sides in the Civil War, the regimental flag held enormous practical and symbolic significance. The regiment was the army's basic military unit; its flag oriented the men, signaled the advance or retreat, and provided a rallying point in moments of disorder. Soldiers came to see deeper meaning in it. They believed the flag was the soul of the regiment.[992]

Simpson waved a flag that had served as the standard in an actual battle and if possible, a battle that was geographically or regionally relevant to his audience. Thus, the New York speech ended with the following:

> Your Fifty-fifth Regiment carried this flag (taking up a war-worn, shot-riddled flag, which was greeted with tremendous cheers); it has been at Newbern, and at South Mountain, and at Antietam. The blood of our brave boys is upon it; the bullets of rebels have gone through and through it; yet it is the same old flag. (Most enthusiastic applause, the audience rising and giving three rousing cheers.) Our fathers followed that flag; we expect that our children and our children's children will follow it; there is nothing on earth like that old flag for beauty. (Long and loud cheering). Long may those stars shine! Just now there are clouds upon it and mists gathering around it, but the stars are coming out, and others are joining them. And they grow brighter and brighter, and so may they shine till the last star in the heavens shall fall! (Great cheering and waving of handkerchiefs and hurrahing).[993]

No Pen Can Adequately Describe the Speech

Several elements of Simpson's "War Speech" should not be disparaged: first, the ability to galvanize a people into the hope and determination that the freedoms afforded by democracy would not be relinquished. Simpson's oratorical performance served as the preeminent proclamation during the

---

991   Ibid., 378.
992   T. J. Stiles. *Custer's Trials: A Life on the Frontier of a New America* (New York: Alfred A. Knopf, 2015) 196.
993   Crooks, 382. Simpson made a mistake as to the regiment, and E. F. Shepard, a Wall Street attorney, corrected him, "The oration closes with a reference to the American flag; and on that occasion, the flag used was the battle flag of the Shepard Rifles, 51st regt. New York Vols., which had its name and some of the battles it, had been in, inscribed upon it. The battles were Roanoke, Newbern, Chantilly, South Mountain, Antietam and Fredericksburg."

Civil War that inspired sacrifice and courage within and by the Northern populace. As sure as Grant's "unconditional surrender" felled Vicksburg and conquered Lee at Appomattox, Simpson's oratory allowed no other alternative, than victory for the North. Second, was the reiteration and reminder that God was in control, and His will would be accomplished however skewed Simpson's interpretation of God's will may have been. The Civil War was a dark time for both the North and South and Simpson, more than any other spokesman, provided light, a pointing of the way, a lifting of the burden for the North. As eloquent as Southern oratory may have been,[994] it is unlikely that the South had anyone of Simpson's equal to arouse a crowd into a fervent pitch, a performance that he repeated with remarkable stamina. If the description in Chillicothe, Ohio, is representative of the War Speech, one cannot question Simpson's ability to enable individuals to believe in God, themselves, and their nation.

> It is said that Bishop Simpson's speech on "The State of the Country," delivered in Walnut Street Church, Chillicothe, at the reunion of the Ohio and Cincinnati Conferences, was one of the greatest of his life, and certainly the surrounding circumstances did much to give it interest. The war was raging; the whole country was in a white heat of excitement. Two large conferences and many citizens were before him. Many of them had near relatives in the army, or in prison or hospital. No pen can adequately describe the speech; no person present can ever forget it. If some Daguerre could have taken the likenesses of the audience showing their attitude, faces, hands, and feet, it would have been a very ludicrous picture, for such was the power of the bishop's logic and eloquence that his hearers seemed to be wholly unconscious of themselves. Ladies threw away their fans and handkerchiefs; men threw their hats in the air, stood erect, and mounted the seats, and stretched out their necks and their hands. When the bishop closed, it was as if

---

994 To be sure, there were flaming Southern orators to stir up Southern patriotism. Mary Chesnut recorded, "Captain Ogden came to dinner on Sunday and in the afternoon asked me to go with him to the Presbyterian Church and hear Mr. Palmer. We went, and I felt very youthful, as the country people say; like a girl and her beau. Ogden took me into a pew and my husband sat afar off. What a sermon! The preacher stirred my blood. My very flesh crept and tingled. A red-hot glow of patriotism passed through me. Such a sermon must strengthen the hearts and the hands of many people. There was more exhortation to fight and die, a la Joshua, than meek Christianity." Mary Chesnut. *A Diary from Dixie: The Civil War's Most Celebrated Journal*, written 1860–1865 by the wife of James Chesnut, Jr., an aide to President Jefferson Davis and a Brigadier General in the Confederate Army. A facsimile of the 1905 edition is edited by Isabella D. Martin and Myrta Lockett Avary (New York: Portland House, 1997) 333-334.

> a great storm at sea had suddenly ceased, but leaving the billows still in commotion-requiring some time for them to settle down to quiet.[995]

Persons are more emotionally vulnerable in times of disequilibrium than in the stasis of equilibrium, and though Gettysburg and Vicksburg seemingly turned the tide, Lee and the South had a way of resurrecting themselves. The Music Hall speech five days before the Presidential election came upon the heels of Cedar Creek, Virginia, October 2, and Hatcher's Run, Southside Railroad, Virginia, October 19, both of them Southern victories. In each of these battles twice as many Northerners as Southerners were killed.[996] The thousands who crammed into the Music Hall were already emotionally wired, and Simpson like any effective communicator, knew where and when to turn on the power switch. He articulated their thoughts, spoke their language, and connected with their deepest longings, giving them hope in the face of their most anguished fears. Without the mediums of cinema, television, and dozens of other communication forms available to us today, preaching served as the dominant art form in which a person could be placed in America's most epic crisis and perceive themselves as individuals of destiny, instruments of God in an apocalyptic showdown, where good would triumph over evil. And most critically, Simpson assured his listeners they were on the side of good.

As opposed to most of Simpson's listeners, Lincoln attended plays, an art form not accessible to the common person living in rural America. The sermon and the stage drama served some of the same purposes, among them the defining, venting, and releasing of emotions. More than any other spokesman, Simpson possessed the undefinable and mysterious

---

995   UMA, Drew University, Crooks papers, "Something Additional," Unidentified newspaper.

996   Mark Hughes. *The New Civil War Handbook* (New York: Savas Beatie, 2012) 105. The North was still smarting from one of the most stupendous blunders ever made in military history, the "Battle of the Crater," July 30, 1864, just outside of Petersburg, Virginia. Union troops dug a mine shaft beneath a Southern battalion, and attempted to obliterate the Southern soldiers with a dynamite blast. The end result was that the Northern troops in charging what they thought to be an incinerated and incapacitated Southern army, managed to shove and knock one another into the "crater," losing 4,500 men. See Richard Slotkin. *No Quarter: The Battle of the Crater, 1864* (New York: Random House, 2009).

orator's intuition, the ability to formulate words and ideas that found receptivity by the cultural zeitgeist. It was the art of arts.[997]

The Cosmic Affirmation

To Northerners, Simpson offered God's smile, a cosmic affirmation consisting of divine intervention and interpretation. Simpson's explicit belief in Providence could see the hand of God at work, and in turn offer coherence to a nation in chaos, torn apart because the sinful South was rebelling. The Union, in Simpson's understanding, had been perpetually set in motion by a God who needed a nation to do his bidding. The God of Simpson's piety, whose most profound revelation was the "warm heart," was immanent and thus understandable. Lincoln's God was far more inscrutable. In defense of Simpson, he offered no smug satisfaction that erased the need for humility and repentance. But he did offer assurance beyond the God that said to Isaiah, "For my thoughts are not your thoughts, neither are your ways my ways." Isaiah 55:8 (NIV) In spite of being subjectively skewed, Simpson wore the prophet's mantle, and in Abraham Heschel's words,

> Authentic utterance derives from a moment of identification of a person and a word; its significance depends upon the urgency and magnitude of its theme. The prophet's theme is, first of all, the very life of a whole people, and his identification lasts more than a moment. He is one not only with what he says; he is involved with his people in what his words foreshadow. This is the secret of the prophet's style: his life and soul are at stake in what he says and in what is going to happen to what he says. It is an involvement that echoes on. What is more, both theme and identification are seen in three dimensions. Not only the prophet and the people, but God Himself is involved in what the words convey.[998]

In a sense, "God could not do without America" was little more than a tautology; God could not do without what was in his omniscience, which he

---

997 With exaggeration, but nonetheless artistic insight, Pat Conroy said of Margaret Mitchell's *Gone with the Wind*, "It involves all the eerie mysteries of enchantment itself, the strange untouchable wizardry that occurs when a story, in all its fragile eloquence, speaks to the times in a clear original voice, and answers some strange hungers and demands of the Zeitgeists." Margaret Mitchell. *Gone With the Wind* (New York: Pocket Books, 2008) xvii.
998 Abraham Heschel. *The Prophets* (New York: Harper & Row, 1962) 6. I know that I have already said that Simpson was not a prophet. He was not a prophet of repentance and revolution, but he was a prophet of hope, at times, unrealistically so.

saw fit to do. In other words, what was in God's wisdom, that is, his perfect perception, became a necessity. But to say that "God cannot do without America" is a different statement than "God could not do without America." The latter interprets the past, which postulates that God could or would not do other than that which He perceived as fit and wise to do. The former statement "cannot," dealing with the present and future, suggests that God paints himself into a corner, or a particular nation is able to paint Him into a corner. The former claims that America's plan coincides with God's plan, which places America and its form of government within God's favor and design, regardless of the nation's character. If the Apostle Paul was correct, that mercy can be given or withdrawn at any time, which God's wisdom deems appropriate, then there is no ongoing obligation of God to a particular people. If such an obligation is postulated, then Simpson's claim resembles the wild assertion of Francis Weyland in 1825: "What nation will be second in the new order of things is yet to be decided but if true to ourselves, we shall be inevitably first."[999] Wayland's "true to us" was an infinite drift from the Puritan covenant with God and with one another. Simpson's theological compass was as faulty as Weyland's.

Whether Simpson said "God could not do without America" or "God cannot do without America" we will never know.[1000] The difference was more than semantic distinctions nuanced by a verb tense. Theologically, "could not do" is more acceptable than "cannot." God's desires become God's needs, because God cannot desire other than what is right, just and proper, and thus, God's desire to use America was a need that issued out of his wisdom, the perfect perspective on human affairs. But to say that God cannot do without America comes perilously close to touting that America had won divine favor via hard work, innovation, ingenuity, and religious decorum, as opposed to a humble and contrite heart. For Simpson, Bushnell, Weyland, and many others, there was an inherent good in America that obligated God to elevate America to the most prominent status among nations on earth. God had irrevocably obligated himself to America, an obligation which replaced the covenant forfeited by Israel. God had moved on to a more worthy recipient of his sovereign grace. America's divine status was as sure

---

999 Mead, 151.
1000 Only the *New York Times* recorded "could not". *The New York Tribune*, Wilson, Clark, Kirby, and Crooks have "cannot."

as the unchanging eternal nature of God. The spreading of Americanism as much as the spreading of Christianity was the answer to the world's problems. Of the American flag, Simpson wrote:

> But those stars are loved not only by us. The world loves them. The day is coming when the matrons of liberty shall hide this flag, as the loyal mothers of the South hid it; and the mothers of Europe will teach their boys the name of Washington, and learn them to love our flag, till it shall be respected and honored to earth's remotest bounds.[1001]

Democracy lends itself to national narcissism and exceptionalism because the voice of the people is the voice of God. The liability of democracy is rarely do the test of truth and acceptance of the majority coincide. The very fact that Christianity in America is the religion of the majority may be the first clue that the "narrow way" as defined by Christ has been perverted. In Geiko Muller-Fahrenholz's observation, "America becomes a God-like reality with the attributes of divine salvation, redemption powers, and, if need be, relentless punishment."[1002] This "divine dimension" was the national apotheosis that Simpson proclaimed, an operative myth ruling the American Church both then and now.

At no point did Simpson hint that America could be lackadaisical, and take God's divine favor for granted. God's smile would become a frown, if America did not continue to give, sacrifice, and, above all, evangelize the heathen. "Devastation shall spread its full waste through our land unless we as Christians learn to do our duty in the name of the Lord. I tell you Christians to learn to do our duty in the name of the Lord."[1003] In Simpson's thinking, it was a given that America would continue to uphold its side of the bargain; forfeiture was not a possibility, much less a probability. James Kirby rightly accuses Simpson's nationalism of evolving into a romantic utopianism as evidenced by his unequivocal proclamation that America was a nation that has in itself the power to elevate its own citizens, and

---

1001   Matthew Simpson, "The Old Flag," *Zion's Herald & Wesleyan Journal* Vol. XXXV, Boston (May 11, 1864) 74.

1002   Geiko Muller-Fahrenholz. *America's Battle for God: A European Christian Looks at Civil Religion* (Grand Rapids: William B. Eerdmans Publishing Company, 2007) 152.

1003   James Kirby, "Matthew Simpson and the Mission of America," *Church History* Vol. XXXVI No. 3 (September 1967) 306. Quoting from Matthew Simpson, "The Empire of Christ," *The Methodist* (September 26, 1863).

to positively influence the surrounding world. Simpson proclaimed, "It is certainly not in God's plan that we should pass away. Then how could the world do without us? The people of all nations look to us. If our country goes down, one-half of the world would raise a wail of woe, and sink lower. God cannot afford to lose the United States."[1004]

As delusional as the myth of America becoming forever God's favorite may have been, Simpson's Protestant nationalism did not diminish his ability to fortify the bastion of America, the ultimate hope of millions of Americans who had fled the crumbling economic and political structures of Europe.[1005] That the myth would later unravel by the greed of capitalism pitted against labor, the rich against the poor and American imperialism against Philippine impotence, made little difference to the steadfastness that Simpson was able to offer a country negotiating the paramount crisis of its existence. More than any other single person, Simpson mined and minted the collective unconscious of the Northern populace and left it firmly convinced that the Union cause would triumph.[1006]

1004   Ibid., 305.

1005   In 1865, theologian Charles Hodge wrote, "The other consequence of the war … has been the sentiment of nationality …. No one can doubt that the sentiment is stronger and more general now than it ever was before." Quoted in Guelzo, *Redeemer President*, 458.

1006   Simpson enabled Northerners to believe they were in rational control of their circumstances. He encouraged them to forge ahead in spite of military setbacks. He provided psychic energy of which Edward Whitmont wrote, "This activity of consciousness–the establishment of control in the world of things through conceptualization, rational thought, and the development of discipline, and the abstractive repression of emotions–is an utterly vital and indispensable phase of psychic development. It leads from psychic primitive infancy to adulthood." Edward C. Whitmont. *The Symbolic Quest: Basic Concepts of Analytical Psychology* (Princeton: Princeton University Press, 1969) 28.

Chapter Thirteen: Hero, Martyr, Friend, Fairwell!

A Deserved Rebuke

Inspirational speech which rallies the troops or champions a cause, cannot afford to be blunted and tamed by details and dialectics. Thus, Simpson primarily concerned himself and the cheering crowds with climbing the mountain rather than strategizing for what awaited them on the other side. The New York speech suggested that the blacks would be shipped back to Africa, but also managed to proclaim one of the most wrong-headed ideas Simpson ever formulated. If the former slaves were colonized in Texas, Louisiana, and southern Arkansas, they would form a shield between the United States and the Mexican dictator, Maximillian. Colonel C. C. Leigh, secretary of the National Freedmen's Relief Association pounced on Simpson with a scathing 1,000 word rebuke: "You did not mean to throw contempt upon a whole people whom God in his wisdom and goodness has made just as they are and just as it pleased him to create them. I know you would not do so cruel and so wicked an act, and yet this will be the exposition that thousands will give of the text."[1007]

Leigh's condemnation clues us as to how far Simpson was removed from radical Emancipation, the kind espoused by Bishop Gilbert Haven, elected to the Episcopacy in 1872. Haven was ten years Simpson's junior, but preceded him in death by four years. Haven argued radical egalitarianism, even to

---

1007   LOC, Simpson papers, Letter, C.C. Leigh to Simpson, November 7, 1864, Container seven.

the point of miscegenation, the amalgamation of the races. In response to Simpson's relegation of the black man to an inferior status, Haven wrote on January 26, 1865, "But we can't expect a Philadelphian, where a captain in the United State Navy is ejected from the cars because of his complexion, to rise to the heights of Boston radicalism in a moment. When he does get his eyes and lips open, with what eloquence, will the great doctrine of human and Christian brotherhood find utterance? The Lord hasten that blessed day!"[1008] We are not confident that the "blessed day" ever arrived. Simpson, in a lame reply to the charge of caste within the Methodist Church, disclaimed "distinction as to color recognized in the Discipline" and "for any official whatever in the Church."[1009] The fact that Simpson worked his way back into the good graces of the South was partial evidence that he would hold the black man at arm's length for the rest of his life. The Knoxville Presiding Elder, John Spence, wrote Simpson, "Our people know you and love you but they repudiate Haven. We are sorry he is to be sent to the Southern work."[1010]

What influence Leigh's letter had on Simpson is difficult to assess. But for sure, Simpson did not do an about face. On December 19, 1865, Simpson was chosen president of the Freedman's Union Commission, an organization which resulted from combining the American Freedman's Aid Commission and the America Union Commission. After six months Simpson begged off, with the rationale that he had too much on his plate, but more likely his resignation was instigated by the Northern Church founding its own relief organization, The Methodist's Freedmen's Aid Society. Within a year the Society had founded fifty-nine schools and had hired fifty-two teachers. Both the students and the surroundings in which they were taught were destitute of the trappings normally associated with formal education. One teacher claimed that his school had "no plaster, paper, or ceilings" and another reported that her students were on "the most friendly relations with pigs that … are visible through the floor … come up and get their long noses in the school water pail."[1011]

1008 William B. Gravely. *Gilbert Haven: Methodist Abolitionist–A Study in Race, Religion, and Reform, 1850–1880* (Nashville: Abingdon Press, 1973) 139–140.

1009 Ibid., 147.

1010 LOC, Simpson papers, Letter, John Spence to Matthew Simpson, September 3, 1872, Container nine.

1011 Walter W. Benjamin, "The Methodist Episcopal Church in the Postwar Era," in

Amazingly, the quadrennial report of the Bishops at their General Conference of 1864 made no mention of slavery. Instead, the Bishops commended themselves for their loyalty to the Northern cause. "Taking her stand on the sure teachings of the New Testament and on our Twenty-third Article of religion with its appended note as the true platform of Christian loyalty, and entirely ignoring all partisan political platforms, she (Methodist Episcopal Church) has given to the federal government her most decided support."[1012] The claim that Methodists had ignored "all partisan political platforms" was the height of ecclesiastical denial. The Committee on Slavery recommended the "extirpation" of slavery by "uprooting it and forbidding it forever." A resolution forbidding slave holding, buying or selling of slaves passed by a vote of 207 to 9, and was sent to the Annual Conferences for passage.[1013] Finally, the Methodist Episcopal Church in America had decided that slavery was a mortal sin, and the holding of slaves carried the threat of excommunication from the Church for both clergy and laity. Sadly, secular government had provided moral leadership for a supposedly sacred community.

The Second Inauguration's Official Preacher

In April, 1864, Matthew Simpson received an invitation to preach in the U. S. House of Representatives, signed by nine Congressmen including Schuyler Colfax and Harry Lane.[1014] House Chaplain William Henry Channing added his endorsement, "Allow me as Chaplain of the House of Representatives, to unite most cordially and earnestly in the invitation extended to you in the above letter." Simpson was not able to fulfill the invitation until he "happened" to be in Washington for Lincoln's Second Inauguration, one of the most momentous weekends in the city of Washington's history. Simpson's sermon on Sunday morning would follow the greatest speech ever given on American soil. "Washington had never seen so many people as those who converged on the Capitol for Lincoln's Second Inauguration. Trains rolled and smoked over the double track of the

---

The History of American Methodism Vol. II, ed. Emory Bucke, 369-370.

1012   *Journal of the 1864 General Conference of the Methodist Episcopal Church* (New York: Carlton and Porter, 1864) 274.

1013   Ibid., 166-167.

1014   LOC, Simpson papers, Letter April no day, 1864, Container seven.

Baltimore and Ohio. Delegations from North and West streamed through the freshly decorated B & O Railroad."[1015] One visitor noted that, "The crowd was almost number-less," and another stood, "on the edge of a great surging ocean of humanity."[1016] An observer estimated that, "At least half of the multitude was colored people."[1017]

Simpson, who stood somewhere in the immense crowd on the afternoon of Saturday March 4, was aware that he had listened to theological profundity crafted in uncommon eloquence. Lincoln's seven-minute speech consisted of seven hundred twenty-three words, twenty-five sentences, and four paragraphs. Simpson's two hour performance on the next day stood the distinct possibility of Edward Everett's fate at Gettysburg, Lincoln's quality obliterating quantity. On Sunday morning, the House chamber was jam-packed with people. It was *the* Sunday morning worship service for the Inaugural visitors, members of Congress and other Washington dignitaries, accented by the presence of Lincoln himself. Simpson recorded the event, "Preached in Capitol House of Representatives to an immense throng–text: 'If I Be Lifted Up.'"[1018] After Lincoln's death Simpson reported to the New York Annual Conference, "The last time in the Hall of Representatives, Mr. Lincoln was there, and I tried to preach Christ, and Him crucified as well as I know, and I have reason to believe it was the last sermon he ever heard."[1019]

According to Thomas Pearne, the simplicity of the Gospel on that occasion was not as pure as Simpson remembered it:

> The inauguration day, Saturday, was dreary, cloudy, and drizzly. Just as Mr. Lincoln took the oath of office, the clouds parted, and sunshine flooded the scene. The next day the bishop preached in the House of Representatives to a most distinguished audience. Senators, congressmen, diplomats, secretaries, judges, generals, admirals, and many others, were present. Floors, galleries, aisles were crowded. In front of the speaker's desk sat Mr. Lincoln. A lady led the singing. Prayer was offered by Dr. Thomas, afterwards killed by the Modocs. The bishop's

---

1015   Ronald White, Jr. *Lincoln's Greatest Speech* (New York: Simon and Schuster, 2002) 24.
1016   Ibid., 30.
1017   Ibid., 32.
1018   LOC, Simpson papers, 1865 *Diary*, Container two.
1019   "The Annual Conferences, New York Conference, Fifth Day Monday April 24," *The Methodist* Vol. VI, No. 18 (May 6, 1865) 138.

text was, "If I be lifted up, will draw all men unto me." He spoke of the power of Christ to diminish war and promote peace, and then, as if recollecting himself, he referred to the Civil War then flagrant, as though it might be considered fatal to his argument, and he added: "I am not much of a believer in signs and omens; but when, yesterday, just as the old Administration expired and the new one began, the rifted clouds let God's sunshine flow, I could not but regard it as an augury of returning peace, and that the war would soon close, and the new Administration would be one of peace." Instantly, as if by electricity, the audience were stirred; they cheered earnestly; many rose to their feet; hats were thrown up; men embraced each other, and wept and shouted. Mr. Lincoln was vigorously rapping the floor with his cane, the big tears chasing each other down his bronzed face. It was a masterly triumph of human eloquence, set on fire by sympathy and Christian patriotism.[1020]

The Good Friday Assassination and Christian Nationalism

On April 16, 1865, American clergyman scrapped their prepared sermons and declared Lincoln a type of Christ, who had been slain on Good Friday, and had entered triumphantly into Richmond, even as Christ entered Jerusalem on Palm Sunday. "As Christ entered into Jerusalem, the city that above all others hated, rejected and would soon slay Him, wrote Methodist Gilbert Haven about Lincoln's Richmond visitation, so did his servant enter the city that above all others hated and rejected him and would soon be the real if not intentional cause of his death."[1021] Lincoln had redeemed America from the sin of slavery and corruption by his own blood and pronounced forgiveness to all offenders.[1022] By transforming Lincoln into a political redeemer, "the sermons of Black Easter became an exercise in the most cruel of ironies, since Lincoln did not believe in the possibility of redemption for himself. But rather than calling this failing to the attention of the Nation, the well-nigh unanimous rush of the clergy was not to criticize Lincoln but to baptize him posthumously."[1023]

1020 Thomas H. Pearne. *Sixty-one Years of Itinerant Christian Life in Church and State* (Cincinnati: Curtis and Jennings, 1898) 161. "Jottings from the Capital," *Hartford Daily Courant*, Hartford, Connecticut (March 8 1865).
1021 Guelzo, *Redeemer President*, 440.
1022 Ibid., 441.
1023 Ibid., 447.

Nationalism consists of a cathexis of ideas and devotions, characterized by both ethnocentric and geocentric pride. Nationalism comes into sharper focus if one particular person incarnates the ideals afforded the Nation. The greater the leader, the less the differentiation between the person and the nation. Lincoln was the man of the people, for the people, and by the people. If the soldiers at Gettysburg had given the last full measure of devotion, he had done the same. His "malice towards none and charity for all" had been sealed by his blood. The close of the Civil War and the death of Lincoln brought America, as defined by the North, to the most cohesive nationalism in its history. In the perspective of Northerners and even some Southerners, America had been put through the refiner's fire and had come through the fiery ordeal forged into the world's greatest nation. Lincoln and the Union government had acted upon the conviction that America would be something other than a Confederacy. The President, who has demanded more analysis, more reference, more reverence, and more hagiography than anyone in the history of our country, was not averse to comparing himself to the prophet Moses who would not live to see the Promised Land and Christ who suffered his agonies in the Garden of Gethsemane before the final triumph. For Americans, Lincoln exemplified what a nation and its leader ought to be at least in the eyes of its citizens. Nationalism necessitates, borrowing language from Mircea Eliade, the "very general human tendency, namely to hold up one's life history as a paradigm and turn an historical personage into an archetype."[1024]

Lincoln, the seer that never said "God told me so," was the ultimate patriot without being a fanatical ideologue. He embodied the rare quality of possessing sufficient certitude to chart a course and enough humility for persons to follow that course. Melinda Lawson describes the patriotism that Lincoln engendered and forged out of persons and states, who knew little about what it meant to be truly a nation. "The Union builders tapped into a repository of nineteenth century values, traditions, and ideals including notions of Christian charity, sacrifice and redemption, ideas of liberal self-interest, and republic virtue, local and partisan identities, free labor tenants, the longing for self and freedom, a profound faith in the founding fathers

---

1024   Donald Capps, "The Myth of Father Abraham: Psychosocial Influences in the Formation of Lincoln Biography" in *Encounter with Erikson*, eds. Donald Capps, Walter Capps, and M. Gerald Bradford (Missoula, Montana: Scholars Press, 1977) 253.

and a providential view of history. The transcendent nationalism that developed during the War was the product of the dialogue and at times the struggle between these disparate voices."[1025] No one proclaimed that "providential view of history" more eloquently, prominently, and persuasively than Matthew Simpson. Methodism's most popular leader had brought the Gospel of Christ and the gospel of America into unison. The agreement worked for all but the most discerning minds.

Simpson Chosen as the Preacher for the Springfield Memorial

Simpson was in Philadelphia when Lincoln was assassinated, and upon hearing the news, he and Ellen took the first available train to Washington, Saturday, April 15. On Sunday afternoon, the Bishop met with the widow and Edwin Stanton. On Monday, Simpson again met with Mary, and at this time, it was decided that Simpson would pray at the White House service, and preach the sermon at the Springfield funeral. "The ceremonies in the East Room were brief and simple. The Reverend Dr. Hall read the burial service. Bishop Simpson of the Methodist Church distinguished equally for his eloquence and patriotism offered a prayer and the Reverend P.D. Gurley in whose church the President habitually attended worship delivered a short address, commemorating in language notably free of courtly flattery, the qualities of courage, purity and sublime faith which had made the dead man great and useful."[1026]

After the Washington funeral, the Bishop chaired the New York Annual Conference. He then went to Evanston, and took a train from Chicago to Springfield on May 3, the evening before the funeral. The local newspaper reported that Simpson was, "Quite unwell, though we hope not so much so as to prevent the fulfillment of the object of his journey."[1027] Simpson stayed with Ninian Wirt Edwards, who married Elizabeth Todd, the eldest sister of Mary Lincoln, in 1862. Ninian was named after his father, who was the

---

1025 Melinda Lawson. *Patriot Fire: Forging a New American Nationalism in the Civil War North* (Lawrence: University Press of Kansas, 2002) 161.

1026 John G, Nicolay and John Hay. *Abraham Lincoln: A History UN* (New York: The Century, 1914) 317–318. Nicolay and Hay should have said that Hall, an Episcopalian, read from the *Book of Common Prayer*.

1027 *Daily Illinois State Journal*, Thursday morning (May 4, 1865).

first and only Territorial Governor of Illinois. The son lived in a large house on the south end of town. In this house, Abraham Lincoln married Mary Todd on November 4, 1842.

On Friday April 24, 1865, Lincoln's casket was placed in a railroad car for a 1,700 mile journey to Springfield, Illinois, its final resting place. Slowly the funeral train made its way first North, then West, stopping at major cities to allow for viewing of the body. In drenching rain and brilliant sunshine the multitudes turned out to honor the martyred President. Elaborate arches of evergreen stretched across the tracks. Bands played funeral dirges; choruses sang mournful hymns; ministers, priests, and rabbis delivered eulogies. In elaborate processionals horse drawn carriages carried the body past buildings draped in black to local state houses, city halls or court houses for display.[1028]

Lincoln's body lay in state in the Illinois Capitol building less than twenty-four hours, arriving at Springfield only the day before the funeral, May 3. Springfield inhabitants were given only the evening of May 3 and morning hours of May 4 to view the body of the man they had bequeathed to America four years earlier to lead the nation. There was a reason:

> The *New York Evening Post*, in its description of the appearance of President Lincoln's remains while lying in the coffin in the City Hall is but a sad reflection of him who so recently filled the Presidential Chair. Those who had thought that the embalmer's art would have preserved his features to us; almost unchanged, will be disappointed. Death will not be cheated of his dread ravages. The eyes of the dead President are sunken, his face is somewhat discolored, sallow about the lower part, dark around the eyes and cheeks; his lips are so tightly compressed that the mouth seems to be but a straight line. It is not the genial, kindly face of Abraham Lincoln; it is but a ghostly shadow.[1029]

The Lincoln Funeral

After the body was placed in a hearse at 10 a.m., Simpson climbed into a carriage. Seven divisions followed the hearse, and Simpson's carriage traveled in the third division which consisted of, "Marshalls, those officiating in the

---

1028   Lawson, 176.
1029   *The Daily Illinois State Journal*: Springfield (May 3, 1865).

funeral, guard of honor, relations and family friends."[1030] Even though the distance between the State House and Oak Ridge Cemetery was only two miles, the procession took over two hours and the actual service began at 1:00 o'clock. "From time to time along the country road, bands broke out with dirges and there were four newly composed 'Lincoln Funeral Marches,' and when the music was silent all that could be heard was the unbroken, ominous, muffled roll of the drums. As in all other cities it was the hypnotic, endless beat of wooden sticks against taut animal skin that conjured up such an unbearably repetitive sound-like the fevered pulsing inside oneself of one's own blood- beat- beat-beat it went on, never faster, never slower and rub-dubbed people's nerves raw."[1031]

Lincoln's body, along with that of his son Willie, was placed in a receiving vault. It had been used before, and would be used some dozen times afterward.[1032] Simpson spoke from a speaker's stand constructed for the occasion, with the temporary tomb to his left. Immediately behind him was a forty-five degree hill almost too steep to climb, but nonetheless, thronged with people, forming a natural sounding board from which Simpson's voice

---

1030   John C. Power. *Abraham Lincoln: His Great Funeral Cortege from Washington City to Springfield, Illinois with a History and Description of the National Lincoln Monument* (Springfield, Illinois: Illinois Journal Company, 1872) 115-121.

1031   Philip B. Kunhardt, Jr., and Dorothy M. Kunhardt. *Twenty Days: A Narrative in Text and Picture of the Assassination of A. Lincoln and the Twenty Days and Nights that followed-The Nation In Mourning, the Long Trip to Springfield.* (Secaucus, New Jersey: Castle Books, 1965) 284–287.

1032   Six months later, the bodies were removed to a temporary grave in Oak Ridge Cemetery, approximately fifty feet behind the initial receiving vault. "Construction began (for the Lincoln Memorial) in Oak Ridge Cemetery in September of 1869, and the stone and brick foundation before year's end. Work on the super structure continued for nearly two years. The obelisk, constructed of brick and steel with granite sheathing, was capped in May, 1871, just as the terrace and interior rooms were being completed. Tad Lincoln's remains were placed within the tomb following his death in July, 1871, and in September of that year, Lincoln's remains, and the remains of his sons, Willie and Eddie, were moved to the unfinished structure." Nancy Hill. "The Transformation of the Lincoln Tomb," *Journal of The Abraham Lincoln Association*, Vol. 27 Issue 1 (Winter 2006), 39-56. Mary Lincoln died on July 16, 1882, and was buried in the Lincoln Memorial with her husband and sons. Lincoln's body was moved twice within the tomb, the last time September 26, 1901. At that time, the casket was opened and the body of the president was identified by his son, Robert Lincoln. See Arthur L. Meriam, "Final Interment of President Abraham Lincoln's Remains at the Lincoln Monument in Oak Ridge Cemetery, Springfield, Illinois," *Illinois State Historical Society Journal* XXIII No. 1, (April 1930) 171-174. Robert Todd Lincoln died July 26, 1926, and is buried with his wife, Mary, in Arlington National Cemetery.

echoed. The ground immediately in front of the vault was flat, the attenders standing shoulder to shoulder. For May 4, the day was unusually hot, and many launched parasols above their heads: "The people stood on tip-toe, occasionally appearing over each other's shoulders. Each one determined if possible, to satisfy himself. There was no crushing or jarring, however–the most rigid order having been observed."[1033]

Those who expected to hear the deep, bass voice of an orator were disappointed. As Simpson passionately waded into the occasion, the how of speech was overcome by the what of speech, and his shrill harshness was forgotten. Someone noted that Simpson's clerical robes seemed to be, "Held together at the seams with big basting stitches. Possibly the Bishop's luggage had been misplaced, but it was obvious that some Springfield housewife had run up this voluminous makeshift garment in a few minutes time."[1034] This observation was strange in that Ellen accompanied her husband to Springfield, and assumed as one of her primary responsibilities in life making her husband presentable. But this was one of the few times Simpson wore a clerical robe, and the garment may have been borrowed.

Concerning the funeral, Simpson recorded two brief, illegible lines in his *Diary*. For the sermon, he utilized a 12-point outline written on two 8 ½ by 5 ¼ sheets of paper.

1. Early poverty and obscurity. His rise shows what may be accomplished.

2. His maternal influence.

3. The outlines of his education.

4. His early struggles and steps

5. His moral position

6. His political life. Ante-president

7. His presidential nomination

8. His presd. acts and life

1033 *Indianapolis Daily Journal* (May 5, 1865).
1034 Kunhardts, 298–301.

9. His death

10. Premonitions

11. His fame

12. Resume of character[1035]

Around 75,000 persons had poured into Springfield, then a town of 15,000 inhabitants.[1036] It was estimated that only one-tenth of them would have been able to find food and lodging. The *Keokuk Gate City*, a newspaper from Keokuk, Iowa, rendered the following melodramatic description:

> The oration of Bishop Simpson was touching, powerful and patriotic and he closed with the statement that vengeance under the existing circumstances must be executed on all the leaders of the rebellion, to which the vast crowd heartily responded by amens and clapping of hands. While the speaker was closing and many were thrilled with his eulogy on Mr. Lincoln, and tears copiously were flowing from most of all, God thundered in the heavens; clouds swiftly gathered and passed over us, and the skies sent forth tears which softly fell in a few drops upon the vault (where lay the sacred remains) and upon the multitude, as if to say the heavens are touched; then all passed off and became clear. Oh, how sublime the thought, when heaven and earth correspondingly weep on such an occasion.[1037]

1035 LOC, Simpson papers, "Lincoln Funeral Notes," Container nineteen. Most of the "points" had "sub-points" beneath them.

1036 "About 15,000 was the population in May 1865, though given the rate that people were moving into town that year, it could've been as high as 16,000. The accepted figure for those who were in town for the funeral on 3–4 May 1865 is about 75,000–which means an average of 1 second per person who walked by his coffin to view his remains in the capitol building. That was a typical average across the country. I mention this because we are fairly sure that the ratio of visitors: population was highest in Spfld of any city for a funeral." Email March 25, 2015, from James Cornelius, Ph.D., Curator, Lincoln Collection, Abraham Lincoln Presidential Library & Museum, Springfield, IL.

1037 Quoted in, *Four Days in May: Lincoln Returns to Springfield*. Compiled and edited by Caroline R. Heath (Springfield: Sangamon County Historical Society and the Illinois State Historical Society, 1965) 4.

The Eulogy

Simpson did justice to the occasion, but did not overdo it. He possessed sufficient wisdom in not attempting to be greater than the man who had led the Nation to its greatest triumph. He determined that no one would think that the eulogist was greater than the eulogized. But nonetheless he had to rise to the occasion. He was not unaware that this one oratorical opportunity would anchor him in history more than any other assignment ever given him. Simpson did not disappoint. For over an hour, graphic and cryptic sentences echoed from the hill behind the tomb. Simpson packed his speech with biblical images which included the funeral procession of Jacob and the death of Moses. "But never was there in the history of man such mourning as that which has accompanied this funeral procession and has gathered around the mortal remains of him who was our loved one, and who now sleeps among us."[1038] Lincoln's death had brought the Nation to a standstill, as no other event would or could have. Lincoln had guided America through its deepest valley, and "Just in the midst of this wildest joy, in one hour, nigh, in one moment the tidings thrilling throughout the land that Abraham Lincoln, the best of Presidents, had perished at the hands of an assassin. And all the feelings which had been gathering for four years in forms of excitement, grief, horror, and joy, turned as a wail of woe, sadness inexpressible, and anguish unutterable."[1039]

Simpson believed that Lincoln had been chosen by God for a particular time and task. God's choice was not regardless of unique abilities particularly needed for an unusual responsibility: "A quick and ready perception of facts; a memory unusually tenacious and retentive; and a logical turn of mind, followed sternly and unwearyingly every task in the chain of thought on every subject which he was called to investigate."[1040] Lincoln possessed unquestionable moral characteristics: honesty, individuality, self-reliance, bravery, and most importantly, the ability to impart courage. Lincoln's greatest act was to give

---

1038 "Funeral Address Delivered at the Burial of President Lincoln at Springfield, Illinois, May 4, 1865, by Rev. Matthew Simpson, D.D., one of the Bishops of the Methodist Episcopal Church," (New York: Carlton & Porter, 1865) 4.
1039 Ibid., 8.
1040 Ibid., 10–11.

"freedom to a race." Simpson spoke with both fairness and equanimity concerning Lincoln's religion, making it neither more nor less than it was.[1041]

> Abraham Lincoln was a good man. He was known as an honest, temperate, forgiving man; a just man; a man of noble heart in every way. As to his religious experience, I cannot speak definitely, because I was not privileged to know much of his private sentiments. My acquaintance with him did not give me the opportunity to hear him speak on those topics. This I know, however, he read the Bible frequently; loved it for its great truths and its profound teachings; and he tried to be guided by its precepts. He believed in Christ the Saviour of sinners; and I think he was sincere in trying to bring his life into harmony with the principles of revealed religion. Certainly if there ever was a man who illustrated the principles of pure religion, that man was our departed president. Look over all his speeches, listen to his utterances. He never spoke unkindly of any man. Even the rebels received no word of anger from him; and his last day illustrated in a remarkable manner his forgiving disposition.[1042]

With the riveting precision of a wordsmith, Simpson sealed and placed closure on the life of the single greatest figure in American history: "We crown thee as our martyr, and humanity enthrones thee as her triumphant son. Hero, martyr, friend, FAREWELL!"[1043]

A Glaring Contradiction

The oration was remarkable for two reasons, something that it did not do and something that it did. First, Simpson did not transfigure Lincoln into a type of Christ. He did not use the words savior, redeemer, and deliverer; at least they are not recorded. The one Christological allusion in the homily was the fact that Lincoln had died on Good Friday and the "loss of Easter itself could not fill or even mollify." In fact, concerning Christianity's triumphant doctrine of the resurrection, the ultimate hope of Christianity, Simpson quoted no classical biblical passages such as John 14 and I Corinthians 15. Simpson did not preach Lincoln into heaven.

1041 Ibid., 15.
1042 Ibid.
1043 Ibid., 21.

Second, towards the end of the eulogy Simpson made a false step, a glaring incongruence, a declaration in complete contrast to the man, to whom for the most part up until now, he had been faithful. After proclaiming the magnanimity of Lincoln's "malice towards none and charity towards all," Simpson inexplicably resolved for himself and the Northern citizenry to punish all leaders who had participated in the rebellion, especially U.S. Representatives and Senators. "Let every officer educated at the public expense, and who having been advanced to high position, perjured himself, and turned his sword against the vitals of his country, be doomed to a traitor's death. This, I believe, is the will of the American people."[1044] Except for "bloody shirt" wavers, vengeance on the South was not the will of the American people, and certainly not the sentiments of the man beside whose grave Simpson stood. He then quoted from Lincoln's "the mystic chords of memory stretching from every battlefield and patriot grave to everything–heart and hearthstone all over this broad land would yet swell the course of union which again touched as surely they will be by the better angels of our nature."[1045] Lincoln had prophesied that goodness, "the better angels of our nature," would triumph for both North and South and the "mystic chords of memory" would again become allegiance to the same flag, and this without retribution. Lincoln died with the firm conviction that the South had suffered enough and it was time for healing to begin. Somehow Simpson's radical optimism for the potential of human goodness escaped him at a moment when he should have proclaimed the forgiveness of Jesus Christ. In what is probably an apocryphal story, it was told that when someone in Tad's presence said Mary Lincoln could not forgive the South, the eleven-year-old son of Lincoln, whose father was now dead, spoke up saying, "Pa would forgive them. He forgave everybody."

As soon as Simpson said goodbye to the past President, he hurried back to Washington to welcome the next President. Two weeks later, Simpson led a delegation of Methodists to the White House. The Washington *Daily Chronicle* reported that:

> The President received them handsomely. Bishop Simpson then presented to him an address from the meeting, accompanied

---

1044　Ibid., 20.
1045　Ibid., 21.

with appropriate remarks, condoling the President on the loss which the nation had sustained, and assuring him of the hearty support of his own Administration by the loyal Methodist public of Philadelphia, consisting of upwards of fifty churches.[1046]

Ironically, the President then assured these ambassadors of peace that punishment of treason was proper, since it was a crime of the highest order. Simpson and his fellow Methodists were then convoyed around the Potomac in ambulances to glory in the victories of George Meade, who welcomed them. Accompanying Simpson were fellow Philadelphians James Long and James Neil, who had furnished the Bishop his home in Philadelphia two years earlier.

Simpson's Civil War Legacy

On April 4, 1864, Lincoln wrote Albert Hodges, "I claim not to have controlled events, but confess that events have controlled me."[1047] It was the most "eventful" time in our nation's history. The events had transformed ordinary men and women into extraordinary individuals. In no period in our nation's history were more persons exalted to the status of heroes and heroines, and granted laurels of messianic mythology, than during the Civil War. Anyone with an ounce of sentiment stands with reverential awe before the Lincoln Monument in Washington, DC, or the sarcophagus of Robert E. Lee at Washington and Lee University, Lexington, Virginia. And though the Civil War legacy of Matthew Simpson is laurelled with a much smaller wreath than the likes of Stonewall Jackson, Ulysses Grant, Clara Barton, and Julia Ward Howe, no clergyman was elevated to greater mythological status than Matthew Simpson. There was something in him and about him, no less than the other Civil War legends that enabled the events to find a ready and able participant uncommon to his particular vocation.

George Frederickson claims that during the Civil War, "The Protestant pulpit was the single most important source of northern patriotic exhortation. As spiritual leaders of a crusade for the Union, the clergy enhanced its professional status attaining a position of public respect that was probably

---

1046 "Visit of Clergymen to the President," Washington: *The Daily Chronicle* (May 19, 1865).

1047 David Herbert Donald. *Lincoln* (London: Jonathan Cape, 1995) In "Introduction."

greater than at any time in the history of the United States."[1048] It may be that the Civil War ensured Simpson's legacy, more than it did any other single clergyman. But the history recorded in Scripture reminds us that elevated status normally does not belong to "prophets." Resonance rather than rejection had transferred Simpson into perhaps the most revered preacher in America.

Simpson did not seek the path laid out for him during the Civil War. The Civil War had grabbed him, and placed him in a position of prominence, no less than it pulled Grant away from his father-in-law's tannery shop in Galena, Illinois. Both of them were instruments, seemingly for the good. But the greatness of their Civil War performance did not extend into the future. Popularity did not transform Grant into a capable President, and neither did the Civil War refine Simpson into the simplicity of a minister of the Gospel. Paradoxically, the Civil War both elevated and entangled the Bishop in the affairs of this life. Recovery for Simpson and the Methodist Episcopal Church would be as difficult as was "Reconstruction" for the South.

Though Simpson's Gospel may have been skewed for one half of a decade, it had not been placed under a bushel, and had not been extinguished, and, even at times, had shed its political encumbrances. In the summer of 1860, he stood before thousands at the Des Plaines Camp Meeting just outside of Chicago, "The mass of humanity stood practically motionless, the hundred or more ministers wept, and shouted for joy, and no one who heard that mighty sermon ever forgot the message or the speaker. It was a day for the giants ...."[1049] In September of 1863, Simpson preached at the Genesee Annual Conference of Batavia, New York, as he preached at all Annual Conferences over which he presided.

> The vast audience made up of all classes, from the most unlettered to the highest cultured, was carried in mass at the will of the people. The sermon was a series of climaxes rising one above the other .... We saw Him (Christ) in his last interview with his disciples as he

---

[1048] George Frederickson. "The Coming of the Lord: The Northern Protestant Clergy and the Civil War Crisis." *Religion and the American Civil War*, eds. Randall M. Miller et al (New York: Oxford University Press, 1998) 118.

[1049] John O. Foster. "Des Plaines Camp Meeting 1860," *Journal of the Illinois State Historical Society* Vol. XXIV (April 1931) 658.

pronounced his parting benediction .... the Savior lifted his mantle from his shoulders and reached it forth while seraphim and cherubim and archangels spring easy to grasp it, but he waved them away .... then turning to the Conference, his face aglow with the light he saw, his frame trembling with suppressed excitement, he described the mantle descending past the waiting throng, and exclaimed, *Brethren, it falls on us.* The effect was overwhelming. The outburst shook the whole audience.

The unknown author of this description recalled that Dr. Israel Chamberlain sat by her side. The man, noted for his "self-control, pure intellect, and calm temperament" responded by "convulsively grasping with both hands the plank on which he sat and shouted at the top of his voice."[1050]

The irony of great preaching in the mid-nineteenth century, was its ability to transcend time and place while, at the same time, reaching those who were defined by a particular time and place. No preacher made more use of a specific time and place, the era of the Civil War, than did Simpson. And yet, he was able to preach in such a manner that made people forget the circumstances in which they were entrapped, from which there was no escape but *up*. Simpson did not forget that his ultimate job was to let people know that they could live their lives *here* because there is another life *there*. For the skeptical and analytical person living in the twenty-first century, all of this sounds a bit magical or mystical, especially if one is not living in a "civil war" and waiting for news from the "front." Notwithstanding his nationalistic agenda, Simpson had not forgotten that the primary craft of his trade was to enable people to know that there is another world concerned about their world, and to bring those two worlds together.

1050   LOC, Simpson papers, three-page report, "Bishop Simpson Presided over the Genesee Annual Conference for the First Time in September, 1863 at Batavia, New York," Container seven. The writer was mistaken. Simpson had presided over the Genesee Annual Conference in 1853 and 1859.

Chapter Fourteen:
The Broken Arrow of Patronage

The Indian Problem in the West[1051]

In the 1851 Fort Laramie Treaty, the U.S. ceded to the Indians, mainly Cheyenne and Arapaho, a huge chunk of land, consisting of present day eastern Colorado, western Kansas, southeastern Wyoming, and southwestern Nebraska. And, why not? Daniel Webster stated in a speech to the U. S. Senate in 1838: "What do we want with the vast, worthless area, this region of savages, and wild beasts, of deserts, shifting sands and whirlwinds of dirt, of cactus, and prairie dogs. To what use could we ever hope to put these great deserts or these endless mountain ranges, impregnable and covered to their very base with eternal snow? What use have we for such a country?"[1052]

In spite of Webster's formidable cranium, he possessed no forte for clairvoyance. He did not foresee the impending war for mineral rights, gold mines, ranch land, and ultimately, railroad right-of-ways. As with many treaties, the U. S. attempted to retract the Fort Laramie agreement and locate the Indians in a dry, barren, forbidding southeast corner of Colorado land along a river gulley known as Sand Creek, a gulch barren of water, unless one dug a hole in its deepest points. On February 18, 1861, ten chiefs, including the Cheyenne's Black Kettle and White Antelope, met with Indian agent

---

1051 Portions of this chapter have been previously published as; "The Sand Creek Massacre: Matthew Simpson and the Broken Arrow of Patronage", *Methodist History* vol. 52:4 (July 2014) 207-230. Used by permission from the General Commission on Archives and History of the United Methodist Church.
1052 Quoted in Linda Kirby. *Heritage of Heroes: Trinity United Methodist Church 1859–1988* (Salt Lake City: Publishers Press, 1988) 5.

Albert Boone and Peace Commissioner F. B. Culver, to sign a treaty which would be highly controversial over the next five years. The controversy lay in "Article Six":

> The Arapaho and Cheyenne of the Upper Arkansas, parties to this Agreement, are anxious that all the members of their tribe shall participate in the advantages herein provided by respecting their improvements and civilization, and to that end, to induce all that are now separated to rejoin and reunite with them. It is therefore agreed that as soon as practicable, the Commissioner of Indian affairs shall cause the necessary proceedings to be adopted, to have them notified of this agreement and its advantages; and to induce them to come in and unite with their brethren, and to enable them to do so, and to sustain themselves for a reasonable time thereafter, such assistance shall be provided for them, at the expense of the tribe as maybe actually necessary for that purpose; *Provided however*, that those who did not rejoin and permanently unite themselves with the tribe within one year from the date of the ratification of this treaty, shall not be entitled to the benefit of any of its stipulations.[1053]

What did "rejoin and permanently unite" mean? How would this stipulation be enforced? Would there actually be a cut-off date, February 18, 1862? The Indians "touched the pen" to the treaty, which they did not understand, other than the vague perception that they had been further disadvantaged and displaced.

Immediately upon arriving in Denver, John Evans stood on the balcony of the Tremont House and to the crowd below emphasized the necessity of railroads for Colorado's growth. The prospect of railroads called for the immediate geographical marginalization of the Indians, an authority vested him by the Sixth Article of the Fort Wise Treaty. Not everyone saw it that way, in particular, William Dole, Commissioner of Indian Affairs in Washington, who wrote Evans recommending "moderation," and accused Evans of "moving too rapidly toward a policy of concentration"[1054] S. E. Brown, United States Attorney for Colorado, backed Dole, ruling that the most prosperous mining sites, and even the territorial capital at Golden City,

---

1053   Charles K. Kappler. Indian *Affairs: Laws and Treaties* Vol. II (Washington: Government Printing Office, 1904) 809-810.
1054   Gary Leland Roberts. "*Sand Creek: Tragedy and Symbol*," unpublished Ph.D. dissertation, University of Oklahoma, 1984, 303.

were off limits to the settlers. Brown even halted surveys for the proposed Sand Creek habitat, never officially called a "reservation."

As we have already seen, the Illinois Methodists began dreaming of a university and selected Evans to serve as the President of the Trustees of North Western University. After three years of much discussion and exploration, a 379 acre farm was purchased twelve miles north of Chicago on the shore of Lake Michigan for the sum of $25,000, which serves today as the site for Northwestern University and Garrett Evangelical School of Theology. Since his election to the Episcopacy, Matthew Simpson had lived in Pittsburgh, where the persistent soot and cold made almost any place else more inviting. As we have already explored, not only did Evans persuade Simpson to move to "Evanston" in 1859, but to accept the "nominal presidency" of Garrett Biblical Institute. The emphasis was on "nominal" rather than "president" and the faculty was soon complaining about the itinerant Bishop's absence and lack of leadership. Itinerancy did not equate to omnipresence.

Simpson and the Appointment of John Evans as Territorial Governor of Colorado

Once the Evanston schools were up and running, Evans needed a new challenge. He approached Samuel Elbert, a member of the Nebraska delegation to the 1860 Republican Convention in Chicago asking for a "territorial appointment," but received no reply. Early on, Abraham Lincoln discovered that he was in political debt to The Methodist Episcopal Church, which more than any single group, other than the Republican Party, had put him in office. The Territory of Washington was the first available political prize, but John Evans thought that to be too far from Chicago. Thus, on October 7, 1861, Lincoln wrote the following to General William Pickering: "You wish to be Governor of Washington. Last spring when I appointed Dr. Jayne, I was greatly pressed to appoint a man presented by the Methodist people through Bishop Simpson & others, and I then said, if I should appoint another Governor of a Territory from Illinois, it should be their man. I do not *know* that their man will accept that to Washington, but it must be offered to him, and if he declines it, you may have it. Your Obt. Servant, A Lincoln."[1055]

John Evans rejected the appointment, and Pickering's governorship of the Washington Territory was confirmed by the Senate on December 19, 1861. What kind of pressure Evans placed on Simpson to run interference for his political ambitions is unknown, but history has preserved two letters from Simpson to Abraham Lincoln on behalf of Evans. Simpson's simple, unadorned, and un-dated note to Lincoln read:

His Excellency A Lincoln President U.S.

Dear Sir:

It will be a matter of peculiar gratification if you, in your wisdom, see fit to appoint Dr. Evans to any of the Western Territories, either Nebraska or Colorado.

His apt would not only gratify me, but his many friends.

Your truly,

M. Simpson[1056]

Simpson did not exaggerate the "many friends." On December 28, 1860, a letter of recommendation was sent to Lincoln from Omaha City, signed by twenty members of the Nebraska House of Representatives, including Schuyler Colfax and Samuel Elbert.[1057] Robert Lumas, editor of the *Nebraska Advertiser*, made sure Lincoln knew that Evans was the choice of "nine-tenths of the Republican Party."[1058] John Evans followed up both

---

1055   Roy P. Basler. *The Collected Works of Abraham Lincoln* Vol. IV (New Brunswick, NJ: Rutgers University Press, 1959) 550.

1056   Simpson to Abraham Lincoln: Department of State, Applications and Recommendations for Office, 1861–69, National Archives. These letters are alphabetized in the order for whom they were written, not by whom the letters were written.

1057   Applications and Recommendations, December 28, 1860.

1058   Applications and Recommendations, January 31, 1861. Also see "Lincoln and the Territorial Patronage: The Ascendency of the Radicals in the West," by Vincent G. Tegeder. Tegeder concludes: "With favorable governors in every one of the territories, well-disposed secretaries, amenable judges, a speculator as customs collector in Washington Territory, and sharp surveyor generals, the radicals were prepared to reconstruct the West for their own benefit and the northern interest which they represented. The radicals could use their territorial allies to promote the supremacy of the Republican Party in the West, to create new

the Nebraska House and Lumas' letter with:

> To His Excellency Abraham Lincoln
>
> President of the USA
>
> Dear Sir:
>
> Please allow the recommendations filed in the department as Governor of Nebraska to be changed to that they may be considered as an application for the office of Governor of the Territory of Colorado and will be much obliged.
>
> Your obedient servant,
>
> John Evans[1059]

Remember that Simpson had personally met with Lincoln on March 8, 1861, on behalf of Evans. Again Simpson wrote Lincoln, this time stating some of Evans' qualifications: "By his business habits, his intellectual power, and his strict integrity, he is well fit for such a position."[1060] On March 15, 1861, Harry Lane sent a letter signed by, "Senators and Representatives from Indiana," recommending "Dr. John Evans of Evanston, Illinois, for appointment as Governor of Colorado Territory."[1061] On the same date, Senator James Harlan, wrote the terse request, "To the President, I must cheerfully recommend the appointment of Dr. John Evans of Evanston to the Office of Governor of the Colorado Territory."[1062] Harlan's appeal was a follow-up to a request that Evans had made six weeks earlier.

> Hon. Jas. Harlan, U.S. Senator
>
> Dear Sir, I heard that the Gov. of Colorado is likely to vacate. If he does, I would like for Mr. Lincoln to know that I would

---

territories and states for their political and economic advantage, to control the disposition of the public domain, and to foster the domination of the Trans-Mississippi Region by northern political, mining, railroad, and other economic interests. In many of their political activities the radicals used the territories as 'pilot plants' for the later reconstruction of the South." Vincent G. Tegeder. "Lincoln and the Territorial Patronage: The Ascendency of the Radicals in the West" in The *Mississippi Valley Historical Review* Vol. 35, No. 1 (June 1948) 90.

1059 Applications and Recommendations, n. d.

1060 Applications and Recommendations, n. d. This letter was also signed by Methodist and Supreme Court Justice, John McLean.

1061 Applications and Recommendations, March 15, 1861.

1062 Applications and Recommendations, March 15, 1861.

be glad to accept the place. There will be a host of applicants I suppose and he may not appreciate my claim unless his attention is called to it. You know all the circumstances and if not too much trouble I would thank you to speak to the President on the subject (if not already too late) before action is had in the case.

Congratulate you upon the ability with which you replied to Mr. Davis.

Very respectfully yours,

John Evans[1063]

On February 19, 1862, twenty-four U. S. Senators, all Republicans, including James Harlan, Harry Lane, Lymon Trumbull, and Samuel Pomeroy signed a letter requesting Lincoln to appoint Evans as Governor of the Colorado Territory.[1064] All of these letters demonstrated how overwhelmed Lincoln felt in responding to patronage requests, often forgetting who had made the request and what offices had been requested. He referred to himself as, "A man so busy, letting rooms at one end of his house that he can't stop to put out the fire that is burning in the other."[1065] Lincoln originally interpreted Evans' rejection of Washington as non-interest in any territorial government. But ultimately, the political pressure bore fruit. Lincoln nominated Evans to the Senate which approved him, and on March 26, 1862, Lincoln signed Evans' appointment as Governor of Colorado and Superintendent of Indian Affairs. This particular decision, which had been highly leveraged by Simpson, would boomerang on the Bishop and leave American Methodism with perhaps the darkest blight on the entirety of its American history. Roberts assesses that Evans' "appointment gave Lincoln an opportunity to pay off a large political debt, satisfied the powerful Methodist lobby within the party, and gave the President a dependable friend in one of the most strategic territories in the West."[1066] To William

---

1063 Applications and Recommendations, January 30, 1861.
1064 Applications and Recommendations, February 19, 1862.
1065 Burlingame, Vol. II, 69.
1066 Roberts, 318.

Seward Lincoln wrote, March 28, 1862, "I believe Dr. Evans has already been appointed Governor of Colorado. If not, let it be done at once ...."[1067]

In the meantime, Simpson and Evans colluded to send John Lewis Smith as a missionary to the Colorado Territory, with the understanding that he would receive his financial support by Evans appointing him "Secretary of the Territory." Harry Kelsey, Jr., in his biography of Evans, questions this recollection of Smith, since Lincoln appointed Samuel Elbert to the office on April 7, three days before the North Indiana Conference convened. At any rate, the appointment of Elbert, also a Methodist led the *Daily Commonwealth* of Denver to suggest that "Evans was favoring Methodists for the spoils of office."[1068]

Evans in Over His Head

Colorado, like most of the West, was an imbroglio of white-red animosity, in which ungovernable Indians resisted a "lying, stealing bureau of Indian Affairs." The combustible situation was just waiting to be ignited by a superintendent who had no idea how to put a stop to the ongoing marauding, murdering, and constant conflict between Native Americans and encroaching whites. Worse, Evans had no "militia" to quell the violence. The Colorado Territory was a mid-19th century Vietnam or Afghanistan with no battle lines and no ability to distinguish the "hostile" and the "friendly" Indians. Even though a militia did not exist, there was a law passed by the territorial legislature which called for all males between 18 and 45 to serve upon conscription, excluding "public officials, Quakers, clergymen, lunatics,

---

1067   Carl Sandburg. *Abraham Lincoln: The War Years* Vol. I, 310. In the "Bancroft Interview," Evans gave no one credit for running political interference. In his perception, he had won the appointment on his own merit. Frank Blair had said to Lincoln, "If you have any friend that you know to be a good businessman, appoint him to that place. I have no one to recommend .... Lincoln told I.N. Arnold to communicate with me (Evans) and see if I would accept the position, if he would appoint me, which he did by telegraph."

1068   *The Daily Commonwealth*: Denver (November 9, 1863) 2. Conveniently, Evans did not remember any ecclesiastical leverage on the Elbert appointment. "I had formed a friendship with Elbert and though I did not have anything against Mr. Gilpin's Secretary of State, I told Mr. Lincoln, that the Secretary of the Territory was a very important officer, and that he must be in harmony with the governor and that I wanted him to appoint Elbert of Nebraska, Secretary of the Territory." "Bancroft Interview," 11.

idiots, and pensioners." The conscription law made no monetary allocation for horses, artillery, or any other kind of provision.

In October of 1862, Evans traveled to Washington to appeal to William P. Dole, to send sufficient federal troops to guard his territory. It was unlikely that the Union, fighting for its very survival, would send troops to put out sporadic fires 2,000 miles away. Longstanding feuds between the Cheyenne, Arapaho, and Utes would just have to work themselves out. According to historian William E. Unrau, "A novice commissioner in distant Washington," had shifted the onus to Governor Evans for an "explosive state of affairs and to find a scapegoat in the event that hostilities became a reality." Evans attempted to enforce the 1861 Treaty of Fort Wise, but there were no resources for settling the Arapaho and Cheyenne on the banks of the upper Arkansas River. Evans was also faced with fixing boundaries, "an unenviable task in a region with traditions of vigilante justice, and petty localism in judicial procedure."[1069]

John Evans and such entrepreneurs as W. A. H. Loveland found themselves at odds with federal policy and vigorously protested. Evans reminded Dole of what was at stake (gold), and hyperventilated, "I beseech you in the name of humanity and our dearest interests, to give us authority to avert this threatened repetition of the Minnesota War." Dole threw up his hands and dumped the whole matter into Evans' lap, permitting him to enact a policy, "as may be found expedient."[1070] What was expedient for the Anglos was not expedient for the Indians. Gary Roberts accurately summarizes the irreconcilable difference:

> The settlers assumed that they must protect themselves because the established authorities seemed unable or unwilling to do so. They assumed that they had an ultimate right to protect themselves under the principle of popular sovereignty. They believed that men must take law into their own hands when the system failed to provide it, because the defense of home and family was the fundamental duty of every man. They wrapped all of these beliefs in a mantle of patriotism, religious rhetoric and manifest destiny.[1071]

1069 William E. Unrau. "A Prelude to War," *The Colorado Magazine* Vol. XLI (Nov. 4, 1964) 311, 308-309.

1070 Roberts, *Tragedy and Symbol*, 150-152.

1071 Ibid., 728.

Enter John Chivington

When Ute Indians stole livestock from a stage station, and Arapaho stole horses from a rancher, Evans beseeched Colonel John Chivington (pronounced Shivington) to "intervene but avoid any collision with the Indians or any cause of ill feeling." Such advice demonstrated Evans' superficial acquaintance with Chivington, his naiveté concerning the evolving fight, and the growing predicament of the Indians who were being disenfranchised and corralled by so-called civilization. Evans was not unaware of the magnitude of his problem. As recently as late August and early September 1862, Sioux Indians of Minnesota had killed some 450-800 white men, women, and children in the approximate time frame of one month.[1072]

The historian is tempted to link Chivington and Evans before Colorado days, because both were from the same area of Ohio, and both entered the Methodist Church about the same time, 1841-1842. But there is no evidence that they knew one another before Evans arrived in Colorado. John Evans was seven years older than John Chivington. Even though born in the same county, and living only fifteen miles apart, a Warren County, Ohio historian has concluded that, "It would appear that the Evans family and the Chivington family were separated by considerable geography (for those times), economics (Evans family fairly prosperous, Chivington's family working farmers, apparently) and religion. There is no evidence that the Chivingtons were active Quakers as were the Evans family …. A possible interference between the Johns could have been business transactions

---

1072   Kenneth Carley. *The Sioux Uprising of 1862* (St. Paul: Minnesota Historical Society Press, 1961). This particular incident resulted in the largest mass execution in the history of the United States. Lincoln authorized thirty-eight of the Indians to be hanged. See Scott W. Berg, *38 Nooses: Lincoln, Little Crow, and the Beginning of the Frontier's End* (New York Vintage Books, 2013). Berg states, "The conventional narrative of the United States-Indian conflict paints the Civil War as a time of suspension, an interim during which the manpower and industrial wealth of the Union had to finish subjugating the rebellious South before the federal government could return its attention to the tribes of the West. But violence between whites and a number of Indian nations was very much a part of the historical fabric of the early 1860s," xiii. Also see Gustav Niebuhr. *Lincoln's Bishop: A President, A Priest, and the Fate of 300 Dakota Sioux Warriors* (New York: HarperCollins Publishers). Niebuhr is referring to Episcopal Bishop Henry Benjamin Whipple.

between the Chivington's and Evans' commercial enterprises."[1073] Chivington arrived in Colorado before Evans, and no doubt, Chivington's Glorieta glory and Methodist credentials impressed the new Governor.

By 1864, the Colorado Territory was caught in the constant throes of Indian vengeance, the Indians' response to marginalization, and the threat of complete extinction. Thirty miles outside of Denver, on June 11, Cheyenne massacred the Hungate family, raping Mrs. Hungate before she died.[1074] In response, Evans decided to distribute an encyclical: "To the friendly Indians on the plains, appealing to all Indians to turn themselves in to Major Colley, U.S. Indian Agent at Fort Lyon, who will give them provisions and show them a place of safety." Thus, friendly Indians would not be killed through mistake. "The families of those who have gone to war with the whites must be kept away from the friendly Indians."[1075] John Evans was going to put out a fire which raged over 100,000 square miles with an ink pen. The entreaty was dated June 27, 1864, and on August 8, the "friendly Indians" responded by murdering 30 persons between Denver and Leavenworth, including a family of ten living at Ewbank Station, "murdered and scalped, and one of the females, besides having suffered the latter inhuman barbarity, was pinned to the earth by a stake thrust through her person in a most revolting manner."[1076]

"The Fighting Parson"

John Chivington distinguished himself at the Battle of Glorieta Pass (Apache Canyon) March 28, 1862, riding among his troops, "wielding a pistol and shouting orders." With his six-foot-four-and-one-half-inch frame decked out in full regimental, the major made a splendid target, but somehow he managed to dodge the numerous Texas missiles that were aimed

---

1073   Furnished by the Warren County Historical Society, Lebanon, Ohio. Author unknown.

1074   "Indians Depredations-Murder of an Entire Family," The Commonwealth (June 15, 1864) included in Scott Williams' *The Indian Wars of 1864 through the Sand Creek Massacre* (Aurora, Colorado: Pick of Ware Publishing, 1997) 40-43.

1075   Ibid., 67.

1076   Report of Department of the Interior, Office of Indian Affairs (Washington: Government Printing Office, November 15, 1864) 254, from the collection of the Prelinger Library, San Francisco, CA 2006.

in his direction.¹⁰⁷⁷ A contemporary stated that "Though wholly unskilled in the science of war, with but little knowledge of drill and discipline, Major Chivington, of Herculean frame and gigantic stature, possessed the courage and exhibited the discrete boldness, dash, and brilliancy in action, which distinguished the more illustrious of our volunteer officers during the war."¹⁰⁷⁸

When John was five years old he lost his dad, a man who instilled in his son a love for God and books. The boy thoughtfully read *Milton's Paradise Lost*, the *Bible*, and the *Book of Common Prayer*.¹⁰⁷⁹ In 1840, Chivington married Martha Rollason, and both of them became Methodists at a camp meeting in southern Ohio in the summer of 1842. According to Clarence A. Lyman, Chivington was converted at Zoar Church, the oldest church in Hamilton, Ohio, in an 1842 revival that boasted of over two hundred conversions.¹⁰⁸⁰ Roberts claims that Chivington as a young man earned his living as a "purse fighter" along the river towns, and "From that roughhouse apprenticeship Chivington found his way into the battle against Satan."¹⁰⁸¹

During the next two years John completed the Methodist "course of study" and began pastoring the Zoar Church of the Goshen Circuit, Ohio Conference. In 1846, Chivington joined the newly organized Masonic Lodge in Butterville, Ohio. In June of 1848, he accepted a charge in Quincy, Illinois. Indeed, Chivington was a man's preacher, demonstrating his machismo when he won a showdown with a federal marshal, who attempted to enact the fugitive slave law on a mulatto girl, whom the pastor and his wife had ensconced in the parsonage. John Chivington throughout his life never backed down from a fight, at least when he thought the cause worth

---

1077 Thomas S. Edrington and John Taylor. *The Battle of Glorieta Pass: A Gettysburg in the West: March 26-28, 1862* (Albuquerque: University of New Mexico Press, 1998) 47.

1078 Reginald Craig. *The Fighting Parson: The Biography of Colonel John M. Chivington* (Los Angeles, Western Lore Press, 1959) 19. Craig's hagiography on Chivington has to be read with caution. Craig was Chivington's great-grandson. However, it is the only full biography on Chivington.

1079 Ibid., 18.

1080 Quoted in Gary Roberts. *Massacre at Sand Creek: How Methodists Were Involved in an American Tragedy* (Nashville: Abingdon Press, 2016) 263. From Clarence A. Lyman, "The Truth About John M. Chivington," unpublished manuscript (Denver: Division of State Archives and Public Records, 1956). Lyman was married to a granddaughter of John Chivington.

1081 Roberts, 116.

defending. Ironically, considering the black mark on his life, Chivington in 1853 became a missionary to the Wyandotte Indians in what is now the general area of Kansas City. He left his imprimatur on Kansas City by helping to found the first Masonic Lodge and became its Grand Master.[1082]

As the "border war" heated up after the Kansas-Nebraska Act, Chivington became a vocal supporter of "free soil," not the "state sovereignty," which had been advocated by Daniel Webster, and ultimately, Stephen Douglas. When Chivington received a threat from pro-slavery elements headquartered in Lecompton, Kansas, warning him not to continue preaching in St. Joe where he was stationed, he laid two pistols on each side of his Bible. Standing in the pulpit, the "Fighting Parson" declared in a deep bass voice, "By the grace of God and these two revolvers, I am going to preach here today."[1083] In 1856, Chivington was appointed Presiding Elder of the Omaha District in the Kansas-Nebraska Conference of the Methodist Church. Chivington was as impressive as a raw pastor as he was a raw soldier. William Goode wrote for the *Western Christian Advocate* in 1854, "Our Wyandotte Mission is prospering under the fearless and faithful labors of Reverend J.M. Chivington. I should think it should take several United States agents to drive him from here."[1084]

A Soldier's Soldier

When South Carolina seceded, a Southern sympathizer declared that one Southerner could whip five Yankees. Chivington retorted that "If you will go out in the town and find four others from the South, I will undertake to thrash the Earth with all five, and settle the matter right here on Ferry Street."[1085] Sometime in September of 1861, Governor Gilpin offered Chivington a commission as a Chaplain, to which the presiding elder responded that he felt, "compelled to strike a blow in

---

1082   Craig, 35.

1083   John Speer. "Sketch of John Chivington," in a report to Fred Martin from an interview with Mrs. John Chivington, Kansas State Historical Society, Topeka, Kansas ((March 11, 1902) 10-11.

1084   Quoted in Wade Barclay. *History of Methodist Missions: Widening Horizons 1845-95* Vol. III (New York: The Board of Missions of the Methodist Church, 1957) 344.

1085   Ibid., 54.

person for the destruction of human slavery and to help in some measure to make this a truly free country. Therefore, I must respectfully decline an appointment as a non-combatant officer and at the same time urgently request a fighting commission instead."[1086] Immediately, Chivington was commissioned a Major of a regiment. Within two months he was stationed at Camp Weld on the South Platte River, two miles north of Denver.

Chivington and his men did not see any action until February 22, 1862, when the First Colorado set out to reinforce Colonel Canby at Fort Union in New Mexico. This trip ended with Chivington distinguishing himself at Apache Canyon, about which a Texas prisoner wrote to his wife, "On they came to what I supposed was destruction; but nothing like lead or iron seemed to stop them, for we were pouring it into them from every side like hail in a storm. In a moment these devils had run the gauntlet for half a mile and were fighting hand to hand with our men in the road." Another Confederate reported that he had "emptied his revolver three times" at the Major (who had a pistol in each hand) and ordered his company to fire a volley at him but "he galloped unhurt through the storm of bullets."[1087] "The Fighting Parson" adumbrated Charles Portis' Rooster Cogburn in *True Grit*. However Chivington is evaluated, for better or worse, he was a leader. Glorieta scholar, William Clarke Whitford, wrote that Chivington in action "became the incarnation of war. The bravest of the brave, a giant in stature and a whirlwind in strife, he had also the rather unusual qualities that go to make soldiers personally love such a leader and eager to follow him into the jaws of death. The admiration and devotion of this man became unbounded. He was their ideal of a dashing, fearless fighting commander."[1088]

Chivington, after returning to Denver, traveled to Washington where he personally met with Edwin Stanton, requesting that his regiment be transferred to the eastern sphere of the war. Stanton denied the request, but offered to make Chivington a Brigadier General training new troops

---

1086   Roberts, *Tragedy and Symbol*, 120.

1087   Craig, 105.

1088   William Clarke Whitford. *Colorado Volunteers in the Civil War: The New Mexico Campaign in 1862* (Glorieta, Mexico: The Rio Grande Press, Inc., 1971) 52. Also see F. Stanley. *The Civil War in New Mexico* (Denver: The World Press, 1960) 194, and Ray Colton. *The Civil War in the Western Territories* (Norman, Oklahoma: University of Oklahoma Press, 1959) 69-75.

in Washington. Chivington replied, "I would rather command the First Cavalry of Colorado than the best brigade in the Army of the Potomac."[1089] Chivington returned to Colorado, but kept the Brigadier General offer in mind. By the time Chivington could get back to Stanton, the Secretary of War changed his mind because John Slough, Chivington's only competition for the generalship, had accused Chivington of attempting to murder him. Slough communicated the accusation to Stanton, a letter that effectively ended Chivington's promotions.[1090] Slough may have been jealous of Chivington's popularity or may have sincerely believed that Chivington fictionalized his success at Glorieta. When Chivington did not immediately return to the main Army after attacking the Confederate "advanced guard," Slough exclaimed that half his regiment had "gone off to hell with a crazy preacher who thinks he is Napoleon Bonaparte."[1091]

As always, mercenary motivations escalated the Colorado tension; disturbances occurred proportionate to the influx of prospectors and ranchers. In the summer of 1863 John Chivington stated, "Colorado in my judgment is not of second importance to any state or territory, to the general government. If protected and kept quiet she will yield 20 million of gold this year and double yearly in years to come, and in view of the national debt I think this important, very!"[1092] In September of 1863, John Evans traveled to the fork of the Arikaree and Republican Rivers to hold a "peace meeting" with the Cheyenne, but the Indians stood him up, and the chagrined Evans stomped back to Denver. Eighteen sixty-four evolved into constant skirmishes between the Indians and whites with Chivington being involved in "three major fights" between April 12 and May 16. In Colorado, several people blamed "old Chivington" for stirring up Indian war, but many instead believed Evans' theory that the Cheyenne were working out a plot "to run the whites out of the country."[1093]

1089   Craig, 142.
1090   Lori Cox-Paul, "'John M. Chivington,' 'The Reverend Colonel,' 'Marry Your Daughter,' 'Sand Creek Massacre,'" *Nebraska History* Vol. 8 No. 4 (Winter 2007) 32.
1091   Roberts. *Massacre at Sand Creek*, 75.
1092   Stan Hoig. *The Sand Creek Massacre* (Norman: The University of Oklahoma Press, 1974) 29.
1093   Ibid., 53.

Simpson and Chivington

Prior to the Colorado disaster, there were several encounters between Simpson and Chivington, but when they were first acquainted is difficult to determine. Chivington was a delegate to the 1856 General Conference at Indianapolis, and even if the two men did not speak to one another, Simpson would have certainly taken note of the most predominant, physical presence at the Conference.[1094] What is clear is that by March of 1862, Simpson was fully aware of Chivington's ministerial and military status, because he presided over the Kansas Conference and "located" Chivington, that is, allowed him to retain his ministerial credentials, while at the same time serving in the military. Obviously the Methodists were not pacifists. On November 1, 1862, Matthew informed Ellen that he met Col. Chivington at the Pittsburgh depot in Chicago.[1095] Somewhere along the way, Chivington had offered Matthew's son, Charles, a job in the Colorado mines, no doubt a clerical position. The father did not want his son going to Colorado, but instead procured him a job with Thomas Carlton at the New York Book Concern. At the end of 1863, Chivington beseeched Simpson for a promotion to Brigadier General.

> Head Quarters, District of Colorado
> Dec. 30, 1863
> My Dear Bishop
>
> I write you at this time to request you to stir up the "pure mind" of the President about my brigadiership. I am informed that you obtained my nomination last winter but my name was left out on the "revised list." If I could get this promotion it would very materially help our plans out here of which I have no doubt Gov. Evans has informed you. We work in harmony. Can you get it? Every officer in this Dist has petitioned for it and all the Colorado officers—serving elsewhere. You will place me under additional obligations, Church matters going on well. Church and seminary are both far on the way to completion. Rev. Mr. Bets is doing well here—we raise

---

1094 *Journal of the General Conference of the Methodist Episcopal Church* held in Indianapolis Vol. III, 1848–1856 (New York: Carlton & Porter, 1856) 5.
1095 UMA, Drew University, Simpson papers, Letter November 1, 1862.

him six hundred and fifty dollars before he had been here a week. Mr. Vincent is doing finely at Central and Black Hawk and will be paid well. Mr. Willard is a trump and will win in any crowd. An extraordinary good preacher and as good a financier as preacher.

Compliments to Mrs. S.
Yours truly,
J. M. Chivington[1096]

It is doubtful that Simpson intervened on Chivington's behalf, and even if he did, Stanton as we have seen, already had his reasons for rejecting the appeal. Chivington mustered out of the Army as a Colonel, January 1865.

Clinton Fisk claimed credit for Chivington's appointment by Samuel Curtis as the Commander of the First Colorado, as he trumpeted his responsibility for just about everything that he interpreted as good which happened on the planet. This is one credit that he later may have wanted erased from his resume.[1097]

Escalating Tension and Explosion

Like most whites, Evans would view the Colorado situation only from an Anglo vantage point. The commissioner of Indian Affairs in Washington concluded from Evans' reports that, "From a careful examination of them I am unable to find any immediate cause for the uprising of Indian tribes of the plains, except the active efforts upon their savage natures by the emissaries from the hostile northern tribes."[1098] On May 18, 1864, Evans appealed to General Curtis, commanding officer of the Department of Kansas at Fort Leavenworth, "Unless a force can be sent out to chastise this combination severely and at once, the delay will cost us a long and bloody war and the loss of a great many lives, with untold amounts of property."[1099] On May 20, Evans apprised Simpson of the escalating crisis:

1096　UMA, Drew University, Simpson papers, Letter December 30, 1863.
1097　UMA, Drew University, Simpson papers, Letter from Clinton Fisk to Matthew Simpson, November 10, 1862.
1098　Hoig., 53.
1099　Ibid., 57.

Denver May 20th 1864

Dear Bishop:

I arrived here with my family last evening, all well. We were somewhat uneasy on account of Indian troubles on the way but had no alarm. It now appears to be the Indians plan to steal all the stock they can safely take without any other depredations or mischief that would excite the earnest attention of the military to their pursuit or punishment. They steal large numbers of horses every few days on the line of our travel and occasionally kill a man. Last Friday evening just before we came by they stole a herd of horses from a train near Julesburgh (Ft. Sedgwick), and killed and scalped the man that was herding them I hope however that there will be more protection & safety on the route soon as attention is being directed to such occurrences as to the above which are too frequent to escape attention. If I would know about the time that you would start I could give you all the information I could gather about the dangers of these events. From what I can learn there will be no danger or difficulty with the Indians here or in the mountains or at any point on the route you are proposing to take through Colorado.

In fact, all the danger is on the road across the plains and that this side of the terminus of the railroad ....

I remain very truly your friend,

John Evans[1100]

On June 14, 1864, Evans appealed directly to Edwin Stanton, Secretary of War, "Indian hostilities on our settlements commenced as per information given you last fall. One settlement devastated 25 miles east of here, murdered and scalped, bodies brought in today" (the Hungate family).[1101] In August he again wired Stanton: "The alliance of Indians on the plains reported last winter in my communication is now undoubted. A large force, say ten

---

1100   UMA, Drew University, Simpson Papers, Letter May 20, 1864. This letter is mystifying. In a year of major speaking engagements, a full slate of Annual Conferences, and a General Conference, was Simpson considering a trip to Colorado? We know that Simpson later invested in Colorado mines, and that he wanted a first-hand investigation of where he was placing his money. No doubt, that dialogue between Evans and Simpson had begun to take place.

1101   Hoig, 60.

thousand troops, will be necessary to defend the lines of hostilities. Unless they can be sent at once we will be cut off and destroyed."[1102] Stanton, to no avail, ordered General William Rosecrans to release the Second Colorado, but Rosecrans was too busy defending Kansas City from Sterling Price's invading Confederates.

In August of 1864, Edwin Stanton granted John Evans permission to create the Third Colorado, a regiment of "one-hundred-day" volunteers. It may have been this one action which implicated John Evans in the Sand Creek Massacre more than anything else. On September 26, John Evans met with Edward Wynkoop, and Wynkoop later recalled that the Governor asserted that the Colorado Third had, "been raised to kill Indians, and they must kill Indians." Evans then asked, "Well, what should I do with the Third Regiment, if I make peace?"[1103] On November 23, Chivington's First Colorado made up of one-hundred regulars and the Third Colorado, consisting of approximately six hundred "one-hundred-day volunteers," left Fort Weld and reached Fort Lyon on November 28, a distance of one hundred fifty miles. It was a remarkable march, considering much of the trip was in snow between six inches and two feet deep. After Chivington was fully provisioned by Anthony, the incarnation of equivocation, Captain Silas Soule passionately remonstrated with both Chivington and Anthony, calling the intended attack on the Sand Creek encampment "murder." Chivington responded that he believed "it to be right or honorable to use any means under God's heaven to kill Indians that would kill women and children and damn any man that was in sympathy with Indians; and such men as Major Wynkoop and myself had better get out of the United States service."[1104] At eight o'clock p.m., over 800 men, including 125 men from Fort Lyon armed with over 135,000 rifle and pistol cartridges, departed for the forty mile hike almost directly north toward Sand Creek.

The next morning at 6 a.m., Chivington and his army stared down on a sleeping encampment of 500 Indians. What happened over the next seven to eight hours varies according to dozens of testimonies that were given

---

1102   Ibid., 68.
1103   *Report of the John Evans Study Committee*, 69. Website: www.northwestern.edu/provost/committees/john-evans-study/study-committee-report.pdf.
1104   Ibid., 143.

before the investigative hearings in Denver: between 70 and 500 Indians killed; only one Indian scalped as opposed to the most sadistic and vulgar atrocities that one human can inflict on another; from mostly only men killed to scores of women and children sadistically mutilated with brains knocked out and sexual organs butchered. What happened in the desolate southeast corner of Colorado, November 29, 1864, would cast a pall over American Methodism, and implicate the intimate friendship between John Evans and Matthew Simpson, a condemnation that has not been absolved to this day.

Defenseless Women and Children

Edwin Stanton ordered an investigation of Sand Creek and the hearings convened in Denver on February 9, 1865, and adjourned on May 30th, seventy-six days later. Samuel F. Tappan, assisted by Edwin Jacoben and George Stillwell, chaired the proceedings. The court attempted to answer three questions: Did Chivington conduct himself according to the recognized rules of "civilized warfare?" Had the U.S. Government made prior commitments, concerning protection of the Indians? Were prisoners and property that were taken properly disposed of? The commission stated its scope and limitations in that it did not intend to try any person, "but simply to investigate and accumulate facts called for by the Government, to fix the responsibility, if any, and to insure justice to all parties."[1105]

The witnesses varied according to their prejudice against or support of John Chivington. There were repeated attempts to assess how many Indians were at Sand Creek, and what proportion of them were women and children. The majority of witnesses assessed approximately five hundred Indians present on the morning of the attack, with two thirds of them being

---

1105 United States Army, Courts of Inquiry, Sand Creek Massacre, 1864, Report of the Secretary of War Communicating in Compliance with a Resolution of the Senate of February 4th, 1867, a copy of the evidence taken at Denver and Fort Lyon Territory by a Military Commission Ordered to Inquire into the Sand Creek Massacre, November, 1864. Washington: Government Printing Office, 1867 Senate Executive Document, November 26, 39th Congress, 2nd Session. Copyright Christopher H. Wynkoop. Hereafter, referred to as Sand Creek Massacre Investigation.

women and children. The preponderance of the testimony estimated that two thirds of those killed were women and children.[1106]

The Damaging Testimonies of Edward Wynkoop and Silas Soule

By far, the most negative witnesses concerning both Chivington and Anthony were Silas Soule, who took the stand first and longest (seven days) and Edward Wynkoop. Both men were convinced that Anthony had double crossed the Indians. Wynkoop recalled, "Previous to the slaughter commencing, he (Chivington) addressed his command, arousing in them by his language all their worst passion, urging them on to the work of committing all these diabolical outrages. Knowing himself all the circumstances of these Indians, resting in the assurance of protection from this government given them by myself and Major S. J. Anthony, he kept his command in entire ignorance of the same, and when it was suggested that such might be the case, he denied it, positively stating that they were still continuing their depredations, and lay there threatening the fort."[1107] Anthony was fully aware of Chivington's intentions, did nothing to dissuade him, and even went with him as a combatant. When Anthony told Soule that "some of those Indians ought to be killed, that he had been only waiting for a good chance to pitch in to them," Soule reminded him of the "pledges" he had made to the Indians. The fort commander responded that the expedition was only for the purpose of following the Indians up, and that Soule should not "compromise himself" by going out.[1108]

After Sand Creek, Soule was appointed "provost marshal" of Denver. Investigating a drunken brawl on April 23, 1865, he was greeted by a bullet to the head, and died almost instantly. Of course, many believed that the killing had been set up by Chivington. Edward Wynkoop was firmly convinced of Chivington's responsibility for Soule's death, though Chivington was not the actual killer, and attempted to do something about it. "I had the pleasure sometime afterwards, of arresting the murderer of Capt. Soule, and sending him in irons to Denver, in charge of Lt. James Cannon, with orders for him

---

1106   Ibid., 14, 110, 112. Sand Creek scholar Gary Roberts concludes that approximately 250 Indians were killed. Roberts, *Massacre at Sand Creek*, XV.
1107   Ibid., 123.
1108   Ibid., 125.

to be turned over to Guy V. Henry, Commander of the Military District. The night the prisoner was incarcerated in Denver through machinations of Col. Chivington and his satellites, he escaped. Lt. Cannon was found dead in his bed the next morning, having been poisoned through the agency of the same demons who had murdered S. Soule."[1109]

The Official U.S. Government Censures of John Evans and John Chivington

While the "investigative committee" met in Denver, "The Joint Committee on the Conduct of the War" (Civil War) met in Washington, March 15-17, to inquire into what exactly had happened at Sand Creek. It condemned both Evans and Chivington before the Denver committee had concluded its business. Ironically, the Washington committee did not interview Chivington, and the Denver investigation did not question Evans. In fact, the congressmen did not personally meet with anyone who was present at Sand Creek, November 29, 1864, other than Scott Anthony and John Smith. The congressmen relied on newspaper articles, depositions, letters, Evans' obfuscation, and "reports and dispatches." Throughout the war the committee consisted of various members, but serving on the committee at the time of the Sand Creek inquiry were Senator Benjamin Wade, Chairman; Senator Charles Buckalew, and Representatives Daniel Gooch and Benjamin Loan. The committee was given liberty to investigate all matters and events in the Civil War, especially if it suspected malfeasance or ineptitude within the Army of the Potomac, and much of the time, was at odds with the President. "Sand Creek" was somewhat of an excursus, the only Indian event investigated by the committee.[1110]

On January 15, 1865, Edward Wynkoop wrote a letter to J. E. Tappan, Acting Assistant Adjutant General, district of upper Arkansas, regretting that he had taken the Indians to see John Evans on September 28, "a mistake

---

1109 See *The Tall Chief: The Autobiography of Edward W. Wynkoop*, ed. Christopher B. Gerboth (Denver: History Colorado, 1993) 100-102. Also C. A. Prentice, "Captain Silas S. Soule: A Pioneer Martyr" *The Colorado Magazine*, Vol. XII, No. 6 (November, 1935) 224-228.

1110 Bruce Tap. *Over Lincoln's Shoulder: Committee on the Conduct of the War* (Lawrence, KS: University Press, 1998) 232.

of which I have sense become painfully aware." Wynkoop condemned both Evans and Chivington:

> Everyone whom I have spoken to, either officer or soldier, agrees in the retelling that the most fearful atrocities were committed, that ever were heard of. Woman and children were killed and scalped, children shot at their mother's breast, and all the bodies mutilated in the most horrible manner. Numerous eye-witnesses have described to me, coming under the eye of Colonel Chivington, of the most disgusting and horrible character, the dead bodies of females profaned in such a manner that the recital is sickening! Colonel J. M. Chivington all the time inciting his troops to these diabolical outrages.[1111]

Evans' testimony was riddled with "I think so," "difficult to say," "I should have to guess," "I gave no orders," "I had no authority," "I have no official knowledge," "that I could not say," "I do not know." The Congressional Committee censured John Evans by concluding that his testimony was "characterized by such prevarication and shuffling as has been shown by no witness they have examined during the four years they have been engaged in their investigations; and for the evident purpose of avoiding the admission that he was fully aware that the Indians massacred so brutally at Sand Creek were then, and had been, actuated by the most friendly feelings towards the whites, and had done all in their power to restrain those less friendly disposed."[1112] The committee's harshest condemnation was reserved for Chivington who,

> Wearing the uniform of the United States which should be the emblem of justice and humanity: holding the important position of commander of a military district, and therefore having the honor of the government to that extent in his keeping, he deliberately planned and executed a foul and dastardly massacre which would have disgraced the veriest savage among those who were the victims of his cruelty. Having full knowledge of their friendly character, having himself been instrumental to some extent in placing them in their position of fancied security, he took advantage of their inapprehension and defenseless condition to gratify the worst passions that ever cursed the heart of man.[1113]

1111 "Massacre of the Cheyenne Indians," Report on the Conduct of the War, 38 Con., 2nd Sess. (Washington: Government Printing Office, 1865) 82-83.
1112 Ibid., 9-10.
1113 Ibid., IV.

Evans Ultimately Indicts Himself

On Aug 6, 1865, John Evans wrote an open letter in response to the accusation of "prevarication" and the Congressional Committee's assessment that the Indians of Sand Creek were "peaceful." In defending himself, Evans only further implicated himself. Almost the entirety of Evans's sixteen-page justification of Sand Creek implied that the Indians got what they deserved. Evans took issue with the committee that "he was fully aware that the Indians massacred so brutally at Sand Creek were then and had been actuated by the most friendly feelings towards the whites."[1114] Evans quoted from a conversation with Robert North on November 16, 1863, in which North had reported "the Comanches, Apaches, Kiowas, the northern band of Arapaho, and all the Cheyenne, and the Sioux have pledged one another to go to war with the whites as soon as they can procure ammunition in the spring."[1115]

Evans attempted exoneration by claiming that he did not have authority to make peace with the Indians. On September 29, 1864, Evans wrote to Major S.G. Colley, U.S. Indian Agent, upper Arkansas that "The Arapaho and Cheyenne Indians being now at war with the United States Government must make peace with the military authorities. Of course the arrangement *relieves* (italics mine) the Indian bureaus of their care until peace is declared with them." After narrating a long litany of Indian atrocities over 1864, Evans concluded that "all this history of war and blood–all history of rapine and ruin–all the story of outrage and suffering on the part of our public–is summed up by the committee and given to the public in one mild sentence, 'some had committed acts of hostility against the whites.'"[1116]

Evans dubiously asserted, "The public documents and files of the Indian Bureau and of my superintendency show consistent and unremitting diligence

---

1114 Reply of Governor Evans of the Territory of Colorado to that part referring to him, of the report "The Committee on The Conduct of the War" headed "Massacre of Cheyenne Indians." Executive Department and Superintendency of Indian Affairs, C.T. Denver, Aug. 6, 1865, 7.
1115 Ibid., 6.
1116 Ibid., 9-10.

and effort on my part to prevent hostilities and protect the people."[1117] From his perspective, Evans was the victim of politically-motivated slander. "Many of these gentlemen were in the city of Washington last winter, endeavoring to affect my removal and were not particular as to the character of the means they employed so that the desired result was accomplished. For this purpose they conspired to connect my name with the Sand Creek battle, although they knew that I was in no way connected with it."[1118] Evans concluded, "I am confident that the public will see, from the facts here set forth, the great injustice done me; and I am further confident that the committee, when they know these and other facts I shall lay before them, will see this injustice, and as far as possible repair it."[1119] Ultimately, Evans indicted himself when he stated to Hubert Bancroft in 1884, "So the benefit of that massacre to the people of Colorado was very great for it ridded the plains of the Indians, for there was a sentiment that the Indians ought not be left in the midst of the community. It relieved us very much of the roaming tribes of Indians."[1120]

Simpson's Intervention for Evans

On June 21, 1865, Simpson performed the marriage of Evans' daughter, Josephine, to Samuel Elbert in Evanston, Illinois.[1121] John Evans was so preoccupied with his political demise that he was not present for the wedding. Even though Simpson was not able to personally talk with Evans during the months leading up to the wedding, he became acutely aware of his friend's crisis. After the wedding, he immediately went to Washington to see President Johnson, but because Johnson was ill, was only able to gain an audience with

---

1117   Ibid., 15.

1118   Ibid., 15.

1119   Ibid., 16.

1120   https://www.popularresistance.org//school-of-theology-display-of-indian-skin-wrapped-book/.
Quoted in "School of Theology Display of Indian Skin Wrapped Book."

1121   I infer that John Evans was not present because the *NW Christian Advocate* reported on Simpson presiding over the marriage and Margaret Evans leaving with the bridal couple for Denver. The reporter did not imply that the Governor, for whom Evanston was named, was in attendance. Also, on June 28, 1865, Simpson wrote to Evans, "As you have heard, Jo's wedding was a remarkably pleasant occasion." "A Marriage Feast," *NW Christian Advocate*, Jun 28, 1865. Evans Mss Collection, History Colorado, Letter, Simpson to Evans, June 28, 1865.

James Harlan. Harlan discussed Evans' situation with Johnson who assured the Secretary of the Interior that "he would do nothing in the matter at present and that if he found it necessary to take any steps; he would consult with him (Harlan) first."[1122]

Harlan communicated this assurance to Evans and in turn, Simpson bolstered Evans' confidence: "I think, however, there is no danger of your removal. You may by intrigue of politicians be so flawed that you will think it wise to resign. But this shall not be if we can help it."[1123] Simpson passed his opprobrium on Johnson: "[H]e is not Mr. Lincoln/he may do well-I hope he will-but I do not yet feel confident in his movements. He does not seem to have a heart."[1124] Simpson closed his letter to Evans, "I hope you will fully realize your highest expectations of financial success. The oil bubble here has bursted. I may wear my long face."[1125]

Over the next several weeks, Evans' political stability deteriorated. The state of affairs prompted Harlan to again approach William Seward on Evans' behalf. Seward informed Harlan that he was satisfied with Evans, but "in view of the published action of the committee on the war, he felt that a change was necessary to prevent attacks on the administration from Congress."[1126] Harlan informed Simpson that according to William Seward, Evans' friends should not "press the administration." But Simpson was not to be deterred, and the first of August, took a second trip to Washington for the purpose of seeing Andrew Johnson. Again, the president was unavailable, and Simpson was so desperate that he ran down William Seward on vacation at Cape May, New Jersey. Seward gave Simpson the same response he had made to Harlan, that he could not continue Evans. The consolation prize would be appointing a Methodist as territorial governor of Colorado of Simpson's and Harlan's choosing (eventually Alexander Cummings) and retaining Samuel Elbert as Secretary. Simpson assured Evans of his on-going place in Colorado's politics and economy. "I cannot speak positively, but I fancy I can form a plan by which

---

1122 Evans Mss. Collection, History Colorado, Letter, Matthew Simpson to John Evans, June 28, 1865.
1123 Ibid.
1124 Ibid.
1125 Ibid.
1126 Evans Mss Collection. History Colorado, Letter, Simpson to Evans, August 4, 1865.

you and your successors can work together, and my cherished hope in your case be carried out."[1127]

William Seward requested Evans' resignation on July 18, 1865, and James Harlan requested his resignation on August 12, 1865. Evans wrote a letter of resignation to Andrew Johnson on August 1, 1865. This series of events demonstrated the lack of communication within Andrew Johnson's cabinet, the question as to whom Evans' was immediately responsible and more practically the unreliability of the United States Postal System.[1128]

What is sad about the ouster, is that Bishop Matthew Simpson expended a good deal of time and energy in enabling his close friend John Evans to save face, but as far as we know, asked no questions about Sand Creek, and never mentioned the event throughout the remainder of his public life, much less express any remorse. Simpson wrote his wife, "On Friday night I went to Washington, but the Prest was sick & I did not see him .... I stayed to see Seward. He will not continue Evans–but will continue Elbert as Secretary. He will appoint Cummings as Governor .... Hope not to have such unpleasant work very soon again, as this Territorial business."[1129] Simpson was relieved that the affair was over, or so he thought.

In the U. S. Senate Chamber, when Senator Samuel Pomeroy from Kansas referred to Chivington as a "Methodist minister," James Harlan inaccurately corrected him, stating that "I have been informed, and I think it is true, that this gentleman was at one time a minister in the Methodist Church, but he was suspended and dismissed from the Church, and he is now not even a member."[1130] In March 1865, Chivington wrote Simpson a vindictive, convoluted and grammatically impoverished letter, arguing that he was still a fully-credentialed Elder in the Methodist Episcopal Church.[1131]

1127   Ibid.
1128   Roberts, *Massacre at Sand Creek*, 154; Evans Mss Collection, History Colorado, Letter, Harlan to Evans, August 12, 1865; Letter, Evans to Andrew Johnson, Aug. 1, 1865.
1129   UMA, Drew University, Simpson papers, Letter August 4, 1865.
1130   Congressional Globe, 38th Congress, 2nd Sess., Part 1, 254.
1131   Denver Colorado Territory, March 9, 1865
        Rev. M. Simpson, D. D. Bishop for the M. E. Church
        Dear Sir:
          You have several weeks since seen the great *lies* that went the rounds of the papers about the Indian Massacres by me and my command, and I should not wonder if you more

than half believed it for I see by the Globe that Mr. Harlan from Iowa gulped it all down and seemed to vie nay to excel "crazy Sumner" wanting swift punishment meted out to us and full credence to talk and even repeated it on the floor of the Senate that it does seem to me must put to the blush any *western man of a half grain* of common sense and a very cursory observation. But for such ignorance and gullibility a man may be pardoned. There is however, a point in his talk to which I list exceptions. That is slander publicly uttered. That I had "years since been expelled both from the ministry and the church." Now sir I want to know if Mr. Harlan has a right as a member of the Church and a Christian Man to give publicity to such a falsehood. I do not care if he had heard it what right had he to repeat it, without some assurance more than double tongued rumor that it was so. Yourself Bp Ames, Bp Clark, Dr. Elliott, Governor Evans, Ayre Dr. Ryan, of the city of Washington in McKendee Church anybody from Colorado or almost anywhere else could have told the gentleman what the probability (at least) was. I am not the man who intends to prepare the way for *apostasy* and to throw off on to my former associates in the Church and ministry as did Mr. Harlan. You will remember soon after his election to the USA, came to the Iowa Conference held at Keokuk resigned his credentials as a minister. You was there and presided at the session at the Conference and how near I have correctly interpreted his purpose in so doing let the indifference he has manifested in the affairs of the Church since that time testify in what instance as he stood up like a true Methodist and demanded justice of the Administration for the people of his Church. I was poor when I went into the Army but did not join with such a determination to blackmail or otherwise make and keep for consumption on my own lusts that I took precaution to retire from the ministry. My conduct has been constantly under the eye of the Church and I'm not expelled and I believe no complaint has been lodged against me at home which is the best place to try to frame a man. In the meantime, I have done all that a man of limited means could for the Church of this Mr. Willard and all the preachers of the Church in Colorado Conference can speak. I preached a good many times in Washington when there lectured on the public grounds near the Capitol and I don't believe I done any discredit to the Church at St. Louis, Leavenworth, Atchison, St. Joseph, Omaha, and other places I have frequently preached since I have been in the Army and that it was acceptable. I infer from the fact that they always want me again and again. Now I must think that if I had been expelled from the Church and ministry "years since" that some of those preachers or people would have learned it and acted differently. Now what I want is for Mr. Harlan to "make the accused honorable." I of course want no fight with Mr. Harlan but then he must do something to repair what he said against my moral and religious character or I shall be found trying to make him do it. He's not through public life yet. I say to the glory of God's grace that my conduct has been above reproach since I have been in the M.E. Church and I shall not at this later day suffer James Harlan or any other man to deal in this way with me. He may get a place in Mr. Lincoln's Cabinet, and if he does, the Church that made him will be none the better off for it unless he changes his course. I happen to know how the Methodist preachers (some of them) in many states feel about his past throwing off on them and their people. I recollect that I heard Justice U. S. McLean say that if he had his official life to live over he would do very differently in this respect to what he did. I will be with Mr. H at his house have given something to the Church and shall have something to spend at his next election. I am outraged in my feelings and this is my excuse for writing as I have. I say these things to you having the most boundless confidence. See Harlan! See what he will do.

Chivington was essentially correct. He was still an official minister in the Methodist Episcopal Church. As the following will show, he was never officially confronted by Matthew Simpson, or any other authority within the denomination which chose to hide his dastardly deed rather than expose it.

The Close Friendship of Evans and Simpson

Simpson's death devastated Evans probably as much as the loss of his four children and first wife. When Evans, who was in New York, was requested to be a pallbearer for the Simpson funeral he responded, "I am overwhelmed with grief. My heart is bowed down under a sense of my own great bereavement in the death of Bishop Simpson. Yes, in the loss of my spiritual father. My most steadfast and intimate friend. My most trusted advisor and wisest counselor for over forty years. I am sorely grieved."[1132]

In May of 1872, Evans was a member of the first lay delegation to General Conference. On May 25, 1871, Simpson wrote, "I hope you will be present at the conf. As I think you ought to be the lay delegate to the general conf. It is very important to have our good men and true to navigate this movement and especially to oppose the wild schemes which a number of the editors are at present endeavoring to foist upon the church."[1133] Throughout their history Methodist Bishops have appointed District Superintendents (until the early twentieth-century called "Presiding Elders," (a practice initiated by Asbury), an authority perennially challenged by factions in the Methodist Episcopal Church (United Methodist Church as of 1968). On November 19, 1875, Simpson wrote Evans, "No other change affecting the episcopacy has any larger following. The advocates of change have avowed such revolutionary tendencies that it is evidently producing reaction. General Conference will be at Baltimore, and I hope you will certainly be there as we will need our heads to keep the church in proper trim."[1134]

J.M. Chivington
LOC, Simpson papers, Letter March 9, 1864, Container eight. LOC, Simpson papers, Letter March 9, 1864, Container eight. LOC, Simpson papers Letter March 9, 1864, Container eight.

1132 Evans Mss. Collection, History Colorado, Letter June 18, 1884.
1133 Evans Mss. Collection, History Colorado, Letter May 25, 1871.
1134 Evans Mss. Collection, History Colorado, Letter November 19, 1875.

Simpson counted John Evans as one of his closest friends, certainly his most trusted financial advisor. On two separate trips to Colorado, Simpson requested to visit the mines in which Evans had invested on behalf of the Bishop.[1135] When Evans sought a financial recommendation, Simpson provided the character reference: "It gives me pleasure to say that I have been acquainted with honorable John Evans, ex-governor, Colorado, for some thirty years. Our friendship during that time has been uninterrupted .... I believe him to be a gentleman of high moral integrity, having been an active member of the Methodist Church, having been a delegate in our last general conference, and he is a delegate-elect to the ensuing one." Like most ecclesiastics of his day, or any other, Simpson gaped at Evans financial acuity. "He has acquired a handsome property, has been president of a Railroad Company, thus; a reputation far more than ordinary financial skill. I would put the most implicit confidence in any statement he might make, in being his honest understanding and judgment in such cases."[1136]

Simpson's admiration was not without its direct financial benefits. Evidently, for Christmas 1880, Evans sent the Simpsons a sizable monetary gift to which Simpson responded, "I regret the delay to acknowledge your great kindness. I rejoice that God has given you, both the means with heart to delight in acts of kindness to your friends. But Mrs. S. as well as myself, were greatly surprised at so unexpectedly and so generous a present."[1137]

There is little doubt about Evans' generosity with his wealth. His gifts to Northwestern over the forty years of chairing its Board totaled over $100,000. He donated as much as half of the funds for the elaborate Lawrence Street Church, by far the most prominent structure in Denver during the 1860s. Of course, he was the main donor to Evans Memorial Chapel, built in 1878 in memory of his deceased daughter, Josephine. Evans earned the label accorded him by the Rocky Mountain Conference: "Layman par excellence."[1138]

1135   Evans Mss. Collection, History Colorado, Letters May 25, 1871, May 14, 1881.
1136   Evans Mss. Collection, History Colorado, Letter to Messrs. Carver, Fowler, and Parks, October 8, 1874.
1137   Evans Mss. Collection, History Colorado, Letter January 18, 1881.
1138   Kirby, 48.

In all likelihood, Evans did not know of Chivington's intentions to travel to Fort Lyon on November 28, for the purpose of destroying the Indian encampment at Sand Creek. Whether Evans could have done anything to prevent it raises a far different question, both psychologically and historically. Does a historian infer complicity when the highest jurisdictional authority knows that a particular outcome is probable? If so, Evans' complicity lies in the fact that he did little to nothing to douse the flame that burst into conflagration at Sand Creek, Colorado, November 29, 1864.

Chivington Maintains His Ministerial Credentials In Spite of His Sordid Past

In 1863, the Colorado Conference was formed, and in 1864, Chivington, in spite of his lack of involvement in church matters, was placed on the Auditing Committee and the Committee on Missions. Evans also served on the Auditing Committee, but how much face to face contact they had is difficult to say.[1139] In 1867, John Chivington was welcomed back into the Nebraska Annual Conference, but was not given an appointment. In 1868, he became an agent of the Nebraska Conference Church Extension Society, but it is unclear as to whether this was a volunteer or paid position. But by 1869, Chivington's Sand Creek baggage along with other shenanigans had caught up with him. No doubt, the events surrounding Chivington had been prime topics of conversation in the 1868 General Conference. Chivington was not present for roll call at either the 1869 or 1870 Nebraska Annual Conferences. The Friday, April 2, 1869, minutes recorded, "The case of J. M. Chivington with the papers therewith, was referred to the Presiding Elder of the Nebraska City District for investigation according to the discipline."[1140] The remainder of the minutes give no evidence that any action was taken in regard to Chivington's relationship to the Methodist Episcopal Church. When the Conference was closed, Chivington was still listed as an Elder. The 1870 Nebraska Annual Conference published minutes reported that,

---

1139   *Minutes of the Colorado Annual Conference of the Methodist Episcopal Church, Second Session,* held at Central, Colorado, October 20, 1864. These minutes were unpublished, and are on file: United Methodist Archives, Iliff School of Theology: Denver, Colorado Annual Conferences of UMC.

1140   *Minutes of the Nebraska Annual Conference of the Methodist Episcopal Church, Ninth Session* (Nebraska City: Price-Miller and Company, 1869) 8.

"J.M. Chivington's case was reported by the P.E. His character passed, and he located at his own request."[1141]

The 1870 written minutes included the tantalizing, following statement, which got edited out of the published minutes, "The documents in the case of J. M. Chivington were received and placed on file." Enough to make a historian salivate, but the "documents" have never been located.[1142] Again

---

1141 *Minutes of the Nebraska Conference of the Methodist Episcopal Church, Tenth Session* at Fremont, March 3- April 2, 1870 (Omaha: Republican Steam Printing House and Book Bindery, 1870) 4.

1142   Karrie Dvorak, Archivist for the Nebraska Conference of the United Methodist Church in an e-mail to the author, April 23, 2014, gives the best explanation, and, in all probability, the last word on the lost Chivington file: "W. B. and Grace Wetherell prepared a history of the Nebraska Methodist Historical Society in 1961. Pages 1-2 discuss the early efforts by members of the NE AC to gather documents relating to their early history. The first such efforts the Wetherells could find from their research were led by the Rev. W. B. Slaughter, a well-respected elder of the NE AC, who announced his intention to gather materials and write a history of Methodism in NE at the 1870 NE AC (at Fremont); note that was the same year that Chivington was brought up on charges and allowed to locate. It's hard for me to imagine that was coincidental, but it might have been; Slaughter could have been thinking about it simply because it was the year before the 10th anniversary of the founding of the NE AC and such anniversaries tend to get people thinking about those things (the NE AC was formed in 1861). Slaughter apparently did collect a lot of material and started to write a history, but he died in 1879 without finishing it (see p. 2). There was no official repository for the records of the NE AC until 1889, when the Nebraska Methodist Historical society ("NMHS") was organized, and Nebr: Wesleyan University (founded in 1887) was named as the official repository for its records. Keep in mind that the NE AC split into 4 separate conferences between 1882-1893; it wasn't until 1924 that they merged back into one conference. So, I think as a practical matter, it was hard to keep track of the records, as there was no official repository designated until 28 years after the NE AC was founded that's a long time for traveling ministers to keep track of records!

Slaughter may well have had the file on Chivington. If so, it may never have been transferred to NWU or the NE AC historian appointed to replace him when Slaughter died may never have rec'd it or he might have thrown it away. Alternatively, the file may never had made its way to Slaughter or anyone else who thought it was worth saving. It was almost 2 decades after Chivington was brought up on charges (in 1870) before the NMHS was created and a repository named. In actual practice, Wetherell's history seems to indicate that NWU didn't really start getting records until at least 1935 (p.11-12), the Discipline didn't officially require the records of the annual conf. to be preserved until 1940 (p.12)."

Because no official repository for records of the NE AC was even created until 1889, my best guess is that Chivington's file was lost or thrown away before folks really started gathering the relevant records for the NE AC. The Wetherell history to which Dvorak refers is, "Mr. and Mrs. W. B. Wetherell, History of the Nebraska Methodist Historical Society, 1961" on file, "Nebraska United Methodist Historical Society", Nebraska Wesleyan University, Lincoln, Nebraska.

the Conference ended with John Chivington listed as an Elder, i.e., in good standing with the Methodist Episcopal Church. Blood runs thicker than cronyism, but does not run further or wider. There will probably never be discovered a letter, nor a recorded action of the Methodist Episcopal Church Board of Bishops, which conveys that a reprimand ousting Chivington, would cost more than it accomplished. Cronyism, which consists of favors, alliances, friendships, and loyalties, that manages sin rather than confronting it, was effective in assuring that the Methodist Episcopal Church did not bring Chivington's sin to accountability and, thus, not its own. There is no evidence that the Methodist Episcopal Church ever stripped its notorious minister of his ecclesiastical credentials. A cronyism of white imperialism and economic ambitions bound Chivington, Evans, and Simpson together. As Simpson made his 1870s Colorado mine trips, he probably did not reflect on the possibility that he was part of the problem in the conflict between whites and Indians.

Chivington left Colorado for twenty years (Nebraska, California, Ohio, Canada, and wherever) with controversy following him almost everywhere he went. The years immediately following Sand Creek were particularly devastating for Chivington, events both beyond his control and of his own choosing. In 1866 his son, Thomas, drowned; in 1867 his two-year-old granddaughter, Lulu, drowned after falling off a Missouri steamboat, which resulted in a frantic but futile effort by her grandfather to save her; the same year his wife, Martha, died while attending a Methodist camp meeting. Then in the impetuosity of neurotic and erotic greed, in order to take advantage of his daughter-in-law's inheritance, he married the twenty-eight-year-old widow, twenty years younger than himself. Amazingly, Bishop Edward Ames performed the ceremony. In April of 1892, Sarah Chivington swore in an affidavit, "May 13th 1868 I was Married to J.M. Chivington by Bishop Ames of the M.E. Church in Chicago. Sarah Chivington."[1143]

Over the next several years Chivington's life was marred by several financial indiscretions, among them forging his name on a bond in order to receive compensation for several horses which his son Thomas had lost to Indians in 1864. Around the same time he was hauled into court for "grossly

---

1143   Cox-Paul, 137.

insulting a lady" by knocking her down on a Washington, D.C. street.[1144] Pathetically, two years before he died, Chivington, as coroner for Arapaho County, Colorado, was accused of stealing $800 from a corpse, which he returned, except for the $182 which he charged for his services.[1145]

Chivington returned to Colorado in 1884, to live out the rest of his years as a respected citizen by the majority of Coloradans and even most Methodists. The older he grew and the whiter his beard, the more dignified he appeared. On June 30, 1884, the *Daily News* reported on Chivington's speaking on the previous Sunday in two different Methodist Churches, "The Hero of Sand Creek Gives His Views on the Theory and Practice of the Christian Religion." Chivington proclaimed, "When Jesus gave that one grand rule 'whatever you would that men should do unto you, do you even so unto them,' He gave them the perfection of moral action. Again, we have the sublime theory in the Scripture of the Common Brotherhood of Our Race. We have the statement that God is no respecter of persons, but that in every nation they that fear God are accepted of him."[1146] Chivington's betrayal of the centrality of the Gospel did not bother the Methodists, or the Baptists, or the Presbyterians, for that matter. As they viewed it, "the brotherhood of mankind" did not include the Indians. Cancer claimed Chivington on October 4, 1894, and six hundred Masons walked through the streets of Denver in honor of their deceased hero.

Sand Creek, at least partially, is what happens when a gargantuan ego becomes marginalized. Persons who were unknown in American society before the Civil War were becoming heroes, their names splashed across American newspapers. The times were momentous, and there was little of importance taking place in Colorado, at least in the perspective of those who were changing history in battles that would become legend in the folklore and consciousness of American history. In Ari Kelman's assessment, "Because Sand Creek took place as the Civil War raged, and because the massacre catalyzed the Indian wars that followed, it seemed likely to be read by future generations as a pivotal chapter in the American story. Chivington, who believed that Sand Creek had been a noble and necessary part of

---
1144   Ibid.,137.
1145   Ibid., 144.
1146   *The Daily News*: Denver (June 30, 1884) 8-9.

winning the West, wanted the episode written into the national narrative as a glorious battle."[1147] November 29, 1864, was written into the "national narrative," but not as Chivington desired.

Simpson's Financial Investments and Conflicts of Interest

With friends in high places, and discretionary monies from his "war speech," Simpson during the Civil War began increasingly to search for investment opportunities. His financial ventures included mines in Colorado, Arizona, and California; land in Bellefontaine, Ohio, oil wells in Pennsylvania and The Whiteside County Land Company, Whiteside County, Illinois, a corporation which was formed with his brother-in-law, George McCullough. Shortly after Evans arrived in Colorado, Simpson inquired of him about the advisability of acquiring lands for orchards. Evans responded, "There are but few places to be had by settling that are watered and they are preparing to irrigate large tracts of places that will be the best when well-watered."[1148]

In the mid-nineteenth century, there was nothing more important for making profitable financial investments than to be able to ascertain the when and where of railroads. The triumvirate of Evans, Harlan, and Simpson, were acutely aware of this economic-geopolitical principle, and on December 17, 1858, Senator Harlan wrote Simpson, "You request me to inform you how things are shaping for the future …. The majority in Congress will not permit the revenue laws to be changed. Hence, no effective specific R. Bill can pass."[1149] Not only did Simpson profit from railroad right-of-ways, but tipped his daughter, Ella, who made a "handsome profit." Simpson was interested in securing profits for both his family, and his denomination. Simpson wrote Gilbert Haven on December 3, 1872, "I see that Gen. Rosecrans has procured the railroad grant from the Mexican government. The Pennsylvania R.R. are at his back, and means business. It seems to me that property will begin to rise and that openings for active usefulness will occur." Simpson urged Haven

---

1147 Ari Kelman. *A Misplaced Massacre: Struggling Over the Memory of Sand Creek* (Cambridge, MA: Harvard University Press, 2014) 9.

1148 LOC, Simpson papers, Letter December 22, 1862, Container seven.

1149 LOC, Simpson papers, Letter December 17, 1858, Container seven.

to secure "the grant," instead of Rosecrans, "as the latter is a strong Catholic, and I fear will work against every Protestant movement."[1150]

Eventually, Simpson's capitalistic pursuits would bring him into conflict with the best interests of the Cherokee Indians, not in Colorado, but in southeastern Kansas. Sometime in 1866, James Harlan, Secretary of the Interior, Simpson's highest and most formidable patronage placement, tipped Simpson regarding a financial opportunity in the American Emigrant Company. Simpson invested $2,500 in a cartel whose sole purpose was to purchase Indian lands, and realize a quick profit, by securing a railroad right-of-way through what is today, Cherokee County, Kansas.[1151] The American Emigrant Company was referred to as a "powerful combination of land grabbers, devising ways and means whereby they might purchase the lands in a body at one-tenth their real value."[1152]

By the authority of a treaty signed with the Cherokee Indians on July 19, 1866, regarding "neutral lands," lands owned but not occupied by Cherokee Indians, Harlan sold for one dollar per acre, 800,000 acres to the American Emigrant Company. What made the sale particularly suspect was first, though incorporated in Connecticut, the American Emigrant Company was headquartered in Des Moines, Iowa, and three of the nine members were from Mount Pleasant, Iowa, where the Secretary of the Interior had served as President of Iowa Wesleyan University. Second, according to some, Harlan had finalized the transaction August 30, 1866, on the night before he left office, a clandestine affair, which earned Harlan accusations of scandal and

---

[1150] UMA, Drew University, Gilbert Haven Papers, Letter, Matthew Simpson to Gilbert Haven, December 3, 1872.

[1151] This was not the original purpose of the company. It was founded in 1864 to attract labor from Europe because of shortage of manpower in the U.S. during the Civil War. "In more than half a dozen European states it established agencies which contracted with workmen and assisted others who were able to pay their own way, at a fee to prospective employers of ten dollars apiece for skilled artisans, six dollars for railroad and agricultural labor, and five dollars for boys and women who would work as domestics and farm workers. American consuls in Europe, at the urging of the Secretary of State, aided this work. During the law's first two years of operation, the commissioner of immigration registered 211 contracts, but the agents of the company inspired many more laborers who emigrated with their own resources." David Montgomery. *Beyond Equality: Labor and the Radical Republicans 1862–1872* (New York: Alfred A. Knopf, 1967) 23.

[1152] Morris Wardell. *A Political History of the Cherokee Nation: 1838-1907* (Norman: University of Oklahoma Press, 1938) 214.

eventually cost him his Senate seat in 1872. The Secretary of the Interior was accused of having, "his clerks up at night, and he was finishing up business at a furious rate. After midnight, Mr. Harlan signed the Neutral Land contract, dating it two days back, and sent it out for record in the department."[1153]

The newspapers poured out their full fury on this betrayal of the Indians and the inflated prices which settlers would pay for the land. The editor of the *Daily Times* in Leavenworth wrote, "I cannot look upon this extraordinary affair in any other light than a most cold-blooded swindle, and a most flagrant violation of the obvious intention and spirit of a sacred trust."[1154] Harlan was called a "pious swindler and the Indian office was described as the seat of an enormous corruption, the fruitful source of Indian wars, the scandal of the government."[1155] Josiah Grinnell, Iowa Congressman, who held a one-tenth interest in the American Emigrant Company, was called a, "blustering, beefy, corrupt, pharisaical foo-foo; he is as much out of place in Congress as a bull in a china shop."[1156] Kansas Senator Samuel Pomeroy though only marginally involved in the transaction, was referred to as "Blow gun and Blatherskite" and his pompous manner earned him a caricature in Mark Twain's *The Gilded Age*.[1157] Contemporary newspaper editor Eugene Ware summed up the matter, "Pomeroy and Harlan enjoyed, in the newspapers at that time, a similar notoriety. Both of them were intentionally devout. Both of them worked under *ministerial* (italics mine) influence to the fullest extent, and both of them were charged with bribe taking and bribe giving, and both of them went out of office under the same kind of cloud."[1158]

1153   *Transactions of the Kansas State Historical Society, 189-1900; Together With Addresses at Annual Meetings, Memorials, And Miscellaneous Papers*, also, *A Catalog of Kansas Constitutions*, and *Territorial and State Documents in The Historical Society* Vol. VI, ed. George. W. Martin, Secretary (Topeka: Kansas Historical Society) 154.

1154   "The Cherokee Treaty," *The Daily Times*, Leavenworth, Kansas (October 17, 1866) 3, on file, Kansas Historical Society, Topeka, Kansas, under Cherokee Neutral Lands.

1155   Paul Wallace Gates. *Fifty Million Acres: Conflicts Over Kansas Land Policy: 1854-1890* (Ithaca, New York: Cornell University Press, 1954) 156.

1156   Gates, 166.

1157   Craig Miner. "Border Frontier: The Missouri River, Fort Scott & Gulf Railroad in the Cherokee Neutral Lands, 1868-1870," *Kansas Historical Quarterly* Volume XXXV, No. 2 (Summer 1969) 106.

1158   *Transactions of the Kansas State Historical Society, 1897-1900*, 154, Kansas State Historical Society, Topeka, Kansas.

When Orville Brown succeeded Harlan as Secretary of the Interior, he voided the deal with the American Emigrant Company and gave the contract to James Joy, a railroad investor from Minnesota at the same price and almost identical terms. In the summer of 1868, the Bishop approached both Harlan and Grinnell, requesting his principal and any interest he may have earned. On July 17, Harlan informed Simpson that Grinnell was, "prepared to return to you your money and interest and $3,000 and he probably will claim better than you could. I could do it if I had not been mixed up with the sale."[1159] He further stated of Cherokee County, "They will build a railroad through it making it worth $5.00 per acre. This would give you a fine profit." Three days later, Grinnell wrote Simpson that he had his money back, $2,500 with interest. "I also have a contract either for cash in hand or note for one year which will make you show after profits by transfer between $3,000 and $4,000 less certain expenses which will bring you not over $5,000 for which I have a promise by Mr. Joy of a, 'ground floor' interest in his R.R. and Sand scheme which promises, I think, two hundred percent."[1160] In other words, if Simpson allowed his money to be used one more year, he would double his investment. (My perception is that Grinnell should have said one hundred per cent rather than two hundred per cent, which in our understanding would be doubling Simpson's money.) It would be a tidy profit.

Methodism Attempts Amends

As for Evans, he never left Colorado except for brief trips back East. Even though he never obtained his coveted Senate seat, he grew richer still by connecting Denver to the Trans-Continental Railroad. Before he died, his fortune had almost been wiped out by over-extension and the 1890s depression. No man was more revered in Colorado than John Evans, who even had a mountain named for him. He died on July 13, 1897. His body lay in state in the Colorado capitol, with most businesses closing out of respect for his life and death.[1161]

1159   LOC, Simpson papers, Letter July 17, 1868, Container eight.
1160   UMA of the E. PA Conference of the United Methodist Church, St. George's UMC, Philadelphia, PA, Simpson papers, Letter July 20, 1868.
1161   Kelsey, 226-229.

When the United Methodist General Conference met in Denver, Colorado, in 1996, the Assembly passed a resolution "That this body of the 1996 General Conference extends to all Cheyenne and Arapahos a hand of reconciliation and asks forgiveness of over 200 persons, mostly women and children, who died in this state where this Great Conference is being held." The Conference laid the blame at Chivington's feet, as one who had "held various pastoral appointments including a District Superintendency." Obviously, the "Resolution" did not trace complicity to John Evans, much less Matthew Simpson.[1162] Such political correctness may assuage guilt feelings, but does not eliminate the solidarity of guilt in which we all stand, as we meet in convention centers, and sleep in hotels, constructed on land which was a century and one half ago, the province of Native Americans.

As increased historical scrutiny was given to Sand Creek over the next two decades, the United Methodist Church came under the conviction that the 1996 resolution, occasioned by the General Conference meeting in Denver, was woefully inadequate. The denomination commissioned Gary L. Roberts, a prominent Sand Creek scholar, to investigate the "massacre," and American Methodism's complicity in the event. The denomination also assigned a "Joint Committee" to work with Dr. Roberts, consisting of "ministers, laymen, historians, and tribal representatives of the Cheyenne and Arapaho Tribes of Oklahoma, the Northern Arapaho Tribe of Wyoming, and the Northern Cheyenne Tribe in Montana."[1163] Roberts' 300-page report, already cited in this book, concluded that Methodists represented the normative nineteenth century bigotry toward the Indians, a prejudice intensified by the capitalistic pursuits and lust for land that preempted any genuine concern for Indian rights. But Methodism's guilt was far more pronounced than culpability by association in the abstract. Many of the major players in the conquest for Colorado were Methodists, such as Samuel Elbert, W. A. H. Loveland, Henry Teller, Jerome Chaffee, and David Moffat. There were accusations that a "Methodist Click" controlled Colorado.[1164]

1162 "Sand Creek Apology," *The Book of Resolutions of the United Methodist Church* (Nashville: United Methodist Publishing House, 1996) 396-397.
1163 Roberts, *Massacre at Sand Creek*, XVII.
1164 Ibid., 233.

Roberts insightfully assesses that the Methodist Episcopal Church became a reflection of society instead of a mirror for society. Methodism was a "white man's" church, "a militant church that represented upper middle class values including the essential goodness of making money."[1165] According to Roberts, Simpson as a key Methodist leader, sanctified the denomination's march into Colorado, a conquest more determined to fill bank accounts than to save the souls of Indians. Roberts aptly titles his last chapter, "The Balance Sheet," and concludes: "The Methodist Episcopal Church embraced the prevailing mind-set of its time, avoided a strong stand against Sand Creek, defended both Chivington and Evans, and played a minimal role in the dialogue over Indian policy in the years that followed."[1166]

Sadly, the books will never be balanced, but Christian eschatology teaches that the accounts of humanity will ultimately be settled.

All of us that luxuriate do so at someone else's expense. At least we possess the distance of history that enables us to condemn others, who lived in different circumstances than we do. On June 20, 1865, newly-elected Bishop Calvin Kingsley wrote Simpson from Denver: "The removal of Governor Evans at this time will be a most unfortunate, if not disastrous affair in this territory. We are just getting a good start in Denver and other important points in the territory, and the Col. and Gov. Evans have been pillars in the church. The persecution of Col. Chivington will probably drive him from the territory, and if the Gov., too, should be removed, it would be a sad day for us."[1167] Sadly, the ecclesiastic did not know that one of the blackest days in Native American history had already come, and would never be gone. As William Faulkner said, "The past is never gone. In fact, it is not even past."

Simpson, Evans and the Collusion of Silence

Northwestern University was fully aware of Faulkner's aphorism, when in the winter of 2013, its administration requested eight scholars to investigate Sand Creek, and more specifically, to identify John Evans' responsibility in the

---

1165   Ibid., 234.
1166   Ibid., 230.
1167   LOC, Simpson papers, Letter June 20, 1865, Container eight.

affair. In attempting to answer the question, "Did Northwestern indirectly or directly benefit from their founder's relationship to Sand Creek?" the thorough 110 page report came to six conclusions, which I summarize: 1. Evans had no prior knowledge and did not plan the massacre. 2. His flawed policy contributed to the massacre. 3. He never confessed any culpability and therefore exhibited deep "moral failure." 4. Rather than Evans profiting from Sand Creek, the incident hurt him both economically and politically. 5. Though the University would not be able to quantify contributions that had accrued to them through policies destructive to Native Americans, the University had economically benefited. 6. The University had ignored its moral failures and they should be corrected.

What the investigation concluded for the purpose of our inquiry is that Simpson and Evans, while serving as board members for Northwestern University, entered into a collusion of silence about Sand Creek.

> No evidence suggests that, when Evans came under fire in Washington as a result of the Sand Creek Massacre and had to resign the governorship, the matter ever came up among the Board members meeting in Evanston. If it did arise in their private conversations, few of his colleagues could have conceived of expressing doubts about his conduct or of asking him to step down. This was not only because of their long-standing friendship with him and appreciation of his service and generosity but also because they probably believed, as he did, that he had done nothing wrong. For proof, they could point not only to his self-defense but also to the strong support he received from many leading politicians and most importantly, from the individual they held in the highest esteem, Bishop Matthew Simpson.[1168]

Whatever the guilt of John Chivington, John Evans, and Matthew Simpson, they incarnated the prevailing white mentality of 1864 Coloradans. The final conquest of the 1803 Louisiana Purchase was the elimination of its original inhabitants. In July of 1865, an investigating committee of Senators James Doolittle, F. S. Foster, and Congressman Lewis Ross, traveled to Denver. On July 21, they held an open forum in the Denver Theatre. Doolittle asked whether the Indians should be placed on reservations or exterminated. "[T]here suddenly arose such a shout, as is never heard unless

---

1168 *John Evans Study Committee*, 95 .

upon some battlefield--a shout loud enough to raise the roof of the opera house: 'Exterminate them! Exterminate them!'"[1169]

Sand Creek was not an anomaly; it was a tragic representation of might makes right, and God favors larger battalions. It was the progress of civilization, a step forward that almost always exposes an ugly posterior branded with greed and selfishness. Money, "the root of all evil," always delineates the oppressor from the oppressed. The Indians, driven out of their natural habitat by professed followers of Christ, were no different than the Chinese who built the Central-Pacific, the West Indies laborers who dug the Panama Canal, the slaves who picked cotton in the South, and pre-union coal miners in West Virginia. Exploitation is one of the most consistent themes within the history of humanity. Gary Roberts concludes that, "The Indians were encircled and the lusty exploitative combination of American settlers and American industry could not be held back for long. The dream of men like John Evans, was careening pell mell into reality, and no group of 'savages' could stand in the way of progress."[1170]

1169 Roberts, *Tragedy and Symbol*, 515.
1170 Ibid., 573.

Chapter Fifteen: All the King's Horses and All the King's Men

The Primary Worry of the Simpson Family

During the war years, domestic life for the Simpsons did not come to a standstill, but was seriously strained. The additional speaking engagements, trips to Washington, journey to the West Coast, and even more extensive travel because of living off the beaten Episcopal path (Evanston), lessened the letters to home, and increased the conflict with Ellen. And, of course, Ellen did not sufficiently communicate. "But why don't you write? Have you your teeth fixed yet? Are you going East before I come? Are you so much occupied with visiting that you cannot get time to write? If so, who are you occupied with? You know at home you ask a thousand and one questions. Now let us ask them …"[1171] She also complained that her husband was not keeping her sufficiently informed, and Matthew responded with a ten-point letter, sermonic form, part of which read, "How could you think I was cold for not writing of our personal matters? I have a deep aversion to bringing myself or family matters before the public …. I suppose my letters would be more interesting if there was more of self and personal affairs but somehow it is not my taste."[1172]

Both husband and wife were frustrated by not being able to sell inherited property in Pittsburgh and a lack of money flow. (Matthew had already informed Ellen in the October 18, 1861 letter, "the *Tribune* and other papers are pitching in to somebody about Pittsburgh for selling bad

---

1171   UMA, Drew University, Simpson papers, Matthew to Ellen, Letter October 18, 1861.
1172   UMA, Drew University, Simpson papers, Matthew to Ellen, Letter August 29, 1862.

houses.") The husband explained: "But, Dearest, whatever you have decided; the failure to sell the lot did not make me disposed and have you stay at home. I had arranged with Dr. Carlton for money–and no money could make me willing to dispense with your company."[1173] Seemingly, Simpson had a running account with Carlton. Carlton asked Simpson if he could charge the $141.53 insurance premium to his (Simpson's) office.[1174]

Charles was the primary worry of the Simpson family. He was beginning to show the symptoms of the nineteenth-century killer, consumption, present-day tuberculosis. The father feared his son's physical condition would be further aggravated by his use of tobacco. In Simpson's estimation, his oldest son had become profligate. In spite of, or because of all of his father's pleading, Charles was living outside of the fold of Christianity. Matthew wrote Ellen, "Nothing but his full conversion will save him. Rather let him fail in business-be sick-or pass away, if need be, than live long and be prosperous and be lost. This thing must have been of long standing. I have no doubt it began in Pittsburgh and was continued in Berea."[1175]

Charles' vocational instability necessitated the father persuading Thomas Carlton to hire him in the New York Book Concern, and in 1863, making arrangements with Clinton Fisk for his son to become the General's personal assistant. Charles had joined the Union Army, and the Bishop was concerned about his son's safety. Fisk responded to the father's plea, "Nothing would give me greater pleasure than to be able to have him associated with myself and make him one of my military family .... I believe him to be better qualified for Asst Adjt Genl, than for any other position and he would doubtless be better pleased with the duties of that position than any other. He should write well and rapidly."[1176] The war provided stability and security for Charles but after his discharge from the Union Army, the father wrote a stern plea:

1173   Ibid.
1174   LOC, Simpson papers, Letter December 30, 1869, Container eight.
1175   UMA, Drew University, Simpson papers, Letter April 19, 1860.
1176   UMA, Drew University, Simpson papers, Letter August 1, 1863.

Washington   Oct 18 1865

Dear Charles:

Resolution is everything on the human side–prayer is everything on the Divine.

Resolve that manfully–pray earnestly. Look to God for the forgiveness of sins and the renewal of your nature. I would sooner have you a new creature in Christ Jesus, than the possessor of all earth's treasures. I hope that you are enjoying yourself well and that you are doing your duty in all things. You do not know how my heart yearns for your happiness and prosperity.

You will be both wiser and happier, if you read two or three chapters in the Bible every morning. Do this, at my request, and by then you will love it for the good which it does you.

Don't neglect any duty, because you have neglected it hitherto, but be faithful to yourself, your friends, and your God. I hope some business arrangements will be found suitable for you, but in the mean times, look up to God and patiently trust Him.

When I return if all things are right, I will try to do what I can to relieve you from embarrassments .... But remember one mistake will fearfully destroy my power.

Love to Maggie and the baby.
May God bless You. Write to me fully.
Yours affectionately,
M. Simpson[1177]

A letter to Ida from San Francisco, gives us a unique glimpse into the Father's personal concerns for his family. "I have climbed many high hills and mountains since I came here, and some of them are so very high that they have snow on them all the time. I had a little boy with me one day, not so big as you, and I played with him in a snow bank with snowballs in July. What do you think of that?" The letter then turned from snowballs to spiritual exhortations. "Say your prayers; love the blessed Savior who died for you, and ask Him to forgive your sins and give you a new heart. You may die like little 'Maggie Evans' (John Evans' daughter), you ought to be good so that you can meet her in Heaven."[1178]

1177   UMA, Drew University, Simpson papers, Letter October 18, 1865.
1178   UMA, Drew University, Simpson papers, Letter September 6, 1862.

Tension between Simpson and McCullough

Simpson, with extra money coming in from speaking engagements, began to search for investments–taking advice from Evans, Harlan, and his brothers-in-law, George McCullough and James Verner. For the most part, wells, farms, or mines, never produced a huge profit, and caused more anxiety than they were worth. Financial entanglements with McCullough strained their relationship. During the McCullough's stay in Iowa City, in order for their son to attend the university, they had been drained of their financial resources. Matthew wrote Ellen, "I am detained here by business matters, and I find that I must go to near Fulton to see about the farm I own, and some claims. I find that matters must be attended to, as I am in danger of losing very considerably. There is no chance of business for Charles here. Things are very dull, and McCullough is in no regular business, but is trading land for goods, and goods for lands."[1179]

McCullough believed matters to be getting out of hand, and desired an accounting from Simpson. Simpson did some calculations for the brother-in-law, and suggested that their attorneys sell the property designated as Whiteside County Lands.[1180] Simpson's suggestion of turning matters over to an attorney sent McCullough into a tizzy. "You know if that course is pursued, it will take years before it can be done, particularly as you depend on lawyers to do all the business and the one you name I have no more confidence in than others and with less judgment and knowledge than many of them. They all will try to do things in the way that they can secure or pocket the greatest amount. My experience with them has been as you know that through their management they done all they could to filch and rob me in every way they could, and the result you know. And you can expect nothing better in this case." In short, McCullough wanted out of the whole mess. "If you feel that you ought to allow me anything, do so. But I want it closed off my mind. And again, I am so anxious to have everything of the business kind settled between us that I want you to say how much you will give me for my interest in the Bellefontaine claim. If it is not the exact

---

1179 UMA, Drew University, Simpson papers, Letter February 7, 1860.
1180 LOC, Simpson papers, Letter November 28, 1864, Container seven.

amount, nor as much as might be had I do not care, so that we can have all matters fixed up between us."[1181]

Simpson had partially bought out McCullough in April of 1858, paying him $6,000 for jointly owned land in Whiteside County, Illinois. Between April of 1858 and April 1872, Simpson purchased nine plots of land, Whiteside County, Illinois, in nine separate transactions. The sum of the investments totaled $9,804. Between February 1862 and November 1872, he sold the same parcels again in nine separate transactions for the total of $21,000, more than doubling his money. Eleven thousand dollars for eighteen land transactions over a fifteen year period was not an enormous profit. We conclude that Simpson was enticed by the fertility of Mississippi River farmland, as he looked from the window of the train traveling between Chicago and Iowa City where McCullough lived. All of the farms were in the vicinity of Fulton, Illinois, four hours directly west of Chicago, purchases convenienced by Simpson living in Evanston.[1182]

The Move to Philadelphia

Perceiving that Simpson was not satisfied with Evanston, a location necessitating extensive travel because of its northwestern location, Methodist Annual Conferences from 1860-1863 besieged him with residential offers. Simpson's popularity would mean prestige for any Annual Conference willing to provide him with a base of operation. Evans did his best to prevent Simpson from leaving Evanston, "The lots fronting the lake are provided; and the plans similar to Dr. Kidder's house, though not so quite large, is agreed upon and unless we get a response to this disapproving, we shall go on with its erection."[1183] The office of G. C. Cook offered the Bishop the opportunity to make Chicago his home; the trustees of Dickinson College, Carlisle, Pennsylvania, offered him the John McClintock mansion (a house

---

1181   LOC, Simpson papers, Letter December 7, 1864, Container seven. I have contacted the Logan County Historical Society in Ohio, and researchers can find no trace of any business transactions by Simpson or McCullough in Bellefontaine.

1182   Information furnished by Harvey Geerts, researcher at the Fulton Historical Society and Dawn M. Young, Whiteside County Recorder, Morrison, Illinois. Copies of all the deeds are in this author's possession.

1183   LOC, Simpson papers, Letter March 10, 1861, Container seven.

where McClintock had lived while professor and still exists), and the Hoyt brothers offered to purchase him a home at a place of his choosing somewhere north of New York City. Annual Conferences normally expressed gratitude to the presiding Bishop for his services, but in the March 18, 1863 Annual Conference, Philadelphians were particularly obsequious, expressing thanks for Simpson's service as "an able and important presiding officer."[1184]

Philadelphia historian Sam Bass Warner claims that mid-nineteenth century Philadelphia suffered from the congestion of poor planning. "The grid street, the narrow house lot, the row house, the interior alley, and the rear yard house or shack, were endlessly repeated. When so repeated however, they lost entirely their eighteenth century character, and took on instead that mixture of druri-ness and confusion which so characterized nineteenth century mass building."[1185] But the 1850s did see some improvements, amenities that appealed to the Simpson family.

> The bare floors, white washed walls, and scant furniture of middle-income eighteenth-century home gave way to wool carpeting, wall paper, and all manner of furnishings. The homes themselves became relatively cheaper, and grew in size from three rooms to four to six rooms, in row houses or flats in row houses. The children slept one to a bed, and indoor toilets became common in their homes.[1186]

In January of 1861, Alexander Cummings beseeched Simpson to make Philadelphia his home.[1187] Finally, Simpson favorably replied to a letter written by Philadelphia pastor James Neil written on April 11, 1863, and the Philadelphia Conference had hit the Episcopal jackpot. A group of laymen headed by James Long and James Neil, acting outside the auspices of the Philadelphia Conference, banded together and purchased the Simpson's a house at 1805-1807 Mount Vernon Street, Philadelphia. This unofficial parsonage committee gave due diligence to the enterprise, a complete

---

1184   UMA, E. PA Conference of the UMC, Old St. George's Church, Philadelphia, Simpson papers, "Resolutions unanimously adopted by the Philadelphia Annual Conference," West Chester, on March 18, 1863, signed by Robert H. Patterson, Secretary, March 27, 1863.

1185   Sam Bass Warner. *The Private City: Philadelphia in Three Periods of Growth* (Philadelphia: University of Pennsylvania Press) 50.

1186   Ibid., 66.

1187   LOC, Simpson papers, Letter, Alexander Cummings to Simpson, January 20, 1861, Container seven.

overhaul of the house. They kept the Bishop apprised of their progress, and also asked him for remodeling advice, but Simpson gave little to no input. The house was not as prestigious as the committee had hoped. James Long wrote on June 2, 1863, "We have not been able to please ourselves fully, nor are we in the choice of the Mount Vernon Street house, but it is the best we can do at the present, and I am glad that it pleased Mrs. Simpson. I hope it will please you, but if it should be thought out of the way, it could be changed for a house more central."[1188]

Pleased or not, the Simpsons lived at 1807 Mount Vernon Street for the next twenty years. The providers adapted the residence as thoroughly as possible to the Bishop's professional needs and to Ellen's aesthetic tastes. "The size of the back building at present including dining room and kitchen is 13 + 29 feet, Dining room is 13 + 16 feet. The second floor now where you contemplate making your study can be divided as you desire, either as the lower story or otherwise-if the partitions are continued up, it will give your study room 13 + 20, or 4 feet to its present length, and the room for your uncle, 13 + 14."[1189] More than anyone else James Long took leadership in buying and readying the home.[1190]

1188   LOC, Simpson papers, Letter, James Long to Matthew Simpson, June 2, 1863, Container seven.

1189   LOC, Simpson papers, James Long to Matthew Simpson, Letter June 24, 1863, Container seven.

1190   James Long was a lay-delegate to the 1872 General Conference and also to the 1881 Wesleyan Conference in London. He, like Simpson's ancestors, was born in Tyrone County, Ireland. After working seventeen-hour days in a grocery store, he was hired by his uncle as General Superintendent in a cotton mill. This ardent Methodist served with Simpson on the Church Extension Society. "For several years he was wholly occupied with the manufacture of cottons, but other business demanding his attention, he was obliged to divide his time accordingly. Having been one of the original subscribers to the stock of the Huntingdon & Broad Top Railroad Company, he was elected, in 1858, a Director of the same, which official station he has continuously held until the present. He was likewise one of the original subscribers to the stock of the Frankford & Southwark Passenger Railway Company (the first laid down in Philadelphia), and is also a Director in the same. He was, in 1865, one of the original founders of the Eighth National Bank, was elected a member of its first Board of Directors, and is now Vice-President of the corporation. He also fills the responsible position of Treasurer of the Penn Mutual Life Insurance Company. In the approaching International Exposition for the Centennial Celebration of American Independence, to be held in Philadelphia in 1876, he has been selected to the very important position of Chairman of the Committee of Cotton and Woolen Manufacturers. As a member of the Board of Education, he is, in all probability, more frequently consulted, and

One problem impeding progress was the residents who still lived in the house. On October 3 Long wrote, "The house was vacated last week. The back building taken down as far as necessary and they are putting up the addition. Brother Miller called this a.m. to know what you desire in respect to the fireplace in your study. It will occupy the center of the partition wall; it will divide your bookcase, but will only be 4 feet wider. Please advise us immediately on this point."[1191] In October the house was receiving its final touches: "There has been more delay in the papering than we expected. It is not papered yet, but according to Mr. Howe's promise, it will all be finished this week. Your friends think it best for Mrs. Simpson to come and have the things fixed that she may think best."[1192] In November, the Simpsons moved to Philadelphia, and were handed a lien-free deed to their new house. The house was fully furnished with a $1,500 gift raised by the Hoyt brothers.

The Simpson home was not a mansion, but a respectable three-story attached, middle-class row house. Eighteen-hundred-seven Mount Vernon Street was forty feet across and approximately sixty feet deep.[1193] The committee had purchased two attached row houses, lots 1805 and 1807. When the Simpson house was purchased, 1805 disappeared from the city addresses. Because it was three stories, the house provided over 7,000 square feet of living space. A publication in 1863, *The Stranger's Guide to Philadelphia* informed that, "Most of the houses in this city are built on a uniform plan being generally three stories high. Within the last few years, however, there has been a decided advance in the style of building, and our streets are now being adorned with edifices that are unrivaled for taste, elegance, and convenience."[1194] The "elegant" houses were one street over on Green Street where Mathias Baldwin, the founder and owner of Baldwin

---

with much greater satisfaction, than any of his colleagues." *The Biographical Encyclopedia of Pennsylvania of the Nineteenth Century* (Philadelphia: Galaxy Publishing Company, 1874) 100.

1191   LOC, Simpson papers, Letter, James Long to Matthew Simpson, August 3, 1863, Container seven.

1192   LOC, Simpson papers, Letter, James Long to Matthew Simpson, October 16, 1863, Container seven

1193   Elvino V. Smith. *1909 Ward Atlas Map*: Atlas of the Eleventh-Seventeenth Ward, 1909.

1194   Quoted in the *Spring Garden History District: A Guide for Property Owners* (Philadelphia: Philadelphia Historical Commission, no date) 4.

Locomotive lived. Only two blocks from Baldwin's home was Baldwin Locomotive Works, a manufacturing complex extending for three blocks, from the south side of Spring Garden Street extending to Callowhill. As opposed to upscale residential areas today, both the Baldwins and Simpsons lived in the vicinity of an industrial complex.[1195]

Some Methodists were troubled by the "large white house" (which was not a large white house) occupied by Simpson. The newspapers did not describe the life of a simple, Methodist preacher.

> His many admiring friends will read with pleasure the following account of the presentation on Thanksgiving Day, of a well-furnished mansion to the Rev. Matthew Simpson, Bishop of the Methodist Church, which ceremony took place at No. 1807 Mount Vernon Street, Philadelphia. The occasion was a happy gathering of the ladies and gentlemen who contributed to the gift and who are efficient members of the church.
>
> The mansion is double, with side parlors each illuminated with six-light chandeliers, a hall and vestibule in the center; extensive back building, the library sitting room reception room, etc., the whole being warmed by means of improved patent heaters and handsomely furnished in all its apartments.[1196]

Looking Older than His Fifty-five Years

Philadelphia, the birthplace of our nation, adequately celebrated its "new birth." Simpson fulfilled his ceremonial duties with his normal forte for public appearances. He offered a formal benediction for the 1865 Fourth of July parade. He fulfilled both private and public duties for the Christian Commission, which had been headed by George Stuart. Simpson pronounced the final benediction for the termination for the

---

1195   According to Architectural Historian, Terry Necciai, the Simpson home was a "typical row house, small, one of many about the same size in the block .... The pink-red wash suggests the houses were all red brick. Email, April 25, 2014 from Terry Necciai, RA, Presentation Architect and Architectural Historian. But keep in mind, the "Housing Committee" purchased two of these houses and combined them. Unfortunately, the Simpson house was torn down to make room for an elementary school. Mount Vernon Street today extends only through the seventeen-hundred block.

1196   "Presentation of a Mansion to Bishop Simpson," *Chicago Tribune* 1860-1872 (Dec. 3, 1863).

Christian Commission, thanking Stuart and the thousands that had assisted in giving material and spiritual comfort to millions of soldiers.[1197] After the hundreds of speeches and parades in Northern cities and villages, Americans would have to face the grim reality that there were now more discontented Americans who were more unhappy than they had been, or would ever be again.

On the second Sunday of June, 1865, Southern Methodist S. S. Headle was warned by Northern Methodists not to preach at Pleasant View, Missouri. When he defied the threat that he would be murdered, a mob which included Henderson McNabb, "a member of the Methodist Episcopal Church in good standing," shot Headle three times which resulted in a lingering, pathetic, seven hour death.[1198] Almost at the same time, the *St. Louis Christian Advocate* reported the death of Green Woods, who had been killed by Northern Methodists in 1862, for ignoring warnings to not preach at a particular place.[1199] Cannon and canister may have achieved a truce at Appomattox, but no white flag would diffuse the hatred and animosity between the North and the South. It would take almost a century for the Northern and Southern Methodist churches, (1844-1939) to reunite, and the Southern and Northern Baptist churches have not declared a truce until this day.

The South had been destroyed. The material, psychological, and cultural wounds seemed untreatable: infrastructure ripped apart, cities burned out, ports obliterated, farms demolished, livestock killed, forests blighted, and human dignity trampled into the dust. Eminent historian, Allan Nevins wrote, "Worst of all was the irretrievable human ruin, physical and moral. Mississippi alone had fully 10,000 orphans; a family there which had not lost a member seemed a rarity; an observer said that half of the adult male population appeared to be gone. The destruction of character and courage, the effect of ruin, camp dissipation and guerrilla warfare was more saddening than poverty or death."[1200] Southern diarist Katherine Edmondson wrote that "the future

---

1197 Thomas Scharf and Thomas Westcott. *History of Philadelphia: 1609-1884* Vol. I (Philadelphia: L. H. Everts & Co., 1884) 829-831.

1198 W. M. Leftwich. *Martyrdom in Missouri* (St. Louis: Southwestern Book and Publishing Company, 1870) 428 – 429.

1199 Ibid., 358–359.

1200 Allan Nevins. *The Emergence of Modern America: 1865-1878* (New York: The Macmillan Company, 1927) 5.

stands before us as dark, forbidding and stern" and "all the bitterness of death without the lively hope of Resurrection."[1201]

Added to the destruction which had already taken place was a precipitous drop in the price of cotton and the loss of 4,000,000 slaves who had worked the land. Reconstruction historian Eric Foner writes, "Southern planters emerged from the Civil War in a state of shock. Their class had been demolished–physically, economically, and psychologically. Thousands of wealthy young men had heeded the Confederacy's call only to die in battle .... The loss of the Confederate lands wiped out the inheritance of generations."[1202] Confederate paper money was hardly worth its weight in dirt.

What Simpson actually thought of the above, we do not know. We should not quickly indict him for a gloating triumphalism. Neither is there any evidence of Simpson's empathy for the South nor deep sorrow for its predicament. We do know what the South thought, at least partially. The *New Orleans Picayune* was no doubt representative of widespread Southern attitudes, when it asserted that Simpson had never lifted his voice against the "mongers of extreme radicalism, to abandon their atrocious schemes for the blood and plunder of a conquered, and unresisting, a much wronged and much robbed people." The newspaper further stated that Simpson "has never so far as we Southerners know, used his grand oratory to enforce the claims of Christian humanity and toleration towards those whom he and his admirers called rebels."[1203] Simpson and many other Northern clergymen were targets of Southern animosity, motivated by fear, that in Charles Reagan Wilson's assessment, "focused especially on the North–its churches, its religious movements, its immigrants, its power in the American nation–as the underminer of Southern religious hegemony. Southerners brooded that the Civil War had unleashed powerful forces which would descend from the North, or perhaps even emerge indigenously, and destroy the Southern Zion they were building."[1204] The antipathy towards the North was stronger after the War than before. The Rebel uniform and flag had

---

1201   Quoted in Bruce Levine. *The Fall of the House of Dixie: The Civil War and the Social Revolution that Transformed the South* (New York: Random House, 2014) 289.

1202   Eric Foner. *Reconstruction: America's Unfinished Revolution: 1863-1877* (New York: Harper and Row, 1989) 129

1203   Clark, *Pulpit and Platform*, 412.

1204   Charles Reagan Wilson. *Baptized in Blood: The Religion of the Lost Cause: 1865–1920* (Athens: The University of Georgia Press, 1980) 10.

become symbols for a sacred society on sacred soil. Southerners were more "Christian" than Northerners because as Christ, they had been crucified. (In fact, the Confederate flag was patterned after St. Andrew's cross.)

The fond hopes for Andrew Johnson reconstructing the South, and in particular, rebuilding Black society by offering federal protection to freed Blacks, who in many ways were still in bondage, quickly dissipated into disillusionment. Johnson's "political apostasy," to the grief of Simpson and the "radical Republicans," included vetoing funds for the continuation of the Freedmen's Bureau, rejecting a "civil rights bill" which would eventually become the Fourteenth Amendment, and an inability to express any sympathy in word or deed for the plight of the Negro. African Americans were faced with a new set of problems, in many ways more complex than they experienced before January 1, 1863. Historian Walter McDougall succinctly writes, "Negros seeking work or expecting a Biblical jubilee clustered in wretched 'dark' towns where malnutrition, smallpox, tuberculosis, and diseases thriving on filth carried off as much as one-third of the population."[1205] Their situation would get worse before it got better.

In the immediate post-war years, racial tension exploded throughout the South, including the Memphis race riot of May 1866 when, "Infuriated white police officers and mobs killed nearly 50 black men, women, and children."[1206] In New Orleans, approximately three months later on July 30, enraged Southerners killed thirty-four blacks and three white radicals, and further injured one hundred persons. General Philip Sheridan referred to the disaster as, "an absolute massacre," and former Vice-President Hannibal Hamlin recorded that he had never witnessed on the battlefield such, "wholesale slaughter and little regard paid to human life."[1207]

News of deconstruction rather than reconstruction traveled to the North via newspaper and telegraph. Early in 1867 a Nashville newspaper described "regulators" who were "whipping, maiming, and killing all Negros who do

---

1205   Walter A. McDougall. *Throes of Democracy: The American Civil War Era: 1829-1877* (New York: Harper, 2008) 503.

1206   Phillip Dray. *Capitol Men: The Epic Story of Reconstruction through the Lives of the First Black Congressman* (Boston: Mariner Books, 2008).

1207   Foner, 263.

not obey the order of their former masters just as if slavery existed."[1208] Northerner John Wesley North intervened when a mob beat a freedman and the Knoxville inhabitants were "amazed that any person should venture to remonstrate against even the murderer of a black man"[1209] Increasingly; the radical Republicans perceived that the only answer to the deteriorating conditions in the South was to get rid of the President. The process would involve Simpson in political maneuvering and ecclesiastical leverage which has not placed him in a favorable historical light.

The Civil War had taken its toll on everyone, Northerners and Southerners, including Matthew Simpson. The Bishop looked older than his fifty-five years. A young Methodist preacher, never having seen Matthew Simpson, was riding on a train in Vermont. In April of 1866, an "elderly man accompanied by a matronly woman" boarded and took a seat close to the novice preacher who described the encounter:

> Both were very plainly dressed. The man wore a slouch hat much the worse for wear, and a brown overcoat sadly faded. His smoothly shaven face and clean white neck-cloth were sufficient indication that he was a preacher--and probably a Methodist. I said to myself: "This good old couple have seen hard times. They are on their way from conference to some little appointment among the hills, or perhaps the old man is superannuated and must henceforth depend on the small stipend of a conference claimant. I will try to cheer them a little." So I took the vacant seat in front of them and said: "Good morning; I suppose you are returning from conference?" "Yes," he meekly replied." And where is your appointment?" "We have no appointment this year." Some conversation followed, in the course of which expressed my sympathy for worn out preachers, and discovered that this plain couple were people of rare intelligence. Approaching a station where I was to stop over, "Five minutes for refreshments," was announced. I rushed out bought a substantial lunch and carried it to my old couple. They received it thankfully. I had also ready in my hand a small amount of money, which I intended to give them at the last moment; but first said: "I should like to know who you are," at the same time handing them my own card.
>
> "My name is Matthew Simpson," replied the old man. I forgot to give my condolence or sympathy.[1210]

1208 Foner, 191.
1209 Ibid., 121.
1210 "An Embarrassing Introduction: How a Young Preacher Made the Acquaintance

So Violent a Break and Continued Bitterness within Methodism

A few naïve souls, particularly in the North, thought that after Appomattox the "plan of separation" would be forgotten or at least annulled, and the Methodist divorce would be immediately reversed. Many in the North believed that the Southern Methodists should repent in sack cloth and ashes, the ashes from the burnt Confederate flag, and show due penance for crimes against the Northern Church and the "stars and stripes" which hung behind its pulpits. But with the vituperation rippling through the churches' publications, both North and South, the animosity became only more vicious. Attempts at pacification in both sacred and secular spheres served only to fan the flames of hatred and entrench cultural proclivities more deeply than they had been before the war. Southern and Northern sectionalism was more galvanized than ever. Nothing unifies a people more than commiseration, and the South had plenty to commiserate. In his classic study, *But There Was No Peace*, George Rable wrote,

> Sacrifice, suffering, and defeat rubbed emotions raw. The physical devastation of four years of fighting could be more easily repaired than the psychological damage. The South drifted outside of the American mainstream–a striking counterpoint to the national myths of success and innocence. The repressive experience of suffering military conquest and occupation and the obsession with lost causes and shattered dreams would shape southern attitudes and actions for many years.[1211]

William Sherman, whose army did more physical damage in America than any other single military unit or movement in American history, understood better than Northern Church leaders that, "ruin, poverty, and distress everywhere and now pestilence adding to the cap sheaf to their stock of misery; her proud men begging for pardon and appealing for permission to raise food for their children; her five million of slaves free and their value lost to their farm masters."[1212] The bottom line for the decade following

---

of Bishop Simpson," *The Milwaukee Sentinel*, Milwaukee, WI: (June 29, 1890) 14.

1211   George C. Rable. *But There Was No Peace: The Role of Violence in the Politics of Reconstruction* (Athens: University of Georgia Press, 1984) 3.

1212   Charles T. Thrift. "Rebuilding the Southern Church," *The History of American Methodism* Vol. II ed. Emory Bucke (Nashville: Abingdon, 1958) 258.

the Civil War is that the South could not understand why the North could not understand the predicament of the "lost cause." Sadly, most "spiritual" leaders, especially in the Methodist Episcopal Church, exhibited no better discernment or Christian character than their secular counterparts. Daniel Whedon, editor of the *Methodist Quarterly Review*, was an exception. He wrote in October 1865, "The missionary who intrudes into their borders will meet with the coldest possible reception. We understand them as holding any minister who comes to establish a pastorate, or Bishops who reside over a Conference in the former slave states, as an aggressor."[1213]

The Northern Bishops, including Simpson, would stubbornly persist in their mission to the South, confiscating both persons and buildings as evidenced by a June 15, 1865 statement that, "they had no authority to originate any proposals or pleas for reconciliation, and as authorized by the 1864 General Conference would establish as much work as possible among both negroes and whites in the South."[1214] Braxton Craven, President of tiny Trinity College in Randolph County, North Carolina, (later to become Duke University) responded, "I will not suppose that Northern Methodists are so self-righteous, so self-confident, or so intolerant as to reject fellowship with the people whom they had striven so hard to retain in the Union."[1215] Lucius Matlack, who served the Northern Church in Virginia, wrote to the *New York Christian Advocate*, "Our occupancy of the territory as ministers of the Methodist Episcopal Church and the organization into circuits and stations is denounced by them as anti-Christian and seditious."[1216] Matthew Simpson was at the top of the Southern hit list. On August 21, 1864, Simpson wrote an open letter, granting authority for Methodist Elder, Calvin Holman, to confiscate churches in East Tennessee. "He is authorized to confer with Generals in Command as to Churches that may be occupied under the direction of orders from the War Department and to receive and use the same as in my name."[1217]

1213   Daniel Whedon. "The Northern and Southern Churches," *Methodist Quarterly Review* (October 1865) 630.
1214   Hunter Dickinson Farish. *The Circuit Rider Dismounts* (Richmond: The Dietz Press, 1938) 262- 263.
1215   Ibid., 263.
1216   Ibid., 269.
1217   LOC, Simpson papers, Letter August 21, 1864, Container seven.

Southern Methodist historian Hunter Dickinson Farish claimed, "In no other denomination had there resulted so violent a break or such intense or long continued bitterness as in the Methodist."[1218] Farish supported his argument with a statistic that though the Methodist Episcopal Church entered South Carolina, it did not gain one white member before the end of the century.[1219] Simpson in disbelief and naivete, muttered that he had not found this condition anywhere else.[1220] Bishop Davis Clark did not help matters when he wrote in the *New York Christian Advocate*, March 8, 1865, "It is well known that McKendree Chapel, by military order has been supplied by a loyal pastor from the old Methodist Church. It is due to truth and candor to say that comparatively few of the Methodists of the Church South in Nashville gave any countenance to its occupancy, or even entered it as a place of worship, the great body of them are traitors ... traitors at heart."[1221]

No such venom came from Simpson's pen or tongue. Even allowing for his "War Speech," he was irenic and pacifistic in personality, especially in the years immediately following the war. Emotionally and spiritually drained by the illness and death of his oldest son, Simpson retained no animosity for the Southern Church. According to Methodist reconstruction scholar Ralph Morrow, it was with reluctance that Simpson gave token permission to fellow Bishop Edward Ames, who persuaded Andrew Johnson to turn Virginia churches over to "ministers and members who remain with and act under the ecclesiastical jurisdiction governing said churches prior to 1861."[1222] Southern and Northern religious factions vied for air space when churches in proximity to one another ramped up their singing while the other preached.[1223] In 1866, mob violence broke out between Southern and Northern Methodists in Maryland and four people were left physically wounded.[1224]

1218   Farish, 25.

1219   Ibid., 79.

1220   Wade Barclay. *History of Methodist Missions: Widening Horizons 1845-95* (New York: The Board of Missions of the Methodist Church, 1957) 318.

1221   Ibid., 41–42.

1222   Ralph Morrow. *Northern Methodism and Reconstruction* (Lansing, MI: State University Press, 1956) 73.

1223   Ibid., 75.

1224   Ibid., 76.

In 1864, The Methodist Episcopal Church set up a beachhead in New Orleans. Of course, New Orleans was a safe place for any Northerner, given the iron hand with which Benjamin Butler ruled the city. Simpson entered the deep South in December of 1866, to hold the Mississippi Mission Conference in New Orleans, December 13-19.[1225] It was an adventuresome trip. "About nine miles from Clarksville on the Mississippi Railroad, we had a frightful disaster. When on a down-grade approaching Budd's Creek, the rails slightly parted, and the tender got off the track. It struck the timbers of the bridge and threw down two or three spans, precipitating baggage and express cars, and two passenger cars, some twenty to thirty feet down, while the locomotive passed over safely. The sleeping car plunged after the others, but the end remained upon the track at an angle of about forty-five degrees." Even though Simpson was only thrown from his berth and slightly bruised, three persons were killed and about twenty others injured.[1226]

Matthew Simpson carried with him a letter of introduction written by Edwin Stanton. This communiqué may represent the most official statement to be found anywhere concerning Simpson's status in America, both politically and religiously.

> Washington City
> November 24, 1866
> General:
>
> It gives me pleasure to introduce to you the Reverend Matthew Simpson who visits New Orleans and perhaps will go to Texas to hold a conference. He is accompanied by his son who is in ill health.
>
> Bishop Simpson is, no doubt, known to you as one of the most eloquent, learned, and patriotic men of our country and age. No one during the war did so much to encourage and strengthen loyal and patriotic sentiments and to sustain the army by appeals to the benevolence of the people.
>
> I commend him and his son to your kindest attention and courtesy, believing that you will take pleasure in contributing to

---

[1225] *Minutes of the Annual Conferences of the Methodist Episcopal Church* (New York: Carlton and Porter, 1867) 5-6.

[1226] LOC, Simpson papers, undated letter to Adam Wallace, editor of the *Methodist Home Journal* sometime in 1867, Container twenty.

their comfort, by any means in your power. If the Bishop should go to Texas, I request you to give him such letters to officers in your command, as may be of service and protection to him there.

With sincere regard I am
Truly yours,
Edwin M. Stanton
Secretary of War

Major General Sheridan
Commander New Orleans[1227]

After arriving in New Orleans, Simpson was convinced that there would be no way to minister in the city without the protection of federal troops. He preached in the Mechanics Institute and noted the walls riveted by bullet holes, which had been incurred during the riots of the previous summer. Simpson was emotionally moved during his ministry to the surrounding "colored" churches. Of the preachers, he stated, "Nearly all had been slaves. Some of them have been severely whipped for preaching the Gospel to their fellow slaves while in bondage, but they rejoiced at being worthy to suffer for the sake of Jesus. The tears rolled down their cheeks as they spoke of their gratitude to God for having permitted them to see a Conference, and to become members of it."[1228] We will never know exactly what Simpson thought about "Blacks," as he was never forthright about their place in American society. We have some indication as to their respect for the Bishop. The "colored employees" of the Department of the Interior gave Simpson a pair of boots "nicely made of the best material, as a token of their appreciation of your character as a friend of the colored race."[1229]

Simpson Recommends the Eccentric John Baldwin

Simpson's most important accomplishment in New Orleans was connecting John Baldwin to Presiding Elder John Newman, in southern

---

[1227] Frank Flower. *Edwin McMasters Stanton: The Autocrat of Rebellion, Emancipation, and Reconstruction* (Akron: The Sandfield Publishing Company, 1905) 373.

[1228] 1867 *Methodist Home Journal*, date unclear.

[1229] LOC, Simpson papers, Letter, James Harlan to Matthew Simpson, March 1, 1866, Container nine. The letter listed sixteen African-Americans who had contributed to the gift for Simpson.

Louisiana. John Baldwin was one of the most fascinating and eccentric persons within the history of American Methodism. In 1842, John Baldwin found himself bankrupt after having invested $15,000 in Josiah Hallbrook's Lyceum Village in Berea, Ohio. Hallbrook's village went under and Baldwin with it. The financial embarrassment drove Baldwin to his knees. He determined to spend one hour daily kneeling in a field on his farm praying for an answer.

> I then and there covenanted with God to not spend a quarter of a dollar in any needless way, but to give all except a bare support for my family and myself toward any cause God might direct, if he would only show me the way out of my troubles. At the end of one month my answer came. Suddenly I was enveloped in light, or I seemed to be; my burden rolled away. I felt that deliverance was at hand; in what way it was to come I knew not, but was certain it was to be shown me. I arose from my knees with abiding faith. At that moment something impelled me, I knew not what, to return to my home, by way of a new route and a longer way that would take me across the river on my farm. Obeying the impulse, I soon found myself across the stream, which at that time was very low, and I could pass over on exposed rocks. Suddenly I noticed a piece of rock that had but recently been broken off. I picked it up and examined its texture and quality of grit. I took from my pocket my knife and in a few moments found by trial that it would put a keen edge on steel. "This," I said to myself, "will make superior grindstones, this is my deliverance," and before the sun went down I had by means of an old ax and some primitive tools, shaped a grindstone in my cellar under the "Old Red House." I hung it and found that it was most excellent grit to sharpen tools.[1230]

After discovering that the answer to his financial plight was not only on his knees, but under his knees, Baldwin made a fortune. At age thirty-four, he perfected a water-run machine for manufacturing grindstones out of the limestone which "just happened" to be on his farm in Berea, Ohio. "Taking a length of soft wood six inches square and four feet long he had it turned on a lathe to a pattern of his own design. Then he traveled on a moonlit night to a Mr. Hoyts, owner of a foundry in Cleveland, and had it cast in the shape of the wooden pattern. Baldwin transported the mandrel home

---

1230   A. R. Webber. *Life of John Baldwin, Sr. of Berea, Ohio* (Cincinnati: Caxton Press, 1925) 45.

the next day."[1231] By developing and perfecting a lathe run by water power Baldwin gained the reputation of manufacturing superior grindstones at a competitive price.

His first educational initiative was a classroom building on his farm, which he named Baldwin Institute. The school opened its doors for students on April 9, 1846, and was the forerunner for today's Baldwin Wallace University in Berea, Ohio. Baldwin was not one to rest on his laurels, and in 1858, headed for Douglas County, Kansas, a location already in the throes of the Civil War. He plotted a town and named it after himself, Baldwin City. Again he built a college building, and gave it to the Methodists who named it after Bishop Osmon Baker, opening its doors in 1859. A fourteen-year-old boy remembered his impression of Baldwin on the Baker campus. "As to his personal appearance and dress, he was very eccentric. He was clad in blue overalls and striped hickory shirt, which was seldom buttoned in its front, and he usually went bare-headed and barefooted."[1232] Baldwin was once thrown off a train because he looked like a vagrant. Before the Civil War, Simpson was aware of Baldwin's ingenuity and philanthropy. Jeremiah Tingley, Simpson's nephew, taught at Baldwin Institute and served as Vice-President from 1858-1860. Simpson had met Baldwin when the Bishop laid the cornerstone for the chapel of Baldwin College in 1860.[1233]

On October 9, 1866, Baldwin wrote Simpson of his desire to further invest in the educational enterprise at Berea, or perhaps a new educational institution in Cincinnati, where Baldwin had established another grindstone business. Simpson responded, "I wish I could see you and converse with you more fully. Do you purpose that the proceeds of your land will be applied wholly in Berea?"[1234] The answer to that question was mostly "yes." According to Baldwin Wallace historian Indira Gesink on January 12, 1866, Baldwin, "donated all the rocks in forty acres of land to B. U., retaining for himself the rights to water power and the land."[1235] For health reasons,

---
1231 Thomas A. Kinney, "John Baldwin and the Grindstone Lathe," *Chronicle of the Early American Industries Association, Inc.*, Vol. 49 No. 4 (General Printing) December 1996, 126.
1232 Webber, 28.
1233 "Baldwin University," *The Daily Cleveland Herald* (September 28, 1860).
1234 Western Reserve Historical Society, John Baldwin papers, Letter October 13, 1866.
1235 Indira Falk Gesink. *Barefoot Millionaire: John Baldwin and the Founding Values of*

Baldwin headed for southern Louisiana in 1867. Simpson wrote an open letter of introduction:

> Mr. John Baldwin of Berea Ohio has for many years been one of the most devoted friends of Christian Education I have ever known. Recently he has taken a deep interest in the education of the Freedmen and of the people of the south, and has contributed largely to that end. He proposes to solicit aid in those enterprises and I most cordially commend him to a benevolent public, as he will most faithfully apply to the cause of education all that he may receive.[1236]

On July 15, 1867, John Newman wrote Simpson, "John Baldwin, Esq. of Berea O, has just concluded the purchase of a plantation of two-thousand acres for our Biblical institute. It is near Franklin, in the most healthy and delightful region in the state. How wonderfully God is leading us on! The beginning will be small, but something worthy of the Church will grow out of this plan, conceived by Mr. Baldwin."[1237] The result was Thompson University on a plantation named "Tillandsia," one of the most beautiful land tracts in Louisiana. Thompson University merged into New Orleans University which today is Dillard University in New Orleans.[1238] John Baldwin was a "sanctified" carpetbagger:

> I embraced entire sanctification in 1818. I have had no property of my own ever since. I am only a steward. I have never taken back that consecration. I have never been able to get any useless piece of furniture for my house, or extravagant clothing for my body. I have a pair of shoes that I have worn for three years, and I expect to wear them one year more; and they only cost $1.50. I felt that I ought to do something for the freedmen, and I told the Lord if he would give me twenty thousand dollars, I would go down south, and buy a plantation, and build a school for the colored people. In less than ten days, I had the money in my hands.[1239]

Simpson may have understated when he said of Baldwin, "He has lived exceedingly plain, and has given very largely in proportion to his means."[1240]

Baldwin Wallace University (Berea, OH: Baldwin Wallace University, 2013) 128.
1236   Western Reserve Historical Society, John Baldwin papers, Letter July 24, 1867.
1237   LOC, Simpson papers, Letter July 15, 1867, Container eight.
1238   Gesink, 138.
1239   Ibid., 140 – 141.
1240   *Cyclopaedia*, 79.

"A Noble and Christian Cause"

From New Orleans, Simpson headed to Houston to establish the Texas Mission Conference, January 3-5, 1867. The Bishop attempted a bi-racial conference, "Ninety men stepped forward as original members of the Conference, "consisting of African Americans, German speakers, and English-speaking European Americans." The diversity experiment lasted only five years, when in 1872, four Conferences were formed, "White, Black, and German," with the African American being split into the "Texas" and "West Texas" Conferences. The two African American Conferences lasted almost a century until 1970, when they were absorbed into other Conferences.[1241]

It was now time to attempt reconciliation between the Methodist Episcopal Church and the Methodist Episcopal Church South. The first moved belonged to the North, and Simpson, who had shattered the amiable "plan of separation" in 1848, would now attempt to repair the damage. The same voice that had served him and the North well during the Civil War, would fail him in Reconstruction. In the thinking of Southern Methodists, no person was more culpable for Northern belligerence than Matthew Simpson. It must have occurred to him as his train rumbled south through the ruin and devastation, that his Southern reception would be something less than enthusiastic. Some radical Republicans believed that Simpson could wave his hand while uttering a few incantations and normality would be restored. Virginia Federal Court Judge John C. Underwood and reconstruction Governor F. H. Pierpoint urged Simpson on to the "noble and truly Christian cause."[1242] The North and South held widely different interpretations as to the word "Christian."

1241 Blog: *Texas Methodist History*, Monday, January 01, 2007-Friday, November 01, 2013, http://txmethhistory.blogspot.com/search?q=simpson.

1242 LOC, Simpson papers, Letter, F. H. Pierpoint to Simpson, n. d. Letter, John C. Underwood to Simpson, May 15, 1867, Container eight.

Chapter Sixteen:
A Withered Olive Branch

The Overture of Simpson and Janes

In May, 1869, E. S. Janes and Matthew Simpson traveled to St. Louis, Missouri, to extend an olive branch to the Methodist Episcopal Church South. "It seems to us that, as the division of those Churches of our country which are of like faith and order has been productive of evil, so the reunion of them would be productive of good. As the main cause of the separation has been removed, so has the chief obstacle to the restoration."[1243]

The Southern Bishops were willing to meet with Northern representatives, but Bishop Robert Paine, chair of the Southern Board, was honest and straightforward in his response.

> It has afforded us pleasure to receive in person your respected colleagues, Bishops Janes and Simpson, deputed by you to confer with us …. And we take this occasion frankly to say that the conduct of some of your missionaries and agents who have been sent into that portion of our common country occupied by us, and their avowed purpose to disintegrate and absorb our societies that otherwise dwell quietly, have been very prejudicial to that charity which we desire our people to cultivate toward all Christians and especially those who are called by the endeared name of Methodists; and their course in taking possession of some of our houses of worship has inflicted both grief and loss on us, and bears the appearance to disinterested men of the world of being not only a breach of charity but an invasion of the plainest rights of property. Thus, the adversary has had occasion to speak reproachfully and the cause of our Master has been wounded by its professed friends.[1244]

1243   John M. Moore. *The Long Road to Methodist Union* (New York: Abingdon-Cokesbury Press, 1943) 55.
1244   Ibid, 59.

The entreaty by the Northerners may have been a "call your bluff" proposal in that Southerners claimed that they had received "no sincere communication pertaining to relations between the Methodisms."[1245] When Simpson and Janes traveled to St. Louis, May 1869, inquiring about the propriety and methodology of reunion, their Southern hosts took the opportunity to remind them of their sins against the South, and that they had no authority to act on the Northern offer of armistice. Attempts at amnesty led only to more animosity as one blamed the other for not making peace. In that there was no public or personal apology from the North, Simpson in the Southern mind remained a pariah. Nothing had changed since the *St. Louis Christian Advocate* had asked on November 23, 1865, "What Southern Conference could ever become so lost to all sense of self-respect and to all feelings of Christian dignity and true manliness as to sit under the Presidency of Matthew Simpson or E. R. Ames?"[1246] Southern Bishop Enoch Morris thought the Northern proposal to be premature and that Simpson's and Janes' words "smoked with a suspicious odor .... Time ought to have been for fumigation to clear away the effluvium of so recently dead policy."[1247] The real problem with the proposal from Simpson and Janes was their assumption that they were in the right and Southerners in the wrong. The latter officially responded,

> We cannot think you mean to offend us when you speak of our having separated from you, and put us in the same category with a small body of schismatics who were always an acknowledged secession. Allow us, in all kindness, brethren, to remind you, and to keep the important fact of history prominent, that we separated from you in no sense in which you did not separate from us. The separation was by compact and mutual; and nearer approaches to each other can be conducted, with hope of a successful issue, only on this basis.[1248]

As African Americans in the South watched their situation deteriorate and the growing resolve of whites to reduce them into forced labor by way of share cropping, peonage, high interest rates of credit for farm supplies,

---

1245 Daniel Whedon. "Spirit of the Southern Methodist Press," *Methodist Quarterly Review* (January 1866) 128.

1246 *St. Louis Christian Advocate* (November 23, 1865).

1247 Enoch Morris "The M.E. Churches North and South," *The Southern Review* (January 1872) 417.

1248 Holland N. McTyeire. *A History of Methodism* (Nashville: Southern Methodist Publishing House, 1886) 681.

deceptive labor controls, convict leasing, and every other inequitable financial arrangement, they turned increasingly to the Methodist Episcopal Church for help. A Freedmen's Bureau superintendent recalled, "I saw one (labor contract) in which it was stipulated that one-third of seventh-twelfths of all corn, potatoes, fodder, etc., shall go to the labourers."[1249]

James Lynch: Simpson's Most Powerful Southern Voice

Simpson in 1867 appointed James Lynch as Presiding Elder of the South Mississippi District. Thaddeus Stevens, then chairing the "Congressional Reconstruction Committee," also appointed Lynch to travel throughout Mississippi and report on both the gains and ills of reconstruction. James Lynch was a curious amalgamation of elitist education, black heritage, radical Republicanism, and Northern Methodism. With impeccable English and showcase handwriting, Lynch wrote to Simpson on December 3, 1868, that he was feeling squeezed, by both the Methodist Episcopal Church, South, and the African Methodist Episcopal Church. Lynch accused white Southern Methodists of "being as unscrupulous as are the legates of the Pope. They tell the colored people that the M.E. Church has become corrupt. That it seeks to make them subjects of taxation in the future to support Church interests." And even though he had high regard for the members of the African Methodist Episcopal Church, they were turning blacks against Simpson's Church by claiming that it had "consumption yet possessed a sufficient leave of life to hinder progress and to teach sectionalism." Lynch begged Simpson to not throw any part of the Presiding Elder's support on the people, since the Northern Church preachers were accused of being only interested in politics and money. To combat the false accusations, Lynch had started a newspaper entitled, *The Colored Citizen Monthly*, "For the purpose of educating the black man on the duties of citizenship and to teach him to regard his manhood and to develop backbone as well as to cultivate temperance and virtue, and as the native capacity of the colored man is so poorly thought of, I desire to make the paper as far as possible, a demonstration of its strength."[1250]

1249   James Anderson. *The Education of Blacks in the South: 1860–1935* (Chapel Hill: The University of North Carolina Press, 1988) 18.
1250   LOC, Simpson papers, Letter December 3, 1868, Container eight.

Among reconstruction blacks, the mulatto, James Lynch, was sui generis, without equal in his hypnotic powers of speech. Born in Baltimore, January 8, 1839, he briefly attended Dartmouth College. After pastoring for a brief time in Illinois and Indiana, A.M.E. Bishop Daniel Payne persuaded Lynch to minister in the Baltimore Conference. Lynch, born a free black, was awakened to racism when he and Daniel Payne, "were expelled from their quarters in the sleeping car of a train to Baltimore because of the protest of a white Tennessean. They were forced to spend the night in the smoker, the car in which black passengers usually rode."[1251] During the Civil War, Lynch labored in South Carolina under the auspices of the A.M.E. Church. But in early 1866, he returned to Philadelphia and for two years served as editor of the *Christian Recorder*. In all likelihood, he, at this time, made contact with Matthew Simpson, and became convinced that he would accomplish a greater good by joining the Methodist Episcopal Church. The Northern Church was, "God's chosen power to lift up my race from degradation."[1252] Simpson shipped him to Mississippi to serve as the Presiding Elder of the Natchez District. Lynch's labors were prodigious and productive, adding about 1,800 members to the M.E. Church rolls during his first year of ministry.

Lynch was critical of the Freedman's Bureau, and wrote Simpson: "It is a remarkable fact that the Freedman's Bureau, in its vast appropriations seems invariably to slight claims pressed by those who are in the interest of Methodism. I think the history of the Bureau will show that it has always given the cold shoulder to Methodism."[1253] Interestingly, Lynch asked Simpson if he should continue in politics. Though he was heavily involved with the Republican Party, Lynch did not shirk his ecclesiastical labors. Between 1868 and 1872, he quadrupled the membership of the Methodist Episcopal Church in Mississippi to over twenty-three thousand.[1254] A contemporary described Lynch's preaching, perhaps the most powerful Black oratory of the post-bellum South:

1251 William B. Gravely, "A Black Methodist in Reconstruction Mississippi: Three Letters by James Lynch in 1868-1869," *Methodist History* Vol. XI No. 4, (July 1973) 4.
1252 Ibid., 7.
1253 Ibid., 14.
1254 Ibid., 17.

> I have heard him paint the horrors of slavery (as they existed in the imagination) in pathetic tones of sympathy till the tears would roll down his cheeks, and every negro in the audience would be weeping; then wiping briskly away his tears, he would break forth into hosannas for the blessings of emancipation, and every negro in the audience would break forth in the wildest shouts. There was a striking peculiarity about this shouting. Imagine one or two thousand negroes standing *en masse* in a semi-circle facing the speaker not a sound to be heard except the sonorous voice of the speaker, whose tones were as clear and wide open, and a spontaneous shout in perfect unison would arise, and swell, and subside as the voice of one then for a moment a deadly silence would follow, and every eye would be fixed on the speaker as he resumed, until all of a sudden the mighty shout would rise again, and again, and so on, at intervals for a period of from one to three hours.[1255]

James Lynch, a model of propriety and political action, a forerunner of Black clergy political leverage in the twentieth century, ran out of strength. He literally worked himself to death and died of pneumonia at the age of thirty-four. Lynch was in the vanguard of Black Southern politics, becoming the first Black Secretary of State in Mississippi and a delegate to both the Methodist Episcopal General Conference which met in Brooklyn, May 1872, and a Delegate to the 1872 Republican National Convention in Philadelphia. In all likelihood, Lynch would have been elected as a U.S. Senator, had he let his name stand with the Mississippi Republican Committee. But he wanted to retain a local presence for the purposes of Reconstruction, and moving to Washington would require resigning his position as Secretary of State to which he had just been elected. He withdrew his name, and Hiram Revels was elected. Unfortunately, Simpson did not mention Lynch in his *Cyclopaedia*.

As a delegate to the Wesleyan-British Conference in 1870, Simpson reported, "The colored people especially have been anxious that we should establish what they term the old mother church among them. I have visited them in nearly all these states: I have seen their eyes and exclamations of joy have I heard as they felt that once more they were in the church of their choice-a church that had always been their friend and that was seeking to

---

[1255] W.H. Hardy, "Reminiscences of a White Mississippian," *Black Re-constructionists: Great Lives Observed*, ed. Emma Lou Thornbrough (Englewood Cliffs, New Jersey: Prentice-Hall, 1972) 127-128. Also see George Sewell. *Mississippi Black History Makers* (Jackson: University Press of Mississippi, 1977).

benefit them again ...." There were two conferences, "composed wholly of colored ministers," and "a large number of others composed partly of colored members and partly of white members; for throughout South Carolina, and Florida, and Georgia, and Alabama and Mississippi, and Louisiana and Texas, the majority of our ministers are colored ministers, there is great prosperity among them and they are beginning to establish schools."[1256] On November 8, 1866, Simpson met with the Board of Bishops in New York City, for the purpose of touting the Freedmen's Aid Society.

> As a suitable channel through which the benefactions of our Church to this object may best reach their design, the Freedmen's Aid Society of the Methodist Episcopal Church has been organized. It is designed to cooperate with our missionary work in the South, and in fact, to supplement that work. There are openings for hundreds of teachers at this moment. Hundreds of teachers are ready to go. The means to send them is only wanting.[1257]

By 1870, the Society had founded fifty-eight elementary schools with one hundred-eighty-five teachers and 2,000 students.[1258]

The Deaths of Charles and Mother Sarah

The crumbling structures of Reconstruction about to come down on his friend Edwin Stanton and the death of his son Charles, along with the normal strains of running ecclesiastical machinery left Simpson overwhelmed, on the verge of a physical and emotional breakdown. He confessed to one of his preachers, March 28, 1868, that "severe affliction" had occupied his mind for some time.[1259] With a premonition of Charles' approaching death, Matthew Simpson purchased a burial lot in South Laurel Hill Cemetery in Philadelphia overlooking the Schuylkill River, May 28, 1867.[1260] During the last year of his life, Charles spent much of his time traveling with his father, eventually spending several weeks in Cuba attempting to restore his health. The father

---

1256 "American Deputation at the British Conferences," New York: *New York Recorder* (August 25, 1870).

1257 Dwight Oliver Wendell Holmes. *The Evolution of the Negro College* (New York: Teachers College-Columbia University, 1934) 104.

1258 Ibid., 205.

1259 LOC, Simpson papers, Letter to H. T. Pease, March 28, 1868, Container eight.

1260 LOC, Simpson papers, *Diary*, May 28, 1867, Container two.

recalled that his son was "quick in his perceptions and movements, learned with great facility and was gentle, amiable, and affectionate in all his ways." He inherited his father's intellectual DNA in that he "was fond of classical studies and made good proficiency, especially in the Greek languages and acquired an excellent literary taste." His vocational history included a stint as "chief bookkeeper at the New York Book Concern" and for a short time he served in the Union Army as "Paymaster with the rank of Major."

Charles passed away in the presence of his wife, father, mother, and sisters on March 2, 1868. Just before expiring he quoted from John 14: "Let not your heart be troubled. In my father's house are many mansions. Blessed be God, there is one for me." The father recalled that his son had wandered from God, but at the Vineland Camp had "renewed his vow of consecration to God. His penitence was deep; he sought earnestly and experienced some measure of divine consolation, but not that full and joyous assurance which he desired. From that period he was steady and uniform in his devotional life, strict attendance to his duties, delighting in public worship and in the holy communion."[1261] In spite of what may have been her aversion to camp meetings, Ellen Simpson was with her son at Vineland, New Jersey, when he made his recommitment to God. Edwin Stanton wrote the following condolence to Simpson, a profound piece of correspondence which made some of the theodicies offered by the Bishop's clergy friends seem superficial.

    Washington City–March 2, 1868
    My Dear friend:

    I sympathize deeply with you and your family in the recent dispensation of providence that has brought mourning to your household. The bereavement, however certain and long expected falling not less heavily when a loved one is called from earth to mansions in the sky.

    To you, I will not presume to offer consolation for you know better than I whence it can come; but I hope it will not be regarded intrusive of me to share your sorrow.

                      With sincere affection,
                      Truly your friend,
                      Edwin M. Stanton[1262]

1261   LOC, Simpson papers, Matthew Simpson: "Memoir of Charles," Container twenty.
1262   Flower, 374.

Sarah Simpson died at her son's Philadelphia home, May 27, 1867, at the age of 86. He had to cancel a railroad excursion party with Senator Wade Cattell, which would have taken him to North Platte, Nebraska,[1263] where he would proceed by stage to Denver and chair the Colorado Annual Conference. He informed John Evans that the unexpected death of his mother as well as other domestic matters required him to cancel the trip, with Edward Ames taking his place. "Her physician called on yesterday morning to see her and while conversing with her and pronouncing her to be much better, she was seized in a moment with a slight convulsion, was wholly unconscious, and in two or three minutes was no more."[1264]

Now that Charles was gone, Simpson would give more attention to his youngest child and only remaining son, Matthew Verner, who would go by the name Verner. Always concerned about his children's spiritual welfare, the father wrote from Knoxville in October of 1869, "I was very glad to receive and was especially thankful to God that your religious experience was so satisfactory. I hope that you will live in the assurance of God's love. You speak of temptation. They are common to man. We cannot escape them."[1265] A year later he wrote the seventeen-year-old, "I want you to be a scholar. You can if you study …. With you pious and studious, I think I can die happy. I want a son to follow me in trying to do something in this world. If I live, you shall have every possible help to get a good education and to prepare for usefulness."[1266] These were big shoes to fill, and a lot of pressure on the oldest son to make something out of himself.

Edwin Stanton and Matthew Simpson Align Themselves against Andrew Johnson

In attempting to fire Edwin Stanton, Johnson had squared off with the former Cadiz inhabitant and Steubenville native. Simpson was anything but a non-partisan bystander in the impeachment hearings. He sided with the

---

1263   Where the railroad ended was a tenuous proposition. On August 27, 1867, Cheyenne warriors destroyed track at Plum Creek, Nebraska. pbs.org/wgbh/americanexperience/features/timeline/terr-timeline.

1264   John Evans Mss. Collection, History Colorado, Letter, May 28, 1867.

1265   LOC, Simpson papers, Letter October 13, 1869, Container three.

1266   LOC, Simpson papers, Letter October 6, 1870, Container three.

radical Republicans which included Thaddeus Stevens. When Stevens heard that Johnson was a self-made man, he responded, "He was glad to hear it because it relieved God Almighty of a heavy responsibility." In response, Johnson declared in his "swing-around-the-circle" that Thaddeus Stevens, Charles Sumner, and Wendell Phillips were intending to assassinate him. In addition, there was a conspiracy "afoot to overthrow the government and set up a military dictatorship."[1267] While Johnson committed "political suicide," Stanton locked himself in the war office, staying there 24/7 for six months.

By the time Stanton moved to Cadiz in January of 1837, Simpson was a professor at Allegheny College, and we have no record of a meeting between the two. We can only conjecture that Stanton and Simpson may have met when the college teacher returned for a visit to Cadiz. Simpson and Stanton would certainly have known of one another. When Stanton ran for prosecuting attorney of Harrison County, the energetic twenty-two year old literally knocked on every door in his district.[1268] Even though by this time Mother Sarah and Uncle Matthew had left Cadiz, there were still a slew of Tingleys, with William Tingley serving as the county court clerk.

In spite of his physical infirmities Stanton was a workaholic, a man about town whom the Cadiz inhabitants referred to as "little Stanton." The moniker referred more to his age than his size, as Stanton stood five foot eight with a stocky build. Though extremely near-sighted so that he peered intently through thick-lens spectacles, he was an attractive youth, "clean shaven, with thick, dark, disheveled hair and good nature when not battling to win a case."[1269] Winning a case called for a different personality, a merciless, acerbic tongue which outwitted just about every lawyer whom he encountered. In squaring off with the opposition, Stanton was referred to as "haughty, severe, domineering, and rude."[1270] His embattled temperament was further complicated by the death of his first child, death of his wife Mary after which he suffered a nervous breakdown, and the suicide of his physician

---

1267   David O. Stewart. *Impeached: The Trial of President Johnson and the Fight for Lincoln's Legacy* (New York: Simon and Schuster, 2009) 71.
1268   Fletcher Pratt. *Stanton: Lincoln's Secretary of War* (New York: W. W. Norton and Company, 1953) 18.
1269   Ibid., 155.
1270   Ibid., 25.

brother. Upon his brother cutting his throat, the distraught Edwin was found out in the woods, his searchers fearing that he too might try to kill himself.

In spite of Stanton's taciturn personality, and at times entirely unpredictable behavior, he and the serene Simpson somewhere along the way became fast friends. Eventually, Simpson was in heavy political debt to the Secretary of War. Stanton yielded to Methodist demands for chaplaincies, named Simpson's son Charles to a commission, and requested the Bishop himself early in 1863 to serve as chairman of a commission to visit forts Monroe, New Bern, Port Royal, and New Orleans, "to examine the condition of the colored people and make suggestions."[1271] Simpson turned down the invitation, but must have experienced some gratification by the offer. To Ellen he wrote, "He (Stanton) offered transportation, assistance, a clerk and fair compensation. I have, however, declined every such proposition."[1272] Throughout his life, Simpson would say no to every vocational offer which did not provide a platform for preaching.

Roger Taney died on October 12, 1864, and Stanton perceived his own attorney skills would best serve as Chief Justice of the Supreme Court rather than Secretary of War. Among several people whom Stanton beseeched to intervene on his behalf to Lincoln was Simpson. Upon Simpson gaining a private audience with the President and arguing Stanton's case, the President responded, "If Mr. Stanton can find a man; he himself will trust as Secretary of War, I'll do it."[1273] Stanton could find no such man and neither could Simpson. Instead, the vacant Chief Justice seat was the perfect opportunity for Lincoln to remove the jealous Samuel Chase from his cabinet, and grant him the highest judicial office in the land.

Because Stanton was responsible for placing Federal troops to enforce Reconstruction in the South, a radical Republican position with which Johnson increasingly disagreed, the President attempted to vanquish the War Secretary. Stanton became the symbolic rallying point, the *cause celebre*, for the impeachment proceedings against Johnson. Stanton and Johnson were at an impasse as the Secretary of War refused to vacate his office at the War Department after the President asked for his resignation. In that a Cabinet

---

1271   Flower, 372.
1272   Ibid., 372.
1273   Ibid., 405.

member was confirmed by Congress, he could not be fired by the President without defying the "Tenure of Office Act." Even though he was acquitted, the President's refusal to abide by this particular point of law caused him to become impotent as the Nation's Chief Magistrate for the remainder of his term.

Simpson recorded in his *Diary* that he spent the evening of January 13, 1868, at dinner with Grant, who had acted as Secretary of War for six months. Being increasingly at odds with Johnson, Grant stepped aside and encouraged Stanton to resume his Cabinet duties. At two a.m. January 14, Simpson was allowed by the posted sentry into Stanton's inner sanctum, where he assured the refugee Secretary that he had the support of both Grant and the "God fearing portion of the people." Simpson recalled that the two of them had a "very long religious talk ... with prayer".[1274] About four a.m. Simpson departed the building. The stubborn Stanton was not to be outdone, and barricaded himself for six months, not resigning until Johnson escaped conviction by one vote. Simpson also recorded that Grant "did not look well."[1275] Simpson would later speak of Stanton,

> I remember once to have visited Washington when there was almost universal gloom. I asked Mr. Stanton what he thought, and I did so because I had found a feeling of almost universal despondency. He expressed himself as unshaken in his confidence of success. I asked him on what he relied; if he had found a general in which he had confidence. After pausing a moment he said, "No; I have no confidence in our generals," and then pausing a moment he said, "And I have no confidence in Congress." And then pausing another moment he said, "I have no confidence but in God. Our cause is right, and he will make it triumph." That strong will was felt in every department of the administration, And when the general in chief had persuaded the President that it was impossible to transport troops to save the army at Chattanooga, Stanton plead and reasoned and succeeded in getting Mr. Lincoln to reverse the decision to which he had been led by the higher officers of the Army, and seizing the railroads, threw his forces through Cincinnati, and Louisville, and Nashville, and reached Chattanooga in time for Hooker's Division to take part in that great combat, where they climbed the mountain side that was shrouded in mists, and where that triumphant battle was gained.[1276]

1274 LOC, Simpson papers, 1868 *Diary*, Container two.
1275 Ibid.
1276 LOC, Simpson papers, Lecture on "True Leadership," Container fifteen.

Stanton Begs Simpson for a Recommendation to a Seat on the U.S. Supreme Court

Stanton appeared ten to fifteen years older than his fifty-four years. The war years and his bout with Johnson had intensified the severe asthma that had plagued him all his life. After Johnson's acquittal, Stanton resigned and returned to Steubenville, but he was too sick (along with being broke) to effectively practice law. His physical liabilities, often prostrating him, did not smother his aspirations for an appointment to the United States Supreme Court. Again, it was Simpson among others who hounded Grant for the fulfillment of Stanton's last wish. Grant rebuffed Simpson, stating that it was his opinion, agreeing with the views of many others that Stanton was not physically up to the task. Nonetheless, Simpson as well as many other Stanton associates persisted, and Grant relented, nominating Stanton for the vacant Supreme Court Chair. On October 2, 1869, Stanton wrote the following groveling letter to Simpson.

> You have been aware of my infirm health during the past year, and will be glad to know that by relaxation from labor, and travel it has very much improved so as to encourage hopes that it may be fully restored to enable me to enjoy some years longer of usefulness. But this may depend upon how I am employed. When I left my private pursuits for the public interest I had the best professional practice in the United States, was rapidly accumulating wealth, & living at ease. My expenses above my salary exhausted my surplus resources and with years advanced, and diminished strength I must toil for my living. There is a vacancy on the Supreme Bench for which I have adequate physical power, & so far as I can judge of my intellect, its powers are as acute & vigorous as at any period in my life—and perhaps more so. General Grant in justice to the Country, to himself & to me, ought to give me that appointment: So far as relates to himself not all his friends in the United States, upheld & advanced him as firmly & successfully during the war as I did in my official acts. There is no man who would uphold the principles of the war on which his usefulness & fame must rest, with more or equal vigor from the Bench. The Bench has now a great part to play in history during his administration, and upon no experienced resolute jurist, can he rely with greater confidence. My appointment would gratify the great mass of republicans, & rally them around Grant—it would be considered as disinterested, un-purchased, and a sure proof of the Presidents loyal determinations. My

residence here in the District is also a recommendation being free from Geographical discriminations. I have said *nothing to General Grant* on the subject and shall not—but I would be glad to have *you* talk with him fully & freely and report to me his views on this question. To me it may in considerable degree be a question of life—it certainly is of health, for I must go to the Bench or Bar. His name & fortune he owed at a critical moment to me. He can preserve me to my family under Providence. I have communicated to you more fully than ever before to mortal man & in confidence you will do what seems right of which you are a better judge than I am. Hoping to see or hear from you soon.[1277]

Grant appointed Stanton and on December 19, Stanton's fifty-fourth birthday, the former War Secretary was confirmed by Congress. Six days later, the new Supreme Court appointee died on Christmas Day, before taking office.

The Failure of Simpson and the Methodists to Oust Johnson

The violation of the "Tenure of Office Act," in that Johnson attempted to fire Stanton without the approval of the Senate, was an excuse for the House of Representatives to impeach the President by a vote of 127 to 47. Thaddeus Stevens and John Bingham (another Cadiz one-time inhabitant) rendered the verdict: "We do impeach Andrew Johnson, President of the United States, of high crimes and misdemeanors in office."[1278] Of course, to throw Johnson out of office would demand a two-thirds vote of the Senate, and the Senate vote just "happened" to take place while the General Conference of the Methodist Episcopal Church met in Chicago during the month of May, 1868. The call for prayer and Simpson's supposedly strong arm tactics on West Virginia's Senator, Waitman Willey, earned the Bishop the sobriquet from Secretary of the Navy, Gideon Wells, "high priest of the Radical Republicans" and Wells further stated that Simpson was a "secular politician of great shrewdness and ability."[1279] In what was probably the most elaborate defense of Andrew Johnson ever penned, George Fort Milton in his *Age of Hate: Andrew Johnson and the Radicals* (1930), further

1277　John Simon. *The Papers of Ulysses Grant* Vol. 20 (Carbondale, IL: Southern Illinois University Press, July 1, 1968-October 31, 1868) 78-79.

1278　Stewart, 153.

1279　*Diary of Gideon Welles: Secretary of the Navy under Lincoln and Johnson* Vol. III, January 1, 1867-June 6, 1869 (Boston: Houghton, Mifflin & Company, 1911) 358.

impaled Simpson on the altar of Republican radicalism by stating that the Methodist petition was "aimed more at Senator Willey than at the Throne of Grace."[1280]

Both the political maneuverings of Simpson and the prayers of the General Conference were ineffectual in that Andrew Johnson conquered his adversaries by one vote. The fervent intercession had not been as effective as the $150,000 bribery fund for Johnson's acquittal, raised by fellow Tennessean, Edward Cooper.[1281] In the end, Simpson and the Methodists were no match for Charles Walker, of "whiskey ring" fame, who bought the acquittal vote of Senator Edmond Ross, the latter who received in the bargain a friend appointed as collector for the Port of New Orleans and another crony as Surveyor General of Public Lands for a Kansas coal company. For whatever reason, God had not chosen to eliminate the graft of American politics. At 8:00 a.m. on May 16, George Pendleton in Chicago received a Washington telegram which read, "We have beaten the Methodist Episcopal Church North, hell, Ben Butler, John Logan, George Wilkes, and impeached President Johnson will win in a vote to be had today."[1282] Historian Roger Burlingame concluded, "Never in our history have ethical guesses and moral judgments been put to so severe a test as in the fifteen or so years following 1861."[1283]

History has given Simpson an unfair rap regarding his action against President Andrew Johnson at the 1868 General Conference. Gilbert Haven, not Simpson, initiated the resolution that directly indicted Andrew Johnson by stating, "It is contrary to the will and word of God that any wicked person or persons should by the people be delegated to any office in said civil government."[1284] Haven moved, "That the General Conference of the Methodist Episcopal Church now in session, solemnly and earnestly invokes upon the Senate of the United States the blessing of Almighty God, that

---

1280   George Fort Milton. *The Age of Hate: Andrew Johnson and the Radicals* (New York: Coward–McCann, 1930) 601.

1281   Stewart, 243.

1282   Victor B. Howard. *Religion and the Radical Republican Movement: 1860-1870* (Lexington: University Press of Kentucky, 1990) 163.

1283   Roger Burlingame. *The American Conscience* (New York: Alfred Knopf, 1957) 307.

1284   *Journal of the 1868 General Conference of the Methodist Episcopal Church* (New York: Carlton & Lanahan, 1868) 152.

they may be guided in the great responsibility now devolving upon them, that tyrannical usurpation may be rebuked, the authority of the law may be maintained against the most dangerous hostility of an Executive who avows his irresponsibilities to its obligation, in that the peace and safety of our fellow-citizens in all the South may be secured."[1285] The Conference was uncomfortable with the specificity of Haven's resolution, and tabled the matter. Two days later, the Bishops took up the issue, and Simpson read the following resolution to the Conference which was more general and allowed God more leeway than had Haven. The following was unanimously adopted by the Conference.

> *Whereas,* painful rumors are in circulation, that, partly by unworthy jealousies, and partly by corrupt influences, pecuniary and otherwise, most actively employed, efforts are being made to influence Senators improperly, and to prevent them from performing their high duty; therefore
>
> *Resolved,* that we hereby appoint an hour of prayer, from nine to ten o'clock. A. M., to-morrow, to invoke humbly and earnestly the mercy of God upon our nation, and to beseech him to save our senators from error, and to so influence them that their decision shall be in truth and righteousness, and shall increase the security and prosperity of our beloved Union.[1286]

Waitman T. Willey had been a student at Madison College when Simpson had briefly attended there in 1828. Willey had intense pressure placed upon him to vote against Johnson, from both his constituency and the West Virginia newspapers. *The Parkersburg Daily Times* addressed both West Virginia Senators: "Gentlemen! Vital issues are at stake: your vote will either bring ruin upon the country or deliver it from the terrible incubus, because of our political and financial distress. It is our firm conviction that the salvation and future safety of the country demand the displacement of Andrew Johnson."[1287] Reportedly, James Harlan wired Simpson, "I fear brother Willey is lost," and Simpson responded, "Brother Willey professes to be a Christian. Brother Willey has a soul to save. He bartered away his soul and impaired the

---

1285   Ibid., 152.

1286   Ibid., 158.

1287   R. W. Bayless, "Peter G. Van Winkle and Waitman T. Willey in the Impeachment Trial of Andrew Johnson," *West Virginia History* (December 1951) 83.

488 | "God Cannot Do Without America"

country. Pray with Brother Willey."[1288] R. W. Bayless concludes that Willey was not proud of his "guilty" vote and the "inveterate collector of newspaper clippings" preserved no reminder of the impeachment proceedings.[1289]

Because the votes were taken alphabetically, Willey's vote was superfluous, since Johnson had already received over one-third of his needed non-guilty votes when the tally reached the V's, George Vickers, the last "not guilty" vote taken. Willey's vote would have been necessary had not his fellow-West Virginia Senator Van Winkle voted "not guilty." Van Winkle's vote occurred four votes ahead of Willey's. Van Winkle and George Vickers, as well as seventeen other Senators, had kept Johnson in office.[1290] Ironically, Vickers, a Maryland Methodist, had saved Johnson's presidency. Simpson and his fellow Methodists at the General Conference had forgotten to beseech God on behalf of Vickers, a Methodist seemingly beyond their persuasion, hopefully not God's.

Simpson Prays at the Republican National Convention

On May 16, 1868, Charles Dyer wrote Simpson, inviting him to speak at the Republican National Convention to be held in Chicago during May 20-21.[1291] Simpson responded "no" to the speaking invitation, but consented to offer a prayer. Due to the on-going General Conference at the same time as the Republican Convention, he probably did not perceive he could give attention to a full-fledged address. To his credit, his intercession was non-partisan as possible at a party-nominating convention. His only error was informing God that "Reconstruction" was going well, but God knew a lot more about what was actually happening in the South than did Simpson. The over one thousand word prayer included,

> While we remember that multiplied thousands have recently fallen in the fierce struggles which have been in our land, we bless Thee that the storm-cloud has passed away; that the voice of battle has been hushed; that peace has been restored to our borders again; and, notwithstanding all our trials, we bless Thy holy name, that Thou hast made us, as we believe,

---

1288   Ibid., 84.
1289   Ibid., 89.
1290   *Congressional Globe,* 40th Congress, 2nd Session, 943- 944.
1291   LOC, Simpson papers, Letter May 16, 1868, Container eight.

stronger and firmer than ever before. As the tree is strengthened by the storms of winter, and prepared for the verdure of coming spring and summer, so we trust Thou has prepared our nation, by the trials through which we have passed, for the glorious future into which we are about to enter ....

> We bless Thee that freedom has diffused its healthful influences over the land, and that the States so lately in rebellion are being successfully reconstructed in peace and prosperity. Hasten the work so gloriously commenced; may there be nothing that shall mar its progress. And, Oh, hasten the moment when all parts of our land shall be firmly and intimately, and fraternally, and perpetually bound together in one common bond of union, and this dear land of ours shall be, as we believe Thou hast designed it to be, a light to all the nations of the earth that shall throw its rays across the Atlantic to Europe, and across the Pacific to Asia, until the dark places of Africa shall have been made glad and the islands of the sea take up the song of praise, and a human brotherhood shall be formed vast as the globe on which we dwell, and sentiments of love, and duty, and adoration shall inspire our common humanity, and prepare it for the glorious assemblage that shall one day convene before the throne of God.

Simpson then led the Convention in the Lord's Prayer.[1292]

Before the Republicans descended on Chicago, it was a foregone conclusion that Grant would be the Grand Old Party nominee. Simpson's prayer did not rain down propriety and charity upon the Convention. Eight thousand people jammed the Crosby's Opera House to witness the nomination of Grant.[1293] "In the Convention itself, the band played the 'Rogue's March' in honor of Johnson and his supporters. Generals Hawley, Sickles, and Logan denounced the seven recalcitrant Senators who had deserted the Party, and led the prolonged cheers with which the soldiers formally nominated Grant as the President."[1294] In Washington, Stanton rushed from the War Office to Grant's office, informing the General of his nomination. The future President made no emotional or facial expression of pleasure or displeasure at the announcement.

1292   https://archive.org/stream/officialproceedi18681880repu/officialprocee. "Full Text of Official Proceedings of the National Republican Convention of 1868."

1293   William B. Heseltine. *Ulysses S. Grant: Politician* (New York: Frederick Unger Publishing, 1957) 119.

1294   Ibid.

Simpson and the Methodists Support Grant

Simpson along with the rest of the Methodists and Republicans believed the Presidential problem would be solved by Ulysses S. Grant. Harlan wrote William Chandler that, "Ninety five hundredths of the members of the Methodist Episcopal Church, perhaps ninety nine hundredths of the traveling ministry are earnest Republicans."[1295] Daniel Lore, editor of the *Northern Advocate*, assessed that, "The Methodist ministers were becoming the most desirable political speakers of the day."[1296] Reconstruction historian Victor Howard concludes that, "In the end, almost all radical Christians supported Grant, but the Methodist clergy and journals were the most active in the canvas."[1297]

Simpson and Grant were not related according to any genealogical records now in existence.[1298] On June 24, 1821, Jesse Root Grant married Hannah Simpson and subsequently named their first son Hiram Ulysses Grant. The Congressman, who recommended the young man to West Point, did not know Ulysses' exact name, and knowing that there was a Simpson back there somewhere, forwarded the name of Ulysses S. Grant. Though some have attempted to attach Simpson to the "S", Grant later claimed that the "S" stood for nothing. We have already noted that Simpson met Grant on his first trip to Nashville in 1864. Immediately following the Civil War, Grant began a habit of hearing Simpson preach whenever possible. On June 26, 1865, Simpson recorded, "Saturday 24 preached at Academy of Music, Philadelphia, and on Sunday at Spring Garden Church with Grant present each time."[1299]

1295 LOC, Simpson papers, Letter June 24, 1868, Container eight. William Chandler had served as an assistant secretary of the U.S. Treasury under Lincoln, and would become a Republican U.S. Senator from New Hampshire.

1296 Howard, 204.

1297 Ibid, 119.

1298 Groh, 490. Also see Edward Chauncey Marshall. *Ancestry of General Grant and Their Contemporaries* (New York: Sheldon and Company, 1869).

1299 LOC, Simpson papers, 1865 *Diary*, Container two.

From the end of the War until his election as President, Simpson called on Grant whenever he was in Washington.[1300] In September of 1868 when Grant learned of Simpson's planned visit to Galena, Illinois, he wrote: "Having a great desire to hear you lecture on the 'future of the Republic,' we must earnestly request that you will, should your health and time permit, favor the citizens of Galena with the delivery, on such evening as may suit your convenience during your present visit to Galena." Simpson responded, "In accordance with your request, I will name tomorrow (Saturday) evening as the only time I will be at liberty to do so during my stay in Galena."[1301] On January 2, 1869, Grant wrote to George Steward, "I visited Bishop Simpson today and learned that he was to preach tomorrow and have arranged to go."[1302]

Perhaps Grant believed he could trust his Cabinet members as well as other government subordinates, just as he had relied on his field officers to carry out his orders. Jay Gould's cornering of the gold market, the whiskey ring, Credit Mobilier, and numerous other scandals plaguing the Grant administration have not placed the Civil War General and Reconstruction President in a favorable historical light. Both Grant's Secretary of War, William Belknap and Secretary of the Interior, Columbus Delano were fired for graft and fraud. Grant's campaign slogan, "Let us have peace" was not working, and the Radicals were almost as disenchanted with Grant as they had been with Johnson. It seemed that Grant was proving Henry Adams' sarcasm, that "the progress of evolution from President Washington to President Grant was alone sufficient evidence to upset Darwin."[1303]

Grant and Simpson, though not blood-related, had inherited the same loyalty gene, a trait that overlooked the inadequacies and failures of their friends. The President gave a government post to a man who had possessed no other qualification other than purchasing fire wood from him after the

---

1300   LOC, Simpson papers, *Diaries*: January 16, 1866, and March 13, 1867. Simpson's *Diary* entries indicate that he developed a pattern of making a lobbying trip to Washington sometime during the early part of each year, especially during the Reconstruction years. For example, Simpson recorded on January 6, 1874, "Went to Washington. Spoke to many representatives and senators." LOC, Simpson papers, 1874 *Diary*, Container two.

1301   Simon, Vol. 19, 84.

1302   Ibid., 102. Grant resided in Galena, IL, between his nomination and his election.

1303   Henry Adams. *The Education of Henry Adams* (New York: Barnes and Noble, 2009) 212.

heavily-drinking, discharged Grant had left California and returned to Illinois before the Civil War. (That Grant would transition from selling wood and almost starving, to the Presidency of the United States in an approximate eight-year span, was even more remarkable than Lincoln having once split wood.) For Postmaster of Nashville, Grant appointed a German butcher because, "When I was a very poor man in St. Louis just before the war, this German butcher furnished meat to my family on credit, and when I needed a loan of $10, $15, or $20, he was my banker without security and without charge of interest."[1304] Simpson had the same relationship to Harlan, Evans, and Grant himself.

James Riley Weaver, the Son Simpson Never Had

On October 27, 1869, Anna Frances Simpson married James Riley Weaver at the Spring Garden Methodist Episcopal Church in Philadelphia, the Methodist Church closest to the Mount Vernon Street house.[1305] Bishop Janes performed the ceremony with the proud father giving his daughter away. He must have reflected on his own wedding, because his daughter, Anna, in facial features, was almost an exact replica of her mother. When it became known that President Grant was to be present, entry cards were sent to the invited guests and, "as it was, and not-withstanding the heavy lines of police, the guests had to pass in through the rear door of the chapel so great was the throng."[1306] The secular press hooted about the "extravagance" of the wedding. *The Washington Express* asked, "Wasn't the wedding at Bishop Simpson's rather gay for a Methodistical arrangement?" The *Daily Cleveland Herald*, asked what early Methodists would have thought, "of the altar covered with flowers, orange trees in full bloom, singing birds and an aquarium of sporting gold-fish, what a bride and maids with sweeping trains, the groom and men in fashionable black, with bouquet in buttonhole, and fautless white chokers and immaculate kids?"[1307]

1304   Jean Edward Smith. *Grant* (New York: Simon and Schuster, 2001) 255.

1305   This church still stands today, but belongs to another denomination.

1306   *In Loving Memory of Anna Simpson Weaver* UMA, Drew University, Simpson papers.

1307   *Daily National Intelligencer and Washington Express*-Washington, DC (November 5, 1869), and The Daily Cleveland Herald-Cleveland, OH (November 1, 1869).

Again, Simpson's relationship with a U.S. President was quid pro quo. During Grant's Inaugural, March 4, 1869, Simpson presented Grant with a gold-headed cane on behalf of the Methodist Women of Baltimore. The wood of the cane was said to be from the estate of General Lafayette in France. Grant joked, "I hope I will have no causation to use it upon anyone"[1308] Simpson pleaded with Grant concerning a consular appointment for his son-in-law, James Weaver, husband of his daughter Anna. Upon being discharged from the Army, Weaver took a job as a professor at the newly-formed West Virginia University at Morgantown. Sometime during the summer of 1869, Simpson wrote Grant the most nepotistic letter of his life.

> Personal. Will you allow me to ask your consideration of a matter personal to myself. My second daughter will in a few months be married to Prof. J. R. Weaver, of West Virginia. He was Capt. in the army--was a prisoner in *Libby* for eighteen months--was breveted Lt. Col,--and is now Professor of Mathematics, Military Tactics & c in West Virginia College at Morgantown. He is a young gentleman of about 28,--a college graduate,--of unblemished character, and should have opportunities of fitting himself for the best literary positions, and hence would be glad to have him reside a few years in Europe. If he could obtain a Consulship that would yield a fair support for him and my daughter for two or three years the plan could be carried out. I do not wish to see him enter political life—nor do I ask for office for him, if he cannot serve the country well, while he can also improve himself, I prefer making this frank statement to you alone. I do not care for a position for him for several months yet—and if in your arrangements no good place can be given him consistently with the public interests, I shall be satisfied with yr decision. If a good place may be obtained and recommendations of Senators or others are desired, I think any number may be obtained. But I prefer making no formal application or be placed on file, unless there is a fair prospect of success. Asking your indulgence for the only application I have ever made for a member of my family, I place the matter in your hands. I ought also to add that I have signed a few applications at the urgent request of friends that I esteem, and in whose success I wd delight, but do not expect to trouble you with many such, as I have declined further representations. With profound regard, and with my sincere desire for your triumphant success .... P.S. If such a position [as] Consul Genl at Frankfort on the Maine cd be procured it wd be very gratifying-

---

1308 *Daily National Intelligencer*-Washington, DC (March 4, 1869).

If the formal application is made it will come from WEST VIRGINIA which I presume will not have many applicants.[1309]

In a flurry of telegrams, Frankfort became Italy, and Italy became Glasgow, and Glasgow became Italy again, and Italy became Glasgow again. Simpson admitted to Grant that he had been "perplexed." The President probably was, too. Finally, on March 4, 1870, Ulysses S. Grant nominated Weaver as Consul to Bringdiai, a small town on the coast of Italy.[1310] *The Daily National Intelligencer and Washington Express* reported, "Come to think of it, we were wrong in saying that President Grant did not make a contribution to the trousseau of Bishop Simpson's daughter, whose wedding he recently attended. He presented her husband with the Consulship of Bringdiai, a little town in Italy, which will be worth a free bridal tour for the young couple over the Continent."[1311]

After only a few months, Weaver was sent to Antwerp, Belgium. Simpson's intercession for his son-in-law continued throughout the next decade. In 1879, Matthew Simpson persuaded Secretary of State William Evarts to appoint his son-in-law to Vienna, one of the choicest plums among American ambassadorships.[1312]

James Riley Weaver was both gifted and industrious. One of ten children from a Pennsylvania farm family, he attended both Allegheny College and Garrett Biblical Institute. His teachers at Allegheny testified that they had never taught a superior student. He enrolled in the Union Army, was captured, and spent seventeen months in southern prisons, mostly Libby outside of Richmond. After his consulship, he became a superlative teacher for thirty-two years years at DePauw, 1885-1917, mainly teaching Political Science. His teaching methodology was dialogical and participatory: "Students are collaborators with the instructor in the investigation of specific subjects. Too much help stultifies the intellect; it must rather be quickened to self-dependence." One of his students headed to Columbia University, which shied from Marx's *Communist Manifesto* and *Das Capital*, but the

---

1309   Simon, Vol. 19, 268-269.
1310   Ibid.
1311   *Daily National Intelligencer and Washington Express* (November 3, 1869).
1312   Kirby, *Social and Ecclesiastical*, 242.

student had already been introduced to Marx by a Republican professor at a small Methodist institution in Greencastle, Indiana. A "model of gentility, a gentleman of the old school," Weaver died at age eighty of heart failure, and is buried in Sandusky, Ohio, the home of his second wife.[1313]

Weaver was the son whom Simpson never had or the kind of son that Simpson desired to have. He was tall, handsome, intelligent, and ambitious. Matthew Verner would not find his vocational legs until after the Bishop's death. And, as we will see in the Epilogue, Simpson pulled every political lever at his disposal for his son to find an occupational niche. Fortunately, for the senior Simpson, his daughter, Anna, did not die until after his death. Her death and the remarrying of his son-in-law would have been an almost unbearable grief.

[1313] Merle Curti. "A Great Teacher's Teacher," *Social Education* Vol. XVIII No. 6 (October 1959) 263-267. Also see "James Riley Weaver Dies at Home," January 28, 1920, on file: UMA, DePauw University, James Riley Weaver papers.

Chapter Seventeen: Anything For a Methodist

An Architectural and Financial Crisis

On Tuesday, May 5, 1868, at the Methodist Episcopal Church General Conference, Simpson read the Episcopal address.[1314] The Bishop, as he stood before the Conference, trumpeted the success of Northern Methodism over the last four years. "The number of members and probationers has increased from 923,394 in 1863 to 1,148,081 in 1867 .... the largest increase which has ever occurred with a single exception, in any quadrenium in the history of the church .... The number of church edifices has increased from 9,430 to 11,121 .... The value of churches in 1863 was 20,130,554 and in 1867, it had swelled to 35,885,439 showing an increase of 15,054,885 or more than 70 percent in four years."[1315] Simpson credited the disproportionate rise in the value of the church property mostly to the substitution of "primitive edifices" with "those more commodious in size and of costlier structure."[1316] He noted that a third Methodist institution of theological education had been added, "by the munificent liberality of Daniel Drew Esquire of New York known as Drew Theological Seminary, (in addition to Boston and Garrett) and located on a beautiful tract of land at Madison, New Jersey."[1317]

One of the "more commodious in size and costlier structures" was the Metropolitan Methodist Episcopal Church, Washington, DC, initiated in the 1852 General Conference by Simpson himself. Simpson had argued for

---

1314   *Journal of the 1868 General Conference of the Methodist Episcopal Church* (New York: Carlton & Lanahan, 1868) 6.
1315   Ibid., 373.
1316   Ibid., 68.
1317   Ibid., 364.

a church of "architectural elegance," one which a visitor could easily find. For Congressmen, a "commodious church was needed," in order to "secure a proper influence upon such persons." Their "intellect and consciences" demanded more than "ordinary means." And even more urgent was, "the Catholics also are about to create a magnificent cathedral on a square of ground which they possess." None of the present churches possessed much architectural elegance, and it was with difficulty for visitors in Washington to find their way to them.[1318]

On the Sunday morning before Grant's inauguration, February 28, 1869, Simpson dedicated the Metropolitan National Church with Grant and Vice-President Schyler Colfax present, as well as other government dignitaries. Yes, it did have rented pews. A Thomas Kelso rented a pew for Grant, who quite frequently occupied it over the next eight years. Grant served as a non-active member of the Metropolitan Church Board and gave $100 toward the construction.(Lincoln had also given $100.) At least for one Sunday, Grant's Methodism was converted into Presbyterianism. On the Sunday after Grant's inauguration, the Presidential family showed up at Metropolitan, but no seat could be found. *The New York Herald*, November 11, reported that before the Sexton could catch up with the first family, the embarrassed and indignant Julia stomped out of the church with her husband and children submissively following. They made their way to First Presbyterian where they were vibrantly welcomed.[1319]

The presidential snub was not the only ill portent for the "National Church." The board, with Simpson's consent, decided they would build the highest spire in Washington. Kelso gave $5,000 to the project, and Julia Grant raised $8,000, which inscribed the latter's name on one of the eleven bells chiming out over the city: "Julia Dent Grant, wife of U.S. Grant, President of the United States of America."[1320] Kelso migrated from

---

1318   Matthew Simpson,"Reasons for Building a Metropolitan Church in Washington." UMA, Drew University, Simpson papers.

1319   William S. McFeely. *Grant* (New York: Norton and Company, 1982) 304.

1320   Lillian Brooks Brown. *A Living Centennial: Commemorating the One Hundredth Anniversary of Metropolitan Memorial United Methodist Church* (Washington, DC: Judd and Detwiler, 1969) 17. On November 25, 1869, Julia Dent Grant sent the following circular letter to the lady members of Metropolitan: "It is the wish of the ladies in Washington, to celebrate the liquidation of our church debt in a suitable manner. We have here fore

Ireland and made a fortune in railroads and insurance. He was President of the Equitable Insurance Society, largest stockholder in the Baltimore Steam Packet Company, as well as the Seaboard and Roanoke Railroad Company.[1321]

Apparently Simpson had not read Francis Asbury's *Journals* sufficiently to know that about nothing was Asbury more sarcastic than spires on a church. When in Charleston he recorded, "There is a holy strife between Bethel's members and Episcopalians who shall have the highest steeple, but I believe there is no contention about who shall have the most souls converted to God."[1322]

In spite of Simpson's plausible argument for a visible church, nature's God sided with Asbury. On July 4, 1874, a storm blew the 240 foot spire six inches off of its vertical axis. On February 1, 1876, a second storm blew the steeple six feet off equilibrium.[1323] What had been a source of solace and stability now became a horror to the surrounding neighbors, the Capital's major threat to life and limb. The steeple, after being stabilized, managed to remain standing until after World War I, during which it flew the American flag. In 1932, the building was sold to the United States Government, and the congregation moved to the corner of Nebraska and New Mexico Avenues, adjacent to American University, founded in 1893 by the Methodist Episcopal Church. The church at its new location is now known as Metropolitan Memorial United Methodist Church.

---

determined, to hold our jubilee in the Metropolitan Church in Christmas Eve. It is our purpose to have President Grant with us on that occasion; and as he is one of the trustees of the church, we propose to present to him the Fifty-thousand dollars, for the Metropolitan, in behalf of you and the other ladies who have aided in this good work. You will therefore, without fail, please report the amount you have collected by December 23rd, 1869, and remit the same by draft on New York to our pastor, the Reverend Doctor J. P Newman, which will be duly acknowledged in our church papers. And we shall be pleased to have you with us on that interesting occasion." Simon, Vol. XX, 73-74. Seemingly, Julia Grant raised far less than the $50,000.

1321   *Cyclopaedia*, 510.

1322   Salter, *America's Bishop*, 238.

1323   This information was taken from a history panel on the wall of The Metropolitan Memorial United Methodist Church, Washington, DC.

In 1879 Kelso's insurance company, the principal lien holder on Metropolitan, was threatening the church with foreclosure. (Kelso had died in 1878.) A Washington attorney, Henry Garnett, attempted an agreement with the church, that if the General Conference did not come up with a feasible financial plan, the church would be turned over to the Baltimore Equitable Insurance Society. The church rejected the proposal.[1324] Simpson received a series of alarming letters from the pastor, H. R. Naylor, one of which read "This morning I received a note from L. A. Crook, Baltimore, stating that the Equitable Insurance Company had ordered its secretary to commence its suit against Metropolitan Memorial Church for ten bonds of $500 each. Others, I presume, will follow."[1325] Simpson was liable for one of those bonds and was threatened with a law suit by the law office of Arthur M. Burton.[1326] He was also being dunned for $480 he had borrowed from the Methodist Aid Society on behalf of Metropolitan.[1327]

On January 3, 1879, Naylor wrote Simpson an adroit letter, a sociological and spiritual observation which not only applied to Metropolitan, but possibly the entire ship of Zion known as the Methodist Episcopal Church. "Instead of being a great life boat saving men, it is their sort of royal yacht beneath whose purple and gold they believe they recline on delightful pleasure excursions. But now royalty has departed and the yacht has lost its gilding and the excursionists much of their zest. Perhaps they may yet become true sailors; who knows."[1328] The 1880 General Conference loosed C. C. McCabe over the land to collect a dollar per brick on behalf of Metropolitan. McCabe played on Evans' emotions. "My second reason was to relieve Bishop Simpson, who felt personally responsible to see this debt paid. It was a great burden which infirming the Bishop's health. I saw it, felt it, and determined to relieve him."[1329]

1324   LOC, Simpson papers, Letters, Henry Wise Garnett to Simpson, July 25, 1879 and August 5, 1879, Container twelve.

1325   LOC, Simpson papers, Letter February, 1879, Container twelve.

1326   LOC, Simpson papers, Letter, Arthur M. Burton to Simpson, July 29, 1879, Container twelve.

1327   LOC, Simpson papers, Letter, The National Farmers and Plantation Bank of Baltimore to Simpson, November 29, 1879, Container twelve.

1328   LOC, Simpson papers, Letter, January 3, 1879, Container twelve.

1329   Evans Mss. Collection, History Colorado, Letter, McCabe to Evans, November 28, 1882.

The church, which had cost a quarter of a million dollars in 1869, retired its debt on "emancipation day," January 27, 1884, with Simpson making one of his last pulpit appearances.[1330]

Simpson's Summer Resort

J. P. Newman, the same person who served as a Presiding Elder in New Orleans (and later a Bishop in the Methodist Episcopal Church) was pastor of Metropolitan when the physical structure was completed, during which time he also served as chaplain of the U.S. Senate. When he was re-appointed elsewhere, he should have surrendered his Senate job to Otis H. Tiffany, the new pastor of Metropolitan. Simpson sided with Tiffany, and the newspapers blew the disagreement out of proportion, attempting to drive a wedge between Simpson and Grant. "Newman, however, was backed by Grant, who it is said, has taken a dislike to Bishop Simpson, because the latter is constantly asking for offices for his friends."[1331] Though in all likelihood, Simpson at times did irritate the President, Grant needed Simpson as much as Simpson needed the President. In that Newman had served as Grant's pastor, he baptized the President just before his death. The choice of baptism and the baptizer was made by the family since Grant was almost or completely comatose when Newman sprinkled the former President on his deathbed.

Besides Metropolitan Church, the other edifice that drew Grant and Simpson together was the cottage purchased for Simpson in 1871. Grant came under the conviction that his favorite preacher needed a reprieve from the hot Philadelphia summers. If Grant was not the primary initiator for both Philadelphia and New Jersey Methodists purchasing a summer retreat for Simpson at Long Branch, New Jersey, he was one of them. On January 18, 1871, Grant wrote New Jersey Presiding Elder Jacob Graw, donating one hundred dollars to the cause.[1332] Grant was extending the same charity that had been extended to him. *The New Yorker* sarcastically editorialized

---

1330   Brown, 7.

1331   "Grant's Spiritual Favorite," *New York Sun* (March 17, 1873).

1332   Simon, Vol. 21, 412. According to Simpson's *Cyclopaedia*, Graw served as a Presiding Elder on two New Jersey districts, the Burlington and New Brunswick. The inclusion of Graw's picture indicated Graw's importance to Simpson, 417-418.

that two questions, "Were you a contributor to either (any) of Grant's three houses?" and "Are you a member of the Dent family or otherwise connected by marriage to General Grant?" would be included on the Civil Service Exam.[1333] (The three homes were Galena, Illinois; Washington, DC; Long Branch, New Jersey; and ultimately a fourth residence in New York City after Grant's Presidency.)

Grant and Simpson summered in Long Branch, New Jersey, America's premier ocean resort, during the peak of its prominence. It was during the 1870s according to historian Randall Gabrielan that, "hotels had sprawled along the shore like wooden boxes on an old Monopoly board while summer cottages built by gentlemen were sprouting around the city .... While large summer houses were surely cottages, some latter 19th-century references called anything in Long Branch not a hotel a cottage, typically the guest buildings rented by hotels to visitors who then dined in hotel halls."[1334] Though Simpson did not own ocean front property, he was only about two hundred yards from the shoreline. His house faced Sea View Avenue, a street which ran perpendicular to Ocean Avenue, the latter running north and south, the length of Long Branch. Sea View was the street closest to the northern-most Long Branch Depot, served by the New Jersey Southern Railroad.[1335] When the Simpson's got off the train they walked approximately fifty yards to their cottage. The Grant's owned ocean front property next door to Philadelphia publisher, George Childs, and only a couple hundred yards from Simpson, on what is now Grant Avenue. There would have been opportunity for them to visit during the summer.

Simpson Endorses Ocean Grove

In July 1870, a group of Methodist entrepreneurs committed to the Wesleyan doctrine of entire sanctification founded a retreat at Ocean

---

[1333] Jean Waugh. *Grant: American Hero, American Myth* (Chapel Hill: University Press, 2009) 126.

[1334] Randall Gabrielan. *Long Branch, New Jersey: Remembering a Resort* (Atglen, PA: Schiffer Publishing Company, 2009) 6.

[1335] F. W. Beers. *Atlas of Monmouth County, New Jersey* (New York: Beers, Comstock, and Cline, 1867) and William S. McFeely. Grant (New York: F. Norton and Company, 1982) 261–262.

Grove six miles south of Long Branch. The Ocean Grove Camp Meeting Association was the immediate mutation of the National Camp Meeting Association for the Promotion of Holiness, which held its first camp meeting at Vineland, New Jersey in July 1867. Out of this association grew the Ocean Grove Camp Meeting Association, which was issued a charter by the New Jersey Legislature to incorporate in March 1870. By the end of the year, 20,000 lots had been laid out and sold, and eight years later its summer population swelled to 18,000. The absence of salt marsh within the immediate vicinity allowed the new township to advertise itself as the only place on the Jersey Shore devoid of mosquitoes. In 1869, Elwood Stokes, an Elder in the New Jersey Conference, became President of the Ocean Grove Association, and in 1893-94, oversaw the building of a 9,000 seat auditorium, which as of this writing, is perhaps the largest wooden tabernacle in the world. Simpson and Stokes knew each other well, and the Bishop thought highly enough of him to include Stokes' picture along with a biographical sketch in his *Cyclopaedia*.[1336] Because on Sundays, all vehicles were banned from Ocean Grove streets until the 1980s, President Ulysses Grant one Sunday in 1875 tied his horse at the chained gates and walked the one half mile to his sister's house.[1337] As for everything that happened in Methodism, it was critical to obtain Simpson's endorsement. In February of 1870, Simpson wrote, "It gives me great pleasure to state that I have visited the grounds of the Ocean Grove Camp Meeting Association and think them admirably adapted for furnishing Christian families a sea-side resort in the midst of Christian influences."[1338]

Simpson and the Founding of John Vincent's Chautauqua

No one sought Simpson's approval more than did John Vincent, founder of Chautauqua at Jamestown, New York, one of the most beautiful settings in America.[1339] The main purpose of the institution was to train Sunday

---

1336 *Cyclopaedia*, 835.

1337 Wayne T. Bell. *Images of America, Ocean Grove* (Charleston: Arcadia Publishing, 2000) 8.

1338 "Endorsement by Bishop M. Simpson," www.loc.,gov/resource/g3814o.ct002342/.

1339 John Vincent wrote Simpson April 24, April 28, June 2, and June 10, 1874, begging him to come to Chautauqua with the desperate plea, "I will do anything you ask." LOC, Simpson papers, Letters, Container eleven.

school teachers. Simpson spoke for its initial conference, August 1874. His presentation was pure Simpson. He asked his congregation to consider an apple: "Each of you could hold in your hand and view it from all sides. But it was different with a mountain, which was so large it afforded a number of different views and approaches. Even more was it even so with knowing God. The shear enormity of God and the limitation of our knowledge prohibited agreement on all points of faith." Simpson's ecumenicity was at its best. "I ask no change in your denomination; keep your own convictions; don't let them stand in your way to Christ or your work for him."[1340] John Vincent recalled the program of that 1874 Chautauqua:

> At the first assembly there were twenty-two lectures on the theory and practice of Sunday-school work; seven upon the authority of the Bible; nine sectional primary meetings; six intermediate; six seniors', superintendents', and pastors' meetings; eight conductors' conferences; twenty-five meetings of normal sections; two teachers' meetings; two model Sunday-schools; four Bible readings; three praise services; two immense children's meetings; six sermons, and other meetings of minor note; also prayer meetings, vesper services and temperance addresses.[1341]

Simpson dedicated the great pavilion at Chautauqua on Saturday afternoon, August 2, 1879, and dedicated a Hall of Philosophy, August 5.[1342] On Sunday morning, August 3, he spoke from Isaiah 6, and focused on the seraphim who cry out to on another, "Holy, Holy, Holy, is the Lord of Hosts. The whole earth is full of his glory." As was often the case during the final years of his preaching, he wandered off into a nationalistic agenda, "And America stands as another seraphim; and Germany stands and the Christian nations all adore him; and by and by, nation after nation shall wheel into line, until representing the nations these spirits stand before the throne and seeing how God has worked out his great problems they cry, "Holy, Holy, Holy, is the Lord of Hosts, the earth is full of his glory."[1343] Simpson could not have known that almost the very moment he was speaking; Kaiser

---

1340   Email from Chautauqua archivist Jonathan Schmitz, Nov 6, 2014.
1341   James McBath. "The Emergence of Chautauqua as a Religious and Educational Institution 1874-1900," *Methodist History* Vol. 20 (October 1981) 4.
1342   LOC, Simpson papers, John Vincent letter to Matthew Simpson, April 24, 1879, Container eleven. This tabernacle still stands today.
1343   LOC, Simpson papers, "Sermon by Bishop Simpson, L.L.D., of Philadelphia," *Chautauqua Herald* (August 5, 1879).

Wilhelm was beginning systematic colonization of southwest Africa, almost completely annihilating the Herero tribe. Even more tragically, the Germans partially borrowed their imperialistic model from America. In 1903, Captain Maximilian Bayer wrote:

> Our Lord has made the laws of nature so that only the strong have a right to continue to exist in the world, and so that the weak and purposeless will perish to favour of the strong. This process is played out in a variety of ways, like, for example, the end of the American Indians, because they were without purpose in the continued development of a world that is striving towards a higher level of civilisation; in the same way the day will come when the Hottentot [Nama] will perish, [it will] not [be] any loss for humanity because they are after all only born thieves and robbers, nothing more.[1344]

By August 1892, the Chautauqua program had taken a decisively secular turn. The program for the season listed, "130 important lectures and addresses, of which 30 are illustrated, 10 musical recitals, 20 concerts and entertainments by musicians and readers, 2 superb tableaux, 4 evenings of fireworks, illuminations and illuminated fleets, 2 prize matches, beside baseball matches, bicycle and athletic exhibitions, and other minor entertainments without number."[1345] William James, who was one of the lecturers at the 1892 Assembly, exclaimed at its end, "What a relief! Now for something primordial and savage, even though it were as bad as an Armenian massacre to set the balance straight again."[1346]

Though neither Ocean Grove nor Chautauqua were Methodist institutions, they were largely supported by Methodists. Into the twentieth-century, the religious emphasis for both locations would fade into the background with an increasing secularization including popular entertainment, political rallies, lectures on almost any subjects, and family recreation. Going the opposite direction was the National Camp Meeting Association for the Promotion of Holiness with a spiritual and theological agenda. The Holiness Association was an attempt to correct the cultural and spiritual drift within Methodism of which both Ocean Grove and

---

1344 David Olusoga and Casper W. Erichsen. *The Kaiser's Holocaust: Germany's Forgotten Genocide* (London: Faber and Faber Ltd) 133.
1345 McBath, 7.
1346 Ibid., 8.

506 | "God Cannot Do Without America"

Chautauqua would become prime examples. (We will return to the National Camp Meeting Association at the end of this chapter.)

Daniel Drew and the Founding of Drew Theological Seminary

Matthew Simpson exhorted as he stood in the pulpit of the elaborate St. Paul's Church in New York City (John McClintock's pulpit) in June of 1866, "Do anything for a Methodist because he is a Methodist …. For myself, I am free to say I have no fault in bringing up my son or my daughters not to be hewers of wood or drawers of water for any other denomination in the land."[1347] As Daniel Drew sat on the platform behind Simpson, he may have decided that he would be the preeminent Methodist "helping Methodists" at least financially. No one ever walked on American soil who more securely compartmentalized the sacred and the profane than did Daniel Drew, a conundrum to both himself and to the Methodists who surrounded him. The thousands of dollars which he gave to Methodist causes spared him close scrutiny.

At this particular point in history, there is no doubt which was the most influential denomination in America, and Simpson its most powerful leader. In 1860 the Methodist Episcopal Church in the North claimed a 29% market share of all religious adherents, while the Baptist only 15%, approximately half as large as Methodism.[1348] No wonder Ulysses Grant observed that there were three great political parties in America, the Republican, the Democrat, and the Methodist Church. To celebrate its centennial the Methodist Episcopal Church issued a medallion with a price tag of $5. Simpson's picture was on one side and an inscription on the other, supposedly quoting Simpson, "Now my young Brethren, I cannot tell which of you will wear the brightest crown, but who sacrifices most to win by the Master."[1349] Why the Methodists did not choose the ultimate sacrificial model, the circuit rider, as its logo is baffling.

1347   From *Zion's Herald* (June 20, 1866) in Walter W. Benjamin, "The Methodist Episcopal Church in the Post-War Era," *The History of American Methodism* Vol. II, ed. Emory Bucke, 319.

1348   Roger Fink and Rodney Stark. *The Churching of America: 1776-1990* (New Brunswick, NJ: Rutgers University Press, 1992) 171.

1349   E. M. Wood. *The Peerless Orator* (Pittsburgh: Pittsburgh Printing Company, 1909) 191.

Drew Theological Seminary was a curious confluence of Cornelius Vanderbilt, Thomas Gibbons, Daniel Drew, John McClintock, and Matthew Simpson. Cornelius Vanderbilt's first employer was Thomas Gibbons, and both of them found themselves in a fight with the Livingstons, a patrician Dutch clan, over the rights to the waterways surrounding New York City. The Livingstons leased what they thought to be their exclusive navigational prerogatives to Aaron Ogden. The contention worked its way through the lower courts and on March 2, 1824, a decision was handed down by Supreme Court Justice John Marshall in the first anti-monopoly case in American history. It was almost impossible for Gibbons to lose, since he was represented by Daniel Webster and the United States Attorney General, William Wirt.

When Thomas Gibbons died, his son William had no interest in the boating business and sold his three ships in February of 1829.[1350] Cleared of his obligations to the Gibbons family, Vanderbilt was now an independent steamboat operator and William Gibbons with the inheritance from his deceased father, which included ridding himself of anything to do with boats, had discretionary money. Gibbons would duplicate his Savannah, Georgia heritage by purchasing a 200 acre tract of land in Madison, New Jersey, and building on it a plantation-style house. Drew historian John T. Cunningham describes William's gift to his wife:

> The mansion was similar to the Carolinas, and Gibbons' own Georgia. Bricks for the mansion came from Benjamin Pierson Lum's brickyard in nearby Chatham. The solid mahogany interior's trim came from Santo Domingo and was hand carved in England. The stout wooden pillars for the front piazza were designed and carved in London. A Mr. Jenkins (a New Brunswick builder) assembled the materials into a house to fit a plantation owner's dreams, at a cost estimated to be $100,000.[1351]

John McClintock and Matthew Simpson leaned on Daniel Drew and persuaded him to be the initial and primary contributor for a "theological seminary" in return for the new institution bearing his name. In 1867, Drew purchased the "Forest" from William Gibbons, and the latter returned

---

1350   T. J. Stiles. *The First Tycoon: The Epic Life of Cornelius Vanderbilt* (New York: Vintage Books, 2010) 75.

1351   John T. Cunningham. *University in the Forest: The Story of Drew University* (Andover, New Jersey: Afton Press, 1972) 37.

to Georgia. Before the two of them converged on Madison, New Jersey, approximately twenty-five miles west of New York City, Simpson and Drew had several opportunities to become acquainted with one another. The Board of Bishops had met in Drew's library.[1352] Simpson was made aware by Thomas Carlton that Drew was one of the contributors to his life insurance policy.[1353] And we remember that Drew had helped throw Simpson a "got well party" in 1859. Simpson reported to Ellen on February 28, 1863, "Last night with Bp. Janes spoke at St. Paul's. They raised $30,000. Drew gave $10,000. Stayed with him at night, had Charlie with me."[1354]

Indeed, the Methodists as led by Matthew Simpson, as much or more than any other person, were determined to be in the education business. Methodist historian Donald Jones calculates that, "From 1865 to 1886 the Methodist Episcopal Church established twenty-eight colleges and seminaries all of which still exist."[1355] Simpson made clear in his Centennial Address at St. Paul's, that the next step in Methodism's growth and progress was education. This was his preeminent and concluding point.

> We want a learning polished and yet sanctified (ministry), whereby we may educate the people and, at the same time, lead them upward to God. God grant that we may now do something worthy of Methodism! And when the year 1866 shall be remembered, among the years of the past, may the pen of the future historian record that among the most notable events was this: That Methodism gave its grandest efforts for the education, not of men and women of a particular locality, not for partial ends, or for personal aggrandizement, but for educating the minds of the masses all over the world.[1356]

Durbin and Simpson Disagree

When the dignitaries, which included all seven Bishops, descended on Madison, New Jersey, and met in the Presbyterian Church on November 6,

---

1352   LOC, Simpson papers, Letter, Edmund Janes to Matthew Simpson, September 23, 1865, Container eight.

1353   LOC, Simpson papers, Letter January 30, 1865, Container seven.

1354   LOC, Simpson papers, Letter February 28, 1863, Container three.

1355   Donald Jones. *Sectional Crisis and Northern Methodism: A Study in Piety, Political Ethics, and Civil Religion* (Metuchen, New Jersey: The Scarecrow Press, 1979) 15.

1356   Crooks, 512.

1868, the two principal speakers found themselves in disagreement with one another. Simpson, with his normative platitudinal espousal of education, sounded as if the need for the formal training of preachers in American Methodism was a foregone conclusion. According to the Bishop, education was necessitated by the new challenges that faced the Church such as Biblical criticism, evolution, and various forms of infidelity, especially those which wrongly interpreted the life of Christ. "I rejoice in the advantage afforded by the location and surroundings of this institution so favorable to esthetic improvement, to the cultivation of the beautiful, which will be given our young men coming from the farm, from the workshop, and from the departments of labor. They will here meet with those forms of culture which will refine and elevate them."[1357]

J. P. Durbin, second only to Simpson in his reputation as a preacher, and speaking immediately after Simpson, questioned Simpson's facile assumptions about an educated ministry. Durbin reminded his auditors that when he had written an article in the *Christian Advocate* July 14, 1834, touting ministerial education, he had received a full frontal assault of negativism. Durbin posed the question, "Ought not some steps be taken to provide a suitable education for junior preachers before they enter extensively into the work of the ministry?" He then argued, "It is necessary to divest ourselves of our prejudices about theological seminaries as we have been accustomed to see and understand them. There was a time when seminaries were chiefly employed in educating young men for the ministry merely as a profession without proper regard to their morals and evangelical piety."[1358] Many disagreed with Durbin then, and in his mind thirty years later, there was still cause for caution. An attender at this auspicious occasion rendered the following observation:

> The two chief speakers of the morning were Dr. John P. Durbin and Bishop Matthew Simpson. Dr. Durbin maintained that the Church in its earlier period had been hostile to the training of preachers in special schools. Bishop Simpson affirmed the contrary, and expressed astonishment that his old friend was not of his opinion. Dr. Durbin instanced his own proposal of special theological training in *The Christian*

1357   Ezra Squire Tipple. *Drew Theological Seminary 1867-1970: A Review of the First Half Century* (New York: The Methodist Book Concern, 1917) 34-35.

1358   *New York Christian Advocate* (July 18, 1834).

Advocate, when he was editor of that paper, and the summary manner in which the proposal was negative. I have forgotten the facts on which Bishop Simpson relied for his proofs. Each of these two eloquent speakers had surprised the other; and the difference in their estimate of the facts was one of the piquant incidents of the day. Which of the two orators was right? In my humble judgment, Dr. Durbin was, unquestionably.[1359]

The Consequences of Drew's Bankruptcy

Daniel Drew could barely read, and was unable to write in a legible, cursive script. The humorous story was told that Drew changed the combination to his safe and when his clerks could not open it, they sent Drew an inquiry asking for the new setting. Drew replied that the combination was the simple word "door." When the clerks again failed to open the safe, the irritated Drew responded that they could open the safe with the letters of "an ordinary house door, barn door, stable door, any kind of door." The clerks again failed and Drew rushed from his house to his office and immediately in the presence of his staff, opened the safe. "There, it opens as easy as an old sack: D.O.A.R.E."!

But Methodism's most munificent benefactor did not have to spell door to open the door to Wall Street. The "jackal" only had to start a rumor on the upgrading or downgrading of a specific stock and "Uncle Daniel," to this day, is still quite possibly the all-time manipulator of Wall Street. Simply by selling and buying stock in America's most prominent railroad, of which he was the major stockholder, Drew could make the stock go up or down. "Daniel says 'up'–Erie goes up. Daniel says 'down'--Erie goes down. Daniel says, 'wiggle-waggle'--it goes both ways."[1360]

In spite of his illiteracy, Drew was more than a financial benefactor to Methodism's first Seminary. He was a hands-on-founder, requiring that John McClintock his New York pastor, be named President, and Randolph Foster, the Professor of Theology. The Methodist Bishops were skittish

---

1359 *Proceedings of the Celebration of the Twenty-First Anniversary of the Founding of Drew Theological Seminary: October 26, 1892* (New York: Hunt and Eaton, 1892) 13. Simpson said of Durbin, "Few men ever equaled him in solid and wide-spread popularity; few have been as equal in ability, fidelity, tact, and industry. He ranked among the first in the church as a pulpit orator, a Christian pastor, an educator, a writer, and administrator." *Cyclopaedia*, 319.

1360 Browder, 115.

about Drew's leverage. Bishop Janes wrote McClintock, "You must advise him about his building. He has very little idea of what is appropriate."[1361] McClintock did not desire the presidency of Drew, a job which he fulfilled only two years before dying on March 4, 1870. His health was already waning, and he had a beautiful home on the Raritan River in New Brunswick, New Jersey, which he would have to vacate. In all likelihood, McClintock doubted his administrative abilities. He was a scholar, not a financial magician possessing the wizardry for performing monetary miracles necessary for an infant educational institution. He was having enough financial problems of his own. He recorded on December 13, 1869, "Lost $5,000 this year, loaned to my brother James, whom he cannot pay. I lost $2,000 also by E. W. McClintock; $5,000 invested with a mine in Benango, CO; $1,000 invested with J. L. Gilden in Ohio; and $2,000 with J. Graden in Colorado. These with interest amount to about $18,500."[1362] In 1867, McClintock reflected upon his acceptance of the Drew Presidency:

> In March, finding that Mr. Drew's centennial gift for Theol. Education was not likely to be consummated soon, unless I shall agree to accept the presidency of the Theological Seminary, to be founded by him, I agreed to do so; my labor to commence in the Spring of the year. The purchase of the Gibbons estate–consummated in June …. In November broke up my beautiful home on the Raritan with great reluctance and moved to the Gibbons mansion so part of my furniture with Drew agreeing to give me what furniture I needed out of the Gibbons house.[1363]

1361 Manuscript Archives and Rare Book Library, Emory University, McClintock papers, Letter February 9, 1866, Container four.

1362 Manuscript Archives and Rare Book Library, Emory University, McClintock papers, *Diary*, December 13, 1869, Container eight. However, McClintock had worked in finance as a young man, but according to former Drew professor Michael Ryan not with a whole lot of flair. "McClintock's childhood came to a rather abrupt close when at the age of fourteen he was made a full-time clerk in the family store. From the standpoint of his parents it was part of his education to learn the mercantile business, but he was plagued by a wandering mind filled with the scenes he had learned to envision from the Songs of Anacreon of the Aeneid of Virgil. Often scolded for not paying attention to details, he was not very happy in the store, although it made it possible for him to accept his first full-time job away from home. He was hired in 1830 at age sixteen as a clerk in the Methodist Book Concern in New York City, where he went to live in the home of a Methodist preacher, the Rev. Samuel Merwin." Michael D Ryan. "John McClintock," *Something More Than Human: Biographies of Leaders in American Methodist Higher Education*, ed. Charles E. Cole (Nashville: United Methodist Board of Higher Education and Ministry, 1986) 144.

1363 Manuscript Archives and Rare Book Library, Emory University, McClintock papers, "Investments," 1867 *Diary*, Container eight.

The man who had the most influence on Drew was neither Simpson nor McClintock, but a relatively unknown Methodist pastor, John Parker, the older man's spiritual advisor.[1364] Parker recalled that, "More than forty times have I met with him alone in prayer, and I felt it was my duty to do so." And it was to Parker in 1857, that Drew first broached the idea of making a significant financial gift to Methodism. In 1865, George Crooks, Charles North, and John McClintock called on Drew in his New York City home, and within five minutes, Drew had stated, "I am willing to give 250 thousand dollars for the endowment of a theological seminary at Carmel, Putnam County, in the state of New York for the use of the Methodist Episcopal Church."[1365] (Drew later doubled his pledge.) Of course, the Methodist clergy that droned around Drew and drooled after his money knew nothing about their benefactor's swindling misrepresentations, if not outright deceit, nor did they bother to measure the distance between Drew's copious repentance on Sunday and his obsession for mammon on Monday.

Had Drew retired from the money game in the late 1860s, he would have fulfilled his one-half-million dollar pledge to Drew and died a multimillionaire. But Wall Street for Daniel Drew was a gambling house to which he was addicted, and the addiction by 1876 left him with liabilities of $1,093,524.82, as against total assets of $746,459.46. There was nothing left but to file bankruptcy. Drew President John Fletcher Hurst knew Daniel Drew would no longer be able to meet his financial obligations to Drew Theological Seminary; thus, the letters of alarm to Simpson as well as the other Drew Trustees.[1366] Plus, Simpson still owed $50 on his pledge to Drew, and it was needed because the faculty was more than one month behind in their salaries.[1367]

The man who had at one time been the "Director of three railroads, the President of two steamboat companies, and a Trustee of three Methodist

---

1364   Browder, 122.

1365   Ibid., 124. Drew's $250,000 was the first pledge to the "Centennial Fund," which eventually raised over $8,000,000. Abel Stevens. *The Centenary of American Methodism: A Sketch of Its History, Theology, Practical System and Success* (New York: Carlton & Porter, 1866) 332. Drew later doubled his pledge to $500,000, a promise he was unable to keep.

1366   OC, Simpson papers, Letters February 11, 1876, and September 25, 1876, Container ten.

1367   LOC, Simpson papers, Letter, A. V. Stout to Simpson, April 15, 1879.

institutions of higher learning" had left Drew Theological Seminary, the primary symbol of Methodism's one hundred year advancement, "on the bubble." The bubble did not burst, and though Daniel Drew's default caused the Seminary to wobble, lack of income did not prevent it from becoming one of the premier theological institutions in late nineteenth and early twentieth century America with the likes of James Strong, John Miley, and Edwin Lewis on its faculty.

Phoebe Palmer Attempts to Push Simpson into Holiness

After Simpson confessed to Phoebe Palmer that he was not "entirely sanctified," she wrote him a six-page letter with the following spiritual advisements: "I do not doubt that your soul and body are laid upon the altar of sacrifice, the promotion of the highest good of the Church of Christ over which the Holy Ghost hath made you overseer .... Believing is an act of obedience and not to believe is to be culpable before God ..." According to Palmer, Simpson had set himself, "wholly apart for the service of the redeemer" and God was obligated to sanctify him or He was a liar. "It seems to me that you've come to the point in your religious career where God requires that this question should be met and answered before you proceed further .... I do not doubt that the main difficulty in your case has been that you have not honored God by steadily relying on his word, believing in your heart that He does not receive you wholly, because you had his word assuring you that He does." Palmer then quoted Matthew 11:12, "The kingdom of heaven suffers violence and the violent take it by force." Palmer emphasized the irony that many persons had been brought into entire sanctification by Simpson's preaching, a state of grace that Simpson himself did not possess.

> I will no longer permit the tempter to hinder you from laying hold upon the promise which makes witness of the blessing of entire sanctification from persuasion that you may not have set yourself apart fully; for the Lord knows the sincerity of your intention and He who has wrought this sincerity of heart assures you in His tender love, that if in anything you be otherwise minded, He will reveal this unto you.[1368]

Palmer's exhortation disregarded the epistemological, theological, exegetical, psychological and, most importantly, the temperamental

---
1368   LOC, Simpson papers, Letter, Palmer to Simpson, n. d., Container thirteen.

separation between herself and her spiritual prey. In Palmer's theological understanding, believing for entire sanctification was an act of the will. Concerning her own experience she wrote, "And by the determination to consecrate all upon the altar of sacrifice to God, with resolve to 'enter into the bonds of an everlasting covenant to be wholly the Lord's for time and eternity,' and then acting in conformity with this decision, actually laying all upon the altar by the most unequivocal Scripture testimony" she was under obligation "to believe that the sacrifice became the Lord's property; and by virtue of the altar upon which the offering was laid became wholly and acceptable."[1369] Unfortunately, Palmer's "resolution" and "determination" sounded remotely Pelagian. Can a regenerated person resolve at any time by an act of the will to be fully devoted to God? Does the grace for entire sanctification come before or after the act of human will? These questions are partially answered by Palmer biographer, Harold Raser, who writes that faith for Palmer was "essentially an intellectual exercise, believing certain propositions to be true–although a dimension of it was trust, since the purpose of the proposition (promises Palmer liked to call them) was to instill confidence in the seeker and lead to action"[1370]

Palmer assumed that Simpson's devotion to the church and tireless ecclesiastical labors equated to the "Redeemer's service." Having to constantly work within an ecclesiastical bureaucracy, which increasingly resembled and reflected the world around it, made it difficult for Simpson to believe that he was serving a church on earth that was "sanctified and cleansed without spot and wrinkle." Phoebe Palmer wrote in her most famed hymn:

> I rise to walk in heaven's own light
> Above the world and sin
> With hearts made pure and garments white
> And Christ enthroned within.[1371]

1369 Phoebe Palmer. *Notes by the Way* (New York: Lane and Scott, 1850) 63.

1370 Harold Raser. *Phoebe Palmer: Her Life and Thought* (Lewiston, NY: The Edwin Mellon Press, 1986) 175. Randy Maddox also argues that Phoebe Palmer adopted an intellectual model for entire sanctification, as "she kept (Asa Mahan's) emphasis that such devotion is possible by a perpetual exercise of will." Randy Maddox. "Holiness of Heart and Life: Lessons from North American Methodism," *Asbury Theological Journal* (Fall 1995) 160.

1371 Phoebe Palmer. "The Cleansing Wave" in *Sing to the Lord* (Kansas City, Missouri: Lillenas Publishing Company, 1993) 528.

Simpson was not above the world, he was in it. Could Simpson operate ecclesiastical and political machinery without sullying his pure and white garments with grease and oil? Palmer and Simpson lived in two different worlds: one of spiritual elitism which gave full time to Godly pursuits and enabling others to do the same, as opposed to fighting in the ecclesiastical trenches, settling church disputes, taking an aggressive stance in the Civil War and applying political leverage as often as he visited the Nation's capital. Constant travel, appointment of preachers, pleading with U.S. Congressmen, defending himself from detractors, and alienating those of a different political, denominational, or cultural allegiance, must have at times made him feel a bit out of tune with the pure will of God. Ralph Morrow referred to Simpson's precarious balance between the secular and sacred as "a kind of purgatory."[1372] His physical and emotional weariness forfeited an assurance of spiritual well-being and at times, left little energy for sufficient attention to his own spiritual welfare.

Not only was Simpson vocationally removed from Phoebe Palmer, but he had knowingly or unknowingly removed himself from the political philosophy of American Methodism's founder, Francis Asbury. Asbury believed that to be involved in secular politics was to skew his divine call and bifurcate his ministry. "As I'm not a man of the world, most of the conversation about it is irksome to me"[1373] When in Washington he wrote, "Company does not amuse, congress does not interest me; I am a man of another world and calling: I am Christ's and for the service of his church."[1374] Of course, Asbury was the head of a fledgling, inchoate, embryonic sect, howbeit, a rapidly growing church, while Simpson was the most powerful leader in America's largest denomination. Simpson no doubt believed that Asbury's "other worldliness" was not his privilege, and was equally cognizant that there was a spiritual price to pay.

What did Palmer mean when she asserted that, "This question should be met and answered before you proceed further?" Should the Bishop stop

---

1372 Ralph Morrow, "The Life of Matthew Simpson by Robert D. Clark" in the *Journal of Southern History* Vol. XXII No. 2 (May, 1956) 240-242.

1373 *The Journal and Letters of Francis Asbury*, eds., Elmer Clark, J. Manning Potts, and Jacob S. Payton (London: Epworth Press, 1958) 2: 129.

1374 Ibid., 497.

believing for salvation? Should he quit the Episcopacy? Should he cancel his preaching appointments? The either-or-ness, holiness or hell, forwards or backwards, growing or backsliding would later earn the "holiness movement" a Pharisaical reputation and cause unnecessary alienation. The holier-than-thou attitudes and spiritual elitism would evolve into denomination-wide contention, which ultimately involved Simpson in an unavoidable and troubling decision. In 1881, a coterie of some of the most eminent sponsors of the "perfectionistic awakening" including John Miley, Daniel Steele, and Asbury Lowry, appealed to the leaders of the Northern Church "to arrange under their own chairmanship a great national convention for the promotion of holiness."[1375] Simpson and his Episcopal cohorts rejected their proposal with the rationale, "It is our solemn conviction that the whole subject of personal experience ... can be maintained and enforced in connection within the established usages of the church."[1376]

Charles White, a Phoebe Palmer scholar, suggests that Simpson grew impatient with the holiness movement, and his faint praise of Palmer in the preface to Wheatly's biography of Palmer was because the Bishop's fashionable wife may have found holiness standards and strictures to be too distasteful.[1377] John Peters interprets Simpson as initially fearing Palmer's "mysticism," as inherited from the French Mystics such as Madame Guyon and Francis Fenelon. But Simpson need not have worried. It was this tendency in Thomas Upham, the prominent mental and moral philosopher, which Palmer rebuked.[1378]

The building tension between the world accommodating Methodism and the fiery holiness proponents would explode into sectarian fragmentation between 1880 and 1910, a denominational fecundity unequalled in any similar epoch within American church history.[1379] Methodists who firmly believed

---

1375   Timothy Smith, "The Theology and Practices of Methodism: 1887-1919" *The History of American Methodism* Vol. II, 620.

1376   Ibid.

1377   White, 43-44.

1378   See Darius Salter. *Spirit and Intellect: Thomas Upham's Holiness Theology* (Metuchen, NJ: Scarecrow Press 1986) 120, 140. Also see Melvin E. Dieter. *The Holiness Revival of the Nineteenth Century* (Metuchen, NJ: The Scarecrow Press, Inc., 1988) 53-54.

1379   In 1949, Methodist historian Elmer Clark wrote, "There are about a dozen groups which may be termed quasi-Methodist sects. These are, and profess to be, Wesleyan in

in the possibility and practicality of entire sanctification found themselves in a wrenching dilemma as whether to stay faithful to the mother church or abandon ship for newer vessels. Nineteenth century American church historian, Timothy Smith wrote, "From the middle 1880s onward, therefore, a lengthy argument raged between those who believed that separate holiness denominations were necessary and those who relied upon associations to carry on the work. The argument was complicated at every stage by the easily revived memory of the excesses of the 'come-outers' and by the fact that radical leaders were usually in the vanguard for succession."[1380]

Palmer's urging Simpson and others to equate trusting for entire sanctification with the *ipso facto* experience of entire sanctification, came under direct condemnation among such Methodist heavyweights as Randolph Foster, Jesse Peck, and Nathan Bangs. Bangs was specifically critical of Palmer's "altar theology."

> Now, it is most manifest that Mr. Wesley considered that the faith by which we are sanctified is inseparably connected with the divine evidence and conviction that the work is done and hence the theory which teaches that we are to lay all upon the altar or surrender up our hearts to God by faith in Christ, and then believe that God has accepted or does accept the offering without our having any evidence of the Holy Spirit that it is accepted, or does accept the offering without having any change in our disposition or any emotion of joy and peace more than we had before, is not sound, is unscriptural, and anti-Wesleyan.[1381]

Palmer's real challenge in convincing Simpson as well as others may have been exegetical, a pragmatic immediatism, what holiness movement historian

---

doctrine; their organizers were for the most part Methodists, and they drew their original members mainly from the Methodist constituency. In addition to all these, there are about two dozen sects which do not bear the Methodist name and did not arise under direct Methodist auspices, but which owe their existence to the Methodist genius. All espouse the sanctification doctrine promulgated by the early Methodist preachers. Thus Methodism is directly or indirectly responsible for over fifty of the existing American sects. These have a combined membership of nearly ten million persons. All may be called perfectionists so far as their official doctrines are concerned, and at least thirty of them still make sanctification one of their central principles." Elmer T. Clark. *The Small Sects in America* (New York: Pierce & Smith, 1949) 59.

1380   Timothy L. Smith. *Called Unto Holiness: The Story of the Nazarenes-The Formative Years* (Kansas City, MO: Nazarene Publishing House, 1962) 35.

1381   Abel Stevens. *Life and Times of Nathan Bangs, D.D.* (New York: Carlton & Porter, 1863) 398.

Melvin Dieter referred to as "autosuggestion" or possible "self-deception," built on an obscure verse taken out of context.[1382] In forbidding swearing, Jesus asked the question: "Ye fools and blind: for whether is greater the gift or the altar that sanctifieth the gift?" (Matthew 23:19 Authorized Version) This one verse was not sufficient to keep Palmer's own personal claim to entire sanctification from tottering. "Let me have the blessing in some such tangible form that the enemy may never be successful in the insinuation that I believe because I will believe, without a reasonable foundation for my faith to rest upon."[1383]

Strangely, though Palmer was so insistent about pinpointing the exact moment of entire sanctification, she like Simpson could not recall the date of her conversion. Walter Palmer wrote to Simpson after his wife's death that this lack of specificity had been disconcerting, "She was converted in a very early age, but could never tell the time. In early life, this caused her much anxiety." Walter made no mention of his wife's experience of entire sanctification (as he chronicled Phoebe's life for the purpose of Simpson's *Cyclopaedia*), though he himself was a definite exponent of the "blessing."[1384]

Simpson and the National Camp Meeting Association for the Promotion of Holiness

On June 13, 1867, thirteen Methodist preachers and laymen met at 1026 Arch Street in Philadelphia, which served as Simpson's office for the headquarters of the Board of Church Extension chaired by Simpson. Among them were W. B. Osborne, J. A. Wood, George Hughes, Alfred Cookman, and John Inskip. They issued a call to the surrounding city and beyond via church bulletins, telegraph and however else, for a camp meeting at Vineland, New Jersey, July 17 through 26. Despite the short notice, thousands descended on Vineland. Thus was born the National Camp Meeting Association for the Promotion of Holiness (to which we have already referred). The invitation stated the new organization's purpose: "Come, brothers and sisters of the

---

1382   Melvin Dieter. *The Holiness Revival of the Nineteenth Century* (Metuchen, NJ: The Scarecrow Press, 1980) 29.

1383   Palmer, *Notes*, 109.

1384   LOC, Simpson papers, Letter, Walter Palmer to Matthew Simpson, December 6, 1876, Container ten.

various denominations, and let us in this forest meeting as in other meetings for the promotion of holiness, furnish an illustration of evangelical union, and make common supplication for the descent of the Spirit upon ourselves, the church and the world."[1385] The emphasis of the Association over the next 140 years of its existence would be "full sanctification," which John Wesley called the "grand depositum" of Methodism, "which God has lodged with a people called Methodists, and for the sake of propagating this chiefly he appeared to have raised us up."[1386]

Vineland was on the West Jersey railroad, thirty miles below Philadelphia. Simpson arrived on Monday accompanied by Alfred Cookman, both of them having participated the day before in the rededication of a church on Cape Island. Upon stepping on the campground Simpson was told that his son, Charles, was seeking to be saved. Simpson immediately made his way to the Kensington tent, and "knelt at the side of his stricken son. He poured tears upon his head, and with up-lifted hands, pleaded as only a father can plead, for his salvation." Because of Charles' salvation, George Hughes, the first comprehensive historian of the Association stated, "No wonder that Bishop Simpson at Manheim and Round Lake preached with such eloquence and power, that thousands were moved."[1387]

Within the year on March 2, 1868, Charles died. He supposedly said before his death, "Mother, I shall bless God through all eternity for the Vineland Camp Meeting."[1388] Charles' salvation initially obligated the father to the Association and he preached at the first three gatherings, Vineland, Manheim, Pennsylvania, and Troy, New York (Round Lake). John Inskip, the first president of the National Camp Meeting Association, wrote Simpson after Charles' death, "Thousands of pious souls will go before the mercy seat and ask the Almighty to pour the light of hope and confidence upon your faith and make the bereavement one of the greatest blessings of your life .... Accept our united and unaffected condolences and both my wife and I will

---

1385 William McDonald and John Searles. *The Life of John Inskip* (Chicago: The Christian Witness Co, 1888) 190.

1386 John Wesley. *The Works of John Wesley* Vol. XIII (Kansas City: Beacon Hill Press, 1978) 9.

1387 George Hughes. *Days of Power in the Forest Temple* (Salem, OH: The Allegheny Wesleyan Methodist Connection, 1975) 169.

1388 Ibid., 193.

pray that God may sanctify all your distress to his glory and your good."[1389]

Though Simpson was not scheduled to preach, he gave an impromptu message on the eighth morning of the Vineland camp. Rev. G. G. Wells preached from Isaiah 6, and after sitting down, the Bishop stepped to the podium. Whether he was requested to speak or not is unclear, but who was going to say "no" to Matthew Simpson? "He was all aglow with the majesty. He declared the nearness of the Baptizer of the New Testament dispensation; that He was at the door, waiting to confer the promised endowment. Waiting in all His fullness …. With these mighty sentences, as they fell from the lips of the honored pleader, there were intermingling cries and shouts all over the ground….The living mass was touched by Pentecostal power …. We would compare it to nothing else than a Gospel avalanche."[1390] Earlier in the week, Simpson led a prayer meeting in the "bower," a brush arbor under which could gather 2,000 people. "In the opening prayer, he pleaded earnestly to the Lord on behalf of the people, invoking upon them abundant spiritual blessing. Rising higher and higher to the throne, he triumphed in his suit."[1391]

American Holiness Movement historian, Melvin Dieter, claims that "The National Camp at Manheim (1868) ranks as one of the largest convocations in American 19th-century religious history, perhaps the greatest in number of attendance at a single meeting until the Moody-Sankey revivals which followed it by a decade."[1392] The dust so filled the air from encroaching wagons that a horse choked and died, and the dust so filled the houses that Manheim inhabitants rejoiced when the holiness crowd got out of town. On Sunday morning, 12,000 stood before the tented platform to hear Simpson preach. *The Daily Spy* from Columbia, Pennsylvania, reported, "The sermon was all that expectations could hope for or the heart could desire. The time occupied in delivery was one hour and 20 minutes, and, although on many heads the sun poured down his fiercest sickening rays, the attention was constant and the interest unflagging. The good bishop opened up a vista of happiness and

---

1389 LOC, Simpson papers, Letter March 1, 1868, Container eight.
1390 Hughes, 103-104.
1391 Ibid., 127.
1392 Dieter, 108.

glory to many anxious souls knowing in heaven they have 'a more enduring inheritance.'"[1393] The Association referred to Manheim as its Pentecost.

> There were those who insisted that at one time they heard a sound, a strange sound, as of a rushing mighty wind and yet as if somewhat subdued and held in check over the prayerful congregation. The writer went to his tent far back from the circle, but God was everywhere. It was an awful season. Souls were wrestling with God. God from the archives of memory was unrolling to many the long list of their sins. Unfaithful church members were looking with a shudder over the dreadful past. The people were face-to-face with God.[1394]

The next year at Troy (Round Lake), New York, Simpson proclaimed, "Dear minister of Jesus, if there is anything you have not given up, now is the time to consecrate fully all to Christ. You need and may have a fresh anointing just now. O Holy Ghost, come now upon us all .... Let us have Him in our hearts and all the glory of His name and ever realize that He saves-that His blood cleanseth, cleanseth, cleanseth, yes, the blood of Jesus cleanseth from all sin."[1395] But Simpson never claimed for himself that the blood cleanses from all sin. Neither did John Wesley, the founder of Methodism and expounder of "entire sanctification;" nor did Francis Asbury, founder of American Methodism, equally insistent that the doctrine of holiness be taught and preached. They may have answered as did the mirthful Peter Cartwright, when sternly asked by Bishop Leonidas Hamline if he was sanctified. He responded, "In spots, Sir, Bishop, in spots."[1396]

Thomas Morris demonstrated the most humility and courage of any ecclesiastical head during the early days of the Association. At Round Lake the seventy-eight-year-old Bishop stepped to the platform and confessed that he had never been sanctified, and if he had, he had not maintained it. "I have been earnestly seeking this grace here; and when the invitation was given at the first meeting, I came forward as a seeker, and when it was again given in the tabernacle, I went forward every time. I have done so, and

---

1393 McDonald and Searles, 280.

1394 A. Mclean and J.W. Eaton. *Peniel: or Face to Face with God* (New York: Garland Publishing, 1884) 240.

1395 McDonald and Searles, 205.

1396 Robert Bray. *Peter Cartwright: Legendary Frontier Preacher* (Chicago: University of Illinois Press, 2005) 202.

expect to keep on seeking until I get it. Ask God in my behalf to give it. Brethren, I want you to pray for me."[1397] Whether Thomas Morris received the second blessing or not is unclear, both in George Hughes' account and John Marlay's biography of Morris.[1398]

No one legitimated the National Camp Meeting Association for the Promotion of Holiness more than did Matthew Simpson. Hughes summed up Simpson's relationship to the Association, "He has been linked in golden and deathless bonds to the Pentecostal advance."[1399] Strangely, he never participated in another Association camp after Round Lake in 1869, though they continued for the rest of his life. Simpson's defection was sociologically, theologically, and experientially motivated, some of which we have explored but do not fully comprehend. Richey points out that Simpson in his *Cyclopaedia* did not include a treatment of the National Camp Meeting Association for the Promotion of Holiness. In short, "The holiness cause was not to be the bishop's thing."[1400]

The White Protestant Establishment as America's Foremost Identity

It would seem in the early part of the 1870s that Providence had a grievance with the Episcopacy of the Methodist Episcopal Church. Three of the seven Bishops died within a fifteen-month span: Edward Thomson, Calvin Kingsley, and Davis Clark, all elected in 1864. Because Kingsley's illness in the summer of 1870 prevented him from chairing the German Conference, Simpson took his place and headed for Europe, Ellen and three daughters with him. A break from the normal routine, escape from the throes of Reconstruction, and visiting historical sites were therapeutic. As always, especially across the ocean, Simpson became sentimentally reflective.

1397   Hughes, 142.

1398   John F. Marlay. *The Life of Rev. Thomas Morris* (New York: Nelson and Phillips, 1875). Marlay writes of Morris, "He never made a profession of Christian perfection; and yet, if to live Christ-like, if always to exhibit the lovely spirit of him, whose was meek and lowly and whose words, actions, and whole deportment were kind, gentle, and attractive, is to have attained to that excellent state of grace then those who knew him best, will concede to Bishop Morris what he did not claim for himself," 392.

1399   Ibid., 169.

1400   Richey, *Methodism in the American Forest*, 71.

In London he recorded, "Thirteen years ago Charles and I stopped at this Hotel. He is gone long time to the spirit world. Does he see me? We joined Dr. McClintock's party. He, too, is gone. How strange that I remain. I am treading on the edge of graves all the time. O, that I may be ready when the Master shall call."[1401]

But Simpson had a whole lot of living to do before the "Master would call." He would return to America for the "laymen's vote," the scandal at the New York Book Concern, his personal and public responses to evolution, and the most relentless lecturing and preaching schedule of his life, and two return trips to Europe. Back in New York on August 28, he wrote Ellen, who was still in Europe, "With all that I have written, and with all that the Church knows of my labors, I am receiving constant applications both for lectures and dedications. The dedications are all *critical* cases–would not ask me, only for *extreme* necessity, etc. I have declined all engagements, however."[1402] The abstinence would not last long.

The one constant through all of Simpson's post-bellum speaking and traveling was the touting of God's plan for America. As he stood in Library Hall in St. Louis, February of 1869, a reporter recorded his impressions of the Bishop giving his lecture, "The Future of Our Country."

> He said he scarcely ever spent ten minutes in the company of the peasantry in Europe without being told that they were saving all they could of their earnings, with the hope of going to America.– This, he said, was implanted in the heart by God. There are vast forests inviting the woodman's axe in Germany; but who thinks of immigrating to Germany? There are unoccupied lands all around Constantinople; but who thinks of migrating to Constantinople? There are as fertile lands in Asia Minor, as the sun ever shone upon; but who thinks of going to Asia Minor? God has turned the eyes of the nations to this country, to carry out His great plans.[1403]

Did Simpson mean that God was placing a desire to come to America that was equal to aspirations for Heaven? Simpson had sharply transitioned from his spiritual forefather John Wesley, who said "I want to know one

---

1401 LOC, Simpson papers, 1870 *Diary*, Container two.

1402 Crooks, 447.

1403 LOC. Simpson papers, "Letter from St. Louis," February 27, 1869, Unidentified newspaper clipping.

thing, how to get to heaven." For Simpson, God was not only placing the American dream in the hearts of those who resided in the United States, but foreigners as well. As Ralph Morrow accurately wrote, "At the height of his fame as a pulpit orator, the Simpson themes were the popular ones of an almost chauvinistic faith in the American future, a bland assurance that 'the Purposes of God are all in harmony with the happiness of man' and a promise that the Kingdom of Heaven was inclining ever closer to earth. In this faith, he was in perfect tune with the middle-class ideals of his day."[1404] And Simpson was also in perfect tune with American Methodism. Dickinson College Professor S. D. Hillman wrote,

> On Methodism rests a solemn responsibility to do its share in civilizing and Christianizing these pagans, the hundred thousand of whom now with us in the West, will increase to millions. So soon as the lines of commerce are fairly established between the Pacific and Asiatic ports. And to Methodism in view of its past history, its present numbers, and its peculiar mission as a Church more than to any other denomination perhaps will come the imperative summons of trust and duty to see to it that the Republic receives no harm from this source.[1405]

Confusingly, American Methodism did not know whether to welcome immigrants, or fear their contamination. But for both Hillman and Simpson, there was no doubt that new arrivals needed to become, if not Methodists, at least, good American Protestants. E. Digby Baltzell argues in *The Protestant Establishment* that in response to Spanish, Portuguese, Polish Jews, Irish, French, and Italian Catholics invading America, there began after the Civil War, an "associationally exclusive establishment of White-Anglo-Saxon-Protestants who dominated the leadership of the nation."[1406] The associations

---

1404   Morrow, *Southern History*, 240–242.
1405   S. D. Hillman. "The United States and Methodism," *Methodist Quarterly Review* (January 1867) 49. Hillman also wrote, "In secular and in religious education, in the broadest diffusion of knowledge among all classes of people, in the distribution, and accumulation of wealth and comforts, in the remuneration and the productiveness of labor, the United States is confessedly the foremost nation of the world. And in their popular education, popular refinement and enrichment, lies the course of our manifest destiny, to which God's good providence has opened the way for the toiling millions this, the genuine American civil policy, has the best words of cheer ever given to men." 43.
1406   E. Digby Baltzell. *The Protestant Establishment: Aristocracy & Caste in America* (New Haven: Yale University Press, 1987) 74.

included social registries, country clubs, private schools, and the Ivy League, city clubs, exclusive suburbs, and yes, summer resorts.

To put it another way, in fear of losing White Protestant identity, the "Wasps" circled the wagons, and though he drove one of the most prominent wagons, Simpson was not the only ecclesiastical driver. Baltzell identifies Phillips Brooks, who was pastoring First Episcopal Church in Philadelphia when Simpson moved there, as one of the most "sensitive barometers of the Brahmin mind and the "favorite clergyman among Philadelphia's Victorian gentry."[1407] Simpson had sufficient help maintaining the white Protestant establishment as America's foremost identify.

Simpson was not unaware of the negative aspects of Methodism's growth and increasing prominence. As impressive edifices were being built in urban centers, and the social standing of Methodists increased, Simpson could not entirely repress his uneasy conscience evoked by Methodism's centennial reflection. As he stood before the New England Conference of March in 1866, he lamented an intensity and intimacy that was being preempted by bigness: "When they met in the country cabins, they never parted without inquiring for each other's welfare." With success came a carelessness about community, a formalism eliminating those who were not strong enough to insert themselves into the new social paradigm. This lamentation would just have to be muted, less it dampen the party. Simpson proclaimed, "The census of the United States, both of 1850 and 1860, show there are more Methodist churches in the United States, than in any other denomination …. When I see the vast family extended from Maine to California, and from the Lakes to the Gulf, I can only exclaim, 'What hath God wrought.'"[1408]

1407 Baltzell, 113.

1408 "Address by Matthew Simpson," New England Methodist Centenary Convention held in Boston, June 4-7, 1866 (Boston: B. B. Russell & Company, 1866) 136-139.

Chapter Eighteen: "He Will Draw You to Your Feet"

The Golden Age of Oratory

However history evaluates Simpson, his foremost legacy is that of a preacher. He preached in an era when elocution was both the primary entertainment for the public and the primary sacrament for the Church. Nineteenth-century Americans flocked to hear a well-known lecturer, and church members gathered by the thousands at Chautauquas and camp meetings to hear their favorite preacher. In the decade after the Civil War, Henry Ward Beecher and Matthew Simpson were the two best-known preachers in America.[1409] Phillips Brooks and Dwight Moody did not capture the public imagination until the 1870s, both Moody and Brooks being two decades younger than Beecher and Simpson. All of these men lived in an era when oratorical speech and the newspaper were the two most influential mediums in America. Oratory was exercised on political platforms, in lyceums, at Chautauquas, in camp meetings, in churches, at holiday celebrations and countless other settings. Lyceum scholar Angela G. Ray writes, "In an oratorical culture, the public lecture hall provided a place for the public communal expression of the desire to leave one's quotidian

---

1409 Gaius Glen Atkins in *Master Sermons of the Nineteenth Century*, which included Thomas Chalmers, William Ellery Channing, and Phillips Brooks, wrote "By the time he was thirty he could probably have been matched in America for power of popular appeal only by Beecher, and Beecher also was in Indiana. An astonishing testimony to Simpson's astounding power began to spread through these back woods and attended him with crescent laudation for forty years." Atkins (1868-1956) was a Congregationalist pastor, who was educated at Cincinnati Law School and Yale Divinity School. Gaius Glen Atkins. *Master Sermons of the Nineteenth Century* (Chicago: Willet, Clark & Co, 1940) 157.

existence for a period of time, to be born along into an unfamiliar setting by a gifted ally, a trusted traveling companion who possessed a special power."[1410]

Simpson's rise to oratorical stardom needs to be understood within the historical period of 1820-1850, which Barnet Baskerville designates as the "Golden Age of Oratory."[1411] Oration was the most popular entertainment medium of the day, advertised and hailed by newspapers as to time and place, and then reported verbatim, with the setting and effects of the speech described in minute detail. When one of the great triumvirate spoke, Daniel Webster, Henry Clay, or John Calhoun, the Senate Chamber or House of Representatives was overflowing with every congressman in his seat. When Harvard student George Tichnor heard Daniel Webster speak he exclaimed, "I was never so excited by public speaking before in my life. Three or four times I thought my temples would burst with the gush of blood …. When I came out, I was almost afraid to come near to him. It seemed to me as he was like the Mount Thor, that might not be touched and that burned with fire. I was beside myself, and am so still."[1412] Play it back to the Shekinah Glory radiating from Moses as he came down from Mount Sinai, or fast-forward over a century to a fifteen-year-old girl at a Beatles or Rolling Stones concert.

Two to five hour speeches were memorized and delivered verbatim. Condemning the Kansas and Nebraska Act, Charles Sumner, May 19- 20, 1856, held forth for five hours, three on the 19th and two on the 20th. As he addressed the Senate "all members were in their seats, galleries, balconies, halls and doorways were packed, despite the ninety-degree heat."[1413] Stephen Douglas accused Sumner of having memorized his speech (as if Douglas didn't) and, "Practiced every night before a glass, with a Negro boy to hold

---

1410　Angela G. Ray. *The Lyceum and Public Culture in the Nineteenth Century United States* (East Lansing: Michigan State University Press, 2005) 182. Edgar DeWitt Jones in reviewing the first eighty years of the Yale Lectures, declared Simpson second only to Beecher in fame and eloquent speech, but "Not even Beecher won such demonstrations from his audiences as did Simpson." Edgar DeWitt Jones. *The Royalty of the Pulpit* (New York: Harper & Brothers Publishers, 1951) 32.

1411　Barnet Baskerville. *The People's Voice: Oratory in American Society* (Lexington, Kentucky: The University Press of Kentucky, 1979) 33.

1412　Ibid., 41.

1413　Ibid., 53.

the candle and watch the gestures." Simpson was not that vain, but he did believe oratory was an art to be practiced and cultivated. "But does the soldier prove less efficient in battle, who has with the greatest care studied his drill? If elocution be studied for display, it is without merit, but if it be pursued to give to truth, greater efficacy and power, it increases the love of the truth .... But is one less assured of the truth, who has not practiced? Whose hands and feet are most in the way? Practiced or unpracticed?"[1414]

Simpson did use the techniques of oratory, in particular the phrase "me thinks." This term invited the auditor into the mind of the speaker, and the world the orator was about to describe. He also utilized "yon" (yonder), as an invitation to imagine a time or place. Henry Clay, the politician most admired by both Simpson and Lincoln, stated of oratory that "It is to this practice of the art of all arts that I am indebted for the primary and leading impulses that stimulated my progress and have shaped and molded my entire destiny."[1415] Simpson believed the same of himself. He would have taken pleasure in the adjectives: erudite, fluent, moving, powerful, and that cherished reference, "a magnificent burst of eloquence." He would also have been piqued, if not wounded, by such assessments as that made by Frederick H. Hedge of Edward Everett, some of which Simpson would have been guilty: extravagant, exaggerated, hyperbolic, overdone sentiment, counterfeit enthusiasm, superfluous verbiage, treacherous, invective, and "all that straining after course affect commonly known as sensation."[1416]

The Deluge of Invitations

Each year, Simpson received scores of invitations to preach at a variety of churches, colleges, associations, camp meetings, temperance societies, political gatherings and situations as varied as the philanthropic causes which defined the crusading Church: the Sabbath School Assembly of the North in Waterloo, Iowa; Wabash College in Crawfordsville, Indiana; Dickinson Seminary in Williamsport, Pennsylvania; University of Michigan Student Christian Association; Wesleyan University in Middletown, Connecticut;

1414 LOC, Simpson papers, Matthew Simpson "Schools of Oratory," Container nineteen.
1415 Baskerville, 36.
1416 Ibid., 91.

Drew Theological Seminary; Union Theological Seminary; Brooklyn Sunday School Union; National School of Elocution and Oratory; the Philadelphia Training School for Feebleminded Children; The Franklin Reformatory Home for Inebriates, countless "Young Men's Associations" (YMCA); and the Republican National Convention, May 25, 1864, an invitation which he did not fulfill, but offered the opening prayer. The State Legislature of Missouri sent a request, signed by the Governor and 28 members of the legislature for "a series of lectures on such subjects as you may be pleased to select."[1417]

Some of the invitations were pathetically desperate. A telegram from Cleveland requested Simpson's "Our Country" lecture with the rationale: "We are in debt and also a suit pending for our church lot."[1418] Other requests almost sounded like extortion. Oliver Hoyt wrote, "I'm glad to inform you that we have made provision to pay the entire debt of our church in Stamford which amounts to $12,000. If my memory serves me correctly, we had a partial promise that if the above purpose was accomplished, we might expect a sermon from you, in honor of the event."[1419] The Bridgeport Methodist Church in Chicago urged Simpson to come "as early as possible to help us cancel the debt of the Bridgeport Methodist Episcopal Church. We intend to be free. Amount of debt: $2,100."[1420] Thomas Carlton, with whom we are already acquainted, amped up the pressure: "Now my dear Bishop, do not say no for I fear if you do, we shall fall short of what we did last year and that would be terrible. I cannot bear the thought of that model church going back. We must advance on the $30,000, if it be only one or two thousand dollars."[1421] Thomas Carlton informed Simpson that his insurance was paid in full, one of the contributors being Daniel Drew. "These your personal friends wanted opportunity to express their friendship and thought

---

1417   LOC, Simpson papers, Letter January 8, 1865, Container eight. During the six month period between January 1 and June 30, 1860, Simpson received thirty-four invitations to preach. Assuming that this six month period is representative of his vocational life, Simpson received more than one invitation per week for most of his tenure as Bishop, 1852-1884. He could accept only a small percentage of these invitations because of church duties and travel distance.
1418   LOC, Simpson papers, Letter January 28, 1865, Container eight.
1419   LOC, Simpson papers, Letter May 16, 1865, Container eight.
1420   LOC, Simpson papers, Letter February 8, 1865, Container eight.
1421   LOC, Simpson papers, Letter January 17, 1860, Container six.

they might do it in this way without offense ... You may send me a draft on Carlton and Porter for the interest for six months on your note."[1422]

They Wept, Shouted, and Danced for Joy

Descriptions of Simpson's preaching and the results abound, exaggerations conceded. When he spoke at the rededication of Wesley Chapel, Washington D.C., in 1882, Charles Parkhurst reported in *Zion's Herald*, "Bishop Simpson was at his best. The audience became plastic under his touch. We were broken and melted until one wept like a child, and often it seemed as if we must cry out to him, Hold! We cannot bear anymore."[1423] When Simpson preached at the Wesleyan Conference in Liverpool in 1857, an observer reported that, "By far the most striking characteristic of his delivery was its spiritual intensity. To borrow Dr. Buckley's words, 'It was a stream of love and light!'"[1424] In Atlanta, January, 1869, "At the close of the ordination service he addressed the candidates in a moving strain of eloquence. Alluding to his visit to the Isle of Patmos, he described the venerable John on his prison isle and after a lengthy description; he concluded with the remark, 'The last time Christ was seen from earth, he was walking among the golden candlesticks, the seven churches of Asia.' The scene which followed no human pen can portray. The whole audience rose. They wept, they shouted, they danced for joy and in his joyous delirium, Father Ross, the old colored preacher, threw his long arms around the Bishop and joined in the general shout of praise."[1425]

Robert Clark accurately contrasted Simpson and Henry Ward Beecher: "Simpson was never without a certain type of intellectuality--his sermons were crowded with facts drawn from history, science, commerce. Beecher drew from these sources, too, but in a more general sort of way, with much less attention to detail; his sermon illustrations were not characterized by an

---

1422   LOC, Simpson papers, Letter January 30, 1860, Container six.
1423   *Zion's Herald* (January 10, 1883).
1424   LOC, Simpson papers, "Bishop Simpson from an English Point of View," Scrapbook D, Container twenty-three.
1425   LOC, Simpson papers, Letter January 27, 1869, Scrapbook D, Container twenty-three.

exactness nor by a force gained through accumulation of fact."[1426] Clark also assessed that unlike Beecher, Simpson "made no attempt to shock the audience by his liberalism, or to entertain them with gentle ridicule and unexpected sallies."[1427] The closest that Simpson came to being directly compared to Henry Ward Beecher was when the two preached two weeks apart at the San Francisco Opera house in 1878. *The San Francisco Chronicle* reported,

> There is nothing in the Bishop's physique of the rubicund or robust usually found in the incumbents of such stations in the Church; nothing suggestive of the good livings and fat slumbers of the church .... But when under the stimulus of oratory the ungainly figure, the uncouth attitude and jesters, the unpleasant voice are all forgotten in the sparkling stream of thought, and the flashes of intellect which carry the entire and unflagging attention of the auditor. Coming immediately after Beecher, the impulse to indulge in comparisons between the two, famed, pulpit orators is natural. So far as the outward graces of oratory go, Beecher is incomparably the superior .... But judging from their sermons in the city, the palm of intellectual depth and grasp must be accorded to the Bishop.[1428]

An attendee at the First Methodist Church on Peachtree Street in Atlanta observed a "tall silver-haired man with slightly stooped shoulders" as speaking with a "peculiar delivery but very attractive, his voice being singularly clear and well-modulated, and his gesticulations easy and very impressive." The writer went on to say, "There were the beautiful narratives to fix the attention, the keen analogies to catch the reason, the flashing rhetoric to delight the fancy and the earnest eloquence to stir the heart."[1429] One of the fullest descriptions given of Simpson preaching was given by a New England auditor, year unknown:

> His height and gently stooping figure suggested a kind of scholarly awkwardness, his features pale, strongly and sharply cut, but by no means classic in their mold, intimated a certain strength of character, but nothing more. The eyelids droop slightly over the sad almost expressionless, leaden blue eyes, deeply sunken under his

---

1426 Clark, *Pulpit and Platform*, 589.

1427 Ibid., 590.

1428 LOC, Simpson papers, *San Francisco Chronicle* (September 16, 1878) Scrapbook D, Container twenty-three.

1429 LOC, Simpson papers, source unknown (January 1880), Scrapbook D, Container twenty-three.

broad lowbrow, which was surmounted by thin slight straight light brown hair slightly tinged with gray. The voice began in a thin, husky, nasal, high pitched and almost feeble tone. The words were slowly but clearly enunciated. There was little in the appearance of the man to indicate the treasure within. For the first fifteen minutes, a stranger would be likely to experience a sense of disappointment. But the eagle was only reserving its strength for an upward flight. As he gradually worked himself into the heart of his subject, as feeling gathered, his quavering tenor voice grew penetrating, resonant, sympathetic and impassioned. The stooping figure became erect; the dull eyes were kindled into a blaze by the long pent-up fire within. His thoughts seemed to play over his face like a luminously radiating atmosphere. The sentences grew short and pithy, and were uttered with an incisiveness and rapidity of enunciation and a peculiar stress of voice upon the final words. Whenever he touched the finer chords of feeling, there was a thrilling melody in his tones like the native music of the land of his Irish ancestors, full of plaintiveness with now and then a kind of wailing tenderness of pathos.[1430]

The following posthumous evaluation, by someone who was not caught up in the hype of a Simpson event, is probably realistic and accurate.

> His manner was characterized by perfect naturalness; that is, according to his nature, and utterly devoid of artificiality. He did not attempt oratorical tricks nor attitudes, nor tones, but spake with entire sincerity, truthfulness and plainness .... He always had his own personal peculiarities, which some young preachers ridiculously imitated, as for instance, the nasal intonation, the habit of squatting or of rising on tiptoes in his most overwhelming periods.[1431]

The Timelessness of Simpson's Preaching

Not many vocations are as culturally bound and sociologically defined as preaching. Presentation and treatment of Scripture varies between races, socio-economic strata, worship forms, denominations, geographical locations

---

1430   Clarence Edward McCarthy. *Six Kings of the American Pulpit* (Philadelphia: The Westminster Press, 1948) 78-79. McCarthy states, "No one in the history of the American pulpit, no one indeed in the history of American oratory seems to have had the power to get an audience to their feet like Bishop Matthew Simpson, the preacher of victorious faith and the greatest of the Methodists. Through a long ministry of more than fifty years, Bishop Simpson demonstrated the singular power to magnetize an assemblage or congregation of human beings and lift them into transports of emotion and enthusiasm." 56-57.

1431   UMA, Drew University, Simpson papers, "An Analysis of Bishop Simpson's Power as a Preacher."

and myriad schools of thought. Boisterous or conversational, expository or topical, deductive or inductive, propositional or narrative, are just a few of the variations that a visitor would expect to find, if she were randomly sampling homiletics as practiced only in the United States. White preaching differs from black, and southeastern Kentucky differs from New York. For some folks preaching is not preaching, if it does not resonate with a particular cadence, rhythm, and volume. In other words, a consensus on the absolutes of preaching does not exist. Preaching is an art form, and opinions are as diverse as the admirers of Rembrandt and the collectors of Picasso.[1432]

In spite of the above relativity, an exegesis of Simpson's sermons renders a timelessness in several characteristics that would reach across centuries and nationalities. Allowing for Simpson's chauvinisms and cultural limitations, and the occasional eisegesis, his sermons were biblical. He gave the background of the text, described the historical context and illustrated Scripture with Scripture throughout the sermon. He constantly referred to Old Testament characters: Adam, Noah, Enoch, Abraham, Isaac, Jacob, Daniel, Solomon and quoted from the Psalms and the Prophets. Often he would ease into a New Testament pericope that was tangential to his main text: the Good Samaritan, the Rich Man and Lazarus, feeding of the five thousand, and references to the Book of the Revelation, one of his most quoted books.

Simpson's preaching evidenced he had given much time to reading the Bible and memorizing Scripture. He possessed both an innate ability and a cultivated gift for rote memorization. When preaching on Moses asking God to show him his glory Exodus 33:18-20, Simpson quoted verse 19, verses 21 through 23; chapter 34, verses five through seven. On "The Christian Ministry," which he preached before the Bristol Wesleyan Conference at Burstyn, August 1, 1870, he quoted a significant portion of Paul's speech to

---

1432 For example, in 1971, Word Incorporated of Waco, Texas, produced *Twenty Centuries of Great Preaching* in thirteen volumes featuring over ninety preachers. The editors listed no specific criteria for their selections other than the preachers had made "an impact on the history of the Christian movement and on the development of preaching." Many of Simpson's contemporaries were included, such as Henry Ward Beecher and Phillips Brooks. Strangely, at least from a homiletical perspective, Simpson was left off the prestigious list, but Billy Sunday and Sam Jones were included. Clyde E. Fant, Jr. and William M. Pinson, Jr., eds. *Twenty Centuries of Great Preaching* (Waco, TX: Word Books, 1971).

the Ephesians in Acts 20. But Simpson mostly utilized snippets of Scripture, allusions to biblical passages throughout his sermon: "A prophet took off his girdle," "speak Lord for thy servant heareth," "I in them and them and thou in me that they may be perfect in one," "If thy heart be as my heart, give me thy hand," "Lo I am with you always even unto death," "O the depth of the riches both of the wisdom and knowledge of God," "O death where is thy sting, O grave where is thy victory?"

Simpson's biblical methodology transcended both time and place. One of his most gripping and imaginative passages treated Paul's declaration, "but none of these things move me." With graphic narrative Simpson placed himself on the inside of the text.

> And I've sometimes fancied that, in vision, I could follow him. I see him yonder. He has been preaching in the city, and they carry him out without the walls. The missiles come thick and fast upon him; he falls bruised and wounded, and his enemies leave him for dead. I go to his side, I lift him up. I wipe the blood away from his face. I look as he catches his breath heavily and now he opens his eyes. I say to him, "Paul, you had better give up preaching. They will kill you. Don't go to the next city; don't take up your next appointment; don't go round your circuit." Just as soon as he is able to recover breath he speaks. I bend my ear to his lips, and he whispers out these words: "None of these things move me." I follow him to another city, and after the sermon they arrest him. The robe is taken off his shoulders; a strong man lays on the lash- "forty stripes save one" -upon his shoulders, and the blood trickles down over his garments, and he is left in a mangled state. I go to him; I place the robe upon his shoulders, and putting my arm affectionately round his neck, I say to him, "Paul, it is time to quit preaching; you are almost dead, and they will kill you;" but the first words he speaks are, "None of these things move me." And again I follow him. He has been "a night and a day in the deep." I see the water dripping from his hair; he is exhausted, and apparently lifeless. I get close by his side, and listen for the first words that fall from his lips, and the third time I hear the same utterance, "None of these things move me, neither count I my life dear unto myself; so that I might finish my course with joy, and the ministry which I have received of the Lord Jesus, to testify the gospel of the grace of God." What a hero! Bonds, imprisonment, scourging, dying itself, cannot change his undaunted spirit. And, last of all, I follow him to the prison in Rome ....[1433]

1433 George R. Crooks. *Sermons by Bishop Matthew Simpson* (New York: Harper & Brothers, Franklin Square, 1885) 74.

Simpson fully incarnated his advice to the students at Yale in 1878: "That the minister may successfully preach the word he must study it diligently."[1434] For Simpson there was an inherent power in the rite of preaching, especially in the quoted Word. The preacher can proclaim, "Thus saith the Lord," because of a divine unseen power so joined to the words of Scripture that they cannot be uttered without fruit.[1435]

Simpson's Biblical Hermeneutic

Simpson left no doubt as to his view on the authority of the Bible. The Scripture gives us direct access to "the thoughts and will of the Almighty."[1436] Though tradition, experience, and reason are important, they are all secondary to the preacher's supreme frame of reference, Scripture. "In theology there can be no new doctrine, for the foundation is in the Bible alone. There may be new turns of thought, more fitting expressions, more pertinent illustrations and even unperceived duties and meanings may be found in the sacred page, but the radical fundamental doctrines are the same. They are like the blessed Savior himself, the same yesterday today and forever."[1437] He made no speculation as to how languages other than English, cultures other than Anglo-Saxon and eras other than the nineteenth century influenced Scripture. Simpson's lectures on preaching espoused no theory of inspiration, and did not interpret whether the human recording of God's communication was verbal dictation, plenary, infallible, inerrant, accurate or culturally informed.

Simpson demonstrated no regard for higher criticism and philosophical idealism, which were only beginning to invade the American church. Neither was he acquainted with hermeneutics popularized by Schleiermacher in the early 1800s, nor Moses Stuart who taught at Andover Seminary from 1810-1852, and who was the first American scholar to take German biblical studies seriously. Even though Simpson could read the original languages,

---

1434 *Lectures*, 103. "The Lectureship on Preaching" at the Divinity School at Yale College was made possible by a gift from Henry W. Sage, an attendee at Henry Ward Beecher's Plymouth Church in honor of the pastor's father, Lyman Beecher. Henry spoke at the first three annual lectures in 1872, 1873, and 1874.
1435 *Lectures*, 102.
1436 Ibid., 109.
1437 Ibid., 115.

Hebrew and Greek, he showed no inclination to deal with linguistic or metaphysical perplexities. Almost all serious biblical scholarship in the nineteenth century took place in Europe, the main exception being Princeton Theological Seminary. Charles Hodge and Benjamin Warfield made Princeton the bastion of "scholastic rationalism." Simpson had no interest in validating the Bible via history, archeology or any other external evidence. In fact, his Uncle Matthew had warned him about using Scripture, "to establish every principle of geology and natural philosophy."[1438] The nephew accepted Scripture by faith, a unique revelation from God, revealing both God's requirements and provision for salvation.[1439]

Scripture and science were of one accord, and any system of thought which disagreed with Scripture was false.[1440] At the same time, Simpson would not have been labeled a fundamentalist in the modernist-fundamentalist controversy that was only beginning to morph into what would be the most critical theological issue of the early 20th century. Simpson fully accepted that there was more than one way to interpret a biblical passage, in that he was charitable to other denominations. The bottom line for Matthew Simpson's approach to the Bible was that it was a *sui generis* book, a one of a kind communication of God to humankind, which separated it from all other literature.

Simpson thoroughly believed in perceiving the "God sense" of the text, what God intended to say in the text.[1441] Though Simpson was not a doctrinal preacher, he was thoroughly theological, though at times erratic. "The true rule is, consider as near as possible what God intended in revealing that portion of his word, and then you will be in line with the thoughts of

---

1438 LOC, Simpson papers, Letter September 7, 1834, Container three. One should not confuse biblical proofs with theistic proofs. Simpson often pointed to nature to establish theism, but he did not use science to prove statements in Scripture or vice versa.

1439 See Gerald Bray. *Biblical Interpretation: Past and Present* (Downers Grove, IL: Inter-Varsity Press, 1996).

1440 For this reason Loral W. Pancake in his analysis of the "Yale lectures" cites Simpson as "representative of traditional orthodoxy," 10. Among several listed as heterodox (liberal) were Henry Van Dyke and Harry Emerson Fosdick. Lorel W. Pancake. *Liberal Theology in the Yale Lectures*, unpublished Ph.D. dissertation, Drew University, 1951.

1441 See Paul Scott Wilson. *God Sense: Reading the Bible for Preaching* (Nashville: Abingdon, 2001).

God."[1442] At no time did he argue against Calvinism for Arminianism or use theological words such as propitiation, eschatology, or foreordination. He understood himself to be a populist preacher, drawing the masses, because he was on the same frequency as the common person, speaking their language. He was using the stethoscope of God's word to hear the heartbeat of the human condition even more assuredly than when he was a practicing physician in Ohio. Even if he was speaking at Yale, even if he was more sophisticated than Peter Cartwright, and even if he did live in Philadelphia, he was still a "Western man." Part of Simpson's popularity was that he was not erudite or pedantic. He never used academic language for the sake of ostentation. And though he utilized Greek and Hebrew for his own understanding of the text, the original languages never decorated the sermon, nor served as window-dressing.

Simpson's Sermons Could Be Seen

Simpson excelled in visual speech. He expressed the invisible through the visible, a consistent stream of allusions to the material world. Hardly any of his sermons are void of references to science, astronomy, geology and botany or the latest mechanical invention. He believed Jesus to be the master illustrator, utilizing analogies to sparrows, sheep, seed, wildlife, vineyards, barns and persons from all walks of life. Christ used visual imagery readily available to anyone, the ingredients of life which are everyday occurrences. "If the Savior thus illustrated his sermons, why should not we? Parable, allegory and metaphor were sanctified by him for our use."[1443] God was an artist painting a "mosaic." Each piece of the painting has no meaning apart from the other pieces. "So I sometimes look upon men. In one sense we are insignificant. What can we do? So very feeble, inefficient, limited. What can we accomplish? And yet when the artist of the universe takes us and places us in the mosaic which the universe shall yet gaze upon with wonder, small as we are, we shall be part of his great design."[1444] God is shaping us even as a gemologist cuts and polishes a diamond. "When a diamond is put into the lathe, it might (if it were conscious) complain, but when its rough edges

---

1442 *Lectures*, 136.
1443 *Lectures*, 149-150.
1444 *Sermons*, 47.

are cut, and from every angle and every part, there sparkles out the glorious light, had it a voice it would then utter its thanks for that which gave it such power to shine. It is so with us."[1445]

Simpson represented the best in phenomenological preaching. His sermons could be seen, felt, heard, and experienced by the congregation. He invited the listener into the inside of the text, so she would experience what happened to the biblical characters in the text. As I have written elsewhere, "Preaching is effective, not to the extent that it informs understanding, but to the extent it forms the consciousness. Phenomenological preaching shifts reality by experiencing or inducing the new reality that it represents. The reality construct of the sermon becomes the reality construct of the hearer. A sermon on grace evokes grace within the consciousness of the listener."[1446] The ultimate test of phenomenological preaching is not what the auditor learns, but what happens to him or her. The purpose of a movie is to make something happen to the viewer, a visceral, gut reaction such as fear, love, nostalgia, and anxiety. Simpson's preaching was cinematographic, before cinematography.

Nature, the planet on which we live, speaks to us daily as to God's plan, power and purpose in our lives. Simpson firmly believed in the direct revelation of Scripture by the Holy Spirit to the ancient writers, but he also had an affinity for natural revelation, or what might be more accurately designated as spiritual truths found in analogies to nature. "I can fancy if a grain of wheat had intelligence and a soul and found itself buried in the cold damp earth of spring without light and heat it might say 'Why am I like this? It is terrible to be underground, terrible to be in the dark. I am likely to decay.' But in a few weeks the sprout is evolved, the blade is spread out, the stock has expanded, the flowers are clad in beauty, the ripe grain is on the ear and then there is the answer."[1447] What was most remembered about Simpson's preaching, while President of Indiana Asbury, "was his ability to paint pictures, to daub and apply his brush with such sharp detail and vivid

---

1445   Ibid., 61.

1446   Darius Salter. *Preaching as Art: Biblical Storytelling for a Media Generation* (Kansas City: Beacon Hill Press, 2008) 134. David Buttrick has been credited for the term "phenomenological preaching," but as far as I can discover in his magnum opus *Homiletic*, he never uses the term. See David Buttrick. *Homiletic: Moves and Structures* (Philadelphia: Fortress Press, 1987).

1447   *Sermons*, 106.

color that the people cried out in pain or anguish, in joy or ecstasy, as they viewed the canvas he had drawn for them."[1448]

Simpson's sermons were replete with the cosmological and teleological arguments for God. Intelligent design surrounds all of us, assuring us of God's providence and wisdom. There was no room for fate, chance or random occurrence even in the most horrendous circumstances. If one has doubts just look at the stars, consider the tides, reflect on the revolutions of the earth, ponder the seasons of the year. The elements of "omnipotence" characterize the individual who is clothed and filled with God's power. "Yonder moon raises the tides of the sea, but there is this observable, that when the moon draws in the same line with the sun, whether at new or full moon the tide is always higher than when it draws at right angles with the sun. The combination of force in the same line gives a much higher result. And so man co-operating with God raises his strength and the tidal wave rushes over the lands around him."[1449] At Yale, Simpson proclaimed, "The knowledge of the currents of the sea and of the air, of the power of steam and of electricity; the very unbraiding of the sunbeams to read what is written between the strands--all these with many others are so many voices of nature crying, 'Prepare ye the way of the Lord.'"[1450] In his sermon "God Reigns over the Earth," Simpson was at his rhetorical best.

> You feel that God reigns. You can look out at night and every star that shines in heaven proclaims that God reigns. You stand in the open air and every breeze that fans your brow proclaims that God reigns. You see the sun rising in the morning and every ray of light that shines from the golden east proclaims that God reigns .... the waves of the sea echo it back, the thunders of heaven roll it out and all earth and sky proclaim that God reigneth.[1451]

Simpson's sermons evidenced his saturation with secular and church history: Luther, Calvin, Zwingli, Wesley, Washington, Franklin, Napoleon, Peter the Great, Stephen the Great, and a host of others paraded through his preaching. The reading of history, especially biography, provided the courage to conquer foes, to transcend circumstances and to do the impossible.

1448   Clark, *Pulpit and Platform*, 177.
1449   *Sermons*, 447-448.
1450   *Lectures*, 208.
1451   Ibid., 347.

> I see that boy as he sits in the corner of the hearth while the pine knots are blazing in the winter fire; associates are about him and the conversation is lively and interesting, but he hears it not; his eye is on the page but his thoughts are not there. Where is he? He is crossing the Granicus with Alexander; he is climbing the Alps with Napoleon; and he is driving into the depths of Russia with Charles VII and he feels heroic emotions stirring within his bosom. An echo comes from his imagination 'what man has done man can do' and unconsciously the boy outgrows the surrounding of the house and the plays of his associates, and there springs up in his heart the desire for fortune and fame.[1452]

Simpson's Christology

Simpson was thoroughly Christocentric. Again, his Christology was non-technical. He offered no theories of the atonement, but was plainly substitutionary. He tendered no theological explanations of the virgin birth, the transfiguration, the resurrection or ascension. He accepted face value the narrated miracles of both Christ and the Apostles. He did believe that part, if not all, the miracles recorded in the New Testament were dispensational. They served a need for the advancement of the early Church, a difference between that age and this, a difference which he did not fully explain. There was no need for such supernatural intervention in the affairs of contemporary humanity.

Simpson was convinced, "that the only way to triumph over the passions and impulses of the heart, the only access to the favor of God and to future, grandeur and glory" comes from telling the story of a crucified Savior.[1453] Faithful preaching is through a personal faith in the atoning merits of Christ, our only sacrifice and mediator. Through Him we enjoy the consciousness of the forgiveness of sins and the assurance of our acceptance with God. He exhorted the students and professors at Yale, "The interest of eternity may to some individuals, rest on the issue of a single sermon and in some form, directly or indirectly every sermon should lead to Christ."[1454] Christology blazed in his sermon, "Glorying in the Cross." He testified, "Now in that cross is my salvation and that is wherein the chief glory consists. I live

---
1452 *Sermons*, 198.
1453 *Lectures*, 32.
1454 Ibid., 127.

because Christ died. I am reconciled to God because Christ bore the load for my sin. I am adopted into God's family because of the death of Jesus Christ."[1455] The following succinctly states his substitutional-penal theory: "He assumes man's place; He pays the penalty and He stands then in such a position that He has the right to ask of God the salvation of man and the covenant is 'He that believeth on the Son shall be saved.'"[1456] The first duty of the minister is to study Christ, his character, his words, his deeds, and above all, his compassion for the world. Christological references abound in Simpson's preaching. The preaching of the cross and the influence of preaching were one and the same. Preaching Christ is the foremost task of the Church.

Simpson's hamartiology and Christology were tied together. The essential problem of humanity is sin and there is only one solution, the blood of Christ. "There are very few of us who have those deep views of sin which we ought to have, the loathing abhorrence of evil, which we ought ever to cherish, but in the cross of Christ is brought out the great abhorrence which God has of sin; the absolute impossibility of his passing it over without punishment and the fact that sin is so contrary to him that the result of it must be death."[1457] To the British Conference in 1870: "Our ministry is a testifying ministry. We urge men to repent; we tell them that if they come to God he will forgive them and in confirmation of what we say we testify that God for Christ's sake has forgiven us. We tell them there is fullness of redemption for them in Christ Jesus and we testify that the blood of Jesus Christ cleanses us from all sin."[1458] In exalting Christ, Simpson sailed into the dawn of rapturous elocution:

> The preacher may speak of nature because all nature shows forth the handiwork of Jesus for all things were created for him and by him and without him was not anything made which was made. So that the pulpit exalts him and carries his message to men, he said, "If I be lifted up, I will draw all men unto me," and our duty as messengers, prophesying for Christ is to lift him up before the people, to tell of his glorious divinity and of his pure humanity, of the boundless compassion and of his

---

1455   *Sermons*, 253.
1456   Ibid., 251-252.
1457   Ibid., 246.
1458   Ibid., 76.

undying love; to tell how he made a sacrifice for the sins of the people, to tell how he has risen triumphantly, and there at the seat of empire at the throne of the universe a brother's heart yearns for our salvation.[1459]

No sermon exhibited and communicated more spiritual intensity and profundity than "I Saw a Great White Throne." It was an archetypical nineteenth century evangelistic sermon, but because of its biblical fidelity, would be relevant today with little revision. Simpson's unction made the redeemed rejoice and sinners repent. The sobriety and ultimacy of the sermon lifted the congregation from this world into the next. The saved "robed in righteousness" and "clad in salvation" will forever be in the presence of God. Those around the throne shall cry out "Praise our God all ye His servants and ye that fear him, both small and great. Then from united assemblage like a river that shall reach the utmost parts of the universe, the chorus shall sound full, clear, and loud as mighty thunderings: 'Alleluiah,' for the Lord God Omnipotent reigneth." To the lost, God will say, "Depart from me ye cursed, into everlasting fire, prepared for the devil and his angels…not only to be banished and separated from God but to be driven into everlasting fire that shall never be quenched."[1460] To be sure, none of the congregation went to sleep.

Simpson's Pneumatology

Pneumatology merited consistent reference within Simpson's preaching, but it was not as prevalent and clear as his Christology. Transformation of character and purity of heart are miracles of the Holy Spirit. The same Holy Spirit that rested upon the Apostle Paul belongs to us today. The impotence and unfaithfulness of the Church is due to a lack of the Holy Spirit. Christ promised the Holy Spirit to his disciples, to those, "who would keep his commandments should have the Spirit within him, that the Comforter should dwell with us and in us; and in acceptable worship there is the answer."[1461] To his auditors at Yale he was clear that, "No man can say he is called to the ministry, but by the Holy Spirit," and no one can do the work of the ministry without the Holy Spirit. The ubiquitous presence of the Holy Spirit, the hope of the world is "the agent of our awakening, justification,

---

1459 Ibid., 395.

1460 Matthew Simpson, "The Great White Throne," LOC, Simpson papers, Container twenty.

1461 Ibid., 444.

and sanctification and without its precious influence there can be no hope and no life for our world."[1462] The church can no more call the world to Christ without the Spirit than could Ezekiel impart life to the valley of bones, one of Simpson's favorite texts. "Here we have the invocation or call for the divine Spirit, as the sole agent of life and power and all preaching fails which is not accompanied with an earnest and public recognition of the absolute need of the divine Spirit."[1463] The primary requisite for preaching is the baptism of the Holy Spirit: "If there is one thing above all others that I have desired for myself, and that above all others I covet for you, young gentlemen, it is this ministerial power, this baptism of fire. Seek more for this than for learning, for wisdom, for oratory; and, above all, more than for any thought of your acceptability or popularity."[1464]

Simpson had read more science and history than he had theology, and thus, his theology was sometimes inconsistent, and at worst, contradictory. Nowhere did he articulate a clear *ordo salutis*, and was often muddled in his concept of grace, a word which he hardly ever uttered. Simpson did not clarify that all goodness, and ultimately salvation, result from God's initiative, an initiative preceding anything good in both individual and corporate affairs. Simpson was glaringly unorthodox when he wrote, "I suppose that there is no human being who has tried to the utmost being, who has tried to the utmost capability of human endurance; in other words, the divine grace does not come in until first we have done all that we can do; it is when our strength shall fail that the God man prevails."[1465] This statement completely missed a central truth in Wesleyan theology: God is the initiator of all things good, not only in the volition and deeds of human kind, but all creation.

Simpson's synergism was decidedly humanistic, almost implying the Holy Spirit is complementary to the human spirit and they act as equal agents. "The power of God once joined to humanity, how much can be accomplished! Now such is the power of the gospel which through Christ is

---

1462   *Lectures*, 120.
1463   Ibid., 214.
1464   "An Analysis of Bishop Simpson's Power as a Preacher," UMA, Drew University, Simpson Papers.
1465   "God is Everywhere," UMA, Drew University, Simpson papers.

preached to us."¹⁴⁶⁶ At times it would seem that faith is something that can be conjured up, the same as willpower. Simpson was not clear that "prevenient grace" precedes faith and both are gifts from God. In order to have faith and the power of the Holy Spirit, Simpson did not stress that grace, the free unmerited gift of God must be operative. "That a man may have the elements of goodness he needs faith and he needs also the operation of the Holy Spirit upon his heart. These are interblended one with the other, but at the same time we consider goodness as the foundation of all Christian character."¹⁴⁶⁷ That Simpson use the word *but* instead of *and* was a semantical difference that makes a difference. Simpson theologically derailed when he spoke of the "tongue of fire as employing the highest efficiency of language," and then followed with the historical examples of Demosthenes, Cicero and Napoleon.¹⁴⁶⁸ (Simpson revered Napoleon.)

Simpson disconnected the power of the Holy Spirit for preaching from the power of the Holy Spirit for sanctified living. "It is the indwelling of the Holy Spirit not for regeneration, not for sanctification, but to use the whole of a purified nature and especially the tongue for aggressive Christian work."¹⁴⁶⁹ He woefully understated the case concerning Ezekiel and the dry bones: "Not waiting until the end of his mission, but on each complemented stage, divine power supplements human power."¹⁴⁷⁰ When Simpson asserted that the baptism of the Holy Spirit does not change the natural characteristics of the minister, but works through them, did he mean the Holy Spirit only enhances innate abilities and imparts no gifts which are not already present?¹⁴⁷¹ In the following, Simpson left some of his Yale students on the outside looking in: "The attainment of this ministerial power should be the object of the most intense desire. I do not suppose that all may be equally robed with it. It is an attribute of divine sovereignty to give it to whomsoever he will and what measure he will."¹⁴⁷² Now, Simpson

---

1466   *Sermons*, 110.
1467   Ibid., 161.
1468   Ibid., 204-205.
1469   *Lectures*, 209.
1470   Ibid., 212.
1471   Ibid., 217.
1472   Ibid., 229.

had gone to the opposite extreme, disconnecting "efficacy in ministry" with the gifts of the Spirit, which are dependent on one's relationship with God. Giving Simpson the benefit of the doubt, there exists a delicate theological tension between Philippians 2:12 and 2:13: "Therefore, my dear friends, as you have always obeyed--not only in my presence, but now much more in my absence--continue to work out your salvation with fear and trembling, for it is God who works in you to will and to act in order to fulfill his good purpose" (NIV).

Simpson, at times, was ambushed by his lack of theological training. In his Yale lectures, he referred to the Holy Spirit as an "it."[1473] Ward M. Lear rightly reminded the Bishop that in seeking the Holy Spirit, he had exhorted his listeners to ask for "it" and pray for "it." This possibly seemed to Simpson as only a semantical miscue, but according to Orthodox theology, Simpson's reference was a serious theological error with practical implications, especially for the Holiness and Pentecostal movements, half-breed children of Methodism. Holiness and Pentecostal exponents when seeking the Holy Spirit, "entire sanctification," were prone to refer to the "experience" as an "it." If an "it," the Holy Spirit is a thing to be possessed. But if a person, He or She, the third person of the Trinity is one with whom a mortal being can have a relationship.

Justification of the Ways of God

Simpson's theodicy was airtight. It admitted of no doubts, no questioning the ways of God, no individuals caught in circumstances beyond their control, and a freedom of the will, somewhat, but not completely detached from grace. In his sermon on Job, "God's Goodness in the Midst of Affliction," Simpson offered common "Christian" interpretations such as suffering is for the purpose of making us better people, God's means for getting our attention and the negative experiences of life for which we will be compensated in Heaven. If we can only understand suffering from the perspective of eternity and/or celestial beings, pain would be more palatable. "Angels see that the very difficulties that beset individuals are for their discipline, to make them better and wiser

---

1473   UMA, E. PA Conference of the UMC, Old St. George's UMC: Philadelphia, Simpson papers, Letter February 20, 1879.

and happier for all eternity than they would be without. If they conceive that the very thing you call ill is the very thing fraught with the greatest possible blessing why should they be sorrowful about it? You cannot understand it: They will see it."[1474]

Simpson admitted of no situation where a person may be faced with the lesser of two evils. "The great lesson dropped into the heart of humanity is that universal happiness will flow only from trying to do right under all possible circumstances."[1475] Simpson exaggerated the claims of the gospel, constructing a utopia light years from the Five Points district in New York and the sod houses on the Nebraska prairies. "Yon man who was steeped in sin and on the very verge of ruin has heard the gospel, and behold he has thrown away the cup; he has tasted of the cup of salvation; he has left his associates and their revelry, and you find him reading the Word of Life, and then the volumes of science and literature; you find him communing with nature; there is a love of the beautiful, the pure and the good manifest in him, his love is smiling with meekness and his grounds are adorned with flowers. There is transformation of taste."[1476] (We will return to the "transformation of taste" later in this chapter.)

Giving Simpson the benefit of the doubt, preaching by its very nature is hyperbolic. Reinhold Niebuhr confessed that the larger the congregation, the more he exaggerated. When Mark Twain was asked his opinion about a particular preacher, he responded, "Well, he exaggerated, but mainly he told the truth." Communication which transforms cannot waffle, equivocate and be dialectically reflective or ambiguous. Most effective preaching does not reflect on the disconnect between clarity and mystery. Affective preaching appeals to the heart, not to the head, the emotions rather than the intellect. Effective preaching must be affective in order to be transformative. For the most part Simpson achieved a balance between rational content and emotional persuasion. At the same time, there is an ethical demarcation, often difficult to locate, between proclaiming the possibilities of grace in this life as opposed to the possibilities which will be realized only in the life

---

[1474] UMA, Drew University, Simpson papers, sermon: "God's Goodness in the Midst of Affliction."
[1475] Ibid., 285.
[1476] *Sermons*, 263.

to come. Though Simpson intended to deceive no one, his triumphalism was often naïve and unrealistic.

For Simpson there was a silver lining in every cloud; the Gospel was a panacea for all of life's circumstances. There was no bewilderment in the face of Americans killing Americans in the Civil War. He sanctified the "hell" of war by recalling:

> I remember the first Sabbath after the terrible conflict commenced. I was called upon in a western city to address a large audience; thousands had gathered, and came inquiring and anxious. I selected as my text: "The Lord reigneth, let the earth rejoice." I thought I saw the end. I had faith in God. I saw beyond the cloud a little streak of light. What trials the nation was called to pass through, yet in the end was recompense.[1477]

Simpson communicated no awareness that children stole bread in the inner-city. Simpson never entered a Civil War prison camp nor visited a coal mine in West Virginia. As he preached, Negroes were being lynched in the South and many southern Blacks were worse off than they were before the Civil War. In 1857, the Society for the Improvement of the Condition of the Poor, New York City, observed, "Crazy old buildings, crowded rear tenements and filthy yards, dark, damp basements, leaking garrets, shops, outhouses, and stables converted into dwellings, though scarcely fit to shelter brutes, are habitations of thousands of our fellow-beings, in this wealthy, Christian city."[1478] In May of 1865, Simpson visited the Five Points Mission, but did not record his observations.[1479]

Simpson theorized that the Church would or should narrow the gap between "the haves" and "the have-nots," but the Bishop neither witnessed nor initiated implementation of such reconciliation. "The pulpit is still greatly needed as the great bond of union between the rich and the poor.

1477 Matthew Simpson. "God's Goodness in the Midst of Affliction." UMA, Drew University, Simpson papers. Remember that Simpson had secured his son, Charles, a job as an adjutant to Gen. Clinton Fisk. He would never have to fire a gun.

1478 Jacob A Riis. *How the Other Half Lives: Studies Among the Tenements of New York* (Cambridge, Massachusetts: The Belknap Press of Harvard University Press, 2010) 15.

1479 LOC, Simpson papers, Letter, Matthew to Ellen, May 7, 1865, Container eight. The notorious slum in New York City had as many as twenty-six people, living in a fifteen-square-foot room. Responding to the agitation of Phoebe Palmer and the Ladies Home Missionary Society, the M.E.C. established a mission at Five Points in 1850. See Charles Edward White. *The Beauty of Holiness* (Grand Rapids: Francis Asbury Press, 1986) 64-65, 218-219.

Few understand the afflictions through which the lower classes pass or the trials which they endure. Little do the upper classes of society know of their suffering and their sorrows, their loss of employment and consequent loss of means of support; their narrow lodgings scanty fare and almost untold anguish."[1480] As he entered the dawn of the Gilded Age, Simpson was either ignorant of, or unwilling to confess that no institution was more socio-economically defined than the Church.

A Utopian Ecclesiology

In no area was Simpson more utopian than in his ecclesiology. The Church militant had already become the Church triumphant; without spot or blemish. The Church was a haven, a place free from temptation. "Nothing that can harm the purity or the peace of society is practiced within those walls; and, not withstanding, on God's holy day, there are multiplied millions to-day in the sanctuaries of the living God, from one end of the earth to the other, there is no practice indulged in, and nothing cultivated which is contrary to purity and peace--to the honor of God and to the safety of men."[1481] The statement would have been true had he changed the word *earth* to *heaven*. Did Simpson mean that no church member coveted the wealth of the affluent person sitting in front of him, or no one envied the talent of the soloist? Did he believe no one attended church for political purposes, and no one desired a compliment on his new horse and carriage, which he parked just outside the front door? It had either been too long since Simpson pastored, or he had not recently read John Wesley's sermon, "The Repentance of Believers." Simpson's ecclesiology was defined by an arrival theology that admitted little of the chaos of a fallen world, and the church in which it existed. Simpson was closer to the truth when he admitted to his Yale audience that in the Church, there should be "the confession of sins, personal, social and national; the deprecation of God's wrath; the prayer for pardon through the atoning merits of Christ, and the expression of trust in the willingness and power of the Great Father to bless and save."[1482]

1480   *Lectures*, 331.

1481   *Sermons*, 281.

1482   *Lectures*, 263. Either Simpson used the wrong word, "deprecation" or the stenographer wrote the wrong word. Though Simpson did not emphasize God's wrath, neither did he minimize it.

Simpson definitely believed that the Gospel can transform society, but he was naïve as to how trenchant preaching would have to be in order to root out systemic evil. Concerning poverty, crime, and cultural conflict, Simpson failed to plumb the complexities of the human condition. His preaching was always positive, perhaps more positive than the contradictions and ironies of human existence merit. He confessed in the early 1880s that a physician in a sick room is quite likely to speak more sanguinely than his own judgment would warrant. Simpson was still a physician, but now engaged in the *curia animarium*, the cure of souls. Physicians are often reluctant to tell the patient just how bad the condition is. As an orator, the speaker was to exude confidence: "The orator who speaks hesitatingly, who is not sure, who talks of doubts and hesitates, seldom convinces." The preacher and politician must be like Napoleon, who "seizes the standard of Austerlitz."[1483] But Simpson did not mention the Napoleon who lost 500,000 men, when he fled Russia in the dead of winter. (He did refer to Napoleon's defeat in another context.) For the dedication of Metropolitan Church in Washington, Simpson trumpeted his post-millennial vision:

> See them coming, one with the other, joining hands and hearts. Hear the song swelling and the joyous acclamation going up; but the perfect shout will not be heard till earth's last son shall join the circle, and then, from redeemed humanity and from bending angels, shall come the voice of triumph that the kingdoms of this world are the kingdoms of our Lord and of his Christ. Oh! I rejoice that there is power in Christianity to give vitality to every human being, and to raise the world quite to the verge of heaven.[1484]

Simpson's Progressive Eschatology and Progressive Nationalism

Simpson may have been the last famed postmillennial preacher in America, though he never used the term "postmillennial." Dwight Moody, whom Simpson mentioned, but as far as we know never met, captivated the

---

1483 Matthew Simpson, "True Leadership," LOC, Simpson papers, Container fifteen. There is no date on this commencement address, but we know it was in the early 80s, because Simpson mentions the death of Garfield.

1484 Matthew Simpson, "The River of Salvation" *The Methodist* Vol. X, No. 11 (March 13, 1869).

popular mind with John Nelson Darby's dispensationalism, a scheme that would be systematized in C.I. Scofield's *Reference Bible*, published in 1909, which made pre-millennial dispensationalism the normative eschatology for most American evangelicals.[1485] Sidney Ahlstrom claims that, "Few religious books equaled its influence.... For millions of people in diverse denominations its dogmatically phrased annotations became an indispensable guide to God's word."[1486] James H. Moorhead explains, "During its heyday in the mid-19th century, postmillennialism represented a compromise between an apocalyptic and evolutionary view of time, between a history characterized by dramatic and supernatural events and one governed by natural laws of organic development." For both Charles Finney and Matthew Simpson, and a host of other evangelicals in between, postmillennialism was a highly cooperative venture which placed as much emphasis on human initiative as it did the sovereignty of God. Moorhead suggests that postmillennialism "failed as a theological paradigm," because it "lost the capacity to address humanity's more primal fears and language and to provide symbols of a transcendent resolution and closure of these issues."[1487]

As the grim reality of urban blight and industrial hardship increasingly gripped American society most of whom was excluded from the prosperity of the Gilded Age, evangelicals adopted an escapist rapture theology. Simpson was a transitional person holding on to the old evangelical order as he squinted through the fog at a new religious paradigm which would be more managerial and capitalistic than anything before. There would be no more sweeping revivals similar to the first and second great awakenings, but the carefully managed and advertised Moody, Sunday, and Graham campaigns which were at one with the Wanamakers, Stewarts, McCormicks, Fields, and Hursts, who supported them.[1488] Both the Church and parachurch

---

1485 When Simpson was in Europe in 1875, he wrote Ellen, "It is astonishing how Smith and Moody and Sankey have stirred the people of England and much of Germany." UMA, E. PA Conference of the UMC, Old St. George's, Philadelphia, letter, n. d. The Smith must have been Robert Pearsall Smith, husband of Hannah Whitall Smith.

1486 Ahlstrom, Vol. II, 280.

1487 James Moorhead. *World Without End: Mainstream America–Protestant Vision of Last Things 1885-1925* (Bloomington: Indiana University Press, 1999) x.

1488 Though Moody had his ministerial start among the orphans and urchins in Chicago, there were some who questioned the ameliorating effects on poverty in his large city campaigns of the 1870s. In April of 1876, Charles Dana, editor of the *New York Sun*,

would become corporations, which calculated favorable returns for time and money expended.

Nowhere was Simpson's progressive nationalism more apparent than in his eschatology; they were almost synonymous with one another. Christianity was advancing and would ultimately claim all the inhabitants of the earth. "Christ is taking the nations one by one. The world is ripening for Christianity. As I see its rapid progress, especially in these last few years, and as I note the events, it seems to me I can almost hear the tread of the angels as they are walking over the earth turning and changing empires as they go, walking along the battlefields, breaking manacles and setting free whole races and nations and I hear them cry as they go, 'All power is given unto Jesus in heaven and in earth.'"[1489] Of course new forms of transportation and communication were enabling the spread of the Gospel and the triumph of Protestantism. Human inventions were a product of God's providence, human means sanctified for divine purposes. "Look at those iron bands which have united the Atlantic and the Mississippi and will soon bind the Mississippi and the Pacific. Look at those telegraph wires on which men whisper and their words ought to be words of light and love. (I thought they were words of battle and trade.) What is all of this? It is Jesus conquering the world."[1490] As he stood before Christ Church in Pittsburgh for its 22nd anniversary, he rhetorically asked:

---

told his readers that Moody's revival had done little to change, "the brokers on Wall Street, the downtown merchants, the Broadway, Bowery, Third and Sixth Avenue shopkeepers, the residents of the fashionable quarters, the politicians of the Custom House and Tammany Hall." Dana found little to suggest that "six months more of revivalism would turn the weedy soil into a Garden of Eden." The *New York Times* noted that the people who attended Moody's campaign at P. T. Barnum's Hippodrome were people of "comfortable circumstances," not the poor. Bruce Evensen. *God's Man for the Gilded Age: D. L. Moody and the Rise of Modern Mass Evangelism* (New York: Oxford University Press, 2003) 120.

1489   *Sermons*, 189.

1490   Ibid., 190. Reinhold Niebuhr scoffed at such notions of progressive Christian nationalism when he took his term as the Yale preaching lecturer in 1945. Of course, Niebuhr had the hind sight of two "world wars" and other disillusions that clouded the "Christian Century." Niebuhr stated, "The development of atomic instruments of conflict aggravated the fears, not only of those who lacked such instruments but of those who had them. The fear of the latter, added a final ironic touch to the whole destiny of modern man. The possession of power has never annulled the fears of those who wield it, since it prompts them to anxiety over its possible loss." Reinhold Niebuhr. *Faith in History* (New York: Charles Scribner Sons, 1949) 7-8.

> Have you thought of it? No railroads outside of Christianity? No great improvements outside of Christianity? Why, if the Mohammadans build a railroad across the Black Sea, it is with Christian's money. If the Suez Canal is built, it is done by Christianity. Christianity develops civilization, improves the nations, joins them together, for the Church though it does not make railroads, nor erect telegraph wires nor tunnel mountains, yet it sends the spirit abroad that accomplishes all these and joins the ends of the earth together.[1491]

Prosperity and the Anglo-Methodist Triumph

Americans celebrated their Centennial with an extravagant world's fair in Philadelphia, the first event of its kind to ever take place. No one would have been more fascinated than Simpson, who had ample opportunity to attend the event, which ran from May 10 to November 10, 1876. Foremost among the exhibits was the Corliss steam engine standing 30 feet high, the most powerful mechanism ever built, providing power for the entire exhibition. There was also a typewriter produced by the Remington-Arins Company and Alexander Graham Bell's telephone. Equally impressive was a 7,000 pound electrical pendulum clock which regulated to the second, 26 smaller "slave" clocks around the building. The master clock represented an age which was now measured by hourly wages rather than organic daylight. Alan Trachtenberg writes that "Measurement of work by units of time was basic to the accounting system of the productive process."[1492] (We will return to the "Centennial Year" in Chapter 20.)

The measurement of time converted skill and muscle into salable hours, a human commodity on the market for the highest bidder. No conversion would provoke more conflict: "The 1880s witnessed almost 10,000 strikes and lockouts."[1493] The inexorable industrial revolution resulted in unresolved cultural dilemmas, conflictive value systems between "machine and garden," the contrast between "mechanical progress and those of pastoral harmony

---

1491   UMA, Drew University, Simpson papers, "Sermon by Bishop Simpson on the Occasion of the Twenty-second Anniversary of Christ Methodist Episcopal Church."

1492   Alan Trachtenberg. *The Incorporation of American Culture and Society in the Gilded Age* (New York: Hill and Wang, 1982) 91.

1493   Ibid., 89.

in a peaceful landscape."[1494] Trachtenberg claims that by the 1880s, "About 45 percent of the industrial laborers held on or above the $500-per-year poverty line; about 40 percent lived below the line of tolerable existence, surviving in shabby tenements and run-down neighborhoods by dint of income eked out by working wives and children."[1495] While Simpson did not condemn trade unions, he suggested that they may "retard the power of the pulpit."[1496] Aaron Abell argues, "As the congregations leaned more and more to the employers' side, the unions urged wage earners to abandon Protestant Christianity."[1497]

Herbert Spencer's social Darwinism provided a paradigm for the demise of the "weak" and the personal triumph of the "strong." Simpson saw no contradiction between the "survival of the fittest" and a biblical view of humanity. Ignoring the depravity of human greed, Simpson proclaimed a gospel of both the individual and society becoming more divine; a common brotherhood that would eventuate into a universal acclamation of God's rule on earth. Simpson declared a Christian pragmatism, formulas for prosperity, if only one believed and acted correctly. This was especially true for Anglo nations. "England rose with the Bible, and has laid her arms around the extremities of the world, gathering an immensity of treasure. Turn to this country, and you will see that just as our fathers worked in harmony with God, he crowned them with glory and when they failed to do what God designed, diversion and strife came in upon them."[1498]

If Simpson observed any contradictions within capitalism, if he contemplated losses in the industrial complex, if he raised any questions about the negative effects of technological advancement, he left no record. Not that Simpson was oblivious to the problems of contemporary society; rather he offered no social gospel, because he espoused no theory of systemic evil. His gospel was individualistic and life's inequities would be rectified eschatologically. "See the poor widow whose children are crying for bread.

1494 Ibid., 52.

1495 Ibid., 90.

1496 *Lectures*, 278.

1497 Aaron Abell. *The Urban Impact on American Protestantism 1865–1900* (London: Archon, 1962) 10.

1498 *Sermons*, 50.

The winter storm rages about; the fuel is exhausted in her fire … a house is prepared for her, that all are hers, that she is a child of God and an heir of glory. She can wipe away her tears and point her children to the Spirit land and she can be happy even in the midst of suffering because she knows that earth has no sorrow that heaven cannot cure."[1499]

Simpson's eschatology displayed his ethnocentric nationalism. American progress was the sine qua non that God was bringing his kingdom to earth. This had been the predominant millennial thought since the Puritans had landed on Plymouth Rock and advocated by persons as diverse as Charles Finney and Ralph Waldo Emerson. God had abandoned apostate Europe for a New Canaan and a more pristine Christianity that would be inhabited by God's "almost chosen people," as Abraham Lincoln referenced America when he stopped in Trenton, New Jersey on his way to inhabit the White House. Robert T. Handy stated of Simpson and his postmillennial kin, "If only one worked harder, witnessed more, gave more, loved more and hated evil more, then perhaps victory would soon come and the voluntary way to a fuller Christian nation would accomplish what all the establishments in history had failed to do."[1500]

Simpson asserted that if one comes from another country, in particular "Mohammedan," stepping on to American shores, the arrivant would feel "another atmosphere heavenly, invigorating, pure-all about him."[1501] In spite of having traveled abroad and taught science, Simpson was anthropologically blind and culturally deaf. "Go among savages and how uncertain is their food, how precarious their livelihood! What poor clothing they wear! Blankets, moccasins, feathers on their head- strange dress! Go among Mohammedan nations; how poor comparatively! How little the comfort of daily life! Their houses compare not with ours; their towns or cities compare not with ours; their trade, their commerce compare not with ours. Who sends out the ships? Who builds the factories? Who have every means of enjoyment? Christian nations."[1502]

1499   Clark, *Pulpit and Platform*, 64.
1500   Robert T. Handy. *A Christian America: Protestant Hopes and Historical Realities* (New York: Oxford, 1971) 114.
1501   *Sermons*. 217.
1502   Ibid., 304.

And which nation was the most Christian? And which denomination was enabling it to be the most Christian? There was no reason for Simpson to write *A Hundred Years of Methodism* in 1876, other than boasting that Methodism was America's most representative and successful denomination. Methodist evangelism historian Mark Teasdale notes Simpson's "synergy between Methodist evangelism and American culture," and then accuses Simpson of nearly "crowing" that "it was the evangelistic zeal of American Methodism that could be thanked for the success of American culture."[1503] No one was more aware than Simpson that in 1876, Methodism had a million more adherents than the next largest denomination, the Baptists. Simpson noted that in 1875, there were 2,875,126 Methodists and 1,815,300 Baptists.[1504] "Moral desolation" would have been the condition of those who migrated into the Western territories, had it not been for the Methodist itinerant.

The Bishop was so caught up in continual progress that he almost forgot the Bible predicts the end of the world as we know it. Simpson evidenced little interest in how the reign of Christ is to defeat evil with a denouement beyond human description. Simpson's constant use of the analogies of nature and his implicit linking of Darwin and evolution with the progress of Christianity makes the following from Perry Miller applicable: "As the cult of nature captured what we may call the higher levels of the American mind, an image of infinite progress bit by bit blotted the ancient expectation. Re-enforced in the second half of the century by Darwinism--or rather, by what optimistic and liberal theologians made out of the *Origin of Species*-- the dominant Protestant mind so yielded itself to the vision of an unchecked progress which was, of itself, to bring about the kingdom of Christ on earth, that eschatology became virtually a lost art."[1505]

To Simpson's credit and his humility, he did not prophecy dates or predict the future, attempting to align contemporary events with biblical references. In his essay, "Thoughts on Heaven," he wrote,

---

[1503] Mark Teasdale, "Growth or Declension: Methodist Historians' Treatment of the Relationship between the Methodist Episcopal Church and the Culture of the United States." *Theological Librarianship* Vol. III No. 2 (December 2010) 36.

[1504] Simpson, *A Hundred Years*, 34.

[1505] Perry Miller. *Errand into the Wilderness* (Cambridge, MA: Harvard University Press, 1956) 235.

We know but little either of matter or mind, and although much of our ignorance may result from neglect, yet with the most constant attention and most constant perseverance, we shall still have to say that we know but in part. If this be true of things present and visible, how much more of things future and invisible? If in things material with the full assistance of our senses we gain but a superficial knowledge–if in things present then we can see the train of sequences as they pass us, but conjecture rather than know–how limited necessarily must be our knowledge of the immaterial in the future.[1506]

Experiential Disconnects

Did Simpson live in the house of his own preaching? Did he exaggerate personal religious experience? In his "Elements of Christian Character," he proclaimed "The man who has the Holy Ghost is a joyous Christian; he is a happy man in all the walks of life; he is happy because God's Spirit is with him. A consciousness that he is the son of God rules his heart."[1507] He then testified, "Now, to have the Spirit is to have this comfort; but what is it to be full of the Holy Spirit? That is the fullness of joy; I take it to be such a consciousness of the indwelling of the Spirit as takes away all fear, all anxiety, and makes one feel at home, if I may reverently use the expression with the divine character."[1508] Is fullness of joy the normative experience for a melancholic personality who is afflicted with salvific anxiety? As he stood before his Yale audience, he let his guard down. "I know your heart because I know my own. I know the afflictions through which I have passed, the deep sadness of my own soul, the doubts which have wrung my spirit; but have you not said as I have said in years passed many a time, I fear heaven is not for me."[1509]

Early in his ministry Simpson had recorded spiritual doubts with frequency. In 1835 as a twenty-four year old, he felt his spiritual pulse and recorded, "Want of personal holiness evidenced by giving way to indolence,

---

1506 Matthew Simpson, "Thoughts on Heaven," LOC, Simpson papers, Scrapbook D, Container twenty-three.
1507 *Sermons*, 165.
1508 Ibid., 166.
1509 Ibid., 290.

not filling of my time spent in the room and family to proper purposes, too much levity of spirit--indulge too much in pleasantry; too little time spent in private prayer, self-examination and religious meditation."[1510] Remember that in late 1852 Simpson had recorded, "For various reasons I am much depressed. My heart greatly needs a deeper work of grace .... My heart is not right." In regard to honest reflection Simpson was being true to Wesleyan spirituality, severe introspection, a sort of soul searching cartography, a mapping of the inner consciousness. As he stood before the British Wesleyan Conference in August, 1870, he confessed:

> A holy minister accomplishes more than one but partially holy, and the voice of God sounds in our ears, "Be ye holy for I am holy." I sometimes say to myself, "If I had always lived where eternal sunshine settles on the head--if I had lived above these clouds and mists--if my experience had been rich and ripe and deep at all times--how many poor souls might have been led to the cross that have not been led there. And then, I say, if there be one cause of deficiency in me that I might have remedied, will not the blood of men be found in my skirts? How can I say "I am pure from the blood of all men?" My dear young ministers keep this in your minds. All the good which you could possibly do by being wholly consecrated to God, and which you fail to do now because you failed of entering into such a relation to him, all that will be sin resting upon you. Why not then seek this higher life?[1511]

A Crisis Impossible to Ignore

The most jarring contradiction which echoed from Simpson was his advocacy for the poor and his obliviousness to their plight. "Not until the minister by some act of kindness, by some manifestation of sympathy by some effort in their behalf gains their confidence, do they open their hearts even to him."[1512] Was Simpson speaking of himself when he stated, "A wall of partition is rising between the capitalist and the laborer, between the higher classes and the lower; and the masses generally identify the minister with the higher classes of society? They contribute chiefly to his support and have

---

1510   LOC, Simpson papers, 1835 *Diary*, Container one.
In 1847, Matthew wrote Ellen: "My heart is so treacherous, so desperately wicked, so apt to lead me astray, that divine greed alone can prepare me for a holy life." UMA, Drew University, Simpson papers, Letter, October 10, 1847.
1511   *Sermons*, 73.
1512   *Lectures*, 331.

much influence in procuring his appointment. His dress, deportment and general habits fit him for association with great society and the masses are liable to feel that he is not one of them."[1513] The answer to this problem was individual conversion, which in Simpson's paradigm as Kirby observes, would cause social problems to disappear and "humanity would be elevated to its proper place in creation .... In this great missionary enterprise the destinies of Protestant Christianity and the American nation were joined."[1514]

More than anything Methodism shaped Simpson as much as he shaped it, a subtle accommodation that John Wesley predicted, and Max Weber so aptly described.[1515] Melvin Stokes and Stephen Conway asked why there was so little resistance to upward mobility in the church and then answer, "The truth is that American Methodism experienced no searing conflicts over the Church's embourgeoisement, because although the early Methodists were poor, they were far from hostile to enterprise and the capitalist ethic."[1516]

But Simpson was not blind to the cultural conflict that was renting the economic fabric of America. He began to suspect that his utopian dream was turning into a nightmare. Up to his death, he made frequent stops in Pittsburgh, his wife's hometown, which was becoming uglier by the day. And though the Haymarket Riot in Chicago, 1886, and the Homestead

---

1513 Ibid., 303.

1514 Kirby, "Matthew Simpson and the Mission of America," 307.

1515 Max Weber displayed John Wesley's prophecy about Methodism as exhibit A for his entire thesis, "I fear wherever riches have increased, the essence of religion has decreased in the same proportion. Therefore I do not see how it is possible, in the nature of things, for any revival of true religion to continue long. For religion must necessarily produce both industry and frugality; and these cannot but produce riches. But as riches increase so will pride, anger, and the love of the world in all its branches. How then is it possible that Methodism, that is, a religion of the heart, though it flourishes now as a green bay tree, should continue in this state? For the Methodists in every place grow diligent and frugal; consequently they increase in goods. Hence they proportionately increase in pride, in anger, in the desires of the flesh, the desire of the eyes, and the pride of life. So, although the form of religion remains, the spirit is swiftly vanishing away. Is there no way to prevent this–this continual decay of pure religion? We ought not prevent people from being diligent and frugal; *we must exhort all Christians to gain all they can, and to save all they can; that is, in effect, to grow rich.*" Max Weber. *The Protestant Work Ethic and the Spirit of Capitalism* (New York: Charles Scribner's Sons, 1950) 175.

1516 Melvyn Stokes and Steven Conway. *The Market Revolution in American Social, Political, and Religious Expressions: 1800-1880* (Charlottesville: The University Press of Virginia, 1996) 287.

Strike in Pittsburgh, 1892, did not take place until after Simpson's death, the conditions for these events were in place long before they happened. A newspaper reporter described the atmosphere and circumstances surrounding the Carnegie Steel Works in Pittsburgh: "A sense of defeat and sullen despair fell over the town, a miasma of dark polluted air. The worker living areas behind the factory were squalid, dingy, gray-framed structures, fifty cent brothels, scruffy children and trash. The roads were unpaved, and there was no sewage system. The area was so unsightly and unsanitary as it shocked me into belief that I was once more witnessing the lowest phases of Chicago's slum life--the worst I had ever seen."[1517] Eighteen eighty-six was, known as the "Great Upheaval, a tsunami of 1,400 strikes against 11,562 businesses."[1518] This unrest had been building since the Civil War, but in spite of the evidence, Simpson still wanted to believe in the unhampered and unfettered advancement of mammon and industrialism, or in Adam Smith's "*laissez-faire*," though he did not evidence having read Smith. It was simply too hard to bite the hand which had fed him. He increasingly viewed the world through the eyes of John Evans, James Harlan and Thomas Carlton.

The Humanistic Inheritance

Kirby is correct in noting that Simpson emphasized the elevation of humanity. But he is wrong to claim that the major subject of Matthew Simpson's theology is man. "Indeed it is not in error to say that his theology is man centered."[1519] Accusing Simpson of being homocentric is an oversimplification. A careful reading of Simpson's sermons and his Yale lectures will reveal a person who is intent on proclaiming Christ in the power of the Holy Spirit. That there are moralistic terms which reflect middle-class values, as Kirby further assesses are due to Simpson's lack of theological depth and a lack of precision

---

1517 Quoted by Richard Ermsburger, Jr., "Andrew Carnegie: Robber Baron Turned Robin Hood" in *American History* Vol XIL, No 6 (February 15, 2015) 34.

1518 Richard White. *Railroaded: The Transcontinentals and the Making of Modern America* (New York: W. W. Norton and Company, 2011) 341.

1519 Ibid., 62. In 1925, future Methodist Bishop and Harrison County, Ohio native Harold Hough wrote the book, *Evangelical Humanism*. He wrote of Wesley, "You cannot call Wesley a humanist in any such sense as was true of Milton. But he did have marks of humanism upon him. And the variety of its interest and the almost exhaustless range of his intellectual curiosity belonged to a humanistic attitude toward life." Lynn Harold Hough. *Evangelical Humanism* (New York: The Abingdon Press, 1925) 149.

in his extemporaneous delivery. If the Renaissance and the Reformation are two sides of the same coin, Protestantism incarnated Michelangelo's David. Almost all American preaching became humanistic after the American Revolution, or certainly more humanistic than the sermons which came from the Puritan divines John Cotton, Increase Mather and Jonathan Edwards.[1520] Both the "Declaration of Independence" and "Constitution" are humanistic manifestos imposing not theocentric responsibilities, but demanding human rights and privileges. The "self" was the center of Thomas Jefferson's universe and God lived on a faraway star, if in the universe at all. Pauline Maier writes, "To justify revolution by 'the eternal laws of self-preservation' or, as others sometimes said 'the first law of nature,' drew upon a politicized religious literature that equated the laws of God with the laws of nature and described self-preservation as 'an instinct by God implanted in our nature.'"[1521] In this "equation" Simpson would have firmly believed. Where Simpson differed from our deistic forefathers is that his God was immanently ubiquitous, almost pantheistic. Their God, after implementing "self-preservation" in human nature, could just leave us alone, and if not, not overly meddle in human affairs. For Washington, Jefferson and their political kin, it was the worship of God that was needed, not God himself.

Moralistic humanism would far more aptly describe Henry Ward Beecher than it would Matthew Simpson. Simpson mentioned Beecher in his *Lectures*, but only in passing as the leader of a large church. In Beecher's sermon, "Conduct, the Index of Feeling," he stated, "If a person can say, I take pains to know what my duty is in Christ Jesus; I take pains to study his life and his words, and I am trying, that is enough to start upon. It is the *trying* (italics

---

[1520] In my perception, Wesley's theology moved towards humanism. Timothy Crutcher examines the role of experience in Wesley's quest for epistemological and theological authority. While Crutcher is mostly positive about Wesley's use of experience, he believes that Wesley was overly pragmatic. "In Wesley's view, our understanding of the Triune God is only there to further our understanding of God's salvation through His Son and sanctification through His Spirit. The result is a tacit theological shift which re-centers Christianity on the Christian rather than on God." Though Crutcher does not use the word humanism, I would argue that Wesley's emphasis on experience lends itself to a subjective humanism. Timothy J. Crutcher. *The Crucible of Life: The Role of Experience in John Wesley's Theological Method* (Lexington, Kentucky: Emeth Press, 2010) 251.

[1521] Pauline Maier. *American Scripture: Making the Declaration of Independence* (New York: Vintage Books, 1997) 87.

his) that is most essential then."[1522] In his sermon, "The Way of Coming to Christ," Beecher proclaimed, "Go to Christ, try this: Begin in earnest. Begin to put your whole life-force into the new ambitions that will arise from this mode of loving God and man. Change the current of your life."[1523] He asked and answered, "How are we to come to Christ? I reply that we are to come to him through a series of moral practical endeavors, to live the life which he has prescribed for us."[1524]

In his sermon, "Morality, the Basis of Piety," Beecher explained that, "These simple moralities, in our circumstances in life, and under the temptations which are brought to bear upon us, will necessitate a determined battle. Some men conquer easier than others. I believe in hereditary tendencies. I believe that an honest man naturally will have honest children."[1525] Beecher went on record that he did not believe in total depravity. "When the claims of God are brought before a man who has trained himself to exact truth, to absolute honesty, to indefatigable fidelity, and to clear moral purity, the transition from the state of morals to the state of true faith and true spirituality is easy and natural."[1526] Obviously, Beecher did not consider self-righteousness as a barrier to humble discipleship. In fact, it would seem that without an innate disposition to follow God, true spirituality was almost impossible. "So far as we can judge by a large induction of facts, there is no action of the divine mind upon the human, except in the line of already established powers and faculties."[1527]

When Beecher spoke at Williams College, a newspaper reported that the commencement speaker had defined, "The end and purpose of life as the doing of good rather than the being of good."[1528] One of Walt Whitman's

---

1522 Henry Ward Beecher. *The Original Plymouth Pulpit: Sermons of Henry Ward Beecher* Vol. II (Boston: The Pilgrim Press, 1870) 32.

1523 Ibid., 11.

1524 Ibid., 29.

1525 Vol. I, 400.

1526 Ibid., 397.

1527 Ibid., 183.

1528 Debby Applegate. *The Most Famous Man in America: The Biography of Henry Ward Beecher* (New York: Doubleday, 2006) 215. William G. McLoughlin places Beecher within a group of "minor prophets" which included Phillips Brooks, Harry Emerson Fosdick, and Norman Vincent Peale, "American prophets of reassurance for a nation desperately wanting to be loved and to love itself." William G. McLoughlin. *The Meaning of Henry Ward Beecher:*

friends told him that, "I heard Henry Ward Beecher last night (or the night before) and the whole sermon was you, you, you, from top to toe."[1529] Pulitzer Prize-winning biographer, Debby Applegate, concludes concerning Beecher's homiletics, "Perhaps it was inevitable that after two decades of promoting 'Free Soil, Free Labor, Free Press, and Free Speech,' Beecher would now take up 'Free Thought.' After his death, Beecher gained a reputation for un-thinking emotionalism, for preaching a 'Gospel of Gush.'"[1530] No one would ever make that accusation of Simpson.[1531]

Preparation and Delivery

Nothing did Simpson stress more to his students than not reading a sermon. He claimed to have never read a sermon from the pulpit in the entirety of his career. "Sometimes I had a line written out here and there, and sometimes a few catch words on a scrap of paper, but which I seldom, if ever carried into the pulpit, and very few of which I ever preserved."[1532] He further claimed that, "If I could have my text firmly fixed in my mind, before sleeping on Saturday night, the plan of the sermon came readily to me on Sunday morning."[1533] The "scraps of paper" may have been true for the later years, but not the earlier. For his sermon on Hebrews 10:25, "Forsaking not

---

An Essay on the Shifting Values of Mid-Victorian America, 1840-1870 (New York: Alfred A. Knopf, 1970) 260.

1529   Ibid., 275.

1530   Ibid., 354.

1531   Another practical difference between Simpson and Beecher is that the latter joined the "Lyceum Circuit," while the former did not. Beecher hired E. S. Wells, who arranged for the preacher to deliver twelve lectures in the "West." Beecher was promised $1,500 per lecture--an exorbitant sum at which the Ohio newspapers scoffed. David Mead. *Yankee Eloquence in the Middle West: The Ohio Lyceum 1850-1870* (East Lansing: Michigan State College Press, 1951) 136.

1532   Ibid., 163. Simpson's memory must have failed him here. In the over-sized scrapbook, Container twenty-four at the LOC, there are 114 sermon outlines, many with copious notes utilized by Simpson. Container nineteen contains the following sermons with detailed notes: "Mighty to Save," "Ascension," "Not Ashamed, " "Oneness," "The Humility of and Exaltation of Christ," "But He Being Dead Yet Speaketh," "The Great Salvation," "Ambassadors for God," "A Voice Was Heard," "And Without Controversy," "The Cross of Christ," "What Think Ye of Christ," "Tarry at Jerusalem," "Christ Crucified," "He Healed All That Were Sick," and "When the Morning Stars Sang Together."

1533   Ibid., 158.

the assembling of yourselves together," Simpson used copious notes. His introduction was written out:

"Introduce with some remarks--to prove Christ a ransom for sin--but yet duty must not be neglected." He then proceeded with a three-point outline:

I. The persons addressed were those who had fled to Christ for refuge.

II. What are the proper assemblies for Christianity?

III. The Design of God in authorizing assemblies of believers.

Under the first division, there are four points; the second division, four points with four points under the first secondary point, and for the third division, Simpson delineated five points. Similar outlines were used for his sermons, "What Think Ye of Christ?" and "Mighty to Save."[1534]

When Simpson's Yale *Lectures* were published in 1879, they met with general acclaim. Charles King commended his hard-lined stance against read sermons by saying, "I think it is a shameful abuse of place and position, to allow readers to be substituted in our pulpits for preachers."[1535] King then objected to Simpson's exhortation to sit down "doggedly" while preparing a sermon. F. Merrick insisted that Simpson should strike out the word "dynamite." (Somehow Merrick possessed a copy of the *Lectures* before publication.) "I think the paragraph would be more impressive without it; and then the imagination keeps connecting the physical idea with the subsequent of this highest of Spiritual powers. I want to keep the thought as free as possible from anything material or earthy."[1536] Simpson did not heed Merrick's advice, but retained the word dynamite, and rightfully so since it comes directly from the New Testament Greek word *dunamis*.

High Spirituality and Low Theology

Whether Simpson was lecturing or preaching he had a unique ability to strike a spiritual chord. A Methodist student at the Yale Divinity School was deeply impressed, "The seats of the chapel are crowded and the aisles

---

1534   LOC. Simpson papers, Sermon notes, Container nineteen.
1535   LOC, Simpson papers, Letter February 2, 1879, Container twelve.
1536   LOC, Simpson papers, Letter January 25, 1879, Container twelve.

filled with chairs the usual crowd of listeners, distinguished divines of various denominations, ladies and laymen show as great interest as the students." The student went on to say that when Simpson testified to his own call to the ministry, the audience was affected to tears. "One of the professors declared, that he had never been so deeply moved."[1537]

When Simpson convert and temperance advocate Frances Willard heard him preach the "Victory of Faith" at the Des Plains camp meeting, she recorded, "I have heard great preachers, Beecher, Talmage, Spurgeon in England .... But to my thought, no flight was ever so steady, so sustained, so lofty, as that of Bishop Simpson's on that memorable day."[1538] This was one of Simpson's most popular sermons, and also one of his most theologically impoverished. (Gaius Atkins chose the "Victory of Faith" as one of his "Master Sermons of the Nineteenth Century.") Simpson utilized natural theology, industrial progress, and human initiative to illustrate faith. Alexander the Great, Napoleon, and George Washington were his primary examples; no George Mueller and William Carey. "Were man to rely on his muscular strength alone, he never could surmount obstacles existing in nature; but he reaches out, seizes mechanical appliances, harnesses the beast of burden, utilizes the cascade, vaporizes water, seizes the sunbeam, and sends his message by electricity. He triumphs when he lays his hand upon and employs for his service the elements about him."[1539] For Simpson and American Protestantism, the faith that comes only by grace would be confused with human initiative and ingenuity.

The "transformation of taste" (page 541) was Simpson at his theological worst. Simpson assumed that the "converted" would salivate for the good in society as society defined the good. Did Simpson really believe that the boy who was reading in the library and who sought fame and fortune (page 555), was following the lowly Galilean? The down side is that Jesus trampled "taste," with the hooves of the donkey which he rode into Jerusalem. Simpson, like most American evangelicals, had read little theology. He was required

---

1537 LOC, Simpson papers, Scrapbook D, Container twenty-three.

1538 Clark, *Pulpit and Platform*, 464.

1539 *Sermons*. 194. Robert Clark argues that Simpson's greatest pulpit triumphs came in the outbreak of the war. The most outstanding of these, "The Victory of Faith", excited "men and women to emotional extravagance which caused even Methodists with their tradition of revivalism to exclaim in wonder." Robert D. Clark. "The Oratorical Career of Bishop Matthew Simpson" in *Speech Monographs* Vol. XVI, No. 1(1949) 14-15.

to read Wesley's sermons for ordination, and as a young pastor, delved into Calvin and read from Lyman Beecher.[1540] Simpson evidenced little to no reading of systematic theology, whether it be contemporary Methodists John Miley or Thomas Ralston. Martin Marty writes, "Formal theology has been the property of a small intellectual elite in the churches. European style, academic theology, had few followers in America before the 1930s …. With the exception of names like Edwards, Bushnell, Rauschenbusch, and Niebuhr in four different eras, few theologians have been widely recognized in the society, including in ecclesiastical culture."[1541]

"He Will Draw You to Your Feet"

In the pulpit, Simpson was a transitional person for Methodism and much of America. He no longer preached on "Brimstone Corner," as the residents of Cincinnati once referred to the location of a Methodist Church. His sermons were polished orations which inspired and encouraged, fit for print. He was not a fire-breathing, anecdote-telling, guilt-inducing preacher. Even though he used no manuscript while preaching, his sermons could be transcribed into smooth and edifying prose after the preaching moment. Consciously or unconsciously, for better or for worse, Simpson had metamorphed into a much different kind of Methodist preacher.

Simpson was born to preach. He loved to preach, making it his first priority among all other pastoral duties, and sometimes even familial. In 1859, when he could have been home with his wife and children on Christmas Day in Evanston, he chose to stay over and preach in New York. James Kirby notes that when he wrote home on Christmas Day, he informed Ellen that he would probably preach in Philadelphia the next evening, and "failed to mention that

---

1540 LOC, Simpson papers, 1836 *Diary*, Container one. In fact, his biographer, George Crooks, points to Simpson's theological weakness, especially the young pastor's perspective that, "children while in infancy ought never to be spoken of as belonging to the Church or making up part of the body of Christ." Crooks, 110. Indeed, Simpson was contradictory in that he was baptized as an infant and would never be re-baptized. On December 7, 1835, the young pastor recorded that he preached on infant baptism, but leaves no indication whether he was for it or against it. One would presume that as a Methodist pastor he baptized infants. LOC, Simpson papers, 1835 *Diary*, Container one.

1541 Martin E. Marty. *Righteous Empire: The Protestant Experience in America* (New York: The Dial Press, 1970) 191

it was Christmas Day, and did not wish Ellen or any of the family members a Merry Christmas." By the time he arrived home on the 29th, he had added three more preaching appointments. It is safe to say that Simpson never turned down a preaching opportunity, no matter how meager the circumstances, if time and logistics allowed. On the Thursday before Christmas he preached in Mamaroneck, New York, "at the home of aged females."[1542]

In spite of, or because of his humility, Simpson was a conflicted man. As Beecher entered his sex scandal problems in the early 1870s, and before Moody began his American crusades in the mid 1870s, Simpson may have been the most adulated preacher in America. There had to be some intentionality in his emotional perorations, sermonic crescendos, and flag-waving. The phenomenal crowd response was both gratifying and guilt-producing. He had not forgotten the admonition of Uncle Matthew, who wrote his twenty-three year old nephew in 1834, "I somehow suspect that very few of the popular pulpit orators will rate high in God's account when the day of reckoning comes; for the question will not then be, how many they pleased, but how many they saved." [1543]

If preaching was an entertainment medium in the nineteenth century, no one did it better than Matthew Simpson. The word "entertain" is derived from the French words, *teneir* to hold, and *entre* between. Simpson held persons between this world and the next, the biblical world and our world, his hearers' problems and God's solution, present turmoil and the promise of future bliss. Entertainment value is difficult to measure and even more difficult to define. Rarely did anyone leave a Simpson event disappointed, though they may have not been able to analyze the source of their jubilation. A memorialist, Jacob Todd, recalled Simpson preaching at the Warren Street

---

1542 James Kirby, "Dearest Ellen: Correspondence between Bishop Matthew Simpson and His Wife" *Methodist History* Vol. XLII, No. 3 (April 2004) 146.

1543 Crooks, 103. In its September 5, 1956 issue, *Christian Century* reviewed Robert Clark's *The Life of Matthew Simpson*. The reviewer wrote, "Above all, it is history of the ecclesiasticizing of the Methodist Church." In spite of ecclesiasticizing not being a word, the assessment was true. The reviewer then wrote, "Paradoxically, Clark shows how close Simpson was to the writings and spirit of John Wesley in his Discipline and Duty, mingled with assurance and Christian perfection to motivate a powerful personality." This observation was curious since Clark expended little ink on Simpson's theology and the actual content of his preaching. The doctrine of "assurance" and "Christian perfection" may have been the two areas where Simpson most distanced himself from Wesley.

Church in Philadelphia. "As he warmed with his subject, he seemed to hold and control his subject as a driver does his team. A number of times as he lifted his long angular arm in gesture, I noticed he lifted a score of people to their feet, and three times he was compelled to stop, until the people could be got quiet enough for him to proceed." Todd went on to say, "They laughed, they cried, they shouted, they leaped, they were intoxicated, they were delirious under the witchery of his magical eloquence."[1544]

A person who had never heard Simpson preach accompanied a friend to a church. On the way to the church the inviter said to the invited, "He will draw you to your feet. I have been magnetized several times and compelled to rise to my feet." The visitor protested and was confident that he had won the wager when he thought that Simpson had reached his oratorical limit. "I had a little difficulty in keeping my seat, but I remembered my pledge, and sincerely resolved to stubbornly sit still if the roof of the building should fly off." Then Simpson soared to his final climax, waving the flag, "and the people sprang to their feet as if drawn by some magnetic force. I forgot all about my promise and ceased to resist the impulse that moved me. It seemed to me that no one with human feelings could withstand the current."[1545]

No one ever earned any money betting against Simpson in the pulpit.

1544 *Journal of the General Conference of the Methodist Episcopal Church*, held in *New York, May 1-31, 1888*. Edited by Rev. David S Monroe, D.D., and Sec. of the Conference (New York: Phillips & Hunt, 1888) 570.

1545 UMA, Drew University, Crooks Papers, anecdote shared with Crooks by an unidentified author, n. d.

Chapter Nineteen: Feuding Friends and Conflicting Paradigms

Suspected Crime at the Publishing House

Many of Simpson's ecclesiastical duties were less than inviting, and he was no doubt depressed as he sat with his fellow Bishops who acted as jurors on January 12, 1871. It was a no win proposition. Simpson had been asked to assign guilt to one or both of his friends. John Lanahan had pastored in Alexandria, Virginia, during the Civil War and served as Simpson's chief informant, keeping the Bishop abreast of the latest political gossip in Washington and how Methodism could gain political leverage. Now, Lanahan, as assistant editor of the Methodist Book Concern in New York City, had accused the one person above him, Thomas Carlton, of fraud, or at least allowing rampant embezzlement and graft by his employees. As the head agent of the New York Publishing House, Carlton served in American Methodism's most exalted financial position. The Publishing House paid the Bishops' salaries, and Carlton had provided perquisites such as Simpson's life insurance policy, a job for his son Charles, and at times loaned the Bishop money.

Lanahan accused Publishing House employees, mainly James Porter and S. J. Goodenough, of purchasing materials never used by the Publishing House, but sold for personal profit on the open market, pocketing the difference between payroll requested and actually paid, and skimming a surcharge paid for paper and ink. Lanahan also obtained evidence that Carlton deposited significant Publishing House funds for long periods of time in his personal bank account, from which he accrued the interest. Lanahan exposed Kate Heath, owner of a "house of prostitution" as being on the payroll, for what purposes he did not say. His sleuthing discovered that part of the muslin designated for book construction had been delivered to her house.[1546] On September 21, 1869, the *New York Times* reported that, "We are credibly assured that the new agent (Lanahan) of the *Methodist Book Concern* has discovered in that establishment great corruption and fraud, incurring losses to the amount of several thousand dollars."[1547]

In 1869, the New York Publishing House moved into an elaborate six-story building at the corner of Broadway and Eleventh Streets. The building was imposing even for New York standards, and symbolized for Methodism another step up in both the financial and religious world. Methodist publishing historian James Pilkington claimed, "Thomas Carlton was widely respected in commercial circles, but also he was Treasurer of the Missionary Society, a bank director, and a stock holder. For purity of character, for his tact, integrity, wisdom, generosity, and friendship he was admired by many. Above all, he seemed to have a genius for handling money."[1548] Pilkington further wrote, "Reminiscent of the early days when Nathan Bangs became Book Agent, the whole tempo of the Book Concern quickened to the touch of Thomas Carlton. In him, Methodist Publishing had an administrator *par excellence*. A financier whose talent was management; he could make men do what he wanted them to do."[1549]

One of the Botchers May Have Been Simpson

One person whom Carlton could not make do what he wanted him to do was John Lanahan. When Lanahan approached Carlton, the head agent shrugged off financial irregularities, and refused to provide Lanahan with receipts, vouchers, and other records which would either verify or refute Lanahan's suspicions. Part

---

1546 Walter Newton Vernon, Jr. *The United Methodist Publishing House* Vol. II (Nashville: Abingdon Press, 1989) 11.

1547 John Lanahan. *The Era of Frauds in the Methodist Book Concern at New York* (Baltimore: Methodist Book Depository, 1896) 174.

1548 James Pilkington. *The Methodist Publishing House: A History* Vol. I (Nashville: Abingdon Press, 1968) 9.

1549 Ibid.

of Carlton's stonewalling was due to the forming of an oil cartel with his fellow employees, Goodenough and Elihu Grant, with capital of over $1,500,000.[1550] Walter Vernon assesses, "In fairness to all concerned--and before the affair was ever made known, it must be said that in the whole drama, everyone closely connected with it in any way botched his part."[1551] As a close friend of Carlton, one of the botchers may have been Simpson. "Consequently, many in and out of the church formed the impression that this group was more concerned with white washing the matter than they were of cleaning it up."[1552] Evidence against Carlton, for some reason never presented by Lanahan, was that in 1865 Carlton drew from the Publishing House funds, $73,000, paid to the "stock holders Mongean, Jenkins, and Company."[1553] If Carlton was not embezzling money, he was at least confusing and complicating his own business with that of the Publishing House, what would in all likelihood be categorized in today's legal lexicon as "money laundering."

No one earned the moniker "Methodist financier" more than did Thomas Carlton. Lanahan defender and Methodist historian James Buckley, stated, "Dr. Carlton, Alderman of Elizabeth, New Jersey, Director of the Shoe and Leather Bank, Director of the Home Life Insurance Company, Director of oil companies, the Crescent Mineral Spring, and I don't know how many more companies, Treasurer of the Missionary Society, and Trustee of various literary institutions, makes a hue and cry that attending to legal proceedings takes his time from the Concern."[1554] Buckley, who was present at the 1872 General Conference, recalled, "Subsequently, a peculiar controversy arose between the agent and the assistant book agent. The latter had demanded access to the books and proposed to take them aside to be investigated by the experts. The agent refused to surrender them for the purpose, and the assistant appealed to the Supreme Court of the State of New York for an injunction to compel him to do so. For this taking the affairs of the church into the civil courts he was suspended and put upon trial before the committee."[1555]

1550   Vernon, 12.
1551   Ibid., 13.
1552   Ibid.
1553   Ibid.,17.
1554   Lanahan, 266.
1555   J. M. Buckley. *A History of Methodists in the United States* (New York: The Christian Literature Company, 1946) 530.

Thomas Carlton exhibited a brooding, almost scowling face with chiseled features, deep-set eyes under heavy eyebrows, hunched shoulders, a large-crooked nose and a menacing countenance crowned with thick black hair as if he could have played Ebenezer Scrooge or some other devious character in a Dickens novel. As we have already seen, Carlton personified the "New York Regency" playing the part of B. T. Roberts' foremost antagonist. No one doubted Carlton's financial acumen. John Robie, editor of the *Buffalo Christian Advocate*, proposed "that the Bishop always take the Treasurer (Carlton) with him wherever he pleads for missions. One will move the heart, the other the dollars."[1556] The Lanahan case was not the first time that Carlton had been accused of "covering up fraud." When it was brought to the attention of the Genesee Conference that one of its ministers had been involved in shady financial dealings, according to B. T. Roberts, "As soon as the complaints were brought before the Conference, one of the leading men of their party, I think it was T. Carlton, moved to lay the whole matter on the table."[1557] Carlton and his minions counter-attacked Lanahan with the following charges:

> 1. Official misconduct and malfeasance
>
> 2. Neglect of official duty
>
> 3. Untruthfulness, irascibility, slanderous disposition, and other objectionable personal characteristics which unfit him for the position of Assistant Book Agent
>
> 4. Insubordination to his official superiors-the Book Committee-and his pledge to them
>
> 5. Want of business qualifications and capacity for the discharge of his official duties as Assistant Book Agent.[1558]

Simpson and his colleagues, their minds befuddled with hours of argument and counter-arguments, numbers thrown at them, impossible to digest on the spot, begged off by claiming, "As Bishops we cannot consider and give official decisions upon such matters as come properly under the jurisdiction of annual conferences when in session or of presiding elders

---

1556 Ibid.
1557 Snyder, 362.
1558 Lanahan, 122.

in the interval of said conference …. We do not judge it proper for us to consider the general fitness or unfitness for the office of any man appointed by the General Conference as editor or agent unless the cause of the alleged unfitness has occurred since his election." The letter was signed by E. S. Janes, M. Simpson, L. Scott, and E. R. Ames.[1559] Carlton personally chose an outside auditor, John Gunn,[1560] who concluded:

> Frequent alterations and changes have rendered the books untrustworthy and unintelligible, because there is no explanation of such alterations. The correctness of the books has been tested by trial balances only once a year; error then disclosed has been allowed to remain without discovery, and consequently the books have not balanced in nearly twenty years. There is a singular lack of uniformity in the manner of keeping some of the accounts, changes being made so frequently, and without explanation or notice upon the books, that the account is rendered unintelligible.[1561]

Gunn then met with Simpson and Janes at the latter's residence in New York, informing them that Carlton had attempted to persuade Gunn to give the report to VanVleck, an accountant likely to glass over the irregularities, and the latter would combine Gunn and VanVleck's conclusions and present them to the General Conference as a single report. Simpson and Janes did not agree with Carlton's proposal and ordered that both men present their individual report to the General Conference.[1562]

Lanahan Arrested

The filth of the dirty laundry became even more embarrassing when Lanahan was arrested and "gruffly" hauled off to jail, because of a slander suit filed by Samuel Goodenough. Lanahan resented not being allowed to write a note to his family before he was "marched off to the sheriff's office in City Hall." The *New York Times* took full advantage of the scoop by comparing

---

1559 Ibid., 158.

1560 This same John Gunn discovered that over a million dollars had been embezzled from the Western Development Company, a financial holding and clearing house for the Central Pacific Railroad. Richard White. *Railroaded: The Transcontinentals and the Making of Modern America* (New York: W.W. Norton and Company, 2011) 200-201.

1561 Lanahan, 199.

1562 Ibid., 190-191.

the arrest of the corrupt Bill Tweed of Tammany Hall infamy, with the incarceration of a Methodist clergyman.

> When Bill Tweed, the biggest rogue of the age, was to be arrested, what did this same Brennan do? Sent him a private note, politely informing him that at a certain hour on a certain day, the Sheriff would humbly wait upon His Highness, hoping that it would not cause him any inconvenience, etc., etc., And yet, when a well-known clergyman is to be arrested in a malicious suit, supported only by ex parte affidavits, he sends two ruffians to insult and degrade him, and this renders himself responsible for an outrage which will excite indignation far beyond the limits of the Methodist Church.[1563]

Friction sparked on the eighth day of the 1872 General Conference when Carlton gave what normally would have been a routine, non-questioned financial report, and Lanahan stood and, "denied ever having authorized or signed said report."[1564] This was such an explosive matter that an investigative committee was created and composed of a representative from every Annual Conference, an intelligence department consisting of seventy-two members. When Lanahan defended himself, he reported that Elihu Grant, Senior Book Keeper of the Concern, had contacted Simpson requesting that the matter should be treated "charitably," and this would be accomplished by securing the services of VanVleck to examine the books and report to the General Conference. Lanahan defended Simpson: "It is needless to say that the proposition was indignantly spurned by Bishop Simpson and that Grant's letter with a suitable reply was transmitted to the Committee."[1565] VanVleck ultimately defended Carlton, and though he glossed over the financial irregularities and attempted to absolve Carlton from wrong doing, not even he could deny the crimes of Carlton's associates.[1566] Although Lanahan had painted Simpson in the best light, the Bishop did not appreciate Lanahan rocking the Methodist boat. Simpson did not obstruct justice, but he desired the whole affair to be swept under the rug. Sin management would be better than sin exposure. He wrote Ellen:

1563   Ibid., 273-274.

1564   *Journal of the 1872 General Conference of the Methodist Episcopal Church* (New York: Nelson and Phillips, 1872) 146.

1565   Lanahan, 268.

1566   *Journal of the 1872 General Conference*, 614.

> Dr. Lanahan, I learn, has again been suspended by the Book Committee and his trial is to commence June 8th. I fear that this time he will be removed, as he entered suit in Court demanding the use of the Books, paper, etc., which the Book Committee and Dr. Carlton wd not give him. He is very impulsive, and very imprudent. I do not know how long his trial may last nor whether it will delay my starting for the West. I think however that it will not last long.[1567]

In the second trial, the majority of the investigative committee found Lanahan guilty of having taken the affairs of the Church into the civil courts, and decided that he should be removed from his office. The recommendation went to Bishops Janes and Ames, since Simpson and Scott had wiggled out of the affair, to render a verdict and a penalty. Janes thought Lanahan to be guilty, and Ames pronounced him innocent.[1568] Because the two Bishops had split, the case of the Methodist Episcopal Church against John Lanahan was dropped.

Simpson Exonerates Carlton

Both Carlton and Lanahan were unseated and replaced by Reuben Nelson and John Phillips. Two years after the General Conference had acquitted him, Carlton died of kidney failure and Simpson preached his funeral. In his *Cyclopaedia*, Simpson exonerated Carlton:

> Between 1868 and 1872, there were rumors of some irregularity and loss through some of the employees. A very earnest and somewhat painful discussion took place respecting the general management. The agents were divided in judgment, and the members of the book committee were unable to agree as to the facts involved. The matter was referred to the General Conference of 1872, and was carefully examined by a large committee, composed in part of men eminent for business ability as well as for integrity. The conclusion arrived at was, "That frauds had been practiced in the bindery by which the Book Concern has suffered loss, but in no other department of the Concern." That there had "been irregularities in the management of the business." But there were no "reasonable grounds to presume that any agent or assistant agent is or has been implicated or interested in any frauds."[1569]

1567 LOC, Simpson papers, Letter to Ellen, n. d., Container three.
1568 Lanahan, 261.
1569 *Cyclopaedia*, 119-120.

Lanahan returned to Washington, D.C., serving as a pastor for Foundry Church where Rutherford Hayes attended. In all likelihood, he again became a critical Washington correspondent for Simpson. Bygones became bygones, as the Simpson family chose Lanahan to be one of the Bishop's pall bearers. After Simpson's death, Lanahan wrote the son, Matthew Verner Simpson:

> My correspondence with my true greatly loved friend, Your honored Father, kind, I destroyed all the letters I received from him. Of this I informed him, when the Book Concern ring boasted falsely, of having one or more of his letters to me.
>
> My rule was, after carefully reading to put them beyond the possibility of accident. All he wrote was honorable to him, but it was best not to have him quoted in that struggle with dishonest men. Most profoundly do I revere & cherish the memory of your dear father. And I am glad to learn that his memoir is to come from so prominent a person as my friend, Dr. Crooks.[1570]

Simpson and Lay Representation Triumph

The revelation of Methodist vice and crime was not the total agenda for the 1872 General Conference. On the opening day of the Denomination's quadrennial meeting, Matthew Simpson stood and made an announcement for which he had dreamed and fought over the last decade. For the first time in the Methodist Episcopal Church, there were lay delegates at the General Conference and some of them were the Bishop's close friends: James Harlan, John Evans, and Washington DePauw. Simpson announced the accomplishment of which he had been the chief architect.

> The last General Conference devised a plan for lay delegation, which was then recommended to the godly consideration of our ministers and people. In connection with this plan, they had directed the Bishops to lay before the Annual Conferences a proposed alteration of the second restrictive rule and to report the result of the vote thereon to the General Conference. In compliance with said action, we laid before each of the Annual Conferences the proposition to alter the Second Restrictive Rule by adding thereto the word "ministerial" after the word "one" and after the word "forty-five," nor more than two lay delegates for any Annual Conference. Every Conference voted on said proposition and the aggregate result is as follows. For the proposed change: 4,915, against the proposed change: 1,597.[1571]

1570 UMA, Drew University, Crooks papers, Letter August 4, 1886.
1571 *Journal of the 1872 General Conference*, 39.

Simpson did not actively advocate lay representation until 1863, but when he finally did, he became its most influential spokesman. Early in the year, Daniel Ross, a New York businessman, wrote Simpson, "We need some distinguished name, and the desires of all the brethren point to you .... I know it is not Methodistical for a Bishop to enter into a progressive movement, but it seems to me that we must carry on the thing bravely or it will fail of success."[1572] Simpson consented to speak at the first Layman's Conference of Methodists at the John Street Church, New York in March and then again May 13-14, 1863 at St. Paul's Methodist Church, New York.[1573] Simpson appealed to history in that Methodism in its beginning had been a lay movement. Class leaders were appointed, stewards were called into action, exhorters were licensed, local preachers were selected, and there came up out of the ranks of the church a body of laymen to spread personal holiness through the church. "And what was the nature of the attack made on Methodism? It was attacked on this very ground–that it was profaning holy things; that it was calling laymen to the exercise of ecclesiastical functions–and if you read the records of those times, and the history of the contents of those times, you will find that Wesley and the early Methodists were charged with this special crime of intruding men into the sacred office who were unfit for the position."[1574] Simpson then referenced a personal habit which he had consistently practiced.

> And while as ministers we are more competent to discuss theological questions than our brethren in the laity. (Shame on us if we were not, when we give our time and hearts to these subjects and claim a divine call.) They are far more competent than we to discuss financial and business questions. In my own business I consult these lay brethren rather than rely on my own judgment. As a minister of the church of Christ, I want in great financial measures, to go to my lay brethren. I want to ask them what they think upon these great subjects and great plans. I want them side by side with the ministry, and I would defer to their judgment and business as their defer to mine in theology.[1575]

1572 Crooks, 415.
1573 Ibid., 416–417.
1574 "Bishop Simpson on Lay Representation," *Zion's Daily Herald*, Vol. 34 (June 3, 1863).
1575 Crooks, 420.

Simpson then turned his appeal into a death bed covenant, a dying wish, or at least he thought he was dying:

> As you know, I went abroad a few years ago, and was taken ill. I doubted whether I should get home. I reached my home, however, and lay sick for a length of time on a bed from which my friends thought I would never rise. I looked over the church. I determined God helping me, if I had strength enough before the dying moment came, to issue an address to the church in this question of Lay Representation.[1576]

Crooks claimed that hostility broke out against Simpson, and some separated themselves from the Bishop fearing guilt by association. Franklin Rand from Boston wrote, "I was at the Layman's Convention: sorry I had no opportunity of seeing you. Indeed, I was almost afraid that my intimacy with lay representation would compromise you with some of the opposing brethren."[1577] Looking back on the decision, Simpson interpreted the constitutional change as a matter of expediency and less of theological or historical conviction. Travel had become more convenient and less expensive, plus "as the church grew in strength and in members, and as property in churches, in educational institutions, in publishing houses, and in other forms was accumulated, a desire became manifest that the laity of the church should have some voice in arranging its general plans."[1578]

Merchant Princes of the Land

Not only could Simpson bask in legislative triumph, but American Methodism continued to show robust growth. Simpson presented the numbers, results that would dwarf any financial miscues in the New York Publishing House. For the preceding quadrennium, 1868-1872, the number of churches had increased from 11,121 to 13,440. The value of churches and parsonages had increased from $41,246,734 to $56,911.900.[1579] For the previous quadrennium, 1864-1868, the value of church properties had increased almost exactly $9,000,000, but for the quadrennium immediately passed, 1868-1872, the value of church properties had grown by

---

1576 Ibid., 425.
1577 Ibid., 427.
1578 *Cyclopaedia*, 530.
1579 *Journal of the 1872 General Conference*, 454.

$15,665,166. The "Pastoral Address" countered with, "the perils attending a large increase of our church members should not be overlooked. We must not relax discipline, sacrifice, and spirituality for more worldly influence and numerical strength."[1580] The Education Committee saw nothing wrong with worldly influence and numerical strength. It responded that, "In 1866 the Methodist Episcopal Church completed her first hundred years, once feeble, she was now strong; still gathering from the poor, she has come to count among her numbers the merchant princes of the land"[1581]

One of those "merchant princes" was Thomas J. Duncan from Pittsburgh, who had willed to Simpson $30,000 nine months earlier which would probably double because of additional property in the bequest.[1582] Duncan became wealthy through oil investments in Pit Hole City, Pennsylvania. Sometime in 1864, he developed respiratory problems, and in August of 1865, he was struck in the head with an errant piece of lumber. The rest of his life was filled with excruciating pain, which at times led to aberrant behavior. Eleven days before he died, he registered his will, liberally taking care of Simpson and the Methodist Church. Relatives disputed the will of the wifeless, childless Duncan, and the combatants paraded no less than seventeen doctors through the court hearings, testifying for or against Duncan's sanity when he filed his will. The court favored the plaintiffs, and it is doubtful that Simpson ever received his $30,000.[1583]

Women's Suffrage, but …

From the 1872 General Conference in New York, Simpson skipped over to St. Paul's and gave a lecture, "The Past Ten Years" subtitled by the newspaper as "The Wonderful Progress of the World Between 1861-1872."[1584] Simpson emphasized material prosperity and intellectual culture. Technological accomplishments, enabled by financial wealth, included the transcontinental

---

1580 Ibid. 445.
1581 Ibid., 702.
1582 "A Windfall for Bishop Simpson," *The Cleveland Morning Herald* (August 5, 1871).
1583 R. Gregory Lande. *The Abraham Man: Madness, Malingering and the Development of Medical Testimony* (New York: Algora Publishing, 2012) 135-136.
1584 Matthew Simpson, "The Past Ten Years," LOC, Simpson papers, Scrapbook D, Container twenty-three.

railroad, the opening of the Suez Canal, and laying of a cable across the Atlantic. But the gloating was far more than technological. America had "overturned monarchies," "set up Republics" and "stood today foremost among the nations of the earth." There had been remarkable discoveries in the North Pole and Africa, not least of which was the finding of David Livingston by a newspaper reporter, Henry Stanley. There was still work to be done, in particular women's suffrage. A newspaper reported that Simpson "had no sympathy with strong-willed women or free love, etc. but for twenty years he had been fervently convinced that intemperance, prostitution, etc., cannot be overthrown until we can command women's influence thereon."[1585] (Did the reporter hear Simpson correctly or did not Simpson believe that Susan Anthony and Frances Willard were strong-willed women?) The newspaper concluded, "The Bishop next pointed out that the proud position in various aspects that America occupies today in the eyes of the world and gave reasons therefore. And we have taken the position within the past ten years. The Bishop closed with a beautiful apostrophe to America."[1586]

Simpson never fully identified with "Women's Suffrage." His argument for the "vote" was more pragmatic than egalitarian. The vote of women would enable America to defeat vice, in particular alcohol. In 1873, he addressed the women's "Constitutional Convention," and argued for a women's suffrage amendment. His argument for equality came from observation. "I have known men with wives more talented, brighter, more able to judge than themselves; better able, therefore to decide upon public business, as well as all the other business that falls to the household." Concerning the result of women being allowed to go to the polls, Simpson made his normative, utopian prediction: "[W]oman's refinement would refine her husband and her brother; that the polls would no longer be as they are now, foul and disgusting places of obscenity and political debotchery, but would through her be exalted into something better."[1587]

Simpson did not accept the invitation of Lucy Stone to become President of the American Women's Suffrage Association.[1588] When Frances Willard

---

1585   Ibid.
1586   Ibid.
1587   UMA, Drew University, Simpson papers, "Woman's Suffrage," February 5, 1873.
1588   LOC, Simpson papers, Letter, Lucy Stone to Matthew Simpson, October 16,

requested to speak on behalf of temperance to the 1880 General Conference, the Bishops responded "no." Frances Willard wrote concerning Simpson and his colleagues, "Grave, dignified clergymen who had always been my friends, look curiously upon me as if I were, somehow, a little daft .... I will not write here the names of the good Bishops, almost as dear to me as my own brothers, who passed by on the other side, not wishing to commit themselves, also not wishing to hurt my feelings at this crisis."[1589]

Regarding abolition, women's suffrage, the holiness movement, and many other issues, Simpson hardly ever moved beyond the proscription of his office. "Lay representation" may have been the one exception. For instance, Simpson's support for the "Ladies and Pastors Christian Union," paradoxically ensured for women both containment and liberation. At the organization's first anniversary meeting in 1869, Simpson stated, "The object of this association is not that woman shall take the pulpit, or engage in any work that may be questionable, but simply to go forward in the discharge of those duties that woman has ever performed, *though not systematically and regularly.*"[1590]

Simpson the Lecturer

In spite of not allowing his name to be listed in the *Directory of the National Literary Association*, a clearing house for lecturers, Simpson found himself besieged by requests. Even though he had pledged to Ellen to resist overtaxing his time and energy, his schedule suggested otherwise. In the last six months of 1867, Simpson received forty-four invitations to lecture. Because of the spottiness of his *Diary*, it is difficult to detect how many of

---

1873, Container nine.

1589   Willard, *Glimpses*, 615-616.
Willard did not allow this slight to diminish her reverence for Simpson. Two years after the Bishop's death, she wrote Ellen,
I remember the wonderful sermons that so influenced my purposes in life; the prayers, unequalled by any ever heard save those in which the Bishop poured out his great heart to God for deliverance to his country, when the Civil War was at its height. I was so wrought upon by one of them that I did what never in my life do I recall having done save then-- lifted my head and gazed upon the face of one who prayed. That face was lofty, wrapted, inspired as ever Hebrew prophet's shone in hours of holiest communIon with Jehovah!) [This insert will become a newly added FN]. UMA, Drew University, Simpson papers, Letter August 1, 1886.

1590   Russell E. Richey, Kenneth E. Rowe, and Jean Miller Schmidt. *The Methodist Experience in America: A History* Vol. I (Nashville: Abingdon Press, 2010) 235.

them he accepted. For the first half of 1871, we learn that, in a twenty-six day span from April 24-May 10, Simpson lectured twelve times, approximately every other day plus preaching on the weekends. During this time he gave only two separate lectures, "Our Country" and "Bismarck and Napoleon." On June 21, 1871 he recorded,

> This day I am sixty years old. How time flies. I am admonished that my day is nearly over. The sun declines, the shadows lengthen. The night cometh. What my hand finds to do, should be done quickly, earnestly, faithfully. Yet health fails, and friends say 'I must rest.' Rest is in the grave. Work the master says, while it is still light, yet I should be prudent. I must watch the body more. I must avoid exposure and fatigue– specially I must seek regularity in sleep & food for my stomach threatens to rebel. But above all, let me learn to be more like Christ–less of self and more of Jesus in thoughts, deeds, work. I commenced reading the Bible again on yesterday, both Old and New Testament. It is the only book that never grows old–that never tire-something new, fresh, living all the time.[1591]

Avoiding fatigue and irregularity in food and sleep were vain resolutions. The constant life of travel did not admit of regularity in much of anything. Keeping in mind that the Bishop was almost always the guest in a home, there was the obligation to regale his hosts with the latest ecclesiastical and political news, until whatever time of night. And, "I must rest," was wishful thinking. There was no diminution in Simpson's schedule. If anything, it increased. He was not able to fulfill the sincere desire that he expressed to Ellen, March 26, 1871: "Often I wish I had no cares, no business, no lectures, and had only to preach the gospel, the glorious gospel."[1592]

One of Simpson's earliest lectures (1856) was, "The Influence of the Bible upon Languages," by which Simpson meant the English Bible. Simpson attempted to answer the question, "Shall there be a time when all men shall utter their thought in a universal, comprehensive tongue." The assumption was that a universal language would be good, but it was not so much the Bible that would accomplish "one tongue," but education. "Provincialism springs up in an ignorant society …. In the South, the Negro population exemplifies the same truth …. but let any of these colored men read & study & you hear from him nothing of the Negro dialect."

1591   LOC, Simpson papers, 1871 *Diary*, Container two.
1592   LOC, Simpson papers, Letter March 26, 1871, Container three.

Simpson traced the division of tongues to the tower of Babel, but did not point to the Day of Pentecost in Acts II as the reversal. The result of sin and ignorance was, "impossible moats– walls and towers," but the walls are falling down. "Language separates us into parties–or preserves old walls of distinction, which also have long crumbled in the dust, thus holding separate those who might unite in efforts for mutual elevation." In other words, the old walls symbolically still existed.[1593] Of course, this transition would not be as simple or as Anglo as Simpson interpreted history and thus, prophesied. He concluded with the following illustration: An Eastern prince sent an ambassador to the Queen of England to inquire, "What is the secret to England's greatness?" She sent the prince a Bible with an attached note, "This is the secret of England's greatness."[1594]

A frequent lecture was entitled "The Crescent and the Cross." Obviously, Simpson accented the differences between Mohammad and Christ. One conquered with the sword and the other with love. The Bishop demonstrated evidence of having read the *Koran* and quoted from it. He criticized Islam for denigrating women and teaching false concepts of immortality. A reporter wrote, "But the heaven of the Prophet was like his earthly career, essentially sensual, and the lecturer gave several humorous citations from the *Koran* on that point. Among them was that all true non-believers go to heaven to be the lovers of seventy thousand houris–while all the earthly wives go to hell." But, Simpson also found positive elements in Islam: "Mohomet cultivated letters and the arts, and his teaching promulgated many great truths of Christianity even going so far as to declare the immaculate conception of Mary long before it was promulgated by the Pontiffs of Rome." (Either Simpson or the reporter was confused at this point. In all likelihood the reporter, because Simpson would have believed in the Virgin birth, but would have not believed that Mary was without sin.) Then Simpson seemed to contradict himself in that,

---

1593 In some ways, Simpson's argument adumbrated Thomas Friedman's *The World is Flat*. According to Friedman, the walls came down (Berlin), and the Windows went up (Microsoft, a universal language) to remove the planet which separates disparate peoples. Thomas Friedman. *The World is Flat: A Brief History of the Twenty-first Century* (New York: Picador/Farrar and Giroux, 2007).

1594 "City and Vicinity: Bishop Simpson's Lecture" (Buffalo: January 24, 1856), lecture: "The Influence of the Bible upon Languages," unidentified newspaper, LOC, Simpson papers, Container fifteen.

"There has been but little art and no science fostered among them ..."[1595] The mosques of Islam are both outstanding aesthetic and scientific achievements.

The lecture on Bismarck and Napoleon demonstrated Simpson's fascination with well-known personalities of history, particularly Napoleon Bonaparte; but in this case Simpson was speaking of the conqueror's nephew, Louis Napoleon. After giving a summary biography on Louis, the lecturer condemned his egocentricity. "He was always pretending to work for the glory of France, when really he was only ministering to his own aggrandizement of honors .... While always appearing to work for the firm establishment of the French government, he was truly fortifying his own throne." Even though Bismarck was profligate in his early years, having fought twenty-one duels, he gradually became controlled by one ruling idea, the unification of Germany. Bismarck's life was exemplified by having saved a drowning man and conspicuously wearing a medal given for the heroic deed. When asked about the medal he replied, "It merely indicates a habit of saving a man's life occasionally."[1596] For us, it merely indicates the lack of entertainment options for the late nineteenth century, not to speak of Simpson's ability to hold an audience with esoteric material. However, Louis Napoleon and Bismarck were contemporaries of Simpson. Thus, Simpson's lecture served as today's "situation room," the opportunity to hear the "spin" of a well-versed and traveled authority.

The response to Simpson's lectures was not always favorable. When Simpson lectured on "The Mission of America" in Boston, the *Boston Daily Advertiser* took him to task. There was too much "buncombe" in the lecture, and the editor was correct in noting that the Bishop's theme should have been announced as *manifest destiny*. What Boston's citizens needed to be taught was "wisdom in this time of their peril; to be told of their dangers and duties rather than of their greatness and virtue; and to learn if possible, some of that prudent self-distrust, which is as far from timidity as it is from foolhardiness."[1597]

1595 "Matthew Simpson: The Crescent and the Cross," *Daily Cleveland Herald* (Feb. 1, 1870).

1596 *Cleveland Morning Herald* (Feb. 9, 1871).

1597 "Bishop Simpson on the Mission of America," *The Boston Daily Advertiser* (November 22, 1867).

A measurement of lecturing success was the size of the honorarium, which was hardly ever contractual or predetermined. The range was anywhere from $25 to $400, and the monetary reward or lack thereof often left Simpson depressed. He expressed his disappointment to Ellen that one effort had netted only $25.75, but rejoiced that at Cincinnati, 1,500 tickets had been sold.[1598] For speaking at Chautauqua, Simpson was promised "Anything you want, $200 and expenses or $300 and expenses, but our committee say we must have you."[1599] Was Simpson supposed to respond, "I think I would rather have $300 rather than $200, because $300 is $100 more than $200?" Another invitation to Chautauqua by John Vincent promised $300 for two lectures, "You to pay your own expenses."[1600]

Off to Europe and the Death of Uncle Matthew

In the summer of 1873, Cora Richardson painted the sixty-two-year-old Matthew Simpson, as he sat in her studio in New York City.[1601] The painting was unveiled for public viewing December 8 at the Academy of Design. It was by far the most flattering portrait of the Bishop ever accomplished. Richardson captured her subject with a visionary gaze, left hand under right breast lapel, his right hand on his Bible as it rested on a table. His hair, parted on the left side, still maintained its youthful reddish glow. His ears are large, nose prominent, eyebrows heavy, lips pursed ready to utter a profound insight. Richardson, by use of color which emphasized a ruddy complexion, captured a serene, dignified composure transcending the swirling aggravations of ecclesiastical duties. The eyes portray wisdom and discernment, the ability to see the possibilities of grace and the progress of humanity, an optimism of high expectations for the Church which he governed and the nation in which he believed. Whatever may have been his daily attire, Simpson was clothed by the artist with a formal cutaway black coat, extended to his knees and starched high collar accented with a thin white bowtie. The *New York Christian*

1598   UMA, Drew University, Simpson papers, Letters, Matthew to Ellen, January 13, 1860, and November 29, 1860.

1599   LOC, Simpson papers, Letter June 4, 1879, Container twelve.

1600   UMA. E. PA Conference of the UMC, St. George's UMC, Philadelphia, PA: Simpson papers, Letter April 21, 1882.

1601   "Portrait of Bishop Simpson," LOC, Simpson papers, Scrapbook D, Container twenty-three.

Advocate "hoped" that the painting "may be brought to some place where it may readily be seen by the Bishop's many admirers."[1602] Where the painting was placed immediately after the New York Exhibition, is unknown. In the 1920s, it was hung in Simpson Hall of the Wesley Building, Seventeenth and Arch Streets, Philadelphia. The painting now resides at Drew University in a small room in Mead Hall, and is seen by very few people.

On the 1875 expedition to Europe, an extensive trip which included fifteen cities, Simpson was impressed by the zeal of the indigenous Methodists.[1603] He reported from Milan: "We held our session for two days during which time we examined carefully the condition of the work at each station and heard from each preacher the report of his labors and of his dangers and persecution. In the smaller places, our preachers are exposed to many hardships and frequently insulted, and they are sometimes in positive danger, but thus far they have graciously persevered." From Milan he traveled to Frankfurt where on Sunday morning he preached to "between two and three thousand people."[1604]

During this trip, shortly after Richardson's stellar portrayal of the Bishop, a photographer captured Simpson sitting with fellow pastors and missionaries in Milan, Italy. This photograph is the most accurate representation of how Simpson actually appeared, of any we have in existence. Dwarfed by a man sitting beside him, thirteen native Italian preachers standing behind the two, Simpson stares into the camera, his right arm resting on the arm of the chair and his left leg over his right knee. He is dressed in a cutaway black, wide-lapel coat, a dark vest beneath, as are most of the others, all of them covered with a light sprinkling of dust. Simpson's face is expressionless. His salt and pepper hair is parted on the left side, combed across his forehead. There is no excess weight on his frame, and his long, boney fingers droop over the chair arm. No ornamentation accented his dress, such as a watch and chain,

---

1602   Ibid.

1603   Matthew Simpson, "Notes of Trip to Mexico 1874, Italy 1875," LOC, Simpson papers, Container fifteen. Simpson's itinerary included Liverpool, Antwerp, Paris, Florence, and Milan, several towns in Switzerland, Frankfurt, Prague, Uppsala, Stockholm, and Copenhagen. Simpson chaired the Germany and Switzerland Conference in Heilbronn, Württemberg July 8-14, 1875. *Minutes of the 1875 Annual Conferences* (New York: Nelson and Phillips, 1875) 81-82.

1604   "Notes of Trip."

which were then fashionable. Short, black boots adorned his feet, and a white collar with a white bow tie graced his neck.[1605]

While in Milan, the Bishop received sorrowful news that must have been somewhat expected. The telegraph from Ellen simply read, "Uncle died today. What shall we do? Pittsburgh all well. January 28, 1874."[1606] The nephew instructed that the body be sent from Allegheny, Pennsylvania to Philadelphia, where his funeral would be held at the Simpson residence, 1807 Mount Vernon Street. The ninety-eight-year-old man had been the single most influential person in his nephew's life. On June 28, 1836, the young Pittsburgh pastor had expressed sincere gratitude to his Uncle.

> Surely you cannot think I could forget, while this heart beats or this mind acts, one who has been so long the object of my warmest regard, one who "raised the tender mind," who gave me what little intellectual culture I may possess, and to whose precepts which have placed me where I am. Can I forget that uncle who nursed me frequently in his arms, sang to me in gleeful mood, turned my infant mind to science, supplied me with books, introduced me to public life, filled my mind with moral and religious sentiments, followed me from home with prayers and his fondest wishes, and, to use his own expression, felt that "his life was bound up in the lad's life?" Can I forget that uncle? No, Never, "while life or thought or being lasts or immortality endures."[1607]

Uncle Matthew moved to Cincinnati circa 1842 with his niece, Hetty, and her husband, George McCullough. When the McCullough's moved to Baltimore during the Civil War, Uncle Matthew with his sister-in-law, Sarah, moved to Philadelphia to live with the Bishop, where he stayed for approximately ten years. For some reason, Uncle Matthew after the death of Sarah, his sister-in-law, moved to Allegheny County to live with Sarah Kennedy.[1608] To George Crooks, the Bishop's biographer, she recounted the

---

1605   UMA, Drew University, Simpson papers, photo on file.

1606   LOC, Simpson papers, Telegraph: Ellen Simpson to Matthew Simpson, Enero (January) 28, 1874, Container nine.

1607   LOC, Simpson papers, Letter January 28, 1836, Container three.

1608   I have not been able to identify this Sarah Kennedy. She was married to Billy Kennedy, a participant at the Bishop's funeral. I suspect she was a granddaughter of William Simpson, brother of James and Matthew. William died young, 1823, leaving a widow and six sons of whom we know nothing. Uncle Matthew had a soft spot in his heart for the widows of his deceased brothers, Groh, 439. Bishop Matthew Simpson was very fond of this Sarah, having written letters to her and all four of her children. On November 7, 1865

last hours of Uncle Matthew's life.

> And now, with sacred love and with feelings of deep reverence, do I speak of the last hours of our dear Uncle Matthew. Yes, I can truly say, that his last days were as peaceful and tranquil, as had marked his whole life of almost a century.
>
> About 5 o'clock of the afternoon of Uncle's death, my children were sitting around his chair as they were want to do, when returning from school, in order to have his assistance in their next day's lessons.
>
> It was on this afternoon that one of them read aloud, a scientific article by Proctor. Incoming to a long technical word which she mispronounced, Uncle stopped her, and gave her the proper pronunciation.
>
> After that, he requested them to sing "Rock of Ages." When singing the last verse, he opened his eyes, and looked long and earnestly at each one of them, closing them again, without speaking. At 7 o'clock, the same evening, uncle was asleep in Jesus. We did not think death was near, for he suffered none and his mental facilities were bright and clear.[1609]

No doubt, emotions and memories flooded the Bishop's consciousness as he remembered the spiritual and intellectual influence of the foremost mentor in his life. Simpson telegraphed Nathaniel Holmes in Pittsburgh to take care of the details in transporting the body to Philadelphia. The nephew had last visited his uncle on February 3, 1873. He recorded no content of the conversation.[1610] No one was a greater friend in time of need than Nathaniel Holmes. Simpson was seldom in Pittsburgh that he did not

---

he wrote, "The letter you sent to me at Canton in which I told you I had not received, after I left they received it and sent it to me two days after you left Phila. It told me all as you said about poor Evelyn's sickness. I wrote two letters to her but got no answer to either. On February 24, 1870 he wrote, "I had intended to write to all your children at intervals, and having written to Inez some time ago, I thought it is about time I should write to Arthur, thus intending to take them seriatim, but yesterday I received a letter from Tempie and am closing one from Essie. I was so glad I thought I would sit down this very minute and write an answer of thanks to each of the little darlings that had all adorned my heart but thought again I will put it off til tomorrow came, and I must write but just then a letter from Arthur arrived in which he tells me he has found a Saviour and has joined the church." UMA, Drew University, Simpson papers, Letters from Matthew Simpson to Sarah Kennedy, November 7, 1869, and February 24, 1870.

1609   UMA, Drew University, Simpson papers, Letter from Sarah Kennedy to George Crooks, August 16, 1888.

1610   LOC, Simpson papers, 1873 *Diary*, Container two.

call on Holmes.[1611]

Simpson's trips to Europe always confirmed, at least for him, the superiority of Protestant America. Nations that had rejected Christianity were failing, especially those adopting "Mohammedism." As he stood before a Boston congregation in November of 1875, he declared that "nothing had been yet found able to elevate the world, and form the permanent basis of government except Christianity ..." Frightened Catholicism was retreating as the spiritual armies of Protestantism demonstrated their superior ability to elevate and to educate. "No Protestant state had gone over to the Catholics, but many Catholics states had turned to Protestantism."[1612] The survival of Catholicism in America was not due to its existence as a viable religious option, but due to Catholic emigration. If it occurred to him that his Scotch-Irish ancestry had something to do with his religious development, he did not mention it. He had much reason to reflect on his spiritual heritage in the ensuing year after the death of his Uncle.

The Evolution Explosion

In 1859, Charles Darwin dropped a bomb on Christianity from which it has never recovered. Darwin, who had earlier trained for the ministry, a great intellect and perhaps the foremost botanist, zoologist, and anthropologist of the nineteenth century, did not intentionally target Christianity. The 1859 best seller, *Origin of Species*, had little to say about the origins of human kind, and made only faint allusion to the "creation story." The author argued for natural selection, survival of the fittest, and why instincts and other innate traits allow some to live and while others perish. "Looking still more remotely to the future we may predict that owing to the continued and steady increase of the larger groups, a multitude of smaller groups will be utterly extinct

---

[1611] LOC, Simpson papers, *Diary* entries for February 13, 1869, March 19, 1880, June 23, 1880, and Jan. 11, 1883, Container two. This Nathaniel Holmes was the son of the senior, who died in 1849. The first Nathaniel Holmes was Simpson's parishioner at Liberty Street Church in Pittsburgh. Of him, Simpson wrote: "Shortly before leaving Ireland, he was converted, and being industrious and frugal, he gradually improved his property until he established a banking-house in 1822, which has been continued by his sons and grandson without interruption and without having suffered in its credit in any of the financial revulsions through which the country has passed." *Cyclopaedia*, 448.

[1612] "A Sermon by the Rev. Bishop Matthew Simpson," *Boston Daily Advertiser* (November 4, 1875).

and consequently that of the species living at one period, extremely few will transmit descendants to a remote futurity."[1613] While in this first work, Darwin did not deny the Judeo-Christian understanding of human origin, he left no room for God's design or providence. In Darwin's paradigm, the influence of nature left little or nothing to divine influence; nature's law had replaced nature's God. "As species are produced and exterminated by slowly acting and still existing causes, and not by acts of miraculous creation …. To my mind it accords better with what we know of the laws impressed on matter by the Creator, that, the production and extinction of the past and present inhabitants of the world should have been due to secondary causes like those determining the birth and death of the individual."[1614]

In his *Descent of Man*, 1871, Darwin published what he thought were the inductive and logical conclusions of his extensive observations on both animal and plant life. "We thus learn that man is descended from a hairy, tailed quadruped, probably arboreal in its habits, and an inhabitant of the Old World. This creature, if its whole structure had been examined by a naturalist would have been classed among the quadrumana, as surely as the still more ancient progenitors of the Old and New world monkeys."[1615] And from where did the monkey come? "This animal seems to be more like the larvae of the existing marine Ascidians than any other known form."[1616]

Darwin admitted the problems of his theory: animals are not moral creatures, possess no language, do not quest for immortality, and are intellectually deficient. Darwin's basic answer to these critical issues was that deficiencies would have been apparent in primitive human kind, barbarian races that exhibit the primeval beliefs of savages. "The idea of a universal and beneficent creator does not arise in the mind of man, until he has been elevated by long continued culture."[1617] It must have occurred to Darwin, who was a genius, that his answer raised more questions than it resolved for his "common origin." Why are Homo sapiens the only species to have

---

1613   Charles Darwin. *Origin of Species* (New York: Barnes and Noble Classics, 2014).
1614   Ibid., 383.
1615   Charles Darwin. *The Descent of Man* (Amherst, New York: Prometheus Books, 1998) 632.
1616   Ibid., 632.
1617   Ibid., 636.

evolved into a language speaking, art producing, soul searching creature? Obviously time and space, not to say knowledge, do not allow us at this point to adequately respond to Darwin. Our purpose is to examine Simpson's response to the largest wrench which had been thrown into the cogs of the smooth running wheels of nineteenth century American Christianity. Even if Darwin was not correct, evolution's erosion on Christianity was, and remains, a historical fact.

Simpson Missed a Critical Opportunity

Simpson had taught natural science and throughout life collected clippings on geology, zoology, ornithology, and ongoing scientific discoveries. The man who lectured on Islam and Christianity, Romanism and Christianity, Progress and Christianity, never gave one lecture on Evolution and Christianity. Simpson was a polymath who possessed a curious mind with a desire to learn everything about everything. And if he desired fame, he missed a critical opportunity.[1618] The ecclesiastic who may have been best equipped of all American clergymen to speak on "evolution," at no time and no place did he render a systematic treatment of Darwin's thesis. He could only throw out uninformed references, tacit opinions on an issue that he had not bothered to investigate. When standing in the Grand Opera House in San Francisco in 1877, Simpson declared:

> But then they tell me that the system of evolution does seem to overturn Christianity. If it be true that things were evolved from some first types, how can it be that the Bible is true? But the Bible doesn't tell me exactly how things were evolved. I don't say evolution is true or untrue. There's a great deal about it not proved, and if I were in a jury

---

1618 Simpson could have gained publicity by accepting Robert Ingersoll's challenge to a debate, "Colonel Ingersoll is reported to have recently said that he would be willing to enter into a debate with such a man as Monsignor Capel, but with a no less representative, person. Were he to discuss with a Methodist, he would choose Bishop Simpson. 'I do not care to enter a discussion of this kind,' said Bishop Simpson. 'Not that I am afraid to meet Mr. Ingersoll in argument, but I think such controversies are productive of no good. I would refuse to meet any other man on the same grounds. I have passed this much of my life without entering into such matters,' he said, as he ran his hand through his snowy hair, 'and I hardly think I will do so now. My duties are active; the demands upon my time are imperative; so, even if I felt the inclination, it would be next to impossible for me to enter into controversy. Such a thing can be answered on paper better than with speech.'" *The Atchison Globe*, Atchison, KS (February 25, 1884).

box I would give the old Scotch verdict "not proven." I don't deny it but I've not seen the matter proven but suppose it true. Here's a watchmaker who makes a perfect watch. There are so many jewels, the wheels are all jeweled and it is a wonderful piece of machinery. Suppose the artist could not only produce that watch, keeping such excellent time, but suppose further he can produce a watch that will make other watches, and every watch it makes be better than the preceding--a more perfect timepiece --why it would exalt my ideas of the skill of the artist. And so they tell me the theory of evolution: that God made certain types of first creatures, and they have been evolving and producing better ones and better ones until man is evolved, and man is getting higher and more intellectual. Well now, if that is true, if my father and God did all that, he is more grand and glorious even than I had conceived the idea of.[1619]

For a fundraising service at Roberts Park Church in Indianapolis on November of 1879, the newspaper headlined the event, "His View of the Scriptural Origin of the Doctrine of Evolution." The newspaper reported that an "immense congregation" attended, making "necessary the placing of chairs in the aisles and all the vacant spaces available." Simpson announced his text as I Corinthians 13:12. "For now we see through a glass darkly, but then face to face, now we know in part then shall we know even as we are known." The text provided the springboard for Simpson to say,

> My friends that are so anxious that Christianity shall be considered a failure because it has not yet conquered the Earth are lavish of time on all other subjects. They are very certain that man sprang from monkeys and monkeys from something lower down. There has been a law of evolution that has brought up everything out of the very lowest. Well, I am not saying there is not. It is not my purpose to attack that system at all. But if in the great workings of God, the facts are that ever since the records of men, there is no evidence of man's frame having changed one particle, and in all historic time there is no evidence of a monkey growing into man nor one animal into another–I am not saying they never do– but if in 6,000 years there has not been any change–and yet my friends tell me there were these great changes–why not give us a little more than 1800 years to change the face of this whole world and to change man intellectually and raise him to the highest possible degree?[1620]

1619   LOC, Simpson papers, newspaper article, "Work and Mission of Christianity: No Conflict between Science and Religion" Scrapbook D, Container twenty-three.

1620   LOC, Simpson papers, "Roberts Park Church Sermon: Yesterday's Morning Service by Bishop Matthew Simpson: His Views of the Scriptural Origin of the Doctrine of Evolution," Scrapbook D, Container twenty-three. The newspaper caption misrepresented Simpson. He did not argue for the "scriptural origin" of evolution.

Had one listened carefully to the above sermon, the listener may have concluded that evolution and the spread of Christianity were opposite sides of the same coin: "Christian thought is permeating the world. I read of the advancement of man from the animal to the intellectual, from the child is developed intellect and spirituality .... They may start their cars in another direction, and for another purpose; but they all point in the same direction. The world is becoming more like Christ."[1621]

On "Emancipation Day," (retirement of debt) January 27, 1884, at Metropolitan Church in Washington DC, though Simpson did not mention evolution, he declared, "Science was like the handmaid of Christianity. The light of science was like the dawn of day. It was the handmaid of religion and the precursor of religion."[1622] What did Simpson mean by the "precursor of religion?" Could an auditor have concluded that science was the foundation of knowledge rather than Scripture? In all probability, Simpson had not read any recent science, in particular, primary sources such as Darwin, Spencer and other seminal thinkers of the late nineteenth century. In response to Darwin, Simpson could have said that animals can bury their deceased, but do not build monuments; they can howl but do not compose music; they can remember, but do not create narratives; can be devoted to their masters, but do not enter into corporate worship; and they are naturally ornamented, but do not decorate themselves with clothing or jewelry. Had Simpson read Darwin, he would have known that the creation story as founded in Genesis 1-2, is fundamentally incompatible with the last line of *The Descent of Man*. "We must however acknowledge, as it seems to me, that man with all of his noble qualities with sympathies which feel for the most debased, with benevolence which extends not only to the other men but to the humblest living creature, with his God-like intellect, which but penetrated into the movements and constitution of the solar system–with all these excellent powers–man still bears in his bodily frame the indelible stamp of his lowly origin."[1623]

1621   Quoted in Kirby, *Ecclesiastical and Social Thought*, 286.
1622   "The Day of Jubilee-The Metropolitan ME Church Celebrates Its Deliverance, Eloquent Bishop Simpson on the Prophecies," LOC, Simpson papers, Scrapbook D, Container twenty-three.
1623   *Descent*, 643.

Broad and Catholic Views

Had Darwin changed the word "lowly" to the word "divine," Christianity and Darwin's evolution could have been forever dancing in a symphonic rhapsody. But unfortunately, Simpson had unwittingly steered the ship of Zion into a tumultuous storm for which he could not, or would not, provide a compass to navigate between two worlds that were oceans apart. At the 1875 New Jersey Annual Conference Simpson stated, "Originally the only test of Methodism was a desire to flee from the wrath to come and a desire to be saved from their sins, and today Methodism stands on the most liberal form of the Christian Church."[1624] Liberalism would have not been true of American Methodism in 1875, but seemingly Simpson was leading his mother denomination in that direction. It is no wonder John Vincent said to him, "You are so broad, bishop, in your views, so catholic, so full of humanity that we cannot afford to lose you."[1625] *The Washington Standard* stated of Simpson, "The Bishop is a gentleman of culture and ability and one of the ablest representatives of the interests and increasing influence of the Methodist Church. He has enlarged ideas of humanity in its varied phases and interests, has traveled much, is a keen observer of men and things, and is evidently one who believes the mind is the standard of man."[1626]

The suction of Simpson and Methodism into modernity was inevitable. When the world which surrounds an individual changes, cognitive dissonance intensifies, leading to personal anxiety. Accommodation becomes almost a psychological, if not a spiritual necessity. James Hunter states, concerning the accommodation of a Christian, "Given a major collision of his view of reality with an alien conception in the absence of social conditions that confirm his own beliefs, it is highly probable that his beliefs will be compromised."[1627] Simpson exhibited little to no ability or desire to think analytically about

---

[1624] LOC, Simpson papers, "Methodist Conference: Annual Meeting of the New Jersey Annual Conference," Scrapbook D, Container twenty-three.

[1625] LOC, Simpson papers, Letter, Vincent to Simpson, sometime in 1874, Container nine.

[1626] LOC, Simpson papers, Scrapbook D, Container twenty-three.

[1627] James Hunter. *American Evangelicalism: Conservative Religion and the Quandary of Modernity* (New Brunswick, New Jersey: Rutgers University Press, 1983) 13.

evolution. Had ecclesiastical duties sterilized the inquisitive mind, that in an earlier day delighted in collecting fossils, studying plant life, and igniting the scientific curiosity of his Allegheny students? There were other contemporaries who were struggling to reconcile the survival of the fittest with biblical creationism such as Louis Agassiz and Asa Gray. There is no evidence that Simpson read from either of them.

Whether one is standing in the gap between feuding friends or competing paradigms, the gap can be a lonely place, especially if one is attempting to act and speak with integrity and, at the same time, maximize the benefits of the institution which he represents. Simpson was standing on the edge of the new frontier of Christianity, "modernism." How was one to maintain biblical integrity and keep the institution that paid him to be their primary spokesman, in lockstep with society? The territory would prove as rough as the Rocky Mountain Divide.

Chapter Twenty:
The Ideal Christian Gentleman

America's Centennial Celebration in Philadelphia

Whenever Simpson had represented Methodism as a fraternal delegate at some ecumenical event or international gathering of Methodism, the ensuing General Conference heard about it, much to Simpson's satisfaction. In the 1876 Quadrennial gathering at Baltimore, Jay Rothweiler reported on Simpson's address to the Evangelical Association which had met the previous October in Philadelphia. "It is due that I should say, that the Brethren were especially pleased and greatly encouraged by the address of Bishop Simpson, which was so rich in thought, sympathetic in love, and inspiring for Christian hearts."[1628] Such reports were music in the Bishop's ears. He collected every newspaper clipping that he could find on his speaking engagements, and placed them in "scrapbooks." He referred to this process, which also included filing his letters and signing church documents as "arranging his papers," an oft evening activity.[1629]

Not only was Simpson feeling good about himself, but American Methodism had reason to boast on the nation's one-hundredth birthday. "In the infant Church had been provided a doctrine, a polity and a spirit singularly fitted to the exigencies of the rising State and destined to contribute largely to its order, unity, and progress. Gladly admitting the great usefulness of other

---

1628   *Journal of the 1876 General Conference of the Methodist Episcopal Church* (New York: Nelson and Phillips, 1876) 234.

1629   LOC, Simpson papers, 1880 *Diary*, February 19, 1880, Container two. On August 31, 1883, Simpson recorded that he, "arranged papers in a trunk." This may have been a premonition of his death.

churches and attempting no exact estimate of the usefulness of Methodism, we believe that God has given to it honor at this hour, that by its direct and indirect influence upon the natural sentiment and character, it has been a prayerful auxiliary to the Republic, and perhaps the indispensable condition of its success."[1630] Seemingly, Methodism had bought into a syllogism: God could not do without America; America could not do without Methodism, and hence, God could not do without Methodism. Methodism needed only to worry about being up-ended by the Roman Catholic Church. "Methodism must be both warned by the aggressions, and instructed by the plans of Romanism. If we keep our children in our own schools, they will lose neither in ability nor availability. They will not be likely to sink into nunneries, or to wander into skepticism."[1631] As if the convent was a high temptation for Methodist youth, and the Catholic Church majored in skepticism.

As Philadelphia's most prominent clergy citizen, Simpson was a natural to pray the dedication prayer at the Nation's Centennial Celebration. And no one anticipated the event more than the Bishop of America's largest denomination. As early as 1873 Simpson had stated, "And that celebration of the 4th of July, 1876, will, I think, give a new impulse to the cause of liberty all over the Earth. Strangers shall carry back to their lands, tidings of our civilization, of the happiness of our people, of our increased wealth, of what a Republican government can do to promote the prosperity of its people."[1632] The older Simpson got, the more nationalistic he became.

The dignitaries, who included President Grant, met at George Childs' home, at the intersection of Walnut and 22nd Streets in Philadelphia. Childs was the publisher of the *Public Ledger*, Philadelphia's most prominent newspaper. Childs ran his daily with a strict moral code, refusing liquor ads and avoiding tabloid sensationalism, while granting ample space to religious items.[1633] He purchased the cottage for Grant at Long Branch, and in all likelihood, donated to Simpson's summer home as well. Childs purchased

---

1630   1876 *Journal*, 408.

1631   Ibid., 411.

1632   *Milwaukee* (WI) *Daily Sentinel* (April 11, 1873).

1633   Charles R Deacon. "George Childs" in *A Biographical Album of Prominent Pennsylvanians: First Series. Statesmen, Military Officers, Journalists, Educators and Prominent Persons Recently Deceased* (Philadelphia: The America Biographical Publishing Company, 1888) 357-361.

and dedicated a stained-glass window to Simpson at Simpson Memorial Church in Long Branch, New Jersey.[1634] When Childs claimed that his office had been enriched by a thousand associations, the first person he mentioned was Matthew Simpson.[1635] Among the guests who had received hospitality in the Childs home were Charles Dickens, Matthew Arnold, Cornelius Vanderbilt, Herbert Spencer, Henry Longfellow, Ralph Waldo Emerson, and Ulysses Grant. Childs accompanied Simpson, when 5,000 members of the Grand Army of the Republic had crowded into Philadelphia's Academy of Music Hall in December, 1879. Grant had just returned from Europe, and reported to the cheering throng: "There is no country where the energetic man can by his own labor, and by his own industry, ingenuity and frugality, acquire competency as he can in America."[1636] In 1883, Simpson requested financial help from Childs for an "industrial school for colored young men in Atlanta."[1637]

For the opening convocation of the 1876 Centennial Celebration in Philadelphia, Frank Leslie's *Illustrated Newspaper* depicted a speaker stand on which stood the dignitaries. The artist sketched Simpson gesturing a blessing, Grant with hat off, bowed behind him. Simpson took full advantage of the opportunity, praying a prayer of over one thousand words. He interceded for America's government, the officials of the Centennial Committee, and international visitors. He thanked God, "for valuable discoveries and multiplied inventions; for labour saving machinery, relieving the toiling masses—for the books and periodicals scattered like leaves of autumn over the land; for art and science; for freedom to worship God according to the dictates of conscience; unfettered by the trammels of the State."[1638] And then sounding the note of progress, but also with an awareness of a building tension within American society, Simpson petitioned, "May the new century

---

1634 This church still stands, but belongs to another denomination. The stained glass inscription reads, "To the memory of the beloved Bishop Simpson. Born June 21, 1811, died June 18, 1884. The gift was from his friend, George W. Childs."

1635 George W. Childs. *Recollections by George W. Childs* (Philadelphia: J. B. Lippincott & Company, 1890) 68.

1636 Ibid., 135-136.

1637 LOC, Simpson papers, Letter July 6, 1883, Container thirteen.

1638 Matthew Simpson, "Prayer for 1876 Centennial," LOC, Simpson papers, Container fifteen.

be better than the past .... May capital gains and labor be freed from all antagonism by establishment and application of such principles of justice and equity, as shall reconcile diversified interests and bind in imperishable bonds of all parts of society." And then in a crescendo that combined the best of George Handel and John Winthrop, Simpson raised his voice with oratorical eloquence that did not disappoint:

> We beseech thee, Almighty Father, that our beloved Republic may be strengthened in every element of true greatness until her mission is accomplished by presenting to the world an illustration of the happiness of a free people with a free church, in a free State under laws of their own enactment and under rulers of their own selection, acknowledging supreme alliance only to the King of kings and Lord of lords, and as thou didst give to one of its illustrious sons, first to draw the electric spark from heaven, which has since girded the globe in its celestial whispers of "Glory to God in the highest, peace on earth and good will to men," so to the lastest time may the mission of America, under divine inspiration, be one of affection, brotherhood and love for all our race; and may the coming centuries be filled with the glory of our Christian civilization; and unto thee, Our Father, through Him whose life is the light of men, will we ascribe glory and praise, now and forever. Amen.[1639]

Simpson's inaugural prayer did not pass without criticism. One Methodist brother complained that Simpson had not mentioned the name of Christ.[1640] A writer from the *New York Sun* critiqued the prayer for its lack of biblical reference and an abundance of flowery language "We have examples of prayer in the scriptures, but it is evident that Bishop Simpson has too ornamental a mind to be able to model his involuntary style upon theirs."[1641]

Over the half-year span, May 10 through November 10, the fair drew 9,000,000 visitors. According to the promoters, "The most lasting accomplishment of the Exhibition was to introduce America as a new industrial world power, soon to eclipse the might and production of every other industrialized nation, and to showcase the city of Philadelphia as a center of American culture and industry." (From the latter part of 1875 through January 28, 1876 Dwight Moody had drawn over 1,000,000 people

---

1639   Ibid.
1640   LOC, Simpson papers, Letter of Austin D. Heyerman to Matthew Simpson, May 19, 1876, Container ten.
1641   As quoted in the *Daily Rocky Mountain News*, Denver (May 27, 1876).

in 210 meetings at the Freight Depot in Philadelphia.) The enthusiasm of the attenders at the Centennial would wane due to an oppressive heat wave which killed over 100 people in Philadelphia during the summer. On July 26, the news reached Philadelphia that George Custer and his men had been annihilated in a battle which would become known as "Little Big Horn."

Did it occur to any of the Centennial visitors that the latest technology which they celebrated had killed Custer? Custer had been the most galant and skilled cavalry commander of the Civil War, commissioned a General at the age of twenty-three for his daring leadership. *Harper's Weekly* filled a front page with Custer commandeering his horse and wielding his sabre, defying death and even serious injury. On July 25, 1876, in the barren southeast corner of the Montana Territory, Custer's two hundred soldiers killed to the last man, could have taken care of one thousand Lakotas, and Cheyenne warriors, had the Indians battled with the ancient artillery of bow and arrows. But the Indians were armed with rifles for which they had bartered or stolen. It's unlikely but not impossible that Simpson was examining one of Eliphalet Remington's most advanced rifles on display at the Centennial Hall, while Custer took rifle bullets to the chest and left temple. In the brief decade between the end of the Civil War and the Centennial celebration, Custer's Calvary charges had become antiquated.[1642]

The historical assessment of the Centennial Fair at Philadelphia has been divided. One of its architects observed, "Restless, happy crowds are flitting from point to point, and the whole looks like a fairyland and incantations seen, something that we wish would never pass away." Russell Lyon wrote three quarters of a century later, "Critics look back upon the Centennial Exhibition as an architectural and artistic calamity that produced not a single new idea, but was rather the epitome of accumulated bad taste of the era that we called The Gilded Age, the Tragic Era, the Dreadful Decade or the Pragmatic Acquiescence--depending on which epithet you thought searing."[1643] *Harpers Weekly*, on July 15, quoted Japanese Fukui Makoto, "The first day crowds come like sheep, run here, run there, run everywhere. One man start, one more thousand follow. Nobody can see anything, nobody can

---

1642 See C. J. Stiles. *Custer's Trials: A Life on the Frontier of a New America* (New York: Alfred Knopf, 2015). (Note Stiles' subtitle.)

1643 Website: libwww.library.phil.gov/cencol/exh-testimony.htm.

do anything. All rush, push, tear, shout, make plenty noise, say damn great many times; get very tired, and go home."[1644]

Rutherford Hayes and Simpson

Rutherford Hayes, while he was President of the United States, confessed that he was a Methodist because, "Every night he slept with one of that persuasion."[1645] But like Lincoln and Grant, Hayes never joined a church and never testified to conversion to Christ. However, his turning to God seemed to be more identifiable than that of Lincoln or Grant. During the Civil War, Hayes was wounded several times. A musket ball fractured his arm; a Minie ball hit him in the head and dropped harmlessly to the ground; and when lightning struck him leaving him unsinged, a fellow soldier remarked, "It was my fortune to be near him a good many times, when it seemed that only an Unseen Hand was his shield."[1646] Hayes came to believe in the "Unseen Hand" and recorded, "But will I not take refuge in the faith of my father's at last? Are we not all impelled to do this? The great abyss, the unknown future—are we not happier if we give ourselves up to some settled faith …. am I not more and more carried along, drifted towards to surrendering to the best religion that the world has yet produced?"[1647]

Metropolitan Church claimed the Hayes, but when *Harper's Bazaar* portrayed the first family at church, they were seated in Foundry Church. Biographer Ari Hoogenboom reminds us that for a "non-church member and non-professor of religion," Hayes gave "inordinate" attention to the church. He hardly ever missed church, attended revivals, served on the board of Ohio Wesleyan University, and stretched his finances in order to pledge "a quarter of what the Methodist Church raised toward its debt for its new building" in Fremont, Ohio, where the family settled after the Hayes

---

1644   *Harpers Weekly* (July 15, 1876). Simpson was influential enough to almost single-handedly shut the fair down on Sundays. LOC, Simpson papers, Letter ,Joseph Hawley to Matthew Simpson, May 20, 1876, Container ten.

1645   Ari Hoogenboom. *Rutherford B. Hayes: Warrior and President* (Lawrence: University Press of Kansas, 1995) 384.

1646   Harry Barnard. *Rutherford B. Hayes* (Newtown, Connecticut: American Political Biography Press, 1954) 218.

1647   Hoogenboom, 223.

Presidency. We do not know where and when Hayes and Simpson first met. Both were from Ohio, and lived in Cincinnati at the same time when Simpson was an editor and Hayes an aspiring, well-known attorney.

Hayes was a capable President, a person of integrity, and according to recent biographers has not received his due from historians. He attempted to reform the Civil Service system, implementing a competitive exam to eliminate a patronage system predicated on the spoils of office. He also removed Federal troops from the South, trusting whites to restore blacks their "God-given rights and legitimate place in society." This optimism would turn into disillusionment. Thus, Hayes became unpopular with the radical Republicans and temporarily, even Simpson himself. Simpson favored a third term for Grant.[1648] But to Simpson's delight, Hayes refused to serve alcohol in the White House, which earned his wife the moniker, "Lemonade Lucy." When Garfield restored the serving of alcohol at State Dinners, Hayes accused his successor of lacking the grit to face fashionable ridicule and further declared that, "The American who drinks wine is in danger of becoming the victim of drunkenness, licentiousness, and gambling."[1649] Hoogenboom assesses that, "Protestant ministers particularly liked Hayes for his temperance and anti-slavery views. In addition, his opposition to public aid for parochial schools had frustrated Roman Catholicism in Ohio, and his upright character helped

---

1648 Gilbert Haven had gone public with his opinion that Grant should run in 1876. When a reporter pressed Simpson on the issue, the Bishop made clear that Grant was not a member of a Methodist church, but simply an attendant at "one of our places of worship. The Methodist denomination neither asked nor expects anything of him." The reporter asked, "From your standpoint, do you think that Methodists as a people are in favor of a Third Term?" Simpson responded, "That I cannot say; I never made any inquiries leading to that point. All I can say is that should President Grant be re-elected, the people will have done wisely." *St. Louis Globe-Democrat* (December 14, 1875). Simpson denied having said, "Should the President be re-elected, the people will have done wisely." LOC, Simpson papers, an unidentified Philadelphia newspaper, Scrapbook D, Container twenty-three. My conclusion is that Simpson said something to make the reporter infer that he was for Grant. In 1872, the rumor was spread that Simpson was for Horace Greeley, about which Simpson received several letters of inquiry. To a newspaper reporter Simpson made clear, "I am not and never have been in favor of Mr. Greeley for President. If I am spared, I expect to vote for General Grant, believing that our country needs an unchanged policy for four years longer." "Bishop Simpson for Grant "*The Cleveland Morning Daily Herald*, Tuesday October 1, 1872.

1649 Hoogenboom, 458.

the country forget the corruption of the Grant regime."[1650] After it became clear that Grant was not going to be the Republican nominee, the Protestant minister who particularly liked Hayes was Matthew Simpson; it was a mutual admiration society. When Hayes visited the Simpson home in Philadelphia on November 28, 1879, he described the Bishop and his family as the Victorian ideal of hearth and home.

> I spent Thanksgiving Day—yesterday--at Bishop Simpson's, 1807 Mount Vernon Street in Philadelphia .... At Bishop Simpson's, met the family and Lucy and Fanny (who had proceeded me) A happy home; a cheerful, pious family--a family of good works and most lovable character. The Bishop and his son Barney (Varney, Matthew Verner) met me at Broad Street Depot at midnight or near it. Mrs. Simpson is a warm-hearted and motherly lady who is full of good works. A home for aged women and now for orphans are her pet hobbies. The fair is the interest of the orphans. Mrs. Bowie (Buoy) a married daughter, wife of a Methodist Episcopal preacher in Harrisburg, was visiting her parents. Two sweet daughters, a blonde and a brunette, young ladies, complete the family. The Bishop's eloquence and success are due to a tender, sincere nature, great modesty, good culture, and sound common sense. These high qualities added to unshaken faith in Christianity and its vast importance, make him a man of great power in the pulpit and in private life. He possesses unusual love and capacity for hard work.[1651]

Hayes added that he accompanied the Bishop for a money raising service on Thanksgiving Day in Frankfort, where, "The Bishop preached a hopeful sermon." In the President's honor, boys from the orphanage did a military drill in front of Simpson's house. The Presidential party and the Simpsons spent the evening "at the crowded fair in the Great Hall hand-shaking and great enthusiasm."[1652] The fund-raising event (a yearly extravaganza for the Methodist orphanage) netted $12,000, and on Saturday evening, Matthew Verner and Sarah Elizabeth accompanied Lucy Hayes on a return train trip to Washington.[1653]

1650   Ibid., 384.
1651   Charles Richard Williams. *Diary and Letters of Rutherford B. Hayes* Vol. III (Columbus: The Ohio State Historical Society, 1926) 578–579.
1652   Ibid., 579.
1653   *Philadelphia Inquirer* (December 1, 1879).

The Favorite Preacher of American Presidents

How was Matthew Simpson the favorite preacher of three successive, elected Presidents who did not profess Christian conversion and were quite nebulous in their theology?[1654] Some said that Hayes read the Bible as if it was Shakespeare, not divine revelation. In all likelihood, Lincoln did the same. Simpson was non-doctrinaire in his preaching and was non-evangelistic, in that in his later years, he seldom called men and women to instantaneous conversion and entire sanctification. He did not impose the Wesleyan order of salvation on his preaching, and held little resemblance to early Methodist circuit riders who were "hunters of souls." It was not that Simpson never mentioned Hell or sin, but the fear of God was not the predominant theme of his preaching. Unlike Wesley's "Veterans," and Asbury's troops, Simpson was non-offensive and possibly even more civil if he spotted a dignitary in his congregation. He chose not to dwell on human depravity, but on human potential and progress. Simpson's sermons were uplifting, and his auditors left with enough conviction that they had fulfilled the penance of attending church, but never with the convincement that they were hanging over the brink of damnation. As Hayes said, "The Bishop preached a hopeful sermon."

As Simpson traveled from city to city and especially when he was in Washington, DC, he hardly ever gave an altar call, which had been the primary sacrament in early American Methodism. Confrontational preaching of calling men and women to a verdict, the dichotomous nature of the gospel, was largely absent from Simpson's homiletical paradigm. For sure, Simpson invited people to Christ, but his invitation was a general appeal, and normally not distinctly oriented to "praying through" which had been the staple of revivalistic Methodism. He never manipulated people with a high pressured sales pitch, to come forward and be singled out as a wayward sinner. In fact at times, it was difficult to tell the difference between his lecturing and preaching. And even more importantly, it was impossible to separate Simpson's personality from his preaching. In plain language, Simpson was a nice person. He exuded the grace of acceptance

---

[1654] Andrew Johnson was not elected to the Presidency.

and affirmation to almost everyone he met. An artist who painted Simpson, (who cannot be identified) said of his subject:

> In my interviews with Bishop Simpson, which sometimes necessarily much extended, I felt at home as I have seldom, if ever been able to feel in the presence of clergymen, especially clergymen of note. I am naturally timid, and am apt to feel oppressed in the presence of others. I had none of this feeling whatever when with this grand old man. I felt him to be a warm, loving friend. I forgot his greatness in his kindliness. And his goodness no more oppressed me than that of my mother's. I cannot explain it wholly, but it gave him a power over me, I will never cease to feel. Can we clergymen do better than seek to master that secret of this noble old bishop?[1655]

Some preachers assume a different personality out of the pulpit than in it. They are far more comfortable before thousands than when conversing with one or two people. The introvert, who shied away from people while growing up in Cadiz, had learned the art of social intercourse. Simpson was gracious both in public discourse and private conversation. Mary Wheeler recalled being in the Simpson home shortly before the Bishop died:

> Mrs. Simpson had invited the Methodist ministers' wives of our city to her own beautiful home, and with the Bishop, seemed to be trying to out-tire each other in making it a banquet of love and joy and inspiration to all present. It was a season long to be remembered. As the Bishop stood at the table with Mrs. Bishop Kingsley at his right hand, conversing with her, I was impressed with his saintliness. He seemed on the verge of heaven, and the words came to mind: "Touch me not, for I am not ascended yet to your Father and my Father."[1656]

Wheeler added, "No man was ever more loved in his own city. He was emphatically the man, whom people delighted to honor." Department Store mogul John Wanamaker recalled in 1905 that Simpson, "Was in his time--Philadelphia's greatest citizen, take him all in all."[1657] Wanamaker also recalled that as a boy, he had been impressed by the Bishop saying that

---

1655 "The Kindliness of Bishop Simpson," *The Metropolitan Pulpit and Homiletic Monthly* Vol. II, ed. I. K. Funk (New York: The Religious Newspaper Agency, 1878) 319–320.

1656 Mary Sparks Wheeler, "Reminiscences of Bishop Simpson," LOC, Simpson papers, Scrapbook D, Container twenty-three. In light of this scene taking place at the 1336 Arch Street mansion, I detect an attempt to display *nouveau riche*.

1657 UMA, Drew University, Simpson papers, Letter of John Wanamaker to Rev. L. H. Thomas, July 10, 1905.

it was, "a terrible thing to let conscience grow hard, for it soon sears as with a hot iron. At first it is like the freezing of a pond; the first film is scarcely perceptible. But if it keeps on hardening the ice, becomes so solid you can drive a wagon over the solid water. So with conscience, it films over gradually." Wanamaker recalled that Simpson had, "Helped many of us boys by his plain, sensible counsels. Any boy, who has such a friend and only one such counselor, will find it to be a life-long blessing."[1658] A eulogist, Jacob Todd, said of Simpson, "There was a subtle magnetism in the name that attracted you to him."[1659]

The Colorado Iliffs

One of those people attracted to Simpson was Lizzy Iliff, widow of the Colorado "Cattle King" John Wesley Iliff. In March, 1879, C. C. McCabe wrote Simpson, "I had the very great privilege of traveling with Mrs. Iliff from Pittsburgh to Chicago. She spoke of you and your family with such love and reverence, that I verily believe she would do anything that you might suggest …. She loves you more than anybody else in the world."[1660] Less than three months later, Simpson received a letter from Lizzie Iliff, "I direct that my executors invest in the interest-bearing bonds of the Government of the United States, the sum of Fifty Thousand Dollars. I hereby devote to found a professorship in a school of Theology to be established in the state of Colorado under the patronage of the Methodist Episcopal Church." Matthew Verner was currently visiting the Iliffs. Mrs. Iliff reported to his father, "He started down to the Cattle Range Tuesday morning to rough it a little and take part or rather see the Roundup."[1661]

1658   John Wanamaker, "Our Old Friend Bishop Matthew Simpson: Highly Valued by Abraham Lincoln," UMA, Drew University, Simpson papers.

1659   *Journal of the 1880 General Conference of the Methodist Episcopal Church* (New York: Phillips and Hunt, 1880) 568.

1660   LOC, Simpson papers, Letter March 1, 1879, Container twelve. Charles Cardwell McCabe was the fundraiser for the Church Extension Society which Simpson chaired. McCabe referred to himself as the, "Great American Champion Beggar." His biographer called him the "Grand-Field-Marshall of Methodism." McCabe was elected to the Episcopacy in 1896. See Frank Milton Bristol. *The Life of Chaplain McCabe: Bishop of the Methodist Episcopal Church* (New York: Eaton and Mains, 1908).

1661   LOC, Simpson papers, Letter May 21-22, 1879, Container twelve. According to Donald Oglesby, Iliff shipped over 30,000 head of cattle in a single year from Colorado to

"God Cannot Do Without America"

The above influence not only proved beneficial, but risked liabilities. Such was the case when, in 1882, Simpson invested $600 in the Isabella Silver Mining Company of California. He had been told by the company that it would invest a percentage of its profits in East Tennessee Wesleyan University at Athens, Tennessee. A Professor Caldwell from the University had visited the "wildcat mine," and after assaying the ore, had determined that the mines were rich. Simpson's venture encouraged several others to invest money that was lost in worthless mines. Simpson concluded that the ore had been "salted" before being re-examined. He then claimed that to those who had inquired of him about the mines, he had responded, "Never invest in a mine any money that you are not prepared to lose."[1662]

No one typified the conflict between range Indians and ranchers more than did John Iliff. Even though Iliff owned 60,000 acres, no parcel was larger than 350 acres. The 100 plots of land were all proximate to water and excluded Indians from the resources most important to their survival. The cattle king not only froze out competitors, but also prevented Indian occupation of lands on which they had previously depended. The Indians "now saw surrounding ground taken and held by men who could call on whatever power to keep it." As Elliot West reminds us, "Rarely can two cultures choose two unique visions at the same place at the same time."[1663] There is no evidence that Simpson was anguished that one of the cultures was ruthlessly and torturously being extinguished.

After chairing what would be the last Annual Conference of his life in Huron, South Dakota, October 11, 1883, Simpson doubled back to Denver where he had spent much of the summer.[1664] On December 27,

---

Chicago. Iliff died of kidney disease February 9, 1878 at the age of 46. Before his death, he indicated to Lizzie, who was his second wife, that he desired for a "theological school" to be built in the area. It was a strange request since, according to Oglesby, John Wesley Iliff was not a member of any church. See Donald Oglesby, "J. W. Iliff: Cattle King of Colorado," unpublished M.A. thesis, Western State College of Colorado, 1953.

1662 "Bishop Simpson's Experience in Wildcat Mines," *Daily Evening Bulletin*: San Francisco (February 13, 1883).

1663 Elliot West. *The Contested Plains: Indians, Gold Seekers, and the Rush to Colorado* (Lawrence: University of Kansas Press, 1998) 353.

1664 On his last Episcopal tour, Simpson chaired the 1883 Iowa Annual Conference in Burlington, IA, Sept. 5-10; the Des Moines Annual Conference, Clarinda, IA, Sept 12-17; the Upper Iowa Conference, Marion, IA, Sept. 19-24; the NW Iowa Annual Conference,

1883, he performed the marriage of Elizabeth Iliff to his colleague, Bishop Henry Warren. A newspaper reported that Simpson's "voice and manner" evidenced his "intimate relationship with both bride and groom." The guests were received at the Iliff mansion, where awaited them in the dining room a long table decorated with

> a band of cardinal plush edged with ferns and the most delicate flowers. The center piece was a ship carved out of lid ice, the little craft being completed of all the rigging. All around the wonder were banks of flowers, while on either side of the center pieces were the words Warren-Iliff in white primroses. The table was further ornamented with flat bouquets and traceries of smilax. The crystal and silver as well as the china were rich and costly and the bouquet seemed in admirable style. The menu included everything that taste could suggest and money procure.

The reporter also described the attire of the bride:

> The bridal toilette, from Worth, was of silver satin brocaded with pale blue. The side revers were of rose point lace and the front was of ruffles of the same costly material. The corsage was cut surplice fashion and the plastron, yes, was fastened with silver buttons. The bonnet to match was of gold braid with point lace and pale blue tips and pompons. Her ornaments were superb diamonds, a bar of brilliante with a pendant diamond ball. Solitaire earrings completed the magnificent costume.[1665]

In a manner that had never been precedented in American Methodism, if not all American Christianity, monetary privilege had been wedded to ecclesiastical power. Coincidentally, on the day that Matthew Simpson died, "Mrs. Elizabeth Iliff Warren offered a gift of $100,000 to endow a school of theology as a graduate department of the University of Denver.[1666] All of this led to one of the most bizarre and shameful events in the history of American theological education. In 1893, a Methodist minister, R. M. Barns, presented to Elizabeth and Henry Warren as well as other members of the Iliff Board, a book written in Latin by Johann Lorenz von Mocheim

---

Le Mars, IA Sept. 26-30; MN Annual Conference, St. Paul, MN, Oct 3-8; Dakota Mission Annual Conference, Huron, SD, Oct. 11-15. *Minutes of the Annual Conferences of the M.E. Church: All Conferences of 1883* (New York: Phillips& Hunt, 1883).

1665   "Check-mate: The Queen Takes the Bishop—A Brilliant Game on the Colorado Chess Board—The Marriage of Bishop Warren and Mrs. Iliff, the Cattle Queen." Article courtesy of Iliff School of Theology Archives, Denver.

1666   J. Alton Templin, "John Wesley Iliff, and Theological Education in the West," *Methodist History* 24:2 (January 1986).

entitled *Institutionum Historiae Christianae Compendium* (History of Christianity). The book was bound in the skin of an Indian, purportedly provided by the Revolutionary War hero, Daniel Morgan. This gruesome trophy of American colonialism may have served as a fitting exclamation mark on Methodism's flagrant imperialism of the nineteenth century. It stayed on display in the Iliff Library until enraged students successfully lobbied for its removal in 1974.[1667]

Cyclopaedia

At the 1880 General Conference, Simpson brought the Episcopal address. With sadness he reported on the deaths of Janes, Ames, and Haven. All of them were some of his closest friends. Although Methodism was still growing; its trajectory was beginning to attenuate, with an actual loss in the value of church property over the last four years. Simpson attributed this trend to "the drop in the price of real estate."[1668] Numerical gain had been 119,743 members (1876-1880), though in the previous quadrennium 159,236(1872-1876).[1669] But Methodism could take pride in its aesthetic advance. "When we survey the whole country, we find the membership is annually enlarging, its edifices are not only increasing in number, but in taste and commodiousness."[1670] In reference to the seminaries Boston, Garrett, and Drew, he stated: "We regret to say we have suffered considerable loss through accidents or the change of terms, but we are gratified to add that our friends are coming to the rescue, replacing their endowments by generous gifts and showing how deep an interest the Church feels in the education of its young ministers."[1671]

Simpson warned against ministers aspiring for political office: "Ministers are, indeed citizens, and have all the rights of citizenship, but the work of

---

1667   Tink Tinker (Washashe/Osage Nation). "Redskin, Tanned Hide: A Book of Christian History Bound in the Flayed Skin of an American Indian: The Colonial Romance, Christian Denial and the Cleansing of a Christian School of Theology," *Journal of Race, Ethnicity, and Religion* Vol. 5, Issue 9 (October 2014).
1668   *Journal of the 1880 General Conference* (New York: Phillips & Hunt, 1880) 406.
1669   *Journal of the 1876 General Conference*, 398.
1670   *Journal of the 1880 New York General Conference*, 416.
1671   Ibid., 412.

the ministry is so momentous, it demands all the energies and all the time of the strongest minds and hearts."[1672] He then set the bar high for himself and his colleagues: "The Bishops should be men of pure personal life, deep piety, earnest devotion to the doctrines and economy of the Church, and self-sacrifice and sympathetic spirit, of comprehensive views, of fair culture and willing to be in labors 'more abundant.'"[1673] No doubt, Simpson was of "fairer culture" than, say, Bishops William McKendree and Robert Roberts. The former had worn a red flannel shirt and the latter had lived in a log cabin. Simpson also suggested that a Bishop should be "removed as far as possible from all questions of locality and partisanship."[1674]

During the Conference Bishop Fallows, the fraternal delegate from Canada commented that, "When Southey's 'Life of Wesley' was written, English High-churchmen said sneeringly, "The book is too big a book for the importance of Wesley. What would these English croakers have thought if they could have seen Simpson's 'Cyclopaedia of Methodism,' and Daniels' superbly illustrated 'History of Methodism'?"[1675] Yes, in 1878, Simpson's *Cyclopaedia of Methodism* did appear; it was a singular achievement, the most exhaustive single book concerning the people, places and events of both British and American Methodism. How exactly Simpson had time to oversee its compilation is difficult to ascertain, other than he had much help multiplying many errors. After listing fifteen people who had assisted in the process including his son-in-law, C. W. Buoy, Simpson admitted that he was aware that "in the collection of matter from so many sources, as well as in copying and preparation, and in passing through the errors, some errors may have escaped notice." He insisted that the errors were, "Generally of a minor moment, and can be corrected in the next edition."[1676]

The mistakes were minor except for the individuals about whom the mistakes were made, and for them the errors became major. Jacob Sleeper, of whom Simpson or someone else wrote a long article, complained that

---

1672   Ibid., 415.
1673   Ibid., 417.
1674   Ibid.
1675   Ibid., 527.
1676   Preface of the *Cyclopaedia*, March 9, 1878, no page number.

Simpson had not credited him for service as Mayor of Boston.[1677] J.B. Good corrected the many mistakes that Simpson had made about Jacob Albright and the Evangelical Association. "When I say there are grave errors in it, I know where of I affirm." Good had lived in the same neighborhood as Albright, and had prepared a biographical sketch for the denominational publication, *The Messenger*.[1678] After listing all of his accomplishments, L. C. Holliday (and probably others) was surprised and disappointed that his name had been left out. Holliday wrote, "But when I saw such names as Hayden, Hays, J. R. Eddy, De La Martyr, I thought there might be a screw loose somewhere, and under that feeling I availed myself of the privilege of personal friendship, to write you a personal note, for I knew that I had done more for the Methodist Church than a regiment of such men."[1679]

On the whole, given his schedule, responsibilities and age, Simpson in spite of his errors, left a 1,000 page tome, on which historians have relied, though cautiously, for the last 125 years. Again as Richey notes, the *Cyclopaedia* was another celebrated milestone in American Methodism. "Simpson imaged the dramatic change of Methodism's social location with the large number (close to four hundred) of engravings, many to be sure of ministers living and dead, but some of rich Methodists, imposing collegiate halls, and cathedral churches. To Simpson, the Lord was rewarding the Methodists—his favored common people—for their diligence, and they were sharing their success with their church."[1680]

The First World Methodist Ecumenical Conference

The most important action of the 1880 General Conference involving Simpson, was a resolve to hold "an ecumenical conference of Methodism in City Road Chapel, London, the middle of August, 1881."[1681] The "General Ecumenical Committee" would consist of two sections: first, "British and Continental" and second, the "Western." Simpson served as the main contact

---

1677   LOC, Simpson papers, Letter June 9, 1879, Container twelve.
1678   LOC, Simpson papers, Letter February 1979, Container twelve.
1679   UMA, E. PA Conference of the UMC, St. George's UMC, Philadelphia, Simpson papers, Letters June 7 and June 13, 1878.
1680   Richey et. al, *The Methodist Experience*, 225.
1681   *Journal of the 1880 General Conference* (New York: Phillips and Hunt, 1880) 427.

person for the western side of the Atlantic. In May of 1879, Simpson explained that he had not the means of convening the committee, but expressed his "concurrence in the views of the British Committee as to the subjects and limits of discussion."[1682] Simpson, then the senior American Bishop both by age and length of service, brought the opening address. He stood before 400 delegates representing twenty-six different denominations under the canopy of Methodism, including delegates from the African Methodist Episcopal Church and the Colored Methodist Episcopal Church of America. By far, the largest group was the Methodist Episcopal Church of America with 114 delegates, rivaled only by the Wesleyan Methodists of Great Britain with 86 delegates. Several of Simpson's lay friends were present including Washington DePauw, James Long, Oliver Hoyt, and Clinton Fisk.

Simpson took as his text, "The words that I speak unto you they are spirit and they are life." Simpson identified with his audience by stating, "How easy is it by a few sentences to detect the style of Johnson or Macaulay, or Carlyle." But Simpson made it clear that he was not entering into a reductionism, by declaring, "Valuable as unquestionably are the works of literature, science, and art, Christ's words pertained to none of these. They are of a prior and higher realm."[1683] The sermon was full of analogies to nature: "Gravitation that controls all the grosser elements," "the lodestone imparts its mysterious touch to the needle," "the limitless realms of space," "nebulae become worlds," and "stardust clusters of systems." Simpson exhorted, "Think of animal life and all of its species. It is said that 320,000 species have been classified and probably the half has not been found. In what strange varieties and what singular forms does this life exist! Life in the branches of mass, life in the drop of water; vegetable life below the surface of the earth's unturned soil, life in every layer or drop of the sea. In summer heat the very dust of the earth seems alive and the air is full of living beings."[1684]

There were Biblical allusions, Moses, Ezekiel, Lazarus; also Church history references, Huss, Tyndale, Wycliffe, and Luther. "Great reforms have always been preceded and accompanied by the study of God's word." There

---

1682 *Report of the Proceedings of the First Ecumenical Methodist Conference held in City Road Chapel, London, September 7, 1881* (London: Wesleyan Conference Office, 1881) vi.
1683 Ibid., 3.
1684 Ibid., 5.

was no better example of this than Methodists who were called, "Bible moths and Bible bigots."[1685] The history of Methodism was a word-centered Church that brought persecution by the establishment. God "helped Wesley to arouse a slumbering world. Though abused by the Press, though derided in books and pamphlets, though caricatured on the stage and by the pencil, though persecuted and his life endangered by mobs, some of which we are sorry to say were headed by priests, who were never rebuked or censured by their bishops, he kept on his way rejoicing."[1686]

The peculiarities of Methodism had been lay preaching, class meetings, family prayer, belief in the possible salvation of all men, and the common people having gladly heard Methodist preachers. Methodism had grown and progressed without communal favor, large-landed estates, great wealth, and special assistance from scholars or educational institutions. What Methodism exemplified was sacrifice and perseverance. The early preachers, "braved winter's cold and summer's heat, swam streams and threaded forests, endured persecution and reproach to save their fellowmen.[1687]

Simpson attempted to argue the unity of Methodists which was a stretch. It was a gross exaggeration, if not a misrepresentation, to declare, "All over the world Methodist theology is a unit. Nor secondly, is there any radical difference in usages? The class meeting, the prayer meeting, the love feasts, the watch night though more or less strictly observed, are known everywhere in Methodism."[1688] Simpson must have been aware that it was "less" rather than "more," especially in America. Simpson emphasized that Methodism could still be identified by the way it prayed, preached, sung, and rejoiced like Methodists.[1689] "Does not the world say, They are like Methodists?" This may have been Simpson's desire, but was not the present trend or future projection. "Like Methodists" would increasingly identify only those schismatic and aberrant fringe groups who held on to Jeremiah's "old paths." He was correct in noting the catholic spirit of Wesley and quoting Wesley's famed, "Is thy heart right as my heart is with thine? If it

---

1685 Ibid., 9.
1686 Ibid., 10-11.
1687 Ibid., 16.
1688 Ibid., 17.
1689 Ibid., 17.

be so, give me thy hand." Some would wonder if Wesley has been taken out of context in this quote or it was a *faux pas* that was to harvest theological and moral pluralism.[1690] The conclusion was as Simpsonesque as the end of a sermon could climax, a vivid, imaginative analogy:

> It is said that in the manufacture of Gobelin tapestry the workman sits at the back of the material, and does not see the figures which he is making, nor can he conceive how his small corner may be connected with the rest. He must implicitly follow the directions before him; a single error on his part will mar the beauty of the work. Brothers, so we work. We sit on the earthly side of the fabric—the beautiful side is turned towards heaven. We see not fully our own work, but there are eyes that every moment behold the pictures which we form; and in the day of eternity we shall see as we are seen. Let us follow the pattern, and do glorious work for Christ. Then when heart and flesh shall fail, we shall be able to say with the dying Wesley, "The best of all is God is with us."[1691]

Methodism's Distinguishing Doctrines Muted

Simpson made only indirect references to the distinguishing doctrines of Methodism, such as entire sanctification, the direct witness of the Spirit, and prevenient grace. He recalled that the "Holy Club" had read "the Spirit itself beareth witness with our spirit that we are the children of God"[1692] and "Wesley became the earnest and unwearied herald of a free and full salvation."[1693] Simpson excelled in history and science, but floundered in theology and philosophy. He absorbed history like a sponge, but demonstrated little evidence of mastering doctrinal nuances. Kirby is correct in noting that

---

1690   Winthrop Hudson observed that this "dictum" by Wesley saved Methodism from the theological witch hunts and heresy trials which plagued Presbyterians and other denominations at the turn of the century. "... the Methodists as a result of their continuing emphasis upon the centrality of heart religion had developed no sharply defined theological position. To the extent that they held to any external test of fellowship, their stress was upon morality rather than dogma." Winthrop S. Hudson. *Religion in America* (New York: Charles Scribner's Sons, 1965) 278. Hudson was simplistic at this point. More accurate was Colin Williams who argued that though Methodism is malleable around the edges, and lends itself to ecumenicity, there were cardinal doctrines (original sin, prevenient grace, justification by faith, etc.,) that were very important to Wesley and early Methodism. Colin Williams. *John Wesley's Theology Today* (Nashville: Abingdon Press, 1960).

1691   Ibid., 20.
1692   Ibid., 9.
1693   Ibid., 10.

Simpson illustrated, "The general lack of intellectual or theological interest, which characterized American Protestantism."[1694]

J. P. Newman spoke on "Scriptural Holiness and the Special Fitness of Methodist Means of Grace to Promote It."[1695] (All the speakers were assigned topics.) According to Newman, "Holiness is the readjustment of our whole nature, whereby the inferior appetites and propensities are subordinated and the superior intellect and moral powers are restored to their supremacy; and Christ reigns in a complete renewed soul."[1696] Newman did not use the terminology of "entire sanctification," "second blessing," nor did he give any instruction as to how holiness fit into the Wesleyan order of salvation. Washington DePauw testified, "Glory be to Jesus! The blood hath cleansed. The blood of Jesus Christ can cleanse from all sin and it doth cleanse."[1697] Simpson's friend, the American glass manufacturer from New Albany, Indiana, had gifted the Conference with a camp meeting moment. Washington DePauw, for whom DePauw University would be named, had experienced "entire sanctification" at one of the early gatherings of the National Camp Meeting Association.[1698]

It was left to J. W. McDonald to state the reality of Methodist preaching on holiness. "Various ideas of entire sanctification have crept into the churches .... What we want is that by some effort, we should come to a clear definition of this important doctrine, and I, for my part, would be very glad to see half a day devoted to the discussion of this question."[1699] The half a day was not granted, and had it been, it would have not yielded unanimity

---

1694 Kirby, *Social and Ecclesiastical*, 314.

1695 *Report of the Proceedings of the First Ecumenical Methodist Conference*, 139.

1696 Ibid., 141.

1697 Ibid., 151.

1698 George Hughes reported: "But the next day Brother Inskip captured him (Washington DePauw) by inviting those who desired to be all that Christ would have them be,' to kneel at the altar. He was constrained to accept the invitation which was given in such a loving manner as to be well-nigh irresistible. He went down into the straw; and, as he did so, it seemed to go from under him, and the ground too. He continued to go down, down, down,--but soon struck rock. He wrote to his wife, and told her what the Lord had done for him. He never expected to testify that he was sanctified; but, oh! He had found something *wondrously grand!* He was a witness for Jesus now, and trusted he should be forever." Hughes, 281.

1699 *Report of the Proceedings of the First Ecumenical Conference*, 151.

of thought any more than would the next half century. It was left to Bishop Simpson to have the final say in the conference which had lasted fourteen days, September 7-20. A stenographer reported of Simpson,

> For his part, if it were possible, he loved Methodism more than ever; he had loved it from his infancy; he received the love of it from his mother, by whose hand he was taken to the class meeting, whose prayers he heard; he had mingled with Methodists, and while he had never had controversy with brethren of any other denomination--he thought he loved them all--his heart was endued with such love that the prosperity and success of Methodism was dearer to him than his own life.[1700]

Simpson's Tribute to an Assassinated President

It was convenient for James Russell Lowell, the American Ambassador to Great Britain, to have Simpson on hand for an oration on behalf of the dead President. On September 24, after Lowell's tribute to Garfield, the Bishop stood before 3,000 persons, mostly Americans, and verbalized the familiar mantra that he had proclaimed so many times before: "I take no exception to the habits or customs of other lands; it would neither be fair nor generous to do so, but I do feel that in our land a poor young man has opportunity which no other under heaven can afford him. President Garfield rose from a boyhood of poverty to a life of culture, and did not stop until he was placed at the head of a great nation."[1701] The entire audience stood with prolonged cheers when Simpson stated, "Kings and Princes gather round his bier, the Queen of the greatest empire in the world drops a tear of sympathy with his widow, and lays a wreath upon his tomb. God bless Queen Victoria for her womanly sympathy and her queenly courtesy."

Simpson stirred the emotions of his crowd when he romanticized, "I passed today the monuments of Wellington and Nelson and it seemed to me that the heads of heroes were bowed in grief. As I passed Westminster Abby, also, it seemed to me that the holy dead of past ages looked down with a greater solemnity and were waiting to be joined in that upper circle by the hero of the western land."[1702] No American could have strummed the

---

1700   Ibid, 603.
1701   Crooks, 459.
1702   Ibid., 460.

heart strings of his auditors more artistically than did Matthew Simpson at London's Exeter Hall. Even though the "holy dead" at Westminster Abbey can hardly look down, since they are buried in the floor, the facts of the matter were of little importance to the collective sorrow of national mourning. Simpson's sentimentalism begged the question, "Would David Garrick and Geoffrey Chaucer really want to participate in that 'upper circle?'"

The death of James Garfield provided Simpson with what Crooks referred to as his "last flash of his peculiar electric power."[1703] The President had died on September 19, in Long Branch, New Jersey, while Simpson was in London. Obviously, the death had not been unexpected, since Garfield had been shot in the back by a deranged office seeker, Charles Giteau, on July 2nd. It was not the bullet that brought death, but the crude medical care, entirely ignorant of germ theory and the necessity of sterilization. To put it another way, the doctors killed him.[1704]

We do not know when Simpson and Garfield first met, but we learn from Garfield's *Diary* that the two of them had intersected before the latter became President. At the Philadelphia Centennial, Garfield did not bother to stick around to hear Simpson pray, "As I had Bishop Simpson's prayer and the other speeches in print before their delivery, I did not care to listen and after the singing Crete and I went into the art gallery"[1705] On February 9, 1879, Garfield recorded,

> In company with James Mason, attended the Foundry Church and listened to a very able sermon from Bishop Simpson. He made a point which I have not heard before, in proof that men after death were conscious of affairs, instancing persons arising from death and being restored to relatives, but especially instancing the cases of Moses and Elias in (Matthew 17:3, Garfield did not know the reference) one who had passed away from the earth 900 years before, the other 1,400 year before. Yet on their return, they talked of Jerusalem and deeds which Christ should accomplish there in language intelligible to the apostle. The Bishop said it was fortunate they had not forgotten the Hebrew language after a lapse of so many centuries.

1703   Ibid.

1704   Candice Millard. *Destiny of the Republic: A Tale of Madness, Medicine, and the Murder of a President* (New York: Anchor Books, 2011).

1705   Harry J. Brown and Frederick R. William. *The Diary of James A. Garfield* Vol. III (Lansing, Michigan: Michigan State University Press, 1981) 290.

Garfield further added, "I received a note from the President inviting Crete and I to dinner with Bishop Simpson and wife. We accepted and had a very pleasant dinner with a number of friends."[1706]

Physical Collapse in San Francisco

Entering his seventies, the body of Matthew Simpson was worn out. Incessant preaching, traveling, and chairing Annual Conferences as well as writing duties imposed on an already weak constitution, had killed him. Simpson's downhill physical slide began in San Francisco in 1880 when he awoke on Sunday, September 12, chilling and unable to eat. After treating himself with "electricity," he made his way to a crowded church with the thought that he would preach himself out of his illness.[1707] A newspaper reported that, "Bishop Simpson arrived early, walking up the aisle alone, and kneeling devoutly for some time for silent prayer in the pulpit. Then he sat quietly with a large overcoat buttoned around him." Rutherford and Lucy Hayes entered the church at 11:00 a.m., and the congregation acknowledged their presence by standing.[1708] Before seating herself, Lucy knelt at the pew while her husband bowed his head on the back of the pew in front of him. Within ten minutes of beginning his sermon, Simpson's "face, always pallid, assumed a white hue, bleaching like his hair …. The Bishop was seized with retching and appeared to be suffocating. He grasped the pulpit with both hands." Simpson requested the congregation to sing a couple of verses of a song and perhaps he would sufficiently recover to continue his sermon. Instead, he tottered and fell backwards into his chair.[1709] In all likelihood, the man who had felt chest pain for much of his life had suffered a major heart attack.[1710]

1706   Ibid., Vol. IV, 180.

1707   LOC, Simpson papers, 1880 *Diary*, Container two.

1708   The Hayes family, along with other guests, including William Sherman who planned the trip, left for California, August 26. The party of nineteen people arrived in San Francisco on September 9, and eventually covered the distance between Puget Sound in the Washington Territory and Los Angeles. They arrived back in Fremont, Ohio, on November 1st, in time for the President to cast his vote for James Garfield. It was an amazing trip for $575.40. Hoogenboom, 440–446.

1709   Taken from the *San Francisco Chronicle* by the *St. Louis Globe-Democrat* (September 22, 1880).

1710   The *Daily Alta California* (September 13, 1880) reported that the Bishop had suffered from a "malarial congested chill." Clark, *Pulpit and Platform*, 595.

For over two weeks, Simpson was prostrated in San Francisco, and left by train, Tuesday, September 28th. He stopped in Denver to see the Evans, departing October 6. After a brief stop in Pittsburgh to visit his brother-in-law, James Verner, he arrived in Philadelphia, October 12, having recovered much of his strength. He felt well enough to meet with the Episcopal Board in Madison, New Jersey on October 28. The ill portent did not slow him down. Christmas Day of 1880 found him arranging his papers and writing letters.[1711]

Unofficial Chaplain to the United States Government

During the last five years of his life until six months before he died, Simpson kept a full slate of Annual Conferences except for the fall of 1880, when scheduled to go to China. Ellen became sick in California, the trip was cancelled, and then Matthew collapsed, as described above. His last trip to the Deep South was in the winter of 1880. Obviously, his Southern status had changed. On a January evening he preached at First Methodist Church on Peachtree Street to a packed house.[1712] The Board of Bishops must have assessed that Simpson was too weak to travel, was nearing death, and scheduled no Annual Conferences for him in 1884.

On January 27, 1884, Simpson preached the "Emancipation Service" (debt retirement) at Metropolitan Church in Washington, D.C.[1713] He announced as his text Isaiah 42:4. Christ "Shall not fail nor be discouraged till He has set judgment in the earth and the aisles shall wait for his law." The pericope provided a proof text for Simpson's post-millennial eschatology and his paradigm of constant and continual progress. Never mind that the text was a promise made to Israel. Christ's words composed the "familiar maxim of the civilized world." Further, "The triumphs of art, by which the races of men are brought together face to face, are steadily diminishing the number of tribes or nations and hastening the time when the sword will be a plowshare and a spear a pruning hook indeed and the art of war be forgotten." The reporter praised Simpson's effort, "For above an hour Bishop Simpson enlarged his

---

1711 LOC, Simpson papers, 1880 *Diary*, Container two.

1712 LOC, Simpson papers, 1880 *Diary*, Container two.

1713 "Georgia: Simpson Preaches Two Powerful Sermons," LOC, Simpson papers, Scrapbook D, Container twenty-three.

argument for Christ's coming reign with instances, enforced it by arguments and illustrated it by anecdotes which held vast crowds spellbound, so that his discourse, which was a long one, seemed short."[1714]

The reporter sent from Chicago must have been assigned to cover only Simpson. "There is a conference near, but Bishop Foster is to attend that. He (Simpson) did not attend the Methodist's preacher's meeting Monday evening …. He did not, in the Old Methodist style, put up with some preachers or in a private dwelling but in a nice hotel, kept by good people it is true, but where politicians easily congregate." Simpson, "was an invited guest at President Arthur's State Dinner, where there was said to have been six wine glasses per plate".[1715] The reporter did not imply that Simpson imbibed.

Simpson, a simple Methodist preacher, who once had run around barefooted in the village of Cadiz, had stood face to face with six successive Presidents of the United States.[1716] Possibly no American clergyman, not even Billy Graham, ever had more access to the White House and the Congressional corridors of power, than Matthew Simpson. When J. P. Newman was Chaplain of the Senate, he observed Simpson casually moving among the Senators.[1717] (Simpson did not need a special invitation to enter the Senate floor.) It may not be too far-fetched to claim that Simpson was the unofficial Chaplain to the United States' government.

The Bishop's Last Sermon

The last sermon which Bishop Simpson preached was at People's Church in Boston, February 10, 1884. The Church was the dream and design of John Hamilton, a Methodist Elder who envisioned an ecumenical house of worship devoid of class and racial distinction. The Church was dedicated over an eight-day period, and tickets were issued for admission to each service. A stenographer recorded Simpson's sermon, and the Bishop edited it; thus, his last literary effort as well as spoken. Ironically, Simpson was the first preacher chosen in a convocation dedicated to combating recent

---

1714   *The Christian Cynosure: Chicago* (February 21, 1884).
1715   Ibid.
1716   The Presidents were Lincoln, Johnson, Grant, Hayes, Garfield, and Arthur.
1717   UMA, Drew University, J. P. Newman papers, *Diary*, December 19, 1871.

trends in church architecture that catered to the rich and excluded the poor. According to Hamilton, "Empty churches eloquent with pride possess more of the form than the power of Godliness."[1718]

Simpson chose as his text Isaiah 9:6, "For unto Us a Child is born, unto us a Son is given, and His name shall be called, Wonderful, Counselor, the Mighty God, the Everlasting Father, The Prince of Peace." The sermon was entitled, "Christ and His Church." The word "wonderful" provided a fifteen-minute exaltation of the attributes and deeds of Christ, but for the word "Counselor" the preacher provided a unique exegetical twist: "So the Church in its stage, follows a Counselor. It is a teacher. The second state of the Church opens schools, seminaries, colleges, universities. It educates the people in science, in art, in literature."[1719] Simpson proclaimed that the "Mighty God" had hushed the seas so that he would show, "He was the Lord of the ocean, and that by human power, travel on the ocean was to be made as safe and easy as on land. He seemed to hold in his hand, all the issues of the coming commerce to all the world. Our messages, telephone communication, substitutes the service of the messenger boys."[1720]

True to his millennial optimism, the old preacher proclaimed, "If we try to save every man on Earth, we will not engage in war, strife will be done away; discord will not reign; the sword will be beaten into plow share, and Christ shall reign triumphant, the Prince of Peace forever."[1721] A reporter wrote, "The discourse will be cherished as a memorial, and considering the preacher's age and pressing infirmities, will be marvelous in its clearness of vision and equal flights of eloquence." The observer further added, "The Bishop was himself to the last. Gentle as a child yet as magnificent as an archangel; brilliant in intellect and warm in heart, coming down to the lowest while mounting in a chariot of flame to the very heavens, when shall

---

1718   John Hamilton. *The People's Church Pulpit* (Boston: The People's Church, 1885) xii.

1719   Ibid., 9.

1720   Ibid., 17.

1721   Ibid., 21. The People's Church (Temple) retained its identity until it merged with Broomfield-Tremont Methodist Episcopal Church in 1922 to form Copley Methodist Episcopal Church. The site of John Hamilton's dream is now occupied by the Salvation Army Headquarters of Boston. No doubt, Hamilton would have been pleased. Methodist Church Records, Massachusetts Boston University School of Theology Library. www.bu.edu/sthlibrary/archives/collections/neccah/records-files-state/ma-records/

we see his like?"[1722] That was not John Hamilton's memory. He wrote to George Crooks that Simpson was "so feeble that his eloquence was pathetic rather than exhilarating or arousing."[1723]

In this last sermon at The People's Church, Simpson explained a hermeneutical shift that had taken place in his own life. "As I grow older, I see more and more of the Spirit of Christ, as it seems to me, actively at work in the world, and passages of scripture that I used to consider as being merely spiritual in their character, I have learned to consider in referring also to the natural interest of the world."[1724] Simpson did not mean that his preaching was void of soteriological proclamation. To his Boston audience he declared, "And if there is one of us who has felt a doubt about Christ's receiving us, and his willingness to save us, let us take heart and courage by this declaration, and let us go to him and we shall find in him a perfect Savior."[1725]

Simpson had not dismissed the message of salvation, but during the post-bellum years, he had increasingly interpreted Scripture in the light of human progress, humanity's ability to control nature. One definition of work is, "changing nature." The more an individual can change nature by way of technology, the less s/he needs God to change it. The transition which had occurred in Simpson's preaching was from what God is doing in the biblical text to what humankind is doing in the text. And the humankind that Simpson had in mind was the American Anglo-Saxon race. Simpson increasingly read Scripture through a nationalistic lens, and this imposed on the Bible a message which was not only skewed, but diametrically opposed to the lowly Galilean who proclaimed, "The meek shall inherit the earth." For Simpson, the technologically advanced would inherit the earth, and no country was as technologically advanced as America. As early as 1867 he had asked, "What is all of this? It is Jesus conquering the world. The iron, the steam, and lightening are his; he made them all long before man found

---

1722   LOC, Simpson papers, "Rev. D. Sherman-The People's Church Pulpit," Scrapbook D, Container twenty-three.
1723   UMA, Drew University, Crooks papers, Letter March 6, 1890.
1724   Hamilton, 15.
1725   Ibid., 14.

out their powers. God has placed them in the world. All power is His, and he has given them to us that the earth may be converted to God."[1726]

The Simpson's Purchase a Mansion

In January of 1882, Simpson made one of the most confounding decisions of his life. He purchased a 15,000 square foot mansion from Margaret Myers, widow of Nathan Myers.[1727] The purchase price was $40,000, over one million dollars in today's currency. The house, 1334-36 Arch Street, stood two doors from the Arch Street Methodist Episcopal Church. The front of the brick home was accented with four arched windows across the first level, six arched windows on the second floor and three dormers on the third. A portico rested on top of the twelve-foot arched entrance, with wide stairs and curved banisters leading into the house. Magnificent crown molding separated the second floor from the third floor. It seemed that Simpson was determined to prove his detractors right. "He lived in a mansion." The Simpson house epitomized the ascendency of a profession which, at one time, had determined to be the, "filth and off-scouring of the earth."[1728] The house overwhelmed Ellen. Of course, hundreds of guests had to be entertained, and the showplace had to be in presentable condition. Matthew wrote his wife: "I am sorry you have so much anxiety with company and with the cares of the house."[1729] But the husband was pleased with his new digs. To Sibbie he wrote, "This is the first letter which I have written in my new library. My books are only partially on the shelves, but the shelving is in, and the carpet is down. I have my large office desk near the window, and my table and turning case near me. I hope to be able to write more comfortably than for some time past."[1730]

1726 Matthew Simpson, "Jesus Conquering the World," *Vermont Chronicle*, Bellows Falls, VT (June 15, 1867).

1727 The house was fifty feet wide and one hundred feet deep, five thousand square feet on each floor. Plot found in *Atlas of the 6th, 9th, & 10th Wards of the City of Philadelphia from Private Plans, Actual Surveys & Official Records* (Philadelphia: Elvino V. Smith, C.E., 1908).

1728 Deed is on record at Philadelphia City Hall. The house was torn down in the 1920s, and the property is now occupied by a private parking garage.

1729 UMA, Drew University, Simpson papers, Letter September 20, 1882.

1730 UMA, Drew University, Simpson papers, Letter January 17, 1882.

Women in Ministry

The last cause which Simpson championed was the right of women to minister in and for the Church. But the word "champion" is possibly too strong, because Simpson provided no theological or biblical rationale for the equality of women. He was not nearly as radical as Phoebe Palmer, who in 1859 wrote *The Promise of the Father*, basing her argument on the second chapter of Joel.[1731] As had been his rationale for women suffrage, he was pragmatic in that women had much to offer especially in terms of missionary service. Before the Women's Foreign Missionary Society in New York he stated, "God is intending evidently that women shall do something in this age more than in the past .... I think I see in this society an answer to the great question, 'What shall women do?'"[1732] At the 1872 General Conference Simpson argued for the formation of the Women's Foreign Missionary Society, which was accomplished. Edward Ames disagreed with Simpson, claiming that women as opposed to men, would realize for Methodism only a three-fourths return on the financial investment. What algorithms Ames used is not clear.[1733]

On January 22, 1884, before the First M. E. Church in Baltimore, Simpson advocated a "college for women," which would be built with a bequest by Baltimore pastor, John Gocher. The "Women's Educational Association" within the M E Church was created, which eventually led to the formation of the Office of Deaconess in 1890.[1734] For the entirety of his Episcopal office, Simpson was not in the vanguard of "women in ministry," and at no time argued for women in the pulpit. On several issues during Simpson's life, it was important for crusaders to gain the Bishop's tacit

---

1731   Phoebe Palmer. *The Promise of the Father* (Salem, Ohio: Schmul Publishers, 1981).
1732   Rosemary S. Kelly. "Creating a Sphere for Women," *Historical Perspectives on the Wesleyan Tradition: Women in New Worlds* Vol. II, eds. Rosemary Skinner Kelly, Louise L Queen, and Hilah F. Tomas (Nashville: Abingdon, 1982) 259
1733   Wade Barclay. *History of Methodist Missions: Widening Horizons, 1845-1895* Vol. III (New York: The Board of Missions of the Methodist Church, 1957) 144.
1734   Mara T. Brannon, "A Partnership in Equality," *Historical Perspectives on the Wesleyan Tradition: Women in New Worlds* Vol. II, eds. Rosemary Skinner Kelly, Louisa L. Queen, and Hilah F. Tomas (Nashville: Abingdon, 1982) 259.

approval, if not his proactive and full endorsement. Not until 1956 did the United Methodist Church fully ordain women, a full century behind the radical Holiness groups which broke away from the Methodist Church.[1735]

Valedictory

The 1884 General Conference meeting at Philadelphia seemed providential. Had it been held elsewhere, Simpson would have not been able to attend. God had allowed Simpson's last public appearance to be a benediction on American Methodism. The Church had made him, and over the last three decades, more than any other person, he had made the Methodist Episcopal Church. As Simpson stood before the Conference, it was apparent that he was at death's door. His face had lost the color of life, his skin hung on an emaciated body, his voice trembled, and his walk tottered. To find in the annals of American Methodism, a more lavish expression of gratitude, than that which the 1884 General Conference extended to their most cherished leader, would be unlikely. The delegates expressed their admiration in a 600 word resolution, part of which read:

> Resolved, 1) That this General Conference desires to express and to place upon the record, voicing the heart of the Church, and, as it believes of universal Methodism, and to a large extent of the people of this country, its deep and ever-increasing affection for Bishop Simpson, its entire confidence in his judgment and piety, its profound respect for his practical wisdom and the blended dignity and simplicity of his personal bearing, its admiration of his eloquence, and its sense of the benefits conferred upon the Church and the Nation by his spotless reputation and beneficent career. Resolved, 2) That we recognize in the peculiar qualities of his mind and the attributes of his eloquence, an excellent gift of God to the Methodist Episcopal Church, in that the power of his oratory has not consisted in meretricious ornaments or deceptive artifices, but in the outflow of a soul yearning to do men good, and in the warmth of a heart able to respond to an unusual extent to those sentiments of love and pathos which the Gospel inspires, and which have caused him to burn with a holy ardor, and enabled him to impart a heavenly unction to the vast congregations to whom the Gospel as preached by him has indeed been a ministry of reconciliation.[1736]

1735 Connor S. Kenaston. "From Rib to Robe: Women Ordination in the United Methodist Church," *Methodist History* 53:3 (April 2015) 162-172.

1736 *Journal of the 1884 General Conference of the Methodist Episcopal Church* (New York: Phillips & Hunt, 1884) 257.

At the close of the Conference, Simpson addressed American Methodism for the last time. His farewell, which lasted approximately five minutes, included the following: "It is true that there is a larger proportion, I think, of youthful members than we have had in former General Conferences; but it is exceedingly gratifying to me, as I feel that the shadows are gathering around me and others, to see young men truly cultured and devoted to the cause of Christ, able to come forward and take the reins of the Church, and guide it so successfully onward. May God be gracious to them, and make them greater than the fathers!" And then Simpson, with a pathos that only a dying man could muster, intimately expressed, as if he was a general departing from his troops after the final battle:

> And now brethren, a word personally. I have no words to express the gratitude of my heart for the many courtesies and the kindly utterances you have made. They will be embalmed in my heart forever. Whatever the future may be, whatever of time and strength I may have, all belong to the cause of Christ. And, may we go forward from this time, dear brethren, to try to do more vigorous work than we have ever done. May we have the spirit of deep consecration. May we pray for a more powerful outpouring of the Holy Spirit. May we look for revivals all over our country, until multiplied thousands shall be converted to God. And now, dear Brethren, in closing this service, and bidding you farewell, I pray that God may be with you, and protect you in your journeyings to your respective homes. May you find your families in peace, and safety, and prosperity, and may God ever pour upon you the riches of his grace![1737]

Death and Funeral

After the benediction of the 1884 General Conference on May 28, it was almost as if Simpson had lived to pronounce his final blessing upon the whole of American Methodism. In hopes that Simpson would recover, his family had made plans to spend the summer at Clifton Springs, New York.[1738] But on Saturday, June 6, his gastroenteritis had worsened, and prominent Philadelphia physicians were called to assist the family doctor, Lewis D. Harlow. His strength failed him quickly. Confined to bed, he

---

1737   Ibid., 291.

1738   Henry Foster had founded a water-cure sanitarium at Clifton Springs, New York, and Simpson was an honorary member of the Board. Simpson had also spent time there in July 1881, for the recovery of his health. Foster attended Simpson's funeral. www.thespringofclifton.com/About-Springs-of-Clifton.html.

survived for three more weeks, for the most part maintaining full awareness, but enduring intense physical suffering. During these last days, no one but his immediate family, except for a few select visitors, was allowed to see him. His son-in-law, Charles Buoy, provided pastoral care and gave updates on the Bishop's physical condition. On June 11 when Buoy probed his father-in-law's spiritual consciousness, the Bishop responded, "I am a sinner saved by grace. O, to be like Him! O, to see Him as He is!" When Buoy asked Simpson, "Is Jesus precious?" the old preacher exclaimed, "Precious! Precious! To you who believe, He is precious! O, the wonderful possibilities beyond." The next day, June 12, he exclaimed, "My Savior! My Savior!" Simpson then quoted from Isaiah 3: 2, "When thou passest through the waters, I will be with thee; and through the rivers they shall not overflow thee." On Friday June 13, when Buoy verbalized the lines of a hymn:

> Oh, would he more of heaven bestow, And let the vessels break Savior!
> And let our ransomed spirits go, To grasp the God we seek,
> In rapturous awe on him to gaze, Who bought the sight for me,
> And shout and wonder at his grace, Through all eternity.

Simpson repeated the last two lines,

> And shout and wonder at his grace, Through all eternity.

On Sunday, June 15, Ellen quoted from Charles Wesley's hymn: "Jesus, lover of my soul," and her husband repeated the last line, "O, receive my soul at last." In his closing hours, before yielding to a coma on Sunday morning, he embraced Ellen and verbalized, "My dearest, my dearest." Sibbe recalled, "Ma said to him, 'Pa, if you go away, you will come back to me again,' he replied, 'I do not know what God's order will be as to that, but affection never dies.' She said, 'I cannot live without you." Oh, yes,' he answered, 'for these girls.' After this, he was quiet and said but little. Very soon his mind began to wander."[1739] He then spoke his last words, "My Savior, My Savior," and fell into a coma, dying three days later, Wednesday, June 18, at 8:40 a.m. American Methodism's most renowned preacher and leader in the entirety of its history, besides Francis Asbury, had passed to his eternal reward.

1739 UMA, Drew University, Crooks papers, Letter, Sarah Elizabeth Simpson to George Crooks, March 7, 1890.

James Morrow, a local Methodist pastor whom the family had allowed into the death chamber, testified that, "Bishop Simpson died as he lived–as a conqueror." A few moments after Simpson expired, Alpha Kynett and James Long stepped into the room and closed his eyes.[1740]

The funeral was held six days after his death, Tuesday, June 24, at the Arch Street Church, Philadelphia Methodism's most architecturally splendid facility, only approximately one hundred feet from the Bishop's residence. Simpson had dedicated the Arch Street church in November of 1870. It was distinguished by its one hundred-twenty feet spire and north-gable stained-glass window, sixteen feet wide and thirty-two feet high. The Gothic arched ceiling rose fifty feet from the floor. The pulpit was made of "white statuary marble, ornamented with various colored marbles, in what is called the renaissance Gothic order of architecture. It stands on a carved, black walnut platform, making a striking contrast between the snowy whiteness of the marble and the heavy dark base. The marble, on which the entire building is constructed, is of a beautiful whiteness and is very hard." In preaching the dedication sermon, Simpson described his architectural philosophy which he had gifted to, if not imposed on, American Methodism. "The log building in the wilderness maybe as acceptable to God as the more imposing pile in the centers of civilization. But the house of God should always be equal to the grandest edifices built for the residences and businesses of those surrounding. If they were not so, they would not be the fullest signification the 'House of God's glory.'"[1741]

At 2:00, the Reverend W. C. Robinson met with the family for prayer at the Simpson home. Twenty Philadelphia police officers were brought in for crowd control and to allow the family and officiates to walk unmolested to the church. A rope was stretched between the church and the house so that the hundreds outside would not press in on the family. Tickets had been issued to those who were allowed to sit on the main floor, and then the balcony was

---

1740 *Southwestern Christian Advocate*, New Orleans (July 3, 1884). There is a disagreement as to the last spoken words of Simpson. The *Southwestern Christian Advocate* recorded them to be, "Yes! Yes! Glory Be to Jesus!" I suspect the claim that he embraced Ellen could be apocryphal. Alpha Kynett, a Methodist Elder, was "Corresponding Secretary" for the Church Extension Society, and, thus, lived in Philadelphia. *Cyclopaedia*, 522.

1741 "The Arch Street Methodist Episcopal Church Dedication Services," *Philadelphia Public Ledger* (November 18, 1870).

opened for the small portion of the remaining crowd who were able to obtain a seat. Hundreds stood around the inside perimeter of the church. It was packed until not another person could find standing room.[1742]

Ellen Simpson, a person of strength and dignity, walked with her son, Matthew Verner Simpson, followed by daughters Ida and Sibbe Simpson, Ellen's brother, James Verner and wife, Charles' two children, George McCullough, Jr. and his wife, and a cousin, David Simpson and wife. The coffin was carried or followed by eleven pallbearers including James Harlan, John Evans, Clinton Fisk, George Crooks, and John Lanahan. The casket was placed on a catafalque at the front of the church, with two large wreaths on each side bearing the inscriptions "Father" and "Husband."[1743] The family had spared no expense in saying goodbye. The body was dressed in a suit of black broadcloth such as the Bishop usually wore, and rested in a casket of Florida red cedar, covered with black velvet, with rows of silkentine molding and black satin. Along the sides and at the ends were handles of oxidized silver, tipped with gold. The top was hinged with lock and key, and tufted with satin. The plate was of oxidized silver inlaid with gold, and bore the following inscription:

BISHOP MATTHEW SIMPSON
BORN
JUNE 11, 1811
DIED
JUNE 18, 1884

The casket rested on two black cloth-covered pedestals, under which was a "black Smyrna rug." Over all was a canopy of cloth and satin lined with white, supported by columns of polished mahogany. Black curtains were draped back to these columns by silk cords and tassels; and heavy tassels hung from the corners.[1744]

1742 According to Arch Street United Methodist Church Historian Dale Shillito, the church presently seats 920. With extra chairs and allowing for standing room, possibly 1,200 could have packed into the church. Another 2,000- 3.000 stood on the outside of the church during Simpson's funeral.

1743 Funeral description is taken from the Philadelphia *North American* (June 25, 1884), the New Orleans *Southwestern Christian Advocate* (July 3, 1884), and the New York *Christian Advocate* (July 3, 1884).

1744 "Funeral Services of Bishop Simpson," *The Christian Advocate*: New York (July 3,

The service lasted two hours, three to five p.m. While all the Bishops participated in the service, Bishop Randolph Foster who had served as both President of North Western University and Drew Theological Seminary brought the main sermon. Foster emphasized that Simpson was a, "progressive, if not a radical on some points in our church life and history, the wisdom of which was questioned by the majority of his brethren, but events have justified his conclusions." Those progressive elements in particular were in the areas of church architecture and lay representation. Of course, Foster recalled Simpson's patriotism and his relationships with Lincoln and Stanton. Simpson would be most remembered for his preaching. "But it should be said that while his sermons were more popular than scientific, for the masses rather than critical ears, they were of the very highest order of pulpit utterance, not simply unctuous, but luminous and rich with the best Christian thought, and often enriched with the finest scientific illustrations and invariably with the revealed thought of God." Foster further stated of Simpson, "One of the noted peculiarities of his influence was the marked power he had over great men. No man has lived among us who has been as influential with the great leading minds of our Country, in professional and political life; and it is doubtful that any have a more conservative power for our holy Christian faith." But Foster, an orator in his own right, could not preach the funeral of America's greatest preacher without being carried up into a flight of elocution himself:

> He sees "face to face." We hover about the grave. He basks in the refulgence of the eternal sun whose glory lightens the city of our God. We mourn; he rejoices. We shiver under the shadow of the farewell. He has emerged exultantly into the warmth of the heavenly welcome. It is too much to expect of us, in the fresh grief of the separation; but if we could see as he now sees, and know as he now knows, our sobs would be changed into shouting and our lamentations into anthems. But we shall be forgiven our tears, badges of weakness and sorrowing love, but we come to where "tears shall be wiped away from all faces," and there shall be no more death, neither sorrow nor crying. Until then farewell, beloved of our soul! Our paths lead on, and the open portal waits for us. The days will not be many when we shall join you again. You know now what it all means; we shall know Brothers all, I cannot refrain; I seem to hear him calling; his tall celestial form dilating, with face aflame and finger pointing to a weary, writhing, sinning, sorrowing world; I seem to hear

---

1884).

his words ringing down through the side rail arches; it is his own voice, still tender, appealing, and pathetic--he is still pleading for humanity. There is a deeper pathos, a more profound and serious earnestness. The new light of eternity has given higher value to the transcendent problems. He has learned the deeper meaning of the soul, its perils, its wants, its salvation or loss forever, of eternity, its immense and awful issues; the woes and sorrows and dangers of a perishing world. He pleads with us, urges us, and entreats us to a deeper consecration, a holier zeal, a more consuming earnestness. He pleads with the Church, with you, his chosen whom he put honor, with the great host of God's elect in every fold, for the consecration of your property, persons, and influence, entire power, to bring the world quickly to Christ. Shall we not hear the voice once so welcome, more potent now from his pulpit in the skies, and go forth from this holy house to renewed diligence in the great Master's work?[1745]

Everyone that was someone was present at Simpson's funeral: mercantile moguls John Wanamaker and Oliver Hoyt, George Stuart, former President of the Christian Commission, Pennsylvania Governor Robert E. Pattison, Governor W. A. Porter from Indiana, and almost all of the clergy and many other dignitaries from Philadelphia. None of them had ever heard a more elaborate eulogy, some of it accurate and much of it exaggerated. But no one could have been more concise and correct than Pastor David Moore, who 2,000 miles away in Denver, Colorado, at Evans Chapel, said of the Bishop's death, "Society mourns, because it has lost its ideal Christian gentleman."[1746]

The casket was re-opened for family and friends to view the body immediately after the service. It was left open until 10 p.m., so that the hundreds, who were unable to get into the church for the actual service, could file by the body of Philadelphia and Methodism's most illustrious citizen. The next morning, June 26, at 9:00 a.m., the family returned to the church, and after briefly tarrying at the open casket, said a final farewell. The coffin was then placed in a hearse and taken to South Laurel Hill Cemetery. After a brief service led by Bishops Bowman, Foster, and Andrews in the presence of approximately 200 persons, the coffin was lowered into a vault at 11:00 a.m.[1747]

1745 Funeral oration from *The Christian Advocate*: New York (July 3, 1884).

1746 "Made In Memory: Services over the Death of the Late Bishop Simpson in All of the Methodist Churches Yesterday," The *Rocky Mountain News*: Denver (June 23, 1884). David Moore was, at this time, serving as President of the University of Denver. In 1900, he would be elected Bishop.

1747 *The North American*: Philadelphia (June 26, 1884).

Epilogue and Reflection

The Biography Squabble

The Bishop's possessions at the time of death were modest, but he had not died in poverty, acquiring an estate of $93,083.11.[1748] Simpson recorded his will in June, 1875, leaving all of his worldly belongings to his wife, Ellen. But on May 26, 1881, Simpson filed a codicil, which allotted $50,000 for the endowment of a Bishop's Chair in Philadelphia; that is, there would be on-going financial support for the residential Bishop of the Philadelphia Conference.[1749] Interestingly, Simpson's two largest investments reflected his relationship with John Evans: $16,000 in the New York, Chicago, & St. Louis R.R., and $18,000 in Denver real estate.[1750]

The bodies of Bishop Simpson, sons James and Charles, would not have to wait the final summons for their first upheaval. Soon after the Bishop's funeral, Ellen set in motion the building of a mausoleum. The Simpsons needed a final resting place in keeping with their status in society and Church. Ellen purchased a ninety-foot-in-diameter lot in the Highlands section of West Laurel Hills Cemetery, Philadelphia, which was founded in 1869. By February 15, 1887, the tomb was readied, and the bodies of the Bishop, his two sons, mother Sarah and Uncle Matthew, were removed from South Laurel Hills Cemetery and reinterred in the Simpson lot in West Laurel Hills. Ultimately, fourteen people were buried in the Simpson mausoleum, including Ellen and her seven children.[1751]

1748   Matthew Simpson Will, Register of Wills Office, City Hall, Philadelphia, PA.
1749   Dale Shillito researched the Minutes of the 1884, 1885, 1886, 1887, and 1888 Philadelphia Annual Conferences, and found no reference of any money left by Simpson to the Philadelphia Annual Conference. Letter from Dale Shillito to Darius Salter, April 1, 2016.
1750   Register of Wills Office, City Hall: Philadelphia, PA.
1751   Buried in the tomb are Matthew Simpson, Ellen Verner Simpson, Matthew Verner Simpson, Charles Henry Simpson, Sarah Elizabeth Simpson, Ida Simpson, Uncle

After securing a proper burial place, the family searched for a biographer. Writing a Simpson biography in a manner that would please the family, while maintaining integrity and exhibiting literary prowess, was far more complicated than building a shrine to house the Bishop's corpse. Ellen decided on George Crooks, a family friend who taught at Drew, a man of academic stature who had written the biography of John McClintock. After McClintock died, Crooks was Simpson's choice for the presidency of Drew Theological Seminary, but the Drew Board elected Randolph Sinks Foster.

The biography project proved trying for all concerned. The family members possessed less material on the patriarch than they assumed, and Crooks was left with a research project that demanded more time and energy than he predicted. Crooks attempted to revise the $1,500 agreed upon price to $5,000 and four years of quarreling ensued between Crooks and the Simpson family. Caught in the calumny and attempted arbitration were Ellen, the Simpson siblings, Harper Brothers, Charles Buoy, Clinton Fisk, and George Crooks. In the beginning, Ellen made it clear that she did not want to be entangled in any disagreement, desiring to defer the issue to Harper Brothers. She wrote Crooks:

> I may entertain the thought of sharing the royalty which the Harpers have contracted to pay me. I am very sorry there should

Matthew Simpson, Mother Sarah Tingley Simpson, Anna Simpson Weaver, Ella Simpson Buoy, Charles W. Buoy, Emma L. Simpson, James V. Simpson, and an urn holding the ashes of Eva Nelson Simpson. The newspapers gave a full description of the Simpson tomb. "The structure is cruciform, 18 ft. 6 in. wide, 22 feet 6 in. long. And 24 ft. 6 in. to the top of the crosses, which capped each gable end. The entrance to the mausoleum, an arched doorway, would be closed in the summer by a perforated, bronze gate of elegant design and superior workmanship, and in winter by a door of heavy carved oak. Light will fall into the interior through windows of cathedral stained glass, one in the rear, three on each side, and one over the entrance, each illustrating some religious fact or story. On each side of the entrance are polished tablets for epitaphs or the names of the silent occupants of the tomb. Supporting the arch of the doorway are columns of polished Quincy granite. In the center of the interior will stand the sarcophagus of white marble, which will contain the mortal remains of the deceased Bishop. This is 8 ft. 6 in. long, 3 ft. 10 in. wide, and 4 ft. 3 in. in height, with marble columns at each corner supporting the top which is an imitation of the roof and the mausoleum. In the projecting wings are catacombs intended to receive the remains of members of the Bishop's family. Of these there are four on each side to which will be fitted marble slabs with bronze handles which will bear the names and the age of their occupants. The floor will be laid with blocks of alternate black and white marble tiling." "Bishop Simpson Mausoleum," *The Atchison Daily Globe* (February 15, 1887). As of this writing, the mausoleum is in a sad state of disrepair.

have been any misunderstanding between us, but feel that any further compensation which you request as justly due you should be met by the publisher. When I made the contract with the Harpers, I was to be relieved of expenses in the preparation of the work, and I do not think, I should be brought into the question.[1752]

The crux of Crooks' argument which he sent to Ellen on January 8, 1889, consisted of the following:

> The letters placed in my hands by you, covering these latter years are mostly rubbish. They are not the Bishop's letters at all, but letters written to him by hundreds of persons on matters which can be of no use to his biographer. There is not a scrap of writing as far as I now remember which touches on his influence with President Lincoln and Secretary Stanton .... I will add to the above, it has cost me $500 to secure the restoration of my sight which was impaired by my exertion to get the book out in the autumn of 1888. I continued at the work of writing and revising when I should have given it up. But, I was so solicitous that the book possibly should be done both for the publisher and yourself that I disregarded the warnings of my physician.[1753]

Ellen held her ground. She assured Crooks of her "best motives at heart," and reminded him of their long friendship. "Still I feel this great amount is larger than I can feel just in assessing; and cannot, therefore, agree to your proposition as it now stands."[1754] Son-in-law Charles Buoy jumped into the fight (July 2, 1889), but after making no progress turned the matter over to Clinton Fisk, who was now President of the East Tennessee Land Company with an office at 175 West 58th Street, New York.[1755] Fisk became the arbitrator between Crooks and the family. Ultimately, Ellen Simpson agreed to pay an extra $1,000, making her part of the financial arrangement $2,500, with the remainder to be collected by "royalties from Harpers."This final offer was contingent on the release of the book by Easter of 1890.[1756] Crooks met his deadline, and the *Life of Bishop Matthew Simpson* hit the market in February, 1890. In 1894 the family was still trying to retrieve the

---

1752 UMA, Drew University, Crooks papers, Letter November 14, 1884.

1753 UMA, Drew University, Crooks papers, Letter January 8, 1889.

1754 UMA, Drew University, Crooks papers, Letter February 1, 1889.

1755 UMA, Drew University, Crooks papers, Letter, Charles Buoy to Clinton Fisk, July 2, 1889.

1756 UMA, Drew University, Crooks papers, Letter, Ellen Simpson to Clinton Fisk, December 6, 1889.

Simpson papers from Crooks. As I stated in the "Introduction," there is an autobiographical piece that has never been recovered.

Ellen's Influence

Ellen lived thirteen years after the death of her husband, dying in Philadelphia, on Sunday December 19, 1897. "Her death was directly due to a general breaking up of the nervous system, but the end was undoubtedly hastened by the recent death of her son-in-law, Rev. Charles Buoy, at whose home she was when she breathed her last," or so the newspaper said.[1757] Ellen Simpson was a cosmopolitan lady in a cosmopolitan city, serving on the boards or committees of no less than ten organizations, including one of thirteen women, representing the thirteen colonies for the 1876 Centennial Committee. She founded an orphanage, chaired the board for the Methodist Episcopal Home (for the aged), which became known as Simpson House, still in existence today.[1758] Ironically, she also involved herself with the Indian Rights Association.

The Gilded Age was defined by a surge of religious philanthropy, especially in Philadelphia. The most prominent Methodist institutions were a home for the aged (Simpson House), a hospital, of which Matthew Simpson was the first president, and an orphanage. Ellen was involved with the founding of all three endeavors. Methodist historian Kenneth Rowe writes: "Inspired by recently-published accounts of Wesley's liberated women, emboldened by their experience as nurses, workers, and single heads of households during the Civil War, freed by a growing list of household conveniences, women in Bishop Simpson's Methodism, began to push the boundaries of acceptable female behavior."[1759] As to the orphanage, Rowe states, "Ellen Simpson, wife of the ME Church's most visible and powerful Bishop and President Lincoln-confidant, helped mobilize the energy

---

[1757] "Mrs. Ellen Simpson Dead," *The North American* (December 21, 1897).

[1758] David R. Adam. *A Second Century of Ministry: A History of Simpson House* (Simpson House: Belmont Avenue, 1990).

[1759] Kenneth E. Rowe, "Three Great Charities: Philadelphia as a Cradle of Methodist Healthcare Initiatives in Victorian America," *Journal of the Historical Society of the EPA Conference* (2011) 26. Rowe claims that Ellen Simpson worked in tent hospitals during the Civil War, which were prevalent in Philadelphia, but I can find no documentation of Ellen's involvement. She likely made some token appearance to care for wounded soldiers.

to build the best known of the nineteenth century Methodist homes for children, The Methodist Episcopal Orphanage in Philadelphia."[1760] This institution, located adjacent to Simpson House, is no longer under the auspices of the Methodist Episcopal Church, and presently serves as a day school and provides temporary housing for indigent families.[1761]

The most visible monument today, of Ellen and her Methodist sisters' philanthropy, is Simpson House, Fairmount Park in Philadelphia. At its construction in 1898, it was a state-of-the-art building, and today serves as an assisted-living residence for senior citizens. Unfortunately, what was once an attractive and contemporary design is today a stark, foreboding Gothic building, which could serve as a *misse in siene* for a horror movie, illuminated by a few lightning bolts on a dark night.

Ellen Simpson was a harbinger for defining the role of a Methodist preacher's wife. She symbolized Methodism's shifting role within American society, even more than did her husband. Without Ellen's societal pretensions and upper class socio-economic background, for better or worse, Matthew Simpson would have been a different person. Primarily because of Ellen, the husband and wife transitioned the Methodist Episcopal Church from the "nobodies" into the "somebodies" of American society. Ellen defined the "queen of the parsonage," as opposed to the no-frills wife of a poor preacher, barely putting bread on the table. More than any other two individuals within nineteenth-century American Methodism, through word and deed, Methodism's "first couple" made loud and clear that one could be a prestigious person in one of America's most prestigious cities, and still represent the meek and lowly in the Kingdom of God. Emblematic of the "new" Methodist in housing, clothing, manners, and a dozen other ways, Matthew and Ellen Simpson personified dual allegiance to God and mammon.[1762]

1760 Rowe, 34.

1761 Though it is no longer directly owned and controlled by the United Methodist Church, The Methodist Home for Children is largely supported by Methodists. Its mission statement reads, "The Methodist Services System provides life enriching programs to children, adults and families as they face the challenges of limited resources, increased poverty, homelessness, disabilities and deficits in education. We provide early childhood education, school age programs, housing services, supports for families, mental health and counseling services, and nutrition programs from pamphlet – courtesy of the Methodist Home for Children, Philadelphia, PA."

1762 Interestingly, Winthrop Hudson in his *Religion in America*, referred to Matthew

Ellen had endured hard times, and had been a tower of strength, defying both the ill-health of her husband and the ecclesiastical pressures of America's largest denomination. Matthew Simpson could not have chosen a more graceful and efficient helpmeet. She defined who and what a Methodist parson's wife should be, a socialite in the community and a tireless worker in the church. At the same time, no one was less surprised than she, when the couple moved into 1334 Arch Street, one of Philadelphia's most handsome mansions. She had hedged her bets, like many other late nineteenth century American Protestants, that the Kingdom of God does not disallow having both a mansion here and a mansion "there." One Philadelphia historian wrote, "She is actively engaged in furthering the interest of the 'Silk Culture Association,' and notwithstanding these many outside industries, Mrs. Simpson is essentially a 'home woman.'"[1763] Ellen Holmes Simpson had combined civic pride with experiential piety, a delicate balance between domestication and societal sophistication, no mean achievement.

Ellen left the Long Branch house and its contents to the three daughters, Ella, Sarah, and Ida. The four children, including Matthew Verner, were to sort through their mother's belongings at 1334 Arch Street, choosing what each desired, the rest of the property sold, and the proceeds equally divided among the four children. In case of their decease before Ellen's death, property was to be distributed to Ellen Verner Weaver and Ida Blanche Weaver, children of Anna Weaver, and to Gertrude Conrey and Charles Henry Simpson, children of the deceased son, Charles Henry Simpson.[1764]

The family's relationship to and residence in the Arch Street house, remains one of the most mysterious elements within the Simpson family story. Why did Matthew and Ellen Simpson move to 1334 Arch Street only two years before the Bishop's death? Ownership of the house is not

---

Simpson only in regard to his wife: "As early as 1856 the stringent rule prohibiting the use of specific items of ornamentation in dress were reduced in the Discipline to a general admonition, an admonition that was not sufficiently rigorous to deter Bishop Matthew Simpson's wife from appearing in ruffled silk, expensive lace, and fine jewelry." Winthrop S. Hudson. *Religion in America* (New York: Charles Scribner's Sons, 1965) 343.

1763   J. Thomas Sharf and Thomas Westcott. *History of Philadelphia: 1609-1884* Vol. II (Philadelphia: L H. Everts and Company, 1884) 1700.

1764   "Ellen Simpson Will." Monmouth County Surrogate Court, Monmouth County Hall of Records, Freehold, New Jersey: Books 128–129, p. 136.

evidenced in the wills of Ellen and Matthew Simpson, or in any of the wills of the children. A deed abstract indicates that the house was transferred to seven family members in January of 1899 (four children and three grandchildren) from Ellen Verner Weaver.[1765] We can only conclude that the deed is incorrect, and should have indicated Ellen Verner Simpson rather than Ellen Verner Weaver, the daughter of James Riley and Anna Simpson Weaver. On September 15, 1919, the house was sold by Ellen Simpson Buoy, Sarah E. Simpson, and Ida Simpson to Edward W. Johnson. Sadly for us, the transformation of Arch Street, Philadelphia, in the name of progress, destroyed the Bishop's last residence in 1928.[1766]

Matthew Verner Simpson

The Bishop remained anxious that Matthew Verner would make something out of himself. Until his death, the father used his connections

---

1765   Department of Records, Deed Abstracts, City Hall: Philadelphia.

1766   In writing the history of Arch Street United Methodist Church, Philadelphia, Dale Shillito has graciously furnished me the following information on the Arch Street house:

> "Ellen H. Simpson died on December 19, 1897, and Sarah lived there through 1898. Ellen's heirs, who included the entire family, filed an abstract for the house at 1334-36 Arch Street in January 1899. Ida and Sarah are shown to have moved to 1518 Arch Street in 1899. In 1905, the sisters are listed at 918 Pine Street. There were 2 other Simpson siblings alive during this period, Matthew Verner (1853-1923), a Philadelphia lawyer married to Emma Lathers, who died in 1915, and Ella (184?-1927), who was married to Rev. Charles Buoy. Neither name appears in Arch Street membership records. Neither Ella nor Matthew Verner is believed to have lived at 1334-36 Arch Street during this period, so it may be assumed that when Ida and Sarah moved in 1899, the family rented out the house to others.
>
> In 1908, a surveyor's evaluation of the property explained that the contents of the house included items from an auction that sold furniture, crockery and cut glass. In 1919, Ella Buoy, Sarah and Ida sold the house to Edward Johnson, a speculator who resold it within a few months.
>
> In 1922, the Evening Bulletin Company purchased the first 4 properties on the 1300 block of Arch Street and the following year built a 7 story Annex Building. The Bulletin Co. acquired the remaining residences on the block in order to construct a truck loading dock for hauling newspapers. Henry Gross, who bought the house from Edward Johnson, sold it to the Bulletin Company in 1923. In 1928, the former residence of the Bishop at 1334-1336 Arch Street was torn down."

on behalf of his son. In November, 1876, he contacted Remington's Armory in Ilion, New York, requesting a job for Matthew Verner. Simpson had, in all probability, made contact with Eliphalet Remington, when the latter displayed his typewriter at the 1876 Centennial in Philadelphia. The request came up empty. As late as June, 1883, Simpson contacted A. G. Porter, former Governor of Indiana, strangely requesting that Porter contact the Governor of Pennsylvania, for the latter to appoint Matthew Verner Commissioner of Deeds.[1767] There is no evidence that Matthew Verner received the appointment. Matthew graduated from Middletown Wesleyan University, Middletown, Connecticut in 1875, eventually passing the Bar Exam in Philadelphia.

In the early part of 1884 just several months before he died, Matthew Simpson secured for his son a job in the administration of Charles F. Warwick, an attorney who had just been elected as the City Solicitor. [1768]Matthew Verner fulfilled the job as Assistant City Solicitor along with several other attorneys until Warwick was elected Mayor on the Republican ticket in Philadelphia in 1896. The City Solicitors office provided legal consultation for the city of Philadelphia. According to the Wharton School of Finance and Economy in 1893, "the duties of the solicitor were to draft all bonds, obligations, contracts, leases, conveyances and assurances which might be required of him by ordinance of Councils. He was to commence and prosecute all actions brought by the 'mayor, aldermen or citizens' on behalf of the corporation, and to defend all suits brought against the city. He was to furnish opinions on all subjects submitted to him by the mayor or Councils, and 'to do every other professional act incident to the office' when required by the mayor or by ordinance."[1769]

On June 19, 1883, almost exactly one year before the Bishop died, the Simpsons attended an important occasion. It may have been more relief than celebration when Matthew Verner married Emma Lathers of New

---

1767   UMA, Old St. George's UMC: Philadelphia, Simpson papers, Letter from Ilion, New York, Office of Remington's Armory, November 1876, and Letter from A. G. Porter to Bishop Simpson, January 4, 1883.

1768   LOC, Simpson papers, Charles Warwick letter to Matthew Simpson, March 28, 1884, Container thirteen.

1769   "The City Government of Philadelphia: A Study in Municipal Administration," *Politics and Economics* Vol II (Philadelphia: June 1893) 81.

Rochelle, New York. It was a society-page reception, attended by some 700 guests, including Noah Brooks, Abraham Lincoln's former press correspondent, and the Governors of both Rhode Island and New York.[1770]

Richard Lathers' grandfather served as an Anglican priest in a small Irish parish. The family immigrated to South Carolina, date unclear, and Richard established "mercantile" businesses in both Georgetown, South Carolina, and New York. Lathers eventually became president of the Great Western Marine Insurance Company. He continued to deal in just about all imports–exports which existed: cotton, rice, sugar, molasses, hemp, hay, silk, spices, coffee, tea, etc. Lathers moved to New Rochelle, New York, in 1847, where he became Warden of Trinity Church and also was elected as a member of the Episcopal Convention of the Diocese.[1771] The church still exists today as an active congregation and is served by the sanctuary in which the Simpsons were married. The Lathers' house, *Winyah Park*, named after the Episcopal parish in Georgetown, South Carolina, and designed for

---

[1770] "Description of a New Rochelle Wedding" copied from an editorial in *The Hour*, New Rochelle (July 7, 1883). "A pleasing indication that not everyone in the country has exchanged natural manners for city artificiality was offered at a wedding at New Rochelle, a few days ago—namely, at that of Colonel Lather's daughter, Emma, to the son of Bishop Simpson, of Pennsylvania, so that there was no lack of money to restrict formality and ostentation, but the festivities were, nevertheless, entirely modest and appropriate to the surroundings of a rural home. The ceremony at the church was as simple as possible, according to the Episcopal ritual; the rector of the Church Rev. Charles F. Canedy, D.D. was not 'assisted' by any high dignitary nor by anyone else, and the six bridesmaids, all rich and accomplished young ladies, were simple and inexpensively attired in white. The church was profusely decorated with flowers, but all these were peculiar to the season and the locality, not a single exotic being among them; daises, ferns, and roses predominated, and over the bride's head hung an enormous wreath of daisies, plucked from her father's own meadows. The guests numbered nearly a thousand; there were a dozen carriage-loads of fashionable people from the city, but the bride's father, loyal to the people among whom he had lived, saw to it that all of his old neighbors were invited, no matter if they happened to have less money than culture. As the house was two miles from the church, every carriage in the vicinity was pressed into the old colonel's hospitable service, and any ladies and gentlemen from the city did not hesitate to avail themselves of the ordinary stages. As the guests approached the home, they did not behold two heavy closed doors; on the contrary, every door and window was wide open, and everyone, on stepping from the carriages, was received on an immense veranda, gaily decorated with flowers, and as they entered the house they saw flowers in profusion on every table, mantel, bracket, and other places where flowers could be placed. There was no frantic struggling for refreshments; late-comers saw hundreds of people comfortably seated on the verandas and served with salads, strawberries, and ices."

[1771] South Carolina Historical Society. *The Discursive Biographical Sketch of Colonel Richard Lathers: 1841-1902* (Philadelphia: J. B. Lippincott, 1902).

the family by Alexander J. Davis, received the first architectural design prize at the New York World's Fair of 1853-1854.[1772] Unfortunately, the house burned to the ground in 1897, after the Lathers no longer owned it.

No doubt, the Bishop gaped at the seventy original oil paintings, mostly imported from Europe, as well as over forty reproductions hanging in the endless rooms throughout his in-law's mansion. Forty eighteenth and nineteenth-century framed engravings also decorated the walls. The Bishop had lived long enough to witness his son, Matthew Verner, marry into Southern aristocracy and wealth, prosperity that had originated in the most representative slave state within the Confederacy. As he reveled in the opulence, was the father of the groom panged by a glaring disconnect, or did he simply bask in a fitting climax to his and Ellen's societal ascension?

Verner was best known as a choir master showcasing a sixty-voice select choir at various city and church functions, as well as minister of music in his local Methodist Episcopal Church. Until his wife's death in December 1915 at age 57, the couple lived in an elite three-story home, 3720 Walnut Street, where they were known to have receptions for the well-to-do of Philadelphia. On February 11, 1917, Verner bought a larger home at 3805 Walnut Street, in which he invested much money. The house is now owned by Pennsylvania University and serves as a fraternity house. The house was built by "Will Decker, although the hands of Willis Hale and Frank Furnace could be suggested by the heavy, highly-individualistic detail. Fine exuberant, probably late witnesses of the vigorous design spirit of the High-Victorian Era."[1773] Philadelphia historian E. Digby Baltzell claims that Walnut Street between Broad Street and the Schuylkill River was the most fashionable area in Victorian Philadelphia. Philadelphia inhabitant George Wharton Pepper nostalgically recalled, "To mention Walnut Street to an Old Philadelphian was to awaken memories of a departed glory."[1774]

Six months after his wife's death, Matthew Verner married Eva Nelson Groff, born January 13, 1893, to Ella and William Groff, Harrisburg,

---

1772   Ibid., 36.

1773   Pennsylvania Historic Resource Survey Form, Office of Historic Preservation, PA Historical & Museum Commission.

1774   E. Dibgy Baltzell. *Philadelphia Gentlemen: The Making of a National Upper Class* (New York: The Free Press, 1958) 185.

Pennsylvania. On the date of marriage, June 26, 1916, she was almost 40 years younger than her husband.[1775] Eva was a twenty-three-year-old, dark-eyed, dark-haired beauty of whom the Simpson family did not approve. The age difference was so apparent that three hotels turned them down on their wedding night, or so the story goes. To escape the disdain of his sisters and the Philadelphia winters, Matthew Verner and Eva moved to California in the early part of 1922. In April of the same year, the couple toured Europe including Holland, Germany, Switzerland, France, and Italy. On his passport application, the husband fudged his wife's age as 30, when she had only recently turned 29. At the time of their European vacation, Matthew Verner was a dapper-looking 68-year-old, with the facial features of his father, but considered more handsome.

Matthew Verner died September 22, 1923, age 70, while he and Eva were still living in Pasadena, for the purpose of enjoying a climate which might be of some help to Matthew Verner's health. There is no record of her remarrying. Eva Nelson Simpson lived for 57 years after her husband's death, and took, at least, five trips abroad during her lifetime, continuing to live in southern California for the rest of her life. After dying, December 5, 1980, her ashes were placed in the Simpson mausoleum where her husband was buried. Matthew Verner Simpson left the 3805 Walnut Street house to his wife in his original will, filed January 9, 1922. A codicil recorded almost three months later, "revoked" the leaving of the 3805 Walnut Street property to Eva Nelson Simpson, for reasons to which we are not privy.[1776]

The Daughters and Final Distribution of the Estate

In 1876, Ella Simpson married thirty-five year old Charles Wesley Buoy, a member of the Philadelphia Conference of the Methodist Episcopal Church. Buoy graduated from Dickinson College, and DePauw conferred the Doctor of Divinity on him in 1886. He was in poor health most of

---

1775   Email sent from Kevin Crain (KCrain@cityofpasadena.net) on Wednesday, August 19, 2015. According to Dave Adam, Simpson House historian, Eva Nelson Simpson was the black sheep of the family. This information was relayed to him by a niece of Eva Nelson Simpson, Josephine Duebler. Not only was Eva nearly forty years younger than Verner, she had replaced the socialite wife, Emma Lathers.

1776   Office of Wills, City Hall, Philadelphia, PA.

his life, having to resign pastorates in Salisbury, Maryland, and Denver, Colorado. In spite of his physical liabilities, Buoy managed to build two Methodist Episcopal churches in the Philadelphia Conference, Trinity and Church of the Covenant. Buoy was scholarly in his approach to ministry and served as an able assistant on his father-in-law's *Cyclopaedia*. His eulogist described him as "winsome in manner, aesthetic in taste, scholarly in argument; he was above everything else, a gospel evangelist and a faithful preacher of righteousness. He valued education. Perhaps his most permanent monument is the Conference seminary at Dover, Delaware at his appeal and has been enriched by his library since his death." (One would assume that Buoy inherited Matthew Simpson's library and Dover, Delaware was its destination.) Buoy died in November of 1897 at fifty-six years old.[1777]

On October 4, 1895, Anna Simpson Weaver, living in Greencastle, Indiana, with her husband-professor James Riley Weaver, died from an operation for breast cancer. The details are not clear, but after surviving one operation, she went into "shock" after a second surgery, expiring in an Indianapolis hospital at 6 p.m.[1778] Her body was shipped by train to Philadelphia and buried in the family mausoleum. She had the looks of her mother and the brains of her father. She attended Pittsburg Female College where she graduated as Valedictorian, displaying oratorical flair by delivering an essay "An Odd Wonder or Two in the World of Literature." Anna was a capable musician in both instrument and song. Simpson was proud of his Diplomat-College Professor Son-In-Law, James Riley Weaver. As I have suggested, he represented for the Bishop, more than did Charles and Matthew Verner, the beau ideal of a son.[1779] Anna left two children, Ellen Verner and Ida Blanche.

Ella outlived her husband, Charles Buoy, by thirty years, dying in 1927 at the Simpson summer home in Long Branch. She bore no children and thus

---

[1777] *Minutes of the Annual Conferences of the Methodist Episcopal Church- Spring Conferences* (New York: Eaton and Mains, 1898) 103-104. This school is presently Wesley College in Dover, Delaware. In visiting the school, I found only one set of books that had been given by C. W. Buoy, Luke Tyerman's *Life of Wesley*. One of the books had Sibbie Simpson's name in it.

[1778] *The Banner Times*, Greencastle, Indiana (October 5, 1895). On file, DePauw University.

[1779] UMA, Drew University, Simpson papers, "In Loving Memory of Anna Simpson."

bequeathed $10,000 to her niece, Ellen Verner Weaver, who was to draw five percent each year until her death. The $10,000 was then to be deposited in an endowment fund at Simpson College in Indianola, Iowa. She also endowed a bed with $5,000 at the Methodist Episcopal Hospital in Philadelphia.[1780] The last two sisters to die were Ida and Sarah Elizabeth, neither having ever married. Ida died in October of 1933 at 78, Philadelphia, and was buried in the family mausoleum. Other than the codicils for Sarah Simpson's will, the wills of the last two sisters were identical, to be determined by the last sister living.[1781] At the time of her death, Ida was serving as the president of the Methodist Episcopal Orphanage.

Sarah Elizabeth (Sibbie) was the last of the children to die, February 29, 1936, leaving an estate of $450,000. The bulk of the estate was not in Philadelphia, but Pittsburgh, in the form of two properties, 613 Liberty Avenue, and 614 Penn Avenue, which were valued at $280,000 by a Pittsburgh appraiser.[1782] The properties were left to Simpson College in Indianola, Iowa, the only college in America named after Matthew Simpson. In total the College received approximately $300,000 designated as the "Bishop and Mrs. Simpson Endowment Fund." There is historical evidence that the College received the properties, but no scholarship, building, or anything else other than the name of the college itself, as of this writing, has the name Simpson attached to it.

Upon learning that a possible gift may be coming from the Simpson family, John Hillman, President of Simpson College, faithfully courted the Simpson sisters. When Ella, Ida, and Sarah attended the General Conference in 1920, Des Moines, Iowa, Hillman chauffeured them to Indianola some twenty miles south for a campus tour.[1783] Hillman dined with Ida and Sarah at the General Conference in Kansas City in 1928. When Hillman thanked the two sisters for the $10,000 bequest provided by Ida Buoy who was

---

1780 "Ella Simpson Buoy Will," Monmouth County Surrogate Court, Monmouth County Hall of Records, Freehold, New Jersey: Book 131-133, p. 447.

1781 "Sarah Elizabeth Simpson Will," Monmouth County Surrogate Court, Monmouth County Hall of Records, Freehold, New Jersey: Book 127, p. 323.

1782 Register of Wills and Agent of the Commonwealth, Allegheny County, Pittsburgh, PA, 2nd Floor, City-County Building, February 16, 1937.

1783 Joseph W. Walt. *Beneath the Whispering Maples: The History of Simpson College* (Indianola, Iowa; College Press, 1995) 325.

no longer living, one of the sisters responded, "We might as well tell you now that there is more, much more coming to the College. We have some valuable property in Pittsburgh that came to us from our Mother, which she had from her Father." Ida or Sarah added, "We have investigated and feel that it will do as much for Christian education as any place we can put it, and that the College was named for our Father. We hope you won't ask us to turn it over (as) an annuity. We are not in a hurry to go to heaven, but we hope you will still be at Simpson when we are gone."[1784] Whenever Hillman was in Philadelphia, he called on the Simpson sisters.

Sarah Elizabeth bequeathed $100,000 to American University for the construction of a "Hall of Nations," dedicated to the study of international affairs and social science. Henry L Stimson, Secretary of War under William Howard Taft, Franklin Roosevelt, and Harry Truman, and Secretary of State under Herbert Hoover, to accept the chairmanship of the advisory committee which would plan the new building and academic department.[1785] The plan never came to pass. One hundred thousand dollars went to the university, but the money was dispersed in operational expenses.[1786] No building or program at American University remains as a reminder of the Simpson gift.[1787]

1784 "Notes" recorded by John Hillman and provided by the Simpson College archives. The June 7, 1937 Simpson College Board of Trustees Minutes read, "The Board was advised that we are now including in the listed assets of Simpson College the Pittsburg business property which accrued from the Simpson estate in Pittsburgh at the tax valuation of $280.000. It was reported that a residuary amount estimated at $20,000 is expected in addition to the Pittsburgh property."

1785 *The Washington Post* (January 8, 1936).

1786 Email from American University Archives, September 15, 2015.

1787 The requirement for the 1613 Liberty Street property being left to American University was predicated on the school remaining "under the control and management of the Methodist Episcopal Church." Will of Sarah Elizabeth Simpson, Will Book 2, 295. American University believed the requirements set by the Simpson will to be overly restrictive; thus, it forfeited claim to the Pittsburgh property by signing a quit claim deed, April 29, 1967. Allegheny County Department of Real Estate, Pittsburgh, Pennsylvania, Deed Book Vol. 4402, 85-87. Liberty and Penn Avenues come together at a forty-five degree angle in a high rent district approximately two miles from city center. When the two avenues intersect Stanwix Street, they form an almost perfect triangle.

The triangle surrounded by high rise office complexes is one of the most expensive locations in the city of Pittsburgh. Land which was at one time bought by James Brown and James Verner for $1,747 is now so valuable that it would be impossible to place a price tag on it, no doubt in the millions. Interestingly, the intersection of Penn and Liberty Avenues

Sarah Elizabeth Simpson also left $50,000 to the "Board of Temperance, Prohibition, and Public Morals of the Methodist Episcopal Church, now operating (in) the Methodist Building at 100 Maryland Avenue, Washington, D. C., as a memorial to father and mother, Bishop and Mrs. Matthew Simpson."[1788] The memorial no longer exists. No doubt, the money evaporated just as did temperance, prohibition, and public morals.

Sarah Elizabeth lived at Rittenhouse Square, an elite area of Philadelphia. "A building boom began by the 1850s and in the second half of the nineteenth century; the Rittenhouse Square neighborhood became the most fashionable residential section of the city, the home of Philadelphia's 'Victorian aristocracy.' Some mansions of that period still survive on the streets facing the square, although most of the grand homes gave way to apartment builders after 1913."[1789] In one of these apartments Sarah Elizabeth lived, and when she died, was the last of the Simpson children deposited in the West Laurel Hills mausoleum.

George and Hetty McCullough moved to Denver, Colorado in 1872, and began investing in real estate. Hetty died in 1880 and George in 1881. When Simpson visited Denver which was often, he never recorded any contact with the McCulloughs. Strange, since Hetty was the last surviving member of his immediate family. One wonders if the strained relationships between the Simpsons and McCulloughs continued because of past business disagreements. The McCulloughs had seven children including George, Jr., who lived out his life in Denver, becoming wealthy in continued real estate development.[1790]

---

almost exactly parallel the Allegheny and Monongahela Rivers. Ft. Duquesne stands on this promenade where the history of Pittsburgh began about one thousand feet from where Brown and Verner built their brewery.

1788   Will of Sarah Elizabeth Simpson.

1789   www.visitphilly.com/museums-attractions/philadelphia/rittenhouse-square-park/.

1790   *Sketches of Colorado: being an analytical summary and biographical history of the state of Colorado as portrayed in the lives of the pioneers, the founders, the builders, the statesmen and the prominent and progressive citizens who helped in the making of Colorado* Vol I (Denver: The Western Press, 1911) 393. http://tree: ancestrylibrary.com/tree/11798064/person/1604888938/print. Also see "George McCullough," in *History: City of Denver, Arapahoe County, and Colorado* (Chicago: O. L. Baskin & Co., 1880) 517-518.

Blindsided by Modernity

Matthew Simpson was a great man, if one defines greatness by doing one thing especially well; great if one defines greatness as exerting influence over a wide array of people; great if one defines greatness by gaining access to the corridors of public and political power; great if one defines greatness by attaining the highest political office in the organization to which one belongs; great if one defines greatness by championing progressive measures in an institution that by its very nature is conservative; great if one defines greatness by leading an organization to a numerical best among ecclesiastical institutions.

The above criteria for greatness could be applied to an athlete, a corporate executive, a politician, and a myriad other vocations. They represent a cultural paradigm for success, and in particular, American success. But Matthew Simpson claimed to fulfill a profession defined by a sacred text, a text which is *sui generis*, one of a kind and counter-cultural. At least it is counter-cultural, as partially inherited from the Hebrews and defined by Jesus Christ. In fact, one might argue that if an individual meets the standards of success set by a materialistic culture, s/he has failed to represent a Kingdom which is not of this world.

It seems unfair to criticize Simpson for his headlong rush into modernity. He had no access to dozens of scholars who have analyzed modernity's lost side of the ledger such as Gregg Easterbrook's *The Progress Paradox,* Neil Postman's *Technopoly,* Sven Birkirts' *The Guttenberg Elegies,* James C. Scott's *Seeing Like a State,* and Marshall Berman's *All That Is Solid Melts Into Air.* These authors have, in turn, quoted from scores of other writers who have analyzed and documented the down side of living in a Wal-Mart, Styrofoam, cyberspace laterally-connected, fossil-fuel driven, and increasingly depersonalized world.

But it is not unfair to critique Simpson by the text which he claimed to have faithfully represented and proclaimed. This particular text teaches that the accumulation of goods quickly reaches the law of diminishing returns. And the law of inverse proportion as to satisfaction arrives more quickly than we realize. In hindsight and only in hindsight, do we possess the perception that intangible values are more important than tangible possessions? Without quoting from the sacred text, in this case the Bible, (but it could be a text from Buddhism, Confucianism, Taoism, or Hinduism) most spiritual writings teach that what really counts in life are peace, contentment, reconciliation, and a clear conscience. In other words, is an Amish community more salubrious than the community in which I live?

At what point do the bureaucratic provisions of sewer systems, utility services, electronic media, manufactured food and everything else that modernity offers, transgress the laws of quietude, contentment, and healthful relationships? Not to even mention a faithful representation of Simpson's theological father, John Wesley who said, "Things eternal are much more considerable than things temporal; things not seen are as certain as the things that are seen. (John Wesley's Covenant Service). Truly amazing, 3,000 years ago a Hebrew leader noted: "The length of our days is seventy years or eighty if we have the strength, yet their span is but trouble and sorrow and they quickly pass and we fly away." (Psalms 90:10 NIV) The average length of life for a person living in an antibiotic, antiseptic, and MRI-defined world has negligibly increased, if at all. Paradoxically, Methodism's advance in society's "improvements" did little to quench Simpson's personal angst about himself, his family, and the haunting realization that the increasing quantity of his Church was decreasing in quality.

And part of Simpson's depression may have come from the dilemma that all preachers face: the task of enabling persons to feel better about themselves as opposed to a truthful, honest, and realistic view of themselves. John Crossan, in *The Historical Jesus: The Life of a Mediterranean Jewish Peasant*, has argued that Jesus was a cynic.[1791] At least we know, if we believe the Bible, that Jesus said to the Pharisees (and there is something Pharisaical in most of us who claim to be Christian), "Woe to you teachers of the law and Pharisees, you hypocrites! You are like whitewashed tombs which look beautiful on the outside, but on the inside are full of dead men's bones and everything unclean." (Matthew 23:27NIV) Such denunciations would have overwhelmed and crippled Simpson's delicate constitution and negated his

---

1791 John Crossan. *The Historical Jesus: The Life of a Mediterranean Jewish Peasant* (San Francisco: Harper of San Francisco, 1991).

political aspirations. Thus, he adopted a theology which equated human goodness with human achievement. The ideal person for Simpson was a solid churchman who, through perseverance, ingenuity, and Christian faith, had reversed his fortunes in life. "The Victory of Faith" for Matthew Simpson, no less than for Horatio Alger, was equated more with the American way than the crucified way. Why Simpson could not detect a sharp dichotomy between the communities as described in Acts chapter 2 and America's most blatantly materialistic and avaricious era is beyond comprehension. But it should not be surprising, since this tension is absent from most of the American Church at the time of this writing.

The problem and issues which defined Matthew Simpson in the nineteenth century are still the dominant characteristics of the twenty-first century American Protestant Church. We refuse to believe Marshall McLuhan's prophecy which is becoming increasingly true, "We will not own technology, but it will own us." Thus, along with everyone else, we rush to attain the latest gadget offered by one of several techno behemoths ruling the world. The American Church reflects a society exponentially trading such intangible qualities as loyalty, community, friendship, tradition, and identity, for the tangible benefits of expediency, efficiency, mobility, technology, and above all, a vast array of commodities labeled "conspicuous consumption." Defining life by "more is better," while the Christian Church claims moral superiority to its neighbors, may be the height of self-deception. Our "Christian nation" boasts of the highest homicidal rate and largest incarceration population of any industrialized nation on earth.

Simpson's Nationalistic Agenda

To argue that Simpson was America's most articulate spokesman for nationalism during the Civil War is much different than claiming Simpson led the nation in a nationalistic agenda which would morph into a cohesiveness and unity of purpose, not yet experienced by America in its brief existence. After all, if a nation establishes a sovereign federal government in one location, a national bank, an income tax and a standing army all in a brief four-year period, its self-understanding has been drastically transformed, not to speak of a war, which necessitated and eventuated into America becoming the largest industrial power on the face of the earth, as well as completing an iron road from the Atlantic to the Pacific in 1869. The Pennsylvania Railroad assumed that when the Civil War ended, business would drop off, but unexpectedly, discovered that in 1865 its business had more than tripled its 1860 revenue. "Between 1870 and 1900, the national wealth quadrupled, rising from 30,400 million to 126,700 million and doubled again by 1914-reaching 254,200 million."[1792]

Underlying the post-Civil War nationalist fervor was America's new identity, or one might say it was "born again." The result of Lincoln's obstetric language in the Gettysburg Address as Garry Wills has reminded us in his Pulitzer Prize winning analysis of Lincoln's "few appropriate remarks," 272 words: "Up to the Civil War, 'the United States' was invariably a plural noun: 'the United States are a free government.' After Gettysburg, it became a singular noun: 'the United States is a free government.'"[1793]

Our founding fathers would not have been surprised by American expansion, a relentless conquering of Indians, Mexicans, and anyone else who stood in the path of "progress." A strong national state from sea to shining sea was their goal and intention from the very beginning. European pride, Christian zeal, and capitalist greed became components of the American creed, "the right of discovery" regardless of who was there first. The North American continent was a gift from God, no less than Canaan was a gift to the Israelites. The first colonial charters claimed a preemptive right to any and all American territory, which enabled our Revolutionary forefathers to create a Leviathan state, "clad in the garments of the social compact. It took seventy-five years of controversy and four years of bloody warfare, however, to make good on the paradox."[1794] For an "ecstatic nation," according to Brenda Wineapple's fluid prose, "To the white settlers, ranchers, and prospectors, to the magnates and to the men seated at their hardwood desks in the Capitol, to the readers of newspapers, the illustrators of magazines, and the investors

---

1792   Baltzell, 110.

1793   Garry Wills. *Lincoln at Gettysburg: The Words that Remade America* (New York: Simon and Schuster, 1992) 145.

1794   R. W. VanAlstyne. *The Rising American Empire* (New York: Oxford University Press, 1960) 4.

on Wall Street, to all of them, westward settlement indicated progress--imperial progress, evolutionary progress, material progress."[1795]

Simpson faced a question that Christianity has not adequately answered throughout its 2,000 year history. Since religion is one of cultures foremost components, how does one claim to possess a superior and exclusive religion without claiming a superior culture, and thus, a superior nation? To ask the question another way, is ethnocentrism a corollary, an inescapable hubris of one who lives within a "Christian nation?" At first glance, the problem is tantamount to building two mountains without a valley. But a second more profound observation may yield a confession that the "Church" for the most part, has not exemplified or actualized the religion of Christ. This was the case for the Apostles who, to the very end of Christ's earthly ministry, believed that Jesus was about a nationalistic agenda. Though there are eras and persons throughout the last 2,000 years who have managed to disentangle the kingdom of this world from the Kingdom of Christ, e.g. John Woolman and Roger Williams, the church for the most part has demonstrated the confusion of Pope Leo III when he crowned Charlemagne emperor of the "Holy Roman Empire," Christmas Day, 800. Obviously, Leo III was not reading the Sermon on the Mount for his job description, no more than was Matthew Simpson.[1796]

As many have pointed out, including Wilcomb Washburn, "The New Testament might have been understood and honored by the Indian of the Americas, had it been preached as it was on the shores of Galilee. But by the time the American Indians came face to face with the doctrine of Christ, it had hardened in a mold of bigotry, intolerance, militancy, and greed, which made it the mortal enemy of the Native Americans."[1797] Because United States Indian policy rarely favored Native Americans, the 138 million acres of tribal land in 1887 was reduced to 48 million by 1934.

1795   Brenda Wineapple. *Ecstatic Nation: Confidence, Crisis, and Compromise, 1848-1877* (New York: HarperCollins Publishers, 2013) 557.

1796   After examining two centuries of British colonialism throughout the world, Brian Stanley concludes that "Christianity is inherently an imperial religion in the sense that it claims that the revealed truth of God was incarnated uniquely in the person of Jesus Christ." Brian Stanley. *The Bible and the Flag* (Leicester, England: Apollos, 1990) 184.

1797   Wilcomb E. Washburn. *Redman's Land/Whiteman's Law: A Study of the Past and Present Status of the American Indian* (New York: Charles Scribner Sons, 1971) 4.

Matthew Simpson presided over an ecclesiastical culture which witnessed America becoming the world's most predominant power. No one articulated America's ascendency more than did the leading Bishop in America's largest denomination. He raised no questions concerning any conquest, confiscation, military action, or collateral damage. Is it fair to suggest that Matthew Simpson was the preeminent preacher for America's "bully pulpit" during and immediately after the Civil War? Edward Said encapsulates the American epoch over which Simpson presided. "This century (19th) climaxed 'the rise of the West,' and Western power allowed the imperial metropolitan centers to acquire and accumulate territory and subjects on a truly astonishing scale. Consider that in 1800, Western powers claimed 55% but actually held approximately 35% of the earth's surface, and by 1878 the proportion was 67%; a rate of increase of 83,000 square miles per year."[1798]

American nationalism, the right to rule by divine mandate and to impose our will on the rest of the world, comes at an increasingly greater price for basically two reasons. First, today, there is no "Cemetery Ridge, " as at Gettysburg, which provides a battle line, as we discovered in Vietnam, Afghanistan, and scores of other hot spots where we can hardly distinguish the good guys from the bad guys. Second, larger battalions no longer win because bombs and missiles inflict the same amount of damage, whether fired by a nation of 300,000,000 or a country of 3,000,000. Doing right is not done because it is the right thing to do. Morality is required not because of love but because of fear, as Freud argued in his *Civilization and Its Discontents*.[1799] In a world of nuclear threat, our Christian nation with its Messianic pretentions, operates not so much by the maxim of Jesus, "Do unto others as you would have them do unto you," but by "Be careful what you do unto others because they might do the same unto you."

"Christianity" without Kingdom values as defined by Christ, results in a tragic reductionism, a deceptive and seductive plot with white middle-class Americans saving and ruling the world. This delusional narrative with American imperialism as its centerpiece, exalts an unjust God, who would condemn billions of his creation who just happen to have been born in

---

1798 Edward Said. *Culture and Imperialism* (New York: Alfred A Knopf, 1999) 7-8.
1799 Sigmund Freud. *Civilization and Its Discontents* (New York: W. W. Norton & Company, 1989).

China, India, Saudi Arabia, or some other "non-Christian" country. Without the graces of humility and contrition, we as Americans cannot Biblically and theologically discern that ISIS and American militant evangelicalism are opposite but similar sides of the same apocalyptic coin. In an age of nuclear angst and global warming, the horrific and stupendous symbolism in the book of the Revelation moves beyond imagination into the realms of reality and plausibility. If it is possible for humanity to "hasten the day," no nation will be held more accountable than the United States. We launched ourselves into the twenty-first century with a unilateral exclusivism as the following from Strobe Talbott reminds us: "More than any of his predecessors, he (Bush 43) adhered to an uncompromising and extreme variant of American exceptionalism—a form of nationalism that ascribes to the United States superior qualities, universal values, global interests, unique responsibilities, and a divine dispensation to use its might on behalf of what its leaders deem to be right."[1800]

As I bring this project to a close, we have just inaugurated the 45th President of the United States. His campaign theme "Make America Great Again," emphasized building a wall between Mexico and the USA, increasing military spending, a caustic perspective on the Muslim community, disengagement from the North Atlantic Treaty Organization, and higher tariffs on countries perceived as an economic threat. Donald Trump stated in his inaugural speech, "From this day forward, it is only going to be America first, America first." (The Washington Post, Jan. 20th). New York columnist David Brooks opined that the Inaugural "offered a zero-sum, ethnically pure, backward-looking, brutalistic nationalism." (David Brooks, "After the Women's March," included in the Kansas City Star, January 26th, 2017).

I did not or would not use the word brutalistic on Simpson's nationalism. Only time will tell if Trump proves to be the most ethnocentric and protectionistic President we have ever experienced. I suggest Simpson's nationalism was underscored by a naive nativism, as opposed to Trump tapping into a simmering populist anger suited to his blustering business persona, but ill-suited for a cyber-connected, global community teetering on the precipice

---

1800   Strobe Talbott. *The Great Experiment: The Story of Ancient Empires, Modern States, and the Quest for a Global Nation* (New York: Simon & Schuster Paperbacks, 2008) v.

of a nuclear holocaust. It is not with gratitude that I now realize that Matthew Simpson's life history is more relevant than I originally envisioned.

The Theological and Sociological Critique

In no way could I have objectively and neutrally evaluated the life of Matthew Simpson. I, like him, am a Wesleyan male preacher, trying to make sense of the Gospel within a middle-class, materialistic, racially-divided church. Unlike him, I live on the other side of the logical and historical outcomes of isogenics, nuclear power, and the "global village." But I cannot exonerate Simpson simply because I did not walk in his shoes or live in his time and place. No doubt, I would have been as culturally blind and deaf as he. As a Southerner, my racist attitudes and cultural proclivities have been ameliorated, but not completely erased. It seems to me that Christianity offers the possibility of wisdom not attained by time and experience, as well as transcendence over the prevailing zeitgeist. The Kingdom of God offers an experience of grace, the possibility of being better without having to learn to be better by trial, error, and hindsight. As C.S. Lewis reminded us, the real miracle of Christianity is not so much that bad persons can become good, but that good persons can become better. Unfortunately, the trajectory of Simpson's life testified more of entrenchment than transcendence.

The question remains, "Did Simpson, by reading Scripture, offer a clear alternative to the American way of life?" Did he ever suggest, much less emphasize, that God's dreams may differ from the normative corporate and individualist aspirations of Americans? But, how can I condemn Simpson, when I myself am a card-carrying professional in a Protestant denomination, which like most other American churches, has only hardened and reified cultural proclivities? Little has changed since the days of Matthew Simpson. Racism, imperialism, and materialism still top the list of any sociological and spiritual critique of the American Protestant Church.

As an academician gazing through history's rarefied air, I find it difficult to forgive Simpson for bowing before the shrine of technology, offering unqualified paeans of praise for education, his myopic interpretations of progress, his cultural blind-sidedness concerning minorities, and the unregulated accumulation of wealth at the expense of laborers who worked in brutal conditions under the tyranny of starvation. He had to have known that the city of Pittsburgh, which he passed through more than any other place on earth, because of friends and relatives, had become the inferno which represented Hell more than either Birmingham or Manchester, England. In Pittsburgh, before Simpson died, men stripped down to their waists standing over vats of molten iron and opened the doors of Bessemer furnaces to shovel in coke making $1.50/day, while losing forty pounds in three weeks' time.

The above situation would lead to the "Homestead Strike" in July of 1892, with twelve strikers and two Pinkerton men killed. Andrew Carnegie claimed to be ignorant of the events that were taking place at the Carnegie Steel Works in Homestead, while he sharpened his golf game on his personal golf course, next to his mansion, Siskou Castle in Scotland, a monstrosity that made Sterling and Campbell Castles look like hovels. But, allow me to go lightly on both Matthew and Andrew, less some future historians look back and detect the incongruities and inconsistencies in my own life. I continue to be blind and impotent in the face of systemic evil which is as black and satanic as Matthew Simpson ever faced. I am hedging my bets that a much stronger microscope or telescope will be required to find me, but the attempt to escape accountability may be futile.

Throughout the manuscript I have acted as a judge. It will be left to the reader to decide if I have been fair, equitable, and just. But just as the reader, I have viewed Simpson through a prism composed of perspectives that have been either inherited or accumulated through life's experiences. All of us see through our own lens, a skewed perspective which led Henry Steele Commager to exclaim: "No, the historian is not God; he is a man and like other men, he confesses most of the temptations that affect his fellow men, consciously or unconsciously he's always taking sides."[1801]

I side with Matthew Simpson. I have attempted many of the things which he did, and even allowing for the exaggeration expressed by friends and contemporaries, he did these things much better than I have done them. Simpson, whatever he felt on the inside, exhibited a charismatic

---

1801 Henry Steele Commager. "Should the Historian Make Moral Judgments?" *A Sense of History: The Best Writing from the Pages of American Heritage* (New York: American Heritage Press, Inc., 1985) 470.

and magnanimous personality. For the most part he left people better than he found them, always communicating "I can help." Simpson possessed a common sense perspective, exhibiting wisdom and accuracy, concerning the events and people who surrounded him.

The Protestant nationalism which Simpson championed did not begin July 4, 1776, but October 31, 1517, a revolution in seeing and thinking. Political science scholar Ernest Gellner wrote, "The stress of the Reformation on literacy and scripturalism, its onslaught on a monopolistic priesthood (or, as Weber clearly saw, its universalization rather than abolition of priesthood), its individualism and links with mobile urban populations, all make it a kind of harbinger of social features and attitudes which, according to our model, produce the nationalist age."[1802] The European nations merely adapted to this revolution, but America's founders built its new house entirely from its premises. If there were cracks in the foundation at the 1876 Centennial celebration over which Simpson as much as any other person presided, they were barely visible. The tectonic shifts of the next one hundred years has left America's original edifice in shambles, certainly unrecognizable by the culture in which this author lives and writes. If these liabilities occurred to Methodism's most prominent leader and Philadelphia's most prominent citizen, Simpson kept his doubts to himself. For him and the majority of Americans, Protestant nationalism was God's finest achievement over the last two thousand years.

Historical Responses and Consequences

Simpson's interpretation of the Church and its role in society yielded historical consequences. Allow me to risk over-simplification, which all categorization does, and suggest that the American Protestant Church and beyond, basically splintered into four groups, with many sub-groups under each of the four. The first group followed Simpson, satisfied with Gilded Age religion and its pretentions. These people built grand edifices for worship and went to church wearing fur coats, and top hats, driving a fine carriage which would later be traded in for a Packard or Cadillac. If someone

---

1802   Ernest Gellner. *Nations and Nationalism* (Ithaca, NY: Cornell University Press, 1983) 40-41.

suggested that the poor needed attention, the nouveau bourgeoisies threw a Christmas party at Madison Square Garden, wore tuxedos and gowns, while they sat in box seats and watched the 20,000 urchins below, scramble for food and presents. When a wealthy church observed a deteriorating neighborhood around them, the church simply moved. "If elite churches wanted to remain fashionable, i.e., filled with gay parties and ladies with feathers, and 'mousseline-de-lame dresses,' they had to move with their congregations, and this principally meant relocating further uptown."[1803]

The second group fell within the category of liberal theology and the "Social Gospel." Its adherents, or perhaps we should say, those whom others have labeled as "Social Gospelers," attempted a thoughtful response to biblical criticism, evolution, urban blight, and the labor capital conflict which would explode in the 1890s and continue with no abatement into the twentieth century. Unfortunately, because some of those who touted a serious social response to inequities within American society, were not all that concerned with Church doctrine, the "Social Gospel" was written off by evangelicals, and particularly by Fundamentalists. The stereotyping of such men as Walter Rauschenbusch and Washington Gladden has been one of conservative religion's most blatant theological miscues over the last one hundred years. Those of us who wore, "What would Jesus do?" bracelets in the 1980s, need to know that a guy named Charles Sheldon wore one a century earlier. He led his congregation in attempting to define and act out exactly what would Jesus have done in Topeka, Kansas or anywhere else, for that matter.

The third group, Fundamentalism, whom we have already mentioned, did an about-face, a one hundred-eighty degree turn away from modernism, post-millennialism, and in particular, any mode of thought that would suggest the "day" in Genesis 1, may be other than a twenty-four hour period, or the Tower of Babel, Genesis 11, may be a myth, which explains differences of languages and culture around the globe. Fundamentalists put no stock in the suggestion that an Old Testament historian meant 50,000 Israelites when he said 500,000 Israelites. While this group made a valuable contribution by forthrightly and faithfully addressing theological issues, it also became characterized by brittle thinking and a certitude which prevented dialogue

---

1803   Sven Beckert. *The Monied Metropolis: New York City and the Consolidation of the American Bourgeoisie, 1850 – 1876* (New York: Cambridge University Press, 2001) 60.

with paradigms other than its own. By adopting dispensationalism, rapture theology, and attempting to match events within the world with obscure prophecies in Scripture, Fundamentalists became obsessed with how the world would end, rather than how it can be fixed.

The fourth response was represented by Pentecostal and Holiness groups, which were dissatisfied with what they perceived to be spiritual deadness, betrayal of theological norms, worldly accomodationalism, and a passive acceptance of class stratification, as if all were ordained by God. Some of these groups eventuated into denominations, such as the Church of God–Anderson, Indiana; the Christian Missionary Alliance, the Church of the Nazarene, and the Salvation Army. Two years before Simpson died, the Army landed on American shores.

Parabolic for our narrative was Phineas Bresee and the founding of the Church of the Nazarene.[1804] Like many young Methodist preachers in the 1860s and 1870s, Bresee idolized Simpson. Simpson ordained Bresee as both a Deacon and an Elder. When Bresee pastored in Iowa, he was one of the leading founders and early fundraisers for Simpson College in Indianola, Iowa. In 1883, Simpson granted Bresee a letter of transfer, from the Iowa Conference to the fledgling Southern California Conference, where Methodism had barely gained a toe hold. Bresee's ministry was so successful that the Conference built a "Methodist tabernacle," in which Bresee could preach to 2,000 people, and was so plain and unadorned, that its total cost was only $10,700.

Shortly after beginning ministry in the "tabernacle," Bresee became a Presiding Elder, and gave leadership to the building of Simpson Tabernacle in Pasadena. This edifice would become known as the most elaborate church on the west coast, resembling the interior of a New York City opera house, seating 2,500 people, on cushioned chairs. In 1892, Bishop John Vincent (Yes, the same Chautauqua Vincent who hounded Simpson) appointed Bresee as pastor of Simpson Tabernacle. Unfortunately, shortly after Bresee arrived, so did the 1893 Financial Panic, which overwhelmed both the pastor and the heavily-indebted church. For the first time in his life, the 54-

---

[1804] Carl Bangs. *Phineas F. Bresee: His Life In Methodism, The Holiness Movement, and The Church of the Nazarene* (Kansas City: Beacon Hill Press, 1995).

year old Bresee had met an ecclesiastical crisis which he could not negotiate. Simpson Tabernacle would be sold to the Unitarians and managed to survive as a building, used for both sacred and commercial purposes, until after World War II, when it was destroyed.

In 1892, Bresee began pastoring the Boyle Heights Methodist Episcopal Church, but by this time his focus had changed. He began giving more attention to the Holiness Movement, and at the same time was drawn to the Los Angeles poor, who were not being reached by the main-line denominations. In the early part of 1895, Bresee left his Methodist pastorate and joined a downtown mission in Los Angeles. For some reason never historically understood, Bresee fell out of favor with the mission leadership, and was dismissed while he was away at the Des Plaines, Illinois Camp Meeting, sponsored by the National Camp Meeting Association for the Promotion of Holiness.

In October of 1895, Bresee founded the Church of the Nazarene. (The denomination added the word "Pentecostal" in 1907 and then removed it in 1919.) The Church of the Nazarene is the largest Wesleyan-Holiness denomination in the world. No doubt, Bresee's disillusionment with Simpson Tabernacle, somewhat directed this unfolding of events, but to what extent is only conjecture. What we do know, is that the Church of the Nazarene was a normative sectarian break with a denomination that had become something other than what its founders, John Wesley and Francis Asbury, envisioned and desired. Phineas Bresee, for whatever reason, adopted a vision for the Church which was diametrically opposed to the Bishop he had once idolized. He recalled,

> We were convinced that houses of worship should be plain and cheap, to save from financial burdens and that everything should say welcome to the poor. We went feeling that food and clothing and shelter were the open doors to the heart of the unsaved poor, and that through these doors we could bear to them the life of God. We went in poverty, to give ourselves--and what God might give--determined to forego provision for the future and old age, in order to see the salvation of God while we were yet here. God has not disappointed us. While we would be glad to do much more, yet hundreds of dollars have gone to the poor, with loving ministry of every kind, and with it a way has been opened up to the hearts of men and women, that has been unutterable joy. The gospel comes to a multitude without money and without price, and the poorest

of the poor are entitled to a front seat at the Church of the Nazarene, the only condition being that they come early enough to get there.[1805]

The Church of the Nazarene over a century later is at the same place spiritually, sociologically, and theologically, where Simpson left the Methodist Episcopal Church in 1884. The aberrations and peculiarities of the Church of the Nazarene's Holiness ancestors have long ago been finely sand-papered into societal acceptance. Paradoxically, the more successful religious groups are, the greater the failure. Throughout history, the church has been energized by polarization. As it wins and assimilates the other, it resembles the other. The distance of polarization has collapsed, and the church has worked itself out of a job. Matthew Simpson was successful. He headed a phalanx of sermons, hymns, magazines, tracts, biographies, and architecture that shaped nineteenth century identity. By the time he died, his denomination was being shaped by the world's identity as much or more than it was shaping the world's identity. Flipping of the equation was seemingly unavoidable. As David Hempton concludes, "Methodism at its heart and center had always been a profoundly counter-cultural movement. It drew energy and personal commitment from the dialectic arising from its challenge to accepted norms in religion and society. It thrived on opposition, but it could not long survive equipoise."[1806]

Final Legacy

The serendipities of this kind of project are encounters with people I had never met: Uncle Matthew, Charles Elliott, John Baldwin, Anthony Bewley, James Lynch, Martin Ruter, William Milburn, and a host of others. The more I learn about Abraham Lincoln, the more I am impressed. And, I can never visit with that first generation of Methodist itinerates that I am not amazed at their courage, sacrifice, humility, and commitment to a single cause.

I have been challenged by the life of Matthew Simpson, as flawed as his vision may have been. The windows into his soul which he provided, only

---

1805　Timothy L. Smith. *Called Unto Holiness* (Kansas City: Nazarene Publishing House, 1962) 114.

1806　David Hempton. *Empire of the Spirit* (New Haven, Connecticut: Yale University Press, 2005) 201.

accented his authenticity. He left the world a better place than he found it. He lived in a time when preaching really mattered, and he stepped up, to borrow the words of Mordecai in the Book of Esther, "For such a time as this." As we have argued, no clergyman in America took fuller advantage of the events which surrounded him. Unfortunately, he allowed the events to skew his message, a message that made little distinction between the Kingdom of God and the Kingdom of America. This confusion still warps us today, especially the American Protestant Church.

Simpson never completely shook off condemnation by the South. In the early 1880s, word got out that he was still belittling the Southern church for intemperance, worldliness, spiritual lackadaisicalness and bigotry. James H. Worman, Professor of Modern Languages at Vanderbilt, wrote him a lengthy letter, refuting the charges, arguing that the Southern Methodists were as Christian as their Northern counterparts, perhaps more so. "The assertion is made that you as well as some of our other Bishops, who our people revere, have publicly declared that the Church South is indifferent to temperance, cold to religion, unmindful to the poor, inimical to the black man, and unfriendly to the North." Without mincing words, Worman charged Simpson with the responsibility of reconciling the North and the South: "It is your high commission to undertake the task and I am sure as a man of justice, and of truth, you will certainly not refuse the task to crown a life already bearing so many friends. You are loved in the South, and the people are grieved because you fail to understand them."[1807]

In 1867, just two years after Lincoln's assassination, Congress empowered a Commission to design and raise funds for a monument in the city of Washington, commemorating Lincoln's life and in particular, the

---

[1807] UMA, Old St. George's UMC: Philadelphia, Simpson papers, Letter December 6, 1883. James Worman's tenure at Vanderbilt was short-lived. He came to Vanderbilt the same year as he wrote the letter to Simpson. He resigned in the latter part of 1885. Vanderbilt was in the throes of a theological and biblical controversy, as were most confessional schools in the late nineteenth century. Vanderbilt historian, Paul Conkin writes, "To add to the woes of September, 1885, Professor James H. Worman did not show up for his modern language classes and then shortly thereafter submitted his resignation. He had come to Vanderbilt only in 1883; a native of Berlin, Worman had engrossed his students in the German language. He cited poor health and the agitated condition of the campus as reasons for his leaving." Paul C. Conkin. *Gone with the Ivy: A Biography of Vanderbilt University* (Knoxville: The University of Tennessee Press, 1985) 73.

Emancipation Proclamation. The sculptor, Clark Mills, best known for his equestrian statue of Andrew Jackson that stands in Jackson Park across from the White House, drew up plans for a bronze monument which would sit on the northeast corner of the Capitol grounds. Mill's monument would have featured thirty-six different figures, ascending on multi-level tiers, Lincoln at the peak, signing the Emancipation Proclamation. Occupation with Reconstruction pre-empted any possibility for sufficient funds, and the plans were laid aside, awaiting an initiative which would not take place until the turn of the century.[1808] Since James Harlan chaired the original committee, it is not surprising that Matthew Simpson was to be one of the thirty-six, not exactly a short list.

Before the Harlan Commission expired, Mills had already cast a mold for a life-size statue which Ellen purchased for $1,500.00.[1809] In 1902, a bronze statue of Simpson was cast from the Mills mold, and erected in Fairmount Park, as the identifying monument for Simpson House and all the philanthropic causes to which Philadelphia Methodism gave birth in the nineteenth century. Simpson's solitary pose points upward and outward to thousands of Philadelphians who daily pass him and have no idea whom the statue represents, much less what Simpson is attempting to say. His long index finger, partially bent, points to something in the future, a future which he attempted to describe but failed to accurately predict. The voice that uncritically praised technology as he wrote with a cartridge ink pen would have never imagined the word processing on a laptop which has turned my life into a living nightmare. But I am confident that Simpson is pointing to something more transcendent and eternal than the latest app on the latest iPad.

It is not surprising that the voice that once represented Philadelphia and all of the North during the Civil War would be forgotten. But that a preacher, posing as a historian such as myself, would not attempt to resurrect his memory, should be surprising. I could think of no one, not only more deserving of a statue, but also a biographical resurrection than Matthew Simpson. Preachers are in the resurrection business, at least, if resurrection is modestly defined.

1808   Jay Sacher. *The Story and Design of an American Monument* (San Francisco: Chronicle Book, 2014) 24-25.
1809   See James E. Kirby, "The Bishop Who Almost Stood with Lincoln," *Journal of the Historical Society of the EPA Conference* (1968).

"God Cannot Do Without America"

Whether God willed the North to win the Civil War is not a question to be posed by a historian. Matthew Simpson more than any other person, made the North believe God would enable its troops, champion its cause, and justify its values. The conviction that the government located in Washington, D.C. with Lincoln at its helm would triumph is the legacy of Matthew Tingley Simpson, Bishop of the Methodist Episcopal Church.

Bibliography

The following abbreviations are used:

E. PA.—Eastern Pennsylvania Conference
LOC—Library of Congress
UMA—United Methodist Archives
UMC-United Methodist Church
WCA—Western Christian Advocate

Secondary Sources

Abell, Aaron Ignatius. *The Urban Impact on American Protestantism: 1865-1900* (London: Archon, 1962).

Adam, David R. *A Second Century of Ministry: A History of Simpson House* (Philadelphia: Simpson House, 1990).

Ahlstrom, Sydney E. *A Religious History of the American People* (Garden City, NY: Image Books, 1975).

Anbinder, Tyler. *Nativism and Slavery: The Northern Know Nothings and the Politics of the 1850's* (New York: Oxford University Press, 1992).

Anderson, James D. *The Education of Blacks in the South: 1860-1935* (Chapel Hill, NC: Univ. of North Carolina Press, 1988).

Applegate, Debby. *The Most Famous Man in America: The Biography of Henry Ward Beecher* (New York: Doubleday, 2006).

Armstrong, Karen. *Fields of Blood: Religion and the History of Violence* (New York: Alfred A. Knopf, 2014).

Atkins, Gaius Glenn. *Master Sermons of the Nineteenth Century* (Chicago: Willett, Clark, 1940).

Baldasty, Gerald J. *The Commercialization of News in the Nineteenth Century* (Madison, WI: University of Wisconsin Press, 1992).

Baltzell, E. Digby. *Philadelphia Gentlemen: The Making of a National Upper Class* (Glencoe, IL: Free Press, 1958).

_____. *The Protestant Establishment: Aristocracy & Caste in America* (New Haven: Yale University Press, 1987).

Bangs, Carl. *Phineas F. Bresee: His Life in Methodism, the Holiness Movement, and the Church of the Nazarene* (Kansas City, MO: Beacon Hill Press of Kansas City, 1995).

Barclay, Wade Crawford. *History of Methodist Missions: Part II: Missions of the Methodist Episcopal Church, 1845-1939 in Two Volumes* (New York: Board of Missions of the Methodist Church, 1950).

Barker, John Marshall. *History of Ohio Methodism: A Study in Social Science.* (Cincinnati: Curts & Jennings, 1898).

Barnard, Harry. *Rutherford B. Hayes, and His America* (Newton, CT: American Political Biography Press, 1954).

Barnes, Gilbert Hobbs. *The Anti-slavery Impulse, 1830-1844* (New York: Harcourt, Brace and World, 1964).

Baskerville, Barnet. *The People's Voice: The Orator in American Society* (Lexington: University Press of Kentucky, 1979).

Barr, Helen, Elena Zaccaria, and Georgie Reed. *A Verona Album, 1871-1971: One Hundred Years of Memories* (Verona, PA: self-published, 1971).

Bascom, H. B., and R. Sutton. *The Methodist Church Property Case: Report of the Suit of Henry Bascom, and Others, vs. George Lane, and Others, Heard before the Judges Nelson and Betts, in the Circuit Court, United States, for the Southern District of New York, May 17-29, 1851* (Richmond: Published by John Early, for the Methodist Church, South, 1851).

Baughman, John J. *Our Past, Their Present: Historical Essays on Putnam County, Indiana* (Greencastle, IN: Putnam County Museum, 2008).

Beckert, Sven. *The Monied Metropolis: New York City and the Consolidation of the American Bourgeoisie, 1850-1896* (Cambridge, UK: Cambridge University Press, 2001).

Bell, Wayne T. *Images of America: Ocean Grove* (Charleston, SC: Arcadia, 2000).

Benjamin, Walter W., "The Methodist Episcopal Church in the Postwar Era," the *History of American Methodism* Vol. II, ed. Emory Bucke (New York: Abingdon, 1964) 315-393.

Berg, Scott W. *38 Nooses: Lincoln, Little Crow, and the Beginning of the Frontier's End* (New York: Pantheon Books, 2012).

Billington, Ray Allen. *The Protestant Crusade, 1800-1860: A Study of the Origins of American Nativism* (New York: Rinehart and Company, 1952).

Boucher, John Newton, and John W. Jordan. *A Century and a Half of Pittsburg and Her People* (New York: Lewis Pub., 1908).

Brands, H.W. *The Age of Gold: The California Gold Rush and the New American Dream* (New York: Doubleday, 2002).

Brannon, Emora," Partnership of Equality" in *Historical Perspectives on the Wesleyan Tradition: Women in New Worlds* Vol. II, eds. Rosemary S. Kelly, Louise Queen, and Hilah Thomas (Nashville: Abingdon, 1982) 132-147.

Bray, Gerald Lewis. *Biblical Interpretation: Past and Present* (Leicester, England: Apollos,1996).

Bray, Robert C. *Peter Cartwright, Legendary Frontier Preacher* (Urbana, IL: University of Illinois Press, 2005).

Bristol, Frank Milton. *The Life of Chaplain McCabe: Bishop of the Methodist Episcopal Church* (New York: F.H. Revell, 1908).

Broadus, John Albert, and Jesse Weatherspoon. *A Treatise on the Preparation and Delivery of Sermons* (New York: Harper & Row, 1944).

Browder, Clifford. *The Money Game in Old New York: Daniel Drew and His Times* (Lexington, KY: University of Kentucky, 1986).

Brown, Candy Gunther. *The Word in the World: Evangelical Writing, Publishing, and Reading in America, 1789-1880* (Chapel Hill: University of North Carolina Press, 2004).

Brown, Lillian. *A Living Centennial: Commemorating the One Hundredth Anniversary of Metropolitan Memorial United Methodist Church* (Washington: Judd & Detweiler, 1969).

Brueggemann, Walter. *Finally Comes the Poet: Daring Speech for Proclamation* (Minneapolis: Fortress Press, 1989).

Buckley, J. M. *A History of Methodists in the United States* (New York: Christian Literature, 1946).

Buoy, Charles Wesley. *Representative Women of Methodism* (New York: Hunt & Eaton, 1893).

Burin, Eric. *Slavery and the Peculiar Solution: A History of the American Colonization Society* (Gainesville: University Press of Florida, 2005).

Burlingame, Michael. *Abraham Lincoln: A Life* (Baltimore: Johns Hopkins University Press, 2008).

Burlingame, Roger. *The American Conscience* (New York: Alfred A. Knopf, 1957).

Burrows, Edwin G. and Michael L. Wallace. *Gotham: A History of New York City to 1898* (New York: Oxford University Press, 1999).

Buttrick, David. *Homiletic: Moves and Structures* (Philadelphia: Fortress Press, 1987).

Cannadine, David. *Mellon: An American Life* (New York: A.A. Knopf, 2006).

Cannon, William, "Education, Publication, Benevolent Work, and Mission," *The History of American Methodism* Vol. I, ed. Emory Bucke (New York: Abingdon, 1964) 315-393.

Carley, Kenneth. *The Sioux Uprising of 1862* (St. Paul: Minnesota Historical Society, 1961).

Carman, Harry J., and Reinhard H. Luthin. *Lincoln and the Patronage* (New York: Columbia University Press, 1943).

Carter, Marcia, and Carol Spiker. *200 Years of Methodism in Cadiz, 1811-2011: And the 200th Birthday of Bishop Matthew Simpson* (Cadiz, OH: Scott United Methodist Church, 2011).

Carton, Evan. *Patriotic Treason: John Brown and the Soul of America* (New York: Free Press, 2006).

Carwardine, Richard, "Trauma in Methodism: Property, Church Schism and Sectional Polarization in Antebellum America." in *God and Mammon: Protestants, Money, and the Market, 1790-1860*, ed. Mark A. Noll (Oxford: Oxford University Press, 2002) 195-206.

——————————. *Lincoln: A Life of Purpose and Power* (New York: Alfred A. Knopf, 2006).

Clark, Christopher. *Social Change in America: From the Revolution through the Civil War* (Chicago: Ivan R. Dee, 2006).

Clark, D. W. *Life and Times of Rev. Elijah Hedding* (New York: Carlton & Phillips, 1855).

Clark, Elmer T. *The Small Sects in America* (New York: Abingdon-Cokesbury Press, 1949).

Clark, Robert D. *The Life of Matthew Simpson* (New York: Macmillan, 1956).

Clinton, Catherine, "Abraham Lincoln: The Family That Made Him, the Family He Made" in *Our Lincoln: New Perspectives on Lincoln and His World*, ed. Eric Foner (New York: W.W. Norton & Company, 2008) 249-266.

Coggeshall, William Turner. *The Poets and Poetry of the West with Biographical and Critical Notices* (New York: Follett, Foster & Company, 1860).

Collins, Kenneth J. *The Theology of John Wesley: Holy Love and the Shape of Grace* (Nashville, TN: Abingdon, 2007).

Colton, Ray Charles. *The Civil War in the Western Territories: Arizona, Colorado, New Mexico, and Utah* (Norman: University of Oklahoma Press, 1959).

Commager, Henry Steele, "Should the Historian Make Moral Judgments?" in *A Sense of History: The Best Writing from the Pages of American Heritage* (New York: American Heritage Press, Inc., 1985) 461-472.

Commemorative Biographical Record, Harrison County, Ohio (Chicago: J. H. Beers and Company, 1891).

Conable, Francis W. *History of the Genesee Annual Conference of the Methodist Episcopal Church: From Its Organization by Bishops Asbury and McKendree in 1810 to the Year 1884* (New York: Phillips & Hunt, 1885).

Connor, Elizabeth. *Methodist Trailblazer, Philip Gatch, 1751-1834: His Life in Virginia, Maryland, and Ohio* (Rutland, VT: Academy Books, 1970).

Cooke, C. *Discourse on the Life and Death of the Rev. Asa Shinn: Delivered May 22, 1853, in the First Methodist Protestant Church, Pittsburgh, Pa* (Pittsburgh: W.S. Haven, 1853).

Craig, Reginald S. *The Fighting Parson; The Biography of Colonel John M. Chivington* (Los Angeles: Westernlore Press, 1959).

Crooks, George Richard. *Life and Letters of the Rev. John McClintock* (New York: Nelson & Phillips, 1876.

———.*The Life of Bishop Matthew Simpson of the Methodist Episcopal Church.* (New York: Harper & Brothers, 1890).

Cross, Whitney R. *The Burned-over District: The Social and Intellectual History of Enthusiastic Religion in Western New York, 1800-1850* (Ithaca: Cornell University Press, 1950).

Crossan, John Dominic. *The Historical Jesus: The Life of a Mediterranean Jewish Peasant* (San Francisco: Harper, 1991).

Crutcher, Timothy J. *The Crucible of Life: The Role of Experience in John Wesley's Theological Method* (Lexington, KY: Emeth Press, 2010).

Cunningham, John T. *University in the Forest: The Story of Drew University* (Florham Park, NJ: Afton Pub., 1972).

Cushing, Robert. *History of Allegheny County PA* Vol. VII (Chicago: A. Warner & Company, 1889).

Deacon, Charles R., "George Childs," in *A Biographical Album of Prominent Pennsylvanians,* (Philadelphia: American Biographical Pub., 1888) 357-361.

Delgado, James P. *To California by Sea: A Maritime History of the California Gold Rush* (Columbia, SC: University of South Carolina Press, 1996).

Dieter, Melvin Easterday. *The Holiness Revival of the Nineteenth Century* (Metuchen, NJ: Scarecrow Press, 1980).

Donald, David Herbert. *Lincoln* (London: Jonathan Cape, 1995).

"Dr. John Evans." *Historical Review of Chicago and Cook County and Selected Biography* Vol. 2, ed. A. N. Waterman (Chicago: The Lewis Publishing Company, 1908).

Dray, Philip. *Capitol Men: The Epic Story of Reconstruction through the Lives of the First Black Congressmen* (Boston: Houghton Mifflin, 2008).

Drinkhouse, Edward Jacob. *History of Methodist Reform, Synoptical of General Methodism, 1703-1898; with Special and Comprehensive Reference to Its Most Salient Exhibition in the History of the Methodist Protestant Church* (Baltimore, MD: Board of Publication of the Methodist Protestant Church, 1899).

Du Bose, Horace M. *Life of Joshua Soule* (Nashville, TN: Publishing House of the M.E. Church, South, Smith & Lamar, Agents, 1911).

Duffy, John. *The Healers: A History of American Medicine* (Urbana: University of Illinois Press, 1979).

John Early. *The Methodist Church Property Case* (Richmond: John Early, 1851).

Eckley, H. J. and William T. Perry. *History of Carroll and Harrison Counties, Ohio* (Chicago: Lewis Pub., 1921).

Edrington, Thomas S. and John Taylor. *The Battle of Glorieta Pass: A Gettysburg in the West, March 26-28, 1862* (Albuquerque: University of New Mexico Press, 1998).

Elliott, Charles. *The Life of the Rev. Robert R. Roberts, One of the Bishops of the Methodist Episcopal Church* (Cincinnati: J.F. Wright and L. Swormstedt, 1844).

_____, and Leroy M. Vernon. *South-western Methodism: A History of the M E. Church in the South West from 1844 to 1864* (Cincinnati, OH: Poe and Hitchcock, 1868).

Erikson, Erik H. *The Life Cycle Completed* (London: W.W. Norton & Co., 1998).

_____. *Young Man Luther: A Study in Psychoanalysis and History* (New York: Norton, 1958).

Esarey, Logan. *A History of Indiana from Its Exploration to 1850* (Indianapolis: W.K. Stewart, 1915).

Evensen, Bruce J. *God's Man for the Gilded Age: D.L. Moody and the Rise of Modern Mass Evangelism* (Oxford: Oxford University Press, 2003).

Fatout, Paul. *Indiana Canals* (West Lafayette, IN: Purdue University Studies, 1972).

Ferril, William Columbus. *Sketches of Colorado: being an analytical summary and biographical history of the state of Colorado as portrayed in the lives of the pioneers, the founders, the builders, the statesmen and the prominent and progressive citizens who helped in the making of Colorado* Vol. I (Denver: The Western Press, 1911).

Feldman, Jay. *When the Mississippi Ran Backwards: Empire, Intrigue, Murder, and the New Madrid Earthquakes* (New York, NY: Free Press, 2005).

Finke, Roger, and Rodney Stark. *The Churching of America, 1776-1990: Winners and Losers in Our Religious Economy* (New Brunswick, NJ: Rutgers University Press, 1992).

Fish, Carl Russell, "The Rise of the Common Man." in *A History of American Life*, ed. Mark Carnes (New York: Simon and Schuster, 1996) 517-615.

Fleming, George Thornton. *History of Pittsburgh and Environs: From Prehistoric Days to the Beginning of the American Revolution* (New York: American Historical Society, 1922).

Flower, Frank Abial. *Edwin McMasters Stanton: The Autocrat of Rebellion, Emancipation, and Reconstruction* (Akron, OH: Saalfield Publishing Company, 1905).

Folk, Patrick H., "McKendree College: The First 100 Years," in *McKendree College History, 1928-1978* (Paducah, KY: Turner Pub., 1996).

Foner, Eric. *Reconstruction: America's Unfinished Revolution, 1863-1877* (New York: Harper & Row, 1988).

Ford, Henry A. and Kate B. Ford. *History of Cincinnati, Ohio, with Illustration and Biographical Sketches* (Cleveland, Ohio: L. A. Williams and Company, 1881).

Forrest, Earle R. *History of Washington County, Pennsylvania* (Chicago: S.J. Clarke Pub., 1926).

Frederickson, George, "The Coming of the Lord: The Northern Protestant Clergy and the Civil War Crisis." in *Religion and the American Civil War*, ed. Randall M. Miller (New York: Oxford University Press, 1998) 110-130.

Freud, Sigmund. *Civilization and Its Discontents* (New York: W.W. Norton, 1989).

Friedman, Thomas L. *The World Is Flat: A Brief History of the Twenty-first Century* (New York: Farrar, Straus and Giroux, 2007).

Gabrielan, Randall. *Long Branch, New Jersey: Remembering a Resort* (Atglen, PA: Schiffer Publishing Company, 2009).

Gates, Paul Wallace. *Fifty Million Acres: Conflicts Over Kansas Land Policy: 1854–1890* (Ithaca, New York: Cornell University Press, 1954).

Gellner, Ernest. *Nations and Nationalism* (Ithaca, NY: Cornell University Press, 1983).

Gesink, Indira Falk. *Barefoot Millionaire: John Baldwin and the Founding Values of Baldwin Wallace University* (Berea, OH: Baldwin Wallace University, 2013).

Gienapp. William E., "Politics Seem to Enter into Everything: Political Culture in the North, 1840-1860," in *Essays on American Antebellum Politics, 1840-1860*, eds. William E. Gienapp, et. al. (College Station: Texas A. & M. University, 1982) 14-60.

Giglierano, G. L. and Deborah Overmeyer. *The Bicentennial Guide to Greater Cincinnati: A Portrait of Two Hundred Years* (Cincinnati: The Cincinnati Historical Society, 1988).

Gilkey, Elliott. *The Ohio Hundred-Year Book* (Columbus: Fred J. Heer, 1901).

Gladwell, Malcolm. *Outliers: The Story of Success* (New York: Little, Brown, and Company, 2008).

Goodwin, Doris Kearns. *Team of Rivals: The Political Genius of Abraham Lincoln* (New York: Simon and Schuster, 2005).

Gordon, John. *The Scarlet Woman of Wall Street* (New York: Weidenfield and Nicholson, 1988).

Gravely, William B. *Gilbert Haven: Methodist Abolitionist–A Study in Race, Religion, and Reform, 1850–1880* (Nashville: Abingdon Press, 1973).

Groh, Waunita Farrier. *Simpson Sons and Daughters: 1735–1986* (Punta Garda, FL: Waunita Farrier Groh, 1987).

Grotzinger, Laura A., ed. "The Mutual Rights of the Ministers of the Methodist Episcopal Church," in *Guide to the Archives of the Western Pennsylvania Conference of the United Methodist Church* (Pittsburgh: Western Pennsylvania Conference, 1988).

Guelzo, Allen. *Abraham Lincoln: Redeemer President* (Grand Rapids: William B. Eerdmans Publishing Company, 1999).

Gunter, W. Stephen. *The Limits of Love Divine: John Wesley's Response to Antinomianism and Enthusiasm* (Nashville: Abingdon, 1989).

Halttunen, Karen. *Confidence Men and Painted Women: A Study of Middleclass Culture in America: 1830-1870* (New Haven: Yale University Press, 1982).

Hamilton, John. *The People's Church Pulpit* (Boston: The People's Church, 1885).

Handy, Robert T. *A Christian America: Protestant Hopes and Historical Realities* (New York: Oxford University Press, 1971).

Hanna, Charles. *Historical Collection of Harrison County in the State of Ohio* (New York: privately printed, 1900).

_____. *Ohio Valley Genealogies: Relating Chiefly to Families in Harrison, Belmont and Jefferson Counties, Ohio, and Washington, Westmoreland, and Fayette Counties, Pennsylvania* (Baltimore: Genealogical Publishing Company, 1968).

Hardy, W.H., "Reminiscences of a White Mississippian," in *Black Re-constructionists: Great Lives Observed*, ed. Emma Lou Thornbrough (Englewood Cliffs, New Jersey: Prentice-Hall, 1972) 127-128.

Harmon, Nolan, "The Organization of the Methodist Episcopal Church, South" *The History of American Methodism* Vol. II, ed. Emory Bucke (Nashville: Abingdon, 1964) 86-143.

Harper, J. Henry. *The House of Harper: A Century of Publishing in Franklin Square* (New York: Harper, 1912).

Haskins, Charles Homer and William Isaac Hull. *The History of Higher Education in Pennsylvania* (Washington: GPO, 1902).

Hatch, Nathan O. *The Democratization of Christianity* (New Haven: Yale University Press, 1989).

_____, "The Puzzle of American Methodism," in *Methodism and the Shaping of American Culture*, eds. Nathan O. Hatch and John Wigger (Nashville: Abingdon, 2001) 23-40.

Heath, Caroline R., ed. *Four Days in May: Lincoln Returns to Springfield* (Springfield: Sangamon County Historical Society and the Illinois State Historical Society, 1965).

Heitzenrater, Richard P., "Great Expectations: Aldersgate and the Evidences of Genuine Christianity," in *Aldersgate Reconsidered*, ed. Randy L. Maddox (Nashville: Kingswood Books, 1990) 49-91.

Hempton, David. *Empire of the Spirit* (New Haven, Connecticut: University Press, 2005).

Herberg, Will. *Protestant, Catholic, Jew: An Essay in American Religious Sociology* (Garden City, New York: Anchor Books, 1960).

Heschel, Abraham. *The Prophets* (New York: Harper & Row, 1962).

Heseltine, William B. *Ulysses S. Grant: Politician* (New York: Frederick Unger Publishing, 1957).

Hinkle, M.M. *The Life of Henry Bidleman Bascom* (Louisville: Morton and Griswold, 1854).

Hoe, Robert. *A Short History of the Printing Press and of the Improvements in Printing Machinery from the Time of Gutenberg up to the Present Day* (New York: Robert Hoe, 1902).

Holmes, Dwight Oliver Wendell. *The Evolution of the Negro College* (New York: Teachers College-Columbia University, 1934).

Holt, Michael. *Forging a Majority: The Formation of the Republican Party in Pittsburgh 1848-1860* (New Haven: Yale University Press, 1969).

_____. *The Rise and Fall of the American Whig Party: Jacksonian Politics and the Onset of the Civil War* (New York: Oxford, 1999).

Hoogenboom, Ari. *Rutherford B. Hayes: Warrior and President* (Lawrence: University Press of Kansas, 1995).

Hough, Lynn Harold. *Evangelical Humanism* (New York: The Abingdon Press, 1925).

Howard, Victor B. *Religion and the Radical Republican Movement: 1860-1870* (Lexington: University Press of Kentucky, 1990).

Howe, Daniel Walker. *Making the American Self: Jonathan Edwards to Abraham Lincoln* (Cambridge, MA: Harvard University Press, 1997).

_____. *What Hath God Wrought: The Transformation of America, 1815–1848* (New York: Oxford University Press, 2007).

Howe, Henry. *Historical Collections of Ohio* Vol. I (Columbus: Henry Howe and Son, 1891).

Hudson, Winthrop S. *Religion in America* (New York: Charles Scribner's Sons, 1965).

Hughes, George. *Days of Power in the Forest Temple* (Salem, OH: The Allegheny Wesleyan Methodist Connection, 1975).

Hughes, Mark. *The New Civil War Handbook* (New York: Savas Beatie, 2012).

Hunter, James. *American Evangelicalism: Conservative Religion and the Quandary of Modernity* (New Brunswick, New Jersey: Rutgers University Press, 1983).

Huntzicker, William E. *The Popular Press: 1833-1865* (Westport, CT: Greenwood Press, 1994).

Hurt, R. Douglas. *The Ohio Frontier, Crucible of the Old Northwest, 1720 to 1830* (Bloomington: Indiana Press, 1998).

Jamison, Kay. *Manic Depressive Temperament and the Artistic Temperament* (New York: MacMillan, 1997).

Jewett, Robert, and John S. Lawrence. *Captain America and the Crusade against Evil: The Dilemma of Zealous Nationalism* (Grand Rapids: William B. Eerdmans Publishing Company, 2003).

John, Richard R. *Spreading the News: The American Postal System from Franklin to Morse* (Cambridge, MA: Harvard University Press, 1995).

Johnson, Paul E. *A Shopkeeper's Millennium: Society and Revivals in Rochester New York 1815–1837* (New York: Hill and Wang, 1978).

Jones, Arthur E. Jr., "The Years of Disagreement: 1844–61," *The History of American Methodism* Vol. II, ed. Emory Bucke (New York: Abingdon, 1964) 144-205.

Jones, Donald G. *The Sectional Crisis in Northern Methodism: A Study in Piety, Political Ethics and Civil Religion* (Metuchen, New Jersey: The Scarecrow Press Inc., 1979).

Kantor, Alvin R. and Marjorie S. Kantor. *Sanitary Fairs: A Philatelic and Historical Study of Civil War Benevolences* (Glencoe, Illinois: S.F. Publishing, 1992).

Kaplan, Fred. *John Quincy Adams: American Visionary* (New York: HarperCollins, 2014).

Kelly, Rosemary S., "Creating a Sphere for Women," in *Historical Perspectives on the Wesleyan Tradition: Women in New Worlds* Vol. II, eds. Rosemary Skinner Kelly, Louise L. Queen and Hilah F. Thomas (Nashville: Abingdon, 1982) 246-260.

Kelman, Ari. *A Misplaced Massacre: Struggling Over the Memory of Sand Creek* (Cambridge, MA: Harvard University Press, 2014).

Kelsey, Harry, Jr. *Frontier Capitalist: Life of John Evans* (Denver: State Historical Society of Colorado & the Pruett Publishing Company, 1965).

Kirby, James E. *The Episcopacy in American Methodism* (Nashville: Kingswood Books, 2000).

Kirby, Linda. *Heritage of Heroes: Trinity United Methodist Church 1859–1988* (Salt Lake City: Publishers Press, 1988).

Lamon, Ward Hill. *Recollections of Abraham Lincoln: 1847–1865*, ed. Dorothy Lamon (Chicago: A.C. McClurg and Company, 1895).

Land, R. Gregory. *The Abraham Man: Madness, Malingering and the Development of Medical Testimony* (New York: Algora Publishing, 2012).

Lawson, Melinda. *Patriot Fire: Forging a New American Nationalism in the Civil War North* (Lawrence: University Press of Kansas, 2002).

Leftwich, W. M. *Martyrdom in Missouri* (St. Louis: Southwestern Book and Publishing Company, 1870).

Letts, J. M. *California Illustrated: Including a Description of the Panama and Nicaragua Routes* (New York: R. T. Young, 1853).

Levine, Bruce. *The Fall of the House of Dixie: The Civil War and the Social Revolution that Transformed the South* (New York: Random House, 2014).

Logan, Mary Simmerson Cunningham. *The Part Taken by Women in American History* (Wilmington, DE: Perry Nalle Publishing Company, 1912).

Maddox, Randy. *Responsible Grace: John Wesley's Practical Theology* (Nashville: Kingswood Books, 1994).

Maier, Pauline. *American Scripture: Making the Declaration of Independence* (New York: Vintage Books, 1997).

Manhart, George B. *DePauw through the Years* Vol. I (Greencastle, IN: DePauw University, 1962).

Mann, Horace. *The Republic and the School: Horace Mann on the Education of Free Men*, ed. Lawrence A. Cremin (New York: Teachers College, Columbia University, 1957).

Marlay, John F. *The Life of Rev. Thomas Morris* (New York: Nelson and Phillips, 1875).

Marty, Martin E. *Righteous Empire: The Protestant Experience in America* (New York: The Dial Press, 1970).

Mathews, Donald. *Slavery and Methodism: A Chapter in American Morality, 1780–1845* (Princeton: Princeton University Press, 1965).

Matlack, Lucius C. *The Anti-Slavery Struggle and Triumph in the Methodist Episcopal Church* (New York: Phillips and Hunt, 1881).

Marsh, Daniel L. *William Fairfield Warren* (Boston: Boston University Press, 1930).

Marshall, Edward Chauncey. *Ancestry of General Grant and Their Contemporaries* (New York: Sheldon and Company, 1869).

Marston, Leslie. *A Living Witness* (Winona Lake, Indiana: Light and Life Press, 1960).

Marti, Donald B., "Rich Methodists: The Rise and Consequence of Lay Philanthropy in the Mid-Nineteenth Century" in *Rethinking Methodism*, eds. Russell E. Richey and Kenneth E. Rowe (Nashville: Kingswood Books, 1985) 159-166.

Maxwell, William Quentin. *Lincoln's Fifth Wheel: The Political History of the United States Sanitary Commission* (New York: Longman, Green & Company, 1956).

May, Henry F. *The Enlightenment in America* (New York: Oxford University Press, 1976).

McCarthy, Clarence Edward. *Six Kings of the American Pulpit* (Philadelphia: The Westminster Press, 1948).

McDonald, William and John Searles. *The Life of John Inskip* (Chicago: The Christian Witness Co, 1888).

McDougall, Walter A. *Throes of Democracy: The American Civil War Era 1829-1877* (New York: HarperCollins, 2008).

McFeely, William S. *Grant* (New York: F. Norton and Company, 1982).

McLean, A. and J.W. Eaton. *Peniel: or Face to Face with God* (New York: Garland Publishing, 1884).

McLoughlin, William G. *The Meaning of Henry Ward Beecher: An Essay on the Shifting Values of Mid-Victorian America, 1840-1870* (New York: Alfred A. Knopf, 1970).

McPherson, Edward. *The Political History of the United States of America during the Great Rebellion* (Washington, DC: Philp & Solomons, 1865).

McPherson, James. *Battle Cry of Freedom* (New York: Oxford, 1988).

McTyeire, Holland N. *A History of Methodism* (Nashville: Southern Methodist Publishing House, 1886).

Mead, David. *Yankee Eloquence in the Middle West: The Ohio Lyceum 1850-1870* (East Lansing: Michigan State College Press, 1951).

Mead, Sidney E. *The Lively Experiment: The Shaping of Christianity in America* (New York: Harper and Row Publishers, 1963).

Menking, Stanley J. *200 Years of United Methodism: An Illustrated History* (Madison, New Jersey: Drew University, 1984).

Merk, Frederick. *Manifest Destiny and Mission in American History: A Reinterpretation* (New York: Alfred A. Knopf, 1963).

Merry, Robert W. *A Country of Vast Designs: James K Polk, the Mexican War and the Conquest of the American Continent* (New York: Simon and Schuster, 2009).

Millard, Candice. *Destiny of the Republic: A Tale of Madness, Medicine, and the Murder of a President* (New York: Anchor Books, 2011).

Miller, Perry. *Errand in the Wilderness* (New York: Harper & Row, 1956).

Milton, George Fort. *The Age of Hate: Andrew Johnson and the Radicals* (New York: Coward-McCann, 1930).

Mitchell, Margaret. *Gone With the Wind* (New York: Pocket Books, 2008).

Moltmann, Jurgen. *The Coming of God: Christian Eschatology* (Minneapolis: Fortress Press, 1996).

Montgomery, David. *Beyond Equality: Labor and the Radical Republicans 1862–1872* (New York: Alfred A. Knopf, 1967).

Moore, Edward. *A Century of Indiana History* (New York: American Book Company, 1910).

Moore, John M. *The Long Road to Methodist Union* (New York: Abingdon-Cokesbury Press, 1943).

Moore, William F. Moore and Jane A. Moore. *Collaborators for Emancipation: Abraham Lincoln and Owen Lovejoy* (Chicago: University of IL Press, 2014).

Moore, R. Laurence. *John Wesley and Authority: A Psychological Perspective* (Missoula, MT: Scholars Press, 1982).

Moorhead, James H. *American Apocalypse: Yankee Protestants and the Civil War* (New Haven: Yale University Press, 1978).

_____. *World without End: Mainstream America–Protestant Vision of Last Things 1885-1925* (Bloomington: Indiana University Press, 1999).

Morrow, Ralph. *Northern Methodism and Reconstruction* (Lansing, MI: State University Press, 1956).

Muller-Fahrenholz, Geiko. *America's Battle for God: A European Christian Looks at Civil Religion* (Grand Rapids: William B. Eerdmans Publishing Company, 2007).

Myers, Edward H. *The Disruption of the Methodist Episcopal Church, 1844-1846: Comprising a Thirty Years' History of the Relations of the Two Methodisms* (Nashville, TN: A.H. Redford, Agent, 1875).

Nassau, David. *Andrew Carnegie* (New York: The Penguin Press, 2006).

Nevins, J. Allan. *The Emergence of Modern America: 1865-1878* (New York: The Macmillan Company, 1927).

_____. *Ordeal of the Union* Vol. II (New York: Charles Scribner's Sons, 1947).

Nevin, Alfred E. ed. *Encyclopaedia of the Presbyterian Church* (Philadelphia: Presbyterian Encyclopaedia Publishing Co., 1884).

The New Encyclopedia Britannica Vol. 6 (New York: Encyclopedia Britannica, 2002).

Nicolay, John G. and John Hay. *Abraham Lincoln: A History* Vol. X (New York: The Century, 1914).

Niebuhr, Gustav. *Lincoln's Bishop: A President, A Priest, and the Fate of 300 Dakota Sioux Warriors* (New York: HarperCollins, 2014).

Niebuhr, Reinhold. *Faith and History: A Comparison of Christian and Modern Views of History* (New York: Charles Scribner's Sons, 1949).

Norwood, Frederick A. *From Dawn to Mid-day at Garrett* (Evanston: Garrett Evangelical Theological Seminary, 1978).

_____. *The Story of American Methodism* (Nashville: Abingdon 1974).

Norwood, John Nelson. *Schism in the Methodist Church: 1844* (Alfred University: Alfred, New York, 1923).

Oakes, James. *Freedom National: The Destruction of Slavery in the United States, 1861–1865* (New York: W.W. Norton & Company, 2013).

Oberholtzer, Ellis Paxson. *Philadelphia: A History of the City and Its People-A Record of 225 Years* (Philadelphia: The S.J. Clarke Publishing Company, 1912).

Olusoga, David and Casper W. Erichsen. *The Kaiser's Holocaust: Germany's Forgotten Genocide* (London: Faber and Faber Ltd, 2011).

Otis, F. N. *History of the Panama Railroad and the Pacific Mail Steamship Company* (New York: Harper & Brothers, 1867).

Packard, Jerrold M. *The Lincolns in the White House: Four Years that Shattered a Family* (New York: St. Marten's Press, 2005).

Paludan, Phillip Shaw. *The Presidency of Abraham Lincoln* (Lawrence: University of Kansas Press, 1994).

Park, Clyde W. *Mount Auburn Methodist Church: The First Hundred Years, 1852-1952* (Columbus: Historical and Philosophical Society of Ohio, 1952).

Patterson, Lyman R. *Copyright in Historical Perspective* (Nashville: Vanderbilt University Press, 1968).

Peters, John L. *Christian Perfection and American Methodism* (New York: Abingdon, 1961).

Phillips, Clifton and John Baughman. *DePauw: A Pictorial History* (Greencastle, Indiana: DePauw University, 1987).

Pilkington, James. *The Methodist Publishing House: A History* Vol. I (Nashville: Abingdon Press, 1968).

Pinson, William M. and Clyde E. Fant. *Twenty Centuries of Great Preaching* (Waco: Word, 1971).

Pollard, Edward. *The Lost Cause: A New Southern History of the War of the Confederates* (New York: E. B. Treat and Company, 1867).

Potter, David. *The Impending Crisis: 1848–1861* (New York: Harper and Row, 1976).

Power, John. *Abraham Lincoln: His Great Funeral Cortege from Washington City to Springfield, Illinois with a History and Description of the National Lincoln Monument* (Springfield, Illinois: Illinois Journal Company, 1872).

Pratt, Fletcher. *Stanton: Lincoln's Secretary of War* (New York: W. W. Norton and Company, 1953).

Price, Carl F. *Wesleyan's First Century: With an Account of the Centennial Celebration* (Middletown, CT: Wesleyan University, 1932).

Pridmore, J. *Northwestern: A History* (Evanston, Illinois: Northwestern University Press).

Rable, George C. *But There Was No Peace: The Role of Violence in the Politics of Reconstruction* (Athens: University of Georgia Press, 1984).

_____. *God's Almost Chosen Peoples: A Religious History of the Civil War* (Chapel Hill: The University of North Carolina, 2010).

Raser, Harold. *Phoebe Palmer: Her Life and Thought* (Lewiston, NY: The Edwin Mellon Press, 1986).

Ray, Angela G.. *The Lyceum and Public Culture in the Nineteenth Century United States* (East Lansing: Michigan State University Press, 2005).

Redford, Alfred. *The Methodist Episcopal Church South* (Nashville: A. H. Redford, 1871).

Reiser, Catherine E. *Pittsburgh's Commercial Developments: 1800–1850* (Harrisburg: Pennsylvania Historical and Museum Commission, 1951).

Remini, Robert. *Henry Clay: Statesman for the Union* (New York: W. W. Norton and Company, 1991).

Richey, Russell E. *Formation for Ministry in American Methodism* (Nashville: The General Board of Higher Education and Ministry, The United Methodist Church, 2014).

_____, "History as a Bearer of Denominational Identity: Methodism as a Case Study," in *Perspectives on American Methodism: Interpretative Essays*, eds. Russell E. Richey, Kenneth E. Rowe, and Jean Miller Schmidt (Nashville: Press, 1993) 480-497.

_____. *Methodism in the American Forest* (New York: Oxford University Press, 2015).

_____, Kenneth E. Rowe, and Jean Miller Schmidt. *The Methodist Experience in America: A History* Vol. I (Nashville: Abingdon Press, 2010).

Ridgeway, Henry. *Life of Edmund S. Janes* (New York: Phillips and Hunt, 1882).

Riis, Jacob A. *How the Other Half Lives: Studies Among the Tenements of New York* (Cambridge, MA: The Belknap Press of Harvard University Press, 2010).

Roberts, Gary Leland. *Massacre at Sand Creek: How Methodists Were Involved in an American Tragedy* (Nashville: Abingdon Press, 2016).

Robson, Charles, ed. *The Biographical Encyclopedia of Pennsylvania of the Nineteenth Century* (Philadelphia: Galaxy, 1874).

Reid, Ross D. *Lincoln's Veteran Volunteers Win the War* (Albany, New York: Albany State University of New York, 2008).

Rubin, Julius H. *Religious Melancholy and Protestant Experience in America* (New York: Oxford University Press, 1995).

Ryan, Michael, "John McClintock (1814-1870)" in *Something More than Human: Biographies of Leaders in American Methodist Higher Education*, ed. Charles E. Cole (Nashville: United Methodist Board of Higher Education, 1986) 141-157.

Sacher, Jay. *The Story and Design of an American Monument* (San Francisco: Chronicle Book, 2014).

Said, Edward. *Culture and Imperialism* (New York: Alfred A Knopf, 1999).

Salter, Darius. *America's Bishop: The Life of Francis Asbury* (Nappanee, IN: Evangel Publishing House, 2003).

_____. *Preaching as Art: Biblical Storytelling for a Media Generation* (Kansas City: Beacon Hill Press, 2008).

_____. *Spirit and Intellect: Thomas Upham's Holiness Theology* (Metuchen, NJ: Scarecrow Press, 1986).

Sandberg, Carl. *Abraham Lincoln: The War Years* Vol. III (New York: Harcourt, Brace, and Company, 1939).

Sanford, Charles. *The Quest for Paradise: Europe and the American Moral Imagination* (Urbana, IL: University of Chicago Press, 1961).

Scharf, J. Thomas and Thomas Westcott. *History of Philadelphia: 1609-1884* Vols. I & II (Philadelphia: L. H. Everts & Co., 1884).

Schlesinger, Arthur, Jr., ed. *The Almanac of American History* (New York: Barnes & Noble, 1993).

Sewell, George. *Mississippi Black History Makers* (Jackson: University Press of Mississippi, 1977).

Shannon, Fred Albert. *The Organization and Administration of the Union Army: 1861–1865* Vol. I (Cleveland: The Arthur H. Clark Company, 1928).

Schenk, Joshua. *Lincoln's Melancholy: How Depression Challenged a President and Fueled His Greatness* (New York: Houghton-Mifflin Company, 2005).

Sheppard, Robert Dickinson, and Harvey B. Hurd. *History of Northwestern University and Evanston* (Chicago: Munsell Publishing Company, 1906).

Shotwell, Walter Gaston. *Driftwood: Being Papers on Old-Time American Towns and Some Old People* (Freeport, New York: Books for Libraries Press, Inc., 1966).

Silberstein, Hessler. *Cincinnati: Then and Now* (Cincinnati: The Value Service Education Fund, 1982).

Simpson, Helen A. *Early Records of Simpson Families* (Philadelphia: J. B. Lippincott & Company, 1927).

Sims, Charles. *The Life of Rev. Thomas M. Eddy* (New York: Phillips and Hunt, 1880).

Slotkin, Richard. *No Quarter: The Battle of the Crater, 1864* (New York: Random House, 2009).

Smith, Ernest Ashton. *Allegheny: A Century of Education 1815–1915* (Meadville, Pennsylvania: The Allegheny College History Company, 1916).

Smith, George G. *The Life and Times of George Foster Pierce* (Sparta, GA: Hancock Publishing Company, 1888).

Smith, H. Shelton, Robert T. Handy, and Lefferts Loetscher. *American Christianity: A Historical Interpretation with Representative Documents* Vol. 2 (New York: Scribner's Sons, 1923).

Smith, Timothy L. *Called Unto Holiness: The Story of the Nazarenes-The Formative Years* (Kansas City, MO: Nazarene Publishing House, 1962).

_____. *Revivalism and Social Reform in Mid-Nineteenth Century America* (New York: Abingdon Press, 1957).

_____. "The Theology and Practices of Methodism: 1887-1919" *The History of American Methodism* Vol. II, ed. Emory Bucke (Nashville: Abingdon, 1958) 608-627.

Smith, William Ernest. *The Preston Blair Family in Politics* Vol. II (New York: Macmillan Company, 1933).

Smith, William Henry. *The History of the State of Indiana from the Earliest Explorations by the French to the Present Time: Containing an Account of the Principal Civil, Political and Military Events from 1763 to 1903*, Vol. 2 (Indianapolis, IN: B. L. Blair Company, 1897).

Snyder, Howard A. *Populist Saints: B.T. and Ellen Roberts and the First Free Methodists* (Grand Rapids: William B. Errdmans Publishing Company, 2006).

South Carolina Historical Society. *The Discursive Biographical Sketch of Colonel Richard Lathers: 1841-1902* (Philadelphia: J. B. Lippincott, 1902).

Southey, Robert. *The Life of Wesley* Vol. I (New York: W.B. Gilley, 1950).

Spellman, Norman W., "The Church Divides," *The History of American Methodism* Vol. II, ed. Emory Bucke (Nashville: Abingdon, 1958) 3-85.

Spring Garden History District: A Guide for Property Owners (Philadelphia: Philadelphia Historical Commission, no date).

Stamp, Kenneth M. *America in 1857: A Nation on the Brink* (New York: Oxford University Press, 1990).

Stanley, Francis Louis Crocchiola. *The Civil War in New Mexico* (Denver: The World Press, 1960).

Stevens, Abel. *The Centenary of American Methodism: A Sketch of Its History, Theology, Practical System and Success* (New York: Carlton & Porter, 1866).

_____. *History of the Methodist Episcopal Church in the United States of America* Vol. III (New York: Eaton and Mains, 1864).

_____. *History of the Methodist Episcopal Church in the United States of America* Vol. IV (New York: Eaton and Mains, 1864).

_____. *Life and Times of Nathan Bangs* (New York: Carlton and Porter, 1863).

_____. *The History of the Religious Movement of the Eighteenth Century Called Methodism* Vol. IV (New York: Carlton and Porter, 1858).

Stewart, David and Ray Knox. *The Earthquake That Never Went Away: The Shaking Stopped in 1812, But The Impact Goes On* (Marble Hill, Missouri: Gutenberg-Richter Publications, 1993).

Stewart, David O. *Impeached: The Trial of President Johnson and the Fight for Lincoln's Legacy* (New York: Simon and Schuster, 2009).

Stiles, T. J. *Custer's Trials: A Life on the Frontier of a New America* (New York: Alfred A. Knopf, 2015).

_____. *The First Tycoon: The Epic Life of Cornelius Vanderbilt* (New York: Vintage Books, 2010).

Stille, Charles. *Memorial of the Great Central Fair for the U.S. Sanitary Commission* (Philadelphia: United States Sanitary Commission, 1864).

Stokes, Melvyn and Steven Conway. *The Market Revolution in American Social, Political, and Religious Expressions: 1800-1880* (Charlottesville: The University Press of Virginia, 1996).

Stout, Harry S. *Upon the Altar of the Nation: A Moral History of the Civil War* (New York: Viking Adult, 2006).

Strickland, W.P. *The Life of Jacob Gruber* (New York: Carlton & Porter, 1860).

Sutton, Walter. *The Western Book Trade: Cincinnati as a Nineteenth Century Publishing and Book-Trade Center* (Columbus: Ohio State University Press, 1961).

Swaney, Charles Baumer. *Episcopal Methodism and Slavery with Sidelights on Ecclesiastical Politics* (New York: Negro University Press, 1969).

Sweet, William Warren. *Circuit Rider Days in Indiana* (Indianapolis: W.K. Stewart, 1916).

_____. *Indiana Asbury-DePauw University, 1837-1937: A Hundred Years of Higher Education in the Middle West* (New York: Abingdon Press, 1937).

_____. *The Methodist Episcopal Church and the Civil War* (Cincinnati: The Methodist Book Concern, 1912).

Talbott, Strobe. *The Great Experiment: The Story of Ancient Empires, Modern States, and the Quest for a Global Nation* (New York: Simon & Schuster Paperbacks, 2008).

Tap, Bruce. *Over Lincoln's Shoulder: Committee on the Conduct of the War* (Lawrence, KS: University Press, 1998).

Taylor, Bob Pepperman. *Horace Mann's Troubling Legacy: The Education of Democratic Citizens* (Lawrence: University Press of Kansas, 2010).

Taylor, George. *The Transportation Revolution: 1815-1860* (New York: Rinehart and Company, 1951).

Thrift, Charles, "Rebuilding the Southern Church," *The History of American Methodism* Vol. II, ed. Emory Bucke (Nashville: Abingdon, 1958) 257-314.

Tippey, Worth Marion. *Frontier Bishop: The Life and Times of Robert Richford Roberts* (Nashville: Abingdon, 1958).

Tipple, Ezra Squire. *Drew Theological Seminary 1867-1970: A Review of the First Half Century* (New York: The Methodist Book Concern, 1917).

Trachtenberg, Alan. *The Incorporation of American Culture and Society in the Gilded Age* (New York: Hill and Wang, 1982).

Trostel, Scott D. *The Lincoln Inaugural Train* (Fletcher, Ohio: Cam-Tech Publishing, 2011).

Trueblood, Elton. *Abraham Lincoln: Theologian of American Anguish* (New York: Harper & Row Publishers, 1953).

Turner, Frederick. *The Frontier in American History* (New York: Dover Publications, 1996).

Tuveson, Ernest Lee. *Millennium and Utopia: A Study in the Background of the Idea of Progress* (New York: Harper & Row Publishers, 1964).

_____. *Redeemer Nation* (Chicago: University of Chicago Press, 1968).

VanAlstyne, R. W. *The Rising American Empire* (New York: Oxford University Press, 1960).

Vernon, Walter Newton, Jr. *The United Methodist Publishing House* Vol. II (Nashville: Abingdon Press, 1989).

Versteeg, John M. *Methodism: Ohio Area, 1812-1862* (Nashville: Parthenon, 1962).

Walker, Charles Manning. *History of Athens County, Ohio* (Cincinnati: Robert T. Clark and Company, 1869).

Walt, Joseph W. *Beneath the Whispering Maples: The History of Simpson College* (Indianola, Iowa: College Press, 1995).

Wardell, Morris. *A Political History of the Cherokee Nation: 1838-1907* (Norman: University of Oklahoma Press, 1938).

Warner, Sam Bass. *The Private City: Philadelphia in Three Periods of Its Growth* (Philadelphia: University of Pennsylvania Press).

Washburn, Wilcomb E. *Redman's Land/Whiteman's Law: A Study of the Past and Present Status of the American Indian* (New York: Charles Scribner Sons, 1971).

Waugh, Jean. *Grant: American Hero, American Myth* (Chapel Hill: University Press, 2009).

Webber, A.R. *Life of John Baldwin, Sr. of Berea, Ohio* (Cincinnati: Caxton Press, 1925).

Weber, Max. *The Protestant Work Ethic and the Spirit of Capitalism* (New York: Charles Scribner's Sons, 1950).

Webster's American Biographies (Springfield, MA: G. & C. Merriam Company Publishers) 80-82.

Weisberger, Bernard. *The American Newspaperman* (Chicago: The University of Chicago Press, 1961).

West, Elliot. *The Contested Plains: Indians, Gold Seekers, and the Rush to Colorado* (Lawrence: University of Kansas Press, 1998).

White, Charles Edward. *The Beauty of Holiness* (Grand Rapids: Francis Asbury Press, 1986).

White, John, Jr. *The American Railroad Passenger Car* (Baltimore: The Johns Hopkins University Press, 1978).

White, Richard. *Railroaded: The Transcontinentals and the Making of Modern America* (New York: W. W. Norton and Company, 2011).

Whitford, William Clarke. *Colorado Volunteers in the Civil War: The New Mexico Campaign in 1862* (Glorieta, Mexico: The Rio Grande Press, Inc., 1971).

Whitmont, Edward C. *The Symbolic Quest: Basic Concepts of Analytical Psychology* (Princeton: Princeton University Press, 1969).

Williams, Colin. *John Wesley's Theology Today* (Nashville: Abingdon Press, 1960).

Williams, Robert C. *Horace Greely: Champion of American Freedom* (New York: New York University Press, 2006).

Williams, Scott. *The Indian Wars of 1864 through the Sand Creek Massacre* (Aurora, Colorado: Pick of Ware Publishing, 1997).

Williams, T. Harry. *Lincoln and the Radicals* (Madison: The University of Wisconsin Press, 1941).

Williamson, Harold F. and Payson S. Wild. *Northwestern University: A History 1850-1975* (Evanston, Illinois: Northwestern University, 1976).

Wills, Garry. *Lincoln at Gettysburg: The Words that Remade America* (New York: Simon and Schuster, 1992).

Wilson, Charles Reagan. *Baptized in Blood: The Religion of the Lost Cause: 1865–1920* (Athens: The University of Georgia Press, 1980).

Wilson, Erasmus. *Standard History of Pittsburg, Pennsylvania* (Chicago: H.R. Cornell and Company, 1898).

Wilson, Paul Scott. *God Sense: Reading the Bible for Preaching* (Nashville: Abingdon, 2001).

Winapple, Brenda. *Ecstatic Nation: Confidence, Crisis, and Compromise, 1848-1877* (New York: HarperCollins, 2013).

Winger, Stewart. *Lincoln, Religion, and Romantic Cultural Politics* (DeKalb, Illinois: Northern Illinois University Press, 2003).

Wood, E. M. *The Peerless Orator* (Pittsburgh: Pittsburgh Printing Company, 1909).

Primary Sources

Adams, Henry. *The Education of Henry Adams* (New York: Barnes and Noble, 2009).

"Address by Matthew Simpson," New England Methodist Centenary Convention held in Boston, June 4-7, 1866 (Boston: B. B. Russell & Company, 1866) 136-139.

Annual Conferences of the Methodist Episcopal Church 1852–1855 Vol. V (New York: Carlton and Porter, 1855).

Basler, Roy P., ed. *The Collected Works of Abraham Lincoln* Vol. VII (New Brunswick, New Jersey: Rutgers University Press, 1959).

Beecher, Henry Ward. *The Original Plymouth Pulpit: Sermons of Henry Ward Beecher* Vol. II (Boston: The Pilgrim Press, 1870).

Beers, F. W. *Atlas of Monmouth County N.J.* (New York: Beers, Comstock, and Cline, 1873).

Brooks, Noah. *Washington DC in Lincoln's Time* (Chicago: Quadrangle Books, 1971).

Brown, George. *The Recollections of Itinerant Life Including Early Reminiscences* (Cincinnati: R.W. Carroll and Company Publishers, 1866).

Brown, Harry J. and Frederick R. William, eds. *The Diary of James A. Garfield* Vol. III (Lansing, Michigan: Michigan State University Press, 1981).

Caldwell, J. A. *Caldwell's Atlas of Harrison County* (Condit, Ohio: J. A. Caldwell, 1875).

Chesnut, Mary. *A Diary from Dixie: The Civil War's Most Celebrated Journal*, written 1860–1865 by the wife of James Chesnut, Jr., an aide to President Jefferson Davis and a Brigadier General in the Confederate Army. A facsimile of the 1905 edition is edited by Isabella D. Martin and Myrta Lockett Avary (New York: Portland House, 1997).

Chevalier, Michel and T. G. Bradford. *Society, Manners and Politics in the United States Being a Series of Letters on North America* (Boston: Weeks, Jordan and Company, 1839).

Childs, George W. *Recollections by George W. Childs* (Philadelphia: J. B. Lippincott & Company, 1890).

Cist, Charles. *Sketches and Statistics of Cincinnati in 1851* (Cincinnati: W.H. Moore & Co, 1851).

Clark, Elmer T., J. Manning Potts and Jacob S. Payton, eds. *The Journal and Letters of Francis Asbury* (London: Epworth, 1958).

Combe, George. *Notes on the United States of North America, during a Phrenological Visit in 1838-40* (Philadelphia: Carey & Hart, 1841).

Congressional Globe, 40th Congress, 2nd Session.

Crooks, George R., ed. *Sermons by Bishop Matthew Simpson* (New York: Harper & Brothers, Franklin Square, 1885).

Cumock, Nehemiah. *The Journal of the Rev. John Wesley* Vol. II (London: The Epworth Press, 1938).

Darwin, Charles. *The Descent of Man* (Amherst, New York: Prometheus Books, 1998).

_____. *Origin of Species* (New York: Barnes and Noble Classics, 2014).

Dickens, Charles. *American Notes* (Hazelton, Pennsylvania: The Electronic Classic Series, 2007).

The Doctrines and Disciplines of the Methodist Episcopal Church (New York: B. Waugh and T. Mason, 1832).

Ella Simpson Buoy Will, Monmouth County Surrogate Court, Monmouth County Hall of Records, Freehold, New Jersey: Book 131-133.

Ellen Simpson Will, Monmouth County Surrogate Court, Monmouth County Hall of Records, Freehold, New Jersey: Book 128–129.

Finley, James. *Autobiography of Reverend James B. Finley* (Cincinnati: Methodist Book Concern, 1872).

General Conference Journal of the Methodist Episcopal Church held in Indianapolis, Indiana, 1856 (New York: Carlton and Porter, 1856).

Gerboth, Christopher B., ed. *The Tall Chief: The Autobiography of Edward W. Wynkoop* (Denver: History Colorado, 1993).

Goodwin, Thomas. "Reminiscences of the Early Days of Indiana Asbury University," *Semi-Centennial Reminiscences and Historical Addresses: 1831-1887*(Greencastle, Indiana: DePauw University, 1887).

Gregory, George. *Elements of the Theory and Practice of Physic* (Philadelphia: Towar and Hogan, 1829).

Hudson, Thomas M. *Life and Times of Rev. Thomas M. Hudson* (Cincinnati: Hitchcock & Walden, 1871).

James Verner Deed–DBV 249, page 553, on file at Oakmont Carnegie Library, Oakmont, PA.

Jobson, Frederick. *America and American Methodism* (London: James S. Virtue, 1857).

Journal of the General Conferences of the Methodist Episcopal Church Vol. II, 1840, 1844 (New York: Carlton and Porter, 1856).

Journal of the General Conferences of the Methodist Episcopal Church, Vol. III, 1848-1856 (New York: Carlton & Porter, 1856).

Journal of the General Conference of the Methodist Episcopal Church: 1860, held in Buffalo, New York, edited by William Harris (New York: Carlton and Porter, 1860).

Journal of the 1864 General Conference of the Methodist Episcopal Church (New York: Carlton and Porter, 1864).

Journal of the 1868 General Conference of the Methodist Episcopal Church (New York: Carlton & Lanahan, 1868).

Journal of the 1876 General Conference of the Methodist Episcopal Church (New York: Nelson and Phillips, 1876).

Journal of the 1880 General Conference of the Methodist Episcopal Church (New York: Phillips and Hunt, 1880).

Journal of the 1884 General Conference of the Methodist Episcopal Church (New York: Phillips & Hunt, 1884).

Journal of the General Conference of the Methodist Episcopal Church, held in New York, May 1-31, 1888. Edited by Rev. David S Monroe, D.D., and Sec. of the Conference (New York: Phillips & Hunt, 1888).

Kappler, Charles K. *Indian Affairs: Laws and Treaties* Vol. II (Washington: Government Printing Office, 1904).

Lanahan, John. *The Era of Frauds in the Methodist Book Concern at New York* (Baltimore: Methodist Book Depository, 1896).

Lee, Luther. *Debates of the Methodist Episcopal Church General Conference: 1840-1844* (New York: O. Scott, 1844).

Lunt, Cornelia Gray. *Sketches of Childhood and Girlhood* (Evanston, Illinois: self-published, 1925).

"Massacre of the Cheyenne Indians," Report on the Conduct of the War, 38 Con., 2nd Sess. (Washington: Government Printing Office, 1865).

Matthew Simpson Will, Office of Wills, City Hall, Philadelphia, PA.

Matthew Verner Simpson Will, Office of Wills, City Hall, Philadelphia, PA.

McClintock, John. "Discourse on the Day of the Funeral of President Lincoln," Wednesday, April 19, 1865, recorded by J. T. Butts (New York: Press of J. M. Broadstreet and Sons, 1865).

"The Methodist Home for Children," (Philadelphia: self-published, 2013). Pamphlet is available on site.

Minutes of Annual Conferences of the Methodist Episcopal Church for the Years Vol. III 1839-1845 (New York: T. Mason and Lane, 1840).

Minutes of the Annual Conferences of the Methodist Episcopal Church of 1860 (New York: Carlton and Porter).

Minutes of the Annual Conferences of the Methodist Episcopal Church of 1867 (New York: Carlton and Porter, 1867).

Minutes of the Annual Conferences of the Methodist Episcopal Church- Spring Conferences of 1898 (New York: Eaton and Mains, 1898).

Minutes of the Colorado Annual Conference of the Methodist Episcopal Church, Second Session, held at Central, Colorado, October 20, 1864. Unpublished, provided by Iliff School of Theology.

Minutes of the Indiana Conference of the Methodist Episcopal Church 1844-1851. These Minutes have been typed from the original manuscript copies by the Northern Indiana Conference Historical Society, UMA, Drew University.

Minutes of the Nebraska Annual Conference of the Methodist Episcopal Church, Ninth Session (Nebraska City: Price-Miller and Company, 1869).

Minutes of the Nebraska Annual Conference of the Methodist Episcopal Church, Tenth Session at Fremont (Omaha: Republican Steam Printing House and Book Bindery, 1870).

Minutes of the Rock River Conference of the Methodist Episcopal Church (Chicago: Northwest Advocate Office, 1853).

Minutes of the Twenty-Second Session of the Rock River Conference of the Methodist Episcopal Church (Rockford: Register Steam Printing Establishment, 1861).

Niven, John. *The Salmon P. Chase Papers, Journals: 1829-1872* Vol. I (Kent, Ohio: The Kent State University Press, 1993).

Ohio Sesquicentennial Celebration: 1813-1963 (Freeport, Ohio: The Sesquicentennial Historical Committee, Harrison County, Ohio, 1963).

Palmer, Phoebe. "The Cleansing Wave" in *Sing to the Lord* (Kansas City, Missouri: Lillenas Publishing Company, 1993).

_____ . *Notes by the Way* (New York: Lane and Scott, 1850).

_____. *The Promise of the Father* (Salem, Ohio: Schmul Publishers, 1981).

Pastoral Records of the Western Pennsylvania Conference of the United Methodist Church: 1784-2013 (Pittsburgh: Commission on Archives and History, 2013).

Pearne, Thomas H. *Sixty-one Years of Itinerant Christian Life in Church and State* (Cincinnati: Curtis and Jennings, 1898).

Proceedings of the Celebration of the Twenty-First Anniversary of the Founding of Drew Theological Seminary: October 26, 1892 (New York: Hunt and Eaton, 1892).

Proceedings of the M.E. General Conference held in Indianapolis, Indiana (Syracuse: L. C. Matlack, 1856).

Reply of Governor Evans of the Territory of Colorado to that part referring to him, of the report "The Committee on The Conduct of the War" headed "Massacre of Cheyenne Indians." Executive Department and Superintendency of Indian Affairs, C.T. Denver, Aug. 6, 1865.

"God Cannot Do Without America"

Report of the Debates in the General Conference of the Methodist Episcopal Church Held in the City of New York, 1844. Robert West, Official Recorder (New York: G. Lane and C. B. Tippett, 1844).

Report of Department of the Interior, Office of Indian Affairs (Washington: Government Printing Office, November 15, 1864) from the collection of the Prelinger Library, San Francisco, CA 2006.

Report of the Proceedings of the First Ecumenical Methodist Conference held in City Road Chapel, London, September 7, 1881 (London: Wesleyan Conference Office, 1881).

Reynolds, Grafton T. *Manual of the Pittsburgh Conference of the Methodist Episcopal Church* (Pittsburgh: Pittsburgh Conference, 1928).

Roberts, B. T. *Why Another Sect* (New York: Garland Publishing Inc., 1984).

"Sand Creek Apology," *The Book of Resolutions of the United Methodist Church* (Nashville: United Methodist Publishing House, 1996).

Sarah Elizabeth Simpson Will, Monmouth County Surrogate Court, Monmouth County Hall of Records, Freehold, New Jersey: Book 127.

Simon, John. *The Papers of Ulysses Grant* Vol. 20 (Carbondale, IL: Southern Illinois University Press, July 1, 1968-October 31, 1868).

Simpson, Matthew, ed. *Cyclopaedia of Methodism: Embracing Sketches of Its Rise, Progress, and Present Condition with Biographical Notes and Numerous Illustrations* (Philadelphia: Lewis H. Everts, 1881).

_____, "Funeral Address Delivered at the Burial of President Lincoln at Springfield, Illinois, May 4, 1865, by Rev. Matthew Simpson, D.D., one of the Bishops of the Methodist Episcopal Church," (New York: Carlton & Porter, 1865).

_____. *A Hundred Years of Methodism* (Hunt and Eaton, 1876).

_____. *Lectures on Preaching* (New York: Nelson and Phillips, 1879).

Smith, Elvino V. *Atlas of the 6th, 9th, & 10th Wards of the City of Philadelphia from Private Plans, Actual Surveys & Official Records* (Philadelphia: Elvino V. Smith, C.E., 1908).

_____. *Atlas of the Eleventh-Seventeenth Wards* (Philadelphia: Elvino V. Smith, C.E., 1909).

Smith, Henry. *Recollections and Reflections of an Old Itinerant* (New York: Carlton and Phillips, 1854).

Tarkington, Joseph. *The Autobiography of Joseph Tarkington* (Cincinnati: Curtis and Jennings, 1899).

Taylor, William. *Seven Years of Street Preaching in San Francisco, California* (New York: Nelson and Hunt, 1875).

Townsend, George. *Washington: Outside and Inside* (Hartford, Connecticut: James Betts and Company, 1874).

Wakeley, J.B. *The Patriarch of One Hundred Years: Being Reminiscences, Historical and Biographical of Rev. Henry Boehm* (New York: Nelson and Phillips, 1875).

Wallace, Charles B., ed. *Excerpts from the Harrison Telegraph of Cadiz, Ohio 1821, 1823, 1828, 1832* (Cadiz, OH: The Harrison County Historical and Genealogical Society, 1994).

Welles, Gideon. *Diary of Gideon Welles: Secretary of the Navy under Lincoln and Johnson* Vol. III, January 1, 1867-June 6, 1869 (Boston: Houghton, Mifflin & Company, 1911).

Wesley, John. *A Plain Account of Christian Perfection* (Kansas City, MO: Beacon Hill Press of Kansas City, 1966).

_____. "The Cause and Cure of Earthquakes," *The Works of John Wesley* Vol. VII (Kansas City: Beacon Hill Press of Kansas City, 1978) 386-399.

_____. *Works* Vol. IXX, ed. W. Reginald Ward (Nashville: Abingdon, 1990).

Western Cincinnati Directory and Business Advertiser for 1850-1851, second annual issue (Cincinnati: C. S. Williams College Hall, 1850).

"The City Government of Philadelphia: A Study in Municipal Administration," in *Politics and Economics* Vol II (Philadelphia: Wharton School of Studies in Politics and Economics, 1893).

Williams, Charles, ed. *Diary and Letters of Rutherford B. Hayes* Vol. III (Columbus: The Ohio State Historical Society, 1926).

Willard, Frances E. *Glimpses of Fifty Years: The Autobiography of an American Woman* (Chicago: H. J. Smith and Company, 1889).

_____. *Writings Out of My Heart: Selections from the Journal of Frances E. Willard ,1855-96* (Chicago: University of Illinois Press, 1995).

Young, Norman. *Church Records: Western Pennsylvania Conference of the United Methodist Conference* (Pittsburgh: Western Pennsylvania Conference, 2013).

Archives

"An Analysis of Bishop Simpson's Power as a Preacher," UMA, Drew University, Simpson papers.

"Andrew Johnson Order," issued January 23, 1865, UMA, Drew University, Simpson papers.

"The Arrival of Dr. Simpson at Greencastle," LOC, Simpson papers, Container twenty.

"Bancroft Interview" on file, Northwestern Archives, Northwestern University: Evanston, Illinois.

"Bishop Simpson and the Widow's Son," UMA, Drew University, Simpson papers.

"Bishop Simpson from an English Point of View," LOC, Simpson papers, Scrapbook D, Container twenty-three.

"City and Vicinity: Bishop Simpson's Lecture" (Buffalo: January 24, 1856) LOC, Simpson papers, Container fifteen.

"The Day of Jubilee-The Metropolitan ME Church Celebrates Its Deliverance, Eloquent Bishop Simpson on the Prophecies," LOC, Simpson papers, Scrapbook D, Container twenty-three.

"Description of Person," LOC, Simpson papers, Container twenty.

"Georgia: Simpson Preaches Two Powerful Sermons," LOC, Simpson papers, Scrapbook D, Container twenty-three.

Iliff School of Theology, "Check-mate: The Queen Takes the Bishop—A Brilliant Game on the Colorado Chess Board—The Marriage of Bishop Warren and Mrs. Iliff, the Cattle Queen." Article courtesy of Iliff School of Theology Archives, Denver.

"In Loving Memory of Anna Simpson Weaver," UMA, Drew University, Simpson papers.

"Isaac Layfort probate file," Harrison County Ohio Historical Society, Cadiz, Ohio.

"James Riley Weaver Dies at Home," January 28, 1920: UMA, DePauw University, James Riley Weaver papers.

Jeffries, A.C, "A Bishop Speaks for Lincoln," LOC, Simpson papers.

"John Evans: Builder of Evanston and Northwestern University." *Evanston Review,* Northwestern Archives, Evanston, IL.

McConnell, William, *Scrapbook,* Harrison County, Ohio, Historical Society.

"Methodist Conference: Annual Meeting of the New Jersey Annual Conference," LOC, Simpson papers, Scrapbook D, Container twenty-three.

Minutes of the March 19, 1846, Board of Trustees Meeting, Indiana Asbury University, UMA, DePauw University.

Minutes of the July 18, 1848, Board of Trustees Meeting, Indiana Asbury University, UMA, DePauw University.

Nutt, Cyrus. *Journal,* UMA, DePauw University.

Patterson, Robert H., UMA, E. PA Conference of the UMC, Old St. George's Church, Philadelphia, Simpson papers, "Resolutions unanimously adopted by the Philadelphia Annual Conference," West Chester, on March 18, 1863, signed by Robert H. Patterson, Secretary, March 27, 1863.

Pepper, Reverend C. W. "Bishop Simpson's Oratory", LOC. Simpson papers, Scrapbook C, Container twenty.

"Portrait of Bishop Simpson," LOC, Simpson papers, Scrapbook D, Container twenty-three.

"Portraits of Our English Delegates," LOC, Simpson papers, Scrapbook A, Container twenty-one.

Reed, J.C. "The War of the Rebellion," UMA, DePauw University, Detzler papers.

"Rev. D. Sherman-The People's Church Pulpit," LOC, Simpson papers, Scrapbook D, Container twenty-three.

"Roberts Park Church Sermon: Yesterday's Morning Service by Bishop Matthew Simpson: His Views of the Scriptural Origin of the Doctrine of Evolution," LOC, Simpson papers, Scrapbook D, Container twenty-three.

Scaife, Charles Papers, Manuscript Division-Heinz Center, Pittsburgh, PA.

Simpson, Matthew, "Address Delivered upon the Author's Installation as President of the Indiana Asbury University." (Indianapolis, IN: University Board of Trustees, 1840).

_____, "Address to E. Simpson," LOC, Simpson papers, Container fifteen.

_____, "Address to Hetty McCullough," LOC, Simpson papers, Container twenty.

_____. *Autobiography*, LOC, Simpson papers, Container fifteen.

_____. "Extracts on Calvin," LOC, Simpson papers, Container seventeen.

_____, "God's Goodness in the Midst of Affliction," UMA, Drew University, Simpson papers.

_____, "God is Everywhere," UMA, Drew University, Simpson papers.

———, "The Great White Throne," LOC, Simpson papers, Container twenty.

———, "Hints of Self-Examination," LOC, Simpson papers, Container nineteen.

———, "Influence of the Bible upon Languages," unidentified newspaper, LOC, Simpson papers. Container fifteen.

———, "The Lover's Farewell," August 21, 1830, LOC, Simpson papers, Container fifteen.

———, "Memoir of Charles," LOC, Simpson papers, Container twenty.

———, "Notes on Bishop Roberts," LOC, Simpson papers, Container sixteen.

———, "Notes on Family History," LOC, Simpson papers, Container twenty.

———, "Notes of Travel and Reading," 1856-62, LOC, Simpson papers, Container one.

———, "Notes on Trip to California," LOC, Simpson papers, Container fifteen.

———, "Notes on Trip to Europe," LOC, Simpson papers, Container fifteen.

———."Notes of Trip to Mexico 1874, Italy 1875," LOC, Simpson papers, Container fifteen.

———, "The Past Ten Years," LOC, Simpson papers, Scrapbook D, Container twenty-three.

_____, "A Plan of Appointments for Pittsburgh and Allegheny town: 1834-1835," LOC, Simpson papers, Container twenty.

_____, "Portraits of Our English Delegates," LOC, Simpson papers, Scrapbook A, Container twenty-one.

_____, "Prayer for 1876 Centennial" LOC, Simpson papers, Container fifteen.

_____, "Reminiscent Lines of Matthew Simpson Jr. on His Nineteenth Birthday," LOC, Simpson papers, Container fifteen.

_____, "Rev. Dr. Elliott" by Bishop Simpson, LOC, Simpson papers, Container twenty.

_____, "Schools of Oratory," LOC, Simpson papers, Container nineteen.

_____, "Things to be Got," LOC, Simpson papers, Container eighteen.

_____, "This Must Be Love," LOC, Simpson papers, Container fifteen.

_____, "Thoughts for Health and Comfort," LOC, Simpson papers, Container nineteen.

_____, "Thoughts on Heaven," LOC, Simpson papers, Scrapbook D, Container twenty-three.

_____, "To Susan Snowdrop," January 14, 1832, LOC, Simpson papers, Container fifteen.

_____, "True Leadership," LOC, Simpson papers, Container fifteen.

718 | "God Cannot Do Without America"

———————, "What I Should Refrain From," LOC, Simpson papers, Container nineteen.

———————, "Woman's Suffrage," February 5, 1873, UMA, Drew University, Simpson papers.

Smith, John, "Address at DePauw," June 12, 1887, UMA, Drew University, Crooks papers.

"Something Additional," UMA, Drew University, Crooks papers, Unidentified author.

Speer, John, "Sketch of John Chivington," in a report to Fred Martin from an interview with Mrs. John Chivington, Kansas State Historical Society, Topeka, Kansas (March 11, 1902).

Tingley, Joseph, "Reminiscences," March 25, 1887, UMA, Drew University, Crooks papers.

———————, "Random Recollections," UMA, Drew University, Crooks papers.

Transactions of the Kansas State Historical Society, 1897-1900; Together With Addresses at Annual Meetings, Memorials, And Miscellaneous Papers, also, *A Catalog of Kansas Constitutions, and Territorial and State Documents in The Historical Society* Vol. VI, ed. George. W. Martin, Secretary (Topeka: Kansas Historical Society).

Verner-Brown property at Penn Avenue and Liberty Street, Pittsburgh, PA, traced from Vernon-Brown ownership to Simpson College ownership, Allegheny County, Pittsburgh, Pennsylvania, Department of Real Estate Deed Books, Vol. 37, Vol. 61, Vol. 1210, Vol. 2374, and Vol. 4402.

Wannamaker, John, "Our Old Friend Bishop Matthew Simpson: Highly Valued by Abraham Lincoln," UMA, Drew University, Simpson papers.

Wheeler, Mary Sparks, "Reminiscences of Bishop Simpson," LOC, Simpson papers, Scrapbook D, Container twenty-three.

Wood, Amanda, "Recollections of Amanda Wood," March 25, 1887, UMA, Drew University, Simpson papers.

Wrenshall Journal, microfilm: Manuscript Division-Heinz Center, Pittsburgh, PA.

Newspapers

Advance Leader (June 6, 1946). Courtesy of Oakmont Carnegie Library, Oakmont, PA.

"American Deputation at the British Conferences," New York: *New York Recorder* (August 25, 1870).

"The Arch Street Methodist Episcopal Church Dedication Services," *Philadelphia Public Ledger* (November 18, 1870).

"An Embarrassing Introduction: How a Young Preacher Made the Acquaintance of Bishop Simpson," *The Milwaukee Sentinel*, Milwaukee, WI: (June 29, 1890).

"A Sermon by the Rev. Bishop Matthew Simpson," *Boston Daily Advertiser* (November 4, 1875).

"A Windfall for Bishop Simpson," *The Cleveland Morning Herald* (August 5, 1871).

"Baldwin University," *The Daily Cleveland Herald* (September 28, 1860).

"Bishop Simpson Mausoleum," *The Atchison Daily Globe* (February 15, 1887).

"Bishop Simpson for Grant," *The Cleveland Morning Daily Herald* (October 1, 1872).

"Bishop Simpson on Lay Representation," *Zion's Daily Herald*, Vol. 34 (June 3, 1863).

"Bishop Simpson on the Mission of America," *The Boston Daily Advertiser* (November 22, 1867).

"Bishop Simpson's Experience in Wildcat Mines," *Daily Evening Bulletin*: San Francisco (February 13, 1883).

"Bishops as Partisans," *New York Christian Advocate & Journal* (November 4, 1867).

Brown, William J., "Dr. Simpson and the Fugitive Slave Law," *Indiana State Sentinel*, Indianapolis (January 7, 1851).

Cadiz Republican, Cadiz, Ohio (January 17, 1878).

"The Cherokee Treaty," *The Daily Times*, Leavenworth, Kansas (October 17, 1866) Kansas Historical Society, Topeka, Kansas, under Cherokee Neutral Lands.

The Daily Cleveland Herald-Cleveland, OH (November 1, 1869).

Daily National Intelligencer and Washington Express-Washington, DC (November 5, 1869).

Daily Republican, Monongahela City, PA: Vol. 4, No. 954 (June 23, 1884).

"Description of a New Rochelle Wedding" copied from an editorial in *The Hour*, New Rochelle (July 7, 1883).

"8th Illinois - Calvary," *Northwestern Christian Advocate* (November 23, 1861).

"Funeral Services of Bishop Simpson," *The Christian Advocate*: New York (July 3, 1884).

"Grant's Spiritual Favorite," *New York Sun* (March 17, 1873).

"The Great Central Fair," *The Philadelphia Inquirer* (June 8, 1864).

"Jottings from the Capital," *Hartford Daily Courant*, Hartford, Connecticut (March 8 1865).

"Made In Memory: Services over the Death of the Late Bishop Simpson in All of the Methodist Churches Yesterday," *Rocky Mountain News*: Denver (June 23, 1884).

"Matthew Simpson: The Crescent and the Cross," *Daily Cleveland Herald* (Feb. 1, 1870).

"Methodist Foreign Missions: The Appropriation for the Next Year to be $750,000 -Liberia and South America," *New York Times* (November 7, 1882).

"Mrs. Ellen Simpson Dead," *The North American* (December 21, 1897).

Pokas, Betty, "Hopewell Project to Create Noise," *The Times Leader*, Martins Ferry, Ohio (May 6, 2012).

Presbyterian Banner, New York (March 6, 1880).

"Presentation of a Mansion to Bishop Simpson," *Chicago Tribune* 1860-1872 (Dec. 3, 1863).

"Sermon by Bishop Simpson, L.L.D., of Philadelphia," *Chautauqua Herald* (August 5, 1879), LOC, Simpson papers.

Simpson, Matthew, "The Destroyer," *WCA* Vol. XVI, No. 29 (July 18, 1849).

_____, "Doings of Congress," *WCA* Vol. XVII, No. 10 (March 6, 1850).

_____, "Emancipation," *WCA* Vol. XVI, No. 31 (August 1, 1849).

_____, "The Empire of Christ," *The Methodist* (September 26, 1863).

_____, "The Fugitive Slave Bill," *WCA* Vol. XVII, No. 41 (October 9, 1850).

_____, "Fugitive Slave Law–Resistance," *WCA* Vol. XVII, No. 46 (Nov. 13, 1850).

_____, "The Great Western Thoroughfare," *WCA* Vol. XVI No. 9 (February 28, 1849).

_____, "The Intolerance of Rome," *WCA* Vol. XVII No. 5 (January 29, 1851).

_____, "Jesus Conquering the World," *Vermont Chronicle*, Bellows Falls, VT (June 15, 1867).

_____, "Liberia Mission," *WCA* Vol. XVII, No. 5 (January 30, 1850).

_____, "The New Year," *WCA* Vol. XIII, No. 1 (January 1, 1851).

_____, "The Old Flag," *Zion's Herald & Wesleyan Journal* Vol. XXXV, Boston (May 11, 1864).

_____, "Political Explanation," *WCA* Vol. XII, No. 43 (October 23, 1850).

_____. "Political Exultation," *WCA* Vol. XV, No. 33 (November 22, 1848).

_____, "The Property Question," *WCA*, Vol. XV, No. 24 (September 20, 1848).

_____, "Reading Sermons," *WCA* Vol. XV, No. 17 (August 2, 1848).

_____, "The Religious Newspaper," *WCA* Vol. XVII, No. 5 (Jan. 29, 1851).

_____, "The Religious Press and Politics," *WCA* Vol. XVII, No. 14 (April 3, 1850).

_____, "Salutary" *WCA* Vol. XV, No. 18 (August 2, 1848).

Smith, Charles W., "Bishop Simpson's Greatest Oratorical Triumph," *Pittsburgh Christian Advocate* (June 22, 1911).

Thumb, Rupert B., "History of Education in Cadiz from the Beginning of the Town," *Cadiz Republican* (March 30, 1911).

"Twelve Bishops Have Left the Western Book Concern for the Episcopate," *Cincinnati Enquirer* (May 23, 1900).

"Visit of Clergymen to the President," Washington: *The Daily Chronicle* (May 19, 1865).

Journals

Barbee, David, "President Lincoln and Dr. Gurley," *The Abraham Lincoln Quarterly* Vol. V, No. 1 (March 1948) 3-24.

Bayless, R. W., "Peter G. Van Winkle and Waitman T. Willey in the Impeachment Trial of Andrew Johnson," *West Virginia History* (December 1951) 75-89.

Brown, Irving Frederick, "Indiana Asbury University: A History," *Bulletin of DePauw University*, Vol. X, No. 4 (November, 1913).

Cannon, William, "The Pierces: Father and Son," *Methodist History* Vol. XVII, No. 1 (October 1978). 92-112.

Carwardine, Richard, "Methodist Politics and the Coming of the American Civil War," *Church History* Vol. 69 (September 2000) 578-609.

Clark, Robert D., "The Oratorical Career of Bishop Matthew Simpson." *Speech Monographs* 16, no. 1 (1949) 1-20.

_____, "Bishop Matthew Simpson and the Emancipation Proclamation," *Mississippi Valley Historical Review* Vol. XXXV (September 19, 1948) 263-271.

_____, "The Medical Training of Matthew Simpson: 1830-1833," *Ohio State Archeological and Historical Quarterly* Vol. LXI, No. 4 (October 1952) 371-379.

Cox-Paul, Lori, "'John M. Chivington,' 'The Reverend Colonel,' 'Marry Your Daughter,' 'Sand Creek Massacre,'" *Nebraska History* Vol. 8, No. 4 (Winter 2007) 126-137, 142-147.

Curti, Merle, "A Great Teacher's Teacher," *Social Education* Vol. XVIII, No. 6 (October 1959) 263-267.

Foster, John O., "Des Plaines Camp Meeting 1860," *Journal of the Illinois State Historical Society* Vol. XXIV (April 1931) 654-670.

Gatke, Robert M., "Ketturah Belknap's Chronicle of the Bellfountain Settlement," *Oregon Historical Quarterly* Vol. 38, No. 3 (September 1937) 265-299.

Gravely, William B. , "A Black Methodist in Reconstruction Mississippi: Three Letters by James Lynch in 1868-1869," *Methodist History* Vol. XI, No. 4, (July 1973) 3-18.

Grimsley, Elizabeth Todd . "Six Months in the White House," *Journal of The Illinois State Historical Society* (October-January 1926-1927) 42-73.

Hillman, S. D. "The United States and Methodism," *Methodist Quarterly Review* (January 1867) 29-49.

Keller, Ralph A., "Methodist Newspapers and the Fugitive Slave Law: A New Perspective for the Slavery Crisis in the North," *Church History*, Vol. 43 No. 3 (September 1974) Cambridge England: Cambridge University Press on behalf of the American Society of Church History, 319-339.

Kenaston, Connor S., "From Rib to Robe: Women Ordination in the United Methodist Church," *Methodist History* 53:3 (April 2015) 162-172.

Kinney, Thomas A., "John Baldwin and the Grindstone Lathe," *Chronicle of the Early American Industries Association, Inc.*, Vol. 49, No. 4 (December 1996) 125-129.

Kirby, James E., "Dearest Ellen: Correspondence between Bishop Matthew Simpson and His Wife," *Methodist History* Vol. XLII, No. 3 (April 2004) 135-147.

_____ , "Matthew Simpson's Diary," *The Journal of San Diego History*, Vol. 29, No. 3 (Summer 1983) 107-114.

_____ , "The McKendree Chapel Affair," *Tennessee Historical Quarterly* Vol. 25 (Winter 1966) 360-370.

_____ , "Matthew Simpson and the Mission of America," *Church History* Vol. XXXVI, No. 3 (September 1967) 299-307.

_____ , "The Bishop Who Almost Stood with Lincoln," *Journal of the Historical Society of the EPA Conference* (1968) 41-47.

_____ , "A Missionary Journey to Oregon," *Oregon Historical Quarterly* Vol. 102, No. 4 (Winter 2001) 454-478.

Kisker, Scott, "Methodism Abroad: Matthew Simpson and the Emergence of American Methodism as a World Church," *Methodist History* Vol. LII, No. 1 (October 2014) 4-20.

Leonard, Ira M., "Rise and Fall of the American Republican Party in New York City: 1843-1845," *New York Historical Society Quarterly* Vol. L (April 1966) 151-192.

Mackey, Alexander , "The Life of Matthew Simpson by Robert D. Clark," *Pennsylvania History* Vol. 23, No. 4 (October 23, 1956) 535-536.

Maddox, Randy L., "Holiness of Heart and Life: Lessons from North American Methodism," *Asbury Theological Seminary Journal* (Fall 1998) 151-172.

_____ , "Wesley's Understanding of Christian Perfection: In What Sense Pentecostal? "Randy L. Maddox's Response to Laurence Wood," *Wesleyan Theological Journal* Vol. 34, No. 2 (Fall 1999) 78-110.

McBath, James, "The Emergence of Chautauqua as a Religious and
    Educational Institution 1874-1900," *Methodist History* Vol. 20
    (October 1981) 3-12.

Meriam, Arthur L., "Final Interment of President Abraham Lincoln's
    Remains at the Lincoln Monument in Oak Ridge Cemetery,
    Springfield, Illinois," *Illinois State Historical Society Journal*
    Vol. XXIII, No. 1 (April 1930) 171-174.

Miner, Craig, "Border Frontier: The Missouri River, Fort Scott & Gulf
    Railroad in the Cherokee Neutral Lands, 1868-1870", *Kansas
    Historical Quarterly* Vol. XXXV, No. 2 (Summer 1969) 105-129.

Morris, Enoch, "The M.E. Churches North and South," *The Southern Review*
    Vol. X, No. 22 (April 1872) 382-421.

Morrow, Ralph, "The Life of Matthew Simpson by Robert D. Clark," *Journal
    of Southern History* Vol. XXIII, No. 2 (May 1956) 240-242.

Nast, William, "Dr. Schaff and Methodism," *Methodist Quarterly Review* 31
    (1857) 428-436.

Noll, Mark. "John Wesley's Doctrine of Assurance," *Bibliotheca Sacra*
    (April 1975) 161-177.

Norwood, Frederick, "Reinterpreted Bishop," *Christian Century* Vol. 73,
    No. 36 (September 5, 1956) 1024-1025.

Peck, Jesse T., "The General Conference of 1844," *Methodist Quarterly
    Review* Vol. 7 (April 1870) 165-189.

Reynolds, Donald E., "Reluctant Martyr: Anthony Bewley and the Texas
    Slave Insurrection Panic of 1860," *Southwestern Historical Quarterly*
    96:3 (January 1993) 345-361.

Rowe, Kenneth E., "Three Great Charities: Philadelphia as a Cradle of Methodist Healthcare Initiatives in Victorian America," *Journal of the Historical Society of the EPA Conference* (2011) 23-41.

_____, "Building Monumental Methodist Cathedrals in America's Capitol City, 1850-1950" *Methodist History* 50:3 (April 2012) 171-178.

Sledge, Robert W., "Till Charity Wept–1844 Revisited," *Methodist History* 48.2 (January 2010) 92-112.

Smith, Elizabeth M., "William Roberts: Circuit Rider of the Far West," *Methodist History* Vol. 22 No. 2 (January 1982) 60-74.

Stowell, Daniel W., "Murder at a Methodist Camp Meeting: The Origins of Abraham Lincoln's Most Famous Trial," *Journal of the Illinois State Historical Society* Vol. X, No. 3–4 (Fall–Winter 2008) 219–234.

Teasdale, Mark, "Growth or Declension: Methodist Historians' Treatment of the Relationship between the Methodist Episcopal Church and the Culture of the United States." *Theological Librarianship* Vol. III, No. 2 (December 2010) 34-44.

Tegeder, Vincent G., "Lincoln and the Territorial Patronage: The Ascendency of the Radicals in the West" *The Mississippi Valley Historical Review* Vol. 35, No. 1 (June 1948) 77-90.

Templin, J. Alton, "John Wesley Iliff, and Theological Education in the West," *Methodist History* 24:2 (January 1986) 67-81.

Tinker, Tink., "Redskin, Tamed Hide: A Book of Christian History Bound in the Flayed Skin of an American Indian," (Watashe/Osage Nation). *Journal of Race, Ethnicity, and Religion* Vol. 5, Issue 9 (October 2014) 1-43, 124-130.

Watkins, Samuel W., "The Causes and Cure: Methodists and the New Madrid Earthquake 1811–1812," *Methodist History* (July 1992) 242-250.

Wedon, Daniel. "Spirit of the Southern Methodist Press," *Methodist Quarterly Review* (January 1866) 124-130.

Wilson, Clarence True, "Bishop Matthew Simpson: The Man Who Inspired the Emancipation Proclamation," *Current History* (October 1929) 99-106.

Wilson, Major, "Ideological Fruits of Manifest Destiny: The Geopolitics of Slavery Expansion in the Crisis of 1850," *Journal of the Illinois State Historical Society* Vol. LXIII, No. 2 (Summer 1970) 132-143.

Unpublished Dissertations

James Edmund Kirby. *The Ecclesiastical and Social Thought of Matthew Simpson* (Unpublished Ph.D. dissertation, Drew University, 1963).

Oglesby, Donald, *J. W. Iliff: Cattle King of Colorado* (Unpublished M.A. thesis, Western State College of Colorado, 1953).

Pancake, Lorel W. *Liberal Theology in the Yale Lectures* (Unpublished Ph.D. dissertation, Drew University, 1951).

Reinhard, James Arnold. *Personal and Sociological Factors in the Formation of the Free Methodist Church 1852–1860* (Unpublished Ph. D. dissertation: The University of Iowa, 1971).

Roberts, Gary Leland. *Sand Creek: Tragedy and Symbol* (Unpublished Ph.D. dissertation, University of Oklahoma, 1984).

Stark, David Thomas. *The Peculiar Doctrine Committed to our Trust: Ideal and Identity in the First Wesleyan Holiness Revival, 1758-1763*. (Unpublished Ph.D. dissertation, University of Manchester, 2011).

Magazines

The American Pulpit Magazine, American Magazine Company Vol. VI (1887) 629. Courtesy of the Harrison County, Ohio, Historical Society.

Clark, Robert D., "Matthew Simpson, the Methodists and the Defeat of Samuel Bigger," *Indiana Magazine of History* Vol. 50, No. 1 (March 1994) 22-33.

Ernsberger, Richard, Jr., "Andrew Carnegie: Robber Baron Turned Robin Hood," *American History* Vol. XLIX, No. 6 (February 15, 2015) 32-41.

"The Kindliness of Bishop Simpson," *The Metropolitan Pulpit and Homiletic Monthly* Vol. II, ed. I. K. Funk (New York: The Religious Newspaper Agency, 1878) 319–320.

The Annual Conferences, New York Conference, Fifth Day Monday April 24," *The Methodist* Vol. VI, No. 18 (May 6, 1865).

Moore, Bishop David, "Bishop Simpson–A Centennial Appreciation," *Pittsburgh Christian Advocate* (June 29, 1911).

Posey, Walter Brownlow, "The Earthquake of 1811 and Its Influence on Evangelistic Methods in the Churches of the Old South" in *Tennessee Historical Magazine* (January 1931) 107-114.

Prentice, C. A., "Captain Silas S. Soule: A Pioneer Martyr" *The Colorado Magazine*, Vol. XII, No. 6 (November 1935) 224-228.

Simpson, Matthew, "The River of Salvation," *The Methodist* Vol. X, No. 11 (March 13, 1869).

Stevens, Abel, "Bishop Ames," *National Magazine: Devoted to Literature, Art, and Religion*, Vol. VII (July-December 1855) 385-389.

Unrau, William E., "A Prelude to War," *The Colorado Magazine* Vol. XLI (Nov. 4, 1964) 299-313.

Wallace, Charles B., "Meteors and Consequences," *The Jimhinker* Vol XL, No. 1 (April 2010).

Websites

SCO Home–SCO Former Justices. John Mills Goodenow, http://www.supremecourt.ohio.gov/SCO/formerjustices/bios/goodenow.asp

"Benjamin Tappan," *Biographical Directory of the United States Congress.* http://bioguide.congress.gov/scripts/biodisplay.pl?index=t000039
http;//www.ohiohistorycentral.org/w/Wright,_John_C.?rec=423

http:www.ourcampaigns.com/NewsDetail.html?NewsID+49165

http://www.genealogybank.com/gbnk/newspaper/doc/v2%3A12A7E3496BF...h%2BBarclay%3B%2BSt.%2BClair-street%3B%2BCalamitous%5D/print.html

"The Underground Railroad," Levi Coffin, http://www.nationalcenter.org/UndergroundRailroad.html

Report of the John Evans Study Committee, 69. Website: www.northwestern.edu/provost/committees/john-evans-study/study-committee-report.pdf.

libwww.library.phil.gov/cencol/exh-testimony.htm.

Methodist Church Records, Massachusetts Boston University School of Theology Library.
www.bu.edu/sthlibrary/archives/collections/neccah/records-files-state/ma-records/

www.thespringofclifton.com/About-Springs-of-Clifton.html.

www.visitphilly.com/museums-attractions/philadelphia/rittenhouse-square-park/.

Joel Hawes, "Lectures Addressed to the Young Men of Hartford and New Haven."
http://catalog,hathitrust.org/apl/volumes/oclc/1189231.html.

Biographical and Historical Catalogue of Washington and Jefferson College, 20.
http://archive.org/stream/biographicaland00eatogoog/biographicaland00eatogoog_djvu.txt

Fertility and Mortality in the United States, EH. Net Encyclopedia, Economic History Association.
http://eh.net/encyclopedia/article/haines.demography

Blog: *Texas Methodist History*, Monday, January 01, 2007-Friday, November 01, 2013,
http://txmethhistory.blogspot.com/search?q=simpson.

https://archive.org/stream/officialproceedi18681880repu/officialprocee.
"Full Text of Official Proceedings of the National Republican Convention of 1868."

Index

A

Abbott, Benjamin 250, 294

Abell, Aaron 554

Adams, Henry 491

Adams, John 374

Adams, John Quincy 160

Agassiz, Louis 596

Ahlstrom, Sidney 221, 551

Akiskal, Hagop 101

Albright, Jacob 614

Alden, Timothy 115, 117

Alger, Horatio 654

Allegheny College 115-122

Ames, Edward 137, 139, 146, 153-155, 162-163, 181, 207, 231-232, 255-257, 266-267, 272, 283-284, 291, 308, 317, 320, 332-333, 347, 433, 438, 464, 474, 480, 575, 577, 612, 627

Andrew, James Osgood 167, 169-176, 178, 180

Anshutz, George 66

Anthony, S.J. 424, 426-427

Anthony, Susan 582

Applegate, Debby 563

Armstrong, Hannah 310

Armstrong, William Duff 310

Arnold, Matthew 601

Arthur, Chester 314, 623

Asbury, Francis 17, 227, 499, 521, 630, 664

Atkins, Gaius 565

B

Baily, William H. 267

Baker, Osman 232, 468

Baldwin, John 466-469, 665

Baldwin, Matthew 456-457

Baldwin, Samuel 333, 335

Baltzell, E. Digby 524-525, 646

Bancroft, Ashley   286

Bancroft, Hubert   430

Bangs, Nathan
68, 134, 216, 233-235, 517, 572

Barnes, Albert   209

Barnes, Gilbert   94, 159

Barns, R.M.   611

Bascom, Henry   51-53, 70, 346

Baskerville, Barnet   528

Bayer, Maximilian   505

Bayless, R.W.   488

Beebe, Walter   19

Beecher, Henry Ward
2-3, 129, 137-138, 153, 305,
527, 531-532, 561-563, 567

Belknap, Ketturah   264

Belknap, William   491

Bell, Alexander Graham   553

Benton, Thomas   223

Berry, Lucien   154, 180, 256

Bewley, Anthony   266-268, 665

Bigger, Samuel   138

Bingham, John   485

Bishop, James   286

Black Kettle   407

Blair, Frances   319-321

Blair, Montgomery   319

Bohler, Peter   279

Bond, Thomas   161, 189

Boone, Albert   408

Bowen, Jesse   318

Bowman, Thomas   312, 634

Boyle, Richard   318

Bragdon, C.P.   290

Brands, H.M.   259, 265

Bresee, Phineas   663-665

Brooks, David   658

Brooks, Noah   312, 645

Brooks, Phillips   525, 527

Brooks, Preston   271

Brown, Candy Gunther   195

Brown, George   70

Brown, James   75-76

Brown, John   270, 301-302

Brown, Orville   443

Brown, S.E. 408-409

Brown, William J. 222

Brueggemann, Walter 95

Buchanan, James 301

Buckalew, Charles 427

Buckley, James 573

Buoy, Charles
324, 613, 630, 638-640, 647-648

Buoy, Ida 649

Burke, William 43-44

Burlingame, Roger 486

Burton, Arthur M. 500

Bushnell, Horace 209, 374, 384

Butler, Andrew 270-271

Butler, Benjamin 331, 465, 486

Butler, Richard 39

C

Calhoun, John 187, 528

Callahan, George 39

Calvin, John 107

Cameron, Simon 315, 317, 319

Campbell, Willie 198

Canby, Colonel 419

Cannadine, Daniel 243

Cannon, James 426-427

Cannon, William 106, 249

Carlson, F.S. 318

Carlton, Thomas
228, 293-294, 298, 421, 450, 508, 530-531, 560, 571-577

Carnegie, Andrew 660

Carton, Evan 301

Cartwright, Peter
155, 175, 272, 310, 521, 538

Carwardine, Richard
161, 189, 250

Cattell, Wade 480

Chaffee, Jerome 444

Chamberlain, Israel 405

Chandler, William 490

Channing, William 323, 391

Charlemagne 656

Chase, Salmon
223, 239, 317, 319, 322, 325, 328

Chaucer, Geoffrey 620

Chautauqua 503-506

Chevalier, Michael 65

Childs, George 369, 502, 600-601

Chivington, J.M. 266, 351, 415-428, 436-440, 444-446

Chivington, Sarah 438

Chivington, Thomas 438

Cist, Charles 199, 203

Clark, Davis 464, 522

Clark J. 188

Clark, Robert 4, 135, 189, 309, 531

Clay, Henry 214-216, 528-529

Coffin, Levi 226-227

Cogburn, Rooster 419

Colfax, Shuyler 239, 391, 410, 498

Colley, S.G. 429

Comegys, C.H. 317

Comfort, Silas 172

Commager, Henry Steele 660

Conable, C.S. 300

Conrey, Gertrude 642

Conway, Stephen 559

Cook, Valentine 42-43

Cooke, Charles 85-86, 110

Cookman, Alfred 518-519

Cooper, Edward 486

Cooper, Samuel 128-129, 139

Cotton, John 561

Cowgill, John 123

Cramer, John 334-335

Craven, Braxton 463

Crawford, D. E. 318

Crook, L.A. 500

Crooks, George 3, 59, 285, 322-323, 329, 379, 512, 578, 580, 589, 625, 632, 638-640

Crossan, John 653

Culver, F.B. 408

Cummings, Alexander 283, 316, 318, 328, 431-432, 454

Cunningham, John T. 507

Curry, Daniel 205

Curtin, Andrew J. 328

D

Daily, William 188, 255-256

Dana, Charles 376

Darby, John Nelson 551

Darwin, Charles 591-595

Davidson, C.D. 256

Davis, Alexander J. 645-646

Davis, Jefferson 331

Decker, Will 646

Delano, Columbus 491

Dempster, John 290

DePauw, Washington 578, 615, 618

Dickens, Charles 601

Dieter, Melvin 298, 518, 520

Dixon, James 190-191

Dole, William 408, 414

Doolittle, James 446

Dorsey, Dennis 67-68

Douglas, Stephen 218, 268, 312, 418, 528

Doyle, Elizabeth 75

Drake, Daniel 198

Drew, Daniel 103, 286, 354, 497, 506-508, 510-513, 530

Dumond, Dwight L. 220-221

Duncan, Thomas J. 581

Durbin, John P. 308, 509-510

Dyer, Charles 488

E

Early, John 179

Eddy, Thomas 153

Edmondson, Katherine 458-459

Edwards, Edward 154

Edwards, Jonathan 561

Edwards, Ninian Wirt 395-396

Elbert, Samuel 409-410, 413, 430-432, 444

Eliade, Mircea 394

Elliott, Charles 49-51, 63, 88, 123, 134, 188-191, 204, 208-209, 211, 225, 267, 343, 433, 665

Elliott, John 286

Emerson, Ralph Waldo 555, 601

Emory, John 68, 83, 89

Everett, Edward 392, 529

Evans, John 87, 139, 228, 286-290, 309, 315, 349, 366, 408-409, 411-416, 420-425, 427-436, 438, 440, 443-447, 451-453, 480, 492, 500, 560, 578, 632, 637

Evans, Josephine 430, 435

Evarts, William 494

F

Falconer, John 286

Fallows, Bishop 613

Farish, Hunter Dickinson 464

Farrar, B.G. 331

Fatout, Paul 151

Faulkner, William 445

Fenelon, Francis 516

Finley, James 41-42, 174

Finney, Charles Grandison 93-95, 159, 209, 292, 296, 551, 555

Fish, Carl Russell 196

Fisk, Clinton 311, 319, 322-324, 422, 450, 615, 632, 638-639

Fleming, George 75

Floy, James 273-274

Foner, Eric 459

Foss, A.C. 285

Foster, F.S. 446

Foster, John 288

Foster, Randolph 510, 517, 633, 638

Frederickson, George 403

Freud, Sigmund 657

Furnace, Frank 646

G

Gabrielan, Randall 502

Garfield, James 605, 619-621

Garnett, Henry 500

Garrett, Augustus 289-290

Garrett, Eliza 289

Garrettson, Freeborn 294

Garrick, David 620

Garrison, William Lloyd   160

Gee, A.A.   336

Gellner, Ernest   661

Gesink, Indira   468

Gibbons, Thomas   507

Gibbons, William   507

Gillette, Francis   317

Gilpin, Governor   418

Giteau, Charles   620

Gladden, Washington   662

Gocher, John   627

Gooch, Daniel   427

Good, J.B.   614

Goode, William   418

Goodenough, S.J.   571, 573, 575

Goodenow, John Milton   37

Goodwin, Doris Kearns   314

Goodwin, Thomas   127-129, 148-149

Gould, Jay   491

Graham, Billy   551, 623

Grant, Elihu   573, 576

Grant, Ulysses S.   239, 334, 404, 483-485, 489-494, 498, 501-503, 506, 600-601, 604-606

Graw, Jacob   501

Gray, Asa   596

Greeley, Horace   199-200, 312

Gregory, George   54-55

Grimsley, Elizabeth Todd   312

Grinnell, Josiah   442-443

Groff, Ella   646

Groff, Eva Nelson   646-647

Groff, William   646

Gruber, Jacob   89

Gunn, John   575

Gunter, Stephen   248

Gurley, P.D.   395

Gurnee, Walter S.   288

Guyon, Madame   516

H

Hale, Willis   646

Hall, Rev. Dr.   395

Handel, George   602

Handy, Robert 6, 555

Hamilton, John 623-625

Hamlin, Hannibal 460

Hamline, Leonidas 232, 521

Hammond, Charles 38

Harding, Francis 167, 169-170

Harper, James 164-166, 352

Harlan, James 145-146, 228, 318, 348, 411-412, 431-433, 440-443, 452, 487, 490, 492, 560, 578, 632, 667

Harlow, Lewis D. 629

Hatch, Nathan 234, 237

Haven, Gilbert 221, 271, 389-390, 393, 440-441, 486-487, 612

Hay, John 314, 319

Hayes, Lucy 606, 621

Hayes, Rutherford 314, 578, 604-607, 621

Hazelton, Edward 75

Headle, S.S. 458

Heath, Kate 572

Hedding, Elijah 160, 232, 250-251

Hedge, Frederick H. 529

Hempton, David 665

Henry, Guy V. 427

Herberg, Will 225

Herndon, William 100-101

Heschel, Abraham 383

Hibbert, Billy 294

Hill, James 150

Hillman, John 649-650

Hillman, S.D. 524

Hoe, Robert 201

Hodge, Charles 537

Hodges, Albert 403

Hogan, John 333

Holliday, L.C. 614

Holman, Calvin 463

Holmes, Nathaniel 70, 75, 120, 590

Hoogenboom, Ari 604-605

Hoover, Herbert 650

Hoover, J.W. 334-335

Howard, Victor 490

Howe, William Walker 201

Hoyt, Mark 371-372, 456

Hoyt, Oliver 371-372, 456, 530, 615, 634

Hoyt, William 372, 456

Hudson, Thomas 66-67

Hughes, George 518-519, 522

Hughes, John 312, 316

Hull, J. H. 256

Hunter, James 596

Hunter, William 120

Hurst, John Fletcher 512

Huss, John 280

I

Iliff, John Wesley 609-610

Iliff, Lizzie 609-612

Indiana Asbury University 123-153

Inskeep, Thomas 43

Inskip, John 518-519

J

Jackson, Andrew 313-314, 319, 666

Jacoben, Edwin 425

James, William 505

Jamison, Kay 95-96

Janes, Edmond 295, 365, 473-474, 492, 508, 511, 575, 577, 612

Jefferson, Thomas 326, 374, 561

Jobson, Frederick 274-275

John, Richard 201

Johnson, Andrew 335-336, 430-432, 460, 464, 480-482, 484-489

Johnson, Paul E. 93-94

Jones, Arthur, Jr. 206

Jones, Donald 196, 221-222, 508

Joy, James 443

K

Keller, Ralph 223

Kelman, Ari 439

Kelsey, Harry Jr.   413

Kelso, Thomas   498-500

Kennedy, Sarah   589-590

Kidder, Daniel   318

Kingsley, Calvin   445, 522

Kingsley, Charles   335

Kirby, James Edmund, Jr.   4-5, 173, 385, 559-560, 566-567

Klingaman, William   325

Kobler, John   40-41

Koenig, Frederick   201

L

Lamon, Ward Hill   326

Lanahan, John   315, 319-320, 322, 329, 571-578, 632

Lane, George   293, 317

Lane, Harry   391, 411-412

Larrabee, William C.   139, 146, 180

Lathers, Emma   644

Lathers, Richard   645

Latta, William   208

Lawson, Melinda   394

Lear, Ward M.   546

Lee, Luther   160-161

Leibnitz, Gottfried   331

Leigh, C.C.   389

Leo III   656

Leslie, Frank   601

Letts, J. M.   259

Levitt, Joseph   159

Lewis, C.S.   659

Lewis, Edwin   513

Lewis, Sinclair   224

Liberty Street Church   66, 85-88, 109, 184

Lincoln, Abraham   1, 99-101, 214, 217, 287-288, 309-315, 318-337, 366, 368-369, 372, 376-378, 391-403, 409-413, 482-483, 529, 555, 604, 607, 633, 645, 655, 665-668

Lincoln, Mary   312, 395-396, 402

Lincoln, Tad   402

Lincoln, Willie   397

Loan, Benjamin   427

Logan, John   486

Long, James 403, 454-456, 615

Longfellow, Henry 601

Longstreet, A.B. 177

Lore, Daniel 490

Lorenz von Mocheim, Johann 611

Lovejoy, Elijah 175

Lovejoy, Owen 330-331

Loveland, W.A.H. 414, 444

Lowell, James Russell 619

Lowry, Asbury 516

Lumas, Robert 410-411

Lunt, Cornelia Gray 330

Lunt, Orrington 286, 288-290, 330

Luther, Martin 296

Lyman, Clarence A. 417

Lynch, James 475-477, 665

Lyon, Russell 603

M

Madison College 49-51, 117

Maier, Pauline 561

Makoto, Fukui 603

Marlay, John 522

Marrow, Ralph 515, 524

Marshall, James 262

Marshall, John 507

Marston, Leslie 299

Marty, Martin 566

Mason, James 620

Mather, Increase 561

Matlack, Lucius 463

Matthews, Donald 222

McBean, John 31-32, 53, 56, 58

McCabe, Charles Cardwell 313, 500

McClintock, John 236, 249, 272-274, 278-281, 284-285, 316, 320, 329, 506-507, 510-512, 638

McCormick, Francis 39-40

McCoy, Mrs. George 108, 128

McCullough, George 79, 128, 196, 246, 440, 452-453, 589, 632, 651

McDonald, J.W. 618

McDougall, Walter 269, 460

McGuffey, William   196

McKendree, William   613

McLuhan, Marshall   654

McPherson, James   268-269

McNabb, Henderson   458

Meade, George   403

Merrick, F.   564

Merrill, Samuel   138

Metropolitan Memorial United Methodist Church   87, 239, 353, 497-501, 595, 604, 622-623

Metzger, James   310

Milburn, William   278-279, 665

Miley, John   513, 516, 566

Miller, Perry   556

Mills, Clark   666-667

Milton, George Fort   485-486

Moffat, David   444

Moody, Dwight   527, 550, 567, 602-603

Moore, David   634

Moore, Jane   330-331

Moore, William   330-331

Moorehead, James   8, 551

Morgan, Daniel   612

Morgan, Edwin   271

Morris, Enoch   474

Morris, Thomas   205-206, 521-522

Morrow, James   631

Morrow, Ralph   464

Morse, Samuel   200

Muller-Fahrenholz, Geiko   385

Murray, Nicholas   209

Myers, Margaret   626

Myers, Nathan   626

N

Napoleon, Louis   586

Nast, William   237-238, 318

National Camp Meeting Association for the Promotion of Holiness   98, 503, 505-506, 518-522

Naylor, H.R.   500

Neil, James   403, 454

Nelson, Reuben 577

Nevins, Allan 271, 458

Newman, John 466, 469, 501, 618, 623

Niebuhr, Reinhold 547

Nolley, Richmond 39

North, Charles 512

North, John Wesley 461

North, Robert 429

Norwood, J.N. 189

Nutt, Cyrus 123, 126, 138, 147, 266

O

Oakes, James 323

Ocean Grove Camp Meeting Association 503, 505

Ogden, Aaron 507

Olin, Stephen 173, 175

Osborne, W.B. 518

O'Sullivan, John 200

P

Packard, Jerrold M. 311

Paine, Robert 473

Palmer, Phoebe 98, 513-518, 627

Palmer, Walter 518

Paludan, Phillip 314

Parker, A.G. 143

Parker, John 512

Parkhurst, Charles 531

Pattison, Robert E. 634

Payne, Daniel 476

Pearne, Thomas 392

Peck, George 187, 206, 236

Peck, Jesse 207, 517

Pendleton, George 486

Pepper, George Wharton 646

Phillips, John 577

Phillips, Wendell 481

Pierpoint, F.H. 470

Pelagius 208-209

Peters, John 516

Pickering, William 409

Pilkington, James 572

Poisal, John 285

Polk, James K. 214-215

Pomeroy, Samuel 412, 432, 442

Porter, A.G. 644

Porter, James 571

Porter, W.A. 634

Portis, Charles 419

Potter, John F. 301

Price, Sterling 424

Puleo, Stephen 271

Q

Queen Victoria 619

R

Rable, George 271, 462

Ralston, Thomas 566

Rand, Franklin 580

Raser, Harold 514

Rauschenbusch, Walter 662

Ray, Angela G. 527-528

Ray, James 151

Reagan, Ronald 375

Reed, J.C. 365

Reed, L.P. 332

Remington, Eliphalet 603, 644

Remington, Stephen 70

Remini, Robert 215

Revels, Hiram 477

Rice, Nathan 208

Richardson, Cora 587-588

Richey, Russell 522, 614

Roberts, Benjamin Titus 293-300, 306-307, 574

Roberts, Gary 414, 412, 417, 444-445, 447

Roberts, Robert 63, 69, 116, 294, 613

Robie, John 574

Robinson, Thomas 70

Robinson, W.C. 631

Roche, J.A. 285

Rollason, Martha 417

Rosecrans, William 424, 440-441

Ross, Daniel 579

Ross, D.L. 285

Ross, Edmond 486

Ross, Father 531

Ross, Lewis 446

Rothweiler, Jay 599

Rowe, Kenneth 640

Rubin, Julius H. 98

Ruter, Martin 117-118, 665

S

Said, Edward 657

Sanford, P.P. 169

Schaff, Phillip 237

Schleiermacher 536

Scofield, C. I. 551

Scoles, Curtis 64

Scott, Dred 319

Scott, Levi 232, 335, 575, 577

Scott, Orange 160

Scott, Winfield 241

Seagar, D.S. 299-300

Sellers, Henry 68, 83, 88-89

Seward, Fredrick 328

Seward, William 301, 324, 328, 413, 431-432

Sheldon, Charles 662

Shenk, Joshua 100-101

Sheridan, Philip 460, 465-466

Sherman, William 462

Shinn, Asa 68-69

Simpson, Anna 197, 492

Simpson, Charles 182, 197, 199, 245-247, 277-281, 421, 450-451, 478-480, 519, 637, 642

Simpson, Charles Henry 642

Simpson, David 632

Simpson, Elizabeth 63-64

Simpson, Ella 197, 440, 642, 647-649

Simpson, Ellen Verner 109, 118, 125-126, 182-184, 196-198, 244-245, 251-252, 344, 449-450, 626, 637-643

Simpson, Hetty   50, 79, 124, 196, 246, 589, 651

Simpson House   361, 640-641, 667

Simpson, Ida   451, 632, 642-643, 649-650

Simpson, James   11, 14-17, 632

Simpson, Jimmy   182-184, 637

Simpson, John   20

Simpson, Matthew Tingley   14, 17, 20-29, 43-45, 50, 57, 63, 79, 86-87, 100, 102, 110, 120-122, 128, 137, 163, 179, 183, 197, 341-342, 537, 567, 588-591, 637, 665

Simpson, Matthew Verner   480, 495, 578, 606, 609, 632, 642-647

Simpson, Sarah   17, 29-31, 79, 128, 163, 197, 480, 637

Simpson, Sarah Elizabeth (Sibbie)   606, 626, 630, 632, 642-643, 649-651

Sleeper, Jacob   613

Slicer, Henry   318

Slough, John   420

Smith, Henry   42

Smith, John L.   228, 256, 413, 427

Smith, Timothy   5-6, 298, 517

Smithfield Street Church   66, 68-71, 85, 117

Snyder, Howard   295, 297

Soule, Joshua   173, 176-177, 180

Soule, Silas   424, 426-427

Spence, John   390

Spencer, Herbert   554, 601

Spencer, O.M.   318

St. Clair, Arthur   66

Stanton, Edwin   324, 332-333, 395, 419, 423-425, 465-466, 478-485, 489

Steele, Daniel   516

Stevens, Abel   134, 233-235, 272-274

Stevens, Thaddeus   475, 481, 485

Stevenson, A. C.   123

Steward, George   491

Stiles, T.J.   380

Stillwell, George 425

Stimson, Henry L. 650

Stokes, Elwood 503

Stokes, Melvin 559

Stone, Lucy 582

Stout, Harry 375

Strong, George Templeton 242

Strong, James 513

Stuart, George 457

Stuart, Moses 536

Sumner, Charles 270, 301, 481, 528

Sunday, Billy 551

Sunderland, Byron 326

Sunderland, La Roy 106

Sweet, William Warren 195

Syle, Edward W. 221

T

Tabor, Joseph 206

Taft, Alphonso 196

Taft, William Howard 196, 650

Talbott, Strobe 658

Taney, Roger 300-301, 320, 482

Tappan, Benjamin 37

Tappan, J.E. 427

Tappan, Samuel F. 425

Tarkington, Joseph 128-129

Taylor, A.B. 202

Taylor, Nathaniel 209

Taylor, William 262, 284

Teasdale, Mark 556

Teller, Henry 444

Tennent, Gilbert 296

Thomas, George 333

Thompson, Edward 231, 522

Thoreau, David 218

Tichnor, George 528

Tiffany, Otis, H. 501

Tingley, Jeremiah 30, 468

Tingley, Joseph 27, 33-34, 43, 44, 73, 119, 126, 156-157, 202, 317

Tingley William 27, 43, 48, 63, 73, 79, 481

Tocqueville, Alexis de   100

Todd, Elizabeth   395

Todd, Jacob   567-568, 609

Tomlinson, Joseph   123

Townsend, George   327

Trachtenburg, Alan   553-554

Trollope, Francis   243

Trueblood, Elton   377

Trumbull, Lymon   412

Trump, Donald   658

Twain, Mark   547

Tweed, Bill   576

U

Underwood, John C.   470

Unrau, William E.   414

Upham, Thomas   516

W

Wade, Benjamin   427

Walker, Charles   486

Wallace, David   129, 151

Wanamaker, John   608-609, 634

Ware, Eugene   442

Warfield, Benjamin   537

Warner, Sam Bass   454

Warren, Henry   611

Warren, William   281-282

Warwick, Charles F.   644

Washburn, Wilcomb   656

Weakly, John   146-147

Weaver, Anna   642-643, 648

Weaver, Ellen Verner   642-643, 648-649

Weaver, James Riley   492-495, 643, 648

Weaver, Ida Blanche   642, 648

Weber, Max   559

Webster, Daniel   218-219, 407, 418, 507, 528

Weisberger, Bernard   201

Weld, Theodore   159-160

Wells, Gideon   324, 485

Wells, G.G. 520

Wesley, John   46-47, 96-97, 102-103, 279-280, 296, 519,

521, 523-524, 559, 579, 607, 616-617, 653, 664

West, Elliot 610

Weyland, Francis 384

Whedon, Daniel 463

Wheeler, John 146, 207

Wheeler, Mary 608

Whitcomb, James 139-140

White Antelope 407

White, Charles 516

Whitefield, George 296

Whitford, William Clarke 419

Whitman, Walt 562-563

Whittier, John Greenleaf 159

Wiley, Allen 183

Wilkes, George 486

Willard, Frances E. 292-293, 350, 565, 582-583

Willey, Waitman 485-488

Williams, Roger 656

Williamsport Church 109-110

Wills, Garry 655

Wilmot, David 215

Wilson, Charles Regan 459

Wilson, Clarence True 5, 322

Wilson, Erasmus 90

Wilson, Robert 314

Winans, William 172

Wineapple, Brenda 655

Winger, Stewart 377

Winthrop, James 115

Winthrop, John 602

Wirt, William 507

Wood, Amanda 57-58

Wood, J.A. 518

Woods, E.M. 5

Woods, Green 458

Woolman, John 656

Worman, James H. 666

Wrenshall, John 75

Wright, John Crafts 38

Wright, Joseph 315

Wynkoop, Edward 424, 426-428

V

Van Vleck   575-576

Van Winkle, Senator   488

Vanderbilt, Cornelius   507, 601

Verner, Ellen Holmes   74, 78-83

Verner, James   68, 70-71, 74-82, 89, 244, 622

Vickers, George   488

Vincent, John   503-504, 596, 663

Z

Zinzendorf, Count   279

www.ingramcontent.com/pod-product-compliance
Lightning Source LLC
Chambersburg PA
CBHW070712160426
43192CB00009B/1155